HD 70 .G7 C57 1988

Company administration
handbook

SOUTH CAMPUS LIBRARY
Community College of Allegheny County
West Mifflin, Pennsylvania 15122

COMPANY ADMINISTRATION HANDBOOK

Sixth Edition

COMPANY ADMINISTRATION HANDBOOK

Sixth Edition

**Edited by
Derek Beattie**

A Gower Handbook

© Gower Publishing Company Limited 1988
(Chapter 25 is Crown copyright)

All rights reserved. No part of this publication may be reproduced, stored in a retrieval system, or transmitted in any form or by any means, electronic, mechanical, photocopying, recording, or otherwise without the prior permission of Gower Publishing Company Limited

First published in Great Britain by
Gower Press Limited, 1970

Sixth edition published in 1988 by
Gower Publishing Company Limited,
Gower House,
Croft Road,
Aldershot,
Hants GU11 3HR,
England.

Gower Publishing Company,
Old Post Road,
Brookfield,
Vermont 05036,
USA

British Library Cataloguing in Publication Data

Company administration handbook — 6th ed.
 1. Management
 I. Beattie, Derek
 658   HD31

Library of Congress Cataloging-in-Publication Data

Company administration handbook.
  Includes index.
  1. Industrial management—Great Britain—Handbooks, manuals, etc.
 2. Corporation law—Great Britain—Handbooks, manuals, etc.
 3. Corporation secretaries—Great Britain—Handbooks, manuals, etc.
 I. Beattie, Derek.

HD70.G7C57 1987   658'.00941   86-31876

ISBN 0-556-02667-8

Printed and bound in Great Britain by
Billing and Sons Limited, Worcester.

Contents

Editor's preface — xiii
Acknowledgements — xiv
List of illustrations — xv
Notes on contributors — xviii

PART ONE THE CONSTITUTION AND CONDUCT OF COMPANIES

1 The Role of the Company Secretary — 3
Richard Sleight
The secretary's legal status — Basic duties of the company secretary — Significance of the secretarial duties — The Institute of Chartered Secretaries and Administrators (ICSA) — Qualifications and Examinations — Future developments

2 Company Law — 17
V J Gersten
Limited companies — Memorandum of association — Objects of the company — Liability — Capital clause — Articles of association — Membership — Shares — Directors — Secretary — Auditors — Annual return — Borrowing by companies — Unlimited and guarantee companies

3 Maintaining a Company Share Register — 48
Audrey Laird
Certificates — Lost certificates — Maintaining the register — Share capital — Subsidiary books

4 The Conduct of Meetings — 82
Desmond Fitzpatrick

Shareholders' meetings — Kinds of resolution — Notice — Quorum — Chairman — Agenda — Voting — Minutes — Adjournment and postponement — Resolutions in writing — Directors' meetings — Meetings of unlimited and guarantee companies — Meetings of debenture holders — Secretary's duties in connection with a board meeting — Agenda for the first board meeting after incorporation — Specimen board resolutions — Organization and procedure for an annual general meeting — Specimen notices for meetings of shareholders — Meetings in a winding-up

PART TWO   ACCOUNTING AND FINANCE

5 The Annual Accounts — 121
W P Ridley

Accounting requirements of the Companies Acts — Standard presentation — The directors' report — Judging a company from its accounts — Profit and loss account for Pangloss PLC — Return to shareholders — Trading prospects — Balance sheet for Pangloss PLC — Inflation accounting

6 Sources of Finance — 137
Stephen Badger

Why capital may be required — Type of capital required — Long-term finance for unlisted companies — Going public — Long-term finance for listed companies — Methods of issue with a listing — Other methods of supplementing cash flow — The overall capital structure

7 Taxation — 154
J C Craig

Returns and assessments — Adjustment of profit and computation of amount liable to tax — Allowable expenses — Relief for increase in stock values — The necessary book-keeping — Capital allowances — Losses — Advance corporation tax — Groups of companies — Capital gains tax — The company as a tax collector — Close company disabilities — Contrast between limited company and partnership — Changes in personal and corporation tax — Definitions of some phrases used in the corporation tax rules

8 Value Added Tax — 177
Richard Service

Legislation — Charge to VAT — Time of supply — Place of supply —

Contents

The tax invoice — Rates of tax — Discounts — Retrospective adjustments — Bad debts — Secondhand goods — Input VAT — Accounting for VAT to Customs and Excise — Default surcharge — Repayment supplement — Serious misdeclaration — Interest on VAT assessments — Retention of records — Groups — Divisions — Cash flows — Appeal procedures — Professional advice

9 Managing Mergers and Acquisitions   **188**
Peter A Verreck
Definitions — Reasons for mergers — Programme — People and mergers — Management and mergers — Checklist

PART THREE   COMMERCIAL FUNCTIONS

10 The Law of Contract   **203**
Alan Hobkirk
Essential elements of a valid contract — Contractual capacity — Remedies for breach of contract — Transfer of ownership and responsibility for accidental loss or damage — Contracts in restraint of trade — Supply of Goods (Implied Terms) Act 1973 — Unfair Contract Terms Act 1977 — Supply of Goods and Services Act 1983

11 Negotiation   **227**
P D V Marsh
Nature of the negotiating process — Planning the negotiation — Negotiating area and the influence of time — Negotiating teams — Opening stages — The follow-up — Negotiating psychology — Negotiating tactics — Checklist: contract dispute

12 Debt Collection   **251**
Guy Vincent
Debt collectors — Solicitors — Legal action — Court action — County court proceedings — High Court proceedings — Enforcement of judgment debts — Moratorium — Insolvency

13 Intellectual Property Rights   **263**
Colin Jones
Patents — Invention — Patent specification — What a patent is — Validity of patents — Employees' inventions — Infringement of patents — European patent law — Patenting procedure in the UK — Patenting procedure in Europe — Community Patent Convention — Foreign patents — The International Convention — Licensing —

Existing patents — Trade marks and service marks — Designs and copyright — Marking — Functions of patent and trade mark agents — Costs

14 Fair Trading — 291
Malcolm Carlisle
Restrictive trade practices — Consumer protection — Direct action against individual traders — Codes of trading practice — Proposals for statutory orders — Consumer credit — Criminal law statutes — Civil law statutes

PART FOUR   OFFICE ADMINISTRATION

15 Managing the Modern Office — 307
Ronald G Anderson
The changing scene — Convergence — Evolution of office equipment — Computers — Methods of selection

16 Reducing Office Costs — 318
Robert C Appleby
Philosophy of cost reduction — The O & M function — Work measurement — Incentives — Reducing the cost of space — Office automation and cost reduction — Saving time — Ask the staff

17 Setting Up a New Office — 335
Rod Revell
Establishment of requirements — Building assessment — Furniture — Implementation — Continuing administration

18 The Role of O & M — 359
J M Alastair Gibson
When is an O & M department necessary? — Why should O & M be necessary? — Organizing an O & M department — Using consultants

19 The Design and Control of Forms — 368
Rod Revell
Forms control — Forms design — Ease of completion — Ease of use — Ease of handling

20 Data Processing — 385
Philip Goacher
The hardware — Using a computer — Paying for a computer — Developing applications — Computing staff — Computer Service Bureaux — Small or large computers? — Future developments

Contents

PART FIVE   THE COMPANY AND ITS EMPLOYEES

21 Employment Law   397
F W Rose
Sources of law on employment and its enforcement — Contracts of employment — Form of the concluded contract — Race Relations Act 1976 — Sex Discrimination Act 1975 — Maternity rights — Equal Pay Act 1970 — Vicarious liability — Independent contractors — Termination of contract — Indefinite contracts — Disciplinary procedure — Reasons for dismissal — Constructive dismissal — Remedies for breach of contract — Unfair dismissal — Discriminatory action short of dismissal — Determination of disputes — Testimonials

22 Working Conditions   439
Patricia George
Health and Safety at Work Act 1974 — Health and safety administration and enforcement — The Factories Act 1961 — Offices, Shops and Railway Premises Act 1963 — The Shops Acts — Regulations — Codes of Practice — Employers' liability (compulsory insurance) — Fire Precautions Act 1971 — Notices to be displayed — Notices to be sent to factory inspector or other authority — Registers to be kept — Advice and further information

23 Salary and Wage Management   457
Keith G Cameron
I Salary Management
Need for a salary policy — Job descriptions — Job evaluation — Salary bands/grades — Salary surveys — Use of graphs — Deciding how much to pay — Rate for age — Salary anomalies — Employee benefits — Departmental budgets — Salary reviews

II Wage Management
Designing a company wage policy — Changing a wage structure — Job evaluation — Costing — Financing the wage structure — Designing the wage structure — Incentive element — Added value — Productivity agreements — Single status — Communication — Supervisory structure — Example of a wage policy statement — Checklist: changing a wage structure — Auditing the pay system

24 Employee Benefits   503
Peter Mumford
Attracting staff — Keeping and motivating — Basic salary — Benefits and salary — Company car — Pensions — Loans and mortgages —

Discounts on goods and services — Meals and entertainment — Gifts and special bonuses — Health insurance — Sabbaticals — Training and development — Share ownership — Keeping up to date

25 National Insurance 515
 Information Division, Department of Health and Social Security
 Who is covered by the schemes? — National insurance contributions for employees — Benefits — Special duties of employers under the industrial injuries scheme — Powers of inspectors — Sources of information

26 Administering Redundancy 533
 Peter Mumford
 Employment Protection Act 1978 — What is redundancy? — Lay-offs and short-time working — Proof of redundancy — Selection — Notice of redundancy — Consultation — Compensation — Rebates to employers — Insolvency — Appeals — Alternative employment — Tribunal awards — Company policy — Corporate planning — Employment services and agencies

27 Employee Relations 549
 J L Cookson
 Trade union recognition — Arrangements with trade unions

28 Industrial Relations Law 561
 F W Rose
 Trade union membership — Advisory, Conciliation and Arbitration Service (ACAS) — Legal status of an employers' association — Legal status of a trade union — Collective agreements — Significance of labour relations law — Trade unions and industrial action — Conduct protected against legal action

29 Industrial Training 577
 Derek Torrington
 The need for training in companies — Administering the training function — Training for different categories of employee — Training methods

PART SIX   THE MANAGEMENT OF PHYSICAL ASSETS

30 The Administration of Commercial Property 593
 Philip Westwood
 Factors affecting the selection of a building — Professional advice —

Acknowledgements

The publishers wish to thank the following for permission to quote their work:

The prime source for Chapter 23, Salary and Wage Management, is two booklets in the Industrial Society's 'notes for Managers' series, *Salary Management* and *Changing a Wage Structure.*

Chapter 19, The Design and Control of Forms, contains material from *Cernach's Work Study in the Office,* by Rod Revell, published by Anbar Management Publications, Wembley, London.

Editor's Preface

It is six years since the fifth edition of this Handbook appeared. In that time the scope of the company secretary's work has not radically changed. What has changed very considerably has been the nature of the information he or she requires to carry out the work efficiently. The previous edition recognized the rapidly-increasing importance of the electronics revolution; this edition confirms that many time-honoured methods of working are now obsolete.

A few chapters, such as *The Conduct of Meetings*, required only updating to incorporate changes in law and regulations. Others, such as *Industrial Relations Law*, while keeping the same framework, now reflect the massive development of this aspect of the law in recent years. *Data Processing* and *Managing the Modern Office* (formerly *Managing Office Equipment*) have been completely rewritten, while other chapters have had to be extensively revised (and in some cases re-named). The chapters on *Company Law, Taxation, Employment Law* and *National Insurance* are, in effect, rewrites in the light of changes in legislation and of decided cases since the last edition.

The law stated in this edition is as at 1 July 1987.

Derek Beattie

Illustrations

Figure

3.1	Return of allotments form	50
3.2	Share certificate	53
3.3	Indemnity for lost certificate	54
3.4	Shareholder's change of address	55
3.5	Letter of request	58
3.6	Statutory declaration by next of kin	60
3.7	Indemnity by next of kin	61
3.8	Power of attorney	62
3.9	Dividend mandate	64
3.10	Request for designation or redesignation of account	65
3.11	Stock transfer form	67
3.12	Talisman Sold Transfer	72
3.13	Talisman Bought Transfer	74
3.14	Rectification of transferee details	75
3.15	Split receipt	77
3.16	Suggested headings for transfer book	80
5.1	Profit and loss account format	123
5.2	Presentation of taxation details	124
5.3	Balance sheet format	125
5.4	Abbreviated profit and loss account of Pangloss PLC	131
5.5	Earnings, dividends and retentions of Pangloss PLC	132
5.6	Performance ratios for Pangloss PLC	132
5.7	Abbreviated 1985 balance sheet for Pangloss PLC	133
6.1	Uses of funds by individuals and institutions	141
6.2	Selected sources of capital funds for industrial and commercial companies	142
7.1	Example of a corporation tax computation	156
7.2	Entries to make in the tax accounts	162

7.3	Example of allowances for expenditure on industrial buildings	163
7.4	Example of normal loss relief	166
7.5	Example of terminal loss relief	167
7.6	Example of set-off of ACT	169
7.7	Simplified example to show that sale as a going concern is better than liquidation where assets have appreciated	171
11.1	Strategy selection for bid submission	234
11.2	Strategy selection for bid procurement	235
11.3	Utility function of union negotiator	236
11.4	Expected value of offers to union negotiator	237
11.5	Bargaining zone in management – union negotiation	237
11.6	Influence of time on negotiation	239
11.7	Dos and don'ts for negotiator handling opening stages	241
16.1	Path to improving effectiveness	320
16.2	Activity sampling	324
16.3	Activity sampling	325
16.4	Management controls	327
16.5	Choices available in work measurement	328
17.1	Creation of a block layout	338
17.2	Relationship diagram	339
17.3	Characteristics of office layout	340
17.4	Typical open-space or landscaped office	341
17.5	Typical open-plan office layout	342
17.6	Environmental standards	345
17.7	Building assessment	348
17.8	Office floor for a company headquarters	349
17.9	Open-space layout	350
17.10	Cellular office layout	351
19.1	Spacing for computer printers	375
19.2	'Sales by department' form	377
19.3	'Sales by department': alternative sheet method	377
19.4	Example of boxed input	379
19.5	Vertical boxed input	379
19.6	Example of two-part form	380
23.1	Job questionnaire	463
23.2	Ranking chart	466
23.3	Job evaluation matrix	467
23.4	Example of comparative questionnaire	469
23.5	Salary structure	470
23.6	Comparison of old and new salary structures	472
23.7	Merit-based salary review form	476
23.8	Scattergram of total earnings (excluding overtime) related to job evaluation points	483

Illustrations xvii

23.9	Example of a wage structure of the Philips premium pay plan type	487
25.1	Rates and earnings brackets for 1986/87	519
26.1	Redundancy statistics	534
31.1	Typical long-term maintenance programme	620
33.1	Line and staff functions within the transport services activity	643
33.2	A simple organization for a small company	643
33.3	Transport services organization for a medium-sized company	644
33.4	Transport services organization for a large group of companies	645
33.5	Standing costs and running costs of various types of vehicle	649
33.6	UK speed limits for goods-registered vehicles	650
33.7	Example of a tachograph chart	654
33.8	Layout of a simple monthly vehicle costing record	666
33.9	Example of a vehicle operating cost record sheet	668
33.10	Form for reporting vehicle defects	672
34.1	Bomb-threat checklist	716

Notes on Contributors

Ronald G Anderson (Managing the Modern Office) is a former Senior Lecturer at West Bromwich College of Commerce and Technology and also at Walsall College of Technology. He worked for many years as an accountant in general business. He is a Fellow of both the Institute of Cost and Management Accountants and the Institute of Management Services, and has diplomas in administrative management and organization and methods from the Institute of Administrative Management. His interests cover a wide range of accounting, office administration and all aspects of computing, and he is the author of several books, including *A Concise Dictionary of Data Processing and Computer Terms* and *A Dictionary of Management Terms*.

Robert C Appleby (Reducing Office Costs) is Head of Department of Business Studies at Worcester Technical College. He has a BSc in Economics from the London School of Economics, London University. He worked for many years in the North Eastern Electricity Board, particularly in accountancy and organisation and methods. He commenced teaching at West Bromwich College of Commerce and Technology in 1965 and moved to Worcester Technical College in 1970. He is an Associate Member of the Institute of Chartered Secretaries and Administrators. His publications include *Modern Business Administration* (Fourth edition, Pitman, 1986) and revision of *Office Organization and Method* (Mills and Standingford, Pitman, 1986 edition).

Stephen Badger (Sources of Finance) is a Director in the Corporate Finance Department of Morgan Grenfell & Co. Limited. He was educated at Sherborne School in Dorset and Pembroke College, Oxford, where he read Greats. He joined Morgan Grenfell on leaving Oxford and became a director in 1977. He is an Associate of the Institute of Bankers and of the Institute of Chartered Secretaries and Administrators.

Notes on Contributors xix

Keith G Cameron (Salary and Wage Management) is Personnel Director of Currys. A graduate in Social Science, he was formerly Personnel Director of Levi Strauss for Northern Europe and has worked for three other international companies.

Malcolm Carlisle (Fair Trading) has a BA in History from Cambridge. He worked for six years in the Pharmaceuticals Division of ICI, marketing ethical drugs in Europe. For three years he was based with ICI Holland BV. Thereafter he qualified as a barrister and joined the legal Department of Colgate-Palmolive Ltd in 1977 where he became the Deputy Group Legal Adviser. Since 1983 he has been European Legal Counsel with the Kendall Company, Colgate's largest subsidiary.

John Cavilla (The Management and Maintenance of Buildings) is a Senior Lecturer in the Department of Building Economics at The South Bank Polytechnic. Before becoming a full-time lecturer in 1983 he spent some twenty-two years in the construction industry where he gained a wide experience of responsible positions in contracting, environmental services engineering and architecture. He graduated with a BSc (Hons) from the University of Manchester Institute of Science and Technology, and is a corporate member of the Chartered Institute of Building and the British Institute of Management.

J L Cookson (Employee Relations) is Principal Lecturer in Labour Law in the Department of Management at Manchester Polytechnic. After graduating in Law from Cambridge University, he spent four years in private legal practice followed by three years in corporate planning overseas. His particular academic interest is in labour law and its impact on industrial relations at organizational level, on which subject he has lectured extensively in both the public and private sectors of industry. He has acted as Independent Chairman of the Lancashire Health Authority's Conciliation Panel for Dispute Settlement and as an External Arbitrator on collective disputes in the private sector. Publications include *Handbook of Industrial Relations* (Gower, 1972) and *Encyclopaedia of Personnel Management* (Gower, 1974).

J C Craig (Taxation) is a taxation partner of KMG Thomson McLintock, chartered accountants, in Glasgow, where he deals with both personal and company taxation. He is a Member of the Institute of Chartered Accountants of Scotland and a former convener of its taxation committee.

Desmond Fitzpatrick (The Conduct of Meetings) is a company secretary within an international oil company. A graduate in Economics of Newcastle University, he was a visiting lecturer at the City of London Polytechnic from

1975-85 and he now lectures and writes on London's history and architecture. He has been a visiting lecturer at the City University since 1982.

Patricia George (Working Conditions) was Senior Adviser of the Industrial Society's Information and Personnel Advisory Services Department. Miss George is an Associate Member of the Institute of Personnel Management, and is now a Principal Personnel Officer working for Surrey County Council.

V J Gersten (Company Law) is a solicitor in general practice in central London. He was born in Liverpool and, on graduating with an LLB from Liverpool University, lectured for some years in law at Hendon College of Technology.

J M Alastair Gibson (The Role of O & M) is a Vice President, a Fellow and an Institute Medallist of the Institute of Administrative Management and has a Diploma in Management Studies. He is a Fellow of the British Institute of Management and a Member Emeritus of the Association for Systems Management (USA). He was a member of the Institute's Council from 1964-84 and has served as the Vice Chairman and the Chairman of the Institute Council. He has also served as Vice Chairman or Chairman of numerous committees and is currently Chairman of the Editorial Board. He has lectured for the Institute at branches, and at residential courses and has had considerable teaching experience in Glasgow and Sheffield on Institute and other management courses. He is a past Governor of the Management Systems Training Council and has given papers to National Conferences of the Association for Systems Management, the most recent being at Boston, USA in 1983. Mr Gibson, now retired, has had industrial experience in steel tubes, heavy engineering and petro-chemical and animal feeds and is currently a Hampshire County Councillor.

Philip Goacher (Data Processing) began his computing career whilst working in the gas industry in 1966. Since then he has been the Technical Director in a software house (1970-74), Technical Applications Manager at a computer bureau (1974-76), Managing Director of a computing consultancy (1977-83), and Managing Director of the British Computer Society's trading company (1984-86). Currently he is a Director of Wordcraft Limited, a company specializing in word processing and electronic publishing, and the Managing Director of APL Software Limited, a worldwide software marketing company. He is a Member of the British Computer Society and the Institute of Data Processing Managers and is a Fellow of the British Institute of Management.

Alan Hobkirk (The Law of Contract) is an Assistant Director with the

Notes on Contributors

Scottish Vocational Education Council where he has overall responsibility for business education. Previously he was employed as a Principal Lecturer in Law at Slough College of Higher Education where he specialized in commercial and employment law. Having obtained MA and LLB degrees from Edinburgh University, Mr Hobkirk spent several years in the legal civil service before taking up lecturing.

Colin Jones (Intellectual Property Rights) is a partner in a provincial firm of chartered patent agents. After graduating from Cambridge in Mechanical Sciences, he joined Metropolitan Vickers (later AEI and now part of GEC) as a graduate apprentice. After working on steam turbine engineering he entered the patent profession in private practice where he qualified and became a Fellow of the Chartered Institute of Patent Agents. He is a contributor to the *European Patent Handbook* (Longman Professional, 1986) and *C.I.P.A. Guide to the Patents Act 1977* (Sweet & Maxwell, 1984) both of which are published by arrangement with the Chartered Institute of Patent Agents.

Audrey Laird (Maintaining a Company Share Register) is a manager in the Trust and Investment Department of KMG Thomson McLintock, chartered accountants, Glasgow, and has had several years' experience of dealing with company registration work.

P D V Marsh (Negotiation) is Commercial Director of British Smelter Constructions Limited. He was formerly Commercial Director of M.T.S.O. Ltd and prior to that Manager Projects and Operations Co-ordination with the Submarine Systems Division of Standard Telephones and Cables Ltd. Mr. Marsh started his commercial career with the National Coal Board where he became their Chief Contracts Officer. He qualified as a solicitor in 1951 and obtained a BA degree in Management Sciences in 1976. He is the author of *Handbook of Contract Negotiation* and *Contracting for Engineering and Construction Projects*, both published by Gower.

Peter Mumford (Employee Benefits; Administering Redundancy) was a personnel manager in industry and now lectures in management at Brighton Polytechnic. He has been a management consultant for a number of years, specializing in management and organizational development and has worked with a variety of industrial organizations, as well as local government departments. Following his book *Redundancy and Security of Employment* (1978) he has written a number of video scripts for training programmes, including 'Styles of Leadership' and is now devising and writing a series of CBT training programs 'Office Skills' for VPS Interactive.

Rod Revell (Setting up a New Office; The Design and Control of Forms) was born and bred in Liverpool. He started his management services career in 1969 at the age of nineteen, when he worked for a major shipping line. He later moved to the East Midlands where he spent seven years in the distribution industry and three in local government. In 1980 he moved 'down south' into the world of insurance where he is currently employed. He is a Member of the British Institute of Management and of the Institute of Management Services. In addition to O & M and business systems he also has six years' experience as an administration manager, which has enabled him to write the 1986 revision of Harry Cemach's classic *Work Study in the Office* for Anbar Publications. Previously he wrote a handbook entitled *Computers and the Management Services Officer* for the Institute of Management Services.

W P Ridley (The Annual Accounts) is a partner in Wood Mackenzie and Company, a firm of stockbrokers he joined in 1973 after five years as a financial consultant with Merrett Cyriax Associates. He read law at Oxford and became an Associate of the Institute of Chartered Accountants in 1961. He taught in Uganda and at Hendon Technical College before joining the Economic and Investment Research Department of the Bank of London and South America. Between 1965 and 1968, Mr Ridley worked for the Commonwealth Development Corporation.

F W Rose (Employment Law; Industrial Relations Law) is Principal Lecturer in Law at the City of Birmingham Polytechnic and Course Director for the Solicitors' Final Course. Mr Rose has an LLM from Birmingham University and an LLM from King's College, London. He served as Assistant to the Secretary of Associated Iliffe Press Limited before spending a year at the Institute of Actuaries in a similar function. He is an Associate of the Institute of Chartered Secretaries and Administrators and he was called to the Bar at Gray's Inn. He is the author of *Personnel Management Law* (Gower) and has had several articles published in the *Legal Executive*.

Richard Service (Value Added Tax) is a taxation manager in the Glasgow office of KMG Thomson McLintock. Since qualifying as a chartered accountant in 1978, he has specialized in taxation, dealing with all aspects of the subject but with particular attention to VAT. He is also a part-time lecturer in the Department of Taxation at Glasgow University, principally involved in the teaching of the Bachelor of Accountancy degree.

Richard Sleight (The Role of the Company Secretary) is a Fellow of the Institute of Chartered Secretaries and Administrators and a past member of council. He has been assistant to the chief executive of Legal and General Assurance Society, the second largest insurance company in the UK, the secretary to the company, the head of the investment planning department

Notes on Contributors

and subsequently of the corporate planning department. He is currently assistant general manager responsible for personnel planning. He has contributed articles on pensions, employee benefits and other financial subjects to leading newspapers and journals, has broadcast from time to time and writes regularly for the *Guardian* newspaper on these topics.

A J Slinn (Security Policy and Administration) is Editor of *International Security Review*, of *Security Times*, of *Securitech* and of the *International Professional Security Association's Yearbook*. A member of the governing body of IPSA, a member of the American Society for Industrial Security he is also consultant editor to the *Handbook of Security* and has both written and lectured on security topics.

Derek Torrington (Industrial Training) is Senior Lecturer in Personnel Management at the University of Manchester Institute of Science and Technology. Previously he spent fifteen years in the engineering industry and five years at Manchester Polytechnic. Publications include *Successful Personnel Management* (Staples Press, 1969), *Face to Face* (Gower, 1972), *Handbook of Industrial Relations* (Gower, 1972), *Handbook of Management Development*, with D F Sutton (Gower, 1973), *Administration of Personnel Policies*, with R Naylor (Gower, 1974), *Encyclopaedia of Personnel Management* (Gower, 1974), and *Comparative Industrial Relations in Europe* (Associated Business Press, 1978). His major text book, *Personnel Management* was published in 1979 by Prentice-Hall International. He is a Companion of the Institute of Personnel Management.

Peter A Verreck (Managing Mergers and Acquisitions) originally worked in the development of the Australian nickel-mining industry before training as a psychologist. He then worked for a number of years in behavioural analysis for a variety of settings in the the public sector. He has recently returned to the private sector and is currently involved in the restructuring and expansion of a company concerned with energy conservation and control.

Guy Vincent (Debt Collection) is a solicitor and partner in the firm of Bower Cotton & Bower who practise in the Chancery Lane area. His particular interest is litigation and commercial work.

Philip Westwood (The Administration of Commercial Property) is a Senior Lecturer in the Department of Building Economics at South Bank Polytechnic. A chartered surveyor and chartered builder, he holds an MPhil degree in Building Legislation. Before becoming a full-time lecturer he worked for many years for a large building contractor as a surveyor and estimator. He has lectured for a number of years in building economics, building technology and management to surveyors and building technologists. He is currently embarking on a research programme into the adaptation of housing to accommodate the needs of the disabled.

Frank H Woodward (Managing Transport Services) is a Fellow of the Institute of Chartered Secretaries and Administrators, a Fellow of the Royal Society of Arts and a Member of the Chartered Institute of Transport with over thirty years practical experience in all types of fleet operation. Before retiring in 1983, he was the Managing Director of a large industrial fleet of over 3,500 vehicles. An author, journalist and well-known speaker at conferences and seminars, he has written many books on fleet management and finance and on road transport distribution. His latest book is *Controlling Company Car Costs* with Peter N C Cooke (Gower, 1986).

Part One
The Constitution and Conduct of Companies

1

The Role of the Company Secretary

Richard Sleight

THE SECRETARY'S LEGAL STATUS

In 1885, every employee was expected to know his place, not least the company secretary. The classic legal view of the secretary's role was given in that year by Lord Brett, Master of the Rolls, in the case of Newlands *v* National Employers' Accident Association Limited:

> A secretary is a mere servant; his position is that he is to do what he is told, and no person can assume that he has any authority to represent anything at all; nor can anyone assume that statements made by him are necessarily to be accepted as trustworthy without further enquiry . . .

Not only a servant but likely enough a rogue as well!

Yet in spite of the gradual change in the social fabric since then, this view of the secretary's function continued to persist in law, partly perhaps because it provided a convenient excuse for anyone who wished to avoid a contract. In 1900 it was held that a company secretary could not issue notices for a company meeting unless he had the authority of the directors contained in a board resolution. Similarly, five years later, judgment was given that a company secretary had no power to register a transfer of shares if the directors could reject transfers and had not given their consent to this particular transfer. Again, in 1916 (Daimler Company Limited *v* Continental Tyre & Rubber Company (Great Britain) Limited), it was held that a company secretary could not begin legal proceedings in the company's name unless he had the authority of the directors contained in a board resolution.

Surprisingly enough, a similar view of the company secretary's role was expressed in cases coming before the courts as late as 1966. Surprising, because this traditional legal view ran directly counter to commonly accepted business practice and to the very different picture of the secretary's function which emerged from the Companies Acts. In the 1948 Act for example, the secretary is defined as an 'officer' of the company equated in this respect with directors and managers ($s455$). And any 'officer' may be personally liable if certain provisions of the Act have not been complied with ($ss5, 7, 24, 25$ or 30). On a winding-up, it is the secretary, together with other 'officers' of the company who can be proceeded against for misapplication or misappropriation of the company's assets, for misfeasance or breach of trust.

Moreover, the authority and responsibility of the secretary as an officer whose actions can bind the company does not only arise in relation to certain defined events. The responsibility also emerges with regard to the day-to-day functions he carries out. Examples are: issuing share and debenture certificates ($s80$), signing the annual return and certifying the documents attached to it ($ss126(1)$ and $127(1)$), delivering particulars of mortgages and charges for registration ($ss96$ and 97), issuing notices for company meetings ($ss130, 131$ and 132), notifying the Registrar of alterations to the share capital ($ss62$ and 63), and preparing agenda and keeping the minutes for meetings ($s145$).

But in spite of these indications in the Companies Acts, defendants continued to argue successfully that a company contract authorized by a company secretary was not binding on the company. Case law was at last brought into line with modern practice in the case of Panorama Development (Guildford) Limited v Fidelis Furnishing Fabrics Limited in May 1971.

The only unfortunate feature of this case from the point of view of the secretarial profession was that it required a fraudulent action by a company secretary to establish that a company secretary had authority to act on behalf of his company. Here the company, Fidelis Furnishing Fabrics, known to be a company of good repute and credit, entered into a contract with the plaintiff company to hire executive cars to meet important customers and potential buyers at Heathrow Airport. The actual hiring and insurance agreements were signed by the Fidelis company secretary and it later emerged that the cars had not been employed to meet customers but had been used by the company secretary for his own private use.

As in similar cases in the past, the defendant company Fidelis disputed the payment of any hire charges for the cars on the grounds that even if it were agreed that the contract had been concluded with Fidelis and not just with the company secretary of Fidelis acting in his personal capacity, a contract entered into by the company secretary was not binding on the company.

Both the judge of first instance and the Court of Appeal answered that the company secretary's action must be regarded as binding on the company. It was especially (and at last!) remarked that the much earlier cases allocating a humbler role to a secretary had arisen in relation to the Companies Acts as they had stood at the time these earlier cases came to court and that since then the secretary's position and status had greatly increased, an increase that was recognized in the current Companies Acts. Since the case itself was concerned with the administrative operations of the company's affairs, the judgment did not go further than to pronounce the secretary as capable of acting on behalf of the company in these affairs, such as employing staff, ordering cars and 'so forth'. A clear-cut pronouncement on the secretary's authority with regard to other contracts which a company may enter into awaits another case bearing on this aspect.

An encouraging indication of the enhanced status of the company secretarial function occurred in 1978 when Mr John Cockcroft, a Conservative Member of Parliament, presented a private member's bill adopting a long standing proposal of the Institute of Chartered Secretaries and Administrators. Though the bill eventually failed, very considerable publicity and support were obtained for its objective: that company secretaries should be required by law to be professionally qualified.

The 1980 Companies Act has, however, taken matters decisively forward. The secretary's enhanced commercial existence has now become important enough for the law to require directors to pay particular attention to the sort of person appointed as secretary. Firstly they must appoint a person 'who appears to them to have the requisite knowledge and experience to discharge the functions of the secretary'. Perhaps case law will show this requirement, general as it is, to have teeth that can bite. Secondly, the secretary must be professionally qualified or qualified by experience. That is, he must be a member of one of those professional bodies listed in the Act, *or* someone who was the secretary when the Act came into force, *or* who in three of the last five years was a secretary and not merely of a private company.

Among the illustrious professional bodies listed in the Act, members of which may be appointed as secretaries, is of course the Institute of Chartered Secretaries and Administrators — not an exclusive category however as in practical terms it could not be. If you are a professionally qualified accountant or a 'barrister, advocate or solicitor', you are considered fit to be a secretary. Finally, and again to be practical, the directors may appoint someone who 'by virtue of his holding or having held any other position or his being a member of any other body' appears to them to be capable of being a secretary.

Broad as the final requirement is, the very positive step forward taken by the 1980 Companies Act is to recognize in statute requirements for the person who can be appointed as secretary.

Moreover, the Act places a liability on the secretary as well as on the directors, if the company does not comply with a wide range of provisions. This is well in keeping with the wider involvement of the secretary in company management.

All these items are very much within the province of the company secretary. So also are many of the provisions which were enacted in the 1981 Companies Act, with its main impetus the EEC fourth directive on company accounts. Also of particular interest to company secretaries are the provisions relaxing the 1980 Act and enabling companies to purchase their own shares under defined circumstances. But of course the grand consolidating legislation is the 1985 Companies Act.

Thus, in the space of 100 years, the secretary has ceased to be a servant and become a recognized part of management. He no longer has to do what he is told nor can he shelter behind this as an excuse. He is personally liable for the effects of the management decisions he makes and has implemented.

BASIC DUTIES OF THE COMPANY SECRETARY

Having discussed the secretary's legal status as an officer of the company, it is interesting to consider the actual responsibilities he normally undertakes in the modern company. In order to obtain an objective description of the tasks he might actually perform, I quote below from an independent source. It is the job description for the position of company secretary prepared by a leading firm of management consultants. The description is based on an examination of the jobs carried out by the company secretary in 173 UK companies having annual sales varying in size from £600 000 to £500 million and covering the wide fields of commerce, industry and financial services. The description was published in *Executive Remuneration, the United Kingdom* by Management Centre Europe's executive compensation service, Brussels.

Basic function
1 The company secretary serves as secretary of the corporation in accordance with the corporation's charter, by-laws and other legal requirements
2 He arranges for meetings of the board of directors and keeps the minutes of such meetings
3 He signs corporate documents and affixes the corporate seal thereto where proper
4 He attends to corporate notices and correspondence, and conducts relations with shareholders on matters concerning the meetings of the shareholders and general corporate policy

Responsibilities

1. He makes arrangements for and gives notice of all board of directors' and shareholders' meetings
2. He directs the preparation of all minutes, agenda, notices, proxies, waivers of notice and subsequent correspondence in connection with meetings of the directors and shareholders
3. He attends all meetings of the board of directors and shareholders and keeps a record of the proceedings
4. He prepares written minutes of each board meeting and is responsible for providing departments with copies of resolutions or extracts from the minutes, where appropriate
5. He acts as custodian of the seal of the corporation; affixes the corporate seal and attests, signs or countersigns corporate documents when authorized
6. He acts as custodian of corporate documents, contracts, leases, deeds to corporate-owned property, minute books and all general records other than those required to be kept by the treasurer and the controller
7. He attends to corporate correspondence including inquiries from shareholders and the public concerning matters of general corporate policy
8. He keeps a current register of the names and addresses of each shareholder; signs, with the president, certificates for shares of the corporation
9. He maintains general charge of the stock transfer books of the corporation; files all corporate reports as prescribed by federal, state or other governmental authorities
10. He performs special assignments as requested by the president

SIGNIFICANCE OF THE SECRETARIAL DUTIES

The bare list of these secretarial duties needs further examination in order to convey some idea of the significance of the various activities and the purpose of the secretarial role in the modern company or organization. The tasks themselves, as listed in the job description, are covered in detail in other chapters of this book. So also are the governing conditions which control the exercise of these duties. These conditions are contained in statutes and their attaching regulations, in case law, in stock exchange requirements and in the organization's own rules and regulations set out in the memorandum and articles or similar document. What this chapter is concerned to do is to take a wider view and specify the key roles of the secretary in the modern business organization, in the public sector and in the very important area of local government or in the very varied activities which can be loosely grouped together as connected with non-profit-making organizations. In what follows, the word 'company' should be read, as far as the context allows, to include all of these three areas.

Company's legality

The secretary has a broad general responsibility to ensure that the company's actions and the company's existence remain within the law — he is the custodian of the company's legality.

The degree to which he exercises this responsibility will depend on the type of company and its organizational structure. At one end of the scale, a small company operating in a limited sector of the home market whose shares were not publicly held would afford the secretary comparatively restricted tasks under many of the items listed in the job description. On the other hand, simply because of the company's small size, the secretary would probably be very much more involved in the company's business operations.

At the other end of the scale, the large multinational company with operating subsidiaries in overseas countries would almost inevitably generate a large number of problems relating to its various corporate legal existences. Because of the volume of this legal work, it would not be unusual to find the secretarial function supplying centralized legal services to the company with the secretary in charge of the company's legal department.

But whatever the range of secretarial duties under this heading, the exercise of this responsibility is always essential and may sometimes be crucial to the continued existence of the company.

Legal disputes

Board disputes do happen — perhaps more frequently than some suppose. An important implication of the secretary's duty to ensure that the actions of the board are in compliance with the provisions of the law, is that if an occasion did arise when some or all of the directors wished to support a course of action which was not within the law, or the company's own powers, then the secretary would be obliged to make clear the legal implications of the proposed act and if necessary to take a stand against it being carried out. Similar professional and statutory obligations do of course govern the conduct of a company's accountant or the actuary of a life insurance company.

It is interesting to see that this issue is very much a live one in the secretarial profession in India today. In that country, in order to strengthen the ability of the secretary to take such a stand against the board on a point of law, the Ministry of Industrial Development and Company Affairs has considered the practicability of introducing a statutory requirement that a secretary with more than five years' service should not be removable without either a special resolution being passed or the approval of the central government.

Clearly, the business life of an Indian company secretary is a good deal more hazardous than that of his UK counterpart!

Responsibility to whom?

In view of what has been said about the secretary's legal responsibilities, it is clear that he owes part of his duties to the board as a whole. And in so far as the board's powers are exercised by and through the president or chairman, then in practice the secretary's responsibility will be to him. An equally common company structure would place the managing director, chief executive officer, or whatever title he may be known by, as the central person through whom the power of the board is exercised and by whom it is interpreted to the management. In these circumstances, therefore, the secretary would, again in practice, be responsible to him.

But in whatever way the role of president and managing director may vary from company to company or are combined in one individual, the central point to emerge is that the secretary, unlike any other purely executive officer of the company, derives a substantial part of his responsibilities and authority from the board and is in turn responsible to them, through either the chairman or the managing director. Conversely, if the secretary does not derive his responsibilities and authority in this way, although he may be secretary in name, in fact he cannot fully exercise a secretarial function and should more exactly be named as a chief administrative officer of the company.

Independence of the secretarial function

It follows that if the company secretary is to fulfil the complete secretarial role, it is of fundamental importance that in this respect he should be independent of any particular function, department or division within the company. It is worth repeating that the reason for this important principle of independence lies in the fact that the secretarial function relates to the activities of the company as a whole and this is why he is responsible to the effective representative of the board, be he president or managing director.

As corroboration of this view from outside the profession itself, not only is the secretary's independence commonly recognized in business practice but it is widely accepted by management consultants both in the UK and the USA and is implicit in the detailed job specification set out earlier.

It is no contradiction of this argument to say that it is not unusual to find the generalist role of the company secretary combined, in one and the same person, with a specialized function at *board level*. But because it is at board level, the separation of the secretarial function is preserved in, for example, the common combination of financial director and company secretary in one person.

Given this background, the secretary's contribution to his organization's success should stem from his uniquely privileged position — that he is afforded an overall view of the organization's activities. Exactly how this contribution is made will depend on the particular structure of the organization he works for. It may centre on a coordinating role aimed at producing the optimum conditions for board and management cooperation in the running of the company. That contribution may extend into any number of diverse fields including personnel work, public relations, legal work, corporate finance, investment, forward planning and so on. But however extended the secretarial role, one of its characteristic and essential features remains that of a separate function concerned with the affairs of the company as a whole.

THE INSTITUTE OF CHARTERED SECRETARIES AND ADMINISTRATORS (ICSA)

The Institute of Chartered Secretaries and Administrators — ICSA or 'The Institute' — is the one and only body representing the interests of the secretary, whether he is concerned in company work, either as an employee or as a consultant, or whether he is employed in non-company work in, for example, the very wide field of local government administration.

The influence of the Institute is shown by the 45 000 members worldwide with no fewer than 21 000 students. The administrative headquarters are in London where the Secretary and Chief Executive head the staff of 70 with the responsibility of servicing the central governing body, the Council and its Committees, providing the professional services and running the twice-yearly examinations. Most encouraging for the future of the profession and the careers of those who have or are going to be qualified secretaries is the strong marketing impetus being put behind the promotion of the chartered secretary function and behind the concept of professional administration. The strategic long-term plan published in 1986 should secure that the Institute's services keep pace with its members' growing and changing needs.

The recognition of the administrative function in the title of the Institute has been more than justified, when the very diverse business activities of its members are examined. The inclusion of 'administrators' in the Institute's title implicitly recognizes the cross-fertilization of disciplines which had been taking place for some time between the traditional subjects of secretarial knowledge — such as company law, taxation or accountancy — and the growing multiplicity of management knowledge. The title accepts in the fullest sense that it is the management and administrative skills which translate the technical expertise of a specialized field like company law or taxation into usable concepts with a practical application in modern business.

Of all professional qualifications, it is perhaps that of the Institute which

THE ROLE OF THE COMPANY SECRETARY

gives the widest practical conspectus of the business world whether this relates to a corporate or a non-corporate organization. And the evidence for this statement lies in the number of the Institute's members who take the examinations, not because they are intending to undertake a specifically secretarial job but because they want a business qualification which would give them a general acquaintance with the problems facing senior management and boards of directors. Effective and competent generalists are at a premium in today's world.

QUALIFICATIONS AND EXAMINATIONS

What then are the qualifications? Before itemizing the various areas of knowledge covered by the examinations, it is worth re-emphasizing that the subjects are treated from the point of view of top management or the board. This is just as much the case whether the subject relates directly to a board activity or whether it is concerned, for example, in evaluating the role of white-collar unions as a preliminary to framing a personnel policy.

It follows that fundamental to the exercise of the secretarial function should be an ability to see the wood for the trees. In sorting through a very wide range of knowledge, it is essential to see beyond the minutiae of the subject which in company law, for example, can be very involved. The end-purpose is always the effective and practical administration of the business or organization.

Analysing a situation, putting together recommendations and summarizing both clearly and concisely, then seeing that action is taken accordingly and monitoring the results are requirements in the exercise of any management position and the Institute's examinations point the way in this direction. It is alas only too common to find, even at the highest managerial levels, those executives who believe their colleagues or the board of directors prefer to read a fifteen-page report or suffer its equivalent in meeting time when, in ninety-nine cases out of a hundred, one or two pages could succinctly sum up the essence of the situation.

The qualifications designed to prepare the ground for these practical business skills start with basic business subjects: economics, law, statistics and mathematics for business, organizational behaviour with the application of the behavioural sciences to business and office administration/management. The most significant new subject is information technology, still an untouchable topic for too many British managers, with their in-built suspicions of computers, software and the electronic office. The same subject can be continued at a more advanced level in the Management of Systems paper which is one of the eight topics in the last two parts of the examination. Qualifiying in these eight topics requires a standard equivalent to a final degree at a British university.

Students can choose between three different groups for the last eight subjects: either a company secretarial group, or general and financial administration, or local government together with public service administration. The breadth of the syllabus and, by implication, the business disciplines catered for, indicates the wide appeal and use of the Institute's qualification. Throughout the emphasis is on producing an examination suitable to cover the full scope of business knowledge necessary for a top administrator.

It is not surprising that nearly one-half of all fully qualified chartered secretaries employed in the UK work outside the normal commercial or industrial company. They are either employed in the public service — local or national — or in organizations like the nationalized industries, the building societies, the co-operative societies, stock exchanges, trade associations, professional bodies, charitable organizations and many other diverse businesses.

Passing the examinations, which usually takes a minimum of four years' part-time study, is one thing. Qualifying as an associate of the Institute (ACIS) or a fellow (FCIS) is another. These further steps are not achieved until the successful examinee has acquired practical experience by exercising his skills: six years in the case of the associate and eight years for a fellow. In addition, the fellowship requires that if he has not been employed in a secretarial capacity, he must have been employed in a job equivalent to that of secretary or assistant secretary for a minimum of three years in the past ten. The equivalence here is intended to cover the multiplicity of jobs, other than those specifically of a secretarial nature, which might be peformed by a chartered secretarial administrator. Prior to gaining the experience, passing the examinations confers the grade of licentiate, but the requirement of practical experience is strictly enforced. A licentiate is not a member of the Institute and is not allowed to call himself a chartered secretary.

Members of the Institute are especially aware of the rapid and accelerating changes in the business environment. The Institute has responded to the need for further training by providing post-qualifying education on an expanding scale. The twenty years' strategic plan of the Institute mentioned earlier identifies as one of its five objectives the development of post-qualification education to be available to members and non-members alike, starting with updatings through short courses and seminars, later going on to provide more structured and examined advanced level courses and finally taking a longer-term view of the need for members to be able to be responsive and flexible to the changing requirements of the job market: a comprehensive and practical plan.

In a more traditional way *Administrator*, the monthly journal of the Institute, carries on where the examinations and the necessarily circumscribed activities of a particular job leave off. The journal is recognized as one of the leading monthly business periodicals.

The subjects covered by the journal make it clear that today's chartered secretary may be working in an incorporated business, in a part of today's very large public sector or in a non-profit-making organization. The latter might be a trade association, charity, research, educational or social organization, or a public relations service or parliamentary lobby, to name some but not all — a pretty formidable range of activities!

FUTURE DEVELOPMENTS

Looking back on the last dozen years, the structure and effectiveness of industry and commerce in the UK have been rocked by the property and stock market crash of 1974. It may seem a long time ago, but the bankruptcy of Rolls-Royce, the disastrous collapse of Vehicle and General and the traumatic crises of British Leyland and Burmah Oil were not trivial events. Only recently have the last of the straggling wounded who were pulled into the Bank of England's lifeboat at that time, swum off on their own again.

Since 1974 one of the great bull markets of the century has been in progress. Its momentum has been encouraged by the turn-round in the fortunes of British industry. The painful restructuring and bankruptcies which followed the downturn have been replaced by buoyant profits for the survivors.

It is a truism to say that the death or contraction of a large organization is not confined in its effect to the employees who lose their jobs or the shareholders who lose their capital. Customers and consumers may be vitally affected and large sums of public money may be at stake. There is nothing new about these effects. What is different today is the degree of public concern and involvement — and the growing degree of government intervention in part reflecting that concern.

The significance of the Wilson committee appointed by the then prime minister in 1977 to inquire into the role and functioning, at home and abroad, of financial institutions in the United Kingdom and their value to the economy, is that all these issues were brought into focus. More particularly the committee was required to review the provision of funds for industry and trade and to consider what changes might be required in the existing arrangements for the supervision of these institutions and whether the public sector should be extended. Never before had there been such an enormous and closely argued body of evidence assembled to show how the system of providing finance for British Industry and commerce worked and how its results were monitored.

The UK's membership of the Common Market puts these questions in a wider context. The USA has set a pattern for disclosure and Britain is still behind America in what it reveals. But by comparison, European companies are positively Victorian in the prudery with which they conceal their vital statistics.

Moreover, the questions of disclosure lead beyond the financial results of the company to consideration of its corporate goals. Is the function of the modern company simply to maximize profits for its shareholders within the legal limits of the country where it operates? Or should the company have other corporate goals like the interests of its employees — a point which was to be specifically recognized in the now defunct Companies Bill of 1978. Should the company specifically recognize objectives like the long-term satisfaction of its customers or the public interest, however imprecisely this may be defined? By their actions, most companies implicitly pay some attention to these other goals, and a larger and larger number of companies, among them some of the biggest and most successful in the UK explicitly adopt these other than profit-making concepts as part of their corporate philosophy.

Whether or not such thinking is simply realistic self-interest is beside the point. What matters is that this thinking recognizes and seeks to come to terms with new forces in society like the powerful consumer pressure groups typified by the Nader groups in America and the consumer movements in the UK, or with the public interest as represented by the use to which taxpayers' subsidies are put, or with the public's refusal to accept present levels of urban pollution.

Given these modifications of what must always remain the corporate goal — profit — what now becomes the role of the board, hitherto simply and straightforwardly defined as the supervision of management's performance in maximizing the return on the shareholder's capital? Do these wider responsibilities fall squarely on its shoulders as well?

These are not theoretical questions but practical issues whose resolution will have a profound effect on UK companies because European thinking on these matters is crystallizing round a very different type of philosophy from that in the UK. For example, in the UK the non-executive director is considered the most effective guardian of the shareholders' interests. But in West Germany, the two-tier structure of the supervisory board over and above an executive board is common, although it is not entirely clear who, ideally, should appoint the members of the supervisory board nor how, once appointed, they should retain their independence.

In European thinking, two-tier boards are closely connected with the vexed subject of employee participation in management and, again using the West German example, with appointment of worker or trade union representatives to the board. In this country, management and trade unions initially shrank from the idea of employees' representatives on a board. But support or opposition to the proposals put forward by the Bullock committee has since polarized depending on whether a union view or a management view is being expressed. The whole tradition of management staying on one side of the bargaining table and workers on the other is being rethought and replaced by the idea of a joint enterprise where both sides can agree to pursue certain common goals. The increasingly common examples in the UK of Japanese companies operating on a new joint management/employee base could be just the tip of the iceberg.

The 1980 Act incorporated the provisions of the EEC directive regulating the formation of public companies and the maintenance and alteration of their capital, introducing the concept and the reality of the public limited company or PLC. Of special interest to company secretaries, it was this Act which placed the duty, already mentioned, on directors to appoint a qualified person as a company secretary, not unfortunately exclusively a chartered secretary. In 1985 the consolidating Companies Act was put on the statute book, sweeping together previous company legislation.

The trend is clear. Ever more complex legal provisions requiring ever more alert interpreters who, like company secretaries, have to be able to take the broader view. Legislation in the companies' field is only one of the areas having a major impact on the company secretary. The Financial Services Act of 1986 encapsulates the far-reaching changes which are reverberating through the City of London, consequent on the forced abandonment of single capacity in the securities' market. Single capacity enshrined the time-honoured principle of the separation of agent's and principal's functions, between stockbroker on the one hand and market-maker or jobber on the other. The new combination of these two functions within the same organization, largely as a result of the threatened erosion of the Stock Exchange's market basis in the City by overseas competition, heralds one of the biggest structural and business shake-ups that the City has seen, with repercussions for British industry and commerce whose end cannot be forecast. The same wind which was blowing through industry in the 'seventies eventually hit the City in the mid 1980s, with the same potential for greater competition and greater profit as London becomes yet more important as a world financial centre.

Financial services in all their various forms and conducted in many cases by large conglomerates which have to resolve the problems of conflicting interests acting to the disadvantage of the client, are the subject of a vast experiment in self-regulation, which if it is not seen to work satisfactorily will eventually be replaced by legislation. The UK, which pioneered the concept of limited liability, is pioneering the financial services revolution in a more through-going way than any other world financial centre has yet done.

In this rapidly moving scene, the skills of the chartered secretary are more than ever required. What continues to be needed, as a necessary preliminary to moving forward, is the careful definition and analysis of the aims and methods of our present company structure, and the relative responsibilities of employees, management, directors and shareholders. The work to be done requires the skills of lawyers, of accountants, of management consultants and many others. The company secretary needs to be fully aware of these developments if he is to adapt to the changing role of the company. At the same time he has a wide practical experience to contribute, covering many aspects of the problem often from the vantage point of a non-technical view, which should enable him to see the broad significances involved.

In all this the secretarial profession, acting among other ways through the collective voice of the Institute of Chartered Secretaries and Administrators, can be expected to exert an increasingly important influence. It was because of the Institute's initiative that, among other points, provision for a company secretary on the UK model was specifically written into the EEC draft company law statute. No mean achievement, when it is remembered that on the Continent the job of company secretary is usually shared between two or three executives and that there is no exact equivalent to this post. One thing is certain: whatever the future holds, it promises an expanding role for the chartered secretary, in whichever area of expertise he exercises his skills. 'Strategic Directions', the central document issued by the Institute in 1986 on the way forward over the next twenty years, demonstrates that the Institute is fully able to support its members in adapting to change and meeting the future challenges.

2

Company Law

V J Gersten

The law deals with relations between persons — normally human beings — their rights and duties. The economic life of the country depends on the law's extension of the concept of personality to include non-human persons called corporations.

When people associate for a common purpose, the law makes it possible for them to create a separate 'person', a corporation of which they are the members, to carry out that purpose. A corporation can perform many of the economic functions that humans can. It can, for example:

1 Own property
2 Employ people
3 Make contracts
4 Sue and be sued

It can do these things only through the agency of human beings, its members or people appointed by them. The advantage of the corporation is that its existence (and hence its ownership of property or its capacity to carry out contracts or be sued on them) is independent of its members and continues even when its membership changes.

LIMITED COMPANIES

The most common type of corporation is the limited company. The law relating to limited companies had its statutory origin in the Joint Stock

Companies Act 1856. A series of further acts culminated in the Companies Act 1948, but subsequent piecemeal changes have led to the most recent consolidating Act — the Companies Act 1985. In this chapter the 1985 Act is referred to as 'the Act' and when the number of a section is given it refers to a section of the Act, unless otherwise stated.

The Act provides a simple method of forming a corporation, the minimum requirements are:

1 Delivery of a printed document — the memorandum of association — with two witnessed signatures
2 Delivery of a statutory declaration that the requirements of the Act have been complied with
3 Delivery of a statement of nominal capital (on which duty is assessed)
4 Details of first director(s) and secretary and their signed consents to act
5 Payment of a fee

— to the Registrar of Companies. The Registrar then issues a certificate of incorporation which is conclusive evidence of the existence of a separate legal person, a registered company. Its existence continues until either its members or a court terminates it by 'winding up'.

Types of registered company

Section 1(2) of the Act distinguishes three main types of company:

1 Company limited by shares
2 Company limited by guarantee
3 Unlimited company

Most companies are of the first type and throughout this chapter, 'company' will be used to mean 'company limited by shares'.

Advantages of the company structure

The limited company format has been developed to facilitate the aggregation of money to be used for production and trading. The people who supply the money exchange it for shares in the company's capital and thereby become members of the company. The members appoint directors to manage the company's affairs, retaining the right to dismiss a director. The profits that the company makes are available for distribution as dividends to the members.

The aspect of company structure that makes it attractive to investors is that the members are separated, not only from the management of the enterprise but also, by the concept of limited liability, from the disasters of mismanagement.

Shares and limited liability

Each share that a company issues when collecting money from its members has a nominal value which is fixed by the company's memorandum of association.

It is not necessary for a member to pay the company the whole nominal value of a share when purchasing it from the company. If the company accepts less then it can, by making a *call*, require the shareholder to pay the difference between the initial payment and the nominal value.

The amount of money that has actually been paid to the company for its shares is called the paid-up capital.

At the time a company is wound up, a member is entitled to receive an amount, proportionate to his shareholding, of any of the company's money left over after its debts have been paid. This money is known as the equity: it could, of course be zero; the shareholder of a share that was not fully paid up might have a call made on him at the winding-up to help pay the company's debts, but he cannot be asked to pay more than the amount unpaid on his shares. That is the limit of his liability for the company's debts.

The company is distinct from its members

The principle that the company is separate from its members who own its shares cannot be too powerfully imprinted upon the mind of anyone in commerce. The idea is abstract but its practical consequences are only too apparent.

An unfortunate small trader may have to walk to a meeting of company creditors because, having failed to recover his debts from the company, he has had to sell his mini van. He then may be knocked down by the Rolls-Royce belonging to one of the company's directors on his way to the same meeting to explain that the company cannot pay its debts because the harsh economic climate caused it such losses that it had to cease trading. The director may keep his Rolls-Royce but the victim of the accident has no claim against the company. (Any claim for damages for the accident is of course another matter.) The director is not personally liable for the debts of the company even though those debts have been incurred because of recklessness or misjudgement on his part.

The armour plate of limited liability may be pierced only if the director concerned can be proved to have behaved fraudulently, but in practice fraud is extremely hard to prove. The expense and difficulty of proving it makes it virtually impossible for the individual creditor to use it as a method of getting his money back.

Moreover, most business failures are not the result of fraud but of recklessness, incompetence or misfortune. This is of little comfort to the small businessman, and anyone running a small company or a small business of any kind should never give extended credit to a small limited company without taking personal guarantees from the directors of that company. If this is done the individual directors will be liable for the company's debts like any other guarantor of a debt.

Conversely, the officers or other persons dealing with the affairs of a small limited company should make sure that they always deal in the company's name so that it can never be suggested that they were acting in their personal capacities or in some way guaranteeing the credit of the company.

The most famous cautionary student's case dealing with these principles is Salomon v Salomon and Company Ltd (1897), usually known as Salomon's Case. Salomon had a boot-manufacturing business. He created a company called Salomon and Company Ltd in which he was the principal shareholder, and sold his boot and shoe business to it partly for shares and partly for debentures; in other words he transferred his business to the company partly in consideration of a promise by the company (in which he was principal shareholder) to pay money to him secured in such a way as to give him priority over its future creditors. The company went into liquidation, its assets being sufficient to repay his loan but not to repay subsequent creditors to whom the company owed £7000. These creditors received nothing. The company was of course almost wholly owned by Salomon himself, and as he was trading for profit it might be thought unfair that the money which he ought to have had at risk was repaid to him in priority to the money risked by the suppliers who had given the company credit. The case was not as unfair as this suggests, because particulars of the notional loan made by Salomon to the company and the fact that this debt had priority over the claims of subsequent creditors could have been ascertained by checking the register of the company at the Companies Registry. If it is proposed to advance substantial sums of money to a company or to give it extended credit such a check should be made. It is clearly impracticable to do this every time a company is given credit, but the risk of the Salomon situation arising must be borne in mind by any creditor of a company.

Publicity

Because of the limitation on a company's liability to pay its debts, the Act requires it to send a great deal of information about itself to the Registrar.

Time-limits are laid down for filing the information, and severe penalties are provided for in the event of default. It may be of some comfort to company secretaries to know that these time-limits are not enforced with great stringency, and the maximum penalties for default are not normally exacted.

This information may be inspected by anyone and one of the purposes of the publicity is to enable people to judge the company's creditworthiness.

Another purpose is to help people to judge whether a company's shares are worth buying. This leads to a distinction between 'public' and 'private' companies.

Public and private companies

A public company is a company whose shares are on sale to the public at large. A private company *must not* offer any shares or debentures to the public. (s81(1)). A public company must satisfy the following requirements:

1   It must be stated in the memorandum of the company that it is to be a public company
2   Its name must end with the words Public Limited Company (PLC)
3   Its capital must not be less than the authorized minimum currently fixed at £50 000
4   At least 25 per cent of the nominal value of its shares and the whole of any premium must be paid up before allotment

The former requirement that public companies must have a minimum membership of seven has now been abolished. Both public and private companies now need only a minimum membership of two.

Commencing business

Section 117 of the Act provides that a public company cannot do business or exercise any borrowing powers unless the Registrar has issued it with a certificate entitling it to do so or it is reregistered as a private company. To obtain the certificate the company must apply to the Registrar in the prescribed form and deliver a statutory declaration in the prescribed form stating:

1   That the nominal value of the company's allotted share capital is not less than the authorized minimum
2   The amount paid up on the allotted share capital of the company at the time of the application
3   The amount of the preliminary expenses of the company (or, if the precise amount cannot be ascertained, an estimate of the expenses) and the persons to whom any of those expenses have been paid or are payable and
4   Any sum or benefit paid or to be paid to the promoter and the consideration for that payment of benefit

Practical company formation

It is first necessary to choose a name for the company. Until the 1980 Companies Act the name had to be first approved by the Registrar of

Companies. The company's name is dealt with in the next section but it is sensible to check with the Companies Registry that the proposed name is not the same as, or very similar to, the name of an existing company.

Company formation firms. There are many firms who make a business of forming companies and the easiest way to make sure that all the statutory formalities are dealt with is to send the letter approving the name to one of them, telling them for what purpose the company is being formed and asking them to form it. They will then prepare the documents for lodging with the Registrar of Companies and either produce them for signature or form the company taking up the subscriber shares themselves, and then send the documents on with signed blank share transfers. Their fees for doing this vary in relation to their expertise (and the quality of their printing since the law requires that most of the documents be printed) but will not normally exceed £100 plus the appropriate duty.

Unless one has had previous experience of the formation of companies it is not wise to use these organizations direct. It is best to have the company formed through an accountant or solicitor who may use one of the company formation firms for printing and sometimes lodging the documens, but will take into consideration any special requirements of the particular company being formed.

For example, the vast majority of private limited companies are in fact small family businesses. In partnership agreements covering the same type of business, it is usual to provide that in the event of one of the partners retiring or dying the remaining partners shall have an option to purchase the partnership share of the retired or dead partner at a fair valuation, which may be fixed by the partnership accountant or in the event of dispute by some outside arbitrator. If one uses a company formation agency to form a company, they will provide a standard form of articles of association which normally, either by reference to Table *A* (see later) or specifically, includes a provision that the directors have the right to refuse to register transfers. It will not normally include a provision that a shareholder wishing to sell his shares must first offer them to the remaining shareholders at a fair valuation. In the family business type of company this provision is desirable.

There are many other provisions which it might be desirable to insert in the standard form of articles of association and which are not normally inserted by company formation agencies, and the existence of these provisions makes the cost of professional advice well worth while.

Purchase of a company. A cheaper method of company acquisition is to buy one ready made, usually obtainable from the firms that form companies. It is generally possible to purchase an existing company designed to carry on the type of business required at a price considerably less than the fees for forming a new company. It is then merely necessary to change the name of the company, which, once the name has been approved by the Department of Trade, can be done by passing a special resolution. If it is necessary to change the articles of the company this too can be done by special resolution. It would nonetheless be unwise to buy a ready-made company without having its memorandum and articles checked by a professional adviser, and if this is done the ultimate saving will not be very great.

The remainder of this chapter will discuss in more detail the structure of registered companies limited by shares.

The court. The phrase 'the court' in the rest of this chapter means the court that has jurisdiction over the company as defined in *s*512. The High Court has jurisdiction over all companies. County courts also have jurisdiction over companies whose paid-up capital is less than £120 000.

Printed documents. The Companies Acts frequently require documents sent to the Registrar to be 'printed'. The Registrar has indicated that this requirement will be fulfilled if a document is produced by letterpress, gravure or lithography; by offset lithography, by electrostatic or photographic copying; or by stencil duplicating using wax stencils and black ink. However, thermographic, hectographic or dye-line copies will not be accepted.

MEMORANDUM OF ASSOCIATION

Every company must have a memorandum of association which must state (*s*2):

1 The name of the company
2 Whether the registered office will be in England and Wales, or Scotland, or simply in Wales
3 The objects of the company
4 A statement that the liability of members is limited
5 The amount of the nominal capital and its division into shares of fixed amount
6 The memorandum must be signed by at least two persons, called the *subscribers*, in the presence of a witness. Each subscriber must take at least one share and the number of shares he takes must be shown opposite his name.

The form of memorandum is not laid down in the Act but is prescribed by regulations to be made from time to time by the Secretary of State. At present the memorandum must be in the form prescribed by the Companies (Tables A to F) Regulations 1985.

The memorandum defines the company's legal personality and controls its relations with the rest of the world. It is filed with the Registrar, after incorporation, at Companies House where any person may inspect it for a fee of 5p. Any member of the company is entitled to be supplied by the company with a copy of its memorandum for a fee not exceeding 5p. Where an alteration is made in the memorandum every copy subsequently issued by the company must incorporate the alteration.

The name

The regulations as to company names are now contained in *ss*25 to 35 of the Act. Though, in principle, a company can now choose whatever name it likes, certain names are prohibited (*s*26). A company shall not be registered by a name which includes otherwise than at the end of the name, the word 'limited', 'unlimited' or 'public limited company' or their Welsh equivalents; which is the same as a name already appearing in the Registrar's index of company names or the use of which, by the company, would, in the opinion of the Secretary of State, constitute a criminal offence. The approval of the Secretary of State is required for certain other names, including those which would give the impression that the company is connected in any way with Her Majesty's Government or any local authority. Certain names, which are specified under regulations made from time to time, require the approval of the Secretary of State before they are used. They are basically names implying a connection with a professional or official body, such as 'building society', 'chamber of commerce' or 'chartered'.

If, in the Secretary of State's opinion, the name by which a company is registered gives so misleading an indication of the nature of its activities as to be likely to cause harm to the public, he may direct it to change its name and the direction must be complied with within a period of six weeks from the date of the direction or such longer period as the Secretary of State may allow, though the company has the right to appeal to the court, within three weeks of the date of the direction.

Limited. The last word of the name must be Limited (Ltd) (or Cyfyngedig (CYF) if the registered office is in Wales) in the case of a private company; Public Limited Company (PLC) in the case of a public company, so that all who have dealings with the company are aware of its structure. In the case of a company limited by guarantee, the Department of Trade will issue a licence to allow a company's name to be registered without the word limited, if it is satisfied that the company's object is to promote 'commerce, art, science, religion, charity or any profession', and it intends to apply its profits or other income to promoting those objects and prohibits paying any dividend to its members (*s*30).

Change of name. A company may change its name by passing a special resolution in general meeting (see p.87). The same restrictions on the name which is then chosen apply as to the original name.

Publication of the name. The full name of the company must appear, in a conspicuous position, in letters easily legible outside every place at which it conducts business, and outside its registered office (*s*348). Limited may be abbreviated to Ltd (Stacey and Company Limited *v* Wallis (1912)).

The full name must also appear on all business letters, notices, official publications, bills of exchange, promissory notes, endorsements, cheques, orders for money or goods, invoices, receipts and letters of credit (*s*349(1)).

Section 9(7) of the European Communities Act 1972 which came into effect on 1 January 1975 provides that the place of registration, registration number and address of the registered office shall appear on all business letters and order forms. Under the same section, a company exempted from using the word 'limited' in its names must state that it is a limited company on all business letters and order forms.

If an officer of the company issues a cheque, bill of exchange, promissory note or order for goods or money without using the company's name, he is personally liable on it unless the company honours it.

Registered office

Every company must at all times have a registered office. Notice of the address of the registered office must be sent to the Registrar within fourteen days of incorporation. Any change must also be notified within fourteen days.

The memorandum has only to state whether the registered office will be in England and Wales, Wales or Scotland. This determines whether the company will be subject to English or Scottish law and it is not possible to move from one country to the other.

The office of the Registrar of Companies in England and Wales is now at Companies Registration Office, Crown Way, Cardiff CF43 VZ, though facilities for inspection of company records are still maintained in London at 55/71 City Road, London EC1. The Office of the Registrar of Companies in Scotland is at Exchequer Chambers, 102 George Street, Edinburgh 2.

Writs and other documents may be served on a company by leaving them at, or posting them to, its registered office (*s*725).

Checklist of documents to be kept

The following documents must be kept at the registered office and must (except for the minute book) be available for inspection by anyone for at least two hours a day during normal business hours:

1 Register of directors and secretaries — see p.37 (*s*288)
2 Register of charges (*s*407(1)) and copies of the instruments creating the charges — see p.44
3 Minute books of general meetings — (*s*383)

Inspection of the minutes may be refused to non-members.

In addition the following documents must be kept at the registered office, unless the work of making them up is done elsewhere when they can be kept where the work is done:

1 Register of members — see p.32 (*s*353)
2 Register of debenture holders — see p.45 (*s*190)

There must also be kept, either at the registered office or at the place where the register of members is kept the register of directors' interests — see pp. 37-8 (*s*325 and schedule 13).

The last two documents must be available for inspection to anyone for at least two hours every business day during normal business hours.

OBJECTS OF THE COMPANY

The memorandum of association must set out the objects of the company, the purpose for which the company has been incorporated. The objects clause in fact takes up the bulk of the memorandum of association. It normally consists of a very lengthy main objects clause setting out the basic purpose of incorporation, then a large number of subsidiary clauses which are usually standardized and give the company power to buy land, borrow money, acquire other businesses and do anything which is necessary to carry out its main object. The standard form used by company formation agencies usually has a standard form of objects clause, leaving only the main objects clause to be specifically designed for the individual company.

Many of the subclauses in the objects clause would be taken by the courts to be subsidiary to the main objects clause, there merely to ensure that the company has power to do everything necessary to carry on the business described in the main objects clause. However, a declaration frequently appears at the end of the main objects clause to the effect that all the objects specified in any of the subclauses of the objects clause should, except where otherwise expressed, not be limited by reference or inference from the terms of any other paragraph or the name of the company and that all of them should be construed as main objects; and this declaration has been allowed by the courts to be effective. Most standard forms of objects clause drawn up in recent years contain such a declaration.

If a company does anything which is outside the scope of its objects, such action is *ultra vires* (beyond the powers) and void, and the company and its members can take no action to render it valid. The purpose of this part of the law is to protect investors in the company. Investors normally invest in a business which they expect to do well and they are entitled to expect that their money will be used for that business and not for some different business. However, the law proved totally ineffective in achieving this end and merely operated arbitrarily to deprive some classes of creditors, and occasionally employees, of just claims against companies. As a result, in 1962 the Company Law Committee under the chairmanship of Lord Jenkins recommended changes in the *ultra vires* doctrine which have effectively been achieved by the European Communities Act 1972. Section 9(1) (now *s*9 of the Act) provides that in favour of a person dealing with a company in good faith any transaction decided on by the directors is deemed to be one which it is within the capacity of the company to enter into and the power of the directors to bind the company is deemed to be free of any limitation under the memorandum or articles of association. A party to a transaction so decided on is not bound to inquire as to the capacity of the company to enter into it or as to any such limitation on the power of the directors and is presumed to have acted in good faith unless the contrary is proved.

However, the danger that any transaction entered into by a company is *ultra vires* cannot be ignored. The changes in the law reduce the ability of a company to escape improperly from claims made by third parties but do not enable it to enforce an *ultra vires* contract against a third party. Whenever a company proposes to make gratuitous dispositions or to confer benefits such as pensions or bonuses on directors or make donations to charities, company secretaries should check the objects clause to make sure that the transaction is not *ultra vires*.

Changing the objects clause

Under *s*4 the objects clause may be altered for certain limited purposes by passing a special resolution (see pp.87-8) in general meeting. For a period of twenty-one days after the resolution is passed there is an opportunity to apply to the court for the alteration to be cancelled. The application may be made by:

1 The holders of not less than 15 per cent of the company's issued share capital, or of 15 per cent of any one class of that capital
2 The holders of at least 15 per cent of any debentures entitling the holders to object to an alteration of the objects (*s*5)

An objection cannot be made by someone who voted for the resolution. The main ground of objection is that that the alteration does not fall within the categories permitted by *s*4. The court may confirm the resolution either wholly or in part and on such terms and conditions as it thinks fit. It may also adjourn the proceedings to enable a satisfactory arrangement for the purchase of the dissentient shareholders' interests to be made.

LIABILITY

This clause is a statement of the essential point that the 'liability of the members is limited'. The clause may not be altered unless the company is re-registered as an unlimited company following the procedure laid down in ss49-50.

The liability of the members may however become unlimited by the operation of s24. This happens after a company has traded for more than six months with fewer than the minimum number of members. If it then continues to trade with too few members the liability of those members who know it is doing so is unlimited.

The memorandum may, by s306, provide that the liability of directors is unlimited (assuming that directors have to be members). By s307, a company may, if it is authorized by its articles, pass a special resolution to render unlimited the liability of its directors or of a managing director.

CAPITAL CLAUSE

This states the amount of the nominal capital and how it is divided into shares. The shares may be divided into classes with different rights — see Shares, below.

Alteration of the capital clause

By s121(2)(a), a company may, if it is authorized by its articles, 'increase its share capital by new shares of such amount as it thinks expedient'.

The alteration must be made by a resolution at a general meeting s121(4) and a printed copy of the resolution together with a notice of the increase must be sent to the Registrar within fifteen days (s123(1)). The copy resolution must either be printed or in some other form approved by the Registrar (s123(3)).

A company may (again if authorized by its articles and by a resolution passed at a general meeting):

1 Consolidate and divide any of its share capital into shares of a larger amount — for example consolidate twenty shares of 5p each into one £1 share — (s121(2)(b))

COMPANY LAW

2   Convert any paid-up shares into stock or reconvert stock into shares of any denomination (s121(2)(c))
3   Subdivide shares into shares of a smaller amount (s121(2)(d))
4   Cancel shares that have not been taken or agreed to be taken

Notice of any of these four actions must be sent to the Registrar within one month (s122).

Stock

Until the Companies Act 1948, shares had to be numbered. In large companies, this meant that registering transfers of shares was a lengthy process, since the numbers must be given in the shareholder's entry in the register of members. Stock is not numbered because in principle it can be bought and sold in any quantity. Thus if £10 shares are converted into stock, the holder of £100 of stock may sell £57 of it. However, articles usually allow the directors to fix a minimum amount of transferable stock (a *stock unit*). Section 182(2) now allows that, if all the issued shares of a particular class are fully paid up and rank *pari passu* for all purposes, then they need not have numbers. This section has removed one of the reasons for converting shares into stock.

Reduction of capital

A company's creditors are entitled to assume that the capital represented by issued shares is available to meet the company's debts: they are prepared to take the risk that the capital will be lost because of bad management but not that the company will actually give it back to the shareholders. For this reason it has traditionally been made very difficult for a company to reduce its issued capital and such a reduction can only be made with the consent of the court after passing a special resolution (s135). For the same reason s66 of the 1948 Act prohibited a company from buying shares in itself. This was both to stop the company reducing its capital in this way and to stop a company from an undesirable dealing in its own shares which might artificially force up the price. However, a considerable modification of this principle was made in the 1981 Companies Act which permitted both public and private companies to purchase their own shares, provided that the appropriate procedures are followed. The power to purchase its own shares must be contained in the company's articles but such a power is contained in the new Table A(s8(2)). Provisions are now ss159 to 170 of the Act. The 1948 Act did permit a company to issue fully paid-up redeemable preference shares. If redemption of these is made by a payment from profits and not by the issue of new shares the effect would be a reduction of the company's issued share capital. Creditors are protected by providing that a sum equal to the nominal value of the redeemed shares must be transferred from profits to a capital redemption reserve fund, which is then treated as paid-up capital of the company. Similar provisions protect the creditor of a company which has acquired its own shares (s170).

ARTICLES OF ASSOCIATION

A company limited by shares must have a set of articles of association, which govern the management of the internal affairs of the company.

Unless it registers with its memorandum a different set of articles, a company will automatically be governed by the set of articles given in Table A (s8(2)). Table A, a model constitution for both public and private companies, was contained in the First Schedule to the 1948 Companies Act. The 1985 Act (apart from the sentence in this chapter called 'the Act') does not contain a revised Table A, but empowers the Secretary of State to make regulations creating the new Table A which, accordingly, can easily be amended from time to time, without the passing of a fresh Companies Act. The new Table A modifies the old to bring it into line with the changes which have taken place in company law, since 1948. For example, it contains power for a company to purchase its own shares. It is thought, however, that the differences between the old and the new Table A are not sufficient to warrant most companies going to the trouble and expense of using the new Table A.

It is normal for Table A to be adopted by a new company with modifications. It is usual for it to be stated at the commencement of the articles of association that Table A is adopted save as specifically excluded and then to continue with details of the provisions of Table A that are excluded.

If the company does register special articles then the regulations in Table A will still apply in so far as the registered articles do not exclude or modify them (s8(2)).

The company secretary should carefully collate with Table A the articles of the company for which he works, so that he knows exactly what has been excluded and can check whether new provisions have been inserted where necessary to replace the excluded provisions of Table A. Common cases where additions to Table A are advisable are in connection with the powers and duties of directors, the dismissal of directors and the voting rights attached to the shares. The prudent company secretary having found out exactly what the articles of his company are by checking them through with Table A will try to envisage the problems that may arise in his company. Articles of association may be changed by special resolution with few restrictions (see below). It is too late to alter the articles when a conflict between directors or shareholders has already arisen and the articles do not cover the situation.

Companies registered before 1 July 1948

The Companies Acts 1862, 1908 and 1929 each had a Table *A* containing a model set of articles. The Joint Stock Companies Act 1856 had a Table *B*. Companies registered under these Acts automatically took the relevant table as their articles in so far as they did not register modifying articles. These earlier tables continue to be the articles of the companies that adopted them.

Alteration of the articles

A company may alter or add to its articles by passing a special resolution (see pp.87-8) in any way subject to its memorandum and the provision of the Act ($s9(1)$).

The articles constitute a contract between the company and its members but $s9(1)$ allows the company to alter articles against a member's will and even to his detriment, if the alteration is made *bona fide* for the benefit of the company as a whole.

This point was demonstrated in Sidebottom v Kershaw, Leese and Company Limited (1920). Sidebottom held a small number of shares in the company, which was controlled by its directors. Sidebottom therefore received copies of the accounts of the company, which annoyed the directors because Sidebottom was also in business in competition with them. At that time, companies did not have to send their accounts to the Registrar and they were not publicly available. The directors altered the articles of association to enable them to require a shareholder who was also a competitor to sell his shares to a nominee of the directors. The Court of Appeal held that the alteration was valid. The articles may not be altered so as to:

1 Exceed the powers conferred by the memorandum, or conflict with it
2 Be inconsistent with the Act or any other statute
3 Increase the liability of existing members unless they give their consent in writing ($s16$)

MEMBERSHIP

The members of a company are persons who have both:

1 Agreed to be members, and
2 Had their names entered in the company's register of members

The usual way of signifying agreement to be a member is by paying for shares in the company, and the words 'member' and 'shareholder' are synonymous.

Register of members

By *s*352, every company must have a register of members, showing:

1 Name and address of each member
2 The number of shares held, and their numbers if they are numbered
3 The amount paid or agreed to be considered as paid on the shares
4 The date when each member was entered on the register
5 The date that a person ceased to be a member

If the company has more than fifty members then its register must either be in the form of an index or there must be a separate index which must contain sufficient information to enable any member's account to be found in the register (*s*354).

The register must be open for inspection for at least two hours every business day. Members have a right of free inspection. Non-members have a right of inspection but may be charged not more than 5p. Anyone may require a copy of the register and may be charged not more than 10p per 100 words for it.

Who may be a member?

Any person having the capacity to make a contract may be a member. This includes:

1 *Aliens* — a company registered in England will be English even if none of its members are
2 *Bankrupts* — although a bankrupt must exercise his vote according to the direction of his trustee and may not be a director without the permission of the court that adjudicated him bankrupt
3 *A registered company* — if authorized by its memorandum. However, a company may not own any of its own shares unless its articles give it power to do so (see Reduction of capital, p.29) or (*s*23) shares in its holding company. (Company *A* is a *subsidiary* of company *B* and *B* is *A*'s *holding company* if *B* is a member of *A* and controls membership of *A*'s board of directors, or if *B* holds more than half of *A*'s equity share capital — see next section — or if *A* is a subsidiary of another company that is a subsidiary of *B* — *s*736(1))
4 *Minors* — because a contract cannot always be enforced against a minor (see p.207), a company may by its articles forbid minor membership.

Disclosure of interest in shares

Part IV of the Act deals with the disclosure of interests in shares (*ss*198-220). Section 211 requires every public company to maintain a register of interests in shares at its registered office or at the place where the register of members is kept. The rules about its availability for inspection are the same as those for the register of members. Anyone who acquires an interest in what s199(2) refers to as 'the notifiable percentage' of the issued shares that carry a right to vote in all circumstances at a general meeting must notify the company in writing within five days of his acquisition. The 'notifiable percentage' is at present 5 per cent, but provision is made for the alteration of the prescribed percentage by statutory instrument (s201). The company must enter in the register his name, address, the way he acquired the interest, the number and class of shares. The entry must be made within three days of receipt of the notice. Notification and a record in the register is then required of any changes in the interest, up to and including the time when it falls below the one-twentieth mark. Anyone who fails to notify a notifiable interest is guilty of an offence and is liable to imprisonment or a fine, or both (s210(3)). A 'notifiable interest' includes the interest of a beneficiary under a trust, but not the interest of a bare trustee (ss208-9). A person is taken to be interested in any shares in which his family, or the company he controls, is interested.

The Act also deals with the 'concert party', that is, a group of persons who separately acquire small quantities of shares with the intention of later combining their holdings. Sections 204 and 205 require persons acting in concert to disclose their agreement to the company. They are also under an obligation to keep each other informed (s206).

A public company may require information from a person about his interest in the company's shares during the previous three years (s212). The company may be compelled to make such an investigation on the acquisition of the holders of one-tenth or more of the paid-up voting share capital (s214).

Termination of membership

Membership ceases when the name of the member is validly removed from the register of members. This is done when the member *transfers* (usually by sale) all his shares to someone else, or when his shares are *transmitted* to his executors (if he dies) or his trustee (if he is adjudicated bankrupt). The details of transfer and transmission are considered in Chapter 3.

SHARES

Shares may be issued in different classes with different rights of control of the company's affairs, participation in its profits, and repayment of their value and share in surplus assets on winding-up. A simple distinction is often made on the basis of the way annual profits are to be shared.

Ordinary shares entitle their holders to a share of the profits only if the directors think fit and to the extent they think fit. The ordinary shareholders are usually entitled to control the company's activities by voting at a general meeting (see Chapter 4).

Preference shares carry the right to a payment of a fixed percentage of their nominal value in every year that the company makes a sufficient profit. Because the risk of not getting a dividend is less than for ordinary shares, preference shareholders are usually denied the right to vote at a general meeting.

Preferential rights may be extended to the division of the company's assets on winding up. Preference shareholders may have the right to repayment of their capital first. To balance this they are not usually entitled to a share of any surplus assets the company has.

Any mixture of rights is possible: 'non-voting ordinary shares', 'participating preference shares' (eligible for a discretionary dividend in addition to the fixed one) and 'deferred shares' (where all other classes of shareholder must be paid dividends or repaid capital first) have been issued. Precise definitions of the rights of any class will be given either in the memorandum or (more conveniently) in the articles.

Redeemable preference shares are discussed under Reduction of capital (p.29).

Equity shares are those whose rights, either to a dividend or to a share in surplus assets on winding up, are not limited to a specified amount.

Modification of class rights

The rights of each class of share will be defined either in the memorandum or in the articles. If the rights are specified in the memorandum there may also be specification of the way in which the rights can be modified. If this is not included then the rights can be altered only by a scheme of arrangement under $s425$, which must be sanctioned by the court.

When rights of a class are modified in acordance with procedures stated in the memorandum of articles then $s127$ provides that the holders of not less than 15 per cent of the issued shares of that class may apply to the court for the alteration to be cancelled. The application must be made within twenty-one days of completion of the procedure for changing the rights.

DIRECTORS

Members invest money in their company but do not usually run its day-to-day affairs, which are controlled by the directors. Every public company registered after 1 November 1929 must have at least two directors. Public companies registered before then and private companies must have at least one director (s282).

A director is not, as such, an employee or servant of the company, although he may hold office in addition to his directorship (for example, as sales director). A director has no right to be paid for his directorial services unless payment is authorized by the articles — which it normally is, as in Table *A* article 82.

Directors are, in law, agents of the company. Hence if directors make a contract in the name of the company, it is the company — the principal — which is liable on it, not the directors, provided they do not exceed the powers conferred on them by the memorandum and articles. If a director made an *ultra vires* contract (see pp.26-7) then he would be personally liable on it, though the company would probably also be liable.

Directors occupy a fiduciary position both in relation to the members and the employees of the company. If a director makes a contract on his own behalf with the company of which he is a director, then the company may rescind the contract or call upon the director to surrender his profit. Directors are, therefore, required by *s*317 to declare their interests in any matter under discussion (see also p.103-4). With certain limited exceptions loans to directors are prohibited (*s*330) and in the case of public companies can constitute a criminal offence.

Who may be a director?

Anyone, including a company, except:

1   Beneficed clergymen of the Church of England (Pluralities Act 1838)
2   An undischarged bankrupt without the permission of the court that adjudicated him bankrupt (*s*302)
3   Persons disqualified by the court after conviction of certain offences connected with company management (*ss*295-300)
4   The court in appropriate cases can disqualify directors who have been involved in the management of more than one insolvent company within a five-year period or who have been persistently in default in relation to certain requirements of the Act. By *s*301 the Secretary of State must maintain a Public Register of Disqualification Orders

Age limits. Section 293 provides that a person may not be a director of a public company or of a private subsidiary of a public company if he is over seventy. In such companies, a director must retire at the end of the annual general meeting that follows his seventieth birthday.

A company may include a clause in its articles abrogating these provisions (*s*293(7)). Alternatively, a person over seventy may be appointed a director at a general meeting by a resolution of which special notice has been given — the notice must state his age ($s293(5)$).

Appointment of directors

The articles state the procedure for the appointment of directors. The only statutory provisions are:

1 Section 285 — a director's acts are valid even if it is subsequently discovered that his appointment was invalid
2 Section 291 interprets articles that require share qualifications of directors
3 Section 291 ensures that when a meeting is voting on the appointment of directors it votes for each name separately

Removal of directors

Section 303(1) states one of the most important principles of company law:

> A company may by ordinary resolution remove a director before the expiration of his period of office, notwithstanding anything in its articles or in any agreement between it and him

Although no provision in a director's contract of service could prevent his dismissal under this section, he might well be able to sue for damages for breach of his contract if he were dismissed. Special notice (see p.90) is required of the resolution. Special notice is also required of a motion to appoint a director to replace one removed under $s303(2)$, if it is to be moved at the same general meeting.

Publicity about directors

The following information about its directors must be made available by every company:

1 A register of directors and secretaries must be kept at the company's registered office
2 A register of directors' interests in shares and debentures must be kept, either at the registered office or at the place where the register of members is kept
3 Particulars of directors' service contracts must be available for inspection by members
4 The names of the directors must appear on certain documents issued by the company

Register of directors and secretaries (ss288-90)

This register must show, in the case of directors who are individuals:

1 Present forename and surname, and any former forenames and surnames
2 Usual residential address
3 Present nationality
4 Business occupation
5 Any other directorships held. Directorships of wholly owned subsidiaries of the company need not be shown, nor a directorship of the company's holding company if the company is a wholly owned subsidiary
6 If the company is public, or a private subsidiary of a public company, their ages

In the case of directors who are corporations, the register must show the corporate name and registered or principal office.

The register must be kept at the registered office and the requirements for inspection are the same as those for the register of members. The particulars entered in the register must also be sent to the Registrar as must any change in them.

Register of directors' interests

Section 325 of the Act requires every company to keep a register of directors' interests in the company's shares or debentures. The Act requires a director to notify his interests to the company:

1 Within fourteen days beginning the day after he was appointed a director
2 Within fourteen days beginning the day after he acquires an interest

Saturdays, Sundays and a day that is a bank holiday in any part of Great Britain are disregarded when counting the period of fourteen days. Persons who were directors on 27 October 1967 should have registered the interests they held on 26 October before 15 November 1967. Because the definition of 'interest' is so wide (it includes the interests of a director's spouse and infant children), the Act anticipates that there will be occasions on which a director does not know that he has acquired an interest within the meaning of the Act. If a director discovers that he does have a previously unknown interest then he must notify it within fourteen days beginning the day after his discovery.

Within three days beginning the day after the company was notified (but excluding Saturdays, Sundays and bank holidays) it must enter in the register the following information:

1 Name of the director giving the information
2 The information given
3 Date of entry in the register

Entries for each name must be in chronological order. If the register is not in the form of an index then there must be a separate index to the names in the register. Rights of inspection are the same as for the register of members (see Register of members, p.32).

In addition to recording information supplied by directors, the company must itself record the following information in the register:

1 The grant to a director of a right to subscribe for shares or debentures of a company
2 The exercise of such a right

Service contracts of directors

Section 319 of the Act requires the resolution of the general meeting for a contract of service or for services between a director and the company or any company in the group not terminable within or for a term exceeding five years during which it cannot be terminated or can be terminated only in specified circumstances.

The approval of the general meeting is also required for substantial property transactions between directors or their connections and the company. Section 318 of the Act requires a company to allow its members, without charge during reasonable business hours, to inspect a copy of the service contract of every director. (If the contract is oral then a memorandum of its terms must be available for inspection.) There are two exceptions:

1 Contracts requiring a director to work wholly or mainly outside the United Kingdom
2 Contracts that have less than twelve months to run or that can be terminated by the company within the next twelve months without payment of compensation

The copies must be kept (all together) at one of the following places:

1 The registered office
2 The place where the register of members is kept
3 The company's principal place of business, provided it is in the same part of the United Kingdom that the company is registered in

If the documents are not kept at the registered office, then notice of their location must be sent to the Registrar.

SECRETARY

Every company is required to have a secretary (s283(1)). There is only one 'secretary' but the office may be performed by more than one person (for example, by a firm of solicitors). The secretary may be any individual, firm or company; however the Act forbids a company that has a sole director having that director as secretary also (s283(2)). Section 283(4) imposes two further rules to ensure that there is a secretary who is not also the sole director:

1   No company shall have as secretary a corporation whose sole director is the sole director of the company
2   No company shall have as sole director a corporation whose sole director is secretary to the company

Section 286 provides that it shall be the duty of the directors of a public company to take all reasonable steps to secure that the secretary or each joint secretary of the company is a person who appears to them to have the requisite knowledge and experience to discharge the functions of secretary of the company and who

(*a*) on 22 December 1980 held the office of secretary or assistant or deputy secretary of the company; or
(*b*) for at least three years of the five years immediately preceding his appointment as secretary held the office of secretary of a company other than a private company; or
(*c*) is a member of any of the bodies specified in subsection (2) below; or
(*d*) is a barrister, advocate or solicitor called or admitted in any part of the United Kingdom; or
(*e*) is a person who, by virtue of his holding or having held any other position or his being a member of any other body, appears to the directors to be capable of discharging those functions

The bodies referred to in subsection (*c*) above are:

(*a*) The Institute of Chartered Accountants in England and Wales
(*b*) The Institute of Chartered Accountants in Scotland
(*c*) The Chartered Association of Certified Accountants
(*d*) The Institute of Chartered Accountants in Ireland
(*e*) The Institute of Chartered Secretaries and Administrators
(*f*) The Institute of Cost and Management Accountants
(*g*) The Chartered Institute of Public Finance and Accountancy

Apart from certain duties at the beginning and end of a company's life, the

Act imposes only one statutory duty on the secretary. That is (s365(2)), to sign the annual return. This is required to be signed both by a director and the secretary and s284 provides that this requirement is not satisfied if the document is signed by one person who is both a director and the secretary.

The duties of secretary have been defined by custom rather than statute. In general the secretary is responsible for the administration of the company, including some or all of the many topics discussed in this book. The responsible nature of their work is emphasized by the existence of a professional institution, the Institute of Chartered Secretaries and Administrators, with high standards of membership.

The nature of the secretary's work implies that he is responsible for performing many of the jobs that the Act requires of companies and for which fines are possible for default. These include the maintenance of registers and allowing people to inspect them, keeping minutes of general meetings, sending copies of balance sheets, directors' reports and auditors' reports and following the rules about publishing the company's name and those of its directors.

Register of directors and secretaries

This is described on p.37. The details about secretaries that must be included are (if the secretary is an individual):

1 Present forename and surname
2 Any former forename and surname
3 Usual residential address

If the secretary is a corporation, the register must show the corporate name and the registered or principal office. If all the partners in a firm are joint secretaries, only the name and principal office of the firm need be entered.

AUDITORS

Detailed provisions for the keeping of accounts and audit are contained in Part VII of the Act starting at s221.

Every company must appoint an auditor or auditors (s384(1)) whose duties are to examine the company's accounts and make a report on them and on every balance sheet, profit and loss account and set of group accounts that is presented to members. This report must be read to the company in general meeting and must be available for inspection by any member; it must also be sent to the Registrar with the annual return — see next section.

The auditors have a right of access to all books and may require the company's officers to give them any information they think necessary for the performance of their duties. They also have the right to attend any general meeting and receive any notices or communications about it that members are entitled to.

Who may be an auditor?

In general only the following individuals may act as auditors:

1 Members of:
   (a) Institute of Chartered Accountants in England and Wales
   (b) Chartered Association of Certified Accountants
   (c) Institute of Chartered Accountants in Scotland
   (d) Institute of Chartered Accountants in Ireland
2 Individuals whom the Department of Trade has certified as having qualifications similar to the people in category 1 or as having adequate knowledge and experience

Certain other people may be authorized by the Department to act as auditors of a restricted set of companies, by $s13(1)$ of the 1967 Act. The following may not act as auditor of a company:

1 An officer or servant of the company
2 A person who is a partner or in the employment of an officer or servant of the company
3 A body corporate ($s389(6)$)
4 A person who is disqualified from acting as auditor of the company's holding company or any of its subsidiaries ($s389(7)$)

Removal of auditors

The term of office of an auditor is from the end of the general meeting at which he is appointed until the end of the next annual general meeting. He is then automatically reappointed unless:

1 He signifies in writing that he does not wish to be reappointed
2 He is disqualified from acting as auditor
3 The company passes a resolution (which requires special notice — see p. 90) appointing someone else or providing that he shall not be reappointed ($s386$)

If an annual general meeting fails to appoint or reappoint an auditor then the company must, within one week, notify the Department of Trade which has the power to appoint an auditor to fill the vacancy.

If there is a casual vacancy in the office of auditor, the directors may fill it.

The provisions of The Companies Act 1976 (now incorporated in the Act) strengthened the auditors' position and were designed to make it more difficult for improper pressures to be exerted on him by the board. In particular $s390$ provides that an auditor's notice of resignation must be in writing and sent to the registered office of the company and must state either the circumstances leading him to resign or that there are no such circumstances which he considers should be brought to the notice of members.

Remuneration of auditors

Auditors' remuneration (which includes expenses) is fixed by those who appoint them — the directors, the company in general meeting or the Department of Trade, as the case may be.

ANNUAL RETURN

By requiring that every company sends once a year details of its affairs to the Registrar, the Companies Acts ensure that the general public has access to a great deal of information about the activities and management of companies.

The return must be made every calendar year within forty-two days of the annual general meeting ($ss363$ and 365). A company does not have to make a return in the first year of its incorporation. If the second year of incorporation ends before the company has been incorporated for eighteen months, then it does not have to make a return in the second year.

Contents

The matters to be included in the annual return are set out in the Fifteenth Schedule to the Act. The form of the return must be as near as possible to that given in Part II of the Schedule. The contents include:

1 A list of the company's membership on the fourteenth day after the annual general meeting. The list must give the names and addresses of the members, the number of shares held (divided into classes) and the number of shares transferred by the member since the date of the last annual return with the date that the transfer was registered. A complete list is required only every third year. In the intervening two years only changes need be shown
2 A list of all persons who have ceased to be members since the date of the last annual return, giving the same details as in list 1
3 The address of the place where the register of members is kept
4 Details of the share capital of the company

COMPANY LAW

5   Details of the company's indebtedness in the form of mortgages and charges
6   For all persons who, at the date of the return, are directors or secretaries of the company, the information that is required to be in the register of directors and secretaries

The annual return gives information about the membership, management and capitalization of the company. The documents that have to be attached to the report give details of the company's activities during the year. They are:

1   Certified copies of every balance sheet and profit and loss account that has been laid before the company in general meeting since the last return
2   Certified copies of the auditors' reports on the balance sheets
3   Certified copies of the directors' reports that accompanied the balance sheets

The certification is done by a director and the secretary. Preparation of these documents is described in Chapter 5.

Private companies

In addition to the documents mentioned above, a private company must file with its annual return a certificate that it has not issued an invitation to the public to subscribe for its shares or debentures.

BORROWING BY COMPANIES

Every trading company, unless prohibited by its memorandum or articles, has implied power to borrow for the purpose of its business and to give security for the loan. The power is normally exercised by the directors. When lending to a company it is extremely important to check that the purpose for which the loan is made is not *ultra vires* the borrowing company because, with certain exceptions, such borrowing and any security given for it is void.

Securities for borrowing by companies

A company must give a fixed charge over its assets, usually its land. This means that the company cannot deal with the asset charged without the consent of the lender. This is the normal way by which a small private company would secure loans made to it. A company may also give a floating charge that is a general charge over the assets of the company or part of the assets of the company (for example, its stock-in-trade) present and future which does not attach to any particular asset until it crystallizes. This occurs when the company ceases to carry on business, when the company is wound up or when the security is enforceable and the debenture holders or trustees enforce it (see below). A floating charge has the great advantage from the company's point of view of enabling the company to continue to deal with its assets quite freely without the consent of the lender until crystallization.

Registration of charges

Section 407 provides that every limited company shall keep at its registered office a register of all charges specifically affecting the property of the company and all floating charges on the undertaking or property of the company. The register must give:

1 A short description of the property charged
2 The amount of the charge
3 The names of the persons entitled thereto except in the case of bearer securities

A fine can be imposed on any officer of the company knowingly and wilfully failing to comply.

Section 406 provides that every company must keep a copy of all instruments creating a charge required to be registered at its registered office. The copies and the company's register are open to inspection of any creditor or member of the company without fee, and to other persons for a fee not exceeding 5p, for at least two hours a day during business hours. Penalties are provided for failing to comply (s408).

Section 395 provides that particulars of charges created by companies together with the instrument if any, creating them, must be delivered to the Registrar within twenty-one days after their creation. The charges requiring registration are:

1 A charge to secure an issue of debentures
2 A charge on uncalled share capital
3 A charge created by an instrument which if executed by an individual would require registration as a bill of sale (these would cover charges over physical movable assets of the company)
4 A charge on any land or any interest therein
5 A charge on the book debts of the company
6 A floating charge on the undertaking or property of the company
7 A charge on calls made but not paid
8 A charge on a ship or any share in a ship
9 A charge on goodwill on a patent or a licence under a patent or a trade mark or on a copyright or a licence under a copyright

The company is primarily responsible for registration under $s395$ but registration may be effected by the lender and the registration fees recovered from the company. It is of *vital importance* that charges be registered as required by the Act. In addition to penalties provided by the Act for non-registration, $s395$ provides that the unregistered charge is void against the liquidator and any creditor of the company, thus reducing the secured creditor to the level of an ordinary creditor. The court has power to extend the time-limit for registration with certain limitations, principally if the omission to register was accidental and will not prejudice the creditors or shareholders of the company. If a company acquires any property on which a charge already exists, it must register that charge as if it had created the charge itself within twenty-one days after completing the acquisition.

Debentures

Strictly speaking, any document containing an acknowledgement of indebtedness by the company is a debenture. It is defined by $s744$ as including debenture stock bonds and any other securities of a company whether constituting a charge on the assets of the company or not. However, the word is usually used to describe a form of loan to a company giving the investor a security comparable with a share in the company in that it is for a specified sum and is freely transferable like a share. Debentures of this type are normally issued in a series and give a fixed charge over the company's fixed assets and a floating charge on the company's stock in trade and other assets. The security is given by means of a trust deed. The trust deed provides that the company will pay debenture holders the principal money and interest secured by the debenture and gives the trustees a legal mortgage over the company's land and a floating charge over the rest of the company's property. If the company breaks any of the covenants contained in the trust deed, the trustees are given power to take possession of the properties charged to them, appoint a receiver and take all steps which are necessary to protect the interests of the debenture holders.

A debenture holder is a person who has lent money to the company and he is accordingly not, like a shareholder, a member of the company. Moreover, a company can purchase its own debentures without restriction. Interest on debentures may be paid out of capital. A debenture is normally a safer form of investment than an equity share but does not of course carry the same prospect of capital gain because the debenture holder owns no portion of the equity capital of the company. Debentures may be payable either to the registered holder or to the bearer. The registered holder is normally issued with a document under the seal of the company promising the debenture holder to pay the principal sum on a specified day and to pay interest in the meantime on specified dates. Registered debentures are normally transferable in a similar manner to shares.

UNLIMITED AND GUARANTEE COMPANIES

The two other forms of company mentioned at the beginning of the chapter are available for special purposes. Both types of company are subject to all the rules of the Companies Acts unless specifically exempted.

Unlimited companies

Section 7/6 forbids the formation of unincorporated associations of more than twenty people to carry on business for gain. This ensures that large associations are subject to the rules about publication of information that apply to companies and forces them to establish an independent, fixed 'person' responsible for carrying out contracts, rather than a fluctuating and possibly untraceable collection of people.

In some professions, it is considered necessary that practitioners should be liable to the full extent of their means if they make a mistake. The Act and statutory instruments therefore allow association of any number of solicitors, accountants, stockbrokers and related professionals.

If other people wish to demonstrate their confidence in their abilities, they can do so by forming an unlimited company in which, as its name suggests, the liability of members is without limit. This liability, however, does not come into effect until the company is wound up, and it is the company that is initially attacked by creditors.

Because one can be slightly less wary about giving credit to unlimited companies, and because they rarely offer their shares to the public (stock exchanges will not grant quotations to shares in unlimited companies) they are exempted from the requirement of having to make details of their accounts public.

Name. Unlimited companies must not have the word 'limited' in their names.

Share capital. An unlimited company's members are the people it agrees to enter in its register. It can, if it wants working capital, issue shares — even (unlike any other type of company) shares of no par value. Because the basis of an unlimited company's credit-worthiness is the wealth of its members rather than the size of its issued share capital, they are exempted from restrictions on the reduction of share capital and may reduce their share capital at will.

Guarantee companies

The guarantee company format is useful for charitable organizations where goodwill rather than working capital is required from members. The members of a company limited by guarantee agree to pay up to a fixed amount to satisfy the debts of the company when it is wound up. They are rather like the holders of totally unpaid shares, except that the company cannot make calls on them until it is being wound up.

Guarantee companies are usually formed for charitable objects and therefore may apply not to include 'limited' in their names (see p.24).

Guarantee companies are not exempt from any of the requirements for filing information.

3

Maintaining a Company Share Register

Audrey Laird

The job of maintaining a company share register is the responsibility of the company secretary. The work may be done by the company's own staff but, particularly in the case of large public companies, it is more normal for this task to be given to professional registrars.

Throughout this chapter it has been assumed that we are dealing with the ordinary share register of a company, but the procedures are similar for the preference register. Preference shares are generally held by shareholders looking for a safe investment with a steady income, since preference shares rank before ordinary on a break-up of the company and dividends, usually payable half-yearly, have to be met before provision can be made for ordinary dividend. Because the rate of dividend is fixed there is, however, no scope for an increased return and generally the preference register of a company will be very small in comparison with the ordinary.

It has also been assumed that we are concerned with the register of a public limited company; not all the following remarks will, therefore, apply to private companies.

The company's memorandum and articles will state the amount of the initial share capital with which the company proposes to be registered and the division into these different classes.

As well as ordinary and preference shares the company may issue loan stock or debentures and registers will have to be maintained for holders of these stocks who are not, however, members of the company.

The first shareholders of the company are the subscribers to the memorandum of whom there must be at least two who must take at least one share each. Further shares will be allotted in due course to provide the company with working capital and in the case of a private company these will be taken up mainly by the directors and members of their families and associates as it is an offence for a private company to offer shares to the public. A public limited company of course does not have this restriction and its shares may be issued either by means of an offer to the public, sometimes at a fixed price and sometimes by asking applicants to tender, or by a placing whereby the shares are issued to stockbrokers or issuing houses who then allot them to their various clients. If there is a large demand for the shares all applications may not be successful, but if there is a poor response some shares may have to be taken up by the underwriters who are generally involved in a large issue.

Details of all allotments of shares must be sent to the Registrar of Companies on the appropriate return of allotments form (see Figure 3.1). Throughout its life the company may from time to time make further issues of shares, for example, by means of a rights issue when it wishes to raise further cash, and these will be dealt with below.

Once the initial allotment of shares is completed details of the shareholders and their holdings will require to be entered in the company's register. This may take various forms and may be in either manual or computer form. For a very small private company with few shareholders where there are not expected to be many transfers of shares a suitable small register bound up together with other statutory forms, share certificates etc. may be obtained from law stationers. Larger private companies will probably prefer to use a looseleaf register so that shareholders' accounts may always be kept in strict alphabetical order. Note that unless the register is self-indexing a company with more than fifty members must provide a separate index.

Most public companies will have a computerized register. While some of the advantages of a manual register are lost, principally the ability to see the whole history of a shareholding at a glance without having to refer to various computer updates, the time saved in preparation of dividends, etc., more than compensates for these.

A share register should contain details of each member's full name and address, date of becoming a member and of ceasing to be a member, date of allotment or transfer of shares, allotment or transfer number, share certificate number, numbers of shares acquired, disposed of and current balance. Most registers will also record beside the shareholder's name details of dividend mandate, communications address if different from the shareholder's etc.

Shareholders may be registered in a sole name or in joint names. In the latter case communications will normally be sent to the first-named unless all the holders formally request otherwise. A company's articles may limit the number of persons who may be registered in a joint account but in the case

50 THE CONSTITUTION AND CONDUCT OF COMPANIES

Form No. PUC2 (revised)

Return of allotments of shares issued for cash

Pursuant to section 52(1) of the Companies Act 1948 as amended by the Companies Act 1976 and Part V of the Finance Act 1973

PUC2

Please do not write in this binding margin.

For official use   Company number

Please do not write in the space below. For Inland Revenue use only

Name of company

Please complete legibly, preferably in black type, or bold block lettering

Limited*

*delete if inappropriate

Distinguish between ordinary, preference, etc.

You are reminded of the fine(s) imposed on a company by virtue of section 47(7) of the Finance Act 1973 if the relative duty is not paid within one month of allotment

Description of shares†			
A Number allotted			
B Nominal value of each	£	£	£
C Total amount payable on each share (including premium if any)	£	£	£
D Amount paid or due and payable on each share. (Take into account premium if any or part payments made)	£	£	£
E Total amount paid or due and payable (A x D)	£		
F Capital duty payable on E at £1 per £100 or part of £100§	£		

Date(s) of allotment(s)

[made on the _____ 19 ____]*

‡ delete or complete as appropriate

[from the _____ 19 ____ to the _____ 19 ____]‡

The names, descriptions and addresses of the allottees should be given overleaf

If you are claiming credit or relief from capital duty under section 49(5) of the Finance Act 1973 a form No. PUC4 must be completed and attached to this form.

Please tick box if attached

If you are claiming relief from capital duty under paragraphs 9 or 14 of Schedule 19 of the Finance Act 1973, a letter to that effect should accompany this form.

This form should not be used for shares allotted by way of bonus – form PUC7 should be used instead.

Presentor's name, address and reference (if any):	For official use Capital section	Post room

Page 1

Figure 3.1   Return of allotments form

MAINTAINING A COMPANY SHARE REGISTER

Names, descriptions and addresses of the allottees

Name and description	Address	Number of shares allotted		
		Preference	Ordinary	Other kinds
		Total		

Please do not write in this binding margin.

Please complete legibly, preferably in black type, or bold block lettering

Where the space given on this form is inadequate, continuation sheets should be used and the number of sheets attached should be indicated in the box opposite:

I hereby certify that the details entered on this form are correct.

Signed_____[Director] [Secretary]‡ Date_____

‡delete as appropriate

Page 2

Figure 3.1 (*concluded*)

of a company listed on the Stock Exchange the maximum number must be not less than four. Shares may also be held by another company but not by an English partnership as it is not a legal entity. A Scottish partnership may however be registered in the firm name and while trusts will not be registered by an English company they will be accepted by companies in Scotland, unless their articles of association provide otherwise.

The share register must be kept at the registered office of the company or, if the share registration work is done elsewhere, at the office of the registrar. A company registered in England and Wales must however, keep its register in England or Wales while one registered in Scotland must keep it in Scotland. Registrars may be appointed in another country but, if so, the main register must still be kept at the registered office, the registrars maintaining a copy only.

Registers must be open for inspection by a member free of charge or by any other person for a nominal charge. A copy of the register or part thereof must be supplied on request again for a small charge, at present 10p per 100 words.

To allow preparation time for payment of dividends, rights issues etc. a company may close the register, ie not register transfers, provided that the total closure period does not exceed thirty days in a year. Most companies, however, continue to maintain the register as usual at these times but fix a date (the record date) to determine entitlement of shareholders to dividends, rights etc. Companies whose shares are listed on the Stock Exchange should arrange their timetable to follow the schedule of recommended record dates published each year by the Stock Exchange.

CERTIFICATES

Once a person has been registered as a member of the company he is issued with a certificate to that effect. Small companies will generally purchase a book of printed share certificates obtainable at law stationers. A sample of such a certificate is shown in Figure 3.2. All that remains to be done is to insert the name of the company and details of share capital etc. before going on to show the member's name and number of shares held. Larger companies will have their own certificates printed and in the case of companies listed on the Stock Exchange these must comply with the requirements of the Stock Exchange, which include the size (not more than $9'' \times 8''$ or 22.5 cm. $\times$ 20 cm.); a note of the authority under which the company is constituted (e.g. incorporated under the Companies Act 1948); and a note stating that no transfer of the security or any portion thereof will be registered without production of the certificate. As well as the shareholder's name and number of shares, the certificate will require to be dated and the company seal affixed. This may be either the common seal of the company or a special securities seal kept by the registrar which is a facsimile of the common seal with the addition of the word 'securities' and which is used for this purpose only in order to avoid delay in having to send certificates to the company for sealing before issuing. It is no longer common practice for the seal to be attested by the signatures of directors.

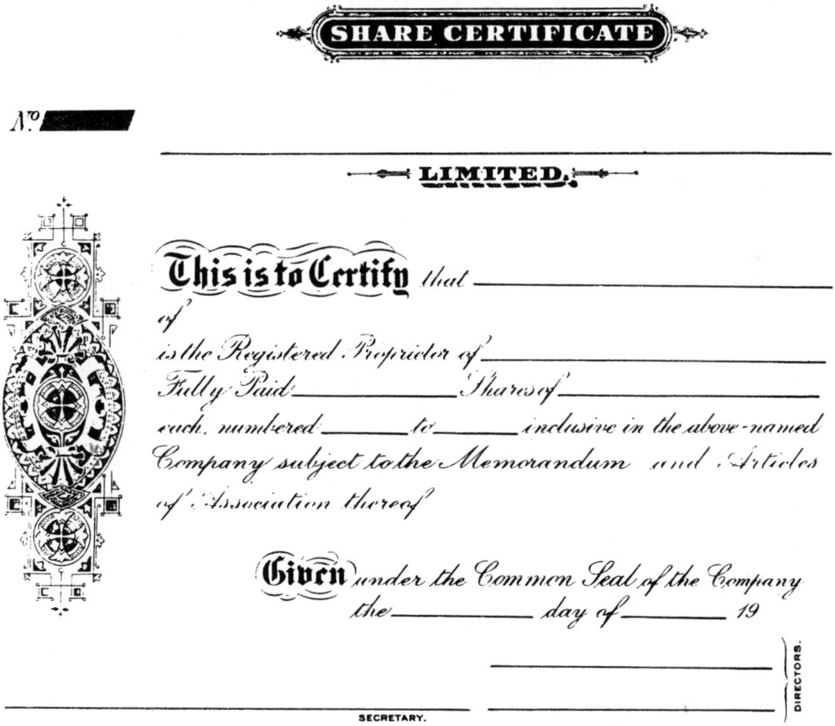
SHARE CERTIFICATE

No.

______________________________ LIMITED.

This is to Certify that ______________________________

of

is the Registered Proprietor of ______________________________

Fully Paid ______________ Shares of ______________

each, numbered ________ to ________ inclusive in the above-named Company subject to the Memorandum and Articles of Association thereof.

Given under the Common Seal of the Company the ____________ day of ____________ 19

______________________________ SECRETARY.

____
______________________________ DIRECTORS.

Figure 3.2 Share Certificate

Certificates should be ready within two months after the date of allotment of shares or receipt of the relevant transfer. For companies whose shares are listed on the Stock Exchange the time limit is two weeks after lodgement of the transfer.

LOST CERTIFICATES

Duplicate share certificates may be issued on completion by the shareholder of a letter of indemnity (see Figure 3.3). In addition to being signed by the shareholder the indemnity should be guaranteed by a bank or an insurance company. As the shareholder will generally be charged by the bank or insurance company for this guarantee companies may be willing to dispense with it if the value of the holding is low. If a certificate is lost in the post between an agent, for example, stockbroker, and the shareholder, most companies will accept an indemnity from the agent rather than the shareholder.

```
The Registrar




              WHEREAS certificate no.            for
              registered in my name has been lost or destroyed and in consideration
              of your issuing a duplicate certificate, I hereby agree to indemnify you
              against any loss which you may incur in consequence of your so doing and I
              undertake to return the original certificate to you for cancellation if it
              should come to hand.


                             Dated this          day of              19    .


                                      .................................


                             We join in the
                             above indemnity ....................................
                             (Bank or
                              Insurance Company)
```

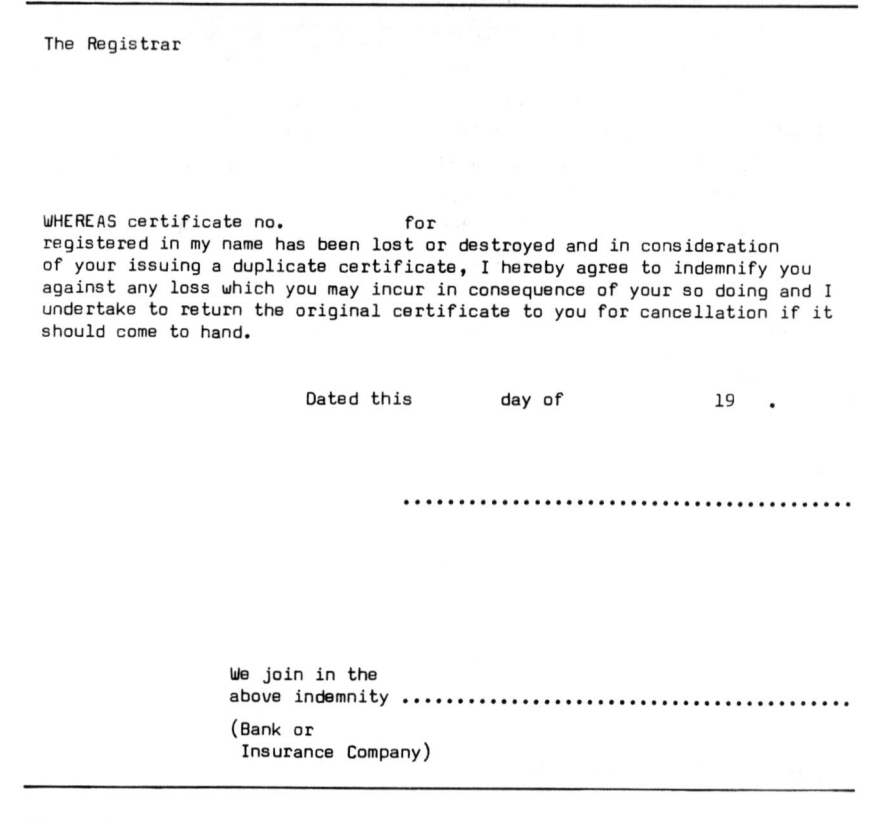

Figure 3.3 Indemnity for lost certificate

On receipt of the indemnity a duplicate certificate marked as such will be issued. If at any time in the future the missing certificate should turn up it should be returned to the registrar for cancellation and the indemnity returned to the shareholder.

MAINTAINING THE REGISTER

The share register will require to be kept up to date as regards both details of

MAINTAINING A COMPANY SHARE REGISTER

members and their shareholdings and also the issued share capital of the company. The following principal changes may occur in connection with shareholders.

Change of address

A shareholder should notify the company of a change of address but many omit to do so. Strictly speaking, when a shareholder's change of address is advised by someone other than the shareholder he should be asked to confirm this in writing (see Figure 3.4), but many companies accept a notification if received from a professional firm (NOT from a member of the shareholder's family). Frequently the first intimation of a change of address is the return by the Post Office of a communication marked 'gone away'. In this case the registrar should endeavour to trace the shareholder, for example, by writing to the bank through which the latest dividend has been cashed by the shareholder.

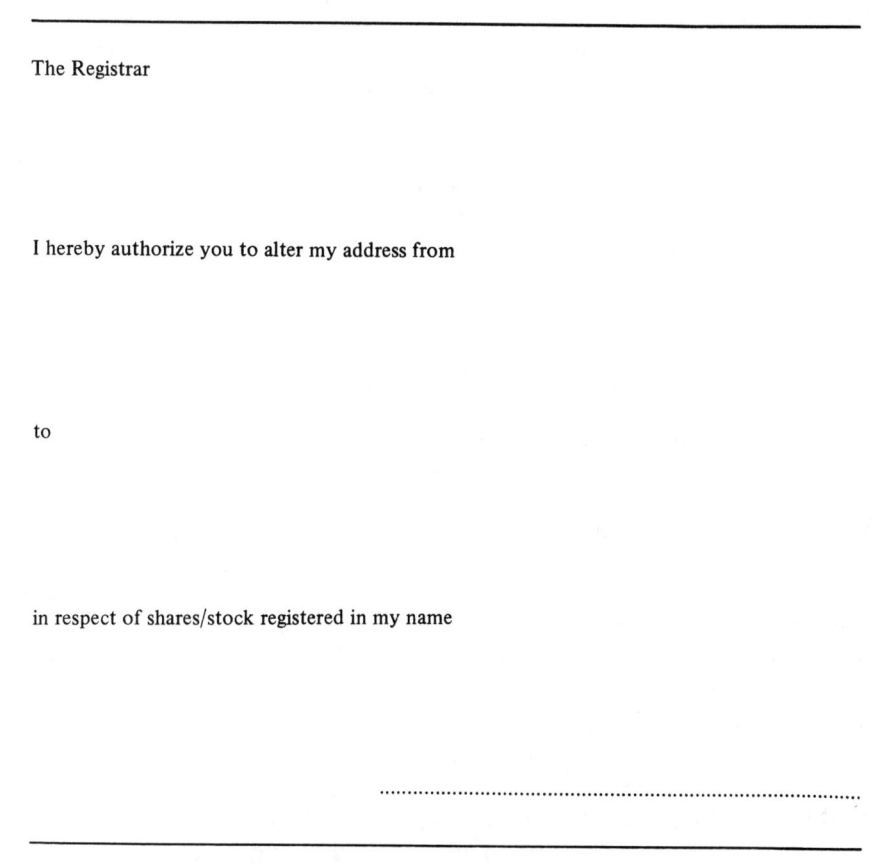

The Registrar

I hereby authorize you to alter my address from

to

in respect of shares/stock registered in my name

....

Figure 3.4 Shareholder's change of address

Change of name

This may occur through marriage in which case the shareholder should be asked to exhibit her marriage certificate. Some (English) companies will accept a photocopy of this, but in Scotland it would require to be certified by the District Registrar. A person may change his name by deed poll which should be exhibited and there is nothing to prevent someone calling himself by any name he chooses. In this case he should be asked to provide the company with a suitable statutory declaration.

Death of a shareholder

In a joint account. When a shareholder in a joint account dies the company is not concerned with his executors as the shareholding now stands in the name of the survivor(s). A death certificate should be exhibited; some companies accept certified photocopies if lodged by a professional firm. In Scotland, however, a copy of a death certificate must be certified by the District Registrar. The death certificate should be stamped with the company stamp to show it has been exhibited and the share certificate should be amended to show the names of the surviving holders. If the deceased shareholder was first-named in the account this will of course entail removing the account to a different part of the register.

If a death certificate is not readily available a probate or confirmation will sometimes be lodged instead. This merely gives evidence of the death and no other particulars should be extracted from it.

Sole name. On the death of a member who is registered as the sole holder a grant of probate is the usual English document to be exhibited. It may be the complete deed, which will have a copy of the will attached, or, as is usual, be an 'office copy' of which sufficient will have been obtained to cover all the deceased's assets and so avoid delay in circulating the probate in turn to several registrars. This office copy merely records the names and addresses of the executors and confirms that they have the right to deal with the estate, without specifying the assets involved. In Scotland, the equivalent document is a confirmation. The complete confirmation will have included in it an inventory of the deceased's assets, but if these are numerous it is usual to obtain certificates of confirmation, one for each of the assets involved. Unlike English office copies of probates these certificates of confirmation each specify the particular asset covered by the certificate and when received by the registrar should be compared with the deceased's holding in the register. If the certificate is for a smaller number of shares than is actually held by the shareholder it will be necessary for the executors to obtain a further confirmation known as an eik so that they may be entitled to deal with the additional shares.

If a shareholder dies intestate or if an executor declines to accept office then in England application may be made to the court to have administrators appointed to deal with the estate. In due course letters of administration will be granted and exhibited to the registrar in the same way as probate. The equivalent term in Scotland is executor's dative.

In all cases the share certificates should be endorsed to record the date of death of the shareholder and to add the names of the executors or administrators described as such. The shareholder's account in the register should be similarly amended but since the holding remains in the name of the deceased shareholder its place in the register is unchanged.

As a considerable time may elapse after a death before probate or confirmation is obtained solicitors will sometimes inform registrars of the death and ask them to retain any dividends etc. to avoid such items being lost in the post.

If the executors wish to have the shares registered in their own names without reference to the deceased shareholder they may complete a letter of request (see Figure 3.5). This document is similar to a stock transfer form and should be signed by the executors and will be accepted by English companies without payment of stamp duty. In Scotland a letter of request attracts the same stamp duty as would a transfer in similar circumstances and must be sent to the stamp office for adjudication before being lodged for registration.

A shareholder may die intestate leaving only a very small estate which would not justify the expense involved in obtaining letters of administration. Provided that the *total* value of the estate, including the shares in question, is not more than £5,000 most companies will agree to register the death and transfer the shares to the next of kin on receipt of the following documents:

(*a*) statutory declaration by next of kin (see Figure 3.6)
(*b*) form of indemnity (see Figure 3.7)
(*c*) death certificate
(*d*) share certificate
(*e*) letter from the capital taxes office confirming that no claim to tax arises on the death

Because of the difficulty which may be experienced in obtaining this last document companies may be willing to dispense with it. In this case a suitable paragraph should be included in the statutory declaration.

Communications

Sometimes shareholders will wish communications to be sent to an agent rather than to themselves and such a request must be obtained in writing from the shareholder.

LETTER OF REQUEST	(above this line for Registrar's use only)
	REQUEST BY EXECUTORS OR ADMINISTRATORS OF A DECEASED HOLDER TO BE PLACED ON THE REGISTER AS HOLDERS IN THEIR OWN RIGHT

TO THE DIRECTORS OF _____

Full name and address of Undertaking.

*Full description of Security. *(See note below)*

	WORDS	FIGURES

Number or amount of Shares, Stock or other Security and, in figures column only, number and denomination of units if any.

(_____ units of _____)

Full name of Deceased. _____ Deceased

late of _____

I/We, the undersigned, being the personal representative(s) of the above-named deceased, hereby request you to register me/us in the books of the Company as the holder(s) of the above-mentioned Stock/Shares now registered in the name of the said deceased.

DATED this _____ day of _____ 19 _____

Signature of Personal Representative(s)

Figure 3.5 Letter of request

Full name(s) and full postal address(es) (including County or, if applicable, Postal District number) of the Personal Representative(s) in the order in which they are to be registered.	
Please state title, if any, or whether Mr, Mrs or Miss.	
Please complete in typewriting or in Block Capitals	

IF AN ACCOUNT ALREADY EXISTS IN THE ABOVE NAME(S) THE ABOVE-MENTIONED HOLDING WILL BE ADDED TO THAT ACCOUNT, UNLESS INSTRUCTIONS ARE GIVEN TO THE CONTRARY.

The Certificate(s) in the name of the deceased if not already with the Company's Registrars must accompany this form.	Stamp or name and address of person lodging this form.

*A separate Letter of Request should be used for each class of security.

Figure 3.5 *(concluded)*

I,

of

do solemnly and sincerely declare that:—

1. I am the   of   deceased ("the deceased") who died intestate on   19   , and that I am the only person entitled to the estate of the deceased.

2. The total value of the estate of the deceased in the United Kingdom, which includes   shares of   each, fully paid, in does not exceed £

3. No capital transfer tax/inheritance tax is payable in respect of the estate of the deceased.

4. I do not intend nor, to the best of my knowledge, does any other person intend to apply for a grant of administration of the estate of the deceased.

And I make this solemn declaration conscientiously believing the same to be true and by virtue of the provisions of the Statutory Declarations Act 1835.

Declared at

the   day of

one thousand nine hundred and

before me

Figure 3.6 Statutory declaration by next of kin

MAINTAINING A COMPANY SHARE REGISTER   *61*

The Directors

In consideration of your Company recognizing me as the sole administrator of the estate of
                                        deceased ("the deceased") without
the production to the Company of a grant of administration of the estate of the deceased, I
hereby agree to indemnify you and the Company from and against all claims, demands, losses,
damages, costs, charges and expenses which you or the Company in consequence thereof may
sustain, incur or be liable for, and I undertake to complete at the request of the Company, such
document or documents as may be necessary to transfer into my name
                    shares of   each, fully paid, in the Company which are registered in the
name of the deceased. I further undertake to obtain and produce to the Company a grant of
administration of the estate of the deceased if so required by the Company.

Dated this   day of   19

Signature:

Address:

Figure 3.7 Indemnity by next of kin

Powers of attorney

A shareholder may appoint an attorney to deal with his affairs, perhaps because of advancing years or because he is resident or travelling abroad etc. A deed will be drawn up known as a power of attorney and sent to registrars for noting in their records. In England there is a fairly standard form based on the Powers of Attorney Act 1971 (see Figure 3.8) which covers all circumstances likely to arise in dealing with securities. If the power varies at

---

Form of general power of attorney (pursuant to Powers of Attorney Act 1971, s. 10)

THIS GENERAL POWER OF ATTORNEY is made this .... day of .... 19...... by A.B. of ....

I appoint C.D. of ....

[or C.D. of .... and E.F. of .... jointly *or* jointly and severally] to be my attorney(s) in accordance with section 10 of the Powers of Attorney Act 1971.

IN WITNESS WHEREOF I have hereunto set my hand and seal the day and year first above written.

Signed, sealed and
delivered by the above-   ....
named A.B. in the
presence of:

Figure 3.8   Power of attorney

all from the standard form it is advisable for registrars to keep a copy of it and to note in a prominent place any unusual features; for example, it may be for a short period only, or cover only certain situations. Powers of attorney will be noted in the same way as communications addresses as communications will be sent to the attorney rather than the shareholder. Note, however, that no reference to an attorney should be made on the share certificate. A general power of attorney is not valid in the case of trustees or executors and, unless the power specifically provides, an attorney may not delegate or appoint a substitute.

MAINTAINING A COMPANY SHARE REGISTER

The short form based on the Powers of Attorney Act described above is not applicable to powers executed in Scotland.

Documents signed by an attorney may be either in his own name or in the name of his principal, for example, AB Attorney to CD, or CD by his Attorney AB.

Dividend mandates

The shareholder's account in the register should contain details of any dividend mandate (see Figure 3.9) completed by the shareholder. This will usually be received from the bank and should bear the bank stamp and details of sorting code and account number. When paying dividends to shareholders' accounts with the large banks most companies use the bulk distribution system whereby instead of preparing individual warrants for all shareholders one warrant is sent to each bank for the total amount of dividends due to the bank's customers. This is accompanied by dividend counterfoils (tax vouchers) for all the relevant shareholders and the bank will then distribute these to its various branches so that the appropriate accounts may be credited.

Mandates may be received in favour of small banks which are not in the bulk distribution system or for building societies or other firms etc. In these cases the normal type of warrant with counterfoil attached will be used, as for shareholders who receive dividends direct.

Designation of accounts

Where the shareholder does not own the shares personally, but holds them in a nominee or trustee capacity, registrars are sometimes asked to add a designation which helps to identify the holding; for example, a person holding shares as a nominee for Mr Andrew Black might wish the designation 'AB Account' added after his name. If the designation does not appear on the original application form or transfer, or if it is desired to amend the designation, the shareholder should be asked to complete the appropriate form (see Figure 3.10). Designations are often requested where shares in a company are held by trustees, as English companies do not recognise trusts, for example, Andrew Black and John White, JG Account. In Scotland a trust clause may be added to the registered name, e.g. Andrew Black and John White, trustees of Mr James Gray's trust. In this case the holding will appear in the register under the name of the trust, i.e. Gray, rather than the name of the first holder as would be the case in England.

A request for designation should be accompanied by the relevant share certificate for endorsement.

64 THE CONSTITUTION AND CONDUCT OF COMPANIES

COMPANY SECURITIES

For Company's use Only

REQUEST for PAYMENT of INTEREST or DIVIDENDS

To: The Secretary or Registrar   *Date* _____ 19 _____

Insert name and address of Company

_____

_____

        Please forward, until further notice, all Interest and Dividends that may from time to time become due on any Stock or Shares now standing, or which may hereafter stand, in my (our) name(s) or in the name(s) of the survivor(s) of us in the Company's books to: —

Full name and address of the Bank, Firm or Person to whom Interest and Dividends are to be sent

_____

_____

_____

or, where payment is to be made to a Bank, to such other Branch of that Bank as the Bank may from time to time request. Your compliance with this request shall discharge the Company's liability in respect of such interest or dividends.

This form must be signed by ALL the Registered Holders, Executors or Administrators as the case may be

(1) *Signature* _____   (3) *Signature* _____

Name in full _____   *Name in full* _____
(BLOCK CAPITALS)   (BLOCK CAPITALS)
Address _____   *Address* _____

Any change of address may be notified by quoting former and present address

(2) *Signature* _____   (4) *Signature* _____

Name in full _____   *Name in full* _____
(BLOCK CAPITALS)   (BLOCK CAPITALS)
Address _____   *Address* _____

NOTE (i) Directions to credit a particular account MUST be given to the Bank direct and NOT INCLUDED in this form.
         (ii) Where the stock is in the name of a deceased Holder, instructions signed by Executor(s) or Administrator(s) should indicate the name of the deceased.

Where the instructions <u>are in favour of a Bank</u>, this form should be sent to the Bank branch concerned for the insertion of the following details: —

Bank's Reference Numbers and Details: —

    (1)   Sorting Code No. _____

    (2)   Name of Bank and
           Title of Branch _____

    (3)   Account Number (if any) _____

STAMP OF BANK BRANCH

Figure 3.9   Dividend mandate

MAINTAINING A COMPANY SHARE REGISTER

Name of undertaking _____

Description of security _____

Amount of stock
or number of
stock units/shares
or other security _____

Full names and
addresses of all
holders

_____

Existing
designation
(if any) _____

New
designation
(if any) _____

I/We, the undersigned hereby request that the amount or number of stock units/shares or other security mentioned above be (delete options not applicable).

(i)   Designated as shown in new designation box.

(ii) Redesignated as shown in new designation box.

(iii) The existing designation be cancelled (please write cancelled in new designation box).

1 .... 2 ....

3 .... 4 ....

This form should be signed by all holders

Bodies corporate should sign by means of authorized signatories whose capacities must be stated.

Date ....

Figure 3.10 Request for designation or redesignation of account

Transfers

Most registration work in a public company will normally occur in the processing of transfers of shares. These may be private transactions, for example, a gift or a transfer to a beneficiary from a trust, in which case the normal white stock transfer form (see Figure 3.11) giving details of both transferor and transferee will be used. On receipt of such a transfer the following points should be checked:

1 That the details of transferor and number and class of shares agree with the certificate and with the share register
2 That the transfer is signed by the member or his attorney, or by *all* the joint holders, or, in the case of a company, that the seal has been affixed and attested
3 That the correct stamp duty has been paid

If the transfer represents a purchase, ad valorem stamp duty is charged and the registrar should be able to see from the amount of the consideration shown on the transfer if this is in line with the current market price and check if the proper duty has been paid. The rate of ad valorem duty on ordinary shares was reduced in the Finance Act 1986 from 1 to 0.5 per cent.

Certain transfers have until recently attracted a nominal 50p stamp duty, for example, transfers to and from nominees, transfers to beneficiaries from trusts etc. Details of the various categories liable to this nominal duty are given on the reverse of the transfer (see Figure 3.11). In this connection the first category relates to holdings in the names of trustees. Any changes in trustees will require a transfer to be executed unless, in the case of Scottish companies, the account is registered in the name of trust in which case it will be sufficient to exhibit to the registrar the appropriate deed of assumption or minute of resignation.

Stamp duty on gifts *inter vivos* was reduced to 50p with effect from 26 March 1985 but as from 1 May 1987 all these categories are exempt from duty.

Transfers to charities are similarly free of duty.

Until recently this type of transfer was also used for Stock Exchange transactions but with the introduction of the Talisman system, which applies to most securities quoted on the Stock Exchange, separate transfers are now prepared for seller and purchaser. The Talisman system has dispensed with the time-consuming need to match sellers and purchasers. Instead, all shares sold through the Stock Exchange go into a pool to be allotted in due course to purchasers. This pool is known as Sepon for which an account will be maintained in the share register but for which no certificates are issued. At regular intervals, for example daily or weekly depending on the volume involved, the Stock Exchange lodges with registrars those transfers signed

STOCK TRANSFER FORM

(Above this line for Registrar only)

Consideration Money £....................	Certificate lodged with the Registrar
	(For completion by the Registrar/Stock Exchange)

Full name of Undertaking.	
Full description of Security.	
Number or amount of Shares, Stock or other security and, in figures column only, number and denomination of units if any.	Words	Figures (units of)
Name(s) of re-gistered holder(s) should be given in full; the address should be given where there is only one holder. If the transfer is not made by the registered holder(s) insert also the name(s) and capacity e.g., Executor(s) of the person(s) making the transfer.	In the name(s) of

Figure 3.11 Stock transfer form

I/We hereby transfer the above security out of the name(s) aforesaid to the person(s) named below *or to the several persons named in Parts 2 of Brokers Transfer Forms to the above security:*

Delete words in italics except for stock exchange transactions.

Signature(s) of transferor(s)

1. ....
2. ....
3. ....
4. ....

Bodies corporate should execute under their common seal.

Full name(s) and full postal address(es) (including County or, if applicable Postal District number) of the person(s) to whom the security is transferred.

Please state title, if any, or whether Mr., Mrs., or Miss.

Please complete in typewriting or in Block Capitals.

Stamp of Selling Broker(s) or, for transactions which are not stock exchange transactions, of Agent(s) if any, acting for the Transferor(s).

Date..............

I/We request that such entries be made in the register as are necessary to give effect to this transfer.

Stamp of Buying Broker(s) (if any)	Stamp or name and address of person lodging this form (if other than the Buying Broker(s))

PLEASE SIGN HERE
(No witness required)

Figure 3.11 *(continued)*

The security represented by the transfer overleaf has been sold as follows:—

..............................Shares/Stock ....Shares/Stock

..............................Shares/Stock ....Shares/Stock

..............................Shares/Stock ....Shares/Stock

..............................Shares/Stock ....Shares/Stock

..............................Shares/Stock ....Shares/Stock

..............................Shares/Stock ....Shares/Stock

Balance (if any) due to Selling Broker(s) _____

Amount of Certificate(s) _____

Brokers Transfer Forms for above amounts certified

Stamp of certifying Stock Exchange   *Stamp of Selling Broker(s)*

Figure 3.11 (*continued*)

FORM OF CERTIFICATE REQUIRED WHERE TRANSFER IS NOT LIABLE TO AD VALOREM STAMP DUTY

Instruments of transfer are liable to a fixed duty of 10s. (50p) when the transaction falls within one of the following categories:—

(a) Transfer vesting the property in new trustees on the appointment of a new trustee of a pre-existing trust, or on the retirement of a trustee.
(b) Transfer by way of security for a loan or re-transfer to the original transferor on repayment of a loan.
(c) Transfer to a beneficiary under a will of a specific legacy of stock, etc. (NOTE—Transfers by executors in discharge or partial discharge of a pecuniary legacy are chargeable with ad valorem duty on the amount of the legacy so discharged unless the will confers on the executors power to discharge the pecuniary legacy without the consent of the legatee.)
(d) Transfer of stock, etc., forming part of an intestate's estate to the person entitled to it, not being a transfer in satisfaction or part satisfaction (i) in England and Wales of the sum to which the surviving spouse has a statutory entitlement under an intestacy where the total value of the residuary estate exceeds that sum, or of the sum due to the surviving spouse in respect of the value of a life interest which he or she has elected to have redeemed, (ii) in Scotland, of any of the monetary rights of the surviving spouse under the provisions of Section 8 (1) (a) (iii), Section 8 (1) (b) or Section 9 (1) of the Succession (Scotland) Act, 1964 as amended by the Succession (Scotland) Act, 1973.
(e) Transfer to a residuary legatee of stock, etc. form part of the residue divisible under a will.
(f) Transfer to a beneficiary under a settlement, on distribution of the trust funds, of stock, etc., forming the share or part of the share of those funds to which the beneficiary is entitled in accordance with the terms of the settlement.
(NOTE—Categories (e) and (f) do not include a transfer to a beneficiary under a will or settlement who takes not only by reason of being entitled under the will or settlement but also
  (i) following a purchase by him of some other interest in the trust property, e.g., a life interest or the interest of some other beneficiary : in such a case ad valorem transfer on sale duty is payable or
  (ii) where there is an element of gift inter vivos in the transaction in consequence of which a beneficiary under a will or settlement takes a share greater in value than his share under the will or settlement : in such a case ad valorem voluntary disposition duty is payable.)
(g) Transfer on and in consideration of marriage of stocks, etc., to either party of the marriage or to trustees to be held on the terms of a duly stamped settlement made in consideration of the marriage. (NOTE—A transfer made to the husband or wife after the date of the marriage is not within this category unless it is made pursuant to an ante-nuptial contract.)
(h) Transfer by the liquidator of a company of stocks, etc., forming part of the assets of the company, to the persons who were shareholders in satisfaction of their rights on a winding-up.
*(j) Transfer, not on sale and not arising under any contract of sale and where no beneficial interest in the property passes, (i) to a person who is a mere nominee of, and is nominated only by, the transferor, (ii) from a mere nominee who has at all times held the property on behalf of the transferee, (iii) from one nominee to another nominee of the same beneficial owner where the first nominee has at all times held the property on behalf of that beneficial owner. (NOTE—This category does not include a transfer made in any of the following circumstances: (i) by a holder of stock, etc., following the grant of an option to purchase the stock, to the person entitled to the option or his nominee; (ii) to a nominee in contemplation of a contract for the sale of the stock, etc., then about to be entered into; (iii) from the nominee of a vendor who has instructed the nominee orally or by some unstamped writing to hold stock, etc., in trust for a purchaser, to such purchaser.)

(1) "I," or "we,"
(2) Insert "(a)," "(b)," or appropriate category.
(3) Here set out concisely the facts explaining the transaction in cases falling within (b) and (j) or in any case which does not clearly fall within any of the categories (a) to (j). Adjudication may be required.

(1) .... hereby certify that the transaction in respect of which this transfer is made is one which falls within the category (2) .... above.

(3) ....

* Signature(s) .... * Description ("Transferor", "Solicitor", etc.)

Date .... 19......

N.B.—A transfer by way of a gift inter vivos is chargeable with ad valorem stamp duty and must be adjudicated.

*NOTE—The above certificate should be signed in the case of (b) or (j) either by (1) the transferor(s) or (2) a member of a stock exchange or a solicitor or an accredited representative of a bank acting for the transferor(s); in cases falling within (b) where the bank or its official nominee is a party to the transfer, a certificate, instead of setting out the terms of the loan, is to the effect that "the transfer is excepted from Section 74 of the Finance (1909–10) Act, 1910." A certificate in other cases should be signed by a solicitor or other person (e.g., a bank acting as trustee or executor) having a full knowledge of the facts.

Figure 3.11 *(concluded)*

MAINTAINING A COMPANY SHARE REGISTER

by the sellers in respect of shares sold which have to be transferred in the first instance into the name of Sepon (these are known as Talisman Sold Transfers or TSTs, see Figure 3.12) and transfers out of the name of Sepon to be registered in the names of the purchasers (Talisman Bought Transfers or TBTs, see Figure 3.13). These are accompanied by a Sepon advice note giving totals of shares bought and sold. The sold transfers are backed up by share certificates in names of the sellers and after making checks similar to those described above the certificate is cancelled, the number of shares sold deducted from the shareholder's account in the register and added to the Sepon account and a balance certificate where applicable prepared in the name of the seller. Similarly, the number of shares on the bought transfers is deducted from the Sepon account in the register and added to the purchasers' accounts if they are already shareholders, or, if not, new accounts are opened. New share certificates are then prepared for the purchasers and sent to the Stock Exchange. At the same time the Sepon advice note is returned, the registrar having inserted the Sepon balance brought forward and the new balance to be carried forward.

Rectification of transferee details

If a stockbroker makes a mistake in a transfer lodged for registration, e.g. by inserting the wrong name or omitting a joint holder etc., he may lodge a rectification of transferee details form (see Figure 3.14). This must be done within three months of the lodging of the original transfer and before a dividend has been paid on the shares.

Certification

Sometimes a transfer accompanied by a share certificate will be received by the registrar with a request that it be certified, ie that the registrar should confirm that a certificate has been lodged in the name of the transferor covering the shares specified on the transfer. This is all that the registrar is certifying – he is not guaranteeing that the person named is in fact the owner of the shares. The registrar will stamp the appropriate box on the transfer with the company stamp on the lines 'Certificate for ..... shares lodged with registrar' and return the transfer, retaining the certificate. The company stamp should be signed or initialled by the registrar. In due course the transfer will be returned for registration with the certification on the transfer taking the place of a share certificate.

Following the introduction of the Talisman system the volume of certifications has decreased substantially. Previously when buyers and sellers had to be matched, if, say, sale of a large holding had to take place to several different purchasers, one transfer would be signed by the transferor and lodged with the registrar, together with the covering certificate and at the same time a broker's transfer (coloured blue) had to be produced and

TALISMAN SOLD TRANSFER

This transfer is pursuant to a Stock Exchange transaction, and is exempt from Transfer Stamp Duty.

Above this line for Registrar's use only

Bargain Reference No.:

Name of Undertaking	Certificate lodged with Registr
Description of Security	*(for completion by the Registr Stock Exchange)*
Amount of Stock or number of Stock units or shares or other security in words	Figures
In the name(s) of	Account Designation (if any)

Name(s) of registered holder(s) should be given in full; the address should be given where there is only one holder.

If the transfer is not made by the registered holder(s) insert also the name(s) and capacity (e.g., Executor(s)) of the person(s) making the transfer.

Figure 3.12 Talisman Sold Transfer

I/We hereby transfer the above security out of the name(s) aforesaid into the name of SEPON LIMITED and request the necessary entries to be made in the register.	Balance Certificate Required for (amount or number in figures)
Bodies corporate should affix their common seal and each signatory should state his/her representative capacity (e.g. 'Company Secretary' 'Director') against his/her signature. 1 _____ 2 _____ 3 _____ 4 _____	Stamp and Firm Code of Selling Broker Date
SEPON LIMITED is lodging this Transfer at the direction and on behalf of the Member Firm whose stamp appears herein ('the Original Lodging Agent') and does not in any manner or to any extent warrant or represent the validity or genuineness of the transfer instructions contained herein or the genuineness of the Transferor's signature. The Original Lodging Agent by delivering this Transfer to SEPON LIMITED authorises SEPON LIMITED to lodge this Transfer for registration and agrees to be deemed for all purposes to be the person(s) actually lodging this Transfer for registration.	Stock Exchange Operating Account Number (if applicable)

⇧

PLEASE SIGN HERE

Figure 3.12 *(concluded)*

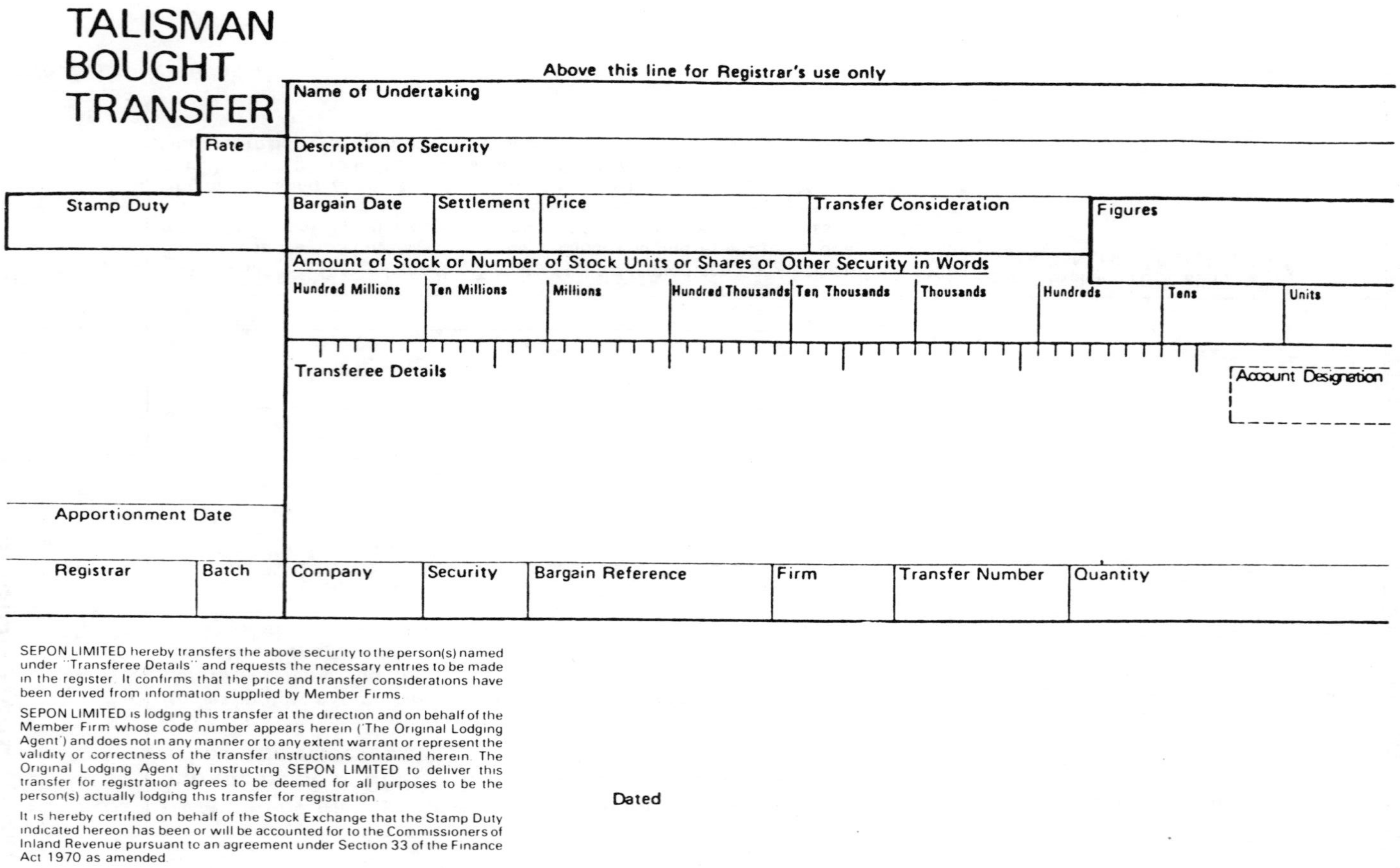

Figure 3.13 Talisman Bought Transfer

MAINTAINING A COMPANY SHARE REGISTER 75

REQUEST FOR RECTIFICATION OF TRANSFEREE DETAILS

Above this line for Registrar's use only

Name of undertaking	
Description of security	
Amount of stock or number of stock units/shares or other security	Words / Figures
Please complete in typewriting or in block capitals	Account designation (if any)
Full name(s) address(es) into which security was incorrectly registered	

PLEASE SIGN HERE ⇨

We hereby certify that as a result of a clerical error this security was registered as above. We request and authorise you to amend the holder's details in the register as under. We confirm that there has been no sub-sale.

Stamp of buying Broker or agent lodging transfer

Authorised signatory whose capacity must be stated   Date ....

Please complete in typewriting or in block capitals	Account designation (if any)
Full name(s) and address(es) into which security should have been registered	

IMPORTANT
THIS FORM MUST BE LODGED AT THE OFFICE OF THE COMPANY'S REGISTRAR TOGETHER WITH THE RELATIVE SHARE/STOCK CERTIFICATE(S), AND ANY REMITTANCE REQUIRED BY THE COMPANY.

IF DIVIDENDS ARE TO BE PAID TO A BANK, OR OTHER THIRD PARTY, A NEW MANDATE MUST BE COMPLETED.

Figure 3.14   Rectification of transferee details

certified for each purchaser before being lodged for registration. Now, with shares sold going into the Sepon pool and purchases being allocated from the pool, this is hardly ever necessary. However, certification is still requested, for example, where a holding is disposed of very shortly after being acquired and before a certificate has been issued.

Certification may also be carried out by the Stock Exchange, in which case the registrar will receive an advice from the exchange together with a certificate for cancellation. Again the certified transfer will later be lodged for registration, but in this instance it will bear the Stock Exchange certification stamp and should of course be checked against the cancelled certificate before being processed.

Stock exchange document service

The Stock Exchange has recently introduced a document service for its members, covering documents such as powers of attorney, probates and confirmations. A stockbroker may send the original document to the Stock Exchange who will check it and issue certified copies to the various registrars involved thus saving some time and trouble.

SHARE CAPITAL

As well as changes regarding shareholders, from time to time there may be changes in the issued share capital of the company which will require to be reflected in the register.

Scrip or capitalization issue

The company may capitalize part of its reserves and turn them into paid up shares to be issued pro rata to existing members of the company. Such shares are often called bonus shares but this term is misleading. Although they are issued without payment, the total value of a member's increased number of shares following the issue will be virtually unchanged, each share now being worth proportionately less than before. This type of share issue is usually made by means of renounceable share certificates. These are similar to normal share certificates but have on the reverse a form of renunciation for use where the shareholder does not wish to retain the new shares, and a registration application form for completion by the person to whom the shares are to be transferred. The renounceable certificates will be issued in the existing shareholder's name with the appropriate number of shares inserted pro rata to his existing holding, for example one new share for every two held. If he wishes to keep the shares no action is necessary on his part other than to keep the certificate in a safe place and in due course the shares

MAINTAINING A COMPANY SHARE REGISTER

allotted will be added to the balance in his account. If, however, he wishes to dispose of them, for example by selling on the market or by way of gift, the form of renunciation should be signed and the certificate will then be passed on to his stockbroker for sale or to his agent dealing with the gift etc. who will complete the registration application form and lodge it with the registrar. If the shareholder wishes to dispose of only some of the new shares or to dispose of them to different persons he must sign the renunciation form and send it to the registrar with a request for split receipts in the amounts required. Each split receipt (see Figure 3.15) must then be completed in the name of the person acquiring the shares and returned for registration. If any split receipts are not returned by the due date the shares will revert to the original allottee.

SPLIT RECEIPT

IMPORTANT.—This document is of value until   , when it ceases to be of any value. If you do not understand how to deal with it you should consult your Stockbroker, Bank Manager, Solicitor, Accountant or other professional adviser immediately.

At the Company's Registrars.

Last day for Splitting	Last day for Registration of Renunciation . . .

INSTRUCTIONS

1. RETENTION OF SHARES BY ORIGINAL ALLOTTEE

If you are the person to whom the Shares comprised in the original Renounceable Cetificate referred to in Form A were allotted and you are retaining the Shares comprised in this Split Receipt you need take no further action and a definitive Share Certificate will be sent to you not later than .

If, however, the Certificate is to be sent to your agent, the name and address of that agent must be inserted in the box at the foot of Form Y and the Split Receipt lodged at the Company's Registrars not later than

2. SPLITTING

If you wish to exchange this Split Receipt for several Split Receipts you must apply to . not later than   '. Your application, accompanied by this Split Receipt, must state the number of Shares to be comprised in each new Split Receipt.

3. REGISTRATION

(a) If you are not the original allottee and the Shares are to be registered in your name, Form Y must be completed and the Split Receipt lodged with   , not later than   . In the absence of such registration the shares can be transferred only by instrument of transfer subject to Stamp Duty.

(b) If you wish to consolidate the Shares comprised in several Certificates (duly renounced where applicable) and/or Split Receipts you or your agent should complete Form Y and the Consolidation Listing Form on one Certificate or Split Receipt (referred to as the Principal Document) and lodge all such documents with   , on or before

4. CERTIFICATES

In all cases of renunciation definitive Share Certificates will be sent by ordinary post not later than   . to the person lodging the Registration Application Form. After   . and pending the issue of Certificates, transfers will be certified against the Register.

5. GENERAL

The surrender of any Certificate or Split Receipt purporting to have been completed and/or signed in accordance with these instructions shall be conclusive evidence in favour of the Company and its Agents of the title of the person(s) surrendering it to deal with it and to receive Split Receipts or a Certificate in exchange. Certificates and Split Receipts sent through the post are sent at the risk of the person(s) entitled to them.

Figure 3.15   Split receipt

Instructions governing the use of this Split Receipt are set out overleaf

Split Receipt No..................

ISSUE OF ORDINARY SHARES OF EACH CREDITED AS FULLY PAID

FORM A

This Split Receipt relates to [ ] Ordinary Shares of each fully paid previously comprised in Renounceable Certificate No. .... which has been surrendered to .... having been duly renounced by the original allottee(s). *Exd.* ....

FORM Y REGISTRATION APPLICATION FORM

To the Directors of:

Registration is requested in the name(s) set out below of the Ordinary Shares comprised in this split Receipt (and in the attached Split Receipts and Certificates (if any) detailed in the Consolidation Listing Form), totalling [ ] Ordinary Shares of 25p each fully paid subject to the Memorandum and Articles of Association of the Company.

Authority is hereby given for a definitive Share Certificate to be sent by post at the risk of the Shareholder(s) to the person or agent lodging this Form.

(1) *Christian Name(s)* .... (3) ....
    (IN FULL)
    Surname ....
    (IN FULL)
    Address ....
    (IN FULL)

(2) *Christian Name(s)* .... (4) ....
    (IN FULL)
    Surname ....
    (IN FULL)
    Address ....
    (IN FULL)

(PLEASE USE BLOCK CAPITALS)   (PLEASE STATE TITLE, IF ANY, OR WHETHER MR, MRS, OR MISS)

Stamp or name and address of person lodging this Form

CONSOLIDATION LISTING FORM	
Serial Number of Principal Document	
Document Nos. (in numerical order)	Number of Ordinary Shares
Total Number of Documents	Total Number of Ordinary Shares
New Certificate No.	

Figure 3.15 *(concluded)*

MAINTAINING A COMPANY SHARE REGISTER

At the end of the renunciation period the new shares will be entered on the register either in the name of the original allottees or in the name of the renouncees. Definitive certificates will be prepared and issued to the renouncees. In the case of shares not renounced the renounceable certificates retained by the original allottees will become definitive.

Rights issue

Rights issues are similar to scrip issues in that new shares are offered to existing holders in proportion to their existing holdings. However these usually arise when a company wishes to raise further capital as, unlike a scrip issue, shareholders must pay to take up the new shares and if they do not wish to do so they may sell the rights in the market. Alternatively they may let the rights lapse and in most cases the company will sell the rights to shares not taken up and distribute the proceeds to those shareholders entitled to them.

Since the new shares are only *provisionally* allotted until such time as the shareholders pay for them it is not appropriate here to issue renounceable certificates. Instead letters of allotment are prepared with details of the number of new shares provisionally allotted and the cost of taking them up. Shareholders wishing to take up the rights return the allotment letters with the appropriate payment and the letters will be receipted and sent back to them to be retained until the new certificates are ready.

As with renounceable certificates, shareholders wishing to sell on the market or gift the shares to donees have to sign the form of renunciation on the allotment letter and there are similar facilities for obtaining splits. Rights issues involve considerably more work than scrip issues since there may be a great deal of splitting and resplitting before the renunciation period comes to an end and of course definitive certificates have to be prepared in the appropriate names for all the shares taken up.

Conversion

As well as ordinary and preference and loan stocks, a company may issue a *convertible* loan stock which starts off life as an ordinary loan stock paying a fixed rate of interest. At various specified times there are opportunities for holders to convert into ordinary shares of the company at a predetermined conversion rate. Shortly before the conversion date the company will send a circular letter to holders reminding them of the forthcoming opportunity to convert. The circular will give details of prices of the ordinary shares and of the convertible loan stock at the latest practicable date so that a comparison can be made of the values and yields and shareholders can decide whether it would be beneficial to convert.

The convertible loan stock certificate will have a conversion notice on the reverse which should be signed if conversion is to take place. The opportunity is usually given at the same time for the holder to nominate someone else to receive the new ordinary shares if he wishes to dispose of them. The signed certificate should then be lodged with the registrar and in due course new ordinary share certificates will be issued.

Other issues

Further issues of new shares may be made as a result for example of a successful bid for another company; in share option schemes whereby employees are given an option to purchase shares of the company at some time in the future at a fixed price; in scrip option dividend schemes operated by some companies whereby shareholders may elect to receive additional shares in lieu of cash dividends. Other types of issues may also arise from time to time. In all these cases, if a company listed on the Stock Exchange is involved, it will be necessary to apply for listing of the new shares to be granted. In addition, as mentioned above, a return of allotments is required to be made to the Registrar of Companies.

With all these issues, it is necessary to ensure that the company has sufficient authorized share capital and power to allot shares in accordance with $s80$ of the Companies Act 1985.

SUBSIDIARY BOOKS

Having dealt with the maintenance of the company share register it should be mentioned that the registrar will almost certainly find it necessary to have additional books in which to record information to back up entries in the register. Where the share register in use is in computerized form, it is very useful to maintain a transfer book (see Figure 3.16) which contains in one volume in chronological order details of transfers registered, new certificates issued, balance certificates issued, balance in Sepon account etc. Where, as is very common now, share certificates are not signed by the directors and the securities seal is used rather than the common seal of the company, a periodic

Date & transfer no.	Transferor	No. of shares	Transferee	New certificate no.
Certificates cancelled	Balance	Balance certificate no.	Sepon balance	Certifications outstanding

Figure 3.16 Suggested headings for transfer book

MAINTAINING A COMPANY SHARE REGISTER

report will be prepared for the board, giving details of transfers registered and new certificates issued. This can readily be obtained from the transfer book which should be reconciled each time entries are made in it.

FURTHER READING

This chapter has given only a brief outline of the work involved in looking after a share register. *Company Secretarial Practice*, the manual of the Institute of Chartered Secretaries and Administrators, published by ICSA Publishing Limited, will be found to be most helpful in dealing with any aspect of company secretarial or registration work.

4

The Conduct of Meetings

Desmond Fitzpatrick

In small private companies, it is often possible and usually quite sensible to minimize the formality connected with company meetings, but in larger companies — especially those under the constant surveillance of the financial press, the Stock Exchange or a shareholders' 'ginger' group — it is important that the procedures are carried out absolutely correctly, if only from the public relations point of view. More important, however, is the fact that under the Companies Act precise provisions regarding meetings have been made for the protection of individual rights and for the benefit of all concerned, and it is obviously the duty of the officers or servants of a company responsible for meetings to see that the rules are carefully observed in the interest of the company, its directors and its shareholders. Meetings have often been set aside by the courts merely because of failure to comply with a particular provision of the Companies Act or with a regulation contained in the articles of association of a company. Such an invalidation would without doubt cause considerable embarrassment to the employee or executive concerned and, of course, much preparatory work carried out prior to the abortive meeting may have to be repeated.

This chapter will refer mainly to companies limited by shares. It is designed to guide readers through the relevant provisions of the Companies Act 1985, which came into effect on 1 July 1985, and serves to consolidate the provisions of the Companies Acts of 1948, 1967, 1976, 1980 and 1981, *inter alia*, and through the provisions of Tables *A-F*, forming the Schedule to a Statutory Instrument, SI 1984 No. 1717, entitled 'Companies (Alteration of Table *A* etc.) Regulations 1984'. This SI consolidated the

Tables, as amended, formerly forming part of the Companies Acts of 1948 and 1980. The Tables set out the regulations for adoption by the various classes of companies. Table *A* is of primary importance, being the form of articles of association for companies limited by shares. Its adoption is, however, optional and many companies adopt articles not based on Table *A* or differing from it to a greater or lesser degree. The regulations in Table *A* should be regarded as model rules rather than as tables of stone!

Companies incorporated before 1 July 1985 may continue to use the former version of Table *A*. The Act also makes provisions for companies limited by guarantee and unlimited companies, but such companies will be ignored for the main purpose of this chapter except in meetings of unlimited and guarantee companies, below. The chapter will not concern itself with chartered or statutory companies since such companies are rare and the regulations governing the meetings will in the main be found or referred to in the charter or statute concerned.

For ease of reading, the numerous decided cases upon which so much of the law of meetings is based and the many references to the Companies Act are not quoted in the body of this chapter. Decided cases are covered in each of the first two books listed for further reading at the end of the chapter; references to the Acts are placed together under headings. As the material under each heading is a summary of the law the actual references in the Act should be consulted for the precise requirements.

SHAREHOLDERS' MEETINGS

Statutory meeting

The Companies Act 1948 provision for statutory meetings was repealed in 1980.

Annual general meeting (*ss*227, 239, 241, 242, 293, 324, 365, 366, 367, 376, 377, 384, 385, 386 and 732 of the Act, and cl.36 of Table *A*)

A shareholders' meeting specifically described as the annual general meeting in the notice calling the meeting must be held by every company to give its shareholders the opportunity to review the progress and the management of the company and to deal with any other matters for which proper notice has been given. An annual general meeting must be held in each calendar year (except in the year of incorporation and the subsequent year provided the first annual general meeting is held within eighteen months of incorporation) and not more than fifteen months must elapse between one annual general meeting and the next. In practice it is always advisable for the annual general meeting to be held about the same time in each year and for a twelve-monthly pattern of procedure to be established quickly, rather than to take advantage of the permitted period of fifteen months between meetings. It only requires three or four annual general meetings, with fourteen or fifteen-month intervals between them, before it will be found that the flexibility offered by the fifteen-month provision in the Act has been whittled away and in the event of any unavoidable delay — in, for example, the production of the accounts — there will be no spare time available to rearrange the programme, with the result that it may be very difficult to comply with all the provisions of the Act. In planning the date for an annual general meeting the provisions regarding time-limits for making up and presenting the accounts (usually at the annual general meeting) should be borne in mind.

If an annual general meeting is not held within the required period, any one member can apply to the Department of Trade and Industry which may call or direct the calling of the meeting, giving such instructions as may be necessary, including a direction that one member present in person or by proxy shall be a quorum. If such an annual general meeting convened by the Department is not held in the year of default it shall not be deemed to be the annual general meeting of the year in which it is held, unless the members by ordinary resolution so agree. If a resolution to this effect is passed, a copy of it must be sent to the Registrar of Companies within fifteen days of its being passed. There is a default fine not exceeding £50 for the company and every officer of the company who does not comply with the provisions of the Act or with any instructions from the Department of Trade and Industry.

Subject to any special provisions in a company's articles of association, any business may be transacted at the annual general meeting, provided appropriate notice has been given. If, for example, it is desired to take the opportunity to make a change in the articles of association or change a company's name, such business is quite acceptable at the annual general meeting, provided the necessary additional formalities have been observed for passing a special resolution. It is however more usual for ordinary business only to be transacted at the annual general meeting. Table *A* for example, limits ordinary business to declaring a dividend, consideration of the report and accounts, election of directors and auditors and fixing the auditors' remuneration. By custom, these matters are normally dealt with at the annual general meeting, although under the Act the presentation of the accounts could take place at an extraordinary general meeting and the articles, as in the case of Table *A*, could provide for dividends to be declared at directors' meetings.

The directors usually hold the initiative in deciding the exact business to be transacted at the annual general meeting, but the Act does make provision whereby members representing not less than one-twentieth of the total voting rights of all members having the right to vote, or not less than 100 members holding shares in the company on which there has been paid up an average sum per member of not less than £100, may, with certain restrictions, requisition the directors in writing to give notice of any resolution which may be properly moved at the annual general meeting and to circulate to members a statement of not more than 1000 words with respect to the proposed resolution. The right to have a statement circulated also relates to a resolution being proposed at any other meeting of shareholders.

The organization and procedure for an annual general meeting will, of course, vary immensely from company to company, but the checklist given below, under Organization and Procedure, will serve for most annual general meetings; it also includes other matters of detail not referred to in this part of the chapter.

Extraordinary general meeting (*ss*368, 370 and 371 of the Act and cll. 6 and 37 of Table *A*)

When it is remembered that the annual general meeting was once known as the ordinary general meeting — that is, the general meeting at which the ordinary business was transacted — it will be easily understood that an extraordinary general meeting is any extra shareholders' meeting held during the year in addition to the annual general meeting. It is quite possible for all business which it may be necessary for shareholders to transact to be carried out at the annual general meeting so that it never becomes necessary for a company to hold an extraordinary general meeting. Calling and holding an extraordinary general meeting obviously involves extra work and therefore, unless the matter is really pressing, it is always preferable to delay any special business (all business other than the four items of ordinary business already mentioned) until the next annual general meeting if at all possible. The alteration of the articles of association, the increase of authorized share capital or a resolution to wind up a company are all items of special business requiring the sanction of shareholders in general meeting and they can just as easily be dealt with at an annual general meeting as at a specially convened extraordinary general meeting.

According to Table *A*, the initiative in calling an extraordinary general meeting, as with the annual general meeting, normally rests with the directors acting as a board. They may convene such a meeting whenever they think it necessary to do so. If there are not enough directors in the United Kingdom to convene an extraordinary general meeting, Table *A* provides that any one director, or any two members, may convene an extraordinary general meeting. If the articles are silent on calling extraordinary general meetings, two or more members holding not less than one-tenth of the issued share capital — or, if the company has no share capital, not less than 5 per cent in number of the members of the company — may convene a meeting. If it becomes impracticable for a meeting to be held in accordance with the articles of association, the court on its own initiative, or at the request of any director or member entitled to vote at the meeting, may order the holding of a meeting with such regulations as it may care to lay down.

Where there are enough directors in the United Kingdom to constitute a board meeting for the purpose of convening an extraordinary general meeting but they do not wish to do so, the Act makes it mandatory upon them to convene such a meeting if so requisitioned by the holders of not less than one-tenth of the paid-up capital which has voting rights — or if there is no share capital by holders representing not less than one-tenth of the total voting rights. Such power to requisition by the shareholders only applies to extraordinary general meetings, as the shareholders' remedy for convening the annual general meeting is through the Department of Trade and Industry.

Any requisition must be in writing, be signed by all the requisitionists, state the object of the meeting and be left at the registered office of the company. The directors must then convene the meeting within twenty-one days of the deposit of the requisition, and in default the requisitionists, or any of them representing more than half the total voting rights of the requisitionists, may convene the meeting providing they do so within three months after the deposit of the requisition. The expenses of the requisitionists in convening the meeting are to be paid by the company and retained from the fees of the directors who were in default.

Class meeting (*ss*127 and 180 of the Act and cl.38(*b*) of Table *A*)

A class meeting is simply a meeting of members whose interests are common. Under Table *A*, for example, the rights attached to a class of shares where there is more than one class cannot be altered by the company in general meeting (usually the ordinary shareholders) unless the members of the particular class concerned have first been given an opportunity of meeting together at a class meeting to sanction the proposed modification by an extraordinary resolution passed at the separate class meeting. Actually, an alternative action is provided by Table *A* whereby the rights attached to a particular class of shares may be varied by a general meeting of the shareholders with the consent in writing of the holders of three-fourths of the issued shares of the class without recourse to a class meeting. In either case the Registrar requires a copy of the extraordinary resolution of the class meeting or of the consent in writing within fifteen days. Where holders of not less in the aggregate than 15 per cent of the issued shares of a class object to a modification of their rights they may, if they did not consent to or vote in favour of the resolution, apply to the court to have the variation cancelled. Any such application must be made within twenty-one days after the date on which the resolution was passed at the class meeting or on which the consent was given. Many schemes of capital reconstruction have passed through the courts in recent years and invariably such schemes require class meetings, which are convened and regulated by the court.

A suggested notice for a class meeting is given later in the chapter.

THE CONDUCT OF MEETINGS

KINDS OF RESOLUTION

Basically there are three kinds of resolution known respectively as ordinary, extraordinary and special resolutions.

Ordinary resolutions

An ordinary resolution is one passed by the method ordinarily adopted by a body of voters under common law when no special rules exist. Such a resolution is passed by a simple majority of those who vote. The removal of a director under the Act is the one occasion in the Act where an ordinary resolution is specifically required. Where on other occasions the Act requires a decision to be made by the company in general meetings, but does not call for a particular kind of resolution, an ordinary resolution is quite sufficient unless the articles of association call for a particular majority. Fourteen days' notice is sufficient for an ordinary resolution, although if the resolution is to be moved at an annual general meeting it would invariably be included in the necessary twenty-one days given in respect of the annual general meeting. The notice for an ordinary resolution need set out only the general nature of the business concerned, although in some instances it is obviously more helpful to members if the exact resolution is given.

Extraordinary resolutions

An extraordinary resolution is called for in four places in the Act — *ss*572, 598, 601 and 640 — all in connection with winding up. Such a resolution is passed by a majority of not less than three-fourths of those who vote. The notice covering the resolution must set out the exact wording of the resolution and must also specify the intention to pass the resolution as an extraordinary resolution. As in the case of an ordinary resolution, fourteen days' notice will be sufficient unless it is to be proposed at an annual general meeting.

Special resolutions

On fourteen occasions in the Act and once in the 1967 Act a special resolution is called for. The notice for a special resolution must set out the exact wording of the resolution and must also mention the intention to pass the resolution as a special resolution. Twenty-one days' notice is required for any general meeting at which a special resolution is to be considered.

Checklist of events requiring a special resolution

1   Alteration of the memorandum:
    (*a*) to change the name (*ss*26(3) and 28)

(b) to change the objects (ss54, 55 and 56)
(c) to make the liability of a director unlimited (s307)
(d) to change a condition that could lawfully have been included in the articles (s17)
(e) to change an unlimited company to a limited company (ss51, 52, 124 and 504)

2 Alteration of the articles (s9)
3 Approval of a director's assignment of his office (s309)
4 Creation of a reserve liability by providing that a portion of unpaid capital cannot be called for until the company is wound up (s120)
5 Payment of interest out of capital
6 Reduction of capital (s135)
7 Declaration that the company's affairs should be investigated by the Department of Trade and Industry (s432)
8 Resolution to wind up (ss517(a) and 572 (b))
9 Sanctioning the liquidator's acceptance of shares as consideration for the sale of the company's assets (s582(2))

A copy of all extraordinary and special resolutions whether passed in general meeting or at class meetings must be filed with the appropriate Registrar of Companies within fifteen days of the meeting at which they are passed. Copies of ordinary resolutions are not required by the Registrar except on the three occasions mentioned in s123 (increase of capital), ss 366, 367, 380 and 572 of the Act.

In addition to the particular majorities required for the three basic types of resolution already mentioned, the articles of association may provide for resolutions to be passed by special majorities.

NOTICE

The following elements should be included in the notice for any shareholders' meeting:

1 Name of company
2 The type of meeting
3 Date, time and place of meeting
4 The nature of any special business — according to Table *A* all business is special business with the exception of declaring a dividend, consideration of the report and accounts, the election of directors in place of those retiring and appointment of an fixing the remuneration of the auditors
5 Exact wording of any special or extraordinary resolution together with

THE CONDUCT OF MEETINGS

a statement specifying the intention to propose the resolution as a special or extraordinary resolution
6 The authority by which the notice is issued
7 The name of the person issuing the notice
8 If the company has a share capital, prominent note to the effect that members may appoint a proxy or proxies who need not also themselves be members
9 Date of notice

These points are illustrated in the specimen notices p.113-15.

Length of notice

The articles of association will invariably set out the length of notice which must be given to shareholders, but in any event it must never be less than that laid down in the Act which requires twenty-one days' notice for an annual general meeting, or any general meeting at which a special resolution is to be considered, and fourteen days for any other meeting in the case of a limited company and seven days for an unlimited company. The Act does, however, provide for shorter notice in the event of:

1 An annual general meeting, if agreement is given by all those entitled to attend and vote
2 An extraordinary general meeting, if agreement is given by a majority of members who between them *also* hold not less than 95 per cent in nominal value of the shares giving the right to attend and vote or if there is no share capital not less than 95 per cent of the total voting rights at that meeting

It would appear that in either of the above cases the consent need not necessarily be in writing.

Means of serving notice

The articles of association should always be studied carefully to ascertain the exact meaning of so many days' notice. Table *A* states that notice shall be exclusive of the day that the notice is served and also of the day of the meeting. It goes on to say that a notice is deemed served twenty-four hours after it is posted. It must be assumed in this case that the twenty-four-hour period applies whether a letter is sent by first or second-class post. The articles may well state that a notice is deemed served at the time it would have been received in the normal course of post and in this case the class of postal service chosen would be taken into account. Yet again, some articles state that the day of posting is the day of service, so it is important that the calculation of the days of notice is worked out most carefully, in accordance with the articles of the particular company, to avoid the possibility of the meeting being set aside through lack of proper notice. If, as in the case of Table A, service is to be by means of post, it has been held that no other manner of service will be valid.

Entitlement to receive notice

Notice must be sent to all entitled to receive it or again a meeting may be invalidated. Table A does provide for accidental omission but it really must be a result of an accident and not of an error. Articles may well provide that preference shareholders (unless their dividends are in arrears) and debenture stockholders (who after all are not members) are not entitled to receive notice. It has been held that if a share carries no rights to vote, by implication it carries no right to attend meetings.

According to Table A it is not necessary to send notice outside the United Kingdom, although most companies with such a clause in their articles do so. In the case of joint holders it is sufficient to send notice to the first named. A copy of all notices to shareholders must be sent to the auditors.

Where a company has bearer shares, it is not possible to dispatch notice by post and meetings would be convened by notice in the press in accordance with the regulations in the company's articles.

Adjourned meetings

No notice need be given for an adjourned meeting unless the adjournment takes place after a period of thirty days from the original meeting.

Special notice

Special notice is not given by the company to the members but by the members to the company. It is required in three sets of circumstances. The Act requires special notice to remove a director before he is due to retire by rotation and to appoint a director who is over seventy years of age. Sections 387 and 388 of the Act require special notice to appoint an auditor other than the one retiring, to fill a casual vacancy for an auditor, to re-appoint a retiring auditor who was appointed by the directors to fill a casual vacancy or to remove an auditor before the expiration of his term of office. These matters are, however, considered to be important enough to warrant shareholders giving them special thought, and under the Act it is necessary for a shareholder who will move the resolution to give the company twenty-eight days' notice of his intention to do so. The directors are then bound to inform the other shareholders of the proposed resolution and also to give the auditors or directors concerned (other than in the case of the appointment of

THE CONDUCT OF MEETINGS

a director who is over seventy) the opportunity to have representation circulated to the shareholders. As far as s379 of the Act is concerned the items of business requiring special notice can all be approved by ordinary resolution upon fourteen days' notice.

Authority to give notice

It is important that a notice is always sent out with the authority of the board or whoever is convening the meeting. Authority to dispatch a notice is usually given to the secretary at a board meeting before notice is dispatched, but it would be sufficient for the dispatch by the secretary without prior authority to be ratified by the board, provided it takes place before the meeting is held.

A notice sometimes includes the expression 'any other business'. This is really meaningless except for the purpose of a general discussion or perhaps moving a vote of thanks. Certainly no resolution can be passed under this heading if proper notice has not been given to shareholders, although if all those entitled to attend and vote are present and agree no prior notice of the resolution need be given.

Notice of meetings is dealt with in ss241, 292, 303, 304, 349(1)(b), 364, 370, 372, 378, 379, 387 and 388 of the Act and cll.38, 39, 45 and 52 of Table A.

QUORUM

The quorum for a meeting is the minimum number of members which must be present before any business can be validly transacted. The quorum for a meeting of shareholders is invariably set out in the articles of association of the company, but in the unlikely event of such a provision not being made the Act provides that two members, personally present, shall be a quorum. Table A makes the provision that two members can be present in person or by proxy. It has been held that only those entitled to vote at a general meeting are qualified to help constitute a quorum.

Table A requires the quorum to be present throughout the meeting. Under Table A, if a meeting has been called and a quorum is not present within half an hour or if the quorum ceases to be present, the meeting stands adjourned for seven days or till some other time if the directors so decide.

CHAIRMAN

If the articles are silent on the question of who takes the chair at meetings of shareholders, the Act provides that the members present may elect a chairman from among themselves.

Who takes the chair?

The articles of association will normally give guidance on who shall take the chair at shareholders' meetings. Table A states that the chairman, if any, of the board shall take the chair. If there is no chairman of the board or he is not present within fifteen minutes after the scheduled time for the meeting, or he is not willing to act as chairman of the meeting, the other directors present shall elect a chairman from among themselves. If no director is willing to act as chairman or no director is present within fifteen minutes, the members present may elect a chairman from among their own ranks.

Casting vote

Under Table A the chairman has a right to demand a poll, and on a show of hands or a poll he has a second or casting vote in the case of an equality of votes.

Chairman's duties

It is at general meetings and particularly at the annual general meeting that the chairman will probably come into closest association with his company's shareholders. In spite of his efficient leadership and management capability as perhaps chief executive throughout the year the members and the press will often judge his effectiveness by the way in which he handles the annual general meeting. It is consequently of the utmost importance that the chairman and his staff should always ensure that he has been adequately prepared to deal with any situation which may arise at the meeting. The following list will serve to remind the chairman of some of his functions and duties in connection with general meetings although he may well delegate some of them to others:

1. To be familiar with the Act and the articles of association especially as regards the right of himself and others to demand a poll and his right to adjourn the meeting
2. To ensure that when the meeting begins it has been properly constituted as regards notice, quorum and his appointment to the chair
3. To ensure that any agenda is followed unless the meeting agrees otherwise, to see that the business remains within the scope of the notice and to decide points of order
4. To maintain order and if necessary to initiate a pre-arranged procedure to have offenders removed from the meeting. The risk of an unruly element entering the meeting is reduced if those attending are screened as they arrive and are asked to sign an attendance sheet. If the number of meetings disturbed by demonstrators increases, the use of admission tickets may soon become a general necessity for shareholders' meetings

THE CONDUCT OF MEETINGS

5   To answer shareholders' questions but to use care that he does not give information not available to all members which could affect the value of their shares
6   To ensure that all who wish to speak have an equal opportunity to do so
7   To be familiar with the mechanics for taking a poll and to be ready to instruct the shareholders in the completion of poll cards
8   To use his casting vote if he is so empowered
9   To demand a poll if he knows of the existence of proxy forms which, if counted on a poll, would alter the result of a vote taken on a show of hands
10 To ensure that minutes are properly drawn up and signed

The chairman's appointment and duties are dealt with in ss370 and 382 of the Act and cll.42, 45 and 46 of Table A.

AGENDA

The task of compiling the agenda for a general meeting is usually left to the company secretary who works very closely with his chairman. The agenda will set out the business already referred to in the notice but in greater detail, showing perhaps the wording of the actual resolutions to be moved and the names of the movers and seconders. The agenda is distributed to those taking part in the meeting and acts as a script so that the chairman, and others concerned, can readily see where they have to speak. If only a few members are expected at the meeting it may be helpful to give a copy to all those present and also to the press.

Items 14 to 25 in Organization and Procedure, below, will serve as a basis for an agenda for any annual general meeting and only a little adaptation will be needed for an extraordinary general meeting.

VOTING

If the articles of association exclude Table A and make no other provision in connection with voting, the Act states that each member shall have one vote for each share of £10 of stock held. This amounts to a poll but does not prevent a vote first being taken on a show of hands under common law when each member present would have one vote.

Right to vote

Table A provides that, subject to any rights or restrictions attached to particular shares, each member personally present shall have one vote on a show of hands and one vote for each share held in the case of a poll. In order to qualify a member for voting, any calls which may be due must have been paid. Preference shareholders are usually deprived of the right to vote unless their dividends are in arrears.

Joint accounts

In the case of a joint account, the vote of the senior (by order of the names in the register of members) who tenders a vote in person or by proxy will be accepted to the exclusion of the votes of any other person named in the joint account.

Members of unsound mind

The vote of a member of unsound mind may be exercised by his committee, receiver, curator bonis or other person appointed by the court.

Deceased and bankrupt members

Under Table *A* the personal representative of a deceased member or a bankrupt who has not taken steps to have his name placed in the register of members is entitled to receive dividends and other advantages but cannot exercise rights of membership at meetings. He is entitled to receive notice of meetings but he cannot vote until he is himself the registered holder of the shares concerned.

Bearer shareholders

The right to vote by a holder of bearer shares must be set out specifically in the articles of the company since Table *A* makes no provision for bearer shares. The articles will probably describe a procedure whereby the owner of a bearer share obtains a certificate of deposit from the bank holding the shares which he in turn lodges with the company. This procedure will give the owner of the bearer share the right to vote.

Show of hands

Most matters at general meetings are uncontroversial and the vote is usually taken on a show of hands. Although this entitles a member to only one vote, regardless of the number of shares he holds, at most meetings this system of voting is acceptable.

THE CONDUCT OF MEETINGS

Polls

It could happen that the result of a vote on a show of hands (when each member receives only one vote and when votes of proxies are excluded) would have been different if a one vote for one share system, including votes of proxies, was adopted. Such an alternative system of voting is known as a poll and according to Table *A* the following persons may demand a poll before, or on the declaration of the results of, a show of hands:

1 The chairman
2 At least three members present in person or by proxy
3 Any member or members in person or by proxy representing not less than one-tenth of the total voting rights of all those having the right to vote at the meeting
4 A member or members holding shares having the right to vote on which the aggregate sum has been paid up equal to not less than one-tenth of the total sum paid up on all the shares with the right to vote

If no provision is made in the articles for demanding a poll, it may be demanded by any one member in accordance with common law principles. On the other hand, if the articles do make provision the requirements must be no more onerous than those set out in the Act, and which are similar to the provisions of Table *A*, except that the chairman is not included among those who can demand a poll and any article is void if it has the effect of making ineffective a demand for a poll by not less than five members who have the right to vote at the meeting.

It has been held that it is the duty of the chairman to demand a poll if he knows of the existence of proxies which, if used on a poll, would have an effect on the result of the vote. The Act provides that on a poll a member need not use all his votes in the same way. This provision enables a shareholder to vote for and against a resolution if, for example, he is holding shares on behalf of more than one person. Bank nominee companies are more likely to makes use of this provision than are individual shareholders. If a poll is demanded it is usually taken on at once, although Table *A* provides that it may be taken at such time as the chairman of the meeting directs, unless it is on the election of the chairman or on the question of an adjournment, in which case it must be taken forthwith.

The important thing, from the point of view of the secretary or other executive supervising shareholders' meetings, is that he should never allow himself to be taken by surprise if a poll is demanded. A good secretary will always prepare himself for a poll, so that when it is actually demanded he knows immediately what he has to do. The following will serve as a procedure for taking or conducting a poll:

1 Be prepared! This means being familiar with the provisions of the

articles of the company. It also means that the necessary staff and materials are always available in case of need

2   Check that the demand for the poll has been properly made

3   Chairman to rule when the poll will be taken — probably forthwith

4   (*a*) If the poll was expected (perhaps a requirement for a court meeting) voting cards can be issued to shareholders as they enter the meeting place showing their holdings which have been extracted from the register of members, or

(*b*) If the poll was not anticipated, preprinted voting cards without holdings can be issued to those present by internal auditors, or

(*c*) Voting lists can be strategically placed round the meeting place for signature

5   Chairman to give clear instructions to the voters. He will, for example, tell the members that they need not fill in the voting card or sign a voting list if they have already given a proxy. He may give simple instructions for filling in the card or finding the way to the voting lists

6   Internal auditors or scrutineers will collect the voting cards or lists and calculate the result by adding the votes cast during the poll to those previously cast by proxy

7   In the case of 4 (*a*), the chairman may be able to declare the result at once. In the case of 4 (*b*) or (*c*), the voting cards or lists should be checked against the register of members and it may only be possible to give a provisional result at the meeting which would be confirmed at a later date in the press

Proxies

The word proxy embraces both the piece of paper authorizing another to act as proxy and also the person who has been so appointed.

Under the Act every shareholder (unless the company has no share capital) has a right to appoint a proxy, regardless of any provision to the contrary in the articles. A proxy need not be a member of the company.

In the case of a private company, the Act provides that a proxy can speak at the meeting (it is interesting to note that the abortive 1973 Companies Bill would have given a proxy the right to speak at the meeting of a public company) but, unless the articles provide otherwise, a proxy can vote only on a poll. A member of a private company can appoint only one proxy. At the shareholders' meeting of a private company a proxy can help form the quorum.

A proxy can join in demanding a poll. According to Table *A* a proxy must be in writing (a form of proxy is given) and lodged at the registered office not less than forty-eight hours before the meeting. Articles could provide for less than forty-eight hours but, according to the Act, cannot require proxies to be lodged with the company more than forty-eight hours before the meeting.

THE CONDUCT OF MEETINGS

A note regarding the time-limit for the deposit of proxies is usually printed on the proxy forms.

Proxies duly deposited with a company prior to a meeting are also valid for an adjournment of the meeting unless the articles of association provide otherwise. Under Table *A* a proxy may be deposited with the company between an original meeting and its adjournment provided it is lodged not less than forty-eight hours before the adjournment. It has been held that a break in a meeting to allow a poll to be taken does not amount to an adjournment allowing further proxies to be lodged, but Table *A* does provide that proxies may be lodged in such circumstances not less than twenty-four hours before the poll is taken.

A very important provision of the Act regarding proxies states that proxy forms must not be sent out by a company to some only of its members (unless they request them in writing) suggesting a name for nomination as a proxy, unless such forms are sent to all members.

Proxies once lodged with the company are revoked in the following circumstances:

1 Notification of the death or insanity of the appointer is received by the company prior to the meeting covered by the proxy
2 The company becomes aware prior to the meeting of a transfer of the shares giving the holder the right to appoint a proxy
3 The company receives a notice of revocation or a further form of proxy within the necessary time-limit before the meeting
4 The appointer of the proxy attends the meeting and votes in person

The Act makes a special provision for a company which is a shareholder in another company. A corporate shareholder may appoint a proxy in the normal way (executed under seal according to Table *A*) but such proxy is in the same position as a proxy appointed by an individual and can only vote on a poll and speak at a meeting of a private company. The Act provides for a company shareholder, by resolution of its board of directors or other governing body, to authorize such person as it thinks fit to represent the corporation at the company meeting. The representative would prove his right to be present by producing a certified extract from the minutes of the board meeting appointing him. Such a representative is entitled to exercise the same powers as an individual member, in that he can vote on a show of hands and speak at a meeting of a private or public company.

Voting is dealt with in *ss*370 and 372-375 of the Act and cll.46-63 of Table *A*.

MINUTES

It is of course a businesslike procedure to keep minutes of general meetings but in fact the Act states that every company must do so. There is no set form, except that Table *A* requires them to include resolutions and proceedings of general meetings and there is no objection to looseleaf minute books being used, so long as proper security arrangements are made to safeguard minutes of past meetings and the unused sheets for the minutes of future meetings. Minutes signed by the chairman of the meeting or by the chairman of the next succeeding meeting are *prima facie* evidence of the proceedings of the meeting. In the case of general meetings it is not usual to leave the minutes of one meeting to be signed by the chairman of the next, as this may involve minutes being left unsigned for twelve months or so. Such minutes are usually signed at the next board meeting.

The minute book of general meetings must be kept at the registered office of the company and must be open to inspection by members, free of charge, for not less than two hours in each working day. There is a provision in the Act entitling members to be furnished with copies of general meeting minutes within seven days of their request at a charge not exceeding 2½p for every 100 words. Because of these inspection provisions it is usual to keep minutes of shareholders' meetings separate from those of board meetings, which are not open to inspection by members. See *ss*382, 383 and 772 of the Act and cl.100(*b*) of Table *A* for provisions concerning minutes.

ADJOURNMENT AND POSTPONEMENT

In dealing with the quorum for general meetings convened by the board it was mentioned that if no quorum is present within half an hour of the scheduled time for the meeting it stands adjourned for a week. Table *A* also provides for adjournment on other occasions and states that the chairman with the consent of the meeting may, and shall if directed by the meeting, adjourn the meeting from time to time and from place to place. There is no power for the chairman to adjourn without the consent of the meeting unless it is to deal with disorder. Only unfinished business can be dealt with at an adjourned general meeting. No notice of the adjournment is necessary unless it is to a date more than thirty days after the date of the original meeting.

For most practical purposes the original meeting and the adjourned meeting are considered to be one meeting, but the Act provides that if a resolution is passed at an adjourned meeting the date of the resolution is the date of the adjourned meeting.

It has been held that once a meeting has been convened it cannot be postponed validly without the consent of all the members concerned. In one case, an annual general meeting was postponed, but, nevertheless, sufficient members to form a quorum met on the appointed day and transacted the business; it was held that their action was valid. The correct action is to hold the meeting as originally planned and then adjourn it, if the majority of those present so agree. See *s*381 of the Act and cl.45 of Table *A*.

THE CONDUCT OF MEETINGS

RESOLUTIONS IN WRITING

In the case of a company with only a few members, Table *A* cl.53 avoids the need to hold a general meeting physically. The resolution or resolutions to be passed are set out on paper, then signed by each of those entitled to attend and vote. The resolution may be set out in several documents of like form, in which case one or more of those who would have been entitled to be present at a meeting will sign each sheet. The resolutions are effective when all the signatures have been appended and the signed resolution is then placed in the minute book as a permanent record. If the resolution passed is one which the Registrar would normally require to have filed with him, a copy of the resolution should be submitted to him within the usual time-limit. Although it is only Table *A* cl.53 which provides specifically for resolutions in writing, it would seem that a resolution similarly signed by all the members of a public company would be quite valid, since, as it must be signed by all the members entitled to attend and vote at meetings, they in effect unanimously alter the articles to provide for a resolution in writing to cover the particular piece of business being transacted. It is doubtful if a court would invalidate such an action even in the case where a meeting is actually called for by the Act or the articles. Again it is interesting that the 1973 Companies Bill provided that a resolution in writing would be statutory for all companies. See *s*380(4)(*c*) of the Act and cl.53 of Table *A*.

DIRECTORS' MEETINGS

There are a number of items of business in the Act or in Table *A* which must be carried out by the directors. For example: 'The directors may make calls ...' or 'The directors may convene an extraordinary general meeting ...' For the directors to do either of these things they must do so as a board at a meeting. Meetings of directors, like other meetings, must be properly constituted and should comply with any specific regulations laid down in the articles. The company secretary would probably be responsible for seeing that the preparations for a board meeting and the procedure at the meeting itself is properly carried out. A suggested procedure for a secretary in this connection is set out on p.104-5.

Notice (cl. 88 of Table *A*)

Under Table *A* board meetings may be summoned by any one director, and the secretary must do so if requested by a director. There are no particular requirements regading the length of notice for a board meeting, and such notice need not be in writing. The important point is that all directors entitled to attend are given a reasonable opportunity to do so, except that directors outside the United Kingdom are not entitled to a notice. As in the case of general meetings, the mere physical presence of directors does not constitute a quorum unless all entitled to a notice are present and agree. It has been held that there is no need for a notice of a forthcoming board meeting to set out the nature of the business since directors have the power to carry out a very wide range of business and should attend prepared for anything.

Agenda

Although there is no need to give formal notice of a board meeting, or indeed any notice at all if meetings are held on predetermined dates, most companies find it helpful to send out a reminder a day or two before the day of the meeting, in the form of an agenda accompanied by papers or reports that are to be considered at he meetings. As in the case of a general meeting, the secretary would consult the chairman about what business is to be carried out and he would compile the agenda accordingly. In some cases a preprinted agenda is used for all board meetings with provision for items to be added to the agenda if necessary. The following would serve as an agenda for board meetings:

Agenda for a meeting of directors to be held on Friday 29 May 1987 at 09.30 at the registered office.

1 Confirmation of minutes of previous meeting (copy herewith)
2 Matters arising:
   (*a*)
   (*b*)
3 Managing director's report
4 Cash position
5 Monthly results
6 Share transfers
7 Personnel
8
9
10 Any other business
11 Date of next meeting

The inclusion of the exact wording of the resolutions to be passed will save time, and a wide margin can be left down the right side to enable directors to take notes. The secretary of the meeting could use his copy of the agenda as a basis for the minutes. An agenda suitable for the first board meeting after incorporation can be found on p.105-6.

THE CONDUCT OF MEETINGS

Quorum ($s370(4)$ of the Act and cll.40 and 41 of Table A)

The quorum for a board is usually set out in the articles of association. In the case of Table A the directors are given power to fix their own quorum, and in the event of their failing to do so specifically the quorum is two directors. Where the directors have the power to fix the quorum but do not do so and no figure is given for that eventuality, as in the case of Table A, it has been held that the quorum will be the number of directors who usually act. In the rare event of the articles making no provision for the quorum a majority of directors must be present before any business can be transacted.

Mere physical presence of a quorum does not constitute a meeting as there must have been an intention to meet which was known to those entitled to attend. Even if a board meeting has been properly called and the appropriate number of directors to constitute a quorum is present, there still may not be a quorum competent to transact business. If the articles are silent on the matter, or if Table A is excluded, a quorum for a board meeting must be a disinterested quorum — which means that none of the directors constituting the quorum may have any interest in the business to be transacted. However, with the advent of the professional director with wide business interests, very little would be done at board meetings if such a restriction were always applicable. In fact articles usually modify this common law rule as does Table A. Table A still acknowledges the principle, but the prohibition does not apply in connection with any arrangement to give a director, or a third party, security or indemnity in respect of money lent by the director to, or obligations undertaken by him for the benefit of, the company in connection with a contract by the director to subscribe for or underwrite shares or debentures of the company, or in connection with any contract or arrangement with any other company in which he is interested only as an officer or shareholder of the other company.

Under the Act every director is obliged to declare at an appropriate meeting of directors the nature of any direct or indirect interests in a contract or proposed contract with the company and consequently the board should always be in a position to know whether or not a distinterested quorum is present for particular transaction.

Chairman (cll.42, 45, 46 and 91 of Table A)

For a board meeting to be properly constituted the proper person must be in the chair, and Table A provides that the board may elect one of their members to take the chair. One director is usually appointed chairman indefinitely or until he retires, but there is no objection to each meeting electing its own chairman. If there is a regular chairman and he is not present within five minutes, the directors present may choose one of their number to take the chair. Sometimes a deputy chairman is elected to take the chair automatically in the chairman's absence. Although, in practice, a deputy chairman would step down if the chairman later arrives he is not bound to do so. The chairman of the board usually presides at meetings of shareholders.

Voting (cl.88 of Table *A*)

Table *A* provides that questions arising at board meetings shall be decided by a majority of votes, and that in the event of an equality of votes the chairman shall have a second or casting vote. Such voting would be on a show of hands, there being no provision for polls and proxies in the case of directors' meetings.

In practice, voting at board meetings is unusual. A board usually works as a well-integrated team pulling in one direction and matters are usually settled without recourse to voting. If there is a constant disharmony among the directors there will probably very soon be a resignation or two followed by suitable payments in compensation for loss of office.

Minutes (*ss*382 and 722 of the Act and cl.100 of Table *A*)

As in the case of general meeting minutes, the Act makes it obligatory that minutes of board meetings must be maintained, but there is no provision for inspection — except by the directors and auditors. There is no need for the minute book to be kept at the registered office. Table *A* is rather more detailed than the Act, and requires minutes of board meetings to cover all appointments of officers made by the directors and to include the names of the directors present at each meeting and minutes of all resolutions and proceedings of the directors.

Board minutes are usually approved at the subsequent board meeting and signed by the chairman of that meeting.

A selection of specimen board resolutions is given on p.106-9.

Resolution in writing (cl.93 of Table *A*)

Most articles, as in the case of Table *A*, make provision for directors to transact business without a physical meeting by the means of all those entitled to receive notice of the meeting signing their name on a written copy of the resolution. This is a useful provision enabling formal business to be done without need to call the directors to a meeting.

Committees (cll. 72, 92 and 93 of Table *A*)

Directors often appoint committees to expedite their work, but before such committees can be appointed the articles should be consulted, as it has been held that a board cannot delegate to a committee unless the articles give them specific power to do so. Such power is contained in Table *A* and any one

THE CONDUCT OF MEETINGS

director can be constituted into a committee. The committee must conform to any regulations laid down by the board and, in the event of no particular regulations being given, it may regulate itself as it thinks proper.

The provisions of Table A regarding the chairman of a committee are the same as those for the chairman of a board meeting. A committee may be formed for any business which does not require the attention of the whole board. The most common committees are transfer committees for dealing with the approval and registration of share transfers and the sealing of new share certificates and sealing committees authorizing the use of the seal on documents other than share certificates. A resolution appointing a committee is given on p.107.

Alternate directors. Clauses 65-69 of Table A provide for a director to appoint an alternate or substitute to act in his absence. Specific provision is often made in the articles of association of a company. The extent of the power of an alternate will be set out in the articles of the company concerned. It is usual for articles which provide, as Table A does, for alternates, to give the alternate the right to receive notice of board meetings and in the absence of the director to whom he is an alternate, to attend and vote at the meetings. It is not usually necessary for an alternate also to be a director in his own right but where he is he may be entitled to vote as an alternate in addition to his own right to vote as a director.

MEETINGS OF UNLIMITED AND GUARANTEE COMPANIES

Unlimited companies ($ss3$, $8(4)(c)$, 49, 50 and 506 of the Act and Table E)

Under ss49, 50 and 506 of the Act provision has been made for the conversion of limited companies to unlimited companies. This provision is of use to smaller private companies that wish to avoid the requirement for all companies to publish their accounts. Companies which re-register as unlimited are not required to file their accounts with the Registrar. Unlimited companies are obliged to adopt articles as near in form as possible to the articles set out in Table E which forms part of the Schedule to SI 1985 No. 1717, and embraces all the regulations of Table A that relate to meetings. Consequently, most of what has been said in this chapter about companies limited by shares applies to meetings of unlimited companies.

Guarantee companies ($ss3$ and 8 of the Act, Table C and Pt. III of Table D)

A guarantee company limited by shares is obliged to adopt articles as near in form as possible to Table D which embraces all the regulations of Table A. It follows that meetings of guarantee companies limited by shares are regulated in the same way as meetings of companies limited by shares.

In the case of a guarantee company without a share capital, Table *C* (or as near as circumstances permit) must be adopted. Table *C* is very similar to Table *A*, as far as meetings are concerned except:

1   Every member has one vote under Table *C*
2   There is no provision for a director to help form the quorum and vote in connection with business in which he has an interest, as there is in certain cases in Table *A*. The quorum must always be disinterested

Inasmuch as some guarantee companies have no share capital, a few of the provisions of the Act, which relate to companies limited by shares, do not apply or are modified:

1   Members of a company without a share capital may appoint proxies who may, however, vote only upon a poll being taken
2   Some of the provisions of the Act (*ss*368, 369 and 373, for example), which require action by certain proportions of the share capital, provide for the qualifications to act being related to a proportion of the voting rights

Apart from these points, the regulations regarding meetings of a guarantee company without a share capital are very similar to those governing companies that have a share capital.

MEETINGS OF DEBENTURE HOLDERS

Debenture holders are not, of course, members of the company but a special class of secured creditors. There are occasions when the debenture holders may wish to meet and such meetings will be covered by the regulations set out in the debenture trust deed, which usually contains provisions regarding meetings, similar in nature to those in the articles of association of the company.

SECRETARY'S DUTIES IN CONNECTION WITH A BOARD MEETING

1   Accumulate papers and items for submission to the next board meeting — bank statements, transfers for approval, reports
2   Consult the chairman and others for any special items to be included in the agenda
3   Draft and reproduce the agenda
4   Dispatch the agenda, which will serve as a notice, to the directors, with

a draft of the minutes of the last meeting and any other papers for consideration at the meeting
5 Prepare board room
   (a) Pads and pencils
   (b) Attendance book
   (c) Agenda for the chairman with special notes if necessary
   (d) Copy of the minutes for chairman marked to indicate matters arising
   (e) Minute book
   (f) Company seal if it is to be used
   (g) Memorandum and articles of association
   (h) Documents for production — bank statement, etc
   (i) Spare copies of papers circulated for consideration
6 At the meeting, quietly draw attention of the chairman to any irregularities; produce documents as required; draft resolutions, if necessary, and take notes for minutes
7 After the meeting
   (a) Ensure documents are properly signed and sealed
   (b) Effect any decisions of the board — dispatch dividend warrants etc.
   (c) Comply with any statutory requirements — returns to Registrar etc.
8 Accumulate papers and items for submission to next board meeting

AGENDA FOR THE FIRST BOARD MEETING AFTER INCORPORATION

Agenda for the first meeting of Directors to be held on Friday 24 July 1987 at 10.30 at 346 Middle Grosvenor Street, London W1.

1 Report incorporation. Production of certificate of incorporation and memorandum and articles of association
2 Report directorate (probably named in articles or appointed by subscribers)
3 Appointment of chairman (cl. 91 of Table *A*)
4 Appointment of secretary ($s283(1)$-(3) of the Act and cl.99 of Table *A*)
5 Appointment of auditors ($ss384$, 385 and 386 of the Act)
6 Fix situation of registered office
7 Appointment of bankers and opening of bank account
8 Adoption of common seal ($s350$ of the Act)
9 Disclosure of directors' interests ($s317$ of the Act)
10 Approval and execution of agreement purchasing business (if any)
11 Dates for subsequent meetings

Some of these items are dealt with in the specimen board resolutions that follow.

SPECIMEN BOARD RESOLUTIONS

Minutes

That the minutes of the board meeting held on 22 May 1987 be and are hereby confirmed.

Interim dividend

That an interim dividend of 10 per cent, less tax, on the ordinary capital of the company, be and is hereby declared payable on 5 June 1987 to shareholders recorded in the register of members at the closing of the books on 22 May 1987.

Approval of new seal on change of name

The secretary reported that as a result of the change of name of company it was necessary to adopt a new common seal. *It was therefore resolved:*

That the seal produced to the meeting, an impression of which shall be made in the margin of the minutes of this meeting, be and is hereby adopted as the common seal of the company and *that* the secretary be and is hereby instructed to ensure that the die of the seal bearing the previous name of the company is thoroughly defaced and destroyed.

Appoint director/managing director/secretary/other officer

That Mr Harold Heath be and is hereby appointed a director/managing director/secretary/other officer of the company.

Transfers

Audit report number 217 dated 13 March 1987 relating to the undermentioned documents was produced, and *it was resolved that* transfers numbered 1241-1283 be passed and that the sealing of new share certificates numbered 4147-4179 in respect thereof be authorized.

Annual/extraordinary general meeting

That the/an annual/extraordinary general meeting be held on Friday 22 May 1987 at Thames House, Victoria Embankment, London EC4, at 11 00, for

THE CONDUCT OF MEETINGS

the ordinary business of the company and/or for the purpose of considering if thought fit passing the following resolution (as a special resolution):
That ....

Execution of lease or other document

That the seal of the company be impressed upon the lease — now produced — by A B Properties Limited to this company in respect of the fourth floor of Kingscote House, Block Street, London EC3, for a period of ten years from 1 January 1987 at an annual rent of £12 000.

Approval of accounts

That the balance sheet as at 31 December 1985 and the profit and loss account for the year ended on that date together with the directors' report — now produced — be approved, that the balance sheet be signed by any two of the directors, and that the directors' report be signed by the secretary of the company.

Appointment of a committee

That pursuant to Article 71 of the company's articles of association a finance committee be and is hereby constituted, that Messrs Nickleby, Dombey and Merdle be appointed members thereof, that Mr Carker be and is hereby appointed secretary and that the following functions be and are hereby delegated to such committee:

1 To consider ....
2 To authorize ....
3 To deal ....

Reporting directors' interests

Pursuant to $s385$ of the Companies Act 1985 a letter was read from Mr T Barnacle dated 27 May 1986 declaring that he is a partner in Overend, Gurney and Co.

Allotment of shares

That 200 shares of £1 each in the capital of the company for which payment in full had been received be allotted to Mr J Smith and that share certificate number 23 in respect of such shares be sealed and issued.

Appointment of alternate director

The secretary reported that a letter had been received from Mr Merdle appointing Mr J Barnacle to act as his alternate director during his absence or inability to act as a director.

(If board approval also necessary.) *It was resolved that* the appointment by Mr Merdle of Mr J Barnacle as his alternate director be and is hereby approved.

Approval and issue of prospectus

That the prospectus of the company which has been considered at this meeting be dated 31 July 1986 and be signed by the directors now present, and sent to each other director named therein for signature by him or his authorized agent and that the same when so signed by all the directors named therein be delivered forthwith to the Registrar of Companies for registration and that immediately thereafter the prospectus be issued and advertised.

Appointment of representative to attend general meetings

That this company being a member of The Island Navigation Co. Ltd hereby appoints Mr J Jones or failing him Mr J Doe (or the secretary of the company for the time being) to represent this company at any general meeting of The Island Navigation Co. Ltd and at any and every adjournment thereof.

Closing transfer books

That the transfer books of the company be closed from 2 March 1987 to 13 March 1987, both days inclusive.

Denumbering shares

That the 15 000 issued shares in the capital of the company which are credited as fully paid and rank *pari passu* in all respects, do have no distinguishing numbers.

Making a call

That a call of £0.10 per share be made upon the members registered in the books at the close of business on 29 May 1987 payable on the 19 June 1987 to Telford's Bank Limited, Threadneedle Street, London EC2.

Forfeiture of shares

That Mr W Glover, the registered holder of 100 shares of £1 each in this company, having failed to pay the instalment of £0.25 per share due on the said shares on 31 March 1987, and having failed to comply with the notice served upon him dated 22 May 1987 the said shares be and are hereby forfeited.

ORGANIZATION AND PROCEDURE FOR AN ANNUAL GENERAL MEETING

Before the meeting

1. Agree date for meeting bearing in mind statutory time-limits and in liaison with those responsible for production of accounts etc.
2. Arrange suitable accommodation well in advance
3. Agree agenda and draft procedure for meeting with the chairman
4. Finalize drafts and arrange printing (after informal approval of board) of
    (*a*) Notice of meeting
    (*b*) Directors' report
    (*c*) Chairman's speech (if desired)
    (*d*) Accounts
    (*e*) Two-way proxy forms (if quoted)
5. Board meeting to formally approve and authorize signing of directors' report and audited accounts, convene AGM and authorize dispatch of notices. (Inform Stock Exchange of any dividend declaration or recommendation if quoted.)
6. Dispatch notices, reports and accounts, and so on — twenty-one clear days — copies to Stock Exchange if quoted
7. Summarize proxy position just before meeting and be prepared for a poll
8. Ensure in advance that a quorum will be present
9. Prime those who will take part — proposers, seconders, stewards, tellers, commissionaires
10. Check accommodation on day prior to meeting — reception area for members, seating, heating, loudspeaker system, parking place for chairman's car etc.
11. Assemble appropriate papers and reference books — register of directors' interests, memorandum and articles of association. Companies Acts, major agreements, general meeting minute book etc

At the meeting

12 Members (in person or by proxy) and press to show admission cards or sign attendance sheets
13 Check that quorum is present
14 Secretary to produce register of directors' interests, read notice (unless taken as read) and auditors' report
15 Chairman to take report and accounts as read
16 Chairman addresses meeting and calls for members to move and second adoption of report and accounts (and dividend)
17 Chairman to invite questions
18 Chairman puts motion adopting accounts to meeting and declares result
19 Chairman refers to election of directors and calls for members to move and second motion(s). Two or more directors may be appointed by a single resolution only if a private company or if no member present objects
20 Chairman puts motion(s) electing directors to meeting and declares result
21 Chairman refers to remuneration of auditors and calls for members to move and second motion. (No resolution needed to reappoint auditors.)
22 Chairman puts motion fixing auditors' remuneration to meeting and declares result
23 Chairman refers to any other motion for which proper notice has been given and calls for members to move and second motion; chairman puts motion to meeting and declares result
24 Members to move and second vote of thanks
25 Chairman responds and closes meeting

After the meeting

26 Prepare minutes
27 Action subsequent to any change of directors — Registrar of Companies, bank, Stock Exchange etc.
28 File resolutions (if any) with Registrar of Companies
29 Pay dividend (if any)
30 Inform press unless present at meeting — and Stock Exchange if quoted
31 Prepare annual return

Protests at annual general meetings

It can no longer be assumed that the annual general meeting of a public company will be the usual thirty-minute formality. It was at annual general meetings in the early 1970s that chairmen of Barclays Bank Limited and Imperial Chemical Industries Limited faced groups of articulate young people, protesting against alleged support for the apartheid policy of South Africa. Shareholders arriving for the meeting were met outside by young people brandishing banners and leaflets and inside others attempted to question the board, move resolutions and generally harass the proceedings so that, in the case of Barclays Bank, the meeting was extended to about three hours. Many other meetings have been similarly disturbed since then.

Recent issues rousing protest have covered such predictable topics as pollution, equal pay, board representation for workers and the shipment and sale of arms but of all issues, that of racial discrimination is likely to be the most emotive in the future. No public company with interests in South Africa, for example, can afford to neglect the possibility that its next annual general meeting may be chosen as a target for protest. Public companies ought to approach future meetings cautiously and a careful review of procedures is now appropriate.

The following reasonable precautions are being taken by some public companies and they should prove sufficient to enable company officials to retain the initiative in currently envisaged situations:

1 Assume that protestors will be present when preparing for a meeting
2 Consider tightening admission procedures so that only shareholders (including, of course, their proxies or representatives) and any other invited persons obtain admission. This obviously will not exclude protestors who are genuine shareholders, nor persons who have become shareholders or proxies merely to obtain admission for protest purposes, but it may well exclude some unwelcome visitors. A small room or separate table at one side of the admission area could be a useful facility for interviewing doubtful cases without impeding the flow of other shareholders. If the formal checking of each person's right to attend appears to be too onerous a task it is worth bearing in mind that even a mere semblance of control may deter some. Other entrances to the meeting place should be sealed off from the outside except that it may help if the platform party and important guests could use a separate and less conspicuous entrance
3 Advise the local police that the meeting is due to take place and agree with them the procedure for obtaining their help if required. One responsible steward should locate in advance the telephone nearest to the meeting place and be prepared with appropriate coin (if necessary) and telephone number so that he can summon instant police help at an agreed signal from the chairman. The presence of a uniformed police officer outside the meeting place may have a tranquillizing effect on some
4 Arrange the seating in manageable blocks so that every seat is reasonably accessible to stewards for the purpose of distributing poll cards, handling microphones and reaching troublemakers

5 Ensure that a good number of well-briefed and strategically placed stewards are seen to be present. Badges help to create an official atmosphere and the more timid protestors may be deterred. Stewards should know the whereabouts of fire buckets and brooms so that they can deal expeditiously with such phenomena as stink bombs
6 Ensure that a competent official is in charge of the amplifying system which ideally should be designed so that the chairman is always in a position to dominate proceedings and that where questioners are provided with individual roving microphones each can be switched off from a control point if necessary
7 Draft the agenda so that formal business is transacted as quickly as possible in the first part of the meeting. By firmly following a carefully worked out agenda a chairman will more easily be able to rule questions out of order if they are not strictly within the scope of the item being dealt with. If an unusually large number of questions are expected it may help to inform the meeting that there will be ample time for general questions at the end of formal business
8 Ensure that the chairman is supplied with necessary facts, figures and possibly prepared statements in advance so that he is in a position to answer all foreseeable questions competently. Some chairmen appreciate an opportunity to rehearse the formal agenda and to answer dummy questions with a few officials present prior to the actual meeting
9 Check that the procedure for conducting a poll is as simple and streamlined as possible. Protestors may successfully demand a poll on every resolution in an attempt to lengthen the meeting and if one poll card is designed to cover all possible resolutions considerable time will be saved in not having to distribute and collect cards at each poll
10 If it is normal practice to reappoint several directors by a single resolution (no one member voting against the initial resolution permitting such action), consider re-electing each director by a single resolution voluntarily rather than be forced to do so by one protestor being unhelpful
11 On the assumption that advance warning has been received, consider the possibility of the chairman inviting representatives of the protestors to meet him privately before the shareholders' meeting. It could be that private assurances from the chairman would satisfy the protestors
12 Bear in mind that some protestors are rational and well-motivated. 11, above, is highly important in the approach to such protestors. Preparedness to talk and the making available of the fullest information will often serve to establish the good faith of the company and so keep protest at an orderly level

A serious factor which must be borne in mind in planning any important meeting is the possibility that the meeting place may be chosen as a target for a bomb or bomb scare causing the meeting to be abandoned before essential business has been transacted. In this connection the services of the company's security officer become essential and in some large companies the security officer has become an important member of the team preparing for the meeting. He will coordinate all aspects of security and safety for the meeting, including the ejection of troublemakers if necessary and the procedure in the event of a speedy evacuation being necessary. He will make himself responsible for surveying the meeting place before the meeting, familiarize himself with all the objects inside and outside, and all means of escape. He will ensure that, as people arrive, no packages of doubtful content are brought in without first being examined. Obviously it could be expensive and embarrassing for a shareholders' meeting to have to break up or perhaps not even get started with the consequence that the meeting would have to be reconvened, and at least one large public company in London has for several years gone to the trouble of booking and preparing a second meeting place to which the meeting could be rapidly adjourned if necessary. From the shareholders' point of view the declaration of the dividend is probably the most important item of business and some companies have taken the precaution of dealing with this item first to ensure that at least that part of the business is dealt with.

SPECIMEN NOTICES FOR MEETINGS OF SHAREHOLDERS

Notice for an annual general meeting

ROBERT ROBERTSON AND SONS PLC

Notice is hereby given that the fifth *annual general meeting of ROBERT ROBERTSON AND SONS PLC* will be held at 20 King's Terrace, Aberdeen, on Thursday 4 June 1987, at 12 30 in the afternoon to transact the ordinary business of the company.

20 King's Terrace
Aberdeen
7 May 1987

By order of the board
Smith and Jones
Secretaries

Any member entitled to attend and vote at the above meeting may appoint one or more proxies to attend and vote instead of him. A proxy need not be a member of the company.

This notice is being sent to all members but only holders of ordinary shares are entitled to attend and vote at the meeting.

Notice for an annual general meeting followed by a class meeting

THAMES AMENITIES LIMITED

Notice is hereby given that the *annual general meeting* of the members of Thames Amenities Limited will be held at Liberty House, Hamsell Street, London EC2 on 10 April 1987 at 10 00, for the following purposes, namely:

1. To receive and consider the accounts and balance sheet and the reports of the directors and auditors thereon
2. To declare a dividend on the ordinary stock
3. To elect directors
4. To appoint the auditors and approve their remuneration

Notice is hereby also given that at the conclusion of the business of the annual general meeting a separate general meeting of the holders of the preference stock of the company will be held for the purpose of appointing a director to represent such holders.

A member of the company entitled to attend and vote is entitled to appoint one or more proxies to attend and vote instead of him. A proxy need not also be a member.

Dated 20 March 1987
Liberty House,
Hamsell Street,
London EC2

By order of the board
J. Hemmings, Secretary

Notice of an extraordinary general meeting

ASSOCIATED SYNDICATIONS LIMITED

Notice is hereby given that an *extraordinary general meeting* of Associated Syndications Limited will be held at the Holt Hotel, Bread Street Chester, Cheshire, on Friday 29 May 1987 at 10 30 in the forenoon, for the purpose of considering and, if thought fit, passing the following resolutions of which that numbered 1 will be proposed as an *ordinary resolution* and that numbered 2 as a *special resolution:*

RESOLUTIONS

1. That the whole of the issued ordinary stock in the capital of the company be converted into fully paid ordinary shares of £0.25 each and that each of the unissued ordinary shares of £1 each in the capital of the company be subdivided into four ordinary shares of £0.25 each
2. That the company's articles of association be altered by deleting '£1' in article 70 and substituting '£0.25' therefor

THE CONDUCT OF MEETINGS

The Rookery
Oak Drive,
Chester, Cheshire
1 May 1987

By order of the board
B A Mackenzie
Secretary

Any member entitled to attend and vote at the above meeting may appoint a proxy to attend and vote instead of him and a proxy need not be a member.

MEETINGS IN A WINDING-UP

Members' voluntary winding-up

1. Board meeting to
   (a) Authorize statutory declaration of solvency (ss577 and 578)
   (b) Convene extraordinary general meeting (s572)
2. Initial EGM (or AGM) to
   (a) Pass appropriate resolution (s572)
   (b) Appoint liquidator (s580)
3. General meeting at end of each year to receive accounts (s581)
4. General meetings at any other time to
   (a) Replace liquidator (s581)
   (b) Empower liquidator to accept shares etc. (s582)
   (c) Transact any other business (ss598 and 601)
5. Final meeting to
   (a) Receive accounts (s585)
   (b) Dispose of books (s640)
   (c) Assign undisclosed assets

The normal provisions about notice and quorum apply in meetings 1 to 4 above. Notice for meeting 5 is governed by s585 — one month's notice in the *London Gazette*. There is no provision for individual notice for meeting 5 although it is usually sent — especially if business is more than that required by s585.

If in a members' voluntary winding-up the liquidator is at any time of the opinion that the company will not be able to pay its debts in full within the period stated in the declaration of solvency, he must summon a meeting of creditors and ss594 and 595 will then apply in place of ss584 and 585. Although creditors' meetings are called, the winding-up remains a members' voluntary winding-up.

Meetings in a creditors' voluntary winding-up

1   Board meeting to
    (a) Convene EGM (s572)
    (b) Convene creditors' meeting (s588)
    (c) Appoint chairman of first creditors' meeting (s588)
    (d) Approve statement for creditors' meeting (s588)
2   Initial EGM (AGM) to
    (a) Pass extraordinary resolution (s572)
    (b) *Nominate* liquidator (s589)
    (c) *Nominate* up to five members of committee or inspection (s590)
3   Initial creditors' meeting held on day of EGM or next day to
    (a) Nominate and *appoint* liquidator (s589)
    (b) Appoint committee of inspection (s590)
4   General meetings of members and/or creditors at end of each year to receive accounts (s594)
5   General meetings of members and/or creditors (or committee of inspection) at any other time to
    (a) Replace liquidator (meeting of creditors, see s592)
    (b) Empower liquidator to accept shares etc. (s593)
    (c) Transact any other business (ss598 and 601)
6   Final meetings of members and creditors to
    (a) Receive accounts (s595)
    (b) Dispose of books (creditors per s640)
    (c) Assign undisclosed assets

In a creditors' voluntary winding-up the provisions about notice, quorum and chairman are a little complicated but may be summarized as follows:

Meetings 1 and 2. Normal provisions
Meeting 3. Notice by post (with notice of meeting 2 (s588(2)(b)) in *Gazette* and at least two local newspapers (s588(2)(c))
Quorum. Three or all if less than three (r.138 of the Companies (Winding-up) Rules 1949).
Chairman. A director (s588(3)(b))

Meetings 4 and 5. Notice. Normal provisions for members; creditors, seven days by post, in *Gazette* and at least one local newspaper (r.129)
Quorum. Normal provisions, for members; creditors, as for meeting 3.
Chairman. If summoned by liquidator, him. If by someone else the meeting elects a chairman (r.133).

Meetings(s) 6. Notice. One month's notice in *Gazette* (s595(2)). No provision in Act for personal notice to members or creditors but usually sent.

Quorum. As for meetings 4 and 5 but if not present appropriate return sent to registrar (*s*595(3)).
Chairman. Liquidator.

FURTHER READING

Handling Protest at Annual Meetings, Conference Board, New York, 1971.
Nelson's Table of Procedures, Longman Professional Publishing, London, 9th edition, 1985.
F. Shackleton, *The Law and Practice of Meetings*, Sweet and Maxwell, London, 7th edition, 1983.
Sir Sebag Shaw and Dennis Smith, *The Law of Meetings*, Macdonald and Evans, Plymouth, 5th edition, 1979.
The City Code on Take-overs and Mergers, The Panel on Takeovers and Mergers, London, 1985.
J. Yelland, *The Conduct of Meetings*, Rose-Jordans, London, 22nd edition, 1982.

Part Two
Accounting and Finance

5

The Annual Accounts

W P Ridley

Anyone interested in the management of a company, whether taking an active part or merely investing capital, needs to have financial information of two kinds concerning the company:

1. Where the capital is invested (shown in the balance sheet)
2. The return earned from the investment (shown in the profit and loss account)

Those in active management can call for financial reports and accounts to be designed according to their own requirements. But, for investors and others, forms of balance sheet and profit and loss account have been laid down by Acts of Parliament. This chapter starts by describing the formal requirements, and then proceeds to discuss other aspects of the accounts, including the interpretation of accounts in order to judge a company's financial performance.

ACCOUNTING REQUIREMENTS OF THE COMPANIES ACTS

The form of the published accounts and the directors' report is set by the Companies Act 1985, which constitutes the Companies Acts 1948–83. They set out what must be included in the profit and loss account, the balance sheet and directors' report (including notes).

The accounts of a company based on this selected information are termed the statutory accounts.

Growth of information required

The information required for the statutory accounts has grown enormously during the past sixty years, owing to pressure from investors and the general public. The pressure from investors for more information has grown with their increasing separation from management in industry and commerce. This separation has led to a need for investors to learn as much as possible of the state of companies, in order to assess the security of their investment. The general public, which in this connection includes creditors and potential investors, are concerned to know how companies are being managed, and whether they are financially sound. (This demand for information becomes especially apparent when public confidence in company administration has been shaken by a well-publicized fraud.) Successive governments have responded to these two pressures in their legislation.

The government itself may wish to have more information made public if it feels this will have a beneficial effect upon industry or commerce as a whole. Thus the publication of export figures by each company, for example, can have the effect of increasing emphasis on overseas sales and thereby stimulating trade. As a result, the successive Companies Acts tend to set increasingly stringent requirements for company disclosure, while accounting standards are continually being tightened to achieve uniformity in reporting.

STANDARD PRESENTATION

The profit and loss account

While there are some variations allowed in presentation, Figure 5.1 shows the information required in a profit and loss account.

Specifically, the objective is to show:

(a) operating income
(b) investment income, splitting income from associated companies from other income
(c) income from ordinary activities separately from extraordinary income charges or tax

In addition, other information has to be given either in the accounts or in a statement attached to the accounts:

1   Directors' remuneration must be given, either in the accounts or in a statement attached to the accounts. All directors' remuneration and past directors' pensions, paid by the company or by any other person, either for their services as directors or for services in other capacities must be

---

1 Turnover
2 Cost of sales (a)
3 Gross profit or loss
4 Distribution costs (a)
5 Administrative expenses (a)
6 Other operating income
7 Income from shares in group companies
8 Income from shares in related companies
9 Income from other fixed asset investments (b)
10 Other interest receivable and similar income (b)
11 Amounts written off investments
12 Interest payable and similar charges (c)
13 Tax on profit or loss on ordinary activities
14 Profit or loss on ordinary activities after taxation
15 Extraordinary income
16 Extraordinary charges
17 Extraordinary profit or loss
18 Tax on extraordinary profit or loss
19 Other taxes not shown under the above items
20 Profit or loss for the financial year

Notes

(a) *Cost of sales: distribution costs: administrative expenses*

These items shall be stated after taking into account any necessary provisions for depreciation or diminution in value of assets

(b) *Income from other fixed asset investments: other interest receivable and similar income*

Income and interest derived from group companies shall be shown separately from income and interest derived from other sources

(c) *Interest payable and similar charges*

The amount payable to group companies shall be shown separately

(d) The amount of any provisions for depreciation and diminution in value of tangible and intangible fixed assets shall be disclosed in a note to the accounts

---

Figure 5.1 Profit and loss account format

shown. Likewise the statement or accounts must show any compensation paid by the company or any other person to past or present directors for loss of office. In addition the statement must show the number of directors who have waived their rights to emoluments and the aggregate amount that has been waived. The chairman's emoluments must be shown separately and also those of the highest paid director if these are in excess of the chairman's emoluments.

The number of directors must be shown, broken down into income groups; that is, the number of directors whose emoluments do not exceed £5 000; the number whose emoluments exceed £5 000 but do not exceed £10 000; and so on for each successive integral number of £5 000. For each of these items, the term 'emoluments' does not include contributions paid by the company for the benefit of directors under any pension scheme.

2 Auditors' remuneration
3 Amount set aside for redemption of share capital and loans
4 Turnover with analysis by geographical market
5 The average number of staff (by category) to be given with the aggregate amount of wages, social security costs and pension costs incurred.

Taxation items. The more detailed requirements about disclosure of taxation items are covered by the layout shown in Figure 5.2.

Taxation based on profits for the year:		
Corporation tax at 35% (including £ previous year £ transferred to deferred taxation) on profits excluding those of associates	x	x
Less relief for overseas taxation	x	x
	x	x
Overseas taxation	x	x
Prior-year adjustments	x	x
Tax on share of profits of associates	x	x
Total tax charge	—	—

Note: No provision has been made for tax, deferment of which is reasonably certain for the foreseeable future.

Figure 5.2 Presentation of taxation details

The balance sheet

Figure 5.3 provides a format for a company's balance sheet. The principles of valuation are also set out.

1 Fixed assets: the amount to be included in respect of a firm's fixed assets is the amount of its purchase price or production cost less provisions for depreciation. Similar principles shall be applied where goodwill or development costs (only rarely to be treated as an asset) are given balance sheet values.

For fixed assets shown at valuations, the year in which the valuations were made must be disclosed. For fixed assets valued during the last financial year, the names or qualifications of the valuers and the bases of valuation they used must be given.

Freehold land must be shown separately from leasehold land, and

THE ANNUAL ACCOUNTS

ASSETS

A Called up share capital not paid (*a*)

B Fixed assets

  I Intangible assets
   1 Development costs
   2 Concessions, patents, licences, trade marks and similar rights and assets (*b*)
   3 Goodwill (*c*)
   4 Payments on account

  II Tangible assets
   1 Land and buildings
   2 Plant and machinery
   3 Fixtures, fittings, tools and equipment
   4 Payments on account and assets in course of construction

  III Investments
   1 Shares in group companies
   2 Loans to group companies
   3 Shares in related companies
   4 Loans to related companies
   5 Other investments other than loans
   6 Other loans
   7 Own shares (*d*)

C Current assets

  I Stocks
   1 Raw materials and consumables
   2 Work in progress
   3 Finished goods and goods for resale
   4 Payments on account

  II Debtors (*e*)
   1 Trade debtors
   2 Amounts owed by group companies
   3 Amounts owed by related companies
   4 Other debtors
   5 Called up share capital not paid (*a*)
   6 Prepayments and accrued income (*f*)

  III Investments
   1 Shares in group companies
   2 Own shares (*d*)
   3 Other investments

  IV Cash at bank and in hand

D Prepayments and accrued income (*f*)

LIABILITIES

A Capital and reserves

  I Called up share capital (*k*)

  II Share premium account

  III Revaluation reserve

Figure 5.3 Balance sheet format

 IV Other reserves
   1 Capital redemption reserve
   2 Reserve for own shares
   3 Reserves provided for by the articles of association
   4 Other reserves
 V Profit and loss account

B Provisions for liabilities and charges
  1 Pensions and similar obligations
  2 Taxation including deferred taxation
  3 Other provisions

C Creditors (*l*)
  1 Debenture loans (*g*)
  2 Bank loans and overdrafts
  3 Payments received on account (*h*)
  4 Trade creditors
  5 Bills of exchange payable
  6 Amounts owed to group companies
  7 Amounts owed to related companies
  8 Other creditors including taxation and social security (*i*)
  9 Accruals and deferred income (*j*)

D Accruals and deferred income (*j*)

Notes

(*a*) This item may be shown under the heading of Assets

(*b*) Amounts in respect of assets shall only included in a company's balance sheet under this item if either
  (i) the assets were acquired for valuable consideration and are not required to be shown under goodwill; *or*
  (ii) the assets in question were created by the company itself

(*c*) Amounts representing goodwill shall only be included to the extent that the goodwill was acquired for valuable consideration

(*d*) The nominal value of the shares held shall be shown separately

(*e*) The amount falling due after more than one year shall be shown separately for each item included under debtors

(*f*) This item may be shown in an alternative position

(*g*) The amount of any convertible loans shall be shown separately

(*h*) Payments received on account of orders shall be shown for each of these items in so far as they are not shown as deductions from stocks

(*i*) The amount for creditors in respect of taxation and social security shall be shown separately from the amount for other creditors

(*j*) The two positions given for this item are alternatives

(*k*) The amount of allotted share capital and the amount of called up share capital which has been paid up shall be shown separately

(*l*) Amounts falling due within one year and after one year shall be shown separately for each of these items and their aggregate shall be shown separately for all of these items

Figure 5.3 *(concluded)*

THE ANNUAL ACCOUNTS

land held on a long lease (one having not less than fifty years to run) must be distinguished from that held on a short lease (having less than fifty years to run).

There must also be shown (i) the aggregate amount of fixed assets acquired during the year; and (ii) the book value at the date of the last balance sheet of fixed assets disposed of during the year.

If the detail to be disclosed is considerable it might best be given on a statement attached to the accounts, reference thereto being made in the balance sheet.

2 Current assets shall normally be valued at production cost or purchase price (which may be calculated on a last in first out or first in first out price or average weighted price). However, where the net realizable value is estimated to be lower than the cost, this lower value will be substituted.

Items requiring disclosure

Other matters to be disclosed in the published accounts (by notes if not otherwise shown) include:

(a) The corresponding figures for the preceding year
(b) The nature and amount, or estimated amount, of any contingent liabilities not provided for; financial commitments (including pensions); charges for other companies
(c) The amount or estimated amount of any contracts for capital expenditure, so far as not provided for, and of any capital expenditure authorized by the directors but not yet contracted for
(d) The bases on which foreign currencies have been converted into sterling
(e) Any special circumstances affecting the company's taxation liability for the current or succeeding financial years

(f) The number of employees (other than directors of the company) whose emoluments for the year (from the company, its subsidiaries or any other person in respect of services to the company or its subsidiaries)

    exceeded £20 000 but did not exceed £25 000
    exceeded £25 000 but did not exceed £30 000
    exceeded £30 000 but did not exceed £35 000

and so on in successive integral multiples of £5 000
(g) The information concerning each of the company's subsidiaries; normally capital reserves and profit or loss for the year
(h) Similar information
  (i) where the company holds equity shares in another company (other than a subsidiary) exceeding one-tenth of the nominal value of the issued equity capital of that other company, or

(ii) where the company holds shares in another company (other than a subsidiary) which, in the investing company's balance sheet, are shown at an amount exceeding one-tenth of the investing company's assets (as stated in its balance sheet)

(i) Under $s5$, a subsidiary has to give the name and country of incorporation of its ultimate holding company

(j) Allotments of shares during the year; outstanding options; amount of redeemable shares; debentures issued redeemed and the amount that can be re-issued. In addition, any financial assistance given by a company for purchase of the company's shares shall be noted

(k) Dividends recommended; any fixed cumulative dividend in arrear

(l) Reserves and provisions at the beginning and end of the year, together with any material movements. Any re-valuation reserve should be shown separately

(m) The amount of any provision for taxation other than deferred taxation shall be stated

THE DIRECTORS' REPORT

The directors' report must accompany the balance sheet and profit and loss account filed with the Registrar of Companies, and must be sent to all members of the company, debenture holders and other interested parties.

The report, which is presented by the board of directors, contains much relevant information concerning a company's activities, and its minimum contents, summarized below, have been considerably extended. It should be especially noted that these minimum contents are required by legislation and are not subject to directors' choice any more than the information contained in the statutory accounts.

Minimum contents

Review. A review of the company's affairs during the period covered by the accounts; particulars of important events that have occurred since the year end; likely future developments; an indication of research and development activities.

Dividends. The amount(s) recommended to be paid by way of dividend.

Reserves. The amount(s) proposed to be transferred to reserves.

Activities. The principal activities of the company and significant changes in these activities.

THE ANNUAL ACCOUNTS

Directors. The names of all directors who acted in such a capacity at any time during the period under review.

Changes in fixed assets. Significant changes in the company's fixed assets. If the market value of land is substantially different from the value shown in the balance sheet, an indication of the difference in value.

Contracts. Contracts with the company (except service contracts) in which a director of the company has an interest; the parties to the contract, the director involved, the nature of the contract, and the nature of the director's interest must be specified.

Arrangements between company and directors. Any arrangement whereby the directors are able to obtain benefits by the acquisition of shares or debentures in the company or any other body corporate.

Directors' interests. Directors' interests (at the beginning and end of each year) in shares or debentures of the company. This requirement is extended to include the directors' spouses and infant children (the directors' 'family interests').

Matters showing the state of the company's affairs. Particulars of any matter required for an appreciation by its members of the state of the company's affairs, so long as in the opinion of the directors the publication of such information would not be harmful to the company.

Relative profitability of different activities. Turnover and profit or loss of each class of business carried on by the company, if such classes differ substantially.

Persons employed. The average number of persons employed in the UK by the company (on a weekly basis) during the year, and the aggregate remuneration paid or payable to such persons in respect of that year. This information is not required where a company has fewer than one hundred employees.

Political and charitable contributions. The amount of contributions, if exceeding £50, given for political or charitable purposes, and the identity of the political party concerned.

Exports. The turnover from exports when the value exceeds £50 000, and a note where no goods are exported.

Previous year. The corresponding amounts in each section for the immediately preceding year.

Employment policy. The arrangements for health, safety and welfare at work and for involvement in the business. Provisions for employment of disabled persons.

JUDGING A COMPANY FROM ITS ACCOUNTS

Reports by a company to its shareholders are regulated in detail by law. As a result, outside assessments of the financial standing of a company are almost inevitably based on the information given in these reports (normally issued annually) rather than on other publications of the company or on its trade reputation. Increasingly it is being realized that this outside assessment is important to the company — in raising finance, whether by loan or equity, in merger discussions with other companies, or in trading negotiations. It is therefore advisable for senior company executives to consider in detail the standards against which their company's financial performance — as set out in the fully audited report to shareholders — will be judged.

PROFIT AND LOSS ACCOUNT FOR PANGLOSS PLC

This chapter takes the abridged accounts of a company called Pangloss PLC to highlight information on which a financial examination is based (see Figure 5.4).

In the year to 31 March 1985, Pangloss earned £1.4m, before a charge of £0.4m for depreciation; depreciation is singled out because it does not represent a direct cash outflow but an accounting adjustment to the value of fixed assets — some of which are likely to have been bought many years before. Therefore when considering the cash resources available to the company both the level of depreciation and retained profits will be taken into account. The trading surplus net of depreciation gives pre-interest profits — an important indicator of company trading performance, see Figure 5.6 — of £1.0m.

Interest charge

The interest charge depends on the amount of loans and overdrafts outstanding, which is an integral part of the financing of the company's assets, rather than of current trading. It is therefore of prime significance to those providing finance whether as lenders or investors. From the point of view of a potential lender, the relation of the interest charge to the level of pre-interest profits gives some indication of the security for loans; in this case with interest at £0.3m he is likely to be deterred by the relatively high ratio of 30 per cent of pre-interest profits (of £1m) already absorbed by interest.

	YEAR TO 31 MARCH 1985	£m
	Trading surplus (before depreciation)	1.4
Less:	Depreciation	0.4
	Pre-interest profits	1.0
Less:	Interest	0.3
	Pre-tax profits	0.7
Less:	Tax	0.3
	Available to shareholders	0.4

Figure 5.4 Abbreviated profit and loss account of Pangloss PLC

From the point of view of the equity investor, this ratio represents the gearing given to the amounts available to ordinary shareholders. Thus if pre-interest profits increase by 70 per cent to £1.7m with interest remaining at £0.3m, pre-tax profits will double to £1.4m, while if they fall by 70 per cent, pre-tax profits will be reduced to nil. So the element of gearing offers both opportunity for increasing the return to shareholders where the company is successful and additional risk if trading returns fall. The degree of gearing that investors are prepared to accept varies according to the industrial risk and this must be borne in mind by the company executive when negotiating loans, overdraft facilities or equity finance.

Tax charge

The tax charge depends not only on the rates of tax ruling in the countries where profits are earned, but also any special allowances or grants offered. Where the charge appears abnormal it will be analysed to ascertain whether this is due to temporary or permanent factors. The tax charge shown for Pangloss however of £0.3m on £0.7m represents a tax rate only slightly higher than normal. This leaves £0.4m available for distribution to shareholders, which will be evaluated by investors with reference to the number of shares issued.

RETURN TO SHAREHOLDERS

Earnings of £0.4m on 2 million shares (see Figure 5.5) are equivalent to 20p per share in Pangloss. The value of the share is normally directly related to

YEAR ENDED 31 MARCH 1985	
Earnings for the year to 31.3.85	= £0.4m or 20p per share*
Recommended dividend	= £0.2m or 10p per share*
Retained profits	= £0.2m
* Issued capital 2 million ordinary shares of £1	

Figure 5.5 Earnings, dividends and retentions of Pangloss PLC

INDUSTRIAL AVERAGE			YEAR ENDED 31 MARCH		
			1983	1984	1985
	(a)	Pre-interest profit (£m)	0.8	0.9	1.0
	(b)	Turnover (£m)	8.0	8.0	9.0
11%		Margin on sales a/b	10%	11%	11%
	(c)	Capital employed (£m)	10.0	11.0	11.0
11%		Return on capital a/c	8%	8%	9%

Figure 5.6 Performance ratios for Pangloss PLC

this figure; thus, if the share price is £2, an investor will consider whether it is reasonable to buy or sell the share given that £2 is equivalent to ten times the earnings attributable to that share (that is a p/e ratio of 10). The dividend must also be considered — for long-term investors, this represents the direct return. At a price of £2, the dividend of 10p per share represents a 5 per cent net return on the investment; because tax is already deducted, the dividend is free of tax up to the standard rate in the hands of the recipient. The 5 per cent return is therefore worth 7.0 per cent in gross terms to the standard taxpayer at current rates of tax. Better returns are offered by an investment in gilts. The investor has therefore to judge whether the trading prospects of Pangloss offer scope for this dividend to be steadily increased.

TRADING PROSPECTS

The record of Pangloss will first be examined to assess the management's abilities to secure satisfactory returns. Figure 5.6 shows the ratios normally applied to the results published in the accounts to judge the management's ability in running the trading of the business.

Performance

Figure 5.6 shows Pangloss's performance measured against sales and capital employed. These criteria are used as a guide to management efficiency, as

THE ANNUAL ACCOUNTS

they allow comparison with other companies in the same industry, as well as to the underlying viability of the company. In this table, pre-interest profit (taken because it excludes interest which depends on the method of funding of the capital employed) has advanced by a quarter from £0.8m in 1983 to £1.0m in 1985; with turnover (up from £8m to £9m) and capital employed (up from £10m to £11m) both rising less fast, margins on sales and return on capital have increased over the period. Margins at 11 per cent in 1985 are the same as for the industry as a whole, which therefore indicates normal trading returns and one without volatile fluctuations; return on capital however at 9 per cent is well below the industry level of 11 per cent, indicating that the amount of capital employed is high compared with other companies in the industry. Moreover, since the return of 9 per cent falls below the general level of interest rates, it is insufficient to justify the use of new capital in the business; indeed disposal of the existing assets or a change of management — whether through merger or staff recruitment — could be justified in these conditions. For the business cannot justify to its shareholders the employment of funds which could be better invested elsewhere. Thus return on capital forms a key element in the financial assessment of a company; capital in this context however has to be carefully defined and this is considered in detail with reference to the Pangloss balance sheet.

BALANCE SHEET FOR PANGLOSS PLC

Pangloss's balance sheet is given in abbreviated form in Figure 5.7.

		£M
Sources of Finance		
Share capital 2 million ordinary shares of £1		2
Retained profits		4
Shareholders' funds		6
Debt finance		
4% Debenture 1986	3	
Bank overdraft	2	5
Total funds		11
Assets Employed		
Fixed assets		
Property	5	
Machinery	1	
Vehicles	1	7
Net current assets		4
Total assets		11

Figure 5.7 Abbreviated 1985 balance sheet for Pangloss PLC

Value of shares

The first point of interest raised by the balance sheet is the book value of the shares. Of the £11m capital employed in Pangloss at the end of the 1985–6 year, £6m is shown to be financed by shareholders' funds giving a book value of £3 each for the 2m shares. (This allows for the assets of the company fetching the £11m shown and thus providing £6m surplus after paying off the debt finance of £5m.)

Scope for raising funds

Secondly the balance sheet gives an indication of the scope for raising further finance. In this case with borrowing at £5m against £11m capital employed, it is unlikely that lenders would be interested in advancing further funds to Pangloss. In addition to checking the company's ability to service the interest charge out of current profits, lenders are concerned with the asset backing for loans. It is rare for a company to obtain half its funds from borrowing. Within the £5m debt the £3m 4 per cent debenture explains the relatively low interest charge given in the profit and loss account. However, since it falls to be redeemed in 1986, it can be considered, with the bank overdraft, as short-term finance; the refinancing of the debenture could well be at a rate of interest of 10 per cent instead of 4 per cent, increasing the interest charge by £180 000 from £120 000 to £300 000. Thus the funding problems of the Pangloss Company are clearly likely to discourage investors; for shareholders will expect to be asked to contribute further equity finance.

Assets employed

However, close attention must also be paid to the assets shown in the balance sheet. For the value attributed to these assets is critical to measuring the efficiency of the company through the rate of return on capital and the potential debt finance that they can secure. In particular the value given to the property must be considered; for if the book figure represents cost or an out-of-date valuation, the current value may be considerably higher provided the property is freehold or on a long lease. The annual report must therefore be examined for details of the basis of valuation of the property; if the up-to-date value of the Pangloss property was for instance £8m against £5m shown, the total assets employed come to £14m; and with pre-interest profits of £1m, return on capital is little over 7 per cent, indicating that higher rewards could be gained by investing the money in gilt-edged stocks. (This assumes the machinery, vehicles and current assets, which include stocks and debtors net of creditors, raise their book value of £6m.) On the other hand the prospect of raising debt finance is clearly less forbidding; not only does property tend to appreciate but legal rights to it can be granted to lenders. As a result up to two-thirds of the value of the property can commonly be raised by debt finance and — provided it is invested at a rate of return that exceeds the interest charge — this offers opportunities for expansion. Property may make Pangloss attractive as a takeover prospect whether on a break-up basis or on the scope for improving the present returns.

Assets other than land have to be treated more cautiously; the value of the plant may be minimal on a break-up basis, while current assets, such as debtors and stock, may not fully realize their book values — particularly if the company does not impose sufficient financial control. The trend of these assets to turnover will therefore be examined closely to see whether normal business standards are being achieved. On a forced realization, these assets may recover much less than their book value if standards have not been maintained.

Other information

There is much other information that can be taken from the report, for instance on the extent of capital commitments, or the subsidiaries and associated companies of the group. These do not however affect the key standards applied to the balance sheet and profit and loss account that have been examined here. These standards are used for assessing the company from several standpoints. For the shareholder the attraction of the company may be measured by the trend in earnings per share. Potential lenders will look at the cover for the interest charge, the proportion of capital funded by loans and the type of security offered. Management will be assessed by the margin on sales and return on capital that it has secured. The significance of the information given in the annual report is therefore of fundamental importance to a company in any assessment of its financial standing and the efficiency of its management.

INFLATION ACCOUNTING

In recent years considerable attention has been paid to adjusting company results to take inflation into account. A simple approach is to charge to the profit and loss account the amount that is required to maintain the real value of the equity base.

However, a more complex approach is to apply adjustments to the profit and loss account that reflect the rate of change of prices experienced by each company in its existing business, rather than the general rate of inflation — as represented, for instance, in the changes in the retail price index. The purpose of this approach is to identify the success of the company in maintaining its business activities rather than providing for the equity base to be maintained.

FURTHER READING

D. Hay and D. Morris, *Industrial Economics: Theory and Evidence,* Oxford University Press, 1979.

M. Firth, *The Valuation of Shares and the Efficient Markets Theory,* Macmillan, London, 1977.

How to Read a Balance Sheet, ILO, Geneva, 1975.

A. J. Merrett and A. Sykes, *Finance and Analysis of Capital Projects,* Longman, London, 1973.

W. Reid and D. R. Myddelton, *The Meaning of Company Accounts,* Gower, Aldershot, 3rd edition, 1982.

L. E. Rockley, *The Meaning of Balance Sheets and Company Reports,* Business Books, London, 1975.

6

Sources of Finance

Stephen Badger

In theory three sources of wealth are available to a company — land, labour and capital. These are not wholly interchangeable, but to some extent the balance in any given company can be changed by the entrepreneur; land can be turned into capital by sale and leaseback (see long-term facilities, below) or a given process can be made more capital-intensive and so generally require less labout (or vice versa). These decisions are within the scope of management, one of whose functions is to optimize the balance between the different factors or production. The first step before raising capital is therefore to ensure that it is really financial capital that is required.

WHY CAPITAL MAY BE REQUIRED

Capital is required to finance the conduct of the business. When a manufacturing business is first established for instance, factory and office premises will be needed and plant and machinery and transport vehicles. These can either be bought outright or hired; in the first case the expenditure represents capital permanently invested in the business (for the second, see medium-term facilities, below). Funds will also be required to finance production from the initial purchase of raw materials to the sale of the finished product to an external purchaser, to pay wages and to meet overheads; these funds are known as working or revolving capital. As the business expands fresh injections of both permanent and working capital will be required. If, on the contrary, it contracts (or is merely run more efficiently) capital will be freed for alternative uses. When the original fixed assets need replacing, more expenditure will be needed. This should have been adequately provided out of profits by depreciation provisions over the life of the assets, but in times of inflation there may well be a shortfall which will need an injection of new capital.

Capital may also be required for acquisitions.

TYPE OF CAPITAL REQUIRED

Capital is conventionally described as short-term, medium-term or long-term. The distinctions are not rigid, but short-term capital may be regarded as any liability repayable within one year; medium-term as being repayable between one and ten years in the future; and everything else as being long-term capital (this covers both the proprietors' ordinary risk capital, or equity, and long-term borrowings, or debt capital). In general, working capital requirements should be financed by short-term capital and capital permanently invested in the business should be long-term. Medium-term capital is useful to give added flexibility and balance to the overall financial structure. Where a project is expected to generate sufficient cash flow to repay the initial investment within, say, seven years, medium-term financing may be appropriate.

This chapter deals primarily with sources of long-term finance (both debt and equity), but sources of short- and medium-term finance are considered in outline.

LONG-TERM FINANCE FOR UNLISTED COMPANIES

The types of finance available to a company that is not listed on a stock exchange are much the same as those for one that is. The difference in the two situations is that the unlisted company is restricted to a narrower range of sources and is likely to incur higher costs, since many potential lenders or shareholders will be unwilling to put up funds if their investment is unlisted and so not marketable. In addition, if the company is private in the legal sense it is not permitted to make any invitation to the public to subscribe for shares or debentures.

In the first place an unlisted company may rely on the permanent capital put up by its promoter and his friends and relations, supplemented by bank borrowings. But in due course, if the company expands faster than retained earnings by themselves allow, there will come a time when these individuals are unable to find all the necessary funds, or they may wish to realize part of their investment. If the company has not yet reached a stage where a public flotation is appropriate, it should be possible to find one or more institutions to put up further capital, consisting either of ordinary shares or a mixture of ordinary and loan capital. A flotation will take place within a few years so the institutions will then be able to realize their investment if they wish. There are a number of specialist institutions providing this kind of finance, such as Industrial and Commercial Finance Corporation, a subsidiary of Investors in Industry, which is owned by the Bank of England and the clearing banks. The merchant banks are also active in this field and insurance companies, pension funds and investment trusts may participate in a placing if the company is large enough.

The wish of Mrs Thatcher's government to encourage the entrepreneur has combined with an increasing appreciation of the profitability of investment made early in a company's life to produce a flourishing venture capital market. There has been a wide proliferation of institutions willing to provide both venture capital in start-up situations and what is sometimes referred to as mezzanine capital at a rather later stage. For example, Equity Capital for Industry, a body originally set up to channel institutional funds into industry, now concentrates almost exclusively on venture capital situations. Most banks now have a venture capital subsidiary and a considerable number of other funds are active in this area, some specializing in high technology business and others operating more generally. Private capital is also tapped for this purpose by business expansion schemes, which take advantage of the legislation allowing the cost of such investments to be charged for tax purposes, and so appeal to investors with high tax rates.

Substantial funds are also available for management buy-outs (MBOs). These are situations where, for instance, a company is willing to dispose of one or more subsidiaries and the existing subsidiary management is willing or even eager to take it over. The managers will put up a relatively small amount of capital with the bulk of it coming from institutions, usually in a mix of ordinary shares, preference shares and loan capital (see types of security, below). But the institutions are prepared to give the management a financial incentive and thus the finance is structured so as to maximize their equity investment so long as they succeed in increasing profits. A number of MBOs have shown very good rates of return and therefore the range of institutions prepared to invest in them has increased. Syndicates have also been set up commanding large amounts of funds so that decisions can be made quickly by the syndicate leaders. There have been examples in the UK of MBOs running into hundreds of millions of pounds, and in the USA the amounts are very much larger again. Some of the privatizations carried through by the government have also involved a sort of MBO with a high percentage of all employees being encouraged to put up at least a small amount of capital – The National Freight Corporation is one of the best examples of this.

Investments in unlisted companies, whether tiny start-ups or large MBOs, all tend to be unmarketable. There will come a time when some or all of the investors in any situation will need to realize their capital. At this stage the company may be taken over by another or it may go public on the Stock Exchange.

GOING PUBLIC

Obtaining a listing on the Stock Exchange is an important step in any company's development. At the end of 1985 there was a total of more than 868 000 companies registered in Great Britain of which about 862 000 were private companies (in the legal sense) and only 2 616 were listed on the Stock Exchange, including nearly 500 overseas companies. Many companies will therefore never reach a stage at which a listing is appropriate, or their proprietors may for various reasons not wish to seek a listing. Taking in new shareholders provides an additional source of capital, but at the same time involves added responsibilities towards those shareholders typified by the Stock Exchange's requirements on disclosure. The interests of 'outside' shareholders may at times differ from those of 'family' shareholders and the future management of the company must reflect the new spread of interests represented.

The reasons for going public are usually among the following:

1 To make the shares marketable and hence more valuable
2 To diversify the family investment holdings and so to reduce the degree of risk
3 To provide funds to meet capital transfer tax liabilities when necessary
4 To make acquisitions of other companies for shares practicable
5 To raise new funds once the resources of the existing shareholders cease to be adequate

This chapter is concerned with the last of these, but it is important to realize that going public does not necessarily involve raising new money for the company – the shares sold to the public are often existing shares sold on behalf of existing shareholders.

There is a small over-the-counter market sponsored by Granville & Co. but to go public on the Stock Exchange a company must either join the Unlisted Securities Market (USM) or else obtain a full listing. The USM caters for smaller companies. Entrants do not need to wait until they can show a five-year record, advertising requirements are less and only 10 per cent of the capital need be made available to the public, often in a placing. It therefore appeals particularly to newer high-technology companies which may well command a high rating. Even so, a high proportion of the money raised is often consumed by the expenses of issue. More substantial companies will tend to apply for a full listing straightaway and the mechanism used for this is an offer for sale. To give an idea of scale, gross issues on the USM in 1985 amounted to £181 million, whereas it can be seen from Figure 6.2 that total corporate issues of ordinary shares exceeded £3.4 billion.

The offer for sale will be made by a merchant bank or a firm of issuing brokers. The offer will be underwritten so that the money will be available even if sufficient public subscriptions are not forthcoming. It is most important for the company's future capital-raising ability that the issue should be successful, which means that it should be fully subscribed, that the shares should open at a premium and that a free after-market should be maintained. To achieve this it is essential that the company should have continuity of good management and attractive prospects and that large shareholders should not continue to sell blocks of shares frequently once the offer for sale is complete. The amount of money that can be raised initially will depend primarily on the present and future profit levels of the company and hence on its ability to pay reasonable dividends on the increased capital: the figures can range from a million pounds to hundreds of millions depending on the size of the company.

LONG-TERM FINANCE FOR LISTED COMPANIES

Once a company has taken the important step of going public it can seek to raise funds from the whole range of investors, both private and institutional, without restriction.

YEAR	PERSONAL USES OF FUNDS			USES OF FUNDS BY FINANCIAL INSTITUTIONS	
	(£ million)				
	Investment in company securities	Life assurance and pension funds	Ordinary shares	Other corporate securities	Land, property and ground rents
1976	−1511	5568	1135	7	1111
1977	−1817	6138	1815	−117	1084
1978	−1152	7333	1924	− 37	1368
1979	−2105	9320	1990	− 61	1365
1980	−2026	10688	2501	− 1	2013
1981	−1648	13270	2540	276	2328
1982	−2525	13996	2707	502	2136
1983	−1086	15244	2089	625	1618
1984	−3048	17059	3488	487	1726
1985	471	17739	6104	1149	1582

Figure 6.1 Uses of funds by individuals and institutions (*CSO Financial Statistics*)

In recent years private investors have tended to an increasing extent to channel their savings through life assurance policies, pension schemes and unit trust purchases rather than make direct investments in securities themselves. Figure 6.1 illustrates that by showing, for recent years, selected uses of funds by the personal sector and by financial institutions (other than the banking sector). This shows that there has been a steady net divestment of corporate securities by individuals with a brief pause in 1985, whereas financial institutions have been substantial net purchasers. They have also increased significantly their rate of investment in property. Any company wishing to raise funds therefore has to try to issue the sort of security that will appeal to this type of investor – primarily insurance companies, pension funds and unit and investment trusts.

YEAR	BANK BORROWING	OTHER LOANS AND MORTGAGES	UK CORPORATE ISSUES		ISSUES OVERSEAS
		(£ million)			
			Ordinary shares	Fixed interest (net)	
1976	2398	439	785	42	6
1977	2966	38	730	−67	102
1978	2939	386	829	−73	−43
1979	4772	616	906	−22	−59
1980	6795	667	902	419	−15
1981	5847	618	1660	738	−34
1982	6563	768	1033	245	−43
1983	1559	725	1872	608	−46
1984	7165	412	1127	249	298
1985	6562	591	3406	860	770

Figure 6.2 Selected sources of capital funds for industrial and commercial companies (*CSO Financial Statistics*)

Figure 6.2 shows some of the ways in which companies have in fact raised finance over the same period. It can be seen from this that bank lending plays a very important role, since banks are the first and often the cheapest source of finance to which all companies turn. Even more important in the overall picture are internally generated funds: the figures in Figure 6.2 must be viewed in the perspective of a total figure for undistributed income adjusted for unremitted profits of £31 576 million in 1985.

Types of security

The types of security usually issued are the following:

1 Ordinary shares

SOURCES OF FINANCE

2   Preference shares
3   Debentures, secured either by a floating charge or a specific mortgage
4   Unsecured loan stocks
5   Unsecured loan stocks with conversion rights or warrants attached
6   Foreign-currency bonds

Ordinary shares represent the equity or risk capital in a business. They entitle their holders to a share of the profits by way of dividend only to the extent that the directors think fit. Thus if the business prospers its ordinary shares may become very valuable, but if it declines they may become valueless. Ordinary shareholders are also usually entitled to control the company's activities by voting at general meetings.

Preference shares carry the right to receive a fixed dividend in every year that the company makes a sufficient profit, but to no further participation unless they are specifically participating preference shares. They may in some cases be redeemable at a fixed future time or at the company's option and they can also be issued on the basis that they are convertible in a specified ratio into ordinary shares of the company, but they will normally only carry full voting rights in special circumstances. Preference shares became relatively unpopular after the tax changes introduced by the Finance Act 1965, but recently they have been used more as a way of increasing the capital base without diluting the interests of ordinary shareholders.

Debentures and loan stocks. The other types of capital are generically referred to as loan capital, which may be either secured or unsecured. Figure 6.2 shows that the use of these instruments has picked up in recent years but still represents a small proportion overall.

A debenture, according to *s*455 of the Companies Act 1948, includes debenture stock, bonds and any other securities of a company whether constituting a charge on the assets of the company or not; but in stock exchange parlance the expression 'debenture' normally means a secured stock, while unsecured loan stock is used to refer to a stock which is not secured. This is the terminology used here.

Unlike shareholders, holders of a debenture or unsecured loan stock are not members of a company, simply its creditors. They are therefore entitled merely to receive the agreed rate of interest (which is normally paid semi-annually) and to receive repayment of capital on final maturity. Their rights will be incorporated in the trust deed constituting the stock which will be made between the company and (usually) a trustee on behalf of the stockholders. It is a requirement of the Stock Exchange that there must be such a trustee if the stock is to be listed. The trustee will normally be one of the insurance companies or investment trusts which specialize in this type of work.

Investors in fixed-interest stocks have historically required a long life to final maturity. In fact most stocks issued in the London market have a term of twenty to twenty-five years, although some medium-term issues have been seen. There is usually a period of five years before final maturity when the company can repay the stock without penalty and the average life of the stock may be reduced by the operation of a sinking fund. Since the creditworthiness of a company, and even the nature of its business, can change materially over an interval of this length the trust deed constituting the stock will impose certain restrictions on the company. These will vary from case to case, but they may include limitations on such things as disposing of more than a certain proportion of the business, changing the nature of the business and giving security. An unsecured loan stock deed issued domestically will also probably contain a permanent limit on the overall borrowings of the company and its subsidiaries and a separate limit on secured borrowings and the borrowings of UK subsidiaries. A debenture deed will not impose a continuing limit but will require the presence of a certain level of cover in terms both of income and of assets before any further issue of another tranche of the stock can be made. In general, debenture stock holders, since their claims are supported by security, will require rather less in terms of restrictions than the holders of an unsecured loan stock who merely rank alongside trade and other unsecured creditors. In either case the trustee will have the power to declare the stock immediately repayable if interest is not paid or if the company defaults on certain other obligations.

Convertible and warrant stocks. These are a compromise between borrowing and equity. A convertible is an unsecured loan stock which initially merely carries a fixed rate of interest but which, on specified dates or within a specified period, may be converted, at the option of the holder, into ordinary shares of the company at a fixed ratio. Warrant stocks are stocks which are not convertible but which are issued together with warrants which entitle the holder to subscribe for ordinary shares of the company at specified times and at a specified price. Convertible stocks have been popular for a long time, but warrant stocks have never really become familiar in the UK domestic market.

The advantage to a company of issuing convertible stock is that for the initial period it can service the stock at a lower rate of interest than would be necessary for a stock that was not convertible; that when it is finally converted the effective price of issuing the resultant shares will be higher than it could have been initially; and that in the interval the interest payments (unlike ordinary dividends) will have been an allowable expense for tax purposes. A warrant stock gives the company a long-term borrowing (at a lower rate of interest than a simple borrowing), and when the warrants are exercised there is a further inflow of cash into the company. Both kinds of stock will impose the same sorts of restriction on the company as an ordinary unsecured loan stock with additional provisions to protect the holders' rights to convert or exercise their warrant rights.

Foreign-currency bonds. Only the very largest companies will want long-term loans in foreign currencies. In the great majority of cases, the UK market will be amply sufficient as a source of capital and in general it is unwise to incur a foreign-currency liability unless one has corresponding assets in that currency. Moreover only the largest companies would be well enough known to attract the interest of foreign lenders. However, in the 1960s a substantial international capital market developed in Eurodollars (US dollars deposited outside the USA, but not necessarily in Europe, and so not subject to any national restrictions on capital flows). A large number of US, and a smaller number of European, companies have taken advantage of this to raise quoted eurodollar loans (both fixed interest and convertible) and there have also been issues in Deutschemarks, French and Swiss francs, eurosterling and artificial units such as the European Unit of Account. Unlike domestic issues, eurobond issues usually have a life to final maturity of not more than fifteen, and in some cases as little as five, years. With the abolition of exchange control in the UK the dividing line between domestic and euro issues in sterling has become blurred and indeed current trends suggest that large companies may find it most convenient to raise long-term funds on an unsecured basis in the eurosterling market.

METHODS OF ISSUE WITH A LISTING

The four chief methods of making an issue for cash on the Stock Exchange are:

1   Offer for sale
2   Rights issue
3   Open offer
4   Placing

Offer for sale

In this case all members of the public are invited to subscribe for the issue by advertisements inserted in the press. The offer is usually made at a fixed price. Sometimes an offer for sale by tender is used where only a minimum price is fixed and applicants decide themselves how much they are willing to pay. A striking price is then fixed at a level at which the issue will be fully subscribed and the shares are issued at that price to all applicants who applied at that price or above. In either case, only a fixed number of shares are available for issue and, if a greater number of applications is received, each application is scaled down proportionately. Priority is sometimes given to existing shareholders or employees who are sent special application forms.

An offer for sale is normally used when a company goes public for the first time, as described earlier. It may also be used in an issue of loan capital where the amount of capital required is very large or where it is necessary to appeal to a particularly wide circle of investors for some other reason. In most cases, however, a placing is preferred because of its speed and simplicity (see below). By comparison an offer for sale involves significantly larger advertising and administrative costs.

Rights issue

In a rights issue new ordinary shares or other securities are offered to existing shareholders of the company pro rata to their holdings. Shareholders can then choose between taking up their entitlement (their rights) by subscribing the set amount per share, or they can sell some or all of their rights in the market if these are quoted at a premium. If they choose to sell, they of course receive money rather than pay it out, but their percentage holding in the company is reduced so that in theory the effect is the same as if they had sold some of their existing shares. From the company's point of view the subscription money will still be received from the purchaser of the rights.

It is a requirement of a listing on the Stock Exchange that new equity shares, or other securities involving an element of equity, should only be issued for cash to existing shareholders of the company in proportion to their holdings, unless they consent otherwise in general meeting, and this has now been given wider application by the Companies Act 1980. As a result, issues of ordinary shares or convertible stocks are normally made by way of rights so that shareholders have the opportunity of maintaining their proportionate stakes in the company.

Open offer

An open offer is an offer of loan capital restricted to shareholders, and possibly the holders of loan capital, of the company making the issue. However, the offer is not made pro rata to their holdings. Each shareholder can apply for as much stock as he wishes or for none; if more applications are received than stock is being issued, each application will be scaled down proportionately. This method of issue is relatively infrequent, but it may be used if it is thought that the stock being issued may attract a large premium and the benefit of this should accrue to shareholders. It is appropriate only where the company has a large number of shareholders, but in that case the effect is very similar to an offer for sale but without the attendant advertising costs.

SOURCES OF FINANCE

Placing

In a placing, stock is offered direct to a relatively small number of large institutional investors who are the principal holders of fixed interest stock; it is therefore a quick and effective method of issue which allows the most precise pricing. Placing for an unlisted company was considered under long-term finance (see p.138-9). Stock Exchange permission must be obtained for a placing with a listing and it is a condition of such permission that a proportion of the stock should be available publicly in the market. As already noted, a placing of new equity issued for cash is only possible with shareholders' consent but, because of its simplicity, placing has become the most usual method of raising loan capital for UK companies.

Underwriting and expenses of an issue

Once a company has decided that it needs money, it will clearly wish to be assured of that money as soon as possible, come what may. Rather than making an issue itself it will therefore go to a merchant bank or issuing broker who, in addition to advising on the documentation and terms of the issue, will arrange for it to be underwritten; that is, the issuing house will undertake to subscribe or find subscribers for the issue on the terms fixed in so far as it is not fully subscribed by the public or shareholders as the case may be. In return for accepting the risk and for its overall co-ordinating work on the issue, the issuing house normally charges a total commission of 2 per cent, 1¼ per cent of which is passed on to the sub-underwriters, that is the institutions who agree to take up different amounts of the issue pro rata to the extent that it is not fully subscribed. In the case of a placing, however, the stock is placed directly with a number of the same institutions. Accordingly, no sub-underwriting commission is required and only a placing commission of perhaps ¾ per cent (varying with the size of the issue) is payable. However, the issue terms will be slightly worse so that the net proceeds receivable by the company will be much the same. The other major expense of an issue of share capital is capital duty levied at a rate of 1 per cent on the value of the shares being issued. Duty is no longer payable on the issue of loan capital but, in the case of a convertible stock, capital duty arises on conversion. By comparison the administrative costs of an issue, especially in a placing, are small.

OTHER METHODS OF SUPPLEMENTING CASH FLOW

The main methods of raising long-term capital with a listing have now been outlined. It remains to consider briefly the various other possible methods of supplementing cash flow, which are of course open to quoted and unquoted companies alike. Some of these can provide relatively long-term finance, but the majority are short-term.

Long-term facilities

These include mortgages, sale and leaseback transactions, and public authority and specialist institution lending. The main sources of mortgage and sale and leaseback finance are the insurance companies and pension funds. In the case of a mortgage loan, a single lender will advance up to two-thirds of the value of a building for a specified term on the specific security of that building—the borrower retains the ownership of the building but his rights are subject to a mortgage charge for the term of the loan. In a sale and leaseback transaction he will actually sell the building (and so forfeit any appreciation in value) in return for a capital sum and at the same time lease the building back for his own use from the purchasing institution for a long period at a specified rent. Other sources of relatively long-term facilities include the Department of Trade and Industry (for specified purposes in development areas and in accordance with such schemes as may be in effect from time to time), local authorities where employment is being created in their areas, and various specialist semi-official organizations such as Investors in Industry, Agricultural Mortgage Corporation and National Research Development Corporation, all of which exist to lend for certain purposes.

Medium-term facilities

These include leasing, hire-purchase, project finance and term loans.

Leasing and hire-purchase are most appropriate for items such as vehicles, plant, machinery and office equipment. In leasing, the ownership of the item remains with the lessor, but the lessee is entitled to the use of it for a specified term in return for regular payments under the lease. A tax-based lease may be particularly attractive to a company with no immediate liability to taxation. In a hire-purchase transaction the purchase price of the item and interest thereon is paid in instalments over a set period, at the end of which ownership of the item does pass to the hirer. There are a large number of finance houses which specialize in these activities.

Similarly, merchant and other banks may undertake to arrange finance for a specific project. This will involve tapping several different sources of finance in accordance with the cash flow requirements of the individual project and is a particularly flexible form of financing.

Finally, banks sometimes engage in medium-term lending for periods up to five or even ten years. A term loan could come from a single bank or it might be syndicated among a number of different banks. It might be at a fixed rate of interest, but it will more usually be on a roll-over basis; that is, with interest fixed periodically at the prevailing rate. In the latter case it is also possible to arrange for drawings to be made in different currencies at different times.

Export finance

The UK government, in common with other major industrial countries, assists UK exporters to finance their contracts with overseas buyers by running an export credit programme which has two purposes: firstly, to provide insurance against political and commercial risks which may affect performance and payment under export contracts; and secondly, to ensure that the terms of any credit offered to overseas buyers of UK goods and services can be made as attractive as possible. The banking system plays a crucial role as provider of funds and of specialist export finance advisory services. The official UK export credit authority providing insurance guarantees and a level of financial subsidy is the Export Credits Guarantee Department (ECGD) which operates as an autonomous government department with a direct reporting line to the Secretary of State for Trade and Industry.

Typical export funding structures

With ECGD support, finance can be made available in several different forms. For short-term transactions a supplier can insure 90 to 95 per cent of his receivables with ECGD and assign the proceeds of his insurance policy to a bank, thereby enabling him to obtain finance from his bank on attractive terms. For transactions attracting medium-term credit (usually the supplies of capital goods), the structure is more complex so as to reduce the impact of deferred payments on the exporter's balance sheet. Under a medium-term supplier credit structure, the supplier would insure deferred contract receivables, evidenced by bills or notes accepted/issued by the buyer, with ECGD. Under a bank facility, the supplier would then be able to sell the bills or notes to his bank who, in turn, is entitled to a 100 per cent unconditional guarantee from ECGD. ECGD has the right of recourse to the exporter in the event that the bank guarantee is called, but the exporter may offset the recourse liability against his ability to claim up to 90 to 95 per cent under his insurance policy. Under this structure, therefore, the supplier carries a continuing residual 5 to 10 per cent financial risk on the buyer throughout the credit period. For larger-sized contracts and major investment projects, the more usual structure is a 'buyer's credit', under which the supplier enters into what is essentially a cash contract. Instead of taking out insurance cover for deferred payments, the supplier is paid by means of disbursements from a loan made available by a bank to the foreign buyer. ECGD provides a 100 per cent unconditional guarantee for the principal and interest due under this loan. ECGD is entitled to take recourse on the supplier in the event of a claim by the bank under the guarantee only in circumstances where the UK supplier is in default under his contract. Although opinions differ on the real extent of this recourse burden (much of the onus of proof of the contractual default lies with ECGD), suppliers would generally agree that they would have no continuing financial risk throughout the credit period as would be the case under a medium-term supplier credit.

The terms available for support of UK export finance transactions vary from straightforward commercial funding for short-term transactions to officially supported interest rates. For transactions involving a credit period of more than two years, the UK authorities acting through ECGD make it possible for exporters to offer the minimum fixed rates permitted by the international consensus on export credit terms subscribed to by OECD member countries. The minimum fixed interest rates currently vary between 8.8 per cent for the poorest category of borrowing country to 11.2 per cent for the richest category. For particular projects in selected markets, it may be possible to obtain even finer 'soft' terms under the 'Aid and Trade' programme administered by the Overseas Development Administration and the Department for Trade and Industry. In cases where an officially supported fixed rate is to be offered to a borrower in connection with a medium-term credit, ECGD agrees with the banks providing the funds that they will receive 'interest make-up' to provide them with:

(a) the difference, if any, between the fixed rate and the cost of funds, and
(b) a margin over the cost of funds

The cost of interest rate support provided by the UK authorities has continued to give rise to concern in recent years, despite a reduction in the overall cost of the scheme due to an increasing alignment between OECD minimum rates and market interest rates. Increasing attention is thus being given to funding medium-term credits from purely commercial financial sources.

If it is thought that finance will be required in connection with an export order, it is advisable to contact a merchant/clearing bank as well as ECGD sooner rather than later in view of the wide range of financing options which may need to be considered and the difficulties which can be encountered in obtaining ECGD support after a firm contract has been struck.

Short-term facilities

These include bank overdrafts and loans, bank acceptance credits, bills of exchange, trade credit, invoice discounting and factoring. Of these, bank overdrafts and loans are the most common and are used universally by companies as Figure 6.2 shows. They may be supplemented by acceptance credits, where a bank undertakes to accept approved bills of exchange up to a certain limit so that the bills can be discounted at the finest rates. Alterntively, bills of exchange can be used as a form of trade credit, whether or not discounted with a bank or discount house, or various arrangements may be made between buyers and suppliers as to the length of credit given in payment for goods. Finally, invoice discounting and factoring are underaken by various specialist institutions. Invoice discounting means financing the collection of specific invoices, at the risk of the selling company. Factoring involves making immediate payment against invoiced debts which are then normally collected at the factor's own risk for an appropriate charge. All these methods have in common that they finance relatively small revolving trade transactions, but in aggregate they provide the finance of a vast amount of business on a continuing basis.

Current trends

The willingness of lenders to lend for long periods will depend on their being able to foresee a reasonable rate of return in real terms. In times of high inflation there is therefore a reluctance to tie up funds in this way except at rates so high as to be unacceptable to many borrowers. Equally, companies may prefer to borrow for relatively short periods in the hope of being able to refinance their obligations later at a lower rate. For these reasons, there has been a considerable shift over the years away from long-term issues to more flexible short-term borrowing. This has been encouraged by the greater availability of bank credit following the new monetary policy adopted by the Bank of England from 1971 onwards in its new approach to competition and credit control.

The banking market has been very competitive and in many cases lending margins have shrunk drastically. The banks have also been active in devising new products to appeal to their customers who are now offered note issuance facilities (nifs) and revolving underwriting facilities (rufs) to supplement the staid overdraft. There is also an active market in swaps both for currencies and interest rates which allow a company to optimize its own position by benefiting from the countervailing position of another party. More recently still, the UK commercial paper has been inaugurated thus allowing companies to obtain funds outside the banking system. It must be said however that many of these instruments are suitable only for the larger listed company and have little relevance for many finance directors.

THE OVERALL CAPITAL STRUCTURE

Before raising any new capital a company should consider what the capital is needed for, whether it is permanent or likely to be repaid out of cash flow within a period and what rate of return it is likely to earn. One can then decide how it can best be supplied. For instance, in the case of an investment with a high degree of risk the best source of finance is likely to be equity (or risk) capital; but, if it is a relatively risk-free long-term investment, loan capital may be more appropriate. If it is a specific project of medium-term duration, project finance should be considered, while for a working capital requirement, bank overdraft facilities are likely to be the answer. In all cases the various methods of supplementing cash flow in other ways must be borne in mind so as to minimize the amount of new capital actually required. Finally, the rate of return must be set against the cost of the capital to ensure that an adequate margin exists to justify the investment.

One of the most important considerations is to preserve a proper balance between debt and equity in the company's financial structure. This relationship is described as the company's financial gearing. If the company's source of income is reasonably stable and assured (such as the rental income of a property company) it is safe for it to be highly geared. However, if it is operating in a cyclical industry (such as machine tools) it is prudent to keep the gearing (that is, the element of borrowing) at a low level, for interest on borrowings has to be paid in adverse as well as favourable times and if a temporary setback combined with high interest charges results in the company making a loss, its overall status will suffer. The degree of gearing will depend both on the absolute amount of borrowing and the extent to which any of this borrowing is at fluctuating interest rates which may rise faster than the company's income. In inflationary times, borrowing at a fixed cost can be most advantageous to a company. But the closer the company gets to what is thought to be an unduly high level of borrowing, the more reluctant lenders will be to provide new funds and the more the equity interest of existing shareholders will be endangered.

The object of company financial management should be to see that the company has adequate funds at the lowest cost consonant with all these factors and so to seek to maximize its earnings for ordinary shareholders.

FURTHER READING

Admission of Securities to Listing, Stock Exchange, London, revised 1984.
R.A. Brearley and C. Pyle, *Bibliography of Finance and Investment*, Elek Books, London 1973.
'Competition and Credit Control', Bank of England, reprinted in *Bank of England Quarterly Bulletin*, June, 1971.
J.H.C. Leach, 'The Weight of New Money—Once Again', in *Investment Analyst*, September, 1975.
J.H.C. Leach, 'The Role of the Institutions in the UK Ordinary Share Market', in *Investment Analyst*, December, 1971.

Merrett, Howe and Newbould, *Equity Issues and the London Capital Market*, Longmans, London, 1967.
'New Capital Issues Statistics', in *Midland Bank Review*, commentary published annually in spring edition.
Report of the Committee of Enquiry on Small Firms (Cmnd 4811), HMSO, London 1971.
Royal Commission on the Distribution of Income and Wealth (Diamond Report), Report No. 2 (Cmnd 6172), HMSO, London, July, 1975.
'The UK Corporate Bond Market', in *Bank of England Quarterly Bulletin*, March, 1981.

The various volumes of evidence given to the Committee to Review the Functioning of Financial Institutions (the Wilson Committee) and published by HMSO may also be of interest.

7

Taxation

J C Craig

The tax law with which we are concerned in this chapter is mainly based on the Income and Corporation Taxes Act 1970, the Taxes Management Act 1970, the Capital Allowances Act 1968, the Capital Gains Tax Act 1979 and annual Finance Acts. The first of these Acts brought together the combined effects of the Income Tax 1952 and subsequent Finance Acts to 1969 with the principal exception of personal capital gains tax; this is now governed by the Capital Gains Tax Act 1979 which consolidated the law on capital gains tax up to 5 April 1979.

Each year, sometimes more frequently, following the budget speech, a Finance Act is introduced, so it is always necessary to look at the accumulated effect of amendments when examining a tax problem.

Interpretation of the law follows the standard pattern of court decisions, and there are now more than two thousand references to decided cases, each of which is normally binding on everyone in similar circumstances, unless reversed by a subsequent enactment or by a decision in a superior court. (Very occasionally the House of Lords will overturn a previous decision of the same court.)

RETURNS AND ASSESSMENTS

Every person who receives income of any kind is under statutory obligation to complete a return of income each year; the senior partner deals with the form for a partnership, and the officers for a limited company. Personal responsibility for making correct returns cannot be avoided even if an agent is employed to complete the return form.

TAXATION

Tax assessment

Assessments for tax are made by local inspectors of taxes in accordance with the return of income and supplementary figures supplied by the taxpayers, including a copy of the annual accounts of a business. Where necessary, an assessment may be altered within six years of the end of the accounting period to which it relates, for example if a mistake is discovered by either the Revenue or the taxpayer. However, there is no time-limit to the correction of assessments which were wrong because of the fraud, wilful default or neglect of the taxpayer. A case heard in 1970 (Rose v Humbles) referred to assessments stretching back to 1942.

Appeals against assessment

Where the taxpayer does not agree with the inspector's assessment, he may appeal in writing within thirty days. Usually the appeal is settled by correspondence or at a meeting with the inspector, with or without professional advice. If agreement cannot be reached the taxpayer may have the appeal heard by either:

1 General Commissioners, who are leading local citizens, unpaid, not civil servants and not specialists in tax, but who hear each case on its merits and aim to give a fair decision according to the facts; or
2 Special Commissioners, who are civil servants concentrating wholly on the complexities of tax and therefore better able to unravel an argument of a complex nature

It tends to be more costly to ask for the appeal to be heard by the Special Commissioners because, though no charge is made, it may be necessary to travel some distance with professional advisers for the appeal to be heard, and it is usually advisable to brief counsel to put the case.

A decision of the commissioners is binding on both Revenue and taxpayer unless it can be shown that the query is based on an interpretation of the law, when permission may be asked to appeal to the High Court in England or the Court of Session in Scotland.

Further appeals may go beyond the High Court to the Court of Appeal and then to the House of Lords, or in Scotland from the Court of Session to the House of Lords, if it can be shown there is still doubt as to whether the law has been interpreted correctly. Occasionally in England an appeal may be taken direct from the High Court to the House of Lords.

Appeals are an expensive, troublesome activity. A good working relationship between the company's management, its auditors who commonly handle the tax returns, and the local inspector of taxes, with the management taking a close personal interest in the tax computations, is recommended as the most practical approach to tax.

(a)
INCOME

Gross trading profit		£700 000
Rent from industrial premises let to tenants		20 000
Interest from bank deposit account		6 000
Dividends from shares held		10 000
Interest from debentures held (gross)		4 000
		£740 000

EXPENDITURE

Depreciation	£26 000	
Salaries, wages, employer's contributions to national insurance and graduated pensions	60 000	
Directors' salaries and fees	10 000	
Bad debts	300	
Specific provision for the bad debt of a named customer	100	
General provision for bad debts	800	
Legal expenses	200	
Rent, rates and insurance	3 000	
Superannuation (company's contributions to an approved scheme)	2 000	
Heating and lighting	1 000	
Travelling expenses	2 000	
Entertainment expenses	600	
Distribution costs	20 000	
Sundry expenses	3 000	
Loss on sale of machinery	1 000	
		130 000
NET PROFIT		£610 000

(b)

Net profit shown in the accounts		£610 000
Add back items not allowable		
Depreciation	£26 000	
General provision for bad debts	800	
Entertainment expenses	600	
Loss on sale of machinery	1 000	
		£ 28 400
		£638 400
Deduct items, either not taxable or taxable under different headings		
Rent	£20 000	
Interest income	6 000	
Dividends	10 000	
Interest	4 000	
		40 000
		£598 400
Less		
Capital allowances (in lieu of depreciation)		28 400
CASE I INCOME		£570 000

Figure 7.1   Example of a corporation tax computation — Profit and loss account
  (a) Adjustment for corporation tax purposes
  (b) Calculation of corporation tax

TAXATION

(c)

Case I income	– business profits adjusted	£570 000
Case III income	– untaxed income from bank deposit interest	6 000
Schedule A income	– rent	20 000
Income received subject to deduction of income tax at source – debenture interest but not dividends		4 000
		600 000
Corporation tax at 35% on £600 000		210 000
		390 000
Dividend income, not liable to corporation tax is not part of the computation		10 000
Remainder, which may be retained or paid out as dividend		£400 000

Figure 7.1 *(concluded)*

Interest on tax assessments

If tax is not paid on its due date, or if unpaid tax is held over for too long pending an appeal, interest will be payable at 11 per cent, not allowable for tax purposes. The rate of interest applying will generally change in line with market fluctuations. In practice it is preferable to avoid this charge by paying tax not in dispute and buying a certificate of tax deposit for the balance. If, after negotiations, the amount of tax in dispute is payable, the certificate can be surrendered in satisfaction of the tax and there will be no interest charges. If the tax is not payable interest will be receivable on the certificate. It can then either be encashed or used to pay other tax liabilities; a higher rate of interest will apply in the latter case.

ADJUSTMENT OF PROFIT AND COMPUTATION OF AMOUNT LIABLE TO TAX

The normal pattern for an industrial or commercial business is to measure and adjust the income from all sources, to arrive at the total on which corporation tax is payable as shown in Figure 7.1.

In making the adjustment of profit to arrive at the amount liable to tax, the starting point is the profit shown in the ordinary profit and loss account. Expenses not allowable must be added back; income which is either not taxable or taxable under a different case or schedule must be deducted, to arrive at the adjusted trading profit assessable under Schedule D Case I (or Case II).

Apart from advance corporation tax paid to the Collector of Taxes following the payment of dividends (dealt with later), the balance of the liability to corporation tax (the 'mainstream' liability) is due for payment nine months after the end of the accounting period, except in the case of companies which carry on the same trade as they did prior to 1965. Such companies may have a longer interval. Normally they pay their mainstream liability on 1 January in the fiscal year following that in which the accounting period ends, unless there has been a change of accounting date.

Rate of tax

The rate of corporation tax is announced for each 'financial year', which runs from 1 April to the following 31 March, in the Chancellor's end-of-year budget. For the financial year 1985, which ended on 31 March 1986, a rate of 40 per cent applies and for financial year 1986 the rate is 35 per cent. For 'small' companies the rate of corporation tax on income is 30 per cent for financial year 1985 and 29 per cent for financial year 1986. For this purpose a company is small if profits do not exceed £100 000 (unless the company has associated companies, in which case a lower level applies); a sliding scale applies to profits between £100 000 and £500 000.

Accounting year

If the company's accounting year spans two financial years in which the percentage differs, the profits are apportioned on a time basis. If, for example, the accounting year ended 31 December 1986, three-twelfths of the profit (for January, February, March 1986) will be taxed at the rate applicable to financial year 1985 and the remaining nine-twelfths at the rate for financial year 1986.

ALLOWABLE EXPENSES

For any expense to be allowable, it must have been incurred 'wholly and exclusively' for purposes of the business. Certain forms of expenditure are disallowed, either by definite statements in the Acts, or as a result of cases decided by the courts. It would be impossible to give an exhaustive list here, particularly as many of them concern only a restricted range of industries, but a selection of the more common ones is given below.

General advice is: when in doubt, check with the detailed tax textbooks; if these do not settle the doubt, claim the expense is allowable and see the inspector's reaction. There is no penalty for this approach provided the true nature of the expense is stated openly and honestly.

Salaries and wages

Salaries and wages of employees and directors are normally allowable in full. However, the deduction allowed for excessive payments to part-time directors is liable to be restricted if the inspector is not satisfied that the amount is reasonable considering the services rendered.

Entertaining

Entertainment expenses are not allowable, except for entertaining overseas trading customers, and even in this case the amount must be reasonable considering the potential business arising. A UK resident agent of a foreign customer is not an overseas customer for this purpose.

'Entertainment' includes gifts of food, drink and tobacco, for example as Christmas presents.

When a senior employee is reimbursed for the cost of entertaining UK customers, the amount is not treated as part of his personal income, but if he is given an allowance to cover entertaining, among other expenses, it becomes part of his earned income from which he cannot deduct any part of the cost of the entertaining.

Bad debts

A general reserve for bad debts is not allowable, but actual bad debts and a specific provision for the bad debts of a named customer are allowable.

Depreciation

Depreciation is not allowable, but capital allowances are given in appropriate cases instead.

Capital expenditure

No kind of capital expenditure is allowable other than by way of capital allowances. Capital profit or loss on the sale of an asset is excluded from the computation of business profit, but may be subject to a separate calculation for capital gains tax.

Legal expenses

Some legal expenses are and some are not allowable, the distinction being broadly that they are allowable if they relate to a transaction of a revenue nature, but not if they are of a capital nature. For example, legal expenses for the preparation of a service agreement for a manager, or the collection of debts, or the renewal of an existing short lease are revenue and allowable, but legal expenses in connection with the purchase of freehold premises or a long lease are capital and are not allowable.

Retirement benefits

Retirement benefits for employees are allowable whether they are direct pensions or contributions to a superannuation scheme approved by the Inland Revenue. A moderate lump sum to an employee on his retirement would be allowable, but an exceptional lump sum to a superannuation fund would be spread forward over future years.

RELIEF FOR INCREASE IN STOCK VALUES

Stock relief was introduced by the Finance Act 1975 and survived in various forms until withdrawn with effect from 12 March 1984.

History

In times of inflation an increasing amount of cash became tied up in trading stock, causing cash-flow problems. To alleviate these difficulties stock relief was introduced. Relief was first granted as a deferment of tax by the Finance Act 1975, and was extended by Finance (No 2) Act 1975. A more permanent relief was provided for in the Finance Act 1976: broadly the taxable profit for an accounting period was reduced by the increase in the value of stock held less a percentage of the Case I or II profit which would otherwise be liable to tax. In any period in which there was a decrease in the value of stock held, taxable profit was increased by the amount of the fall or the amount of unrecovered past stock relief, whichever is smaller.

Because a large potential charge to tax existed in many companies should their stock levels fall, the Finance (No 2) Act 1979 provided that certain stock relief granted be excluded from the amount of unrecovered past stock relief and thus effectively be written off.

In November 1980 a new system was introduced (by the Finance Act 1981) under which relief was given by reference to an 'all stocks' index published monthly by the Department of Industry. The movement in the 'all stocks' index over the period of account was applied to the closing stock of the previous period less a *de minimis* amount of £2 000. If there was a reduction or no movement in the index no relief was granted and no addition made to taxable profits. There was no clawback of relief unless trade ceased or the scale of activities in the company became small in relation to past levels.

Unused stock relief

Unused relief under the Finance Act 1981 may only be carried forward for six years. If it is unused by that time the relief is lost. There are rules for determining the order of set-off of reliefs available in each year. Unused relief under the old systems may be carried forward without time limit.

TAXATION

THE NECESSARY BOOK-KEEPING

Adjustment of profit and computation of tax payable are made outside the double-entry book-keeping system, but settlement of the tax requires three ledger accounts:

1. Corporation tax account (including advance corporation tax and tax credits)
2. Income tax account for unfranked investment income
3. Income tax account for PAYE deducted from employees' income

The foundation for accounts 1 and 2 is that a company suffers corporation tax but not income tax on its own income. Income tax which has been deducted at source from unfranked investment income received by the company may be offset against income tax deducted from payments made by the company, and if a net balance is due by the company it is payable to the Collector of Taxes. If a balance is due to the company it will be treated as a payment to account of any corporation tax due for the period. It is important to keep franked items separate from unfranked, and PAYE separate from both.

The necessary entries are summarized in Figure 7.2.

CAPITAL ALLOWANCES

Capital allowances exist on seven main types of fixed assets used wholly and exclusively for purposes of the business:

1. Industrial buildings
2. Plant and machinery
3. Agricultural land and buildings
4. Mines and oil-wells
5. Capital expenditure on scientific research
6. Patents
7. Know-how

Only the first two types will be considered in detail here.

When any asset which qualifies for allowances is purchased, the year's allowances are given in full for the company's accounting period no matter how late in the period the asset was obtained. This rule may need to be modified where the accounting period is shorter than twelve months.

It is important to consider the overall position before deciding whether or not, or to what extent, capital allowances should be claimed.

Corporation tax account	with double entry in:
Debit:	
(a) Adjustment for overprovision of last year's liability	Profit and Loss (appropriation) a/c
(b) Excess tax suffered on unfranked investment income tax	Unfranked investment income a/c
Credit:	
(a) Estimated tax on the profits for the year now ending	Profit and Loss (appropriation) a/c
(b) Adjustment for underprovision for last year's liability	Profit and Loss (appropriation) a/c
Tax on Unfranked Investment Income Account	
Debit:	
Income tax suffered at source on unfranked investment income received	Unfranked investment income a/c
Credit:	
Tax retained when paying out debenture interest and other annual interest payments	Accounts for debenture etc., interest paid
Where credit is greater than debit, the difference is settled by paying tax to the Collector	Bank a/c
Where debit is greater than credit, the difference is settled by transfer to corporation tax a/c	Corporation tax a/c
Advance Corporation Tax	
Debit:	
Tax credit accompanying franked investment income received	Memorandum only – not passed through books of account
Credit:	
ACT paid when paying out dividends	

Figure 7.2 Entries to make in the tax accounts

Industrial buildings

The nature of the business must be industrial as distinct from commercial, retailing or wholesaling, or professional. Even for an industrial company the allowance is not given for offices and showrooms, except where these form an integral part of a factory and account for less than 25 per cent (10 per cent prior to 16 March 1983) of its whole cost.

The allowances to the first owner are as follows:

1   Initial allowance: this was abolished for expenditure after 31 March 1986 (other than for expenditure in enterprise zones). Previously the rates were as follows:
    After 10 March 1981   75 per cent
    After 13 March 1984   50 per cent
    After 31 March 1985   25 per cent
2   Writing-down allowance of 4 per cent of the cost price (or 2 per cent if the building was erected before November 1962).

In the year of disposal, instead of the writing-down allowance there is a balancing allowance or balancing charge to bring total allowances into line with net cost.

Where the building is sold for more than it cost, the balancing charge cannot exceed the total of allowances already received. (There may, however, be a taxable capital gain in addition to the balancing charge.)

On sale of a factory built before November 1962 there is no balancing adjustment if it is sold after it is fifty years old, and for factories built since November 1962 none after they are twenty-five years old.

Cost price includes: the building, plus the architect's fees, plus cost of tunnelling, levelling and preparing the land; installing main services, fences, perimeter walls and roadways on the site.

It does not include: the cost of land, legal and estate agency fees; preparation of a lease; purchase price of a lease; demolition of a former building.

When a building is demolished, the cost of demolition, is added to the original cost before working out the balancing adjustment.

For the second and subsequent owners, the allowances are equal to the residue of cost spread over the remainder of twenty-five or fifty years. An example is given in Figure 7.3. The importance of distinguishing between land and buildings is vital, with seller and buyer having opposing interests.

Example:

Original cost to first owner, 1977		£10 000
Initial allowance in first year 50%	£5 000	
Writing-down allowance 4% a year for 10 years	4 000	9 000
Written-down value in 1986 (end of year)		1 000
Sell on 1 January 1987 for		7 350
Balancing charge on first owner		£ 6 350

Second owner: residue of cost is £7 350
    balance of 25 years is 15 years
    so annual allowance is £490 a year

Check: £490 × 15 = £7 350

Figure 7.3 Example of allowances for expenditure on industrial buildings

From 12 April 1978 industrial buildings' allowances were extended to apply also to certain qualifying hotels, the rate of initial allowance being 20 per cent, with a writing-down allowance of 4 per cent. With effect from 1 April 1986 the initial allowance was abolished.

Expenditure incurred between 26 March 1980 and 27 March 1983 on small workshops of up to 2500 square feet and expenditure incurred between 26 March 1983 and 27 March 1985 on very small workshops of up to 1250 square feet qualified for an initial allowance of 100 per cent and a writing-down allowance of 25 per cent on any part disclaimed.

Any industrial or commercial structure or qualifying hotel in an Enterprise Zone (an area designated as such by the government) also qualifies for 100 per cent initial allowance; if a reduced allowance is claimed, 25 per cent writing-down allowance is available on the amount of the reduction.

Plant and machinery

Allowances may be claimed by any type of business assessed to trading income under Case I or Case II of Schedule D, or against Schedule A assessments on income from real property, or in respect of assets owned by an employee and used by the employee for his employer's business, or against profits of a trade assessed under Schedule D Case V.

The definition of 'plant and machinery' spreads remarkably widely to include office and canteen equipment, furniture, dry docks and virtually every type of fixed tangible asset which is not 'building'.

The allowances available for plant are as follows:

1. First-year allowances: abolished for expenditure incurred after 31 March 1986 unless incurred before 1 April 1987 on a pre-14 March 1984 contract, but were previously given in the year of purchase at the following rates

	%
After 26 October 1970	60
After 19 July 1971	80
After 21 March 1972	100
After 13 March 1984	75
After 31 March 1985	50

2. Writing-down allowance: any expenditure not qualifying for the first-year allowance and the balance of the previous year's qualifying expenditure after deducting any first-year allowance given is added to the pool of expenditure and a writing-down allowance of 25 per cent is taken on the pool value
3. When an asset is sold or scrapped, its disposal price is deducted from the pool figure on which writing-down allowances are being calculated,

unless sale proceeds exceed cost in which case the deduction is restricted to cost

It is possible for the company to take any smaller amount of allowances and so defer allowances to subsequent years. First-year allowance applies equally to new or secondhand assets unless a secondhand machine is bought from a connected company or transactions are entered into mainly with a view to obtaining a larger allowance, in which case the first-year allowance is restricted.

Private cars do not qualify for first-year allowance unless hired on a short-term basis in the course of a trade, and no capital allowances are given on assets bought for purposes of business entertainment. Details of cars should be shown in a separate 'pool'.

Private cars costing over £8000 (£5000 prior to 12 June 1979) are kept separate from other assets and qualify only for a writing-down allowance at 25 per cent of the written-down value, but restricted to a maximum of £2000 per year, starting in the year of purchase and with a balancing adjustment for the year of sale.

From 1 April 1986 it is possible to elect for separate items of plant to be treated as short-life assets. Each asset forms its own pool of expenditure outside of the general pool. If the assets are still held after four years the residue of expenditure is transferred into the general pool.

For assets acquired on hire purchase, allowances are given on the equivalent of the cash price, and the hire charge is treated as an allowable revenue expense in the years in which it is paid. For assets on straight hire, contract hire or lease, there are no capital allowances but the rental is allowed as a revenue expense in the years in which it is paid.

The lessor will be eligible for capital allowances like any other trader but subject to certain conditions. These are basically that the asset is used for short-term hire in the UK or the asset is used for the 'requisite' period, of four years (or shorter if the asset is sold within four years) by a trader who would have been granted first-year allowance had he purchased the asset himself. If the lessee does not fall into one of these categories the lessor will be entitled to 25 per cent writing-down allowance on the cost of the asset.

Where private cars costing over £8000 are hired a proportion of the rental charge payable by the lessee is disallowable.

Expenditure incurred on the provision of a new ship has a degree of flexibility not available on other assets. The taxpayer is able to postpone allowances and take them in the period in which it is most advantageous.

LOSSES

Setting losses against profits

A trading loss in one accounting period may be set against:

1 Other sources of profit in the same accounting period in which the loss is suffered
2 The trading profit of the immediately preceding accounting period provided that the company was then carrying on the trade
3 Other sources of profit in that preceding accounting period

To the extent that a trading loss has been created by first-year allowances it may be set against profits in the three years preceding the year of the loss, again provided that the trade was then being carried on.

Claims for relief in this way are optional. If they are not made, or if they leave a balance of loss still unrelieved, the remaining loss may be set against the first available future profits from the same trade, but not against future profits from other sources.

The right to carry forward any losses is ended when the trade ceases or a majority of the shares changes hands and there is a major change in the nature or conduct of the trade being carried on. The effect of this restriction has been virtually to end the sale of tax-loss companies.

An example of a normal loss claim is given in Figure 7.4.

PQ Ltd – Accounting period to 23 December annually:

Trading results – 1983 profit		£20 000
1984 loss		60 000
1985 profit		8 000
Unfranked investment income – 1983		5 000
1984		7 000
1985		6 000

Set-off of loss
1 Other income in 1984	7 000
2 Profits in 1983 (£20 000 + £5 000)	25 000
3 Trading profit in 1985	8 000
4 Carry forward against future trading profits	20 000
	£60 000

Losses carried forward may only be set against future profits from the same trade and not other income hence unfranked investment income in 1985 is taxable. Corporation tax payable for the year to 31 December 1983 would be cancelled, or if already paid it will be refunded.

Note the cash flow advantage of submitting promptly the figures for 1984 and the claim for loss relief.

Figure 7.4 Example of normal loss relief

Terminal loss relief

A loss suffered during the final twelve months up to the time a trade is discontinued may be carried backwards and set against the trading profits of

TAXATION

	RS Ltd	TU Ltd
Profit for year to:		
31 December 1981	£40 000	£40 000
31 December 1982	15 000	15 000
31 December 1983	10 000	10 000
31 December 1984 (Loss)	(80 000)	(80 000)
RS closed trade at 31 December 1984		
31 December 1985		5 000
TU closed trade at 31 December 1985		

RS Ltd will have a terminal loss of £80 000 which will successfully be offset to the extent of £65 000 against the profits of 1981, 1982 and 1983.
TU Ltd has no terminal loss because the loss was not made in the final twelve months and so will only be able to use normal loss claims against 1983 (£10 000) and 1985 (£5 000).

Figure 7.5 Example of terminal loss relief

the three preceding years. An example is given in Figure 7.5.

Note particularly that to make a terminal loss claim it is sufficient that the trade has been permanently discontinued. This is not necessarily the same as winding up the company, as a company may have more than one activity and its existence may continue without the discounted trade, or a fresh trade of a different nature may be started after the loss-making enterprise has been discontinued.

Directors' remuneration as it affects loss

It will be seen that skill is needed in arranging a company's affairs in the way to take the best advantage of the many variations of the loss relief rules. For example, even in a small private company it may be sound policy to pay the directors at least a portion of their customary remuneration, even though this makes the loss larger. Otherwise the directors might be without income from which to offset their personal tax reliefs.

Example: Williams is sole director and principal sharehold of WL Ltd. He customarily draws £5000 a year from the company as director's remuneration and leaves the company with no profit to suffer corporation tax. In 1985/86 trade is poor and before paying himself any remuneration there is trading loss of £1000. If Williams forgoes remuneration his personal reliefs will be wasted, so he declares himself £3600 and leaves the company showing £4600 loss (the liability to employer national insurance contributions has been ignored).

His personal income then is £3600
from which he deducts:
Personal allowance £3455
Dependent relative relief 100
3555
£ 45

Income tax payable by Williams will be only:
£45 at 30 per cent = £13.50

The company's trading loss will go forward to set against future trade profits if Williams is confident he can restore the profit-making basis of the trade. His personal reliefs would have been wasted had he not taken any remuneration, as they cannot be carried forward.

ADVANCE CORPORATION TAX

On the occasion when a company pays a dividend (or other distribution to members), it is required to make a payment of advance corporation tax (ACT) to the Inland Revenue. The rate of ACT is fixed annually and applied to the actual or net dividend, but is equivalent to income tax at the basic rate on the gross of the dividend plus the ACT. Payment of ACT is due quarterly and must be made fourteen days after the end of the quarter in which the dividend is paid. When the dividend is paid, the member is given a tax credit for the ACT in respect of the dividend.

Treatment by shareholders

Every individual in the UK who receives a dividend and tax credit can treat the tax credit as if it were a voucher for income tax paid. If he is liable at the basic rate of income tax, no further liability will arise; if he is liable at more than the basic rate, he will be required to pay only at the excess of his higher rate over the basic rate. If his income is so small he pays no income tax, he will recover the tax credit.

Where a company receives a dividend with a tax credit the sum of the two will be treated as 'franked investment income', i.e. income which has already borne corporation tax and therefore income upon which no further tax is payable. The company may set the amount of the tax credit against an obligation to pay ACT in respect of its own dividends, and pay only the balance to the Inland Revenue.

Treatment of ACT by company paying dividends

In respect of dividends paid during an accounting period, ACT is treated as

TAXATION

a payment to account of the corporation tax liability for that accounting period and only the balance, or mainstream liability, is payable nine months after the balance date (or later in respect of certain companies – see Adjustment of profit, above). The ACT must, however, be set against corporation tax on income – it must not be set against tax on capital gains – and the maximum which may be set off is the ACT on a distribution such that the sum of the two is equal to the income charged to corporation tax.

Any ACT not relieved in this way may be carried back for six years and any balance still not relieved may be carried forward. An example is given in Figure 7.6.

Trading profit, Schedule D Case I, year to 31 March 1986	£520 000
Unfranked investment income	20 000
Capital gains £40 000 less excluded £10 000 (see section on capital gains tax, below)	30 000
In May 1985 Z Ltd paid a dividend of £413 000 on which ACT amounted to £177 000	
The mainstream liability is computed: Taxable profits – Income £520 000 + £20 000	£540 000
– Capital	30 000
	£570 000
Corporation tax at 40 per cent	£228 000
ACT for set-off – £177 000 Restricted to tax on 'gross' dividend of £540 000, i.e. to (Since £378 000 + ACT thereon of £162 000 = £540 000)	162 000
Mainstream liability	£ 66 000

Figure 7.6 Example of set-off of ACT

During the year to 31 March 1986, when the rate of corporation tax was 40 per cent and of ACT three-sevenths, Z Ltd had the taxable profits shown in Figure 7.6.

GROUPS OF COMPANIES

There are special concessions in the taxation of groups of companies, their main effect being to reduce or cut out the tax on intercompany transactions within the group. It requires considerable skill to arrange group affairs to take the best advantage of these arrangements, and the administrator should either make a specialized study or else form a regular practice of consulting the group's professional advisers before making transfers of assets or dividends within the group.

For example, for some purposes a 'subsidiary' is one in which the parent company owns more than half the ordinary shares, for others the minimum is 75 per cent of the ordinary shares, and for yet others 75 per cent of the whole equity capital including certain non-commercial loans.

The three main advantages of group taxations are:

Subsidiaries. A subsidiary may pay dividends to its parent company with or without paying ACT thereon. It may be valuable to pay the dividend without ACT when the parent company is not making distributions to its own shareolders, or when it has other sources of franked investment income receivable net and no trading income of its own.

Loss in one company against profit in others. When one company has suffered a trading loss, this may be set off against the profits of any one or more members of the group. It should be noted that this concession does not extend to capital losses and careful planning is essential prior to a disposal where there are capital losses within the group.

Transfers of capital assets. No chargeable gain arises when capital assets are transferred between members of a group. Care is required however when a company which has received an asset leaves the group within six years of the transfer.

CAPITAL GAINS TAX

Companies pay corporation tax on chargeable gains as well as on income, but a proportion of the capital gain is excluded from the assessment at the full rate of corporation tax to bring the effective rate of corporation tax on capital gains down to 30 per cent – the normal rate for individuals. All forms of property are included as assets for capital gains tax purposes, but certain of them are exempt from charge. These include:

1 Wasting assets with a predictable life of less than fifty years, if they are chattels (tangible moveable objects), but excluding assets which have qualified for capital allowances
2 Gains on certain government securities and qualifying corporate bands
3 Winnings from betting or lotteries
4 Gains on discharge of liabilities (for example, the repayment of debentures at less than their issue price)

TAXATION

If assets were acquired pre-April 1965 any part of the gain arising before that date is not taxable.

The list is not exhaustive and does not include assets such as dwelling-houses for which the gain may be exempt if made by an individual. When a capital gain made by a company has suffered tax and the balance is paid out to shareholders, a further round of tax is deducted. For example, if it sells its premises and goes into liquidation the position is as shown in Figure 7.7. This example has been simplified to illustrate the principle, which in an actual company would be clouded but not overthrown by the existence of other assets.

Purchase price of asset, £400 000 – absorbed into the business as a fixed asset, or alternatively the shares are purchased.

The position of the seller is as follows:—

Sell the asset and then go into liquidation:		Alternatively sell the company's shares	
Selling price 1986	£400 000	for	£400 000
Cost price 1965	300 000	Cost price 1965	300 000
Capital gain	£100 000		£100 000
Tax at effective rate of 30%	30 000		
Balance distributed to shareholders	£ 70 000		£100 000
Less: Personal capital gains tax 30%	21 000		30 000
Net gain in the hands of shareholders	£ 49 000		£ 70 000

NB: Indexation allowance has been ignored for the purposes of this example.

If the shares are purchased, the asset will be owned by a subsidiary of the buying company. It may subsequently be sold to the parent company which may declare a dividend to dispose of its capital gain without suffering any tax; alternatively, the proceeds may simply be lent to the parent company.

Figure 7.7 Simplified example to show that sale as a going concern is better than liquidation where assets have appreciated

Underlying capital gains

A company with an underlying capital gain in its assets is always better sold as a going concern than put into liquidation, and to the purchaser it may be a matter of indifference whether he obtains ownership of the valuable assets in the one way or the other. He is not obliged to run the company as a trading concern when he has acquired its shares. The directors of a private company should give thought to the chances of 'retirement exemption' before disposing of their shares. For disposals after 5 April 1985, the first £100 000 (previously £50 000) of gain will be exempt if they are aged over sixty and have been full-time directors for not less than ten years and hold either:

1 Not less than 25 per cent of the voting share capital in own right, or
2 Not less than 5 per cent in own right, and members of immediate family own more than 50 per cent

A proportionate amount of relief is available if the shares have been owned for less than ten years, but more than one year. The exemption is restricted to the underlying chargeable business assets; it is not available in respect of portfolio investments held by the company.

Replacement of assets

Deferment of tax on capital gains may be claimed where the asset has been used only for trading purposes and is replaced by fresh assets, not necessarily of a similar nature, or even serving the same function, if they are of one of the following classes:

1 Land, building, fixed plant and machinery
2 Ships
3 Aircraft
4 Goodwill
5 Hovercraft

It is important that the replacement is bought within twelve months before or three years after the sale of the previous asset. These time limits may be extended at the discretion of the Inland Revenue.

Deferment continues indefinitely if the replacement asset is permanent, but if a 'depreciating' asset is bought deferment will continue only for ten years. If the depreciating asset is sold within ten years and replaced by a fresh permanent asset, the permanence of the deferment is established, but if it is replaced by a fresh depreciating asset the deferment ends immediately.

Depreciating assets for this purpose are assets with an expected life of less than sixty years, ie they are wasting assets, or items which will become wasting assets within ten years. The most common example is fixed plant.

Full deferment is given only where it is requested and where the whole proceeds from sale of the previous asset are used for the purchase of the replacement. Where only a portion of the sale proceeds are used, the amount on which deferment can be claimed is restricted.

TAXATION

THE COMPANY AS A TAX COLLECTOR

Although the company does not itself pay any income tax, it is obliged to serve as an unpaid collector by withholding income tax when making payment of:

1 Wages and salaries, for the PAYE system
2 Annual interest, the most common example being debenture interest

The amount of PAYE deducted in a month has to be passed to the Collector of Taxes on the nineteenth day of the month next following. For example, month from 6 April to 5 May; tax to be paid on 19 May. Income tax on annual interest is payable quarterly, fourteen days after the end of the quarter.

Extension for close companies. When a close company does not pay a sufficient dividend, part of its income may be treated as if it had been distributed by the company and income tax thereon at the higher rates applicable to its members may be recovered from the company.

CLOSE COMPANY DISABILITIES

1 If money is lent to a 'participator' an amount equal to tax at the basic rate on the grossed up amount of the loan is payable by the company. This is repaid to the company as and when the participator repays the loan
2 Where a close company fails to make an adequate distribution out of income, tax may be payable as if such a distribution had in fact been made. The amount of the shortfall in distributions is apportioned to members and the appropriate income tax is computed; this income tax may be paid by the members or by the company

For a trading company the maximum which may be apportioned is its distributable investment income, plus 50 per cent of its estate income abated by the appropriate fraction, namely

$$\frac{\text{Estate income}}{\text{Estate plus trading income}}$$

Estate income of less than the appropriate fraction of £25 000 is disregarded and if less than the appropriate fraction of £75 000 it is reduced by 50 per cent of the difference. In addition distributable investment income is arrived at after deduction of the smaller of 10 per cent of the estate or trading income of £3000.

It is always open to a trading company to justify a smaller distribution, on the grounds that the company needs to retain more of the profit to meet the requirements of its business—to finance improvements, modernization or expansion and to repay short-term loans. Cash required to finance a wholly new trade will be treated as a business expense for this purpose.

Negotiations with a view to ensuring there will be no apportionment of income should be opened by an approach to the inspector backed by a clear statement of intentions such as the forecast of sources and application of funds which forms part of the management accounting routine of most companies.

CONTRAST BETWEEN LIMITED COMPANY AND PARTNERSHIP

Partners pay income tax at graduated rates on the whole of their profit, which is regarded as earned income in their hands, except in the case of a limited (or 'sleeping') partner whose share is normally treated as investment income for tax purposes.

In a limited company, corporation tax is payable on the profit after deducting remuneration of its directors, who are classed as employees. Profit remaining in the company after paying corporation tax is not subject to further tax, but if it is withdrawn as dividend this may be liable to income tax at the higher rates as personal investment income of the shareholder.

From purely a tax viewpoint, there is a distinct advantage in the tax rates applicable to a company compared with personal tax rates. From 1 April 1986 the full rate of corporation tax is 35 per cent, whereas income tax rates for 1986/87 rise from the basic rate of 29 per cent on income of £17 200 to a top rate of 60 per cent on income over £41 200.

There are many powerful legal advantages for running a limited company and these often far outweigh the importance of tax differences. The larger the business and the more involved its ownership, the more important it becomes to operate it as a limited company. Also a company pension scheme for the directors can provide better benefits than a self-employed retirement annuity scheme. On the other hand certain undertakings, such as most of the professions, are not allowed to operate through limited companies.

CHANGES IN PERSONAL AND CORPORATION TAX

From 1973–74, income tax and surtax were replaced by a single unified tax, but the change was one of administration. It did not alter the total tax liability, the only real difference to the taxpayer being that the new high rates of tax on large incomes are payable more promptly than the surtax they replaced, but now only marginally so. Surtax was due nine months after the

TAXATION

year end; higher rates of new unified tax were originally due three months after the year end but this was extended to eight months in 1980.

Changes in the corporation tax system were effected from 1 April 1973 when the system was changed from a 'classical' one (corporation tax on profits, with income tax deducted from dividends) to an 'imputation' one (corporation tax on profits, part of the tax being passed on as a credit to the recipients of dividends). The object of the change was to make the corporation tax on retained profits as heavy as the combined tax on distributed profits. This reduces the incentive to retain profits for reinvestment in expansion of the company's business, the plan being strangely at odds with the then government's supposed encouragement to increase industrial investment.

DEFINITIONS OF SOME PHRASES USED IN THE CORPORATION TAX RULES

Accounting date. The date to which a company makes up its accounts.

Accounting period. The period for which corporation tax is charged. This will normally be a period for which a company makes up its accounts, but it may be a shorter period and must not exceed a year.

Close company. A UK resident company under the control of five or fewer participators, or any number of participators who are directors, or if more than half the company's income could be apportioned for tax purposes among five or fewer participators or among any number of participators who are directors. However, any company in which shares carrying at least 35 per cent of the voting power are held by the public is excluded from the definition, provided such shares have been dealt in and officially listed on a recognized stock exchange within the preceding twelve months.

Participator in a close company. Primarily a person who is a shareholder or has an interest in the capital or income of the company.

Distribution. Any dividend paid by a company, including a capital dividend. It also includes any other distribution out of the assets of a company, whether in cash or otherwise, except for a repayment of capital on liquidation or any amount for which new consideration has been given. Also excluded is a company purchasing its own shares satisfying certain conditions.

Franked investment income. Income from a source which has already suffered corporation tax and is consequently not liable to further corporation tax in the hands of the receiving company. Dividends from UK companies are the most common example.

Unfranked investment income. Income from a source which has not suffered corporation tax and is therefore to be included in this company's total income for corporation tax purposes. Debenture interest from other companies is a common example.

FURTHER READING

The aim in this chapter has been to highlight those aspects of company taxation which appear to be of most consequence to administrators. All the rules are hedged round with ifs and buts which make it imperative to check details before making major decisions.

Useful explanatory booklets may be obtained free from the Inland Revenue; these include Corporation Tax; Capital Gains Tax; Directors' Benefits and Expenses; Capital Allowances on Plant and Machinery and VAT material from Customs and Excise.

The taxation of banks, insurance companies, building societies and other financial organizations, and of agricultural concerns, is outside the scope of this work. The following books may prove useful:

Colin Cretton, *Practical CGT*, Butterworth, London, 1982.
Malcolm Gammie, *Tax Strategy for Companies*, Oyez, London, 1981.
K.J.M. Ritchie, *Official Tax Forms Manual*, Oyez, London.
Whiteman and Wheatcroft on Income Tax, Sweet and Maxwell, London, 1976 (with latest supplement).
Eric L Harvey, *Tolley's Income Tax*, Tolley Publishing Company, Croydon.
Glyn Saunders and John Boulding, *Tolley's Corporation Tax*, Tolley Publishing Company, Croydon.
Patrick Noakes and Robert Wareham, *Tolley's Capital Gains Tax*, Tolley Publishing Company, Croydon.

8

Value Added Tax

Richard Service

VAT was introduced on 1 April 1973 to replace purchase tax and selective employment tax. It was intended to be a broader based tax with a charge to tax arising unless the type of supply was specifically excluded.

Strictly speaking, value added tax is not a tax on value added in the true economic sense. Rather it is a tax on consumption, collected at each stage in the economy, on the difference (broadly) between the purchase price of goods and services acquired to make the product and the sale price of that product. Purchases are called inputs, and the tax which a business pays on buying those inputs is called input tax; sales are called outputs, and the tax which a business charges on its customers is called output tax. The excess of output tax over input tax is payable by the business to Customs and Excise, who are responsible for administering the tax, but if the input tax exceeds the output tax the difference is repayable by Customs and Excise to the business. Assuming that a business is wholly within the VAT system, the business bears no VAT itself but recovers all the tax it pays on its inputs either by way of deduction from its output tax or by way of repayment from Customs and Excise.

LEGISLATION

The primary VAT legislation is the EEC sixth directive adopted on 17 May 1977. Considerable amendments were made to the UK domestic VAT legislation to harmonize UK law with the requirements of the directive from 1 January 1978. It is now an established principle that any conflict between

EEC and UK legislation is to be resolved by preferring the provisions of the EEC directive. The UK has been allowed to 'derogate' in certain specified ways from the EEC directive.

The UK VAT legislation is contained in the following:

1   The Value Added Tax Act 1983 and subsequent Finance Acts (for example 1985, which contains the surcharge and penalty provisions)
2   Statutory Instruments and Orders (for example the VAT (General) Regulations, 1985)
3   Certain parts of the booklets issued by Customs and Excise (for example section VII of *The VAT Guide,* notice number 700)

Guidance as to the meaning of the law is given in VAT tribunal and court decisions. A VAT tribunal is an independent body for resolving disputes between Customs and taxpayers. For further details, see below under 'Appeal procedures'.

CHARGE TO VAT

VAT is chargeable on any taxable supply of goods or services made in the UK by anyone who is, or should be, registered for VAT in the course or furtherance of any business carried on by him. Taxable supplies are all supplies other than those which are exempt from VAT. VAT is also payable on the importation of goods into the UK whether or not the importer is carrying on a business. A registered trader may apply to Customs to defer payment of VAT on imports until the fifteenth day of the month following importation. The VAT paid on importation forms part of the trader's input tax. Registered traders have to account for VAT on payments made abroad for certain services (see 'Place of supply' below).

Supply is defined as including all forms of supply but not anything done for no consideration. Thus VAT has to be accounted for on non-cash transactions (for example, barter). It arises in unexpected circumstances (for example, on charges made to employees for phone calls, on sales of items of plant and on receipts for sales of goodwill or patents if not disposed of along with the business) and is not limited to being charged on what would be regarded as sales or income in accounting terms. If consideration in money or money's worth is received by a trader VAT will be due unless the supply is exempt or outwith the scope of VAT.

A distinction is drawn between goods and services. The most common supply of goods is the transfer of the whole property in the goods either by sale or hire purchase. Further examples may be found in the reference works cited at the end of this chapter. Any supply which is not goods will, almost invariably, be a supply of services. This includes leasing of assets and repair work. A few supplies, such as the transfer of a business as a going concern,

VALUE ADDED TAX

are deemed to be neither goods nor services and therefore not liable to VAT.

A trader has to register for VAT if the value of his taxable supplies in the previous calendar quarter exceeded £7000 or previous year £20 500, or if he anticipates his future taxable supplies in any year will exceed £20 500. These limits are revised annually and details are included in Customs' leaflet *Should I be registered for VAT* (no.700/1).

TIME OF SUPPLY

In order to determine into which VAT accounting period a transaction falls, the time of supply has to be ascertained.

Goods

1. If the goods are to be removed, the basic tax point is the time when they are removed
2. If the goods are not to be removed, the basic tax point is the time when they are made available to the person to whom they are being supplied
3. There are special rules for sale or return and for certain other transactions. A hire-purchase transaction is deemed to be a sale. The construction industry is subject to special rules
4. Where a tax invoice is issued within fourteen days after the basic tax point, the invoice date becomes the tax point unless the taxpayer elects to use the basic tax point instead. The fourteen-day period may be extended by agreement with Customs and Excise
5. If a tax invoice is rendered before the date of the basic tax point or if payment is received in respect of a supply before the basic tax point, the earlier of the invoice date and the payment date becomes the tax point. The taxpayer in this case has no option to elect for the tax point in 1 or 2 above

Services

1. The basic tax point in the case of the supply of services is when those services are performed
2. If a tax invoice is issued within fourteen days after the basic tax point (extendable by negotiation with Customs and Excise), the invoice date is the tax point unless the taxpayer elects to the contrary
3. In other cases, for example, continuous supplies of services, the tax point is the earlier of the tax invoice date and the date on which payment is made for the services. Thus a business can issue a request for payment and delay the tax point until receipt of the payment. Of course the recipient of the supply cannot deduct input VAT until the VAT invoice is issued

Businesses should ensure that where an option is open they choose the best tax point for their accounting and administrative systems.

PLACE OF SUPPLY

Broadly, if goods are supplied within the UK (which, for VAT purposes, includes the Isle of Man) for use in the UK, the supply is taxable. If goods are supplied in the UK and exported, the supply is still taxable, but at the time of export is zero-rated. Goods supplied outside the UK but imported into the UK are liable to VAT at the time of importation. A supply of goods made outside the UK but not imported into the UK is outside VAT altogether; this applies whether or not the goods are ordered from the UK.

The rules regarding the place of supply of services initially only applied to a supply rendered and enjoyed within the UK and services in the UK for the benefit of someone outside the UK. The implementation of the EEC sixth directive on VAT extended the scope of the tax in the UK to include the importation of certain services. Where a taxable person receives, from a person who does not belong in the UK, any of the services listed in Schedule 3 to the VAT Act 1983, except services which would be exempt if supplied in the UK, he is required to account for tax as if he had supplied the services to himself. This is known as the reverse charge on services received from abroad. The VAT accounted for forms part of the trader's input VAT.

THE TAX INVOICE

No special form of tax invoice is laid down but certain minimum requirements have to be met. In particular every tax invoice must show an identifying number, the date of supply, the name and address and VAT registration number of the supplier, the name and address of the person to whom the supply is made, the type of supply (ie sale, lease etc.), a description of the supply, the price for each supply before the addition of VAT, any discount offered and the rate and amount of tax chargeable.

An abbreviated form of tax invoice may be used in some cases; these are small transactions at retail level.

It is not necessary, unless requested, for a retailer to issue a tax invoice. Tax invoices need not be rendered where the transaction is zero-rated. In the case of exempt transactions it is not legally possible to issue a tax invoice.

RATES OF TAX

At present supplies are either exempt from VAT or else subject to VAT at the positive rate of 15 per cent or the zero rate. In order to determine the VAT treatment of a supply one first considers if it is zero rated, and secondly if it is exempt. If it falls into neither of these categories, the standard rate applies. Prior to 18 June 1979 there were two positive rates of VAT, a higher rate on 'luxuries' of 12½ per cent (25 per cent before 12 April 1976) and a standard rate of 8 per cent.

Zero-rated supplies are listed in Schedule 5 to the VAT Act and these are food, books, newspapers, periodicals, news services, fuel (excluding road fuel) and power, the construction of buildings, services to overseas traders, transport, certain drugs and medicines and children's clothing and footwear. In addition, the export of all goods and most services is zero-rated. This ensures that no VAT enters into the price of any export.

Exempt supplies are set out in Schedule 6 to the VAT Act and these comprise most supplies relating to land; insurance; postal services; betting, gaming and lotteries; certain financial services (banking, credit finance); education; health and subscriptions to trades unions and professional bodies.

Whereas VAT is charged on zero-rated supplies, albeit at a nil rate, no VAT is charged on exempt supplies. This distinction is of vital importance when considering recovery of input VAT (see below).

The liability to VAT can depend upon seemingly trivial factors. For example, the sale or granting of a long lease of a building by the person who constructed it will be zero rated; letting the same property for holiday accommodation, standard rated; and most other types of supply exempt.

If there is any doubt as to the appropriate rate of VAT on a particular supply, the law should be carefully considered. Copies of Schedules 5 and 6 are contained in Customs' leaflet no.701/39.

If doubt persists, a ruling from Customs should be sought. This can be obtained from the local VAT office by putting all relevant facts to them. Customs should be asked to put their ruling in writing if the matter is of importance as they do not consider themselves bound by oral rulings.

DISCOUNTS

Where a discount is offered for prompt or immediate payment, VAT should be charged as though the discount will be taken by the person to whom the goods or services are being supplied. If in the event the discount is not earned no recalculation of the VAT should be made. Where a trade discount is offered, VAT should similarly be calculated on the discounted price. Where on the other hand a contingent discount is offered which will be available, for example, when a certain level of purchases have been achieved by the customer, the VAT should be calculated on the assumption that the volume target will not be reached.

RETROSPECTIVE ADJUSTMENTS

Where a downwards movement to the price charged for a supply is made, the VAT on the original invoice will be overstated. VAT should be added to the amount of the credit on a credit note issued to the customer; the VAT must be at the same rate as that originally charged by the supplier. Retrospective adjustments of any kind can be made by the use of the credit-note mechanism.

BAD DEBTS

VAT has to be accounted for to Customs at the time of the supply (tax point), unless one of the retail schemes is operated and the standard method for accounting for takings is adopted. If a customer fails to pay for a supply, no refund can be obtained of the VAT charged unless the customer has become formally insolvent. Note that for companies, bad debt relief may now be claimed where a receiver has been appointed and the assets are insufficient to permit any payment to the ordinary unsecured creditors. Prior to 1 April 1986 no relief was obtained until the company went into liquidation.

SECONDHAND GOODS

In principle secondhand goods are treated in the same way as new goods. There are, however, special schemes for secondhand works of art, antiques, scientific collections, electric organs, firearms, horses and ponies, boats, aircraft, cars, motor cycles and caravans. Provided the trader keeps records as required by Customs he is liable to account for VAT on only the dealer's margin rather than the full sale price.

INPUT VAT

A trader is entitled to relief for input VAT suffered on supplies made to him which he uses for the purpose of making taxable supplies in any business he carries on. Input VAT may never be recovered on supplies which are not for the purposes of the business, for example, repairs to domestic property; or not made to the trader; or on items barred from credit (private motor cars and business entertainment, unless of overseas customers). Capital goods are treated in the same way as any other item and there is no question of spreading the input tax over the life of the asset or indeed in any other way. Thus heavy purchases of plant within a short period may put a business into a temporary repayment position.

VALUE ADDED TAX

Records must be maintained of all taxable inputs, including zero-rated inputs, and a tax invoice must be held in support of the input tax deduction. If, at the end of a return period, not all purchase invoices have been processed, Customs allow an estimated amount to be included in the claim for input VAT provided the estimate is deducted in calculating the input VAT on the next return.

Reference is made above to the distinction between zero-rated and exempt supplies. A business that only makes exempt supplies may not register for VAT and cannot reclaim any of the VAT on supplies made to it. Thus VAT becomes an additional cost of the business. Businesses which made both taxable and exempt supplies are termed partially exempt and usually suffer a disallowance of a portion of their input VAT. If the exempt supplies are made less than any of the following limits (total supplies being supplies net of VAT), all the input VAT may be reclaimed:

£2400 per annum; or
both £96 000 per annum and 50 per cent of all supplies; or
both £192 000 per annum and 25 per cent of all supplies; or
1 per cent of all supplies

Where these limits cannot be met, the standard method of calculating recoverable input VAT is

$$\text{input VAT} \times \frac{\text{value of taxable supplies}}{\text{value of all supplies}}$$

A partially exempt trader may request a method other than the standard one, e.g. direct attribution whereby inputs are attributed as far as possible to taxable or exempt supplies (the former receiving full relief the latter none) and the recovery of the unattributable balance being calculated as above.

Partial exemption is a complicated area but careful planning can significantly enhance the recovery of input VAT.

ACCOUNTING FOR VAT TO CUSTOMS AND EXCISE

Traders have to submit a return to Customs detailing the amount of output VAT charged, the amount of input VAT suffered that is eligible for relief, the total value of outputs and the total value of inputs in the return period. The normal return period is three months although traders with habitual VAT repayments, for example, the food industry, may apply to make monthly returns. The return has to be submitted within a month after the end of the return period and, unless the trader has applied to Customs to pay VAT by credit transfer, the return has to be accompanied by a cheque for any

VAT due. Payment of VAT by credit transfer can be delayed for a further seven days. Traders with habitual repayments will have VAT refunded by credit transfer, otherwise Customs repay by cheque.

It is very important to ensure that the accounting records are maintained in such a form that the tax return can be completed with the minimum of additional work and that VAT returns may be verified by Customs' officers when they make a control visit.

Although accounting for VAT is a burden on most businesses the quarterly return imposes a discipline on the accounting function and should be used as a method of providing up-to-date information for the trader, and thus result in increased efficiency.

DEFAULT SURCHARGE

The Finance Act 1985 introduced several civil penalties, some to replace and some as alternatives to the criminal code. VAT returns due after 1 October 1986 are within the ambit of the default surcharge. A default occurs when a VAT return is submitted after the thirty-day time limit. A second default within a year, ie any one of the four subsequent returns, will trigger the issue of a surcharge liability notice by Customs. Any default within the following year results in the trader suffering a surcharge of 5 per cent of the VAT due on the return that is in default. A further default within a year of the third results in a 10 per cent surcharge. This process continues with the surcharge increasing by 5 per cent steps to a maximum surcharge of 30 per cent. Note that if one VAT return is habitually late each year, for example the return for the period to the end of the company's financial year, the company will receive a surcharge liability notice and will suffer the default surcharge. The notice lapses once four successive VAT returns, or twelve in the case of a trader making monthly returns, are lodged on time. Surcharges are not deductible in computing corporation tax liabilities.

REPAYMENT SUPPLEMENT

In certain restricted circumstances Customs will pay a 5 per cent supplement on the amount of a VAT repayment claim. For this to be paid, the repayment must be due to an excess of input over output tax; the return must be submitted on time; all previous returns must have been submitted and all outstanding tax paid; Customs delay issuing instructions for the repayment beyond thirty days after receipt of the return (extended if there are errors in, or Customs ask reasonable inquiries in relation to, the return); and the amount shown as repayable on the return is not overclaimed by more than £100. The multiplicity of conditions will severely restrict the number of occasions that Customs will be obliged to pay the supplement.

VALUE ADDED TAX

SERIOUS MISDECLARATION

The penalty for serious misdeclaration is expected to apply to return periods beginning on or after 1 July 1988. A company which makes a return seriously understating a liability to VAT, seriously overstating an entitlement to a repayment of VAT or which accepts an assessment seriously understating a VAT liability will suffer a penalty of 30 per cent of the tax which would have been lost if the error had gone undiscovered. A serious misdeclaration occurs where the tax which would have been lost exceeds the lesser of (*a*) 30 per cent (or 15 per cent — see below) of the true amount of tax and (*b*) £10 000 or, if more, 5 per cent of the true amount of the tax. In monetary terms, the limits which trigger the penalty are:

Correct VAT liability	Error exceeds
Under £33 334	30% of correct liability
£33 334 – £200 000	£10 000
over £200 000	5% of correct liability

The 30 per cent limit is reduced to 15 per cent if, in any four-year period within the previous six years, two previous returns after 1 July 1988 contained errors which exceeded 15 per cent of the true tax liability.

INTEREST ON VAT ASSESSMENTS

An interest charge, in addition to any penalty that may apply, is expected to commence on 1 July 1988. The charge will be levied on VAT charged in an assessment made to recover an incorrect repayment of VAT, made in the absence of a return and in certain other circumstances. Interest will be charged at a rate to be fixed by the Treasury, will be payable without deduction of income tax and will not be deductible in computing profits for corporation tax.

RETENTION OF RECORDS

Invoices both in and out have to be retained for a minimum period of six years to enable Customs and Excise to perform their periodical audit of the business's VAT position. Their retention period was increased to six years on 25 July 1985, thus there is no requirement to retain records prior to 25 July 1982. By agreement with Customs and Excise, invoices may be kept in microfilm or any other form. Invoices should be stored and recorded in such a way that the periodical VAT return can be completed without difficulty.

GROUPS

Provision is made so that groups of commonly-controlled companies can be treated as one single VAT-paying entity. Transactions within companies in such a group are then ignored for VAT purposes and a single return is made by the 'representative member' of the group to Customs and Excise. All members of the VAT group are jointly and severally liable for the VAT liabilities of the group. Not all members of a Companies Act group need be grouped for VAT purposes: VAT recovery and the cash flow of a Companies Act group can be improved if the correct selection of companies is made.

DIVISIONS

A company organized in divisions may ask to have each division treated separately for VAT.

CASH FLOWS

The combination of the rules on the tax point and the date on which tax is payable to Customs and Excise gives rise either to cash-flow advantages or disadvantages. Thus a business which secures a long period of credit on its purchases will very likely not have to pay the VAT on the purchase price until after it has received credit for the tax on the purchase. On the other hand, a business which allows long periods of credit on its sales may find that it has to pay the appropriate output tax to Customs before receiving payment of that tax from the customer. If possible maximum credit should be obtained from one's suppliers but minimum credit given to one's customers. Equally important is the most advantageous use of the provisions for tax-point elections.

APPEAL PROCEDURES

Disputes can arise between businesses and Customs and Excise. If agreement cannot be reached with the local VAT office, it is usually prudent to seek a ruling from customs and Excise head office in London. If this does not resolve the matter, an appeal may be lodged to a VAT tribunal. These are presided over by lawyers, and meet in various parts of the country. Their proceedings are held in public and all their decisions are published. Those touching on points of wide interest are issued by HMSO, all others are available for reference and copying at the tribunal centre where the appeal was held. Appeals, on a point of law only, can be made from a VAT tribunal

VALUE ADDED TAX

to the High Court or, in Scotland, the Court of Session or, in Northern Ireland, the High Court of Justice. Appeals proceed thereafter to the House of Lords (via the Court of Appeal in England and Wales). Appeals in England and Wales may be made direct from the High Court to the House of Lords. Court decisions are published in *Simons Tax Cases*. At any stage the tribunal or court may make a reference to the EEC court for a ruling on the interpretation of an EEC directive.

PROFESSIONAL ADVICE

As in other areas of taxation, the taxpayer is at a disadvantage in dealing with Customs and Excise. It is important, therefore, to take professional advice not merely in negotiations with Customs and Excise but also in the handling of appeals.

FURTHER READING

John Price, *Croner's Reference Book for VAT*, Croner Publications Ltd.

P.W. De Voil, *Value Added Tax*, Butterworths.

The above two titles are looseleaf works updated monthly.

The VAT Guide: Customs and Excise Notice No 700, (available free of charge from all local VAT offices.

Other notices and leaflets are available free of charge from Customs and Excise. A full list is contained in their leaflet no.700/13.

Robert Wareham and Eric L Harvey, *Tolley's Value Added Tax*, Tolley publishing Co. Ltd (the current edition of their annual publication should be consulted).

9

Managing Mergers and Acquisitions

Peter A Verreck

Mergers have been likened to marriages with somewhat similar programmes consisting of a period of search, a period of courtship, a solemnisation, a honeymoon period and finally, one hopes, a settling down. In seeking a marriage partner certain inherited and intuitive instincts prevail to create a course of action which follows in general a familiar plan. The individual learns by observation and from experience, while there is no shortage of experts with their own brand of advice.

Despite all this, some marriages fail and the divorce courts are available to put an end to the partnership. The process is not painless and it can be costly and time-consuming. No such comparatively easy disengagement is possible when it is a 'business marriage', although the original causes may be similar, such as ill-matched partners, immaturity, inadequate planning and instruction. The incidence of failed mergers is possibly higher than that of marriages, but the failure can have a much wider and more serious effect on the community.

There is no reliable or accepted method of assessing success or failure of mergers and one must concede that the number of cases of divorce is no guide to the rate of unhappy marriages! It is, however, authoritatively estimated that some 60 per cent of mergers either failed or did not reach expected results: the figure has been put as high as 80 per cent. Which quite simply means that four out of five mergers were either badly planned or badly carried out, while some should never have been contemplated in the first place.

There are no rules for mergers in the concept and planning stage, though there are laws, recommendations and instructions laid down in the public's interest for the remaining stages. A significant factor in many mergers has not been growth by acquisition, as was usually the case, but merger to avoid liquidation or redundancy. Economic forces may create conditions under which positive, if disagreeable, action needs to be taken and which *per se* creates a viable organization.

In the past and under conditions of stress, a number of such mergers are showing some success which it is hoped will be maintained on a return to normality.

A further development of late has been the takeover, sometimes with government approval if not financial assistance, of a company by employees threatened with redundancy or unwanted takeover.

This chapter introduces and comments on the subject of mergers generally, and recommends the study of case histories of both successful and unsuccessful mergers, while stressing the importance of both short-term and long-term planning. There is value to be gained from the expertise of others, including the use of specialist consultants, but even this requires a degree of selective skill. The past few years have seen an increase in the literature on the subject and further reading is advisable. There have also been remarkable, if not totally unexpected, developments over the whole field of acquisitions. Some of these developments have been of a legislative nature, some of a regulatory nature and, in particular, research has been carried out on the aspect of human relations, with case histories being critically appraised.

Few business terms in common usage can cause the reaction that seems to follow the words 'mergers' and 'acquisitions'. This emotional attitude is not confined to any one section of the community and there has been a marked degree of media sensationalism in the step-by-step reporting of a number of cases. An attitude akin to fear has sometimes developed and this is not unreasonable when one appreciates the element of secrecy often necessary in the conduct of negotiations which may have an effect on the lives of many people. It is also unfortunate that much coverage is given to the difficulties and problems of failed mergers and very little to the successes. The general reader could easily believe that the practice of merging and acquiring was a recent innovation, whereas it has been with us in a formal way since the 1862 Companies Act.

Mergers and acquisitions should be seen as a normal process of corporate evolution. If a company is to develop, or indeed remain in being, it must constantly be searching and probing. It can never stand still except for temporary consolidation. It must examine its future closely and in the light of ever-changing patterns of commerce whether local, national or international.

Shareholders and employees have the right to expect that the board of directors are taking all possible steps to protect the company and *inter alia* their security. Planning for merger should be high on the list of priorities and will of itself also prove defensive.

Planning of this nature will be incorporated in the overall corporate plan, and management responsible for outward development through merger or acquisition should also provide defensive tactics. Such tactics do not imply a negative attitude or an admission of defeat. They are an acceptance that the company must be placed in a position of strength if and when it is necessary for the board to report to the shareholders following a takeover offer.

DEFINITIONS

The term 'merger' is used in this chapter in a broad sense to include mergers and consolidations. Both have the object of combining the assets, liabilities, organization, rights and business of one or more units into one corporate body. In a merger the company absorbing the assets and so on, retains its identity, but a consolidation involves the formation of a new company which acquires the assets and liabilities of the constituent companies. The term merger is also used for straightforward acquisitions, as the latter term denotes basically the same operation.

There are various formulae employed in merger situations but for simplicity these can be reduced to the following outlines.

Acquisition by purchase of equity. The acquiring company offers to purchase the capital stock from the owners of the company and is prepared to make payment in cash or other negotiable instrument. The acquired company usually retains a separate identity but is operated as a subsidiary.

Acquisition by purchase of assets. The tangible assets, as well as possible goodwill or patent rights, are purchased and payment is made in cash or in equity of the purchasing company or, much more frequently, in a combination of cash and equity. Liabilities of the acquired company are often assumed by the purchasing company, although it is not uncommon for the latter to insist on the exclusion of certain types of indebtedness. Some cash element is therefore essential in order that the sellers can settle such claims on their own terms.

Takeover bids. Some authorities consider that a 'takeover' is not a merger as it is usually a unilateral process, as the name seems to imply. But it shares with all mergers a loss or change in identity. A form of agreement between the principal shareholders or the boards of directors of both companies has often been reached before the bid is made. The takeover tactic is employed quite often to acquire a controlling interest in a publicly quoted company and bids are made to existing shareholders for their stock at a price usually above that prevailing on the market. The price can be one of many combinations, as in a purchase of assets, and this can make it difficult to assess the true value being offered.

MANAGING MERGERS AND ACQUISITIONS

The directors have a duty to recommend to the shareholders acceptance or rejection of the bid. Further consideration may also be needed if rival bids are made.

Conglomerate mergers. These involve combination of two or more companies engaged in seemingly unrelated activities. On closer inspection the activities may be found to be similar in such areas as production methods but to differ in the type of product and market.

Vertical mergers (or integration). These aim to bring successive stages of manufacture or commercial activity under common ownership. Such a merger might be carried out as a protection against a competitor or to deny him access to supplies essential to his operation. This type of merger may be subject to control via the monopolies legislation.

Horizontal mergers. Involve the unification of two or more companies engaged in similar manufacture, services or perhaps markets. A notable form of this type of merger has been seen amongst brewers in recent years.

Reverse takeover. This is the process by which one company, usually the stronger, is taken over by another but payment in equity gives the seller control of the purchaser. Control may be gained by the management of the purchasing company without of necessity having control of stock. This technique is particularly valuable as a means of obtaining quotation without the considerable cost of going public.

The high incidence of this form of merger is partly due to the number of public companies formed under looser regulations some years ago and which failed to grow in line with the rest of the economy. Others have lost their real objectives possibly by mergers and are now little more than shells. A certain number of companies being used as the 'purchaser' in this form of exercise may have been the outcome of failed mergers.

European merger. A further form of merger has been taking place in EEC countries, and British companies have been involved in a number of such actions. Unfortunately some of these have not proved the success originally anticipated and one reason advanced is the lack of a pan-European form of enterprise.

The Rome Treaty originally sought to curb monopolies while removing trade barriers. A change has taken place since 1969 and the EEC has produced a memorandum which encourages cross-border mergers and has assisted the setting up of a common merger 'marriage' agency to act as a catalyst in bringing together likely partners.

If some transfrontier mergers have not proved successful the reasons could be fiscal, legal, historical or industrial. Regional priorities, high unemployment, political considerations, management and trade union intransigence are some of the reasons advanced for failures.

A number of European firms have demonstrated market success through joint ownership of a common operation across frontiers and with shared responsibilities, for example, Shell, Unilever, Gaevert-Agfa etc. Mutual interest, a willingness to share management and similarity of objectives are some of the reasons for the progress such companies have made and which, incidentally, have also made them powerful competitors of US multinationals.

REASONS FOR MERGERS

It is unfortunately true that the reasons for some acquisitions have seemed obscure, while financial circles have not been slow in accusing certain company directors of going into the market place with a mentality more akin to that of a 'campaign medal collector' or possibly, as one writer caustically remarked, 'adding glitter to the company Christmas tree'.

Assessment of merger success is not easy and certain authorities place the success rate as low as 20 per cent. If correct, this is not encouraging, but it is incontestable that many of the failures would never have been commenced if serious consideration had been given at the early planning stage not only to the reasons for contemplating the merger but equally to the alternatives.

The reasons or motives for seeking a merger or an acquisition are many and there are inevitably more than one for each situation. The following is only a representative list:

1 Diversification, useful because it can cover so much but requires careful consideration in each case
2 Elimination of competition, sometimes a costly process involving questions of monopoly control
3 The acquisition of skilled management or/and personnel
4 The acquisition of production facilities
5 The acquisition of patent rights etc.
6 Gaining greater collateral
7 Improving the rate of growth
8 To avoid seasonal underproduction etc.
9 To exploit a raw material or process
10 To inject profits before further capitalization
11 To rationalize or regulate marketing
12 Cost reductions, mainly of specific functions such as administration
13 To penetrate a protected market
14 For the benefit of tax losses

MANAGING MERGERS AND ACQUISITIONS

15 Asset acquisition and eventual disposal
16 By combining two or more companies to make possible a Stock Exchange listing
17 To obtain a quote by merger with an existing quoted company

PROGRAMME

The need to evolve a programme, as well as the importance of including some form of preparation for merger situations in the company's corporate activity, has already been stressed. Responsibility for this function should be at board level and incorporated in strategic decision making.

The programme can be divided into four stages which in turn are sectional according to the activity contemplated and the various skills or professional acumen required.

Planning

Various alternatives are considered followed by research of the selected choice. This will involve 'undercover' activities and the amount of information obtained will depend on sources. In general much of this stage is concerned with financial data of markets, of products, of weaknesses, of strengths etc.

Approach and negotiations

This follows once the planning stage provides an affirmative response. In theory approach and negotiation could be looked on as two separate stages but in practice they are concurrent. The skills required for successful approach are those of the diplomat and differ from those required for negotiating, which are often those of the financier-cum-psychologist. The planning stage will have revealed some economic data and the accountant will have no difficulty in arriving at a number of options using different formulae, and this knowledge will be useful to set low and high values during early stages of negotiation.

The price to be paid is obviously a vital factor in any negotiation, but many acquisitions have failed to get off the ground because the approach was wrong and too little attention was paid to future organization and the effect on the human side of the enterprise. Asset values seldom seem to have much relevance to the price except where the assets have not as yet started to show any real profitability, such as in the case of a fairly new enterprise or when they could be substantially surplus to requirements and easily realized.

Profit record is currently used and today's trends seem to indicate that the buyer is looking for a return in the range 17 to 24 per cent. Prices based on such easy formulae are more commonly employed when there is general agreement to buy and sell, whereas a good deal of bargaining may otherwise be necessary. The reaction of institutional shareholders and the opinion of the financial press also become vital factors.

Procedural activities

The procedural activities are commenced during the negotation stage but become operational once general agreement has been reached. Competent advice is required as the planning and realization are invariably linked to a tight schedule.

Briefing of accountants and lawyers is essential at an early stage, together with any other experts whose assistance may be required.

On reaching agreement, the proposed contracting parties draw up a simple memorandum stating the basis (or terms), and that such agreement is subject to approval of respective boards and their shareholders. It will also allow for easy access by the buyer to properties, assets, books of account etc. and will possibly stipulate a certain date by which completion is to take place.

Agreement will also have been reached with reference to disclosure and some provision made for operations during the interim period. Those who have been involved with this stage have found that the completion date seemed impossibly narrow, but long-delayed completions can create problems from which the new corporation may suffer long after the merger takes place. Careful planning, efficient communications and wise allocation of responsibilities are the answer.

It is at this stage that a close study should be made of relevant legislation including the Merger and Monopolies Act (1965), the City Code on Takeovers and Mergers (1981), the Industry Act (1975), and the Transfer of Undertakings (Protection of Employment) Regulations (1981).

The procedural stage can now be summed up:

1. Final agreement and contract prepared by legal advisers for the buyer in close touch with those for the seller
2. Au audit of the financial accounts with adjustments made for any variance in accounting practice
3. An examination of deed of title, contracts of service etc., copyrights, debentures, and similar memoranda
4. An investigation of contingent liabilities, of long-term commitments, of possible legal actions, bad debts etc.
5. Some investigation, on behalf of the seller, of the financial situation and prospects of the buyer

Financing

The method to be employed will in practice have been discussed and agreed

MANAGING MERGERS AND ACQUISITIONS

upon at an earlier stage and various methods of carrying out the acquisition have already been mentioned.

It is rare that a suitable financing arrangement cannot be planned to permit the acquisition to proceed. Financing the arrangement is unlikely to be the main consideration, but it should not be assumed that it is going to be straightforward. Each situation involves particular conditions, personal and domestic obligations and special factors.

'Consideration' can take a number of forms and the first that often springs to mind is cash, but this has become less attractive in the UK since the introduction of capital gains tax. This form of consideration raises fewer problems of financing than most because it is relatively simple to raise funds, although advice is essential on the most suitable and economic way of obtaining finance.

The City Code on Takeovers and Mergers should be studied in detail with relevance to cash offers. In particular the City panel decided that an offeror who purchases for cash, through the market or otherwise, holdings of a size which may materially affect the outcome of a bid should, in certain circumstances, be required to offer a cash alternative to the remaining holders.

The panel has specific authority to require a cash alternative in exceptional circumstances where it feels that this is necessary in order to ensure that General Principle 8 of the code is observed. Provision for exemption is made in certain circumstances.

Reference should also be made to the Companies Act with special relevance by a company of its own shares as this is particularly pertinent in the event of a management takeover.

Other forms of consideration could be debentures, loans, preference stock, equity, or a combination of some of these, together perhaps with cash. The issue of convertible preference shares has found favour in certain situations.

Equity holders will prefer to exchange for similar shares and will not favour other forms of stock but personal considerations are important, for instance if there is a need to maintain some kind of assured income which would be available from preference shares or debentures. Again there may also be a wish to remain involved in the running of the business and to participate in any capital growth.

Capital gains tax must remain a prime concern of the vendor. He may appreciate that there is little possibility of total avoidance but will want to postpone payment of the tax.

A further issue will be the strain on the purchasing company's resources and on its borrowing powers if a cash consideration is proposed. Obviously the relative size of companies is to be considered and its future capital requirements, hence the need for planning. The level of anticipated profits should be accurately forecast if new capital is going to incur a servicing charge.

In general, equity consideration is desirable for the acquiring company if profits are likely to be unsteady, while some form of loan stock would be preferable if stable profits are anticipated. If, on the other hand, it is expected that satisfactory profitability will be slow to materialize, the offer of stock with conversion rights might prove attractive.

Mergers have come unstuck because an *ad hoc* solution has been provided to rush a deal through without regard to the financial position of the consolidated group.

PEOPLE AND MERGERS

Takeovers, mergers or acquisitions have been receiving, and continue to receive, growing attention not only from national government but also from the European Commission and Parliament. Much of this interest is concerned with the influence of such activities as they affect the lives of employees and of the public, rathen than with political implications. Apart from the legislative documents already mentioned a study should be made of the Fair Trading Act, of Redundancy Payments Acts and the Contracts of Employments Act 1972 and subsequent amendments. Fuller reference will be found in other chapters of this book. The timing and release of information is particularly relevant; while the City Code is concerned with the mechanics of communication at various stages of acquisition, no mention is made of the employees' interests. The Commission on Industrial Relations however advocates early consultation, though recognizing that there may be practical and ethical reasons for caution.

Trades unions have shown growing concern but have demonstrated a realistic appreciation of the economic necessity for certain mergers. In some cases the short-term interests of their members has taken precedence over long-term security.

In practice, a wise manager will institute a plan which will allow for reasonable communication at both pre- and post-merger stages. The relevance of the information given must be judged from the local standpoint but sensibly should prevent employees, shareholders or public receiving, from a secondhand source, news which affects their lives and their security. Responsibility for the creation and implementation of such a plan of communication should rest with a member of the main board – it is assumed that an efficient company will place the personnel function at that level – and such a plan must cover personnel of both companies, at least at the post-merger stage.

MANAGEMENT AND MERGERS

During the implementation of mergers and acquisitions, problems are met and decisions taken which are often far more complex than most of those

MANAGING MERGERS AND ACQUISITIONS

ordinarily faced by management. Generally there is a lack of previous experience, training is minimal and few companies carry staff qualified to examine, analyse and carry out preliminary investigations, follow-up negotiations and further planning. The help of organizations with specialist skill is often desirable. Banking institutions, including merchant banks and finance houses, are prepared to put at disposal the services of their advisory departments, while certain firms of solicitors and accountants have a considerable background of experience. In some cases it may be helpful to bring in a firm of management consultants but care is required in the selection and definition of the assignment.

Throughout this chapter 'people' have figured prominently and emphasis has been placed on adequate communication and dissemination of information. A satisfactory operation depends on the participant people.

A merger is not merely the acquisition of the assets of another company. The board of the acquiring company has to assume fresh responsibilities as well as new relationships. Will the new team operate efficiently? Will personalities clash? Have they the intellectual capacity to manage a larger unit? Can they accept a more challenging role? These are just some of the questions which should be answered. It is in the board room that strains and tensions become dangerously acute and yet top management's ability to manage mergers is seldom questioned. Some critical reading of published case histories will demonstrate this fact.

Management at all levels is under strain during a merger activity and will come under unusual scrutiny. Their future should be adequately defined from the outset if full collaboration is to be achieved.

CHECKLIST

In conclusion the following checklist provides a reference point for the main considerations when contemplating merger or acquisition. They are not arranged in order of priority as this will depend on the requirements of each individual case.

- Clearly define the objectives
- Examine the alternatives
- Obtain board approval
- Decide how to make the initial approach
- Decide who to approach
- Develop a policy
- Initiate an investigation in depth into major shareholders, connections of officers and directors, financial obligations, capital requirements, production problems, distribution, management succession, labour relations and any other areas peculiar to the

case being considered
Negotiate and exchange preliminary information
Discuss terms
Prepare preliminary agreement
Communicate with auditors, legal advisers, financial advisers, management and staff, trades unions
Set time for completion
Ensure adequate management skills and resources
Initiate training programmes as required
Revise corporate plan and consider post-merger situation
At final agreement conduct a full investigation of the business to be acquired paying particular attention to the following:
- (a) review accounting procedures and reconcile differences in accounting policies and practices
- (b) examine commitments and liabilities (patents, warranties, retirement benefits etc.)
- (c) settle method of financing and tax implications
- (d) study all aspects of all salaried positions to eliminate inconsistencies in structure and policy of the acquirer
- (e) examine critically the new organization structure and in particular boardroom ability

FURTHER READING

P.F. Barrett, *Human Implications of Mergers and Takeovers*, Personnel Management, London.
M. Doctoroff, *Company Mergers and Takeovers*, Gower, 1972.
S. Ellon and T.R. Fowkes (eds), *Applications of Management Science in Banking and Finance*, Gower, 1972.
P.E. Hart, M.A. Utton and G.Walshe, *Mergers and Concentration in British Industry*, Cambridge University Press.
C.S. Jones, *Successful Management of Acquisitions*, Derek Beattie Publishing, 1982.
R. Jones and O. Marriott, *Anatomy of a Merger*, Pan, 1972.
N.R.A. Krekel, T.G. Van der Woerd and J.J. Wouterse, *Mergers—a European Approach to Technique*, Business Books, 1969.
C. Layton, *Cross Frontier Mergers in Europe*, University Press, 1971.
G. Morse (ed.), *Charlesworth and Cain—Company Law*, Stevens and Sons, 1983.
M.E. Porter, *Competitive Strategy*, Collier Macmillan, 1980.
M. Salter, *Diversification Through Acquisition*, Collier Macmillan, 1979.
I. Webb, *Management Buyout*, Gower, 1985.

Gower Handbook of Management, Gower, 2nd edition, 1988.
Management Buy-outs, A Guide, Daily Telegraph, 1982.

HMSO Publications:
City Code on Takeovers and Mergers, 1981.
Industry Act 1975, Part II.
Transfer of Undertakings (Protection of Employment) Regulations 1981.
Report of the Monopolies Commission.

Part Three
Commercial Functions

10

The Law of Contract

Alan Hobkirk

ESSENTIAL ELEMENTS OF A VALID CONTRACT

Six essential elements must be present in any valid contract: offer and unconditional acceptance, genuine agreement between the parties, intention to create legal relations, capacity of the parties, legality and possibility and consideration or form.

Offer

1. May be made to a definite person or a member of a group or even to the world at large
2. Must not be vague, for example, selling a car on 'usual hire purchase terms' was regarded by the court as being too vague in Scammel *v* Ouston (1941)
3. Must be distinguished from an invitation to treat, for example, goods displayed in shop windows
4. Must be communicated to the offeree
5. Must state all the terms of the offer
6. May be terminated at any time before it is accepted by revocation, lapse of time, death or rejection

Acceptance

1. Must be unconditional, otherwise it is regarded as a counter offer (Northland Airliners *v* Ferranti (1970))

2   Must be made within a reasonable or stipulated time
3   Silence cannot amount to acceptance; compare inertia selling methods and the case of Felthouse v Bindley (1982). Felthouse wrote to the owner of a horse, offering £30 for it and saying that if he did not hear from the owner within a day he would assume the horse was his. The owner did not reply to Felthouse but tried to halt the auctioning of the horse by Bindley who refused and sold it. Felthouse sued Bindley for conversion, that is denying his ownership of property. The court held that Felthouse never owned the horse because his offer had not been expressly accepted
4   Must be communicated to the offeror, although the following are exceptions to this general rule
    (a) Acceptance may be implied from conduct
    (b) Communication may be waived by offeror
    (c) Where an acceptance is made by post, the contract is regarded as being completed at the moment of posting, not at the time of receipt by the offeror. The so-called postal rules apply also to telegrams but not to telephones or telex

Genuine agreement between the parties

It is essential that there should be real consent to the contract by the parties to it otherwise there is no *consensus ad idem* or meeting of the minds. Factors such as mistake, fraud, misrepresentation, duress and undue influence may affect the genuineness of consent.

Mistake may involve the subject matter of the contract, the identity of the parties, the nature of the instrument. If the mistake is fundamental, the contract will normally be rendered void. This is a complex topic, however, and there is a great deal of case law involved.

Fraud, if proved, allows the injured party to avoid the contract with or without seeking damages.

Misrepresentation falls into two classes: fraudulent or innocent. Before the 1967 Misrepresentation Act it was more essential to distinguish between the two classes since the remedies available were quite distinct. The position regarding remedies is as follows:

Fraudulent misrepresentation. Here the aggrieved party may either avoid the contract with or without seeking damages or alternatively affirm the contract and seek damages or specific performance.

Innocent misrepresentation. The main remedy is to avoid the contract, but damages may now be awarded even after performance has taken place or after title in goods has passed — Misrepresentation Act 1967.

Misrepresentation and its remedies is another complicated subject and the above outline is only to be regarded as a broad simplification of the position. Duress has been defined as 'actual or threatened violence to or imprisonment of the party coerced' and, at common law, any contract induced by duress is voidable. Undue influence, on the other hand, has been defined as 'pressure on or coercion of a party to a contract, *not amounting* to duress, whereby he is precluded from the exercise of free judgement'. A contract which has been induced by indue influence is voidable at the court's discretion.

Intention to create legal relations

Albeit that an agreement may be in existence this will not be enforced by the courts unless it can be shown that the parties intended it to have a legal effect. There are two main presumptions as regards intention:

1. In domestic or social agreements the court usually decides that there was no intention to create legal relations
2. In business agreements the court presumes that there was such an intention although this presumption is rebutted by express provision such as that which appears on football coupons

Capacity of the parties

This topic is dealt with in more detail in the next section, but suffice it to say at this stage that before an agreement made with the intention of creating legally binding relations can be enforced, it is essential that the parties involved should have had proper capacity to contract.

Legality and possibility

At the time of its formation, it is fundamental that the contract should be capable of being performed; where reasonable to do so, however, future difficulties should be anticipated and provided for in the contract, for example the possibility of delay through labour difficulties — Davis Contractors v Fareham Urban District Council (1956). The contractors attempted to prove that their contract for building houses had been frustrated by bad weather and labour troubles, which had turned their quoted price into a loss, but they failed.

A contract which is illegal at formation is devoid of legal effect; where a contract is legal when made and subsequently becomes illegal because of a change in the law, such a contract will usually be discharged on the ground of frustration.

Contracts may be illegal because they are forbidden either by statute or by common law. Examples of contracts contrary to statute are:

1   Gaming and wagering contracts (various Acts from 1845 onwards)
2   Moneylenders Acts 1900 and 1927
3   Resale Prices Act 1964
4   Trading with the Enemy Act 1939

Examples of contracts contrary to common law are:

1   Contracts for an immoral purpose
2   Contracts interfering with the course of justice
3   Contracts in restraint of trade (see p.220)
4   Contracts to defraud the Revenue

Consideration or form

Apart from contracts incorporated in deeds conforming to certain formal requirements such as being signed, sealed and delivered, the general rule in English law is that unless something of value is given in exchange for a promise or undertaking, the promise cannot be enforced against the promisor. Consideration may be regarded, therefore, as the element of bargain in a contract and at its simplest involves a *quid pro quo*. The classic definition of consideration was given in the case of Currie *v* Misa (1875): '...some right, interest, profit or benefit accuring to the one party, or some forbearance, detriment, loss or responsibility, given, suffered or undertaken by the other'.

The following are some of the principal rules relating to consideration but it is stressed that many exceptions to these rules have arisen over the years as a result of case law decisions:

1   Every simple contract requires to be supported by consideration
2   The consideration must move from the person to whom the promise is made. This rule is to some extent connected with the doctrine of privity of contract which at its simplest means that only those who are parties to the contract acquire rights and obligations under it
3   The consideration must be something beyond the promisor's existing obligations to the promisee
4   The consideration must be legal
5   Consideration must not be past — this means that a promise made in return for some past benefit or service is usually unenforceable. Where it can be shown that services were rendered at the express or implied request of the promisor, however, the courts take the view that this is sufficient consideration to support a subsequent promise to pay. Also by the Bills of Exchange Act 1882 (*s*27), a bill of exchange can be supported by an antecedent debt
6   The consideration must be real but need not be adequate since it is up to the parties to make their own bargain

CONTRACTUAL CAPACITY

The principles relating to contractual capacity will be dealt with below as they affect various groups both of natural and artificial persons who suffer either limitation or impairment in their ability to enter into contractual relations. Particular emphasis will be placed on the position of companies.

Minors

Since the Family Law Reform Act 1969 the age of majority has been reduced from twenty-one to eighteen; anyone below eighteen is classified in English law as a minor. For their protection, minors have limited contractual capacity and although, as a general rule, they can enforce contracts against other people, they cannot have contracts enforced against them. To this general rule, however, there are certain exceptions and the following are examples of contracts which can be enforced against minors:

1   *Contracts for necessaries.* Defined by s2, Sale of Goods Act 1893, as 'goods suitable to the conditions in life of the minor and to his actual requirements at the time of sale and delivery'. The tests both of utility and relativity will usually be applied and, if the goods are deemed necessaries, the minor will be obliged to pay a reasonable price for them and not necessarily the contract price
2   *Contracts for the minor's benefit.* Educational, service or apprenticeship contracts, provided it can be shown that the fundamental purpose of such contracts is for the minor's ultimate benefit — Doyle v White City Stadium (1935)
3   *Voidable contracts.* These are contracts under which a minor usually acquired an interest of a permanent nature, for example acquisition of shares in a company. Unless the minor takes active steps to avoid such a contract during his minority or within a reasonable time of reaching his majority, such a contract will bind him — Steinberg v Scala Limited (1923)

By statute (Infants Relief Act 1874) certain contracts are void and cannot therefore be enforced against a minor. Void contracts include the following:

1   Contracts for the repayment of money lent or to be lent
2   Contracts for goods supplied or to be supplied, other than necessaries
3   All accounts stated — for example, IOUs

Mentally disordered persons

The general rule is that contracts made with persons of unsound mind are valid except in the following cases:

1   If the other contracting party is aware of the mental disability, the contract is voidable at the option of the mentally unsound person. The onus of proof lies with the person claiming insanity and he must prove both that his disability prevented him from understanding the consequences of the transaction and that the other party knew this
2   In cases where the property of the mentally ill person has been placed in the court's control under the Mental Health Act 1959, any contract involving disposal of the property does not bind the patient

Despite the two exceptions above, the effect of *s2* of the Sale of Goods Act 1893 should be noted as regards the supply of necessaries. Section 2 provides that 'where necessaries have been sold and delivered...to a person who by reason of mental incapacity...is incompetent to contract, he must pay a reasonable price therefor'.

Drunkards

Since it is not unknown for contracting parties to facilitate their negotiations by the administration of liberal doses of alcohol, the possible effect of such ministrations on the capacity to enter into binding contractual relations should be understood. The contract is voidable at the option of the party who was drunk if he can prove both that he was incapacitated temporarily through intoxication and also that the other party was aware of this.

The drunkard is liable, of course, if he ratifies the contract when he becomes sober. Again, under *s2* of the Sale of Goods Act 1893, a drunkard is liable to pay for necessaries.

Bankrupts

Although a bankrupt is not devoid of contractual capacity, certain limitations are imposed upon him under the Bankruptcy Act 1914. For instance, it is an offence for him while undischarged and without disclosing his position to obtain credit beyond £10 or to trade under a name different from that under which he was adjudged bankrupt.

In circumstances where, after formation of the contract, one of the parties to it becomes bankrupt, the rights and obligations under the contract pass to the trustee in bankruptcy who in certain circumstances may exercise his right of disclaimer and thereby abandon the contract.

Corporations

The contractual position of the following types of corporation aggregate requires to be considered.

Common law corporations. Such corporations are formed by the granting of a royal charter which sets out the objects. The better view appears to be that a contract with this type of corporation will be binding if it is unauthorized or even forbidden by its charter although in such cases the Attorney General is empowered to initiate proceedings for the revocation of the charter and a member can restrain such contracts by injunction.

Statutory corporations. These corporations are created by special Acts of Parliament which specify their powers. The *ultra vires* doctrine applies to this type of corporation and basically any contract entered into beyond the scope of the defined powers of the corporation will be void.

Registered companies

The contractual capacity of a limited company is governed by the contents of its memorandum of association and to a certain extent its articles of association. In this respect, UK law has been altered by entry into the EEC so as to make our law conform with Directive 151/1968. This is effected by the European Communities Act 1972 (*s*9). There are nine subsections and it is proposed to deal with each:

Section 9(1). To understand the provisions of the subsection it is necessary to examine the *ultra vires* doctrine and the rule in Royal British Bank *v* Turquand as applied up to 31 December 1972:

On the formation of a limited company two documents are necessary: the memorandum of association which is a document of external management and affects the relationship between the company and outsiders dealing with it, and the articles of association — a document of internal management affecting the company's relationship with its shareholders, directors and employees. Both these documents are a matter of public record, and knowledge of their contents is imputed to everyone. A company's capacity to contract is found in the objects clause of its memorandum of association. The objects clause specifies in detail the business that the company is empowered to carry on. There is very little scope for satisfactorily amending the objects clause once the company is incorporated (*s*5, Companies Act 1948). Further, because of the restrictive interpretation by the courts of the *ultra vires* doctrine, it has become the practice to draft the objects clause to provide for the widest possible area of operations. However, in view of the Court of Appeal's decision in Bell Houses Limited *v* City Wall Properties Limited (1966), the need for this practice is not now important so long as the objects clause contains a Bell Houses' type of 'sweeping up' object. Any contracts within these objects are said to be *intra vires* and valid, whereas contracts outside these objects are *ultra vires* and void. Either the company or an outside contracting party can plead that a contract is *ultra vires* and void.

Powers of directors or employees to contract on behalf of a company. A person negotiating with an outsider on behalf of a company is acting as agent for the company whatever his position inside the company. Assuming the contract to be within the powers of the company, the question is how far can the company deny liability if a director, manager or employee negotiates and completes a contract without authority. So far as the outsider is concerned — provided he does not know of the lack of authority — he is entitled to assume that a director, manager or chief officer has ostensible authority to do such acts as would normally be expected to be given to such agents...
Rule in Royal British Bank v Turquand (1856). Until recently a company's secretary was assumed not to have any ostensible authority to bind the company in contract. However, in Panorama Developments (Guildford) Limited *v* Fidelis Furnishing Fabrics Limited (1971) the Court of Appeal held that a company's secretary had ostensible authority to bind his company on contracts connected with the administrative side of the company affairs such as employing staff and ordering cars.

Section 9(1) provides as follows:

In favour of a person dealing with a company in good faith, any transaction decided on by the directors shall be deemed to be one which it is within the capacity of the company to enter into, and the power of the directors to bind the company, shall be deemed to be free of any limitation under the memorandum or articles of association; and a party to a transaction so decided on shall not be bound to enquire as to the capacity of the company to enter into it or as to any such limitation on the powers of the directors, and shall be presumed to have acted in good faith unless the contrary is proved.

From the wording of *s*9(1), it is clear that the effect of the *ultra vires* doctrine and the rule in the Royal British Bank case are modified, but only so far as they affect an outsider dealing with the company in good faith. Neither doctrine has been abolished. As between the company, its directors and shareholders, both doctrines still apply and one can envisage a case where, because of the acts of the directors, a company incurs liability to an outsider on an *ultra vires* contract, it can claim reimbursement from the defaulting directors personally for compelling it to act *ultra vires*. Directors ought to consider the inclusion of an indemnity clause in their contracts of service to exclude their personal liability in this respect.

The effect of *s*9(1) so far as the outsider is concerned can be summarized as follows:

1   Any lawful transaction decided by the directors will be deemed to be within the capacity of the company and within the ostensible authority

of the directors. It seems the outsider can plead *ultra vires*, but the company cannot
2   Although the memorandum and articles are public documents, the outsider is not bound by constructive notice of their contents — and he is not under obligation to find out the objects of the company
3   The outsider is only protected if he deals with the company in good faith. There is a rebuttable presumption that good faith exists and the onus is on the company to rebut it, e.g. by showing that the outsider had actual knowledge that the transaction was outside the scope of the objects of the company or outside the scope of the ostensible authority of the directors. This presumption will be difficult to rebut, as the outsider is expressly relieved of the obligation to inspect and therefore to investigate the capacity of the company or the authority of the directors. One possible way is to show that the outsider was put on inquiry by suspicious circumstances and deliberately refrained from inquiring
4   Even an express prohibition of activities in the memorandum or on the authority of directors in the articles will not exclude a company's liability under the section: '...and the power of directors to bind the company shall be deemed free of restrictions under the memorandum or articles'
5   The transaction must be decided upon by the directors collectively even though acted upon by one of them or by an executive of the company. It thus seems that *s*9(1) will afford no protection to an outsider if the transaction is dealt with by a manager, the secretary or director without the collective approval of the directors; in these cases the original *ultra vires* doctrines and the original rule in the Royal British Bank can still apply

Section 9(2). Again we must examine the law as it stood up to 31 December 1972. The general rule is that a company comes into existence as a legal entity on being incorporated and has no legal personality before incorporation. Therefore it could not enter into a pre-incorporation contract nor could it, after incorporation, ratify such a contract purported to be entered into on its behalf by the promoters or other persons. However, this rule created problems as to what rights or obligations, if any, such pre-incorporation contracts created and the parties that are bound by such contracts. In Newborne *v* Sensolid (Great Britain) Limited (1954), Mr Newborne signed a contract in the name of a company about to be incorporated, adding his name as a director under that of the company. It was held that neither company nor Mr Newborne could be bound by the contract and that it was in fact a nullity. However, in Kelner *v* Baxter (1867), the directors of a company about to be formed signed a contract in their own names 'as agents for' the company whose name was added after their signatures. In this case it was held that the directors were personally liable under the contract as principals. This unsatisfactory state of UK law has now been removed by $s9(2)$ which provides:

> Where a contract is purported to be made by a company or by a person as agent for a company, at a time when the company has not been formed, then subject to any agreement to the contrary, the contract shall have effect as a contract entered into by the person purporting to act for the company or as agent for it, and he shall be personally liable on the contract accordingly.

The effect of this provision is to abolish the decision in Newborne v Sensolid and to extend the decision in Kelner v Baxter to cover all pre-incorporation contracts by making the purported agent personally liable in all cases unless the contract provides to the contrary. However, it seems that the company still cannot ratify such contracts but obviously there is no objection, if it wishes, to the company entering into a new contract on the same terms.

Sections 9(3) and (4). Before the coming into force of these provisions, the Companies Act required the company to file certain documents or information at the Registry of Companies or maintain registers at its registered office containing information of certain of the matters dealt with in the provisions. In other cases the Companies Act required the Registrar of Companies to issue certificates to a company. The effect was to place the onus on an outsider to inquire at the registered office of the company or make search at the Companies Registry to ascertain that certain events had taken place, e.g. a company had been incorporated as a limited company, its memorandum or articles had been altered and so on. Section 9(3) now places a duty on the Registrar of Companies on the receipt or issue by him of certain documents to advertise notice of this fact (stating the name of the company, the description of the document and the date of receipt or issue of the document) in the *London Gazette* for English companies and the *Edinburgh Gazette* for Scottish companies. Such an advertised notice shall constitute 'official notification'. The documents set out in $s9(3)$ are as follows:

1   Any certificate of incorporation of a company
2   Any document making or evidencing an alteration in the memorandum or articles of association of a company
3   Any return relating to a company's register of directors or notification of a change among its directors
4   A company's annual return
5   Any notice of the situation of a company's registered office, or of any change therein
6   Any copy of a winding-up order in respect of a company

7   Any order for the dissolution of a company on a winding-up
8   Any return by a liquidator of the final meeting of a company on a winding-up

The significance of 'official notification' as defined in $s9(3)$ is that the company cannot rely against other persons on the happening of any of the events listed in $s9(4)$

> ...if the event had not been officially notified at the material time and is not shown by the company to have been known at that time to the person concerned or if the material time fell on or before 15 days after the date of official notification and it is shown that the person concerned was unavoidably prevented from knowing of the event at the time.

Consequently the company can only safely rely on the events listed in $s9(4)$ after the expiration of fifteen days of the notice in the *London Gazette*. The events listed in $s9(4)$ are as follows:

1   The making of a winding-up order in respect of the company, or the appointment of a liquidator in a voluntary winding-up of the company; or
2   Any alterations to the company's memorandum or articles of association; or
3   Any change among the company's directors; or
4   (As regards service of any documents on the company) any change in the situation of the company's registered office

Sections 9(5) and (6). The first affects statutory alterations to a company's memorandum and articles — as such statutory alterations are extremely rare it need not affect or concern most of the incorporated companies in the UK. In addition, a second part of the subsection makes available to the public an up-to-date copy of the company's memorandum and articles. Thus, where a company's memorandum or articles is altered after 1 January 1973 and the company is required by $s9$ of the European Communities Act, or otherwise, to file a copy of the document making the alteration, a printed copy of the memorandum or articles as altered must be filed at the same time, e.g. $s10$ of the Companies Act 1948 enables a company by special resolution to alter its articles and $s143$ of the same Act requires special resolutions to be filed within fifteen days of their being passed — such a resolution will be the 'document making or evidencing an alteration in the company's articles' ($s9(5)$) — and it must be filed together with a printed copy of the articles as altered. The provisions in $s9(5)$ do not apply to alterations to the objects clause in a memorandum, since $s5$ of the Companies Act 1948 already imposes on the company the duty of filing a copy of the memorandum as altered when the special resolution is passed to alter the objects clause. Whereas $s9(5)$ deals with alterations to the memorandum or articles made after 1 January 1973, $s9(6)$ provides *inter alia* that where an alteration had been made in a company's memorandum or articles in any manner before the coming into force of the subsection (i.e. before 1 January 1973), and a printed copy of the memorandum or articles as altered has not been sent to the Registrar of Companies, it shall be sent to him within one month after the enforcement of this subsection. This provision applies to all alterations made at any time since incorporation and affects a considerable number of companies both private and public which have made changes in their memorandum (e.g. in the capital clause) or articles since incorporation and have not previously been required to deliver a printed copy of the memoranda or articles as altered.

In default of compliance with $s9(5)$ and (6) the company and any responsible officer thereof will be liable to a fine.

Section 9(7). Under $s201$ Companies Act 1948, unless a company is exempted by the Department of Trade and Industry, it must show on its business letters, trade catalogues, circulars and showcards its directors' names and nationalities if not British — if any director is a corporation, the corporate name must be shown. Section $108(c)$ provides that every company must have its name mentioned with the word 'limited' as the last word of the name (unless exempted by Department of Trade and Industry) in all business letters, notices, official publications, cheques and various other documents or papers. In addition, $s9(7)$ European Communities Act now itemizes the following matters, details of which must appear in 'all business letters and order forms' of a company:

1 The place of registration of the company
2 The company's registered number
3 The address of its registered office
4 If exempt for the use of the word 'limited' in its name, the fact that it is a limited company
5 If, in a company having a share capital, its stationery carries reference to the amount of share capital, such reference must be to paid-up capital — not authorized or nominal share capital

Non-compliance renders the company and any of its officers authorizing the issue of stationery not complying, to a fine not exceeding £50 each.

Section 9(8). This extends the provisions of $s9$ to unregistered companies and certain unincorporated bodies entitled by letters patent to privileges under the Chartered Companies Act 1837.

REMEDIES FOR BREACH OF CONTRACT

The following are remedies which may be available in the event of a breach of contract:

1. An action for damages
2. A *quantum meruit* claim
3. An application to the court for a decree of specific performance
4. Application to the court for an injunction

Damages

An award of damages by the court is intended to be compensatory and not punitive. If a legal right has been infringed, therefore, yet no actual loss has resulted, the court will award nominal damages only. Furthermore, the injured party must take all reasonable steps to mitigate the extent of the damage and he will be unable to claim compensation for loss which is really due to his own failure to act in a reasonable manner after the occurrence of the breach.

Some limitation requires to be imposed on the extent of the defendant's liability for the losses occasioned by the breach and certain rules have evolved as regards remoteness of damage. These rules, which were stated in the leading case of Hadley *v* Baxendale (1854), are as follows. If the results of the breach were:

1. Such as could fairly and reasonably be considered to be the natural consequences of the breach
2. Such as could reasonably be supposed to have been in the contemplation of both parties at the time of the contract

then the resultant damage will be recoverable.

A distinction requires to be drawn between liquidated and unliquidated damages. In the former case, these are damages agreed upon by the parties at the time of entering into the contract. Only the fact that a breach has occurred need be proved and no proof of loss is required. Unliquidated damages are those which are awarded by the court in cases where no damages are provided for in the contract itself, and obviously proof of loss is required.

To be enforceable by the court, however, liquidated damages must be shown to be a genuine pre-estimate of loss and not a penalty inserted as a threat of punishment to follow in the event of a breach. If the court concludes that the prearranged sum is in fact a penalty, it will not be awarded but unliquidated damages based on normal principles will be awarded instead.

The following rules, which were established by the case of Dunlop Tyre Company Limited v New Garage Limited (1915), will normally be applied by the court to determine whether or not a penalty is involved:

1   The words used by the parties are not conclusive
2   The essence of a penalty is a payment which is stipulated *in terrorem* in an attempt to frighten the defaulter into carrying out his side of the bargain. The essence of liquidated damages is a genuine pre-estimate of the likely loss
3   If a single sum is payable as damages for any one of several breaches, varying in gravity, there is presumption that it is a penalty
4   If the sum involved is extravagant or unconscionable it is a penalty

Quantum meruit

The meaning of this expression is literally 'as much as has been earned', and a claim on this basis is for reasonable remuneration distinct from a claim for compensation for loss which would be the basis of an action for damages. The following are the circumstances where a *quantum meruit* claim would be appropriate:

1   Where work has been carried out under a contract which subsequently turns out to be void, as damages cannot be awarded for breach of a void contract
2   Where substantial performance of the contract has taken place
3   Where, although no agreement as to remuneration was made, there was an express or implied contract to render services
4   Where the original contract has been replaced by a new implied contract

The above information is of necessity very generalized since this particular remedy can be used both contractually and quasi-contractually, the latter being outside the scope of this chapter. At its simplest, a *quantum meruit* claim may offer an alternative course to a plaintiff in preference to an action for damages.

Specific performance

This is an equitable remedy which formerly was only available in the courts of equity but which is now available in any court. It is not available as of right and is awarded only at the discretion of the court.

The discretion exercised by the court is not an arbitrary one, however, and reliance will be made on the following established principles:

1   Action must commence within a reasonable time in accordance with the maxim 'delay defeats equity'

THE LAW OF CONTRACT

2 The plaintiff's conduct will also be considered by the court as 'he who comes to equity must come with clean hands'
3 A decree of specific performance will never be granted where damages would be an adequate and appropriate remedy
4 Where the contract is one for personal services, specific performance will not be awarded
5 If it is not possible for the court to supervise the contract, a decree for specific performance will not be granted — for example, the granting of such a decree is very rare in the case of building contracts
6 A promise unsupported by consideration and even if made under seal is not specifically enforceable
7 Where undue hardship would be caused to the defendant, specific performance will not be awarded
8 Where the contract is not binding on both parties — for example, infants' voidable contracts — specific performance will not be awarded

Injunction

Injunction is another equitable remedy which the court may award especially in cases where damages would neither be an adequate nor an appropriate remedy. Its application by the court is governed by the same guiding principles as outlined in the preceding paragraph. There are several forms of injunction: interlocutory, prohibitory, perpetual and mandatory. At its simplest, an injunction is a court order restraining either an actual or contemplated breach of the contract in question.

Limitation Act 1980

In conclusion, it should be noted that there are time-limits within which actions for breach of contract must be initiated. The time-limits are as follows:

Simple contracts. No action may commence after the expiration of six years from the date on which the cause of action accrued.

Specialty contracts. An action cannot be commenced after the expiration of twelve years from the date on which the cause of action accrued. A specialty contract is one made under seal.

TRANSFER OF OWNERSHIP AND RESPONSIBILITY FOR ACCIDENTAL LOSS OR DAMAGE

The underlying purpose of a contract of sale of goods is of course the transfer of the ownership of the goods from seller to buyer. The legal distinction between possession and ownership must be kept in mind — although one of the parties to the contract may have physical possession of the goods, this does not necessarily mean that he is the legal owner. The Sale of Goods Act 1979 sets out various rules regarding the transfer of ownership of the goods and these will be examined later. The reason it is important to know the precise moment of time at which the ownership of the goods passes from seller to buyer is that (a) if the goods are accidentally destroyed, it is essential to know which party has to bear the loss, and (b) in the case of bankruptcy of either party or liquidation of a limited company it is necessary to know whether the goods belong to the trustee or liquidator or not.

The rules governing the transfer of ownership depend on whether the goods are unascertained or specific. Section 16 (Sales of Goods Act 1979) provides that unless and until the goods are ascertained then no transfer of ownership is made to the buyer. Section 17, dealing with specific goods, states that the transfer of ownership will take place at such time as the parties intend it to take place. The parties' intention may be determined from the terms of the contract itself or from the conduct of the parties but recognizing that in many cases such intention will not readily be determinable, the Act in s18 specifies the following rules for ascertaining when ownership is transferred, unless a contrary intention appears:

1   In unconditional contracts for the sale of specific goods in a deliverable state, the ownership is transferred when the contract is made, irrespective of the date of payment or delivery
2   Where sales of specific goods are involved and the seller is bound to do something to the goods to put them into a deliverable state, the ownership does not pass until such thing is done and the buyer has notice of it
3   In sales of specific goods in a deliverable state, where the seller is bound to weigh, measure, test or do some other act or thing with reference to the goods for the purpose of ascertaining the price, transfer of ownership does not take place until such thing is done and the buyer has notice thereof
4   Where goods are delivered to the buyer on 'approval' or on 'sale or return', or other similar terms, the transfer of ownership take place
    (a)   When the buyer signifies his approval or acceptance to the seller or does any other act adopting the transaction
    (b)   If the buyer does not signify his approval or acceptance but retains the goods without giving notice of rejection, then, if a time has been fixed for the return of the goods, on the expiration of such time, and if no time has been fixed, on the expiration of a reasonable time. What is a reasonable time is open to interpretation
5   (a)   Where there is a contract for the sale of unascertained or future goods by description, and goods of that description and in a deliverable state are unconditionally appropriated to the contract, the ownership of

the goods thereupon transfers to the buyer. The consent may be express or implied and can be given either before or after the appropriation

(b) Where, in pursuance of the contract, the seller delivers the goods to the buyer or to a carrier or other bailee or custodian — for example, warehouse owner — whether named by the buyer or not, for the purpose of transmission to the buyer, and does not reserve the right of disposal, he is deemed to have unconditionally appropriated the goods to the contract

Apart from the above rules, the effect of s20 should be noted since it provides that, unless otherwise agreed, the goods remain at the seller's risk until ownership has been transferred to the buyer and furthermore where such transfer does take place, the goods are at the buyer's risk, whether delivery has been made or not. There are two provisos to s20:

1 Where delivery has been delayed by the fault of either buyer or seller the goods are at the risk of the party in default as regards any loss which might not have occurred but for such fault
2 Nothing in the section is to affect the duties or liabilities of either seller or buyer as a bailee or custodian of the goods of the other party. In other words, irrespective of fault, the party who has physical possession of the goods must exercise due care of them

Although the general rule as provided by s20 Sale of Goods Act 1979 is that the risk of accidental loss follows ownership, this is not the case if cif (cost, insurance, freight) contracts where once the goods are delivered to the ship, the risk of loss passes to the buyer. So far as Fob (free on board) contracts are concerned it is usual that once the goods are shipped the ownership and risk passes to the buyer. The effect of the decision of the Court of Appeal in Aluminium Industrie B.V. v Romalpa Ltd [1976] 1 W.L.R. 676, should be noted because of its effect on the reservation of title. The brief facts of the case were that a Dutch company (Aluminium Industrie) sold a consignment of aluminium foil to an English company (Romalpa Ltd), the sale being subject to the Dutch company's conditions of sale one of which was that 'ownership of the material to be delivered will only be transferred to the purchaser when he has got all that is owing to the vendor'. Having taken delivery of a consignment of foil and having sub-sold part of the consignment, Romalpa went into liquidation. The Dutch supplier, who had not been paid, sought to enforce the conditions of sale so as to secure payment prior to distribution of Romalpa's assets to the general creditors. The Court of Appeal ruled that Aluminium Industrie was entitled to:

1 Recover all the unsold foil
2 Trace and recover the proceeds of any sub-sale by Romalpa and in this respect take priority over all other claims

CONTRACTS IN RESTRAINT OF TRADE

At its simplest, a contract in restraint of trade is one in which a person's freedom of action to carry on business or to be employed is restricted. Such contracts may be classified under three distinct heads:

1. Agreements whereby the vendor of a business undertakes not to set up in competition with the purchaser
2. Agreements in contracts of employment which restrict the freedom of movement of the employee after leaving his employer's service
3. Agreements regulating trade and involving restrictive practice

Before considering in more detail the three groups of restrictive agreement outlined above, we must mention the following general rules which apply to all types of restrictive agreement:

At common law, every agreement in restraint of trade is *prima facie* illegal and void.

Despite the initial presumption against validity, however, the court will look into the question of reasonableness and will apply two major tests: (*a*) is it reasonable between the parties to it, and (*b*) is it reasonable from the point of view of the public interest? In the cases of agreements classified under (1) and (2) above, the question of extent — both of time and of geographical area — will be taken into consideration. The person seeking to enforce the agreement will also be required to show that he has given valuable consideration for the promise which he seeks to enforce, even if the contract is under seal.

Agreements in connection with sales of business

Since the purchase price of the business normally includes a substantial sum in respect of goodwill, the court tends to enforce those agreements which are intended primarily to protect a proprietary interest. The question of reasonableness is fundamental and, provided the agreement is no wider than is reasonably necessary to protect the interest, is not against the public interest and is not unreasonably restrictive as regards the party involved, it will be enforceable.

Agreements imposing restraints on employees

The court is usually very reluctant to enforce this type of restrictive covenant and the tests of reasonableness which will be applied are normally much stricter than those involved in agreements between vendors and purchasers of businesses. It is clearly established that a covenant which is concerned primarily with restricting competition after the employee has left his employer's service will be void. Factors such as the type of employment, the area of restraint, the period of the restriction, will all be taken into account by the court. Furthermore the court will normally require to be satisfied that the employee has received some valuable consideration in return for his undertaking to be restricted.

Agreements involving the regulation of trade

Fundamentally, these are agreements between manufacturers and suppliers relating to the conditions under which they will produce, market or fix the price of goods. Unlike the other forms of contracts in restraint of trade, this particular category is very much subject to statutory regulation, in particular the Restrictive Trade Practices Act 1956 and the Resale Prices Act 1964.

In broad terms, the 1956 Act covers agreements under which producers, suppliers or exporters of goods restrict the manufacture, supply or distribution of these goods by means of collective agreements. Unless such agreements are registered with the Registrar of Restrictive Trading Agreements, they will be void. After registration, the Restrictive Practices Court will then consider the validity or otherwise of the agreement.

The Resale Prices Act 1964 prohibits resale price maintenance except where it can be shown to be in the public interest.

Since 1973, restrictive trading agreements come within the province of the Director of Fair Trading and reference should be made to Chapter 14.

SUPPLY OF GOODS (IMPLIED TERMS) ACT 1973

General observation

This Act amends, in certain respects, the Sale of Goods Act 1973. In particular it specifies a number of conditions which will be implied in every so-called consumer contract for the sale of goods. In commercial and non-consumer type contracts, it is still permissible for the implied conditions established by the Act or arising through implication, to be excluded but the exclusion will only be valid if the courts decide that it is fair and reasonable to exclude them.

In deciding whether it is fair and reasonable to exclude the implied conditions regard must be paid to all the circumstances and in particular the following matters:

1 The strength of the bargaining positions of the parties, taking into account suitable alternative products and sources of supply
2 Whether the buyer received an inducement to agree to the exclusion terms

3   Whether the buyer knew or ought to have known of the existence and extent of the exclusion term
4   Whether the exclusion arises from the non-performance of some condition
5   Whether it is reasonable to expect that compliance with the condition would be practicable
6   Whether the goods were manufactured, processed or adapted to the special order of the buyer

Consumer sale is defined as 'A sale of goods (other than a sale by auction or by competitive tender) by a seller in the course of a business where the goods:

1   Are of a type ordinarily bought for private use or consumption and
2   Are sold to a person who does not buy or hold himself out as buying them in the course of business'

Section 13: Sale by description. Where there is a contract for the sale of goods by description there is an implied condition that the goods shall correspond with the description.

Note: The expression 'sale by description' includes all goods whether seen by the buyer or not if he is purchasing an article corresponding to a general description and not a particular one — Beale *v* Taylor.

Description also includes such matters as measuring or method of packing. Re: Moore & Co. Ltd *v* Landauer & Co.
   The section is now augmented by the amending Act providing that 'a sale of goods shall not be prevented from being a sale by description by reason only that being exposed for sale or hire, they are selected by the buyer'.

Section 14(i): Fitness for a purpose. Where the buyer, expressly or by implication, makes known to the seller the particular purpose for which the goods are required, so as to show that the buyer relies on the seller's skill and judgement, and the goods are of a description which it is in the course of the seller's business to supply (whether he is the manufacture or not) there is an implied condition that the goods shall be reasonably fit for such purpose.

Notes: (i)   The 1973 Act includes the condition where 'the circumstances show that the buyer does not rely, or that it is undesirable for him to rely on the seller's skill or judgement'
         (ii) It is no defence to the seller that no ordinary skill and care could have detected the defect — Frost *v* Aylesbury Dairy Co.
         (iii) It is not necessary to rely exclusively on the seller's skill for the

condition to be implied — Cammell Laird & Co. Ltd v Manganese Bronze Co. Ltd

(iv) If both parties contemplated that something is to be done to the goods before use then no implied condition would arise until the thing is done to the goods — Contrast Heil v Hedges with Grant v Australian Knitting Mills Ltd

Section 14(ii): Merchantable quality. Where the goods are bought from a seller who deals in goods of that description (whether a manufacturer or not) there is an implied condition that the goods shall be of merchantable quality. The implied condition does not apply as regards defects brought to the attention of the buyer prior to the contract or where the buyer has examined the goods, as regards defects which such examination ought to reveal.

Notes: (i) Goods are merchantable even though they prove illegal to sell where it is known that the goods are required to be resold — Summer Permain & Co. v Webb & Co.

(ii) The 1973 Act defines merchantable quality as follows: 'Goods of any kind are of merchantable quality... if they are as fit for the purpose or purposes for which goods of that kind are commonly bought as it is reasonable to expect having regard to any description applied to them, the price (if relvant) and all other relevant circumstances'

N.B. The effect of the 1973 Supply of Goods (Implied Terms) Act on guarantees applying to consumer-type contracts is as follows:

1 The seller is always liable for:
   (a) the quality of the product when it is sold
   (b) its fitness for the purpose agreed at the time of sale
   (c) the accuracy of its description
2 If due to an inherent defect, the product fails, it must be replaced or repaired free of charge by the seller and a temporary replacement provided if necessary
3 The seller may be liable for consequential loss if a fault in the product results in damage to the buyer and/or his property
4 The buyer has a right to bring a claim against the seller at any time up to six years from the date of purchase of the product. In a dispute it will be for the courts to decide how long a component or product ought to last
5 The *manufacturer* may offer extra benefits but he cannot alter the buyer's rights against the seller
6 The seller is not normally liable for faults which should have been noticed by the buyer before the purchase was made

UNFAIR CONTRACT TERMS ACT 1977

General observation

This Act makes fundamental and far-reaching changes to the law of contract and tort. Virtually all types of contract are affected including sale of goods, hire-purchase, hire, services, work and labour, manufacturers' guarantees, building contracts etc. It applies not only as between business and consumer but also as between business and business. It deals not only with exemption clauses but also with any clause whereby a party seeks to limit or avoid liability for non-performance.

1. The Act does not apply to contracts relating to:
    Insurance
    Land
    Patents, trade marks, copyright or other intellectual property
    Formation of companies
    Securities
    Carriage of goods by sea except in favour of a consumer
    Employment
2. The Act applies to *business liability:* as against a party dealing in the course of a business or from the occupation of premises used for business purposes — it is immaterial whether the breach is inadvertent or intentional or whether liability arises directly or vicariously. Further the liability is not affected by the other party agreeing to an exclusion term or notice
3. As regards contracts for sale of goods the test of reasonableness referred to herein is as stated in the Supply of Goods (Implied Terms) Act 1973. As regards all other contracts the test of reasonableness is that 'the term shall have been a fair and reasonable one to be included having regard to the circumstances which were or ought reasonably to have been, known to or in the contemplation of the parties when the contract was made'

Subject to the above the Act imposes liability as follows:

A   *In all contracts* (sale of goods or services)

   1. No exclusion or restriction by term or notice of liability for death or personal injury resulting from negligence
   2. Exclusion or restriction of liability for other loss or damage is permitted subject to the reasonable test

THE LAW OF CONTRACT

B   *Contracts for services*

    1   Consumer contracts or where one party is dealing on the other's written standard terms of business
        (*a*)   no exclusion for breach of contract
        (*b*)   no claim for loss or non-performance except in so far as the term satisfies the reasonable test
    2   In consumer contracts consumer cannot be made to indemnify another person in respect of liability of the other person for negligence or breach except in so far as the term satisfies the reasonable test

C   *Contracts for sale of goods*

    1   Consumer contracts: manufacturers' or distributors' negligence for defective goods resulting in loss or damage cannot be excluded by reference to a guarantee of the goods
    2   Exclusion of implied terms in sale of goods as in Supply of Goods (Implied Terms) Act 1973

D   *Contracts for services where ownership of goods pass*

    1   Consumer contracts: no exclusion of implied terms in sale of goods — as in 1973 Act
    2   Non-consumer contracts: exclusion or restriction subject to reasonable test — as in 1973 Act

E   *International goods contracts:*   Act does not apply even where, by the parties' choice, the proper law of the contract is English Law

SUPPLY OF GOODS AND SERVICES ACT 1983

The broad effect of this Act was to codify all existing common-law rights regarding contracts for the supply of a service and to give statutory authority to the rights of the consumer by implying the following terms into every contract for the supply of a service:

(*a*)   that the service will be carried out with reasonable care and skill
(*b*)   that the service will be carried out at a reasonable price unless a price has already been agreed and
(*c*)   that the service will be carried out within a reasonable time unless the time has already been agreed by the parties

Since the passing of the Act the law relating to the supply of goods and services has been placed on a similar footing to the law affecting the sale of goods.

FURTHER READING

A.H. Boulton, *The Making of Business Contracts,* Sweet and Maxwell, London, 1972.
R. Brazier, *Cases and Statutes on Contract,* Sweet and Maxwell, London, 1983.
Charlesworth, *Mercantile Law,* Sweet and Maxwell, London, 1984.
Cheshire and Fifoot, *Law of Contract,* Butterworths, London, 1984.
Smith and Keenan, *Mercantile Law,* Pitman, London, 1982.
J. Tillotson, *Contract Law in Perspective,* Butterworths, London, 1985.
Law of Contract, Financial Training Publications, London, 1985.

11

Negotiation

P D V Marsh

Negotiation is a dynamic process by which two parties, each with their own objectives, confer together to reach a mutually satisfying agreement on a matter of common interest. It demands careful planning and skilful tactics so that each party may extract maximum benefit from the terms of the agreement.

NATURE OF THE NEGOTIATING PROCESS

There are four essential elements of the negotiating process:

1 The process of negotiation takes place within a defined time-scale which will impose limitations on the objectives of the negotiators. This time-scale may extend to include the next occasion on which the parties contemplate doing business
2 Each party will have its own objectives which it must strive to achieve
3 The parties must be motivated towards reaching agreement which is recognized by both as mutually satisfying their essential needs: imposition by the stronger of his will on the weaker, regardless of the latter's interest, is not negotiation
4 The end-product of the negotiation is a matter of common interest: this could be the construction of a new factory, or, in a labour negotiation, the continued existence of the firm as providing a source of worthwhile employment to its employees and of profit to its shareholders

Distributive and integrative bargaining

Distributive bargaining refers to the process in which two parties bargain over the allocation between them of a fixed resource. Their interests are in total conflict since the gain to one is a loss to the other. Bargaining between employer and union over a simple pay increase with no productivity strings attached, or between buyer and seller on the price of an article, are examples of this type of bargaining.

Integrative bargaining describes the situation in which, through a joint exercise by the parties, a solution can be found to a problem which provides both with some benefit.

An example of such a bargaining situation was where a union and management were in dispute because few long-service employees were being promoted. The union proposed that long service be given greater weight in judging promotion suitability; the company stated that it could judge promotion suitability only on the grounds of ability and skill. The solution found was for the company to institute a scheme for helping long-service employees to obtain the necessary skills through further education. Both sides achieved their objective. The union obtained better promotion opportunities for their members; management retained the prerogative of determining the criteria for promotion decisions.

Negotiation as a matter of progressive commitment

Negotiation is an exercise in progressive commitment. As the negotiation proceeds, both parties will leave their initial positions and move towards each other so that, with each move made, the area remaining for further movement is automatically reduced. Only exceptionally will a negotiator be able to increase his area of movement by withdrawing from a position previously conceded, while at the same time retaining his integrity. No position should therefore be established or movement made until the degree to which the company is willing to be committed has been determined.

This would apply, for instance, where a firm is asked to give a budgetary quotation. Whatever figure is put forward will in practice represent the maximum price the firm will be able to obtain. The buyer will only expect the price to move one way from the budgetary figure — and that is downwards.

PLANNING THE NEGOTIATION

Value and scope of planning

Success in negotiation depends primarily on the skill and care with which the negotiating plan has been prepared. Tactics at the negotiating table can help but they too need to be planned in advance. Planning should commence before any offer is made, or responded to, and continue the whole way through the negotiation until final agreement is reached and recorded.

Time must be found at each stage of the negotiating process for the planning effort which is required. Planning involves:

Content — what the negotiation is about, the issues which have to be dealt with and their relationship one to another

The governing rules — the applicable law and the regulations to which both sides are subject

The personalities of the negotiators, their respective attitudes and social pressures to which each will have to conform

Power — where this lies

Time — the time which is available for the negotiation, including any artificial time constraints which either side may seek to impose

Resources both in terms of people, expertise and money which each side is able and willing to devote to the negotiation

Selection of the objective

The starting point for the preparation of any negotiating plan should be an explicit statement of the target objective. Vague generalizations should not be accepted. The objective should be quantified as for example

> Our gross margin after an allowance for contingencies of 5 per cent and based on recovery of full shop costs and overheads should not be less than 30 per cent

The next step is the analysis of the target objective in relation to the three critical factors which will affect is achievement:

1   Strength of negotiating position
2   Competing objectives of other projects
3   Resource requirement and availability

These three factors within the time-scale for an individual negotiation have a single total value so that an increase in the value of one can be secured only at the expense of a decrease in the value of one or both of the others. Negotiating strength can be increased if all competing objectives are abandoned and the whole resources available are concentrated on the one project. Equally, if the resources required are greater than those which can be made available without interfering with other projects, then either a reduction in negotiating strength must be accepted or one or more competing objectives abandoned. What should never be allowed to happen is that the available resources are spread across so wide a range of objectives that the negotiating strength on each is reduced to the point at which success is achieved on none.

Assessment of the negotiating position

Three typical negotiating situations will be discussed:

1 Bid submission
2 Procurement
3 Dispute

The factors which will primarily influence the company's negotiating position in each situation and which need to be considered in preparing the negotiating plan are as follows:

Bid submission
1 Probability of the company being successful
2 Desirability of the company securing the business
3 Resources required both for bidding and contract execution
4 Alternative opportunities open to the company for the employment of its resources

Clearly factors 1 and 2 are interrelated. Thus the company might increase its success probability by taking a lower margin or shortening the delivery, but either of these steps would lead to a reduction in bid desirability since the profit would be less and the risk of penalty greater.

A simple method of presenting the negotiating position to management would be to require the sales department to prepare a quantified assessment of both the success probability and the bid desirability and by taking the product of these two figures arrive at an expected value of the bid. This expected value could then be compared with the norm established by the company for the product line in question.

Two other propositions are put forward:

1 If the bid desirability as a percentage is below some guideline figure established by management then no tender should be submitted, irrespective of success probability
2 If the business desirability is positive then the extent of resource employment which is justified is related directly to the expected value of the bid. The employment of additional resources because the expected value is high is valid only to the extent that these increase proportionately the success probability

Procurement. Three basic procurement situations exist:

1 Continued demand by two or more buyers which is large enough to stimulate competition and maintain two or more suppliers in the market. this may be further subdivided into situations where:
   (*a*)   one major buyer predominates
   (*b*)   no single buyer predominates
2 Continued demand by a single buyer large enough to stimulate competition and maintain two or more suppliers in the market
3 Demand insufficient to maintain more than one supplier in the market or one supplier has established a monopoly

Within the framework of these three basic situations, the buyer can improve or worsen his own negotiating position according to the manner in which he specifies his requirements.

In cases 1(*a*) and 2, the specification is set by the buyer and the suppliers have no alternative if they wish to stay in business but to respond. The buyer should therefore draft his inquiry in such a way that it can be responded to by the maximum number of qualified firms at the minimum economic price level. Reduction in competitiveness will arise if the buyer specifies higher technical standards than are really needed or imposes technical or commercial conditions which can be met only by a limited number of firms.

In the other two cases, the buyer does not possess the negotiating advantage. In 1(*b*), he must accept the specification standards generally prevailing in the industry or else pay a much higher price for a special whatever the total value of his purchasing bill. Again in 3, it is often the buyer himself who contributes towards the monopolistic nature of the supply position, by the detailed descriptive manner in which he defines the item or service required. If he would limit himself to describing the service or function which he wishes to have performed then he would widen the competitive field.

Dispute. There are four elements to the power relationship between the parties. A detailed checklist is given on p.248-50.

Legal. Who has the stronger case and is in a position to go to law?

Financial. Has the client got the money — how long can the contractor afford to wait — how important is the money to either side?

Commercial. Does the client need the contractor in the future because he possesses specialist skills or knowledge of the client's business — does the contractor similarly need the client because he represents a significant portion of the contractor's business which the contractor, at least in the short term, would find it difficult to replace?

Political. Does the contractor possess influence in the client's organization or outside — can he use publicity to his advantage?

It must be remembered that power is the ability of the negotiator to influence the behaviour of others. It involves therefore both the negotiator's own knowledge that he possesses certain power and the other side's perception of this. It is not sufficient for the negotiator to look at the case only from his own viewpoint. The question must be asked both ways around. How does the other perceive your power; how do you perceive his power and how does he perceive it himself? Very often as a negotiator one can become worried over weaknesses in one's own case which arise from knowledge not in the other side's possession. Provided that the negotiator is satisfied that the other has not perceived that weakness then he is in a position to act as if it did not exist. Equally as a negotiator it is no use possessing power which is not appreciated by the other side. Therefore part of one's approach to the negotiation will be at the appropriate moment to reveal the existence of that power factor.

The effect of time. How quickly is a settlement required? The less time that the negotiator can afford to wait the weaker is his position. Time spent in actual negotiations costs money both directly on expenses and indirectly because of the resources involved which cannot be used profitably in other directions. Also the value of any settlement delayed a significant period of time must be discounted back to the point in time at which agreement on those terms or similar could have been reached. It will often be found that the additional face value of the agreement reached at a later date is in real terms worth less than that which could have been achieved much earlier.

The availability of resources. Does the party have the necessary resources in-house or must he engage outside assistance, e.g. lawyers or expert witnesses? It all costs money. Can the party afford to have his own people involved in negotiation or worse in arbitration, instead of getting on with earning profits? Are the people still around with firsthand knowledge of what actually happened? Are there in existence adequate records of what occurred which were made at the time? The strength or weakness of both people and records as witnesses subject to hostile cross examination must be considered.

Choice of negotiating strategy

The two basic negotiating strategies which a party can employ are quick kill and hold back.

Quick kill is the strategy of selecting an offer which the recipient will accept without further negotiation or of responding to an offer by accepting it without bargaining.

Hold back is the strategy of selecting an offer which is sufficiently attractive to the recipient that he will not reject it out of hand, but which at the same time contains a margin for negotiation which is adequate:

1   To enable the party submitting the offer to meet the recipient's anticipated demands
2   To ensure that at the end of the negotiation the party submitting the offer obtains a return which he considers to be adequate

To the recipient, it is the strategy of bargaining with the party or parties submitting offers until terms are secured which the recipient considers to be the most advantageous he can obtain.

Strategy selection for bid submission and procurement. The parties will be in one of the three negotiating states relative to each other:

Party	*Opponent*
Domination	Subordination
Subordination	Domination
Uncertainty	Uncertainty

Domination. This exists:

1   For the seller, if the buyer must so far prefer some feature in the seller's offer that this preference outweighs any advantages which are possessed by the competing offers and this is known to the seller
2   For the buyer, if he knows for certain he will obtain at least two genuinely competing offers either of which would be acceptable to him and this is known to the sellers

The correct strategy for the party to select if he is dominant is quick kill.

Subordination. Subordination exists if the strategy of the person submitting the offer must be that which is dictated by the wishes of the recipient. Two basic examples would be:

1   Tendering to a strict public authority which is debarred by its own rules from post-tender negotiation. The bidder must adopt quick kill
2   Tendering to a purchaser who is known to bargain whatever offer is submitted to him. The bidder in this event must select hold back

Uncertainty. In many negotiating situations neither party will possess enough knowledge to be certain of the competitive situation or the other's intentions. In a state of uncertainty which strategy should each party select?

This position can be represented in a game-theory type matrix as set out in Figure 11.1.

In this matrix the expected value to the seller of the outcome of each combination of his strategy with that of the buyer is determined in accordance with the following equation: EV = Conditional value of strategy if successful × probability of success + conditional value of strategy unsuccessful × (1 — success probability)

		BUYERS' STRATEGIES	
		Quick kill b_1	Hold back b_2
SUPPLIERS' STRATEGIES	Quick kill a_1	$\left.\begin{array}{l}4 \times 0.7 \\ -1 \times 0.3\end{array}\right\}$ 2.5	$\left.\begin{array}{l}4 \times 0.2 \\ -1 \times 0.8\end{array}\right\}$ 0
	Hold back a_2	$\left.\begin{array}{l}6 \times 0.2 \\ -1 \times 0.8\end{array}\right\}$ 0.4	$\left.\begin{array}{l}5 \times 0.7 \\ -1 \times 0.3\end{array}\right\}$ 3.2

Figure 11.1 Strategy selection for bid submission

The values shown are based on the following assumptions:

1 Normal profit margin is £4000. To this is added £2000 as negotiating margin when hold-back strategy is employed
2 Variable tendering costs which would be lost if bid not successful: £1000
3 In $a_1 b_2$ the supplier does not reduce his price, therefore there is a high probability that he will lose the bid
4 In $a_2 b_1$ he has a lower probability of success due to the addition of the negotiation margin
5 In $a_2 b_2$ the success probability of 70 per cent is based on the supplier conceding 50 per cent of his negotiating margin

The seller will select hold back since the expected value of the hold-back strategy is £3600 as compared with £2500 for the quick kill, and hold back maximizes his security against either strategy used by the buyer.

A similar analysis can be prepared for the buyer as shown in Figure 11.2. The buyer estimates the price at which he will have to purchase for each alternative and in the absence of any better information thinks it equally likely that all or a majority of suppliers will adopt a quick kill or hold-back strategy. It is obvious that again the buyer will select hold back.

In a state of uncertainty, therefore, the strategy of both parties should be hold back. Outcome $a_1 b_1$ will *not* be reached by both parties acting

		SUPPLIERS' STRATEGIES	
		Quick kill b_1	Hold back b_2
BUYERS' STRATEGIES	Quick a_1 kill	$40 \times 0.5 = 20$	$42 \times 0.5 = 21$
	Hold a_2 back	$38 \times 0.5 = 19$	$41 \times 0.5 = 20.5$

Figure 11.2 Strategy selection for bid procurement

independently of one another, but only if there is cooperation between them to the extent that both have complete confidence in the strategy which will be selected by the other, so that the situation is no longer one of uncertainty.

Strategy selection for a dispute. Experimental evidence supports the view that within reason the higher the opening offer of the party submitting the claim the better the bargain they will eventually obtain (unless the negotiation finishes in deadlock). But the party must be prepared, in so doing, for a long battle since having pitched his initial demand high he must then concede slowly in order to retain his credibility. It follows that he must be able to absorb the adverse effects of the time costs and discount factor involved, and that the combined effect of these will not be sufficient to offset the nominal extra value of the settlement finally reached. Provided that these conditions can be met then the strategy should be hold back.

An additional reason for selecting hold back would be if the negotiator were concerned that by going for quick kill the negotiators for the other side would be prevented from being seen by their colleagues, or union membership, to have done their job of securing concessions and would accordingly turn hostile or resentful and break off the negotiations, so in an industrial relations situation precipitating a strike.

NEGOTIATING AREA AND THE INFLUENCE OF TIME

Identification of the negotiating area and resistance points

The level of the first offer to the party who submits it is critical in that it establishes the maximum benefit which that party will derive from the negotiation on the assumption that the recipient of the offer behaves rationally and does not make a mistake.

If the negotiating strategy of the party making the offer is quick kill then the initial offer should be put forward at a level which maximizes that party's expected value.

Assume that a union negotiator was putting forward a proposal for an increase in the basic wage rate which is at present £150 per week. He estimates the minimum demand likely to be just acceptable to his members as £8.00 and the maximum he could possibly hope to obtain would be £15.00. The curve of his utility function against possible increases could be of the shape shown in Figure 11.3.

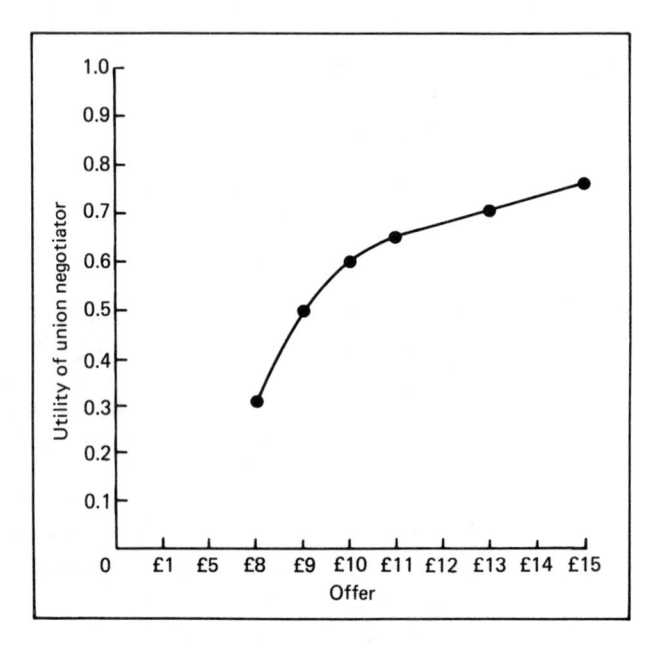

Figure 11.3 Utility function of union negotiator

Increments up to £8.00 are valued very positively; increments over that and up to £9.00 are still valued positively but of rather less importance; over £10.00 each marginal increase becomes of less and less significance. Assume that a strike would have a disutility cost of 3 against the above scale and the negotiator subjectively assesses the probabilities of a series of offers as in Figure 11.4. The final column in the table shows the expected value of each offer to the union negotiator.

If the union leader was bidding on a final-offer-first basis then he would select a bid at £9.00.

If, however, he were expecting to bargain then he would use the above table to establish both his target objective and his points of resistance. Realistically on the above scale these would be:

NEGOTIATION

OFFER	UTILITY	PROBABILITY OF ACCEPTANCE	DISUTILITY COSTS	PROBABILITY OF REJECTION	EXPECTED VALUE
£ 8.00	3	0.9	−3	0.1	2.4
£ 9.00	5	0.8	−3	0.2	3.4
£10.00	6	0.7	−3	0.3	3.3
£11.00	6.5	0.5	−3	0.5	1.75
£13.00	7	0.2	−3	0.8	−1.0
£15.00	7.5	0.1	−3	0.9	−1.95

Figure 11.4 Expected values of offers to union negotiator

Target	£13.00
First resistance point	£10.00
Final resistance point	£8.00

Assuming now the company negotiators similarly assessed their position and came up with the following:

Company preferred level	£9.00
Company maximum acceptable level	£11.00

The negotiating area could then be represented as shown in Figure 11.5.

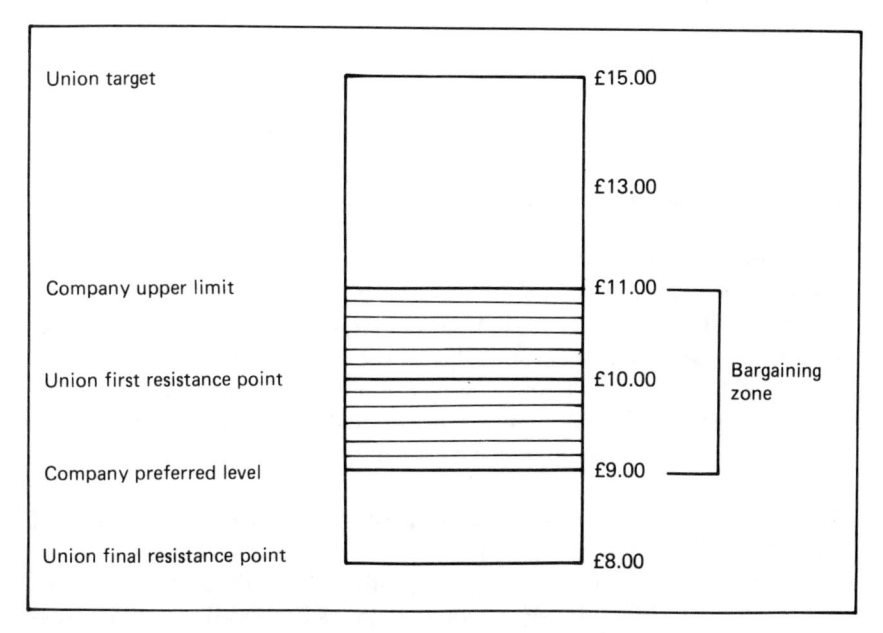

Figure 11.5 Bargaining zone in management − union negotiation

The real bargaining zone would be the hatched area between £10.00 and £9.00 and the likely point of settlement between £11.00 and £10.00. The union could be expected to resist strongly any attempt to reduce below £10.00. As this is below the company's maximum it is probably the minimum figure at which a bargain will be agreed.

Movement within the negotiating area relative to time

The advantage in negotiation lies generally with the party who is under least pressure for reaching agreement by a deadline. Either party can therefore bring pressure on the other by creating an artificial deadline. 'We must have an answer from the company by Friday midnight or we strike', or by deliberately showing that he is not bothered by time, like the sales negotiator who lets the overseas buyer know he has booked his hotel for an indefinite period and has an 'open' return air ticket.

In most negotiations both parties will be aware at some stage that there is a defined time-limit. Over the period remaining it is to the negotiator's advantage:

1 In the initial stages to move as little as possible from his original position. He will gain tactically by keeping the gap deliberately wide and cause his opponent to lose confidence and become uncertain. He must however be prepared to suffer a certain amount of abuse

2 At the penultimate stage:
(*a*) if he is dominant again to make only a minor adjustment to his position leaving it to his opponent to concede, or
(*b*) if he is less than dominant to move sufficiently to persuade his opponent also to move so that at the final stage the gap left between them is such that both will recognize the point at which to coordinate their expectations and reach a bargain

Assume in the example in the previous part of this section the negotiating period left before expiry of the union's strike ultimatum was three days.

Lines A and A' in Figure 11.6 show the pattern as it might be if both sides made the mistake of moving too early. By the end of day one there is only a gap of £2.00 between them and however long the negotiations last a 50/50 split of this seems inevitable. The gap is too small relative to the time left for it to be otherwise. This would mean a final bargain at £11.00, the company's maximum figure.

Supposing however that the company, recognizing that it had only £2.00 to negotiate with and three days to go, increased its offer only marginally at the beginning of day two by £1.00. The position could then be as shown on line BB'. After its initial move the company stays firm until the union drops to £11.00. The company has learnt something of the shape of the union's

NEGOTIATION

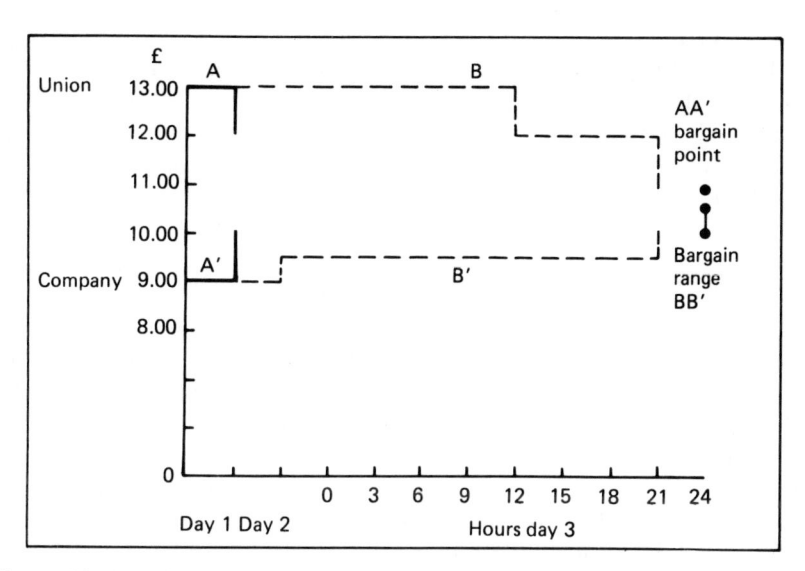

Figure 11.6 Influence of time on negotiation

utility curve through the negotiation and does not believe that the union will use its threat. Finally the company offers £10.00 shortly before the deadline. The union may accept or possibly come back with say £10.50. In either event the company will have made a significant saving.

NEGOTIATING TEAMS

Size and constitution of the team

The following guidelines should be observed in the selection of a negotiation team:

1. The team should never consist of one but equally should not be too large. One person on his own cannot be expected to present his case, listen to his opponents' arguments, develop counter-arguments, take notes and finally achieve the most favourable bargain. He must have support without which any effective negotiating tactics are impractical. At the same time three is probably the maximum number that can function effectively as a negotiating team at any one period
2. The characters who form the team must be compatible and prepared to work together
3. The team should have equal status to that of the opponent's and equal

competence on technical matters such as law, accountancy or engineering
4   Technical experts on a team must be prepared, however senior their personal position may be in the organization, to act only as advisers. Even though they are members of the team it may be preferable for certain negotiating sessions that they remain in the background since their presence may inhibit Opponent from making a commercial deal

Appointment and duties of the team leader

Someone must be selected to act as team leader and there can only be one leader for any negotiation. His authority must be recognized and respected by the other team members even though within their particular functions they may be senior to him in the company hierarchy. The duties of the team leader include:

1   Preparation of the negotiating plan
2   Ensuring the availability of all necessary data, files and so on
3   Conducting the briefing meeting before the negotiation starts: he must allow adequate time for this
4   Ensuring that all necessary authority has been obtained from company management and that individual team members have authority to act for their departments
5   Checking that all administrative and security arrangements appropriate to the negotiation have been made
6   Selecting the negotiating tactics
7   Opening Party's case
8   Responding to Opponent's case
9   Calling on other team members to make their individual contributions but personally summing up after each one
10 Holding further briefing sessions as necessary; revising the negotiating plan and obtaining any additional authority required from company management. The team leader should be the only person who communicates with company management during the course of the negotiation
11 Allowing any necessary concessions
12 Making the final bargain
13 Ensuring a written record of the negotiation is made and agreed with Opponent
14 Signing or initialling the written record
15 Reporting on the negotiation to management. This report should include a list of follow-up action points with the names of those responsible for carrying them out

OPENING STAGES

The objective in the opening stage is to expose the whole of the area which you as the negotiator wish to cover, and to identify the strength of Opponent's case including the degree of his opposition to or acceptance of your ideas. Until this has been done no concession should be made, even if you agree with his point of view, since to do so would deprive you of a bargaining counter which you may need in the future. The table of Dos and Don'ts in Figure 11.7 summarizes the way in which the negotiator should handle the opening of the negotiation.

When a written statement has been submitted by the other side

DO	DON'T
1 Challenge each point asking why he has made it.	Speculate on his reasons or put words into his mouth.
2 Appear ignorant, even if you are not, and let him justify his case.	Try to be clever and show how much you know by answering your own questions.
3 Note his answers and reserve your position.	Agree immediately even if you know you will in the end, no matter how reasonable his proposal. You may need that 'concession' later.
4 Make certain you have fully understood each point and his motives even if this means going over the ground more than once. This applies particularly if your native languages are not the same.	Snatch at what appears to be a favourable bargain or interpretation of his views.
5 Test out the strength of his views on each point so that later on you can assess the probability of his sticking to his position under pressure, and formulate a possible overall bargain.	Be drawn into lengthy arguments on any individual point at this stage in which it may be difficult to avoid offering or accepting a compromise solution on that point alone.
6 Be aware of interrelationship between different contract points and the possible counterarguments which will be developed against you if you succeed or are allowed to do so, on any one. For example, if as a contractor you suggest that the buyer should have a liability for additional costs in which you may be involved, if items supplied by him prove defective, you must expect that he in turn will ask you to accept some measure of consequential liability for defective items of your supply.	Be conscious only of the particular point under negotiation and of the immediate benefits to be derived from succeeding on that point alone.
7 Appear calm and quiet and keep your thoughts to yourself.	Betray your feelings by showing anger, surprise or delight at his remarks.

Figure 11.7 Dos and don'ts for negotiator handling opening stages

	DO	DON'T
8	Correct him if he is proceeding on a false belief as to a factual position for which you are responsible.	Improve his judgement unless it is to your advantage to do so.

When you have submitted a written proposal

	DO	DON'T
1	Limit your answers to his questions to the minimum and seek to persuade him into talking again as soon as possible.	Elaborate at length on your motives.
2	Test out the strength of his objections by seeing if he will withdraw without requiring any corresponding concessions from you.	Concede anything or be drawn into trade-off negotiations before all points have been discussed.
3	Behave generally as described in points 6, 7 and 8 above.	

When no written statement has been submitted by either party

	DO	DON'T
1	Identify all the points to be discussed.	Let the discussions ramble on without any defined order.
2	Cover each point in sufficient depth for both sides to be aware of each other's position.	Concentrate the discussion on one point to the exclusion of all others.
3	Keep the dicussions exploratory—you can confirm your position in writing later.	Be drawn into definite commitments either in the form of making a firm concession or taking up a position from which it will be difficult later for you to withdraw.
4	Behave generally as described in points 6, 7 and 8 above.	

Conclusion of the initial presentation

The initial phase of the negotiation is preferably limited therefore to an overall review and an identification of the differences between the parties. It should end in the establishment of the means by which these differences are to be resolved.

The situation at the conclusion of the initial phase will fall into one of the following three broad categories:

1. The issues will be sufficiently simple and the gap identified between the parties will be sufficiently narrow for the negotiators to move straight into the decision phase
2. The issues will be more complex and/or the differences wider so that further discussions are required on specific issues to be followed by a final bargaining session
3. It will be apparent that the gap is so wide that the result must either be a 'no-bargain' or, if an agreement is to be reached then one, or perhaps both, sets of negotiators must concede further than they are permitted to do by the terms of their negotiating authority. Accordingly before meeting again they must refer back for revised instructions

Figure 11.7 (*continued*)

NEGOTIATION

Follow-up

Resolution of the gap between the parties to the point at which a bargain can be identified may be accomplished in the following ways:

1. Establishment of small working parties from each side consisting of one or two experts to deal with specific issues
2. Each side is assigned to give further study to and prepare draft proposals on the controversial issues. These drafts are then exchanged and used as bases for further discussion between full negotiation teams
3. Through informal contact between the chief negotiators for each side or their respective specialists on an exploratory basis
4. By referring the issue to a third party whose judgement is respected by both sides

These methods are not mutually exclusive. On a major contract negotiation all four may be used.

The principal problem facing the team captain for each side at this stage is to retain overall control. He must identify and make sure all his team are fully aware of:

1. Any issue so vital that the company would prefer 'no-bargain' to conceding from their present position
2. The interrelationship between specific issues, particularly if these are going to be discussed by different pairs of specialists for example inspection, testing and time for delivery, penalty
3. The limits to which at any stage the team leader is willing to be committed on any issue.

Figure 11.7 *(concluded)*

THE FOLLOW UP

The first step for the negotiator is to review the original plan against what he has learnt and decide if there are any modifications. He should not however allow himself persuaded to change too easily.

Time is an important element in the next step. The following axioms apply in a situation in which there is a definite time frame established for the negotiations:

> The higher the initial concession rate of either side relative to time the worst bargain they will obtain. Both sides should therefore initially make only minor concessions or none at all. At some point before the deadline both sides should make a series of moves designed to permit identification of the final bargain which both would be prepared to accept. These moves may be either concessionary or a repeat of earlier offers depending on the bargaining strength of the two sides. The side with the weaker position is the one under greater pressure to reach agreement by the deadline and is the one who has the most to lose if the result is deadlock.

Always keep in mind the overall objective. The negotiator should try gradually to clear a way through to the form of the bargain he wants, without conceding on any major issue.

Consider the use of threats. The severity of the deterrent effect of any threat will depend upon:

1. The extent of the commitment which the issue of the threat makes upon the person making it
2. The belief of the person to whom the threat is made that if he does not give in then the threat will be implemented
3. The injury which would be suffered by the person to whom the threat is made if he accedes, in comparison to the loss he would suffer were the threat to be carried out

Remember that once a threat has been made in sufficiently specific terms then the person making it *must* carry it out if his demands are not met or lose his reputation for credibility. Successive time deadlines in hostage negotiations are an example.

Identifying the bargain

The final bargain will often identify itself from the way in which the demands have been structured. If figures can be brought close enough there is the 50/50 split, but beware of offering it too soon. Figures which have been presented just above or below landmark figures will usually finish up by being rounded up or down.

Bargains, especially when the parties will meet again, will also often depend upon precedents which have been set in other cases. This is one reason why if repeat bargaining is expected on an issue the negotiator may want to take a tough line, even if the amount involved at the time is relatively small.

Recognize when the other side has totally committed itself to a particular position. Total commitment is not easy to communicate especially when one has spent some time in bluffing. One way is to change to a personal role from that of a company employee, but this is only possible when one has already established a personal relationship with the lead negotiator for the other side.

In identifying the bargain it is usually wise to try to avoid policy issues to which the other side may be sensitive or would have difficulty in justifying to their own masters. Getting agreement to a sum of money without specifying exactly its make-up may be much easier.

NEGOTIATING PSYCHOLOGY

Motivations

Security. A negotiator will be concerned that acceptance of any proposition will not expose him to risk of censure. The other side must be able to give him the assurance that his own position is protected. This may mean choosing to concentrate on issues where he is not personally vulnerable. In a contract dispute an extra because of a change which some other person has requested may be easier to negotiate on than a claim based on the engineer or architect's delay in providing drawings or information.

Esteem. People like to think well of themselves and also that others of importance to them in their office or profession think well of them. This must be allowed for by letting them appear to win something otherwise they will be resentful.

Inter-personal relationships

People react in different ways according to the character type with which they are dealing. Inter-personal orientation (IO) is high when a person is responsive to his relationship with another and sensitive as to how the other feels. A person with low IO is interested only in himself and his own interests. A high IO negotiator may either be competitively oriented or cooperative. The selection of the negotiating team should take account of what is known about the character of the lead negotiator for the other side. In general like should be matched against like.

NEGOTIATING TACTICS

Attitudinal tactics

The objective of attitudinal tactics is to reduce the negotiator for the other side's attachment to a particular demand. This attachment is a function of his valuation of that demand and the probability which he foresees of achieving it. Attitudinal tactics therefore can be aimed either at reducing the valuation which he places on the demand or at his expectation of success.

Lowering his valuation can be achieved either by showing him it is not as attractive as he thought or offering him something which he can be persuaded is just as good.

Reducing his estimation of success usually requires that he be convinced of your total commitment to the line which you are taking. This may be achieved by:

Making your commitment simple and direct
Being patient
Putting the statement in writing
Leaving yourself no way out
Sitting back and appearing indifferent to the outcome

Situation tactics

Offensive tactics
1 *Asking questions.* Questions are of different types. Probing questions are designed to discover any weak point in the other's case. They should be framed in a general way. 'Could you please explain why it is that...'. The counter to this type of question is not an answer but another question: 'I am sorry if there is any misunderstanding. Can you please be more specific.' Specific questions are those which are directed towards finding out a particular piece of data. They are a form of attack which is used when one has already detected a certain weakness in the other's position. The rules for framing such a question are:
 (a) keep it short and simple
 (b) do not disclose all the facts
 (c) never suggest an answer
Perhaps the most effective attacking question is simply 'Why?'
2 *Bringing pressure.* This may be achieved either through
 (a) flattery — asking for advice from someone on the other side whom you believe will answer in your favour
 (b) coercion — this is the opposite to flattery and is used to suggest to the member of the other team that the line he is taking is not one which his seniors have followed in the past
 (c) blackmail — suggesting there are powerful friends in the other side's top management or politically who would want you to be successful
3 *Being arbitrary.* Sweet reason may not be the best form of argument under all situations. The firm who is working on a short-term contract which must be completed fast can be irrational in the demands it makes prior to completion, although it loses that power afterwards
4 *Final offer first.* Taking the initiative by making a complete presentation to the other party to which he can make no major objection. Can be extremely effective provided you have done a complete and thorough job of preparation and have limited your case to that which you know cannot be faulted. Carries with it however the risk of causing resentment from the opponent which may lead to an emotional outburst. You must either be ready for this, or if you believe the emotional response will be serious abandon the use of the tactic

NEGOTIATION

5. *Putting on a show of strength.* Deploy a team of experts under the leadership of a senior manager or director whose status level is higher than the other party would normally expect for the type of negotiation concerned. Often used in association with the 'final-offer-first' tactic in order to lend credence to its authority
6. *Making opponent appear unreasonable.* By taking the opponent's line of argument to the extreme, you show that as a matter of principle it cannot be supported. The other party is then put on the defensive and compelled to justify the particular case as an exception to the general rule. You are then in a position to demand acceptance of one of his points as the price he must pay for your agreeing to the 'exception'.
7. *Fishing tactics.* A proposition is deliberately overstated by you to make your opponent respond by disclosing his true position and the reasons why he is adopting that position. After hearing his explanation and going through the argument, you can then make a 'concession' in return for one from the other party
8. *'Good guy – bad guy'.* This is an old trick which can still be effective since the other side cannot usually be sure whether or not a genuine disagreement exists between the two negotiators and if it does then this is something they will wish to exploit. It can be played both ways round. As an example, one negotiator may make a few minor concesssions on points of no consequence and then on the point which does matter he is mildly rebuked by his partner for having given too much away already and told this is one that cannot be conceded
9. *Setting up 'straw issues'.* This refers to always having some points in the case which you do not expect to win on, but which you can use to trade, perhaps as a group, in exchange for the one you really do want.
10. *Demonstrating commitment by reference to authority.* Laws, regulations, company standard instructions, all these can be used to support the negotiator's commitment to a particular point. However the negotiator has to be careful not to undermine his own authority.
11. *The tactical recess* in order to break up a deadlock or avoid tempers rising too high. The negotiator may find an excuse to leave the room, ask the secretary to bring in refreshments, or just suggest a break for fresh air.

Defensive tactics
1. *Keeping quiet.* A minimal response by you to a proposition put forward by the other side to which he is seeking your agreement will often result in his feeling compelled to go on talking and offer more and more justification for his proposal. In so doing he is likely to reveal more of his genuine motivation than he intended and provide you with a basis on which to mount a counterattack
2. *Pretended misunderstanding.* By pretending to misunderstand your

opponent's case, you may again cause him to show more of his hand than he intended. Experts in particular can rarely miss the opportunity to display their knowledge

3 *Yes-but technique.* Rather than an outright denial of a proposition put forward by the other side, which may cause antagonism and a breakdown in communication, you will often obtain better results by indicating that you have some sympathy or support for his position but cannot see its application or relevance to the present negotiation. 'Yes, I see what you mean and there could be a problem here, but I don't see how what you propose will provide any real solution.' The only admission you have made with that reply is that 'there could be a problem' which was probably evident anyhow; otherwise he is back where he started from. At the same time he cannot accuse you of being non-cooperative

4 *Calculated incompetence.* If you do not wish to discuss a particular issue, or at any rate not for the moment, you can deliberately avoid doing so by ensuring that your expert on that subject is not available.

5 *Taking opponent into your confidence.* It is much easier for your opponent to be aggressive and demanding when he is not in possession of sufficient facts. If for example he is insisting that you complete certain work by a date which is impossible to achieve you should table your own internal production or construction schedule and invite him to consider this and see where he could suggest improvements. This at once calms down the discussion and can easily lead to the other side's negotiators becoming supporters of your position against their own management. This same type of tactic can be used in industrial relations negotiations. By taking the union leaders into the company's confidence on such matters as the state of the order book, overseas competition, profit margins, economies being made in staff 'perks', it is made much more difficult for those leaders to press unrealistic wage claims

6 *The counter question.* Don't answer the question you have been asked, ask one back (like the wife who replies to an invitation to attend some social function by saying 'What shall I wear?')

CHECKLIST: CONTRACT DISPUTE

Contractual

1 Has a legally binding contract been formed? By what law is it governed?
2 What are the contract documents?
3 What are the rights given expressly by the contract documents? Note, in answering this question make sure that all the contract documents are looked at as a whole. These may include preliminary correspondence in which representations were made

4   To what extent are these rights supplemented or modified by the general legal system by which the contract is governed?
5   Have the rights available under 3 and 4 been waived either in whole or in part by the conduct of either of the parties?
6   To what extent are the rights available under 3 and 4 exercisable in practice? This will depend upon:
    (*a*)   which court or tribunal has jurisdiction
    (*b*)   whether such court or tribunal is independent or open to influence
    (*c*)   the time which such proceedings are likely to take
    (*d*)   the availability of local lawyers and their freedom to practise in the court or tribunal
    (*e*)   the costs which are likely to be incurred and the extent to which these may be recovered from the other party in the event of the proceedings being successful
7   What is the measure of damages which may be recovered or other legal remedy available?
8   To what extent may any judgment obtained be enforced in practice against the other party? This will depend upon:
    (*a*)   the assets of the other party situated within the jurisdiction of the court or tribunal. If none, can a judgment be enforced within a territory where the other party does have assets by registration without re-examination of the merits of the case?
    (*b*)   any political immunity of the other party from process either in theory or practice
    (*c*)   where the defendant is resident overseas, can any sums awarded easily be transferred or can they be blocked under exchange control or taxation legislation?

Financial

9   What payments if any are outstanding, when are these payable and how are they secured?
10 Is there a performance bond covering the performance of any contractual obligations, if so under what circumstances can it be encashed and by what procedure? Note that a bond can often be cashed by simple notice to the bank without the necessity of the holder of the bond having to prove contractual default
11 What retention monies are held and when are these due to be released?
12 Are there any goods or plant which may be seized or are liable to be seized and either held as security or sold?
13 Are there payments due under any other contract between the parties which may be used as offset?
14 On an export contract, is there any insurance cover against default by the buyer in payment and if so is such cover still valid?

Commercial

Possible action by purchaser

1. Is there another tender from the supplier under adjudication by the purchaser which he may refuse to accept or use as a bargaining counter?
2. Are there other contracts in existence between the parties on which it is possible for the purchaser to claim damages or otherwise strictly enforce his contractual rights?
3. Are there concessions which the purchaser normally allows to the contractor which the purchaser can restrict or suspend?
4. Are there concessions which the purchaser normally allows to the contractor on this and other contracts, for example on inspection and testing, which it would be open to the purchaser to withdraw?
5. Could the purchaser blacklist the supplier for future work and, if so could this extend to associated companies or other firms/administrations with which the purchaser has contact?

Possible action by supplier

1. Could the supplier suspend work even without any contractual right to do so?
2. Is the supplier in a position to refuse to tender for other of the purchaser's requirements?
3. Could the supplier bring pressure through his government, trade association or Member of Parliament?

FURTHER READING

P.D.V. Marsh, *Contract Negotiation Handbook*, 2nd edition, Gower, Aldershot, 1984.

Bill Scott, *The Skills of Negotiating*, Gower, Aldershot, 1981.

12

Debt Collection

Guy Vincent

No matter what type of business one is involved in, a time will come when the normal approaches to a customer to settle his account become exhausted and one has to look elsewhere for collection. Whether a debt can be classified as 'bad' at that stage must depend on the particular circumstances of the case, but it would be prudent to make provision for it to be written off or treated as 'doubtful' once its collection has to be placed in other hands. Once an account has reached this stage the alternatives for collection are either to place it in the hands of a debt collector or to take legal action, for which it is sensible to employ a solicitor.

DEBT COLLECTORS

A multiplicity of debt collection agencies exists, ranging in size from those which form part of large companies dealing with trade protection in general, to those which are little more than individual 'door-to-door knockers'. However, debt collectors do not have the power to issue proceedings in the High Court and if they are unsuccessful in collecting an account by correspondence, telephone, or personal calls, then solicitors will have to be instructed and valuable time might have been lost while the debt collectors have been trying to attempt recovery. The efficiency of agencies does, of course, vary widely as does the efficiency of solicitors. It would seem prudent from a creditor's point of view that, in the event of debt collectors being instructed, a firm that specializes in the creditor's particular trade is employed. A number of trade protection associations exist which operate in certain trades, or for example in the hire purchase or mail order fields.

The fees charged by debt collection agencies vary according to the service provided. Few agencies charge other than a nominal registration fee unless they recover the debt, when they normally charge a percentage of the amount recovered. At this stage the employment of a debt collector can prove expensive as some agencies are known to charge up to 20 per cent in addition to any legal fees incurred on the creditor's behalf. Low rates, however, are often charged where large sums are recovered.

An advantage of using a debt collector is that information is often available (through any relevant trade protection association) which is not available to a solicitor. In addition, most collectors offer a tracing service where debtors have disappeared.

SOLICITORS

If a creditor decides to employ a solicitor it is sensible to choose carefully and it is advisable, in these days of specialization, to select a firm which specializes in this type of work. There are few firms now which involve themselves exclusively in collection work, but those which have specialized debt collection departments can provide a more efficient and, usually, a cheaper service. Most of these firms act for trade protection associations or finance, insurance or factoring companies and the like. Solicitors will charge a fee which is based on the amount of work done, whether the debt is recovered or not. Solicitors are not permitted to charge on a percentage or on a 'no recovery — no fee' basis. The basis of charge is for negotiation between the creditor and the solicitor and some firms specializing in this type of work will be prepared to agree a special rate for undertaking volume business.

It is sensible to seek an estimate from the solicitor. If legal proceedings are contemplated a limited company is obliged to instruct a solicitor if proceedings are to be brought in the High Court. Proceedings in the county court may be brought by a company acting through an authorized agent such as its secretary or a debt collector.

LEGAL ACTION

The first decisions

Whether a debt collecting agency or solicitors are to be instructed certain basic decisions are essential to speed up the work and assist in recovery:

1   Who is the debtor? Is the money owed by a firm, a company or an individual? Any written orders should be checked for the correct title of

DEBT COLLECTION

the debtors and any solicitors instructed should be provided with a copy. if there is no written order or other document from the debtor, or if there is doubt about the proper identity of the debtor, inquiries should be made. These steps should be taken before invoices are dispatched but are often overlooked

2 How much is due? It is wasteful to chase one outstanding invoice only to find others falling due for payment shortly, or indeed already outstanding. It is important to make sure that the amount being pursued is correct. If some payments have been made, and a balance is being pursued, time will be saved if solicitors are provided with a statement of account so that they can deal with any debtor's queries about whether or not they have been given credit for payments made

3 Can or should interest be claimed? If the contract between the debtor and creditor allows the creditor to charge interest on his overdue account, the terms of that contract (through established conditions of trading, or agreed to in some other way) should be brought to the solicitor's attention. Interest can be claimed under contract or by statute. If claimed by statute ($s35A$, Supreme Court Act 1981 or $s69$, County Court Act 1984) the rate and amount must be set out in the claim and the court will decide if this is fair. If interest is claimed, it will usually be allowed from the date that the debt fell due for payment until judgment is obtained. In the High Court judgments themselves carry interest, but in the county court they do not

4 Is the debtor worth powder and shot? If the debtor has no money, it is plainly futile to spend money in chasing him. It is worth making sensible inquiries, or getting solicitors to do so, if there is realistic doubt that the debtor can pay

5 If a debtor is a company, the first question to be answered is what sort of legal action should be taken. Should the debtor be sued or should a winding-up petition be presented? If there is no dispute over the debt and if there are doubts about the solvency of the debtor, that is to say if it appears not to be able to pay its debts as they fall due, it may be sensible to take winding-up proceedings straight away. It is wasteful of time and legal costs to issue a writ and obtain judgment if, at the end of the day, the cupboard is bare. The payment of legal costs of winding-up proceedings is the first distribution out of the funds of a liquidated company and, contrary to common belief, there is no need for a creditor to have sued and obtained a judgment before presenting a winding-up petition. The petition, which will come before the court some six weeks after being presented, can be presented on an existing trading debt provided that it is for more than £750 but most solicitors, for safety's sake, prefer to make a demand under $s518$ of the Companies Act 1985. This notice, which should be delivered at the debtor company's registered office, requires payment of the undisputed

debt within twenty-one days. The Companies Act provides that if no payment is made under such a notice that is sufficient evidence of insolvency for a winding-up petition to be presented. The notice will often have a more salutory effect on a debtor than ordinary legal proceedings. The notice can be by letter and there is no reason why a creditor should not deliver his own notice before instructing his solicitors

COURT ACTION

If winding-up proceedings are not appropriate, solicitors will usually make formal application to the debtor for payment. It is only in exceptional circumstances that he will dispense with a letter before action; firstly because there is a chance that the debtor will respond in some way to a letter and, secondly, because The Law Society advises that a letter before action should be written lest it should be thought that, by not doing so, a solicitor is involving a debtor in unnecessary costs.

Proceedings can be commenced in either the High Court or a county court depending on the amount of the debt. The High Court has jurisdiction throughout England and Wales, but a county court is limited geographically to its particular area. The High Court has jurisdiction for the issue of proceedings up to any amount, but a writ issued for a sum of less than £600 does not entitle the plaintiff to be paid his costs by the defendant, as such a writ is not endorsed with any scale costs. Costs are payable by a defendant in respect of proceedings commenced for sums over £600, provided that they are issued before payment by the defendant. In the High Court judgment for at least £3,000 must be obtained before High Court, rather than the lower county court, scale costs can be ordered. It sometimes happens that a defendant will pay the debt after the issue of the writ but before service upon him; he is still liable for payment of the scale costs of the writ. The county court is limited to the issue of proceedings, in debt recovery cases, of sums up to £5,000. Its general jurisdiction and procedure, are governed by the County Courts Act 1984 and the County Court Rules 1981, as amended.

Despite the limit on costs recoveries in the High Court in actions for smaller debts, many solicitors will advise High Court proceedings for recovery because at present only High Court judgments carry interest, generally, enforcement in the High Court is more efficient and the proceedings can be commenced more quickly.

COUNTY COURT PROCEEDINGS

Proceedings must be brought either:

1   In the court of the district where the defendant resides or carries on business; or

DEBT COLLECTION

2   In that in which the cause of action wholly or in part arose

The action will commence with the issue of a default summons, service of which is normally effected by the county court bailiff, and will be served by post when it can be certified that the defendant will receive it. A default summons may be issued in respect of any debt or liquidated claim (a claim for a specific sum of money ascertained or capable of being ascertained as a mere matter of arithmetic). A form of notice of defence, admission, set off or counterclaim is appended to all summonses when served and an admission or defence must be filed by the defendant within fourteen days of service. If a defence or an admission and offer are delivered in a default action and the offer is not acceptable to the plaintiff, the court will fix a hearing at which it will give directions for the future conduct and hearing of the case. At the disposal of the hearing of an application by the debtor to pay by instalments the plaintiff will be expected to produce evidence of the defendant's means and the onus will be upon him to show that the defendant is able to pay more than the amount of the instalments offered. If no defence or admission and offer is filed, then the plaintiff may enter judgment in default of appearance at which time the whole of the debt becomes payable and the judgment may be enforced.

For certain claims an ordinary summons must be issued. Although served in the same way as a default summons, judgment in default of appearance cannot be obtained if the defendant fails to appear, as the case is given a hearing date and the plaintiff is required to attend and formally prove his debt. Personal attendance may now be avoided by producing proof in the form of an affidavit which is filed with the court prior to the hearing.

A procedure for summary judgment similar to that available in the High Court (set out below) is available in the county court.

HIGH COURT PROCEEDINGS

All proceedings in the High Court are governed by the Rules and Practice Directions contained in the Supreme Court Practice (usually known as 'The White Book'). The High Court is based in London but has District Registries in most cities. Proceedings commence with the issue of a writ of summons which may be served by post or personally. Alternatively solicitors can accept service on behalf of a debtor. Service on a limited company is by post to its registered office and is treated as having been effected on the day after posting. Otherwise if service is by post, or delivery to a defendant's address, it is treated as being effected seven days later.

If the defendant wishes to defend the proceedings, he should file an acknowledgement of service at the court, after which he has fourteen days, inclusive of the day of service, in which to deliver a defence. Should the defendant not acknowledge service, the plaintiff may enter judgment in default after the fourteen days have elapsed from service having been treated as effected. In the event that the defendant acknowledges service he then has a further fourteen days in which to file his defence (i.e. twenty-eight days after service of the writ), although this time is often extended by agreement between the respective solicitors. It is not always necessary for the plaintiff's solicitors to wait these fourteen days for a defence to be entered. Where it is clear that the defendant has no defence he can issue a summons for summary judgment under the provisions of order 14 of the Rules of the Supreme Court. Under this procedure, the plaintiff or his solicitor will swear an affidavit briefly setting out the facts and a summons will be issued and served on the defendant. The defendant is required to file an affidavit setting out the grounds of his defence and if, on the hearing of the summons, the defendant satisfies the court that he has an arguable defence, he will be given leave to defend the action. Otherwise the court will allow the plaintiff to enter judgment for his claim. In circumstances where the court accepts that the defendant has an arguable defence but that it is shadowy the court may only allow the defendant to defend subject to conditions which are usually that the defendant pay all or part of the sum claimed into court.

ENFORCEMENT OF JUDGMENT DEBTS

A party who has successfully obtained a judgment may well find, particularly if there has been no active participation by the defendant in the proceedings, that he has gained only a pyrrhic victory. The court will not take any initiative, in civil cases, to enforce the judgment and it will be for the plaintiff's solicitor to advise the best method of enforcement dependent upon the information available. To assist in coming to a proper conclusion it is obviously desirable to have as much information as possible regarding the defendant's assets. If insufficient information is available, an inquiry agent might be employed to make investigations. If inquiries have not been made before proceedings were started, searches might be made at this stage in the Register of Bills of Sale kept in the Central Office of the Law Courts, in the Land Charges Registry, in the Register of Deeds of Arrangement, in the Register of Bankruptcy Proceedings kept at Thomas More Building, Royal Courts of Justice, Strand, London WC2 or in the Register of County Court judgments kept in London. Information may be revealed from any one of these sources which would avoid further fruitless and time-consuming proceedings. If a defendant company is the subject of winding-up proceedings or an individual is the subject of bankruptcy proceedings, an uncompleted execution against goods would be ineffective and any money recovered by the sheriff will have to be returned to the liquidator or trustee in bankruptcy for the benefit of all creditors.

DEBT COLLECTION

In order to gain information, it is possible to summon the defendant, or in the case of a limited company an officer thereof, before an officer of the court to be examined orally. This sort of examination is inexpensive and, subject of course to the debtor being truthful, can provide information which should guide the judgment creditor on what course to adopt. The court may also order production of any relevant books or other documents.

Execution against goods

There are numerous methods of execution of a money judgment both in the High Court and county court, but the most common method is by means of a writ of execution against goods. In the High Court such a writ is called a writ of fieri facias. The method may be used in both the High Court and the county court (where it is called a warrant of execution) and is generally the most effective, although it will fail where goods belong to third parties, for example where they are subject to hire-purchase agreements or where goods have been sold to the defendant subject to a reservation of title by the supplier concerned. The Sheriff, or bailiff, is bound to treat the writs in the order in which they have been lodged with him, and it is therefore imperative that no time is lost in enforcing a judgment in this way, as it becomes a question of first come first served. Enforcement in the High Court (by sheriff's officers) is generally thought to be more efficient than in the county court (by bailiffs). Perhaps this is because bailiffs are court employees with no direct interest in results, whilst sheriff's officers are paid, in part, by what is called poundage, on recoveries made.

Garnishee proceedings

It is not infrequent to find that, having obtained a judgment, the creditor is unable to enforce it easily. A process is available in both the High Court and the County Court which enables a judgment creditor to attach any unconditional debt owing to the defendant solely, but not necessarily immediately payable. A bank account is obviously liable to attachment, but not a joint account in the names of the defendant and another. Application is made to the court ex parte (that is to say, without the other side present) on affidavit, stating that some other person is indebted to the defendant and that that other person is within the jurisdiction. On this application an order is made attaching the debt due from the third person (the garnishee) and ordering the garnishee to appear before the court to show cause why he should not pay the amount he owes the defendant or so much as will satisfy the judgment debt and costs, direct to the judgment creditor. This order is called an order nisi, and must be served on the garnishee and on the judgment debtor seven days before the hearing of an application to make the order nisi absolute.

Charging

This method of enforcing a judgment may be used to charge the defendant's beneficial interest in any property, stocks, shares, debentures, funds or annuities and any dividends or interest payable thereon.

The Charging Orders Act 1979 now extends the principle to enable a judgment creditor to obtain a charge on land owned jointly by a debtor and a third party, most usually a jointly owned matrimonial property.

The charge does not itself produce any money, in that it does not force the debtor to sell the property charged. If a creditor wants to force a sale, a separate application must be made to the court, at least six months after the charge is made. However, the charge acts as security and if the asset is to be sold then the debt must be discharged provided that the sale realizes sufficient funds.

MORATORIUM

It will not always be the case that a creditor has to pursue the debtor. It will often happen that on the creditor obtaining his judgment, or even before he asks for his money, the debtor will appreciate that he does not have the money to pay his debts. He is therefore insolvent and may come to his creditors for support.

If a debtor only really needs time it is open to him to ask for what is known as a moratorium from all of his creditors. The effect of a moratorium, if granted by the creditors, is to 'freeze' those debts existing at the time for an agreed period. As a moratorium must essentially refer to and be agreed upon by all creditors, its main advantage is that no creditor obtains preference over any other and the business may continue, probably under the general supervision of an independent accountant or committee elected by the general body of creditors.

As a moratorium is an informal arrangement it does not have any statutory requirements. Any formalities would be dealt with, in all probability, at an information meeting of the creditors called to approve the moratorium. At the meeting, creditors should insist upon a proper statement of affairs, deficiency account and list of creditors, and an explanation of why the business has failed. Creditors would then be advised to appoint a small committee from among themselves to investigate the position and make a recommendation to the general body of creditors. For example it can be suggested that a new bank account be opened and the old one frozen pending the period of the moratorium; that all small debts, say those below £50, be paid in full forthwith in order to avoid the possibility of one of them proving difficult and wrecking the scheme; and that a professional trustee be appointed to supervise the running of the moratorium. The object of a moratorium is to ensure equality of treatment to all creditors and perhaps to allow the debtor to trade out of difficulty.

A creditor is not bound to accept an informal arrangement of this kind and, in the case of a company, if he does not wish to accept it he can take steps to present a petition for compulsory winding-up. In the case of an individual he can petition for bankruptcy. If, however, the general body of creditors decides to accept it, the dissenting creditor might find that all the other creditors will oppose a winding-up petition or bankruptcy and defeat him. In order to bind creditors to an arrangement of this nature, a company may present a scheme for approval by the court pursuant to the provision of *s*206 of the Companies Act 1948. A petition for such a scheme provides for the convening of a meeting of creditors at which the creditors present vote either for or against it. A report is made to the court by affidavit by the chairman of the meeting and if three-quarters of those creditors present and voting approve the scheme, the court will sanction it and it will become binding on all creditors. This type of procedure is not recommended however, as it is both costly and long drawn out.

INSOLVENCY

A debtor, if unable to pay debts as they fall due, is insolvent and may have his affairs, including the payment of debts, placed in the control of a third party. If the debtor is an individual or partnership this procedure is known as bankruptcy; if a limited company then it is known as liquidation. The procedures may be triggered either by the debtor voluntarily accepting that he cannot pay his way or alternatively by a creditor petitioning the court to compel bankruptcy or liquidation. A practical consideration for the creditor to consider is whether an insolvency will result in full payment of the debt. If the debtor is insolvent then the assets available will be divided equally between all the debtor's unsecured creditors. There may also be secured creditors, such as a bank, or preferential creditors, such as rates and the Inland Revenue, who are paid in full along with the costs of the insolvency before the unsecured creditors. Once a debtor is made bankrupt or placed in liquidation the creditor may seek bad debt relief on any VAT paid on the debt.

An exhaustive review of insolvency law resulted in the Insolvency Act 1985. Some of the provisions of this Act have been implemented but most are not expected to come into force until 1987. The main impact on debtors will be the revision of bankruptcy procedure and the tightening of company directors' personal liabilities.

Bankruptcy

If the debtor is an individual, or in partnership with others, bankruptcy proceedings on the judgment may be appropriate.

The law and procedure relating to bankruptcy is contained in the Bankruptcy Act 1914, as amended, and the Bankruptcy Rules 1952 (to be replaced by sections of the Insolvency Act 1985). Proceedings may be taken either in the High Court or whichever county court has jurisdiction for bankruptcy purposes.

Before bankruptcy proceedings can be commenced, the debtor must have committed one of a number of statutory bankruptcy offences (s1(1) of the Bankruptcy Act 1914). The most common of these is failure to comply with the terms of a bankruptcy notice within ten days, excluding the day of service (s1(1)(h)). A bankruptcy notice is issued for a liquidated sum and must be based on a judgment debt. If, within the ten days after service, the debtor has failed to pay the sum demanded, the debtor has committed an Act of bankruptcy upon which a bankruptcy petition may be presented. If the petition is accepted by the court, a receiving order is made against the debtor, the effect of which is to vest the debtor's possessions in the Official Receiver in Bankruptcy pending the possible appointment of a trustee in bankruptcy by the creditors.

The Insolvency Act will introduce a statutory demand for payment of an undisputed trade debt within twenty-one days. Creditors will not have to start court proceedings and will be able to petition for bankruptcy if the debt is not paid following the statutory demand.

The debtor is required to submit a statement of affairs to the Official Receiver within seven days of the making of the receiving order and subsequently a public examination is held at which the Official Receiver will, and any creditor may, examine the debtor regarding his financial affairs and conduct generally. The court now has power, if it thinks fit, to make an order dispensing with the public examination (s6 of the Insolvency Act 1976) and in determining whether to make an order it shall have regard, *inter alia*, to whether the debtor has made a full disclosure of his affairs, and the number and nature of his debts.

Within fourteen days of the making of the receiving order, the Official Receiver will summon a meeting of the creditors at which a resolution may be passed either adjudicating the debtor bankrupt or at which a proposal for a composition will be put forward. In the event of adjudication, creditors may also vote for the appointment of a trustee who will then begin the realization of the estate.

A bankrupt suffers severe disabilities until such time as he obtains his discharge. For example, he cannot obtain credit for more than £50 without disclosing that he is an undischarged bankrupt; he may not become a director or the secretary of a limited company; he may not engage in trade on his own account.

The Insolvency Act is attempting to try and avoid 'small bankruptcies'. The court will refuse to make a bankruptcy order if the unsecured debts would be less than 'the small bankruptcy level' yet to be prescribed, or if a creditor has unreasonably refused an offer of payment. The duration of most bankruptcies will be reduced from five to two years. The Act and new rules will introduce various other reforms.

Liquidation

If the debtor is a company and it has concluded that it cannot carry on, liquidation may be inevitable. There are three types of liquidation of limited companies: members' voluntary winding-up, creditors' voluntary winding-up and compulsory winding-up by the court.

Members' voluntary winding-up. Where a company believes itself to be solvent and wishes to cease trading, either for reasons of reconstruction or because the members wish it to close down so that they may realize their investment, a resolution for voluntary winding-up may be passed. A statutory declaration is then filed by the directors which states that a full investigation has been made into the company's affairs and that the company will be able to pay all its debts in full within a period of twelve months. This declaration is called a declaration of solvency and a director making such a declaration without having reasonable grounds for the opinion that the company will be able to pay its debts in full, is liable to imprisonment for a period of not exceeding six months or to a fine not exceeding £500 or to both (s577 of the Companies Act 1985). If the directors cannot make a declaration of solvency, the liquidation must be a creditors' liquidation.

Creditors' voluntary winding-up. The directors will call a meeting of creditors pursuant to the provisions of ss588, 589 and 590 of the Companies Act 1985, if they have reason to believe, or are advised, that the company is insolvent. At the meeting, the creditors will have placed before them a statement of affairs together with a list of the creditors' names and the amounts owed to each of them. Prior to the creditors' meeting, a meeting of the shareholders of the company will pass a resolution for voluntary winding-up and may nominate a liquidator of their own choice to realize and distribute the assets. The main purpose of the creditors' meeting is to endorse the shareholders' resolution and nomination, although this does not always happen as creditors may wish to nominate a liquidator of their own choice as an alternative. The creditors' choice prevails over that of the shareholders. It is not uncommon for joint liquidators to be appointed.

The liquidator's fees are payable out of the assets of the company and are voted to him by a committee of inspection which is normally appointed by the creditors to assist the liquidator. In the absence of a committee of inspection the liquidator will apply to the Department of Trade and Industry for approval of his fees. A liquidator's fees may be fixed in advance at a certain sum or he may retain a percentage of the assets realized and distributed.

Compulsory winding-up. Any creditor may present a petition for compulsory winding-up. Sometimes a company is put into compulsory liquidation even after it has put itself into voluntary liquidation. This has the effect of the Official Receiver being appointed interim liquidator. He can remain liquidator or, if there are assets, a professional liquidator will be appointed by a vote of the creditors. The advantage of a compulsory liquidation is that the conduct of the directors and managers of the company can be investigated by the Official Receiver. If creditors are concerned about how the company has dealt with its creditors, or has created charges or disposed of assets, all of these matters can be investigated.

The various steps available in such an investigation are outside the scope of this chapter.

Various reforms of the winding-up procedure will be introduced by the Insolvency Act. The major change will be to implement the government's view that company directors have operated in a 'mirage of optimism' and have generally been allowed to trade on too long to the detriment of creditors. The Act introduces a new civil offence of wrongful trading and makes it easier to disqualify a director. In certain circumstances a director may be fined or made personally liable for the company's debts. It is hoped that these provisions will make directors more aware of their responsibilities to creditors of the company.

Administration orders and voluntary arrangements

To try to reduce the number of liquidations and bankruptcies the Insolvency Act will introduce a procedure whereby debtors may seek the protection of the court from their creditors in order to implement a scheme designed to pay creditors and trade out of their problems. This will be known as an administration order in the case of a company and a voluntary arrangement in the case of an individual or partnership. Such schemes must be administered by a qualified insolvency practitioner but may be challenged in the courts by a creditor.

FURTHER READING

Alistair Black, *Enforcement of a Judgment*, Longman Professional Practice Notes, 1986.
J.K. Gatenby, *Recovery of Money*, Longmans, 1986.

13

Intellectual Property Rights

Colin Jones

Historically, patents, trade marks and designs were referred to collectively as 'industrial property'. In recent years, it has become usual to refer to 'intellectual property' so as to include more clearly copyright, know-how and trade secrets. All forms of intellectual property can be bought, sold and licensed.

PATENTS

Patents for inventions (until recently 'Letters Patent') have a long lineage in England. They were being granted by the Crown, along with other monopoly rights, in pre-Tudor times, but the first legislative enactment was the Statute of Monopolies of 1623, which made all monopolies void except (under $s6$) those granted for fourteen years (now twenty) in respect of 'any manner of new manufacture'.

The latest in a long series of enactments is the Patents Act 1977 (referred to in this chapter as 'the 1977 Act') which came into force on 1 June 1978. There are still in force some patents ('existing patents') which were granted under the Patents Act 1949 (referred to here as 'the old Act'). Another major change was the coming into force (also on 1 June 1978) of the European Patent Convention (EPC), with the opening of the European Patent Office (EPO) in Munich. A further development is the Community Patent Convention (CPC), which has been signed by the EEC members, but will not come into force for a considerable time because ratification of the EPC and the CPC by Denmark and the Irish Republic will entail amendments to the constitutions of these two countries.

The EPC provides a system whereby a single application at the EPO designating a number of member countries (which will include all the Western European countries when all the signatories have ratified the convention) selected by the applicant will be examined by the EPO and, if accepted, will result in the grant of a bundle of identical patents in the designated countries. The CPC will go further, in that an application at the EPO designating the EEC will (if successful) result in the granting of a single 'Community patent'. Thus, there will be three kinds of patent in the UK:

1. National Patents, granted by the UK Patent Office (UKPO) and effective only in the UK
2. European Patents (UK), granted by the EPO and effective only in the UK (although identical patents in the bundle will be effective in the other designated countries)
3. Community Patents, granted by the EPO and effective as a single entity throughout the EEC

All three kinds of patents are enforceable by the UK courts, but validity of Community Patents will be under the jurisdiction of the EPO with an appeal to a Community Patent Court (COPAC), yet to be established.

INVENTION

An adequate guide to the meaning of 'invention' for present purposes is that an invention is a new article or substance, or a new machine, or a new method or process of carrying out an industrial operation — the word 'industrial' including agriculture and horticulture. Computer programming is not included, but new computer programs now enjoy copyright protection (see p.285).

Further types of activity may, with the advance of technology, become suitable for patenting in the future, and the 1977 Act provides that such new developments can be included within its scope by Statutory Instrument without the need for legislation.

Not all inventions can be *validly* patented; certain attributes are necessary to make an invention 'patentable'. Before considering these, we need to know more about the nature of patents.

PATENT SPECIFICATION

The grant of a patent can be regarded in a sense as a contract between the

INTELLECTUAL PROPERTY RIGHTS

State and the patentee under which the State grants the patentee a twenty-year monopoly in making or using the invention in return for a disclosure to the public of the invention and how to put it into practice. The vehible for this disclosure is the patent specification — a document printed and published by the Patent Office as a prerequisite to every granted patent.

The claim

Besides disclosing the invention, the specification has another essential function: the definition of the area of monopoly to which the patentee claims to be entitled, this being contained in the claims of the specification.

It has long been recognized that to confine the patentee's monopoly exactly to his invention would stultify the whole system, since a competitor could evade the monopoly simply by making an inconsequential variation. The patentee is therefore allowed to include in his monopoly a range of constructions or processes centred on the original invention but in return he must by means of the claims define precisely the scope of the monopoly for which he wishes to have protection and to which he believes himself to be entitled.

A simple example will help to clarify this rather difficult concept. Suppose the invention is a ballcock for a cistern. It is a piece of mechanism which includes a float in the form of a hollow sphere. If the patent monopoly were confined to the exact mechanism as conceived by the inventor, a competitor might be able to evade it quite easily by replacing the sphere by an egg-shaped float or even perhaps a rectangular one. So the patentee does not refer in his claim to a 'hollow spherical float' but to a 'hollow body serving as a float' or perhaps just to a 'float'.

The extent to which the inventor can extrapolate from his original invention is dealt with in the 1977 Act by the provision that the claims must be supported by the matter disclosed in the specification ($s14(5)(c)$), but this can in the last analysis only be a subjective judgment by the tribunal considering the matter.

Explaining the nature and function of patent claims is not made easier by the fact that the word 'invention' is used not only as above to mean the concrete article or process devised by the inventor, but also in the quite different sense of 'the invention claimed' — that is the area of the monopoly. Although these two meanings are hallowed in the legal phraseology of patents and by time-honoured usage generally, the word will in this chapter be used only in the first of the above senses, thus removing at least one semantic obstacle from the reader's path.

WHAT A PATENT IS

We can now consider what sort of thing a patent is. A simple analogy may be helpful. A patent can be likened to a fence erected round an area of technology and bearing the sign 'trespassers will be prosecuted'. The area of technology will be recognizable as the claims discussed above, while somewhere near the middle of the area is the 'invention'.

By way of illustration, let us vary the theme from a ballcock to a chemical process — say a process for making sulphuric acid by passing sulphur dioxide over a catalyst at a temperature of $x°C$. The patentee will probably have been allowed to include in his claims a range of catalysts and a range of temperatures on either side of x. The fence delimits these ranges.

It will be observed that the fence in itself does not prevent anyone from trespassing on the forbidden area, or *infringing* the patent as it is called. But once the fence is crossed the patentee has a cause of action in the High Court claiming damages and (usually much more significant) an injunction to stop the infringer from doing it again.

VALIDITY OF PATENTS

The validity of a granted patent can be the subject of proceedings in the Patent Office acting in a judicial capacity, or the Patents Court, which is a branch of the High Court. If the patent is held to be invalid, it is revoked.

The grounds of revocation under the new Act are of three types:

1   That the invention is not patentable
2   That the patent was granted to somebody who was not the inventor(s) or a person deriving title from him or them
3   That the specification does not adequately tell the expert (in the 1977 Act, 'person skilled in the art') how to put the invention into effect

The state of the art

The fundamental requirements of patentability are concerned with the relationship of the invention to the 'state of the art'. This phrase means the sum total of the knowledge available to the public in the relevant 'art (i.e. technology) at the 'priority date' (see p.272) of the patent. The knowledge can be documentary, e.g. in the technical journals or above all in prior patent specifications (usually referred to for short, but inaccurately, as 'prior patents'), or it can be by virtue of what has been done before (so-called 'prior use'), provided the nature of the use was known to the public, e.g. as a product available on the market.

Under the old Act the knowledge had to exist in the UK to be effective, but under the 1977 Act it can be anywhere in the world. This will not make as much difference as might be thought, because most technical publications, including patent specifications, become available here shortly after publication.

Novelty

The first requirement for patentability is that the invention shall be new. This means that if a comparison is made between the alleged invention and the state of the art, there must be some genuine difference between them. In making the comparison, account must be taken not only of the express wording of the relevant documents, but also any clear implications. The approach is to ask the person skilled in the art what, on a fair reading, the document actually means to him.

Obviousness

The commonest ground of invalidity is probably that the invention is 'obvious and does not involve any inventive step' having regard to the state of the art. This means that while there is some difference between the invention and the prior art, so that it can properly be described as new, the difference is such as would have been obvious to the person skilled in the art such as, for instance, a 'mere workshop variant'. To justify a monopoly, the inventor must have taken an 'inventive step'. This need not be of breakthrough proportions; quite the contrary. In one case it was held that a 'mere scintilla of invention' will suffice. What is certain is that there is no definition of what it consists of. As in the case of the phrase 'supported by' the description in the specification as referred to above, it is a matter of the subjective judgment of the tribunal considering the case. It is possible by a study of the decided cases to arrive at various generalizations to assist in judging particular cases but such a study would not be appropriate here.

There is, however, one criterion which is worth discussing as it enters in one form or other into most arguments on obviousness. Let us take as an example, the mixing of two well-known fungicides. One's first reaction is likely to be that this cannot be inventive, especially as it is generally well known that biocidal agents can be mixed in order to enlarge their 'spectrum' of activity. If, however, the inventor shows that the fungicides have a marked synergistic effect on each other, so that the mixture is more effective than the sum of the components, it is very difficult to say that it was obvious to make the mixture. The incentive was there, but nobody before the inventor thought of doing it. That the invention produces an unexpected advantage is thus often decisive in justifying a finding of inventiveness, although it must be emphasized that it is not an indispensable condition.

What it amounts to is that, if there had been an incentive for some time to come up with the new development but no-one had thought of it before the inventor, it is not possible to regard it as having been an obvious thing to do.

Secret prior use

Prior use which was 'secret' (i.e. the nature of which was not known to the public) is not part of the state of the art, and is not available under the 1977 Act as a ground of invalidity.

The word 'secret' is a little unfortunate, as it covers a normal works operation, provided the public are not admitted. If members of the public had access and could find out what was going on, the relevant activity is part of the state of the art and is available as such under both Acts.

It is fundamental that a patent should not be granted which could stop a person from continuing to do what he was doing before, even if he was doing it 'secretly'. The 1977 Act, recognizing that the secret use is not part of the state of the art, provides that, if a person other than the inventor was using the technology before the priority date of the patent, he shall have a free licence to continue doing so. Thus the patent remains valid and enforceable except against the individual or company who operated the invention before the priority date.

Is the technology an invention?

Patents can only be validly granted for patentable inventions. Before patentability is considered, the question must be asked: 'Is the item of technology in question an invention at all?' To enable this question to be answered, the 1977 Act includes a definition of the sort of technology that can be patented in that section, i.e. $s1$, of the Act which defines the requirements of a patentable invention. We have given a simplified version of this definition above.

Ground of invalidity concerned with the specification

The specification must disclose the invention in a fair and intelligible manner and must reflect the breadth of the scope of the claims; it must not withhold significant information on its optimization, because this information is the consideration for the grant of the patent. Failure to comply with this requirement is a ground of revocation.

The above discussion on validity needs qualifying in view of our determination not to use the word 'invention' in a double sense. To understand the point it may be helpful to return to the analogy of a fence round an area of technology — defined with precision by the words of the patent claim — and think of the area as covering a whole range of articles or processes roughly centred on the invention. Then everything which has to be satisfied by the invention to make the patent valid must also be satisfied by the whole range of variants included in the fenced-off area. It is this which is the main factor in restraining the inventor from claiming too great an area, for the bigger the area, the more chance there is that some variant near the periphery will contravene one of the requirements for validity. In that event the whole claim is invalid — patent claims cannot be like the curate's egg, good in parts.

INTELLECTUAL PROPERTY RIGHTS

EMPLOYEES' INVENTIONS

In the absence of any rule of law to the contrary, an invention, including any patent rights in it at home or abroad, belongs to the inventor or joint inventors. However, an invention made by an employee is the property of the employer if:

1 The duties of the employee might reasonably be expected to lead to the making of an invention, and
2 The invention was made in the course of those duties

The first is a legal question to be decided by the Patent Office or courts considering a particular case. They could, however, be assisted if a job description agreed between the employer and employee included a specific statement that the job was expected to result in inventions.

Compensation to employee inventors

The 1977 Act (*s*40) introduced the concept of awarding compensation to employee inventors in appropriate circumstances.

Entitlement to an award can arise in either of two cases as follows:

1 The invention belongs to the employer and a patent granted in respect of the invention is of outstanding benefit to the employee
2 The invention belongs to the employee and a patent granted in respect of the invention has been assigned or exclusively licensed to the employer

The first case can only arise where the invention was made after 1 June 1978 and the second case can only arise where the assignment or licence was effected after 1 June 1978.

An application for an award can be made by the employee (even if his employment has ceased) to the UKPO or to the Patents Court at any time up to one year after the patent has ceased to have effect and any number of applications may be made. The 1977 Act (*s*41) sets out the considerations which the tribunal must have in mind (such as relative contributions to the success of the invention by the inventor and by others and renumeration or payment already received by the inventor from his employer) in deciding how much compensation, if any, should be awarded.

An employee is debarred from making a claim to the UKPO or the Patents Court for an award of compensation if he is a member of a trade union which has entered into a 'collective agreement' with his employer relating to payment of compensation.

Since time is required before it can be seen that a patent has been an outstanding benefit to the employer, very few applications for compensation awards have yet been made.

Contracts on employee inventions

The 1977 Act overrides the ordinary law of contract in certain cases. Thus, s42 renders unenforceable any contract between an employer and employee inventor which reduces the statutory rights of the employee, if the contract was made *before* the invention. A contract relating to an invention belonging to an employee which was entered into after the invention was made is clearly enforceable, and presumably the same applies to inventions belonging to the employer.

A collective agreement with a trade union relating to employee inventions is enforceable in respect of members of the union only. It appears that non-members retain their full statutory rights under the Act, even if they benefit from the collective agreement, but the tribunal could probably take this into account in awarding compensation.

INFRINGEMENT OF PATENTS

A patent is infringed by anyone who makes, imports, uses or sells an article or machine protected by the patent, or uses a process protected by the patent, or sells the direct product of such a process (whether the process is conducted in the UK or abroad). To decide whether a given article is protected by the patent it is necessary to construe the definition constituted by the patent claim and determine whether the article falls within or without the definition.

British patent law is strict in holding the patentee to the words of his claim but there are two qualifications. The first is that the *de minimis* rule (that the law takes no account of trifles) applies as always. The second is the doctrine of *equivalents* or 'pith and marrow', according to which a man infringes a claim if he substitutes an element of it by an equivalent (as for instance a non-spherical float in a ballcock claim confined to a spherical float) so as to take the pith and marrow of the claim even if it is not within its exact wording. This doctrine grew up in the days before the patentee was required to delineate the boundary of his monopoly by an accurately drafted patent claim. Further reference to this question is made in the section on European Patents.

Court action

If the patentee wishes to go to the limit in enforcing his patent against a supposed infringer, he must issue a writ for infringement in the Patents Court. If he cannot tell from any product sold by the alleged infringer whether what the latter is doing infringes the patent (as in the case of a chemical process, for example) he can ask the court for an order for discovery and inspection on the basis of a reasonable suspicion.

It is routine in an infringement action for the defendant to counter-claim for revocation of the patent on the basis that it is invalid on one or more specified grounds. The question at issue at the trial is therefore whether any valid claim of the patent has been infringed.

What also constitutes infringement?

1 *Contributory infringement.* (This is only a very brief summary of a section of the Act which will prove difficult to interpret.) This applies to patents where the invention essentially involves the use of some unpatented material, substance or article. Section 60(2) of the 1977 Act provides that anyone selling such unpatented material etc. knowing that the customer intends to use it for infringing the patent is guilty of infringement. Section 60(3) makes the additional qualification that if the material etc. is a 'staple article of commerce', the supplier must actually induce the customer to infringe before he (the supplier) can be held to infringe. A typical example would be the issue of a data sheet to customers recommending the infringing use

2 *Pharmaceutical use.* A method or process of treating the human body is not a patentable invention ($s2(6)$). However, the 1977 Act provides that a patent can be obtained for a new pharmaceutical use of a substance and such patent will be infringed by a person supplying the substance for the patented use, even though the use itself, being a treatment of the human body, is not deemed to be an infringement. In other words the pharmaceutical manufacturer can be sued, but not the doctor

Threats

An important practical point in the relationship between a patentee and a person he suspects of infringing his patent is the matter of threats. Under $s70$ of the 1977 Act, anyone who makes unjustified threats to bring proceedings for infringement against somebody, such as a retailer, who is re-selling an article or product, renders himself liable to an action to restrain these threats. The threat need not be spelt out in so many words, provided what is said or written would be regarded as a threat by a reasonable business man. A patentee is free to threaten the manufacturer or importer to his heart's content.

EUROPEAN PATENT LAW

The function of the EPO has been touched on above, and the procedural aspects will be dealt with later in this chapter. At the moment we will deal with the substantive law embodied in the EPC.

The question can be considered quite briefly because the law is mainly confined to matters relating to the criteria for granting and validity of a patent; in other words, what is a patentable invention? It is, moreover, the express intention ($s130(7)$) of the 1977 Act to bring UK law into line with the EPC so far as it is practicable to equate an Act of Parliament with an international treaty. It follows that the EPC law on patentability is essentially as set out above in relation to UK law.

The need to harmonize UK and EPC law is increased by the CPC. Although this convention cannot yet be ratified, the 1977 Act had to make provision for eventual ratification. Since community patents, which will be granted by the EPO under the EPC, will be effective as such in the UK after granting, it is essential that British patent law should be assimilated to the law of the EPC.

PATENTING PROCEDURE IN THE UK

Each country has its own system of patent law and administrative procedure. In broad outline the principles set out in the preceding sections, although directed primarily to the UK and EPC law, are valid for overseas countries, with a few important exceptions which will be referred to later. Administrative procedures, however, differ substantially from country to country. Those obtaining in Great Britain will be considered first.

Priority dates

The first step in obtaining a patent is to file an application at the UKPO. It has always been a special feature of the British system that the application need be accompanied only by a 'provisional' specification, which does not require the inclusion of the monopoly-defining 'claims' and that the application need not be completed until twelve months after the filing date.

For the sake of harmony with the EPC, the 1977 Act has formally abolished provisional specifications, but the substance of the system has been retained by an ingenious device.

Under the 1977 Act, the applicant need only file a description which can be informal; in particular, he does not need to include claims. In fact, the description can be just the same as a provisional specification under the old Act. Such a document serves to establish the applicant's priority date for his invention. But in order to proceed to the granting of a patent, the claims must be filed within twelve months. Alternatively, a new application containing a specification with claims may be filed and this is particularly useful if the applicant wishes to add new matter to his description. If such new application is filed within twelve months of the first application, the priority date established by the latter remains effective. The system is thus essentially the same as the old provisional and complete specifications.

Publication

The specification with claims is published, usually just as it is filed, at eighteen months from the priority date. The specification is printed and indexed in a comprehensive classification system, and copies can be bought at the Sales Branch of the UKPO. It should be noted that this document only fulfils one part of the function of a patent specification — the provision of technical information about the invention. The other function — defining the scope of the claimed monopoly — cannot be fulfilled until the patent has been granted.

On publication of the specification, the Patent Office file of the case becomes open to public inspection, and remains so for the life of the patent and thereafter.

Search and examination

When the claims have been filed and the prescribed search fee (£80) has been paid, the application is remitted to an examiner who makes a search among prior documents (in practice, existing patent specifications) and reports those which are relevant to the invention as claimed in the claims. The applicant then has the opportunity of deciding whether, in the light of the search report, it is worth proceeding to the next step. The sort of considerations which usually arise can be illustrated with reference to our ballcock invention.

Let us imagine that the applicant thinks he is entitled to claim a ballcock with any kind of float, but that (surprisingly) an elliptical float is especially advantageous in some way. The examiner cites a specification describing a ballcock with a spherical float. This clearly destroys the patentability of the broad claim to any kind of float but not of a claim limited to the case in which the float is elliptical. To cater for this (very common) type of situation the law provides that the applicant can make a whole series of claims directed to successively smaller fenced-off areas, each within the confines of the previous one, and that in litigation the validity and infringement of each claim is to be considered separately. In our case claim 1 would include any kind of float and claim 2 would be restricted to an elliptical float; so that on being notified of the examiner's citation, the applicant would simply strike out claim 1 and accept the grant of a patent based on claim 2.

The applicant must make up his mind whether there is enough chance of securing allowance of a claim or claims which are of worthwhile scope, to justify spending the further fee of £100 for *examination* of the application.

If he decides in the affirmative, the case is sent back to the examiner, who determines on behalf of the Patent Office whether, in his view, the prior documents totally destroy the patentability of the invention, in which case he will refuse the application; or whether (as is more likely) there is something left which could be patented, in which case he reports to the applicant, who can amend his claims accordingly. If the examiner is satisfied, usually after some argument to and fro, a patent is granted.

It should be emphasized that acceptance by the examiner is in no way a guarantee of the validity of the claims. In our illustration he could have missed the ballcock specification in his search, so that a patent was granted containing claim 1 as well as claim 2, and this could be challenged in litigation by a defendant who managed to discover the prior specification the examiner had missed. The court would then hold claim 1 invalid but might hold claim 2 valid. If the defendant had made a ballcock with an elliptical float, the court would order an injunction and (subject to a defined discretion) damages for infringement of claim 2, at the same time ordering the cancellation of claim 1.

The patent in its granted form is reprinted, using the same number as the previously published specification but with the letter B added. The letter A is used for the first published version.

Conflict between co-pending applications

It can happen that an Applicant B files a patent application after an application by A for closely similar subject-matter, but during the eighteen months between A's priority date and publication of his (A's) final specification. This is particularly so in intensively research-based industries. We then have the paradox that A's specification was still secret at B's priority date and therefore ought not to count against B, yet patents ought not to be granted to both A and B for the same invention.

To get round this difficulty, both in the EPC and the British 1977 Act, A's specification in our illustration is deemed, during the period before its publication, to be part of the 'state of the art'. However, the prior unpublished specification is only half way to being in the state of the art: it counts against the *novelty* of the later application but cannot be used as a basis for proving *obviousness*.

Adjudication of patents

Under the 1977 Act, the UKPO has jurisdiction over the validity of patents granted both by the UKPO and by the EPO, although, in the latter case, the jurisdiction is confined to the UK part of the bundle. Opposition before grant of a patent has been abolished. Anyone interested in securing the revocation of a patent at any time in its life can apply to the UKPO for revocation under *s*72 of the 1977 Act. There is a right of appeal to a new branch of the High Court called the Patents Court, but appeal from this to the Court of Appeal only lies in respect of particular grounds listed in the 1977 Act (s97(3)).

The Patents Court can also adjudicate on validity at first instance, for example if a defendant in a patent infringement action puts in (as he invariably does) a counter-claim for revocation of the patent.

PATENTING PROCEDURE IN EUROPE

Since procedure under the 1977 Act has been devised to correspond closely with that under the EPC, only a few further points need be added under this heading.

Language

The EPO is an autonomous international organization set up by a treaty (the EPC). It has no connection with the EEC. It is staffed by officials from all member countries.

Patent applications must be filed in one of the official languages: English, French or German. Since the system is accessible to nationals of any country, a large number of applications originate in USA and Japan. More applications are therefore filed in the English language than in either of the other two languages. When a patent is granted, the claims will have to be translated into the other two official languages. Most countries, but not the UK, require that the specification be translated into their national language when this differs from the language of publication of the grant.

Application for a European patent

There are two main differences between procedures in the EPO and the UKPO. The first is that there is no counterpart in the EPO of the British specification without claims. Priority can be claimed in the EPO from a British preliminary specification, but this is part of the International Convention system (see below) rather than a specifically EPC procedure.

Secondly, as mentioned above, the applicant has to 'designate' the countries in which he wishes the European patent, if granted, to be effective, a designation fee of £84 approx being payable for each country, including of course the UK.

Opposition

Although the EPO is basically concerned only with the *granting* of patents, which then revert to the national jurisdictions of the respective designated countries, there is one exception. Within nine months after grant, a

European patent can be 'opposed' at the EPO. This is similar to British revocation proceedings at the UKPO. If an opposition is successful, the European patent as a whole (i.e. in respect of each designated country) is revoked.

Which route: European or national?

If a prospective applicant wants to cover his invention in more than one member country of the EPC, he has the option of applying at the EPO (the 'European route') or of filing separate national applications in each of the countries concerned (the 'national route'). The considerations which arise are as follows:

1 Financial: Obviously the greater the number of countries involved, the greater the financial advantage of the European route. The calculation is complicated because it involves professional as well as official Patent Office fees, and both of these vary from country to country in the case of national applications and it also involves the cost of translation of the granted European patent for those countries where such translation is required. As a rough guide it can be said that there is a break-even point of three or four countries at which the European route becomes less expensive than the national route
2 National patents can be obtained very easily in a number of member countries (e.g. France, Belgium, Italy, Spain). If the European route is chosen, fairly strict criteria for allowing an application will be applied by the EPO, and in any case one would be putting all one's eggs in one basket
3 In the case of a European patent, a single opposition can destroy the patent in all the designated countries
4 The amount of time and effort which has to be spent by the applicant and his patent agent in securing protection in more than one country should be less by the European than the national route
5 British patent agents who are also European patent attorneys can act directly at the EPO, whereas if the national route is used local agents have to be employed for each country

COMMUNITY PATENT CONVENTION

We have indicated briefly the nature of the CPC, which will provide for the granting of a *single* patent for the whole Common Market. This will raise interesting questions of jurisprudence which have not yet been resolved. Procedure under the CPC should fit comfortably into that of the EPO and the UKPO. The main problem will be the cost, since the annual renewal fees to keep the patent in force will be very high.

INTELLECTUAL PROPERTY RIGHTS

Further discussion of the CPC in this book would be premature until ratification by all the member countries takes place, and this may be years ahead.

FOREIGN PATENTS

Nearly all the countries of the world have their own patent offices and fully autonomous patent systems. This includes the members of the EPC, whose national systems will continue to operate in parallel with the EPO. There are two treaties which operate worldwide:

1 The International Convention for the Protection of Industrial Property
2 The Patent Co-operation Treaty (PCT)

The PCT is concerned with providing a single filing and searching facility for all the countries which a patent applicant may wish to cover. This sounds like a simple matter, but in fact the technical and procedural complications are immense and so the PCT is not popular amongst patent agents.

THE INTERNATIONAL CONVENTION

This dates from 1883 and now includes all the industrial countries of the world and many more. We will call it simply 'the Convention'.

The EPC counts as a 'Convention country', on the same footing as each individual European or other member country.

The main provisions of the Convention are:

1 That the laws of a Convention country will be applied equally to citizens of all Convention countries
2 That if a patent application for an invention is filed in one Convention country and within twelve months an application for the same invention is filed in one or more other Convention countries, then such other applications will have the priority date of the first one. Hence it is very desirable for a UK applicant to file foreign applications within twelve months of his British application. Thus if the latter was filed with a preliminary specification, the filing of the claims in the UK normally coincides with the filing of foreign 'Convention applications'
3 If a ship or aircraft, which has on board equipment used for the operation of that craft, temporarily enters a country where such equipment has been patented by a third party, no proceedings for infringement may be taken

If an applicant (usually from abroad) files a Convention application in the UK, he files a certified copy of the original foreign application and this serves to establish his priority in much the same way as a British preliminary specification does for a British applicant in the UK.

Diversity of laws

It is not possible here to touch on the different procedures in different countries and only salient differences in substantive laws can be mentioned.

In the USA and Canada, the inventor's priority does not stem from the date of filing a patent application, but from the date he 'conceived' the invention.

No country except the UK and some of the old commonwealth countries has the preliminary specification system.

The examination to which a patent application is submitted before grant varies as follows:

1   Full examination of all possible grounds of invalidity — for example, the USA, Japan, Germany and other northern European countries including the UK
2   Little or no examination at all — for example, Italy, Belgium, Spain and Latin countries generally. France has provision for an official search, although it is left to the applicant whether to take action on the search report or not
3   Germany, Holland, Australia and Japan have adopted the system of 'deferred examination' whereby the application is not examined unless the patentee or an interested party requests it and pays the appropriate fee within the specified period, failing which the application lapses

There used to be a fundamental difference in the way the UK, on the one hand, and the civil law countries and most of the rest of the world on the other (with USA somewhere in between but nearer the UK) approach the questions of definition of the monopoly area and validity. To take Germany as a typical example, there is no definition of the monopoly area in the claims or the rest of the specification or in any other document. Whether any particular manufacture is within or without the patent can only be a matter of subjective judgment after considering the description and claims in the light of the prior art and any statements made by the patentee to the Patent Office to persuade them to grant the patent. On the other hand, the validity of a patent once issued tends to be taken for granted unless a challenger brings up fresh facts, such as items of prior art which were not before the examiner. This is somewhat the reverse of the British position where the monopoly is tightly defined by the claims and the question of validity is more open. However, in those countries, including the UK, which participated in the Strasbourg Convention on the Unification of Certain Points of Substantive Law on Patents for Inventions, steps are being taken to bring laws on validity and infringement into line.

Renewal fees

In all countries except the USA and Canada, annual renewal fees have to be paid to keep a patent in force. These vary greatly in amount but are generally payable annually and usually increase with the life of the patent. In West and, more especially, East Germany the fees are particularly onerous.

LICENSING

Instead of using his 'fence' to keep out the competition, the patentee may decide to exploit it by allowing one or more parties in for a consideration. A licence in its simplest form is a promise not to sue the licensee for infringement if he enters the forbidden territory. If at the same time the patentee agrees not to let anyone else in, and to stay out himself, the licence is 'exclusive' within the meaning of the 1977 Act. Such an exclusive licensee has most of the rights and privileges of the patentee, including the right to sue for infringement.

If the patentee undertakes to grant no further licences, but does not exclude himself from working the invention, the licence is known as a 'sole' licence. This carries none of the statutory rights of the exclusive licence.

Territory

The effect of a licence is to give the licensee permission to do something which would otherwise be an infringement of the patent. This may be limited to a part only of the technology covered by the patent and to a part only of the UK, though the latter is probably rare in these days. If there are corresponding patents in other countries, the agreement may include a licence in one or more of these countries. A not uncommon arrangement would be to grant a British company an exclusive licence to make, use and sell in the UK and a non-exclusive licence to sell in other countries where there are patents, thus leaving it open for manufacturing licences to be granted to other companies abroad. The licensee does not need a licence to sell in countries where there are no patents, but he may (subject to legal restrictions which obtain in various countries — see below) agree collaterally *not* to sell in specified countries.

Financial arrangements

The consideration for the grant of a licence is normally monetary, and may take the form of a royalty based on use of the invention, an annual minimum payment and/or a down payment. The royalty can conveniently be expressed as a percentage of the sales value of an article, or the product of a process, covered by the patent. If, however, the article is a machine, for example for making shoes, it is difficult to get a fair return by charging a percentage of the value of the machine unless the percentage is an intimidatingly high figure. It is more realistic to charge a small percentage on the value of the shoes made by the machine. Similar considerations arise if the invention is for example a mixture of petrol and an additive present in very small quantities, in which case a royalty based on the value of the petrol has a more realistic appearance than one based on the value of the additive.

If the licence is exclusive, the patentee has a prime interest in ensuring adequate performance by the licensee. This is usually provided for by requiring the licensee to make up the royalty payment to a stated annual minimum payment. The licensee for his part is willing to do this since he is effectively buying a monopoly as well as a right of entry. The licensee may either covenant outright to pay the annual minimum or he may reserve the right not to pay it in which case he submits to a penalty such as termination of the licence or conversion to a non-exclusive one.

A down payment is appropriate if the deal includes the initial transmission of technical information ('know-how') such as drawings, to enable the licensee to commence manufacture.

Miscellaneous terms

If the parties so agree, the licence may permit the licensee to grant sub-licences to third parties.

The question of infringement usually arises during negotiations. There are two quite distinct issues: what is to happen if a third party infringes the licensed patent, and infringement of a third-party patent by the licensee. On the first issue, the licensee is justified in objecting to pay royalty if an infringer is operating for nothing. The agreement can therefore provide that the payment of royalty shall be suspended until either the infringement is stopped by the patentee or the infringer is granted a licence (assuming the original licence was non-exclusive). What is not reasonable in view of the high cost and uncertainty of patent actions is to expect the patentee to covenant to sue an infringer.

The question of infringement of a third party's patent by the licensee is not directly connected with the licence, and the licensor is justified in refusing to take any responsibility. The fact that a licensee's operation is covered by two patents, one of them being the subject of the licence and the other belonging to a third party, is in no way derogatory of the former. A patent gives no right to anyone, even the patentee, to manufacture the subject of the patent, as can be seen if we remember the fence analogy. To revert to the ballcock example, if A gets a patent with a claim worded widely enough to cover any kind of float, but in which the specification describes only a spherical float, and later B discovers that an elliptical float has a special unexpected advantage, B may be able to get a valid patent for that particular variant and this would in no way reflect on the validity of A's patent. If B grants a licence to C there is no reason why B should be responsible for the fact that in operating under the licence C will infringe A's patent. It is up to C to make terms with A (with the sanction of a compulsory licence in the background if A's terms are so unreasonable as to frustrate exploitation of B's invention).

The duration of a licence is normally for the life of the relevant patent and it is provided in the 1977 Act (*s*45) that it shall be terminable by either party when the patent expires.

Know-how and improvements

It often happens, especially if an exclusive licence is contemplated, that the parties agree to transmit know-how and improvements to each other. The point to note here is that an essential part of such an agreement is an exact definition of the technological field. If this is to be coterminous with the fenced-off area of the patent, the agreement should say so; it is not, as is often believed, an accepted meaning of the word 'improvement'. The agreement should also be clear about what rights will accrue in respect of *patentable* improvements. Possibly each party will be able to exploit these in his own territory.

Another important point is the right to use the know-how after termination of the agreement. In the absence of an explicit provision there is no such right, and this can have very serious consequences for the recipient of the know-how.

Know-how licence

Of course, technology does not need to be patented to enable it to be licensed. It is not unreasonable for secret unpatented know-how to be licensed in return for a royalty payment so long as the know-how remains secret. In the case of know-how which is not secret, a single payment or stage payments are more appropriate as all the licensee is doing is saving himself the trouble of seeking out know-how for himself.

Forbidden terms

In English law the parties can negotiate a patent licence (or for that matter any other intellectual property licence) on any terms they please provided it is not in restraint of trade — a common-law doctrine of fairly narrow compass — and (when a patent is included in the licence) does not contravene s44 of the 1977 Act. This provides that the patentee shall not extend his monopoly right by making it a condition of a licence that the licensee shall buy from the patentee unpatented raw material, for example, unpatented phosphoric acid for use in a patented metal-finishing process. This is in fact frequently done, especially by implication, but the patentee is risking the enforceability of his patent if the practice ever comes to light.

In the USA and the EEC this matter comes in the province of the antitrust or competition laws, which are being applied with even more stringent effect to restrict what a licensor and licensee can lawfully agree. It is impossible here to go into any detail on this subject, but readers will be aware of the importance of not falling foul of these laws.

The practice of applying restrictions to licence agreements has been spreading in recent years, especially in developing countries, where the main motives are to foster local development and reduce the payment of royalties to other countries.

EXISTING PATENTS

Existing patents are patents granted under the old Act, i.e. on applications filed before 1 June 1978. Existing patents can be recognized in that their numbers are in the 1 000 000 range whereas patents granted under the 1977 Act are numbered from 2 000 000 onwards. Since the term of a patent is twenty years, the last existing patent is not due to expire until 1998. The law on validity of existing patents differs from that applicable to patents granted under the 1977 Act but it is rare for these differences to be of great significance.

The law on infringement of existing patents, on the other hand, is that prescribed under the 1977 Act as described above, unless the infringement commenced before 1 June 1978. Since, at the time of application for an existing patent, the term of the patent was sixteen years, an existing patent is deemed endorsed 'licences of right' for the seventeenth to twentieth years of its life. This means that anyone wishing to take a licence under the patent must be given one. If the prospective licensee cannot agree terms with the patentee, these will be settled by the UKPO.

TRADE MARKS AND SERVICE MARKS

It has long been part of the common law that if A has a reputation in a trade name or trade mark and B sells his goods in association with the trade mark in such a way as to lead the public to believe that his goods emanate from A, then A has a cause of action against B for 'passing off' his goods as A's. In such an action, A has the onus of proving both the reputation of his mark and the confusion caused by B's use of it.

By the Trade Marks Act 1875 the owner of a trade mark was given a new right: to enter his mark on a Register of Trade Marks, thereby gaining an entitlement to stop anyone else from using the mark, always assuming that the registration was valid. The current registration is provided by the Trade Marks Act 1938.

Under pressure from trade mark agents and persons providing services rather than selling goods and in anticipation of a future Community Trade Mark Regulation, the Trade Marks (Amendment) Act 1984 was passed to provide for registration of service marks. At the time of writing it was expected that applications to register service marks would be filed on or after 1 October 1986.

An essential part of the system is that the registration must be in respect of a specified range of goods on which the owner uses or intends to use the mark or services which he offers or intends to offer, and that the registration is infringed only by use of the mark in connection with goods or services within this 'specification of goods' or 'specification of services'.

The Register of Trade Marks

The Register of Trade Marks is kept by the Registrar, who is in fact the same person as the Comptroller of Patents. As in the case of patents, an application to register a mark is examined to see if it complies with the requirements of the Trade Marks Act. The examination extends to almost the grounds on which a registration could be held invalid. The guiding principle is that the mark must be distinctive (in the sense that it distinguishes the owner's goods or services from those originating or provided elsewhere) either inherently or because past use has in fact made it distinctive. The former is in effect a subjective judgment by the examiner or tribunal considering the matter, while the latter is determined by evidence furnished by persons in the relevant trade. There are, however, two categories which are difficult to register no matter how much distinctiveness is proved, namely words of which the ordinary significance is either a geographical name or a surname ($s9$ of the Trade Marks Act). The opposite of a distinctive mark is one which is descriptive of the goods in question. This fact, coupled with the overriding requirement ($s11$) that the mark must not be deceptive, shows the narrow path which has to be trodden in many cases. For example, 'Silico' for polishes might be held descriptive if they contained silicones but deceptive if they did not.

All goods are divided into thirty-four classes and separate applications must be made for goods in different classes. Services are divided into eight further classes.

Conflicting marks

A further requirement of registration ($s12$) is that the mark must not resemble too closely a mark already on the register for the same or similar goods or services, unless the applicant for registration can prove 'honest concurrent use' of the two marks for a period of some years. In borderline cases the Registrar will accept the consent of the owner of the mark already on the Register as justification for allowing the marks to coexist. Whether the consent is given and if so, subject to what conditions, is a private matter between the two parties, but in practice consent is often given gratis on the assumption that the consenting party may want the same favour from the other on some future occasion.

Opposition and rectification

There is provision for opposition to the registration ($s18$) and for an action to 'rectify the Register' by removing an existing registration ($s26$). One ground of removal which will not have been considered at the registration stage is that the owner had no bona fide intention to use the mark and has not in fact used it; or that he has not used the mark for a continuous period of five years.

Trade mark and service mark use

It is most important that a mark, whether registered or not, should be used correctly if the proprietor is to retain his exclusive rights in the mark.

Specifically, the proprietor should aim to prevent his mark (in the case of a word mark) from becoming a generic name for the goods or services in question. To this end, it is recommended always to use the mark in conjunction with the conventional noun for the goods or services and to write the mark in some special way, such as between quotation marks, in capital letters or in bold letters. The proprietor should monitor the trade press to ensure that any reference to his trade mark which may appear includes a reference to the ownership of the mark.

Licensing

The right to use a trade mark or service mark, whether registered or not, can be licensed by the owner but he must be careful to require the licensee to adopt his standards of quality for the goods in question, since otherwise the public may be deceived, with the result that the owner will lose his rights in the mark. It is advisable in the case of a registered mark to get the official seal of approval on the terms of the licence by making the licensee a 'registered user' under $s28$ of the Trade Marks Act. This has the further advantage that use of the mark by the registered user counts as use for the purpose of $s26$.

International

Trade marks, but not service marks, are included in the International Convention for the Protection of Industrial Property, but the priority period is six months as distinct from twelve months in the case of patents. The trade mark laws and practice of other countries differ from each other about as much as they do for patents, the main point being that in some countries, notably France, there is no concept of ownership of a trade mark until and unless the mark is registered, prior use being of no consequence. Hence a company that has failed to register a valuable mark in France can see it lost to a third party simply by registration.

Discussions have been in progress for some years under the aegis of the EEC for the setting up of a Community trade mark system. It will be at least a couple of years, probably more, before this is finalized and put into operation. As in the case of the EPC, national systems will continue to exist in parallel with that of the EEC.

DESIGNS AND COPYRIGHT

Literary and artistic copyright has a long history and protection for industrial designs has followed in the wake of copyright legislation. The current Designs Act is the Designs Act 1949 with some minor amendments. A design registered under the Designs Act must be in respect of a named article and gives the proprietor the exclusive right to make, import and sell such articles to which that design is applied. The design may be in respect of the 'shape or configuration' of the article (which is usual in the case of three-dimensional articles, such as furniture), or in respect of the 'pattern or ornamentation' (which is more usual in the case of two-dimensional articles, such as wallpaper and textiles). Features of the design which are dictated solely by the function of the article are not protectable under the Designs Act.

The current Copyright Act is the Copyright Act 1956, with amendments. It covers artistic copyright, literary copyright and musical copyright and performing and broadcasting rights. Artistic copyright includes not only artistic drawings, paintings, sculpture and photographs, but also original engineering drawings and this is where copyright is particularly important to the industrialist. Such copyright is conveniently called 'industrial copyright'. By virtue of a recent amendment to the Copyright Act, it has been confirmed that computer programs are protectable as literary works. Copyright other than industrial copyright and computer programs is outside the scope of this handbook.

A design registration is infringed by anyone who, without permission, makes, imports, sells or hires articles to which the same or a similar design has been applied. There need not be any actual copying for infringement to be found. The reliefs available are an injunction to restrain further infringement and damages.

Artistic and literary copyright is infringed by anyone who, without permission, *copies* the author's work or a material part of it and sells the copies. In the case of artistic copyright, it is also an infringement to copy a three-dimensional reproduction of a two-dimensional drawing. This means that a product which has been made or reproduced from original drawings or sketches effectively enjoys copyright under the Copyright Act. 'Original' means that the drawing is not merely a copy of an earlier drawing or of a model. The remedies available are an injunction to restrain further infringement, an account of profits or 'conversion damages'. Conversion damages are equivalent to the value of the infringing articles to the infringer and not just the damage suffered by the copyright owner. For this reason, a mere threat to bring a copyright infringement action will often bring an infringer to heel.

However, care is needed when threatening to bring a design registration infringement action since the person threatened has the possibility of bringing an action for restraint of threats which are unjustified. Unlike threats of patent infringement proceedings, there can be danger in threatening a manufacturer or importer with design infringement.

The Designs Register and filing design applications

The Designs Register is kept by the Registrar who is again the same person as the Comptroller of Patents. An application to register a design is filed at the Designs Registry and must be accompanied by 'representations' illustrating the article to which the design is applied. The representations can be drawings or mounted photographs but, in either case, there must be sufficient views to illustrate the whole of the exterior of the article. Only features which are judged solely by the eye are protectable, so views of the interior of the article must not be included.

The design must be new at the date of filing of the application. Novelty is judged in relation to what was available to the public in the UK before the filing date. Thus, the proprietor of a design must file his application *before* making his design available by publication or by sale of articles to which the design is applied. The application is examined by the Registry and a search confined to previous design registrations is carried out. An opportunity is given to correct formal defects and to reply to any objections.

The registration is dated as of the filing date and lasts for five years, renewable for two further periods of five years each on payment of the prescribed fees.

There is no procedure for registration of copyright. Copyright is an inherent right which arises when the original work is made. The copyright term in respect of most artistic and literary works is for the life of the author and for fifty years after his death.

Licensing

Registered designs and copyright can be licensed in much the same way as patents. An exclusive licence of copyright carries with it a right of the licensee to sue infringers. Whilst an exclusive licensee under a registered design does not have any statutory right to institute infringement proceedings, a true exclusive licence will probably include the right of the licensee to sue. A restrictive condition concerning articles not the subject of a design registration or copyright should be avoided, for fears of running foul of EEC anti-trust laws.

International

Designs are covered by the International Convention (see p.284) but, as with trade marks, the priority period is six months. A design filed under convention is dated as of the priority date, not the filing date.

There are two copyright conventions, the Universal Copyright Convention and the Berne Copyright Union. Each of these conventions in principle extends the copyright under domestic legislation of each member country to nationals of all other member countries. The Berne Union imposes more conditions on member countries as to the content of their copyright laws. The UK is a member of the Universal Copyright Convention but not of the Berne Union. The UK recognizes countries party to either or both of these conventions for the purpose of providing copyright protection under the Act.

Only those countries whose copyright laws follow closely those of the UK provide for 'industrial copyright' protection of the kind described above. On the other hand, many countries have an unfair competition law which can provide remedies similar to those under the UK passing-off law and UK industrial copyright law, except that they do not provide for conversion damages.

MARKING

Since patents, registered designs, trade marks and copyright are exclusive to the proprietor, it is to the benefit of the proprietor that his competitors should know of the existence of those rights. Therefore the proprietor is well advised to advertise that he has such rights by marking the patented product, or article protected by a registered design with the patent or design number or by indicating the number of any trade mark which is registered. Indeed such marking is compulsory in some countries and where marking is not compulsory, failure to mark may result in failure to obtain damages for infringement.

A false claim to protection is, in general, an offence punishable by a fine or imprisonment or both. Accordingly, when an application for a patent, a design registration or a trade mark registration has not been granted, it is necessary to use wording such as 'Patent applied for, No. 86 54321'.

In the case of unregistered trade marks, it is useful to include the marking such as 'ACME is a Trade Mark of PQR Ltd'. This makes it clear that PQR Ltd has staked its claim to the trade mark.

Copyright is somewhat different in that it does not have an identification number and in that it automatically extends to all countries recognizing the relevant convention. The marking in accordance with the copyright conventions consists of the letter C in a circle followed by the year of publication followed by the name of the copyright owner, thus '© 1986 XYZ Ltd'. Failure to use this prescribed marking may mean that, in some countries, no damages can be recovered for infringement.

FUNCTIONS OF PATENT AND TRADE MARK AGENTS

Patent agents have a function in relation to patent law and practice which is analogous to that of solicitors in relation to other branches of the law. Owing to the technological subject-matter involved, a patent agent has to have achieved at least GCE A level standard in a science or engineering subject, and usually has a university degree, before sitting for the qualifying examinations which the Chartered Institute of Patent Agents administers on behalf of the Department of Trade and Industry.

There is a contradiction between the difficulty of the concepts underlying the patent system and the familiarity of its main visible product — the patent specification. In many industries, patent specifications are an important if not main source of information on recent developments and they are constantly handled by technical personnel of all grades. This means that laymen who are familiar with 'patents' (as they incorrectly term patent specifications) as items of technical information are unlikely to learn the underlying concepts of the system but substitute a rough-and-ready version which usually has little relation to reality. There are, in fact, very few matters connected with patent law or practice in which it is safe to proceed without consulting a patent agent.

It is usual for patent agents to include trade marks in their practice, some training in trade marks being necessary in order to pass the patent agent's qualifying examinations. Although this is elementary compared with the training in patents, a patent agent will either have acquired a full understanding by assisting an expert or will employ a fully qualified trade mark agent in his practice.

Unlike the profession of patent agency, that of trade marks is not closed, but there is an Institute of Trade Mark Agents which administers a rigorous examination as a condition of membership. Many patent agents are members of both institutes.

The bread-and-butter work of the patent agent is the preparation of patent applications, the main part of which is the patent specification, for filing in the UK and abroad in accordance with the local procedures; dealing with objections raised by the various examiners and with any oppositions; securing the grant of a patent; and ensuring the renewal fees are paid on it as long as the patentee requires. To do the job properly the patent agent ought to be in direct touch with the inventor in any particular case.

Analogous work arises in relation to trade marks and here the agent should be in *direct* touch with the relevant marketing executive. Trade mark matters sometimes seem simple, but in fact this is deceptive and the agent needs to have direct access to the principle actually involved just as much as he does in patent matters.

Representation before the UKPO in connection with design registration application is also an open profession. Nevertheless, it is usually conducted by patent agents and sometimes by trade mark agents.

The role of the patent agent in copyright questions is purely advisory. Many patent agents develop a substantial expertise in industrial copyright because of the overlap of interests with other intellectual property matters.

European patent attorneys

Professional representatives (practitioners) of any EPC country can act directly at the EPO in contradistinction to the national patent offices which require the representation to be held by a local patent practitioner. Qualification to act before the EPO is by an examination of similar scope to that in the UK, run by the EPO. Qualification leads to membership of the European Patent Institute (EPI).

Most foreign practitioners, when speaking English, call themselves 'patent attorneys'. Recognizing that this could put British agents at a disadvantage when competing for EPO business, e.g. in USA and Japan, Parliament approved the name 'European Patent Attorney' for use by British practitioners qualified to act before the EPO, in $s85(1)$ of the 1977 Act. The same expression was subsequently approved by the EPI for use by all professional representatives, irrespective of nationality and equivalent expressions in French and German have also been approved.

COSTS

The costs of obtaining and maintaining patents contain two components: government fees and professional charges. The Patent Office in each country has to carry out a number of clerical and technical operations on each patent application, the latter requiring skilled manpower, and the objective is to charge applicants and patentees enough to make the Patent Office self-supporting. The fee in the UK for an application is a nominal £10, the search fee is £80 and the examination fee is £100. The patent agent's charges depend on the nature of the job but they are not likely to be less than £250 for a preliminary specification and £350 for an application with claims. Much higher charges may be made for lengthy or complex work.

The costs for foreign applications vary a good deal from country to country. A large fraction of the costs in foreign-language countries goes for translation. An idea of the order of magnitude of the costs and of their range can be given by quoting estimates of £700 for an average case in India, and of £1500 in West Germany.

It is impossible to estimate the cost of prosecuting an application since it depends on the nature of the subject-matter, the procedure of the country concerned and the objections the examiners happen to turn up. The cost can vary from a few pounds in some countries to hundreds of pounds for a difficult USA case.

The annual renewal fees necessary to maintain a patent in force also vary enormously from country to country and over the life of the patent, generally increasing with its age. The UK is in a range of about £76 to £292 exclusive of agent's charges.

Charges for trade mark work follow a similar pattern but on a lower scale, perhaps a quarter to a half of the charge for analogous patent work. Renewal fees are required only at relatively long periods, for example in the UK every fourteen years after an initial period of seven years.

Charges for design registration applications are generally of the same order as those for trade marks.

FURTHER READING

T.A. Blanco White and Robin Jacob, *Patents, Trade Marks, Copyright and Industrial Designs,* Sweet & Maxwell, Concise College Texts, 3rd edition, 1986.
Michael F. Flint, *A User's Guide to Copyright,* Butterworths, 1985.
Patrick Hearn, *The Business of Industrial Licensing,* Gower, 2nd edition, 1986.
Peter Meinhardt and Keith R. Havelock, *Concise Trade Mark Law and Practice,* Gower, 1983.
Jeremy Phillips, *Introduction to Intellectual Property Law,* Butterworths, 1986.
Jeremy Phillips and Michael J. Hoolahan, *Employees' Inventions in the United Kingdom Law and Practice,* ESC Publishing Ltd, 1982.
Brian C. Reid, *A Practical Guide to Patent Law,* ESC Publishing, 1984.

14

Fair Trading

Malcolm Carlisle

Companies are faced with a broad spectrum of fair trading and competition law which has grown up like Topsy over the years. Broadly this law may be divided into two sectors; restrictive trade practices and consumer protection legislation. Clearly such a division is to some extent a convenient simplification, and other matters such as EEC law must be considered. However, it is a division expressed in the Fair Trading Act 1973 itself, which on the one hand contained provisions to give new protection to consumers and on the other consolidated and reorganized restrictive trade practices law.

This chapter will summarize first the restrictive trade practices legislation, which is the UK name for competition law, and then examine the main elements of consumer protection legislation which are designed to ensure that companies trade 'fairly'. It should be pointed out that the UK does not have a well developed law of what constitutes 'fair' or 'unfair' trading between companies. That is a concept recognized in a number of foreign jurisdictions, but it is not one with which this chapter is concerned.

RESTRICTIVE TRADE PRACTICES

The legislation in this field arose after the war from a changing attitude to business arrangements. Before the war monopolies and restrictive practices were not just tolerated but often encouraged as a means of protecting industry and hence employment. Later, a different philosophy developed to the effect that an economy is stimulated better by competition than by protectionism. Hence Parliament has taken action to prohibit a wide range of restrictive or collusive practices and to control monopolies and mergers. The old pre-war attitude is not entirely dead: it may be seen operating, for example, on a European scale in the arrangements made within the European Coal and Steel Community for the steel industry. However, in general, the approach in the UK and the rest of Europe is to encourage competition.

The relevant legislation

A summary of the development of restrictive practices legislation illustrates the piecemeal nature of the law in this area.

Monopolies and Restrictive Practices (Inquiry and Control) Act 1948. Established the Monopolies and Restrictive Practices Commission to which could be referred monopoly situations (then defined as control of one-third of the market).

Restrictive Trade Practices Act 1956

1 Created a Registrar of Restrictive Trading Agreements who was responsible for policing restrictive trading practices. Restrictive agreements were taken out of the Commission's control and made subject to registration. Such agreements were presumed contrary to the public interest and normally had to be referred by the Registrar to the Restrictive Practices Court, which was established by the Act for the purpose
2 The Commission was renamed the 'Monopolies Commission' and retained power to examine monopoly situations referred to it

Resale Prices Act 1964 (RPA 1964). This Act banned minimum resale price maintenance except in respect of goods which were specifically exempted upon application to the Restrictive Practices Court. Today the only goods so exempted are books and medicinal products, and they are the only products on which resale price maintenance may be enforced.

Monopolies and Mergers Act 1965

1 Extended the provisions of the 1948 Act to include mergers, enabling them to be referred to the Monopolies Commission
2 Permitted monopolies in the supply of services as well as goods to be referred to the Monopolies Commission

Restrictive Trade Practices Act 1968. Amended the 1956 Act by (*a*) introducing stronger sanctions, and (*b*) extending the 1956 Act to restrictive agreements in the form of 'information agreements' about goods

Fair Trading Act 1973

1 Repealed and replaced the 1948 and 1956 Acts' provisions as to monopolies and mergers and renamed the Commission the 'Monopolies and Mergers Commission'
2 Extended the restrictive trade practices legislation to restrictive agreements and information agreements concerning services as well as goods
3 Transferred the functions of the Registrar of Restrictive Trading Agreements to the Director General of Fair Trading, a new position created by the Act
4 The Director General was given certain responsibilities for administering the law on monopolies and mergers
5 The Act also contained a number of consumer protection provisions

Restrictive Trade Practices Act 1976 (RTPA 1976)

Resale Prices Act 1976 (RPA 1976)

Restrictive Practices Court Act 1976. Consolidated the legislation in these areas. Minor amendments were made by the RTPA 1977.

Competition Act 1980. Introduced a new procedure whereby the Director General could conduct preliminary investigations into alleged anti-competitive practices, request appropriate undertakings from companies concerned and, failing receipt of such undertakings, make a 'competition reference' to the Monopolies and Mergers Commission to investigate whether a particular course of dealing is against the public interest. The Act enabled the investigation of particular companies rather than just industry sectors. In addition power was given to enable the Monopolies and Mergers Commission to investigate certain public bodies and prices of major public concern.

Broadly speaking this quantity of legislation has produced a situation where:

(*a*) certain restrictive agreements and information agreements relating to goods and services are registrable with the Director General of Fair Trading and must in almost every case be referred to the Restrictive Practices Court, where they are presumed to be against the public interest unless justified
(*b*) monopolies, defined as 25 per cent or more of the market, and mergers involving the acquisition of more than £15 million assets may be referred to the Monopolies and Mergers Commission

(c) the Director General of Fair Trading may investigate practices which appear to be anti-competitive, and
(d) resale price maintenance is banned in all but pharmaceuticals and books

Over and above this UK legislation lie the competitive law provisions of articles 85 and 86 of the Treaty of Rome and the effect of these is discussed below. In many ways they provide a broader and more effective competition law in the UK than does our domestic legislation.

The institutions

The enforcement of restrictive trade practices legislation lies mainly in the following hands.

The Secretary of State for Trade and Industry has powers under the RTPA 1976 to apply the legislation to certain agreements; to exempt other agreements; and to instruct the Director General not to take proceedings on certain registered agreements.

With regard to monopolies and mergers, the Secretary of State can institute inquiries by the Commission and make orders following a Commission report.

The Director General of Fair Trading has the principal role. He is the registrar of restrictive agreements and information agreements and in general he must bring those agreements before the Restrictive Practices Court. He may make most kinds of monopoly reference to the Commission. He may investigate anti-competitive practices and make competitive references to the Commission. He is the 'competent authority' in the UK with regard to the European Commission and he has general investigatory powers.

The Monopolies and Mergers Commission reports on references made to it, which may require merely a factual report or may include a request for recommendations. The references may concern monopolies, mergers, restrictive labour practices (not used to date), anti-competitive practices or public bodies.

The Restrictive Practices Court has both lay and judicial members. Questions of fact are decided by majority and there is no appeal. Questions of law are decided by the judicial members and appeal is open to the Court of Appeal.

The Restrictive Trade Practices Act 1976

The following is a brief summary of this very complex legislation and must inevitably suffer from simplification.

The Act covers restrictive agreements as to goods (Pt II, $s6$); restrictive agreements as to services (Pt III, *s*11); information agreements as to goods (Pt II, *s*7); and information agreements as to services (Pt III, *s*12). The scheme of the Act is similar as to each of these types of agreement, and for convenience we shall discuss mainly the provisions applying to restrictive agreements as to goods and then indicate generally the position as to the other types of agreement.

To be caught by the Act a restrictive agreement as to goods must be an agreement between two or more persons in the UK relating to one of the matters set out in *s*6 broadly as follows:

(*a*) prices actually charged or to be charged
(*b*) recommended prices
(*c*) terms of supply or purchase
(*d*) quantities and descriptions of goods
(*e*) manufacturing processes
(*f*) persons or areas to be supplied

To be deemed 'restrictive' there must be acceptance of a negative obligation restricting a right which would otherwise exist. Such negative obligations must be accepted by at least two parties in the UK. In this context individual (but no corporate) partners in a partnership and companies within one group of companies are treated as a single party.

As examples price notification agreements and many joint venture contracts will be caught.

Section 9 provides that certain *terms and conditions* are to be *disregarded* in deciding whether an agreement falls within the Act. The most important are coal and steel restrictions (a matter left to the ECSC); terms relating exclusively to goods supplied pursuant to an agreement (i.e. an agreement for the supply of goods); terms relating to the application of BSI and other approved standards; restrictions in an employment contract; and certain terms in financing agreements (added by *s*2, RTPA 1977).

Section 28 exempts from the Act the types of agreement listed in Schedule 3, which include certain export agreements and (added by the Competition Act 1980) certain copyright agreements, exclusive dealing agreements and certain know-how and industrial property agreements.

Section 6 will catch certain agreements in which information is exchanged, e.g. price notification agreements. Section 7 empowers the Secretary of State to issue 'calling-up orders' to the effect that the Act shall apply to information agreements which would not otherwise be caught. Section 7 provides that these must be agreements to exchange information about the same matters broadly as are listed in (*a*)–(*f*) above.

However, the only calling-up order to date is the Restrictive Trade Practices (Information Agreements) Order 1969 relating to agreements to give information on

(a) prices charged or quoted or to be charged or quoted; and
(b) terms and conditions on, or subject to which, goods are to be supplied

The provisions of $s9$ disregarding certain terms and conditions apply also to information agreements.

Sections 11 and 12 respectively provide for restrictive agreements and information agreements relating to services to be caught by the Act in similar terms to those set out above. However, as yet no calling-up order has been issued in respect of information agreements as to services and this provision is therefore inoperative at present.

If an agreement is caught by the Act it will normally be referred to the Restrictive Practices Court by the Director General. There is a statutory presumption that the agreement is contrary to the public interest ($s10$) and unless the court can be persuaded otherwise, the agreement will be declared void in respect of its restrictive provisions. In order to justify an agreement before the court the parties must

(a) bring it within one of the 'gateways' provided in $s10$, i.e. eight possible grounds for satisfying the court that the agreement should be permitted, and
(b) satisfy the further provision in $s10$ that the agreement is not unreasonable having regard to the balance between the circumstances pleaded before the court and any detriment to the public

This double test — gateway and balancing provision — is a difficult one to pass. The gateways may be broadly summarized as: protection of public from injury; specific and substantial benefit to the public; necessity to counteract competitive activity; necessity in dealing with a third party enjoying a monopoly position; protection of employment; benefit to export earnings; necessity in the context of another restriction already found to be in the public interest; no material actual or likely adverse effect on competition.

Competition Act 1980

The Competition Act added to the Director General's powers to police restrictive practices. It empowered him to conduct preliminary investigations into a course of action which appears to constitute an anti-competitive practice. If the Director General decides that the practice is anti-competitive he may seek assurances from the parties involved. Often those assurances will be given in order to avoid the risk that the matter will be referred to the Monopolies and Mergers Commission, a 'competition reference'.

The Act also contains provisions for the investigation of the activities of public bodies and of prices of major public interest.

Monopolies and mergers

The law relating to monopolies and mergers is consolidated principally in the Fair Trading Act 1973. Both the Secretary of State and the Director General have powers to refer matters to the Monopolies and Mergers Commission and those matters may fall into four categories:

1. Monopolies in the supply of goods or services or the export of goods, a monopoly being a market share of 25 per cent or more
2. Mergers, where the merger creates a group with 25 per cent or more of the market or adds market share to such an existing monopoly group, or the acquired assets are valued at £15 million or more
3. General references
4. References relating to restrictive labour practices, a power unused to date

Monopolies may arise from the simple market position of a company or group of companies or it may be a 'complex monopoly' arising from agreements or arrangements or trading practices between a number of companies.

The Commission may be charged simply with the preparation of a factual report or be asked to make recommendations for action. While the latter may be persuasive, power to adopt remedies lies solely with the Secretary of State.

Resale Prices Act 1976

This very important Act which consolidated the 1964 Act and subsequent legislation prohibits resale price maintenance, in the sense of enforcing minimum resale prices, unless their enforcement is justified before the Restrictive Practices Court. Terms of contract requiring minimum resale prices are rendered void ($s9(1)$) in contracts for the sale or supply of goods between suppliers and dealers.

Section 9(2) applies to any contract and forbids terms, conditions or undertakings concerning resale price maintenance. It also prohibits publication of express or implied minimum prices. Section 11 prohibits the withholding of supplies as a means of coercing dealers to maintain minimum resale prices. 'Withholding supplies' is given a broad definition by $s12$ to include various forms of discrimination, e.g. sale on less favourable terms as to price, credit or delivery.

Part I of the Act deals with collective arrangements to preserve minimum resale prices.

Section 9(2) contains an important proviso saving the ability of suppliers to publish recommended resale prices.

Section 11 does permit the withholding of supplies in order to enforce *maximum* resale prices.

Section 14 provides for application to the Restrictive Practices Court to exempt specific goods from the Act on any of the following grounds:

1 The quality of the goods would otherwise be reduced
2 The number of resale outlets would otherwise be reduced
3 Prices in the long term would generally rise
4 Goods would be sold by retail in circumstances likely to cause danger to health because of their misuse by the public as consumers or users
5 Any necessary services would cease to be provided or be substantially reduced to the detriment of the public

EEC law — articles 85 and 86

EEC competition law is based on articles 85 and 86 of the Treaty of Rome and since UK accession to the EEC in January 1973 these provisions have been part of UK law.

Article 85(1) provides that 'all agreements between undertakings, all decisions by associations of undertakings and concerted practices which may affect trade between member states and which have as their object or effect the prevention, restriction or distortion of competition within the Common Market' are prohibited. Such provisions are also void (art.85(2)), although in certain circumstances it may be possible to obtain an exemption. In order to facilitate business practice certain common types of agreement have been made subject to block exemption, e.g. exclusive distribution agreements and exclusive purchase agreements. If an agreement comes within the terms of such block exemption no particular application for exemption need be made.

Article 86 deals with abuse of a dominant market position within the EEC and may be involved, for example, in cases of discriminatory or excessive pricing policies.

The Commission of the EEC has been given wide powers of investigation and enforcement and recent examples of high fines imposed on infringing undertakings have illustrated the potential force of its sanctions.

The detailed law which as evolved around these provisions goes well beyond the scope of this chapter. Suffice it to say that it is arguable that the application of articles 85 and 86 to UK law provides a wider and potentially more effective control of anti-competitive practices in the UK than do the provisions of the various UK statutes considered above.

CONSUMER PROTECTION

The second part of this chapter is closely linked to competition law. In his first report (that for 1976) the present Director General recorded the Office of Fair Trading's job as being 'to keep watch on commercial activities in the UK and to protect the consumer against unfair trading practices'. He also commented that it would be quite wrong 'to think of the two main aspects of the Office's activities — competition policy and consumer protection — as separate entities', and that 'consumer interest is an important factor in the work carried out at the Office of Fair Trading concerning restrictive practices'.

DIRECT ACTION AGAINST INDIVIDUAL TRADERS

It is no part of the Director General's functions to take action on behalf of any individual consumer, but he does have power to act against an individual trader — whether a firm or a person — and in doing so, the Fair Trading Act requires him to have regard to the complaints received from consumers or other persons. The Act says that if he has reason to believe that a trader has adopted and is persisting in a course of business conduct which is both detrimental and unfair to the interests of consumers in the United Kingdom he shall use his best endeavours to obtain from the trader a satisfactory written assurance that the business will cease to be conducted in that way. If the trader declines to give such an assurance, or if he gives it but fails to implement it, the Director General may bring proceedings before the Restrictive Practices Court or other appropriate court, breach of whose order would be punishable as an offence (see Pt III of the Act).

The OFT has found cause to require several hundred such undertakings to be given. The cause arises from reports received from members of the public both to the OFT and to local authorities and from note being taken of repeated appearances of a trader in court on charges under legislation designed to protect consumers. Particulars of undertakings given by traders are usually published in the press, and details are contained in the Director General's annual reports.

CODES OF TRADING PRACTICE

The Fair Trading Act includes among the Director General's duties that of encouraging trade associations and similar bodies to establish and implement codes of practice for their members which will contain guidance in safeguarding and promoting the interests of consumers in the United Kingdom. Many trade associations for individual industries in the consumer goods and services fields have been at the receiving end of this encouragement since the Act came into operation, and the OFT will turn towards more industries as time and staff resources become available (see $s124(3)$ of the Act).

There is of course no obligation on any company to join a trade association for an industry in which it operates, and no sanction against a company in membership of a trade association which fails to comply with that association's code of practice other than expulsion from membership. But no reputable manufacturer or trader would wish to ignore a code of practice relating to its business. Moreover, in the event of investigation, a company might be asked to justify its failure to comply with a code of practice accepted by the rest of the industry.

PROPOSALS FOR STATUTORY ORDERS

Like many other Acts of Parliament, the Fair Trading Act authorizes 'the Secretary of State' to introduce draft orders supplementing the Act's provisions. The Fair Trading Act contains detailed procedures for the preparation of orders to deal with what it describes as 'a consumer trade practice' which 'adversely affects the economic interests of consumers in the United Kingdom'.

Action can be initiated by 'the Secretary of State' or any other Minister or the Director General, and takes the form of a reference to the Consumer Protection Advisory Committee (*ss*14 and 17 of the Act). This is a body, created by the Act and appointed by the Secretary of State, whose sole function is to advise on such references — these being whether the trade practice specified in the reference has an adverse effect on the economic interests of consumers in the United Kingdom. On the basis of the CPAC's report, an order may be prepared and, subject to Parliamentary approval, will come into existence (*s*22 of the Act). The order will deal with methods of carrying on business which may well hitherto have been thought to be quite legitimate by firms using them, or it will deal with operations which reputable firms have been finding difficulty in competing with.

Trade associations and similar bodies whose members would be likely to be affected by an order made in this way, and also individual firms, are entitled to — and should — make representations to the CPAC when it is considering a reference made to it.

CONSUMER CREDIT

The Consumer Credit Act 1974 was introduced, in its own words, 'to establish for the protection of consumers a new system of licensing and other control of traders concerned with the provision of credit, or the supply of goods on hire or hire-purchase, and their transactions' and it has always been regarded as a piece of legislation designed to promote both fair trading and consumer protection. It is an Act of immense complexity and has spread its chapter is concerned, all that need be said of it is that any company which has even the remotest involvement in granting, or in advising about, credit facilities for members of the general public should take professional advice on how this Act's requirements affect his company.

CRIMINAL LAW STATUTES

The Trade Descriptions Act of 1968 provides that any manufacturer or trader who in the course of business applies a false trade description to goods, or supplies goods to which a false trade description has been applied, commits an offence. For practical purposes, goods can be regarded as having a false trade description applied to them when they are described in terms (printed or written or pictorial or oral) which would lead a person considering purchasing them to make a purchase which would not have been made had the terms been different and more accurate. The Act also contains provisions about statements of price by the seller of goods and about inaccurate descriptions of services offered. The false or misleading description need not be given only at the point of sale; the Act contains provisions about advertisements also. There are parallel provisions applying to false trade descriptions used in relation to business services or facilities. These provisions are apt to cover the wording of competitions and promotions used to boost the sale of goods.

The Trade Descriptions Act 1968 ('TDA') was amended by the Consumer Protection Act 1987 ('CPA') which repealed section II of the TDA relating to false indications as to prices. Instead, part III of the CPA introduces important new provisions prohibiting 'misleading indications' as to prices. These provisions apply to most businesses, including services, and are designed to protect consumers from any inaccurate or misleading statements about prices. Linked to the CPA is a new Code of Practice for Traders, giving detailed guidelines as to what is and is not allowed. An infringement of the Code of Practice is very strong evidence that there has been a breach of the CPA.

The 1972 Trade Descriptions Act applied to situations in which goods of non-British origin are marketed in the United Kingdom under what the Act calls a 'United Kingdom name or mark'. Its purpose was to prevent intending purchasers from being allowed wrongly to infer that the use of such a name or mark necessarily indicates that the produce is of UK origin. It was made an offence by the Act to fail to show the country of origin prominently when goods of foreign origin are marked here with a UK name or mark on them or associated with them. However, the Trade Descriptions (Origin Marking) Miscellaneous Goods Order 1981, which required origin marking on certain specified goods wherever they were made (including the UK), was withdrawn after EEC protests. Following that decision, the whole of the Trade Descriptions Act 1972 was repealed and replaced by the Consumer Protection Act 1987.

There is also legislation making it an offence to try to sell goods or services by relying on the inertia of the selected customer. With goods, this usually means dumping by some means, so that the selected customer has the choice of sending them back or paying for them and keeping them. With services, this generally arises by providing the selected customer with a note indicating that payment should be made for an offered service and that the service will be provided unless the receiver of the note forthwith acts to reject the offer. Such methods of selling are almost always unfair, but it is remarkable how successful they often are. The relevant statutes (the Unsolicited Goods and Services Acts of 1971 and 1975) were intended to stamp out three well-known rackets — the encyclopaedia racket, the carbon paper racket, and the directory racket.

Company administrators should ensure that there are careful and well-known internal rules regulating which few members of the company's staff have authority to sign even the most innocuous seeming document presented by visitors and similar rules preventing payments being made other than in relation to a duly authorized purchase order issued by the company.

CIVIL LAW STATUTES

The 1893 Sale of Goods Act has been codified in the Sale of Goods Act 1979, which incorporates revisions made by the Supply of Goods (Implied Terms) Act 1973 and the Unfair Contract Terms Act 1977. It has substantially stood the test of time and still largely sets out the basic terms and conditions which any buyer, business or consumer is entitled to expect from any business seller of goods. Every transaction under which goods (or services) are supplied and paid for is in law a contract, and with a very few exceptions (none of which need be considered here) the absence of a document specifying the terms and conditions of the contract is irrelevant for any purpose other than showing that the agrement between the seller and the buyer was on the particular occasion in unusual terms. The principal usual terms, derived from the Act, are that the seller has the full right to provide the buyer with the goods; that if sold by description or sample the goods conform to the description or sample; that the goods are of 'merchantable quality'; and in certain circumstances that the goods go beyond that 'quality' by being suitable for the purpose which the buyer had in mind when purchasing them (see ss12–15 of the 1979 Act).

The changes made by the 1973 and 1977 Acts referred to above are of the greatest importance. For the first eighty years of its existence, the Act included a provision that the parties to a contract of sale could agree to exclude any or all but the first of the 'usual terms' set out above. From about the 1930s sellers, and particularly manufacturers of consumer durable goods, made use of this provision extensively, often by means of what were promoted as 'manufacturers' guarantees'. Many, and indeed most, of these had the effect of taking away the rights which the Act stated to be those of the retail purchaser against the retail seller.

It is no longer possible to agree that those rights should be excluded when the purchaser is a consumer: the consumer's rights are now inalienable.

Broadly speaking, the effect of the 1973 and 1977 legislation is to make void any attempt to take away the consumer's statutory rights. Business men can no longer use so-called 'exclusion clauses' to avoid the consequences of supplying goods which do not comply with the implied warranties as to quality contained in the Sale of Goods Act. There are also provisions in the 1977 Unfair Contract Terms Act which regulate the use of exclusion clauses in other contracts with consumers, for example, contracts for the supply of services.

Further, the 1977 Act protects consumers from unscrupulous indemnity clauses (whereby a trader seeks to require a consumer to indemnify him against loss) and from unreasonable attempts to permit a trader to substitute manifestly different goods or services from those bargained for (a practice once favourite with the holiday trade).

The 1977 Act has application to dealings between businessmen as well as those with consumers. However, in the case of business contracts, the Act generally invalidates only those exclusion clauses which are not reasonable, having regard to the circumstances which were (or ought to have been) in the minds of the parties at the time the contract was made. The Act has particular reference to the reasonability of exclusion clauses contained in standard terms of trade.

The provisions of the 1977 legislation are complex and far reaching. Any business which has not already reviewed its terms of trade in the light of this Act should quickly do so.

In addition to the 1973 and 1977 legislation, which modified the civil law of contract, Parliament decided to enlist the aid of the criminal law in protecting consumers. By virtue of the Consumer Transactions (Restrictions on Statements) Order 1976, as amended in 1978, it has made it an offence to suggest to consumers by means of any form of guarantee, that their statutory rights have been displaced. The point is that, whilst the civil law may, in fact, preserve the consumer's statutory rights, little will be gained if a trader can continue to suggest that those rights have been replaced by his own guarantee. The practical effect of the above Order is that guarantees should be accompanied by a statement to the effect that the consumer's statutory rights are preserved.

Mention should also be made of another civil law statute — the Misrepresentation Act 1967. This was a piece of general law reform rather than of consumer protection legislation, but it is customarily included among items of 'consumer law'.

It is an essential element in fair trading that no party to a transaction will willingly permit another party to bind himself by contract when under an important and relevant misunderstanding. If the misunderstanding has been deliberately created or allowed to persist, there is fraud and the contract can be rescinded. But there are occasions when misunderstanding results from an inadvertent failure to pass information over or from lack of knowledge of what would be a material fact at a material time. On those occasions there is 'innocent misrepresentation'. The law about innocent misrepresentation developed unsatisfactorily through an accumulation of judicial decisions, and so the 1967 Act was passed to restore fairness. It provides remedies for situations which arise when a transaction has been completed but would not have gone through had all concerned known all the material facts at the material time.

The Bargain Offers Order 1979

The Bargain Offers Order was intended to prevent misleading price comparisons being made to consumers. Vague claims such as 'Lowest prices' were to be justified against an objective standard. The Order envisaged justification against a trader's own previous or intended prices; against other traders' actual prices; against genuine sale prices; against different prices charged to different categories of consumer, for example, students or senior citizens, or different terms, e.g. cash price against credit price; or against recommended retail prices. However, the Order was difficult to interpret, gave rise to considerable confusion and was apt to catch innocent as well as misleading price comparisons. The Order has now been repealed and replaced by the Consumer Protection Act 1987.

Codes of practice

The UK has developed voluntary controls over advertising and promotion, in addition to the many statutory controls. In particular, the British Code of Advertising Practice applies to most advertising to the public and is administered by the Advertising Standards Authority (ASA). The British Code adapts the rules of the International Chamber of Commerce's International Code of Advertising Practice. Also administered by the ASA is the British Code of Sales Promotion Practice, which monitors the activities of those conducting consumer promotions.

Both codes rely upon the willingness of practitioners in advertising and sales promotion to submit themselves to the rules.

Radio and television advertising is separately controlled via the Independent Broadcasting Authority's Code of Practice, and by the vetting to which all television advertisements are subjected by the ITCA.

Part Four
Office Administration

15

Managing the Modern Office

Ronald G Anderson

Office management is concerned with the effective use of administrative resources relating to the following primary business activities:

- communication
- typing
- printing
- computing
- copying
- editing
- validating
- filing
- sorting
- merging
- updating of records

Machines of various types are used for these activities and it is therefore essential that managers who are responsible for the procurement and use of office equipment should be fully conversant with the range of equipment available, its initial cost and operating costs. The equipment includes:

- photocopiers
- dictating systems
- telephone exchanges
- laser printers

electric typewriters
word processors
document filing systems
main frame, mini and microcomputers
work stations
intelligent terminals modems
multiplexors
acoustic couplers
front-end processors
terminal controllers
addressing machines

THE CHANGING SCENE

Managers must be aware of the dynamic nature of the external business environment and its effect on the internal administrative environment. They should be 'agents of change' as they are in the best possible position to know the requirements of the systems for which they are responsible. The efficiency of their systems requires constant appraisal; old mechanical equipment or inadequate clerical systems need to be replaced with more modern electronic aids in order to increase the productivity of the administrative function.

Bear in mind that the objective of managing office equipment is an acceptable 'bottom line', i.e. the level of profit, on the profit and loss account. Profit is greatly influenced by the level of administrative costs which are often a high proportion of total costs. The use of electronic equipment can influence the level of such costs by increased productivity and reduced manning levels. Modern offices are becoming predominantly automated and machine-oriented as opposed to the previously high incidence of clerical staff when administrative systems were less machine-intensive.

Modern machines should only replace people or older machines on a planned basis and should not be acquired merely for image-building purposes. As with any other type of investment, they should have an adequate return on the capital outlay either by way of cost savings or the prevention of cost increases. Machines should certainly be considered when the level of activity is increasing beyond the capabilities of present resources, whether of people or machines. Sophisticated machines should be used where necessary to accomplish the required purpose of the system under consideration efficiently and to achieve its objectives.

The velocity of technological change is forever increasing and frequent changes of method are required to maintain or increase the level of productivity. Such changes of method, particularly if sophisticated electronic equipment is to be installed, necessitate the retraining of staff and transferring of displaced personnel to other sections of the business if feasible. It is also important to be aware of what one's competitors are doing in their quest for office efficiency, otherwise a business may lose sales and profits because the price of its products or services are too high compared with those of competitors. Sometimes the organization will need restructuring so that it is compatible with the changing nature of business operations, the type of activities performed and the span of control related to changing manning levels.

CONVERGENCE

Office management is directly related to the management of information flows in a business; for example, a word processor is required mainly for producing edited standardized text in original ribbon print form in the most efficient way. In order to communicate this information speedily to its specific destinations electronic mail facilities may be combined with word processing or microcomputer activities and this eliminates the need for printed reports in many instances. Messages can be viewed on the screen of the work station without the need for printouts, unless they are specifically required in which case they can be printed locally. Such facilities are associated with 'information technology' and 'the electronic office'. Office automation provides the foundation of the electronic office which consists of the 'converging' technologies of computing, word processing and communications mentioned above. Microcomputers are used for the processing and storage of information and the use of spreadsheet and business modelling programs for business planning and problem solving. Information technology also embraces the use of interactive 'Viewdata' database systems such as British Telecom's Prestel and private internal systems. The systems are interactive because once information has been accessed and displayed on the television screen the user can, for example, book hotel accommodation or order goods at a supermarket by means of a keypad. The new technology also includes distributed processing and information systems structured as local area networks, and the use of message switching and digital PABX providing for both voice and data transmission as well as electronic (laser) printing equipment.

EVOLUTION OF OFFICE EQUIPMENT

The philosophy of the electronic office was first adopted in 1947 by J. Lyons, the British catering company, when the viability of using computers for office activities was discussed. Not only did the company apply computers to its office routines and procedures but it actually built its own computer for the task — the 'LEO', an acronym for Lyons Electronic Office, which became operational in 1951. Businesses must respond to change to remain economically viable, or even to survive, in the highly competitive business arena. Electronic technology enables business activities to be conducted in the most efficient manner by reducing the time for information to flow to the various parts of an organization and this is often achieved by the provision of computing power wherever it is most needed.

Long ago, the abacus or counting frame was used for high-speed counting by moving beads along wires on a frame. In the early days of business transactions the most used counting facilities were the human fingers, or digits, the forerunner of computerized digital processing facilities which became known as electronic data processing (EDP) or automatic data processing (ADP). Computerized accounting is now the norm.

Mechanized accounting

The recording of business transactions has undergone evolutionary changes since the Dickensian era. In the larger businesses, to avoid employing armies of clerks, activities began to be mechanized. Electro-mechanical accounting or bookkeeping machines were introduced for posting transactions to ledger cards by keying in the data which was then printed instead of being written by hand. This innovation was referred to as office mechanization and tended to speed up the recording process, enabling several documents to be prepared simultaneously, e.g. payroll, payslip and tax and earnings record.

These accounting machines were later replaced by Hollerith, Powers-samas or IBM punched-card machines which increased the speed of processing and provided greater versatility and flexibility in the accounting systems. The data stored in the punched cards was then processed by various machines such as sorters, collators, tabulators and multiplying punches. All businesses could not justify the use of such facilities, of course, and many small companies adopted simple systems such as spiking unpaid bills on a bill file and removing them when they were paid. This was probably the first ledgerless accounting system.

High-speed calculations

Comptometers were used for high-speed calculations which were very fast in the hands of a competent operator, but rather slow when compared with the modern electronic computers and calculators. Computations were also performed using crank-driven calculating machines and adding/listing machines which enabled the results of calculations to be printed.

Use of computers

Computers subsequently superseded punched-card equipment in larger businesses and microcomputers superseded mechanized accounting machines and visible record computers in the smaller business. A wide range of hardware and computer configurations are available which can be structured or expanded on a modular basis to suit the processing commitment of various organizations. Computers differ widely in size, speed, output capability and cost and it is necessary to select the most suitable combination of hardware, and indeed software, for the proposed applications. The optimum system would be the one capable of attaining the required level of performance for both the current and foreseeable future needs of the business. At the same time its initial purchase and operating costs must be economically justifiable on the basis of the return on the investment. This will avoid having to change the system in a short time scale. To this end computer systems should be selected with a defined migration path to allow for small systems initially, which can be built up by add-on memory modules, slow peripherals exchanged for faster ones and additional network facilities and terminals as required to allow for changes in the business environment, strategy and mode of operation.

Supermarkets

Supermarkets require an efficient and speedy method of capturing and processing transaction data in order to improve the level of customer service and the effectiveness of supermarket operations. Special laser scanners are used for this purpose at check-out points. If the system is linked to an electronic funds transfer system, a data communication link is established to the various banks' computers for credit check inquiries and the transfer of funds.

Real-time systems

Some business systems control operations in real-time, ie whilst the operation takes place. Airline seat reservation systems are an example and they require powerful communication-oriented computers supporting a network of terminals for dealing with enquiries and seat reservations which are immediately updated on the on-line information file. The required hardware also includes tickets and boarding-pass printers and remote communication concentrators. The primary objectives of this type of system are to provide instant information on demand and to eliminate double booking of seats on aircraft. Such systems must respond immediately to enquiries from dispersed booking offices and display the up-to-the-second status of seats. In fact the status changes on the screen whilst it is being viewed, thus providing accurate information concerning the required objectives.

COMPUTERS

Meeting the functional administrative needs of an organization efficiently is not a simple task. Initially it is important to be aware of the structure of the organization and its interfunctional relationships. An organization and communications analysis will determine the inter- and intra-functional information flows and define the communication pattern within the business. The analysis will also define the information which flows between the external and internal environment, e.g. to and from customers and suppliers. It is also necessary to establish the nature of the information flows, the purpose they serve, the action taken from them and the contents of such information. Information should be categorized into essential and non-essential, which will allow the latter to be discarded — there is no point in processing unrequired information more efficiently. In addition it is important to assess the way in which such information can be collected, recorded, processed and communicated.

Large businesses, large computers

Large organizations require large computers with high-speed processing power, whereas medium-sized businesses can function effectively using a minicomputer. At one time small businesses could not justify a computer due to high cost and low volumes of transactions to process, but this situation has now changed. The inexpensive small business computer, costing in the region of £2000–£5000, comes within the financial range of the smallest of businesses – even the one-man business. Although this is only a generalized rule of thumb it is a useful empirical guide for initial considerations. A large computer can cost a large sum even today, mainly because of its speed of operation, communication and multiprogramming facilities including the ability to support many terminals. Minis on the other hand cost far less but are dependent on a number of peripherals. Costs, as a general guide, are in the region of £20 000–£30 000.

Volume of transactions

The number of transactions to be processed is an important factor to consider in the choice of system as it allows an assessment to be made of the type of input device required and the nature of the processing techniques to be established. Relatively low volumes can be handled by a business microcomputer using keyboard data entry, but this is a very slow method of data input. Larger volumes may necessitate the use of a small, medium or large mainframe using a key-to-disk method of data collection and validation. This then enables data to be transferred into the computer at high speed from magnetic disk.

Volume and length of records

Files containing many thousands of records will require a large computer system with high-capacity disk or tape storage and high data transfer speeds. Applications of 500–1000 records may be suitable for the small business microcomputer as the capacity of floppy disks is limited compared to that of hard disks, i.e. Winchester disks. The more powerful business machines can upgrade the system by adding Winchesters as an optional extra. This will increase the storage capacity and the speed with which data is transferred to and from the processor. If an application having many thousands of records was processed on a small business machine using floppy disks the records would have to be stored on several disks.

Benchmarks

In order to assess the total processing time for each application multiply the volume of transactions by the processing time for each transaction. This may be established from benchmark timings which provide a basis for appraising the performance of different computers. The benchmarks provide timings for arithmetic computations, sorting routines, calling sub-routines and handling arrays etc.

Processor characteristics

Processors function at different speeds and have either 8, 16 or 32-bit processors which is an indication of processing power defining the size of numbers, i.e. the number of digits which can be processed at one time. The more powerful processors have greater internal storage addressing capabilities. Whereas an 8-bit processor only has an address bus of sixteen channels which allows up to 64K bytes, i.e. 2^{16} which equals 65536 bytes capacity, a 16-bit processor often has twenty address channels which provides addressing facilities up to 2^{20}, i.e. 1 048 576 or one megabyte. A large internal memory capacity is essential in order to process integrated accounting packages and spreadsheets because of the storage capacity they require to store the programs. The program specification indicates the minimum memory size and other hardware requirements such as the need for two disk drives. Applications with relatively little computational needs but high-volume printout requirements need high-speed printers. The specific devices and their capability are dependent upon the characteristics of the system.

Operating system

The operating system used by any specific computer needs to be assessed. Standard operating systems have a vast amount of software available, whereas those computers with less widely adopted operating systems have a lower software base and their costs are likely to be higher because they are spread over a smaller number of potential users.

Relative costs of hardware and software

The former high cost of computer hardware is now falling, mainly because of the great advances in electronic technology which have reduced the size of computers whilst increasing their performance. Attention is now increasingly being focused on the costs and time involved in developing software. Remember that although hardware costs are falling the labour-intensive task of producing software is increasing and it is necessary for an organization to minimize the problems and costs in software development. Some manufacturers provide *bundled* software, i.e. the costs are included in the quoted cost of the system, but whichever is the case it is essential to assess the total cost of any proposed computer system. Only then can true comparative costs be obtained. Of course, you must also assess the suitability of packages for the proposed systems to be run on the computer. Program generators can also be used for developing programs either by experienced programmers or by non-specialists in the operating departments.

METHODS OF SELECTION

When selecting a computer, as with any other office equipment, the relative strengths and weaknesses of specific models will provide the basis for a short list of three or four models. Compare the specification of selected models with the facilities required and the objectives to be attained by the relevant business systems. A points rating method of selection may be adopted whereby selected attributes are listed and points awarded from a maximum of ten for each attribute in the context of its utility to the business. A points league table may contain the following details:

1 Processor
   (a) number of communication channels
   (b) 8, 16 or 32-bit processor
   (c) memory capacity
   (d) number of peripheral ports for plug-in devices, e.g. serial or parallel centronic ports for printers, terminals and other devices
   (e) speed of processor
2 Operating system installed — industry standard or otherwise
3 Software
   (a) bundled or unbundled
   (b) availability of suitable software for potential applications

MANAGING THE MODERN OFFICE

4   Total purchase, lease or rental costs
5   Degree of manufacturers' support
    (a)   installation support
    (b)   software support
    (c)   staff training services provided
6   Cost of maintenance agreement
7   Programming languages supported
8   Backing storage capacity
9   Multi-user/multi-tasking capability
10 Speed of printer
11 Other options, i.e. COM compatability

Before selecting a computer it is usual to invite a number of manufacturers to tender for the contract. The initial specification supplied to each manufacturer would typically include:

(a) nature of the system
(b) volumes of the various transactions
(c) number of terminals/work stations required
(d) multi-tasking facilities
(e) standby needs
(f) real-time or interactive processing needs
(g) type and content of reports and the frequency of production
(h) details of maintenance contract

Subsequent proposals are based on this information and the details are discussed by manufacturers' sales representatives with the systems staff and executives of the business. Such discussions embrace possible alternative solutions to the needs of the business. It is the prerogative of management to discuss these proposals with their systems staff who will subsequently recommend a specific course of action. The proposals will include a great deal of data relating to the nature and extent of hardware requirements, software support, the level of staff training to be provided and the extent of systems support and equipment maintenance. Detailed cost schedules relating to the various facets of hardware and software and the overall purchase cost will be included. It is important to consider the alternative financing methods available including purchasing, leasing or rental before arriving at a final decision.

Selection of computing technique

It is important before selecting a computer to establish the processing technique most suitable for the business and apart from batch processing other techniques to be considered include distributed processing networks, multi-user and multi-tasking systems.

Distributed processing is facilitated by local area networks (LANs) which consist of a series of interconnected microcomputers. A local area network is designed to serve a business unit such as a factory and its administrative offices, and provides a speedy and effective means of communication between the various departments thus improving the efficiency of administrative activities. Networks often consist of interconnected workstations, intelligent terminals, microcomputers, word processors and electronic mail facilities, together forming a very effective inter-company communication network. LANs provide for the sharing of resources, such as a high-speed printer and high-capacity hard disk, which can be accessed by any authorized user of the network. Networks have different topologies, protocols and methods of data transmission and many include a database supported by a mainframe computer as an integral element of the network. Two-way communication is possible between the various computers in the network for transferring data or messages electronically by electronic mail. Modems can link LANs to British Telecom's telephone system and to gateways to other networks providing facilities for teleshopping, airline seat reservations, viewdata and other on-line information systems.

Value-added networks provide additional services to the normal communication channels by third-party vendors under a government licence. The additional services include automatic error detection and correction as well as 'store and forward' message services, electronic mail and protocol conversions to access different computers and networks. The vendors can provide point to point or switched services on British Telecom and Mercury circuits provided they 'add value' to those circuits.

Store and forward systems provide facilities for the temporary storage of a message in a computer system for subsequent transmission to its destination at a later time. Store and forward techniques allow for routeing over networks which are not always accessible. This will necessitate one or more computer-controlled exchanges or nodes which are able to store messages and then release them when a transmission path is available. Messages for different time zones can be 'stored and forwarded' to the destination during normal daytime by this means.

Multi-user systems

Multi-user computer systems allow several users to gain simultaneous access to a central computer by means of a terminal. The hardware costs of the computer are then shared by a number of users, but must be offset by the cost of the VDU and keyboard for each user. It may sometimes be less costly to have separate rather than shared micros. System degradation is likely to occur at peak processing periods which increases the response time. Some multi-user computers support sixteen terminals or more thus allowing them to access files and programs stored on hard disks and to print output on a high-speed printer. The use of computers in this way is sometimes referred to as 'distributed processing' but is, in effect, distributed access to 'centralized processing'. This feature may be contrasted with network systems which do provide distributed processing because diversified computers are connected together by means of the network and are able to intercommunicate with each other for the transfer of data in addition to performing local processing as a stand-alone system. The individual terminals in a multi-user system cannot communicate with each other. A disadvantage of a multi-user system is that if the connecting cable is severed then the terminal becomes inoperative as it has no link with the computer.

Multi-tasking systems facilitate the running of two or more tasks concurrently and require special software. Microsoft market a package called 'Windows' which opens a window for each application selected. The window can be closed when switching to a different task while the original task is being executed.

In conclusion, it is apparent that the diversity of modern office equipment, with its emphasis on high-technology electronics, underlines the need for effective management in this important aspect of office administration. The costs are considerable and the selection demands an insight into the relative strengths and weaknesses of specific business systems in order to meet the functional needs of an organization.

FURTHER READING

M. Peltu, *Successful Management of Office Automation*, NCC, 1984.
A Planning Guide to Office Automation, Gower, Aldershot, 1984.

16

Reducing Office Costs

Robert C Appleby

The work of an office involves the capture of information, its processing, storage and retrieval. In the past most of this information has been on paper, but this is slowly changing to the medium of magnetic storage, to enable quicker manipulation of the information. The volume of office work is increasing by 1.6 per cent annually in the number of hours worked, which means that over 125 000 more information workers are required each year. The running costs of an office show that:

- 70 per cent of all costs relate to people
- 25 per cent of all costs relate to equipment
- 5 per cent of all costs relate to space/environment aspects

With those figures in mind and the recent estimate that administrative costs are increasing at the rate of 10 to 15 per cent per annum, it is obvious that any reduction in office costs will be a valuable saving. Information is becoming easier to obtain because of new technology and more information is being demanded. For example, there has been a large increase in the number of telephone calls and the quantity of mail sent. There is all the more reason for office activities to be examined closely to see if they are being performed as efficiently as possible. Any increase in productivity may allow the release of staff for other activities.

PHILOSOPHY OF COST REDUCTION

Mechanization

The underlying philosophy behind office cost reduction has evolved greatly over the years. At one time, the predominant aim was mechanization. It was felt that since machines were reliably impersonal, they should be introduced as often as possible.

It is now realized that mechanization as an end in itself may hold severe pitfalls. A company was discovered that possessed fourteen photocopying machines — those fourteen machines were producing 3 000 000 photocopies a year. In fact, photocopiers can present a considerable challenge to those trying to contain administration costs. Some firms put multiple locks on their photocopiers; each lock is released by a key which belongs to a departmental manager who has the relevant photocopying cost deducted from his budget.

Other firms are transferring certain procedures away from their computers on to more simple methods. This is both to save money and also to increase flexibility.

Method study

The next stage in the evolution of cost reduction philosophy saw an emphasis being placed on 'work simplification' and 'method study'. People looked for the 'one best way' of carrying out each task in the office. The search was for greater efficiency. In some instances, however, even this proved insufficient. A work study department in a large organization received a considerable bundle of statistics every Friday from central accounts. A work study engineer filed this information (very efficiently) because he had been told that central accounts were very short of filing space. Meanwhile, the people in central accounts prepared the statistics every week with a Friday deadline. They did this very efficiently; they had been told that the work study department needed the statistics. Thus these statistics were prepared at considerable cost for the sole benefit of the filing cabinet manufacturer.

Effectiveness

The third and final stage in the evolution of cost reduction philosophy is the present emphasis on 'effectiveness'. This has not been accompanied by a rejection of mechanization or work simplification or efficiency in any way. It is rather a further evolution in philosophy. The search for effectiveness follows two paths.

The first path is to look at major items of expense and to ask what benefit is being obtained from each — the cost of each item and its effectiveness. For

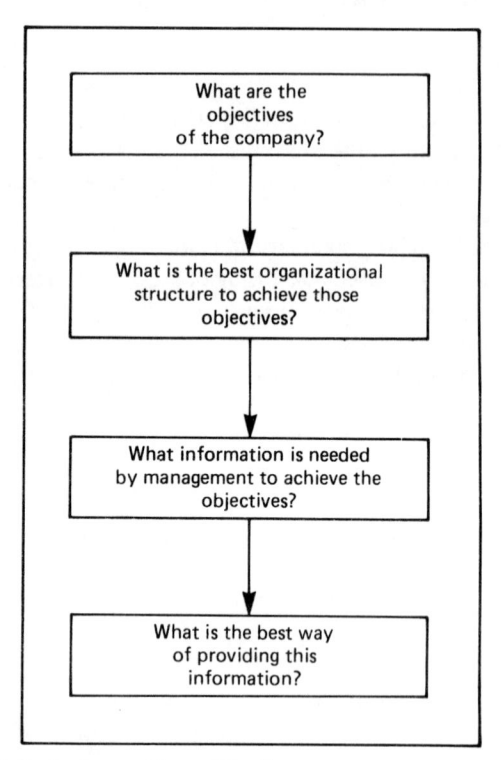

```
┌─────────────────────────────┐
│   What are the objectives   │
│      of the company?        │
└─────────────┬───────────────┘
              ▼
┌─────────────────────────────┐
│ What is the best organizational │
│ structure to achieve those  │
│         objectives?         │
└─────────────┬───────────────┘
              ▼
┌─────────────────────────────┐
│  What information is needed │
│ by management to achieve the│
│         objectives?         │
└─────────────┬───────────────┘
              ▼
┌─────────────────────────────┐
│    What is the best way     │
│     of providing this       │
│        information?         │
└─────────────────────────────┘
```

Figure 16.1 Path to improving effectiveness

example, what do fringe benefits cost us and are they what the employees want? How much did the Management Services department cost and what benefits did we actually gain in return?

The second path is to look at the paperwork in a concern and to regard this paperwork as being a flow of information. We can then ask what information is being provided, what does it cost and at that cost is it worth having? A sales director told the computer manager what information he needed each week; the first week that the computer went on stream it took two men to push on two trolleys all the print-out required. On the other hand, a large car manufacturer charges divisional managers with programmers' time so that value is obtained. This path to improving effectiveness is shown in Figure 16.1.

THE O & M FUNCTION

For many concerns, the main agent for reducing costs will be the O & M group. This being so, it is important that this group should itself be made effective.

Every job that an O & M team is given should have an objective and a set time for completion. For example, the objective might be to reduce the money outstanding on the sales ledger by 7 per cent in forty working days. It is relatively easy to put a standard cost per day to actual working time of the members of the O & M team. If in the above example the cost per day is £x, then forty working days will cost £40(x). The decision to be made then becomes, should we spend £40(x) to reduce the outstanding debtors by 7 per cent? It may be that we would get an even better return by getting the O & M team to tackle a different area.

Certain jobs will be tackled that do not result in any financial savings. Such jobs should still be given a time allocation since this will allow a clear judgement to be made on the job's importance in relation to the cost. We are not restricting freedom of choice — we are however indicating a clear decision that has to be made. Shall a particular job be done if it is going to cost x hundred pounds?

Once a year, the O & M group should present a report. This report will contain:

1 Highlights of the year's work
2 Total cost of the O & M personnel including rent, typing, printing etc.
3 Total of money saved
4 Annual ratio of money saved to money cost

Appendices can show jobs completed in more detail. The method of allocating money saved on any long-lasting improvements must be agreed in advance. A good compromise is to take 100 per cent of the money in the first year, two-thirds in the second year, one-third in the third year and nothing thereafter.

This report should be distributed to top management. As far as the O & M staff is concerned it can become a first-rate piece of 'public relations'. As far as top management is concerned, it acts as a form of control. If an O & M group cannot save every year an amount equal to its cost, does it have any right to exist?

The objectives and organization of the O & M function are treated in detail in Chapter 18.

WORK MEASUREMENT

The basic idea of measuring work is not of itself new. There is a record of an interesting 'oath of allegiance' which a particular work measurement engineer had to take in the eighteenth century. By then, a manufacturer of pins had already used standard times to build up standard costs for his product. By the middle of the nineteenth century, the British Treasury was using work measurement techniques — in Ireland the amount of food received by certain labourers on relief depended upon the amount of work completed in road-laying.

However, what is newer is the application of work measurement techniques to administrative staff. At one time this was perhaps considered undignified for white-collar people. There are several reasons for the change in attitude that has occurred. First, the gap between white- and blue-collar people has changed. Secondly, during periods of wages restraint, government departments have demanded proof of increased productivity before sanctioning pay rises. Thirdly, greater union activity is increasing the incidence of productivity deals.

Work measurement in the office can have many uses. Some of these are:

1 To provide management with the means of knowing the size of staff needed for different workloads. For example suppose that an increase in sales of 50 per cent is expected — how many more staff must be engaged and trained, and what skills will they need?
2 To form the basis of cost comparisons between alternative methods. For example, an entrepreneur was considering setting up a computer-based information service. He then considered the alternative of using straightforward manual methods — a cost comparison was only possible by using work measurement
3 To provide management with the relative costs of obtaining different levels of management information. A chain of retail shops placed 300 000 orders a year with suppliers, many of the orders having several lines. It was the habit to provide buyers with printed details of all purchase orders including standard mark-ups. Was this level of information worth having at the cost involved?
4 To provide a yardstick for personal or group performance. This may or may not then be used for incentive purposes

Work measurement techniques

There are a number of work measurement techniques that can be used in the office. It is very important that flexibility be retained in the choice of technique. Anybody pinning his faith to one technique alone will not be as effective as the person who uses different techniques in different situations. The particular technique to use will depend on:

1 The economics of measurement. A different technique is needed if the group size is four compared with 150 people all performing the same task
2 The use that is to be made of any standards

3   The ease of defining the units of output (for example telephone calls, memos)
4   The size of the units of output (for example a design drawing as compared with a short calculation)
5   The needs of management

The main techniques that are in use are:

Time study. This long-established technique involves the timing of a task as it is being performed. At the same time, an assessment is made of the effective rate of working which is compared with a standard rate. The time actually taken is then converted to the time which would be taken at the standard rate. In factories, a stop-watch is used for timing. It has been found that in offices a wrist watch is usually more appropriate. For example, if a job actually takes one minute when performed by somebody working at 90 per cent performance, then the standard time would be:

$$\frac{90}{100} \times 60 = 54 \text{ seconds}$$

To this time must be added certain allowances for possible contingencies and for personal needs.

Activity sampling. This is the application of sampling techniques to work activities. A number of instantaneous observations are made of people and/or machines over a period of time.

At each observation, a note is made of the activity taking place (for example typing, telephoning, awaiting work). At the end of the study, the percentage of time that a particular activity was observed is a measure of how often this activity is occurring in the office. An example is given in Figures 16.2 and 16.3.

Clerical standard data (CSD). There are certain tasks which occur in a precisely similar manner in many offices (such as using a particular machine). A standard time for a task can therefore be used in such a situation.

Various proprietary systems have been developed to this end, one of which is Clerical Standard Data.

Predetermined motion time system (PMTS). There are certain basic human movements (such as reaching, taking hold, letting go). These movements are used repeatedly in all human activities. A standard time for a task can therefore be built up by using a predetermined time for each of these very small motions.

Various systems have been developed to this end, one of which is Clerical

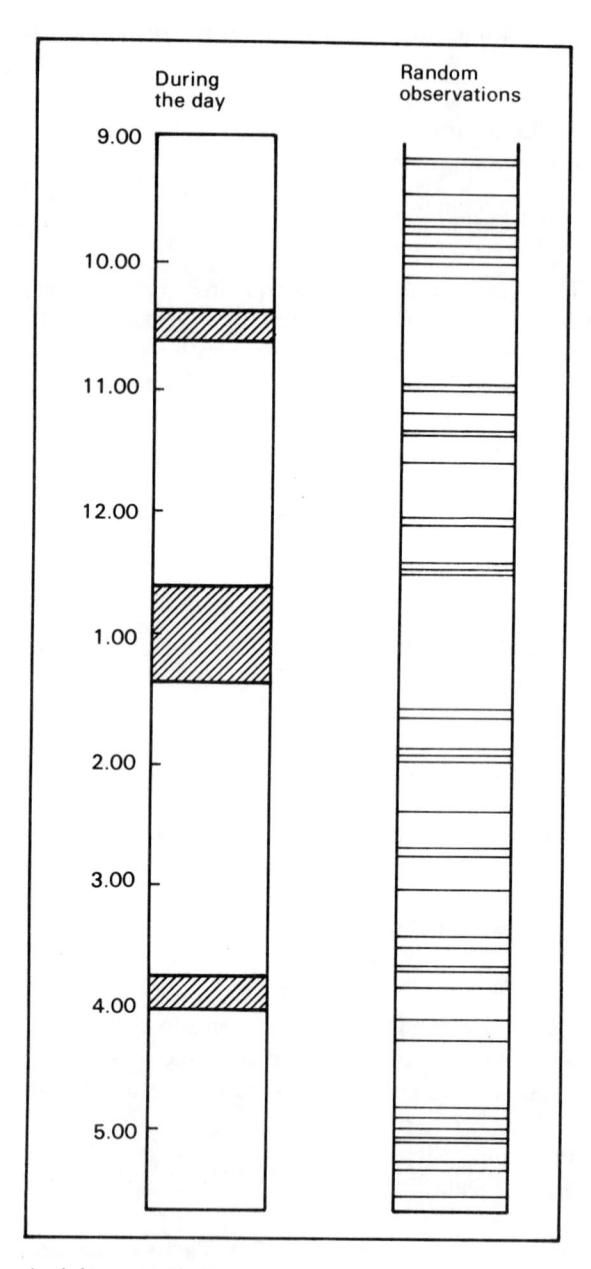

Figure 16.2 Activity sampling

ACTIVITY SEEN	NUMBER OF TIMES SEEN	PERCENTAGE OF TIME SPENT
Awaiting work	78	26
Out of office	12	4
Telephoning	63	21
Meetings	94	31
Dictating	32	11
Reading	15	5
Calculating	6	2
	300	100

Figure 16.3 Activity sampling

MMD. This resulted from an international research project and incorporates the better features of several previous systems.

All the basic standard values for Clerical MMD are contained on a small card. These values are coded. Suppose we wish to time somebody getting up from a desk, moving four paces to a filing cabinet, opening and closing a drawer, returning to the desk and sitting down (ignoring for this example what is done to the filing when the drawer is open).

Moving the chair back from the desk when getting up and moving the chair into the desk when sitting down are covered by the element coded *SCM*. The walk is of eight paces or steps — coded *S*. Opening and closing a filing cabinet drawer is coded as *ODF*. We now have:

ELEMENT	CODE	TIME
Move chair	*SCM*	86
To filing cabinet and return	8*S*	72
Open and close drawer	*ODF*	35
		193

The time is given in milliminutes ($1/1000$ minute), so that the total time is 0.19 minute or nearly 12 seconds.

Presentation of work measurement data

Having selected the combination of work measurement techniques to be employed, the method of presentation must be decided upon. This will depend upon:

1. Nature of the work
2. Variability of the work
3. Length of time that management has been using work measurement in the office
4. Incidence of machinery
5. Needs of management

There are alternative methods of using work measurement techniques, and of presenting the data. The main ones include:

Job values. This is the commonest type of presentation. Using one of the work measurement techniques, a standard time can be built up for a particular job or task. These standard times can then be used to discover the workload for an office.

Categorized work values. The tasks in an office are listed in order of approximate length of time required for each one. This list is divided into a smaller number of groups so that the operations in each group do not differ excessively in amount of time needed. A task in each group is timed precisely to act as a 'benchmark' for the whole group. Each group is allotted a single work value and all operations in a group receive the same time.

Synthetics. This technique builds up the total time for a job by adding together times for parts of the job which have been obtained from various sources. This technique is of particular use when dealing with office machinery. Most managements find that they can build up their own 'synthetics' which are special for their particular enterprise.

Controls

There are a number of ways in which the work measurement techniques can be used. The methods chosen will depend upon:

1. Nature of the work
2. Degree of control contemplated
3. Agreements made with staff associations and unions
4. Need for exact timetables and schedules
5. Needs of management

The alternative methods of control which may be selected include:

Group assessment. Group assessment programmes (such as Group Capability Programme) give a broad supervisory control where a group of people are carrying out a separate clear-cut set of tasks. The need for detailed

REDUCING OFFICE COSTS

standards, which may be needed for individual control, can be reduced by controlling on a group basis. The group should be 4–12 people. Incentives are usually not recommended for group assessment systems.

Short-interval scheduling. This is a method of control based on work standards. The work is divided into batches, each one of which is to be completed in a target time (say, two hours). The batches are distributed to the staff who return for the next batch when the previous one has been completed. The supervisor controls the work flow and individual performances.

Incentives. There are monetary and non-monetary incentives. For both types, work measurement can provide a valid, meaningful basic tool. Incentives are not an inevitable consequence of work measurement.

Management controls. Clerical work measurement must aim to produce a comprehensive and relevant system of management controls. The basic principles for such controls are constant although the precise details vary with the needs of management. A practical example is given in Figure 16.4.

Date	Standard numbers	Actual numbers	Variance	Office: Accounts C		
				Statistics		
				Invoices	Queries	Owing-£
7:9:81	24	26	+2	5700	80	128 000

Figure 16.4 **Management controls**

The choices available in work measurement are summarized in Figure 16.5.

INCENTIVES

We should query incentives on the grounds of cost and effectiveness just as we query other items of expenditure. What are our incentives supposed to be for? To reduce costs, to make people get to work on time, to increase output? Could we attain these ends in other ways at less cost?

Fringe benefits. The question of incentives can be very confused, especially in the field of employee benefits. Employee benefits can add 25 per cent to clerical labour costs; they can include free BUPA, sports clubs, on-site dentists, help with children's education. The whole question of employee benefits is discussed in detail in Chapter 24 but the point being made here is

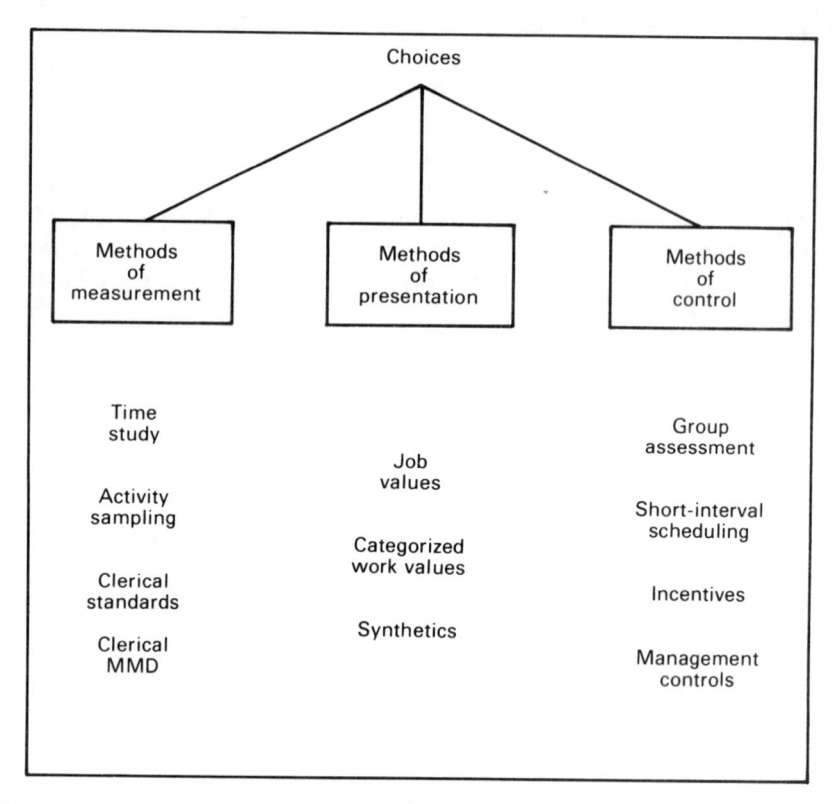

```
                        Choices
              /           |           \
     Methods         Methods         Methods
       of              of              of
   measurement     presentation      control


      Time                            Group
      study                         assessment
                      Job
                     values
     Activity                      Short-interval
     sampling                        scheduling
                   Categorized
                   work values
     Clerical                         Incentives
     standards
                    Synthetics
     Clerical                        Management
     MMD                              controls
```

Figure 16.5 Choices available in work measurement

that they can be expensive. Nowadays, their effectiveness purely as incentives for higher output is considered minimal. They are often retained since they are a sign of good management practice rather than being major incentives.

Campaigns and lotteries. A second group of incentives are those known as 'campaigns'. These have very specific aims, cost relatively small amounts of money and have measurable results. An example in this group is 'zero defects' which is an incentive for people not to make mistakes. This is done by building up the right atmosphere and by motivating people rather than by just giving them money. Another example is that used by a company that holds a lottery every week. Everybody's name goes into the lottery provided that they have an absolutely clean attendance and time-keeping record for the previous week (illness is no excuse). One of the major car manufacturers started the same idea using a car as the prize. In both cases, the firm was convinced that the lottery paid for itself several times over in better time-keeping and reduced absenteeism.

REDUCING OFFICE COSTS

Profit-sharing. A third group of incentives is the 'profit-sharing' idea. The best known of these is probably the ICI scheme in which shares in the company are distributed to employees. Other firms using profit-sharing are the John Lewis Partnership and, in a very different philosophical approach, Scott-Bader. Although once very popular, it is usually admitted nowadays that profit-sharing is not the strongest form of incentive to reduce costs. However, many firms use it as part of their general management philosophy.

Competitions. A fourth group of incentives is the competition. For example, a large firm can offer a prize to the office supervisor that reduces his costs of say, photocopying, by the largest amount. There are some concerns that specialize in running these competitions on behalf of an employer. A travel firm uses one of its package holidays as a prize — the idea of a fortnight's sun-bathing in Majorca can be a powerful incentive. Care must be taken that prizes do not attract income tax — this usually happens if a recipient earns more than a certain amount in his regular job.

Bonuses. The fifth group of incentives is that based on work measurement. It is possible, using clerical work measurement, to set a certain level of output as being a norm. If output exceeds this, the payment of a bonus is made for all extra work. For example, an audio typist may be paid her basic salary for producing 800 lines of typewriting per day. Output above this level can be paid for at the rate of so much per fifty lines up to a maximum of say 1250 lines per day. This type of incentive is particularly appropriate for typists, computer-punch operators and verifiers.

Management. The final incentive is 'management'. Just that. The part played by straightforward management ability and leadership is often overlooked. It is in fact the most important single incentive and motivator.

The field of incentives can now be expressed briefly thus:

	TYPE OF INCENTIVE	OBJECTIVES	AMOUNT OF MONEY INVOLVED	ARE THE RESULTS MEASURABLE?	EXAMPLE
1	Fringe benefits	General	High	No	Sports club
2	Campaigns	Specific	Low	Yes	Zero defects
3	Profit-sharing	General	Medium	No	Trusts
4	Competitions	Specific	Low	Yes	Holidays
5	Work measurement based	Specific	Medium	Yes	Clerical MMD
6	Management	General & specific	Medium	Yes	Personal ability

REDUCING THE COST OF SPACE

There are four basic ways of reducing the cost of office space.

Using space effectively

The first approach is to ensure that the correct number of rooms and people are employed within the office. This assessment will normally be based on the work measurement techniques already described. This is reinforced by looking critically at each function and considering whether it would be better to replace it by outside contracts. For example, should the tea ladies' kitchens be replaced by vending machines? Would the staff prefer luncheon vouchers to the existing canteen facilities? Should bulky files be microfilmed and/or deposited with a firm specializing in paperwork storage?

Lower-cost buildings

The second way of reducing costs is to reduce the cost per square metre of the office accommodation. This involves moving part or all of the staff to a lower-cost building. Such a move is a major event and must be treated with care. The alternatives usually lie between:

1   Moving all or part of the office away from a high-cost area (e.g. central London)
2   Moving into purpose-built offices which are more suitable for one's needs
3   Converting a building (e.g. a modern warehouse) to one's own special needs, provided 'change of use' permission can be obtained
4   Putting widely dispersed offices all together in one location

The feelings of the key staff must be carefully sounded out. Sometimes as few as 15 per cent of staff want to move although senior personnel will usually be willing and flexible.

In this field, a further possibility that should be considered is selling the building and retaining the offices needed on a leaseback basis. The attraction of this manoeuvre depends on the current financial situation.

Reducing cost of furniture

The third way of reducing costs is to get value for money in the field of furnishing, decorations, carpeting, and so on. One firm purchased some very expensive desks and paternalistically congratulated themselves. The staff however were appalled. Not only did they feel that this was wasteful ('I'd rather have it in my salary') but they did not like the new furniture anyway.

It is therefore worth asking people what furnishing they want — in practice, people do not take advantage of this situation. For example, it is usually found that typists in a typing centre are happy with utilitarian desks but do appreciate carpeting or curtains.

Office layout

The fourth way of reducing office costs is in better office layouts. This is a subject about which numerous books have been written but here we are concerned with the cost of various alternatives and their respective effectiveness. One of the current trends is towards open-plan offices instead of having separate 'cells'. An analysis of scores of books and articles on office landscaping leads to the following areas of agreement:

1 The minimum dimension of a landscaped office should be 18m (60ft) in either direction
2 Employees should have a minimum of $4\frac{1}{2}m^2$ ($50ft^2$) per person. For creative work the minimum distance between people should be 4m (13ft)
3 Some background noise is necessary and a level of 55dB is recommended
4 Separate areas should be provided for snacks, vending machines, and so on

It is claimed that open offices save money because of the reduced cost of moving groups of people and the greater feeling of working together.

OFFICE AUTOMATION AND COST REDUCTION

The introduction of modern office technology in recent years has presented a fundamental challenge to managers. In the past many managers considered the office function in terms of a junior supporting role. Office automation in an organization can reduce costs, but it must be done in a logical manner.

The organization must possess or have access to certain knowledge and skills, backed up by experience of real applications and in order to apply this knowledge properly and in the right context, it should be able to diagnose its own systems and procedures. In particular, because of the impact on people, there should be a high degree of awareness of how to manage change in an organization.

Office automation must be tackled in the right order to ensure that maximum benefits are obtained. The order is:

1 Establish functional requirements
2 Identify applications
3 Select technological solutions

Knowledge of technological solutions is often available first and can lead to costly mistakes. Many companies purchased computers or word-processing equipment which failed to meet user or operator needs. There was often insufficient systems analysis and in many cases users and operators were badly trained. Modern office equipment can reduce office costs by:

1. Enabling support staff to become more efficient; for example, productivity increases from word-processing operations
2. Relieving managers from time-consuming and low-level tasks
3. Giving managers access to information more quickly with improved tools of analysis for more effective decision making

It is worth noting that the potential for efficiency savings can be predicted fairly clearly, but it is not easy to convert this potential into clearly stated cost savings, as the cost justification must address organizational as well as technological issues.

Measurement of efficiency and productivity

Productivity may increase because of office automation, but such change may not be easy to quantify. Counting keystrokes is simple but can produce misleading figures. If word processing is introduced, productivity in the form of keystrokes may rise. Text alterations are easier to make once words have been typed, but authors may tend to make more changes, so although quality may be improved, the quantity produced may be lower. Office automation can therefore lead to increased costs with no real increase in output if it is installed without systematic appraisal, although the quality of work may be enhanced by elimination of boring and routine tasks.

SAVING TIME

Reducing the number of meetings

A great deal of time is wasted and the corresponding cost of salaries and expenses in unnecessary meetings. Any saving in the number and extent of meetings can only be productive. Modern technology should be considered, especially by using the telephone to have a meeting. The latest equipment enables each person to 'join' the meeting while still in their office, but one of the drawbacks is that the other participants cannot be seen. The British Telecom system of Confravision allows people from several major cities to be linked together so they can all see each other and talk and there is a facility to show documents. This vision-and-sound conferencing is an improvement on voice conferencing alone, but it also has drawbacks.

Telephone system efficiency

It has been estimated that only two out of three telephone calls reach the required location, the reasons being mainly 'no reply' or 'engaged'. Costs can be reduced by ensuring that:

1 The duration of any call is reduced
2 The call is not made at peak times
3 Calls are monitored by using new electronic systems

It has been calculated that 60 per cent of every telephone call consists of information exchange and 40 per cent of greetings, salutations, goodbyes etc. By using the new equipment an analysis of line usage can be made which will show if the telephone system is adequate for the work required. In addition a detailed analysis of calls logged is possible.

ASK THE STAFF

As has been previously hinted at in this chapter, a potent method of saving costs is to ask the staff what they want. Employee questionnaires are being used by more and more concerns to ask people for their opinions. For example, do people want a sports ground?

One company asked its staff this sort of question. The answer came back that what the men would really appreciate would be a petrol filling station near the entrance — not, it should be noted, to get cheap petrol, but just for the convenience.

Other companies have introduced flexible hours for the staff. For example in Germany, Messerschmitt allow staff to arrive between 7 a.m. and 9 a.m. and leave between 4 p.m. and 6 p.m. The staff clock on and off to make the official working week. When the scheme started it was feared that employees would take advantage of the scheme and 'run into debt' with their hours worked. In point of fact, in the first month, the staff ran up 26 000 hours credit.

SUMMARY

The secrets of reducing office costs can be summarized as follows:

1 Decide what information is needed by management and provide this information at optimum cost
2 Investigate all major items of expenditure and decide on their effectiveness
3 Ask the staff for their help

FURTHER READING

M. Peltu, *Successful Management of Office Automation*, NCC, 1984.
Purcell and Smith (eds), *Control of Work*, Macmillan, 1980.
B.H. Walley, *Handbook of Office Management*, Business Books, 1982.

17

Setting Up a New Office

Rod Revell

Setting up a new office is an infrequent and complex operation for most companies. However, it presents a rare opportunity for creating a major and long-lasting influence on company efficiency and overhead costs. On all these counts, therefore, thorough planning and close management attention are amply rewarded.

A project of this nature should be under the direct control of a senior member of the company to ensure that decisions are taken quickly and that all the cost implications are recognized. For the purposes of control, the project can be split into a number of overlapping stages:

1 Establishment of requirements
2 Building assessment
3 Furniture
4 Implementation
5 Continuing administration

The time required for each stage will vary from project to project, but the same logical sequence should always be followed.

ESTABLISHMENT OF REQUIREMENTS

The first step in the planning operation is to collect together the data on which all else will be based. The ultimate success of the project will depend on a proper balance being reached between individual needs and corporate objectives after a careful analysis of each.

In order to ensure that the information is comprehensive, staff questionnaires and selected interviews can be used. It is very important at this stage to obtain a complete and unbiased picture of the type of work that is undertaken by each individual. Questions should be phrased so as to elicit information in the form which will be most useful. For instance, it is not enough to know that someone is an engineer, an accountant, or a typist. The questionnaires should highlight the activities which are carried out for a significant portion of the time — such as reading, writing, telephoning, meetings and so on. The number of visitors that can be expected and their frequency of arrival is important, as well as the degree of confidentiality of the work that is being performed. Communication patterns should be analysed for departments, sections and individuals, and the need for furniture, storage and equipment should be calculated.

In addition to individual needs, staff numbers today and for at least five years into the future must be established. It should be remembered that these figures need not be the same as those for normal budgeting purposes. It is not unusual for management to reduce budget figures in order to provide a target for each department to aim for. The figures that should be used for office planning purposes should relate to a less restrained estimate of what will actually happen. It is rare to find that a company overestimates its future staff numbers. The penalty of underestimation is that the new offices become overcrowded and inefficient within a relatively short period of time. Forecasts should also be made of the possible changes in company organization, office systems and equipment over this period. It would be unrealistic to expect a high degree of accuracy but the range of options should be identified.

Thus far, the information has been gathered in company terms, which are of little use when looking for or assessing potential new offices. Therefore it must be translated into an accommodation specification. In order to achieve this, a process of analysis must be carried out to determine space requirements, relationship patterns, layout types, service requirements and working environment. All facets of the company's needs must be established and expressed as accommodation requirements. In many cases it is advisable to use professional assistance during this phase, to ensure the most economic solutions.

Space requirements

In order to establish space requirements, a set of standards must be developed for individuals and functions. These should be based on the analysis of a number of factors:

Work content
Furniture and equipment
Storage
Need for privacy
Type of layout
Number of visitors or meetings
Access

Space standards should also be developed for facilities such as meeting areas, common storage, reception, computer and catering. The sum of all these needs is the total net usable space requirement for the company. It is most important that this figure is not confused with the net lettable area quoted for a building. The difference between these figures is discussed in the next section.

Relationship patterns

The relationship pattern within the company can be established by the sequence of steps illustrated in Figure 17.1. A survey is carried out to determine the existing pattern of telephone calls, paper flow and visits. This can be done by individual records, sampling, estimate or observation. The results should be summarized into a matrix which will show the comparative figures. Any major bias resulting from the present location of departments or individuals should be known from the interviews. It is common to find that some personal communication links have grown up for no other reason than that the people are housed in adjacent areas, and conversely that departments which should be working closely together have a weak link as a result of being based on different floors, or in different buildings. Adjustments can be made to the matrix in order to correct this or to reflect company policy. By this means, specific communication links in the new building can be strengthened and others weakened.

The modified matrix should be used to create a relationship diagram (Figure 17.2), which will be the basis for locating activities. The thicker lines denote the stronger relationship links and therefore should be kept as short as possible. In due course, when space requirements have been finalized and the shape and size of the accommodation is known, the relationship diagram is developed into a block diagram allocating space to each department (see Figure 17.1).

Layout types

There are several types of layout in common use which should be considered. The choice will depend on an analysis of departmental and individual needs, with the twin objectives of an efficient office and good staff relations. Figure 17.3 illustrates a means of determining the most appropriate layout. Each

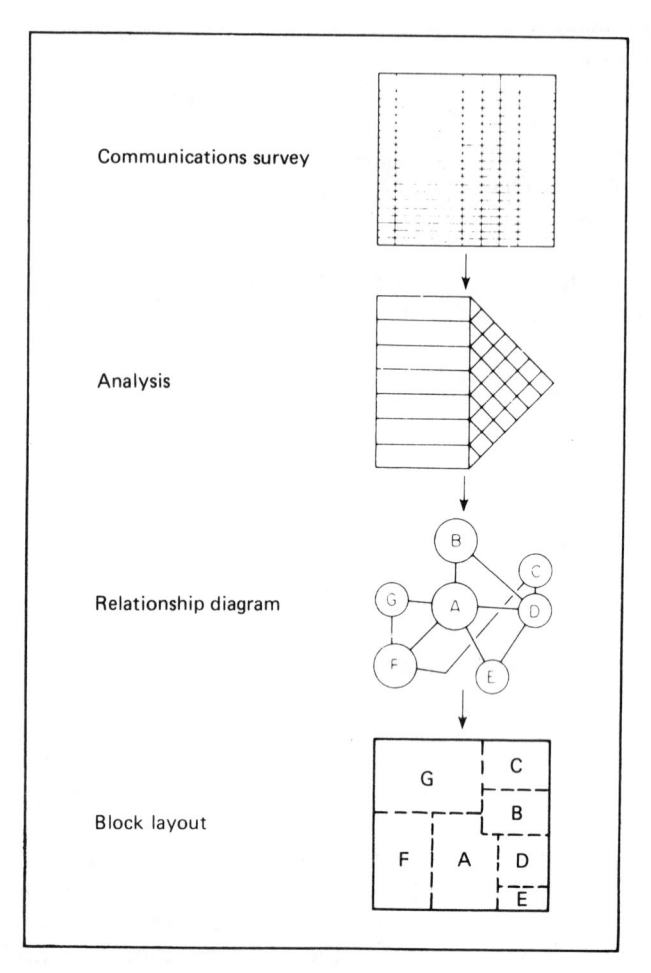

Figure 17.1 Creation of a block layout

layout has a number of advantages and disadvantages and they are graded accordingly. However, each department or function will have a particular set of priorities and these must be matched with the layout factors in the table. Thus an advertising department may well need considerable flexibility and good communications but little privacy, whereas a personnel department would put a very high rating on privacy but might need little flexibility.

The six layouts listed in Figure 17.3 are all in common use in offices throughout the country. A layout which is currently much in fashion is the open-space or landscaped office. This type of layout gives an informal appearance whilst being based on an analysis of departmental requirements. No fixed partitions are used and individuals are grouped by section or

SETTING UP A NEW OFFICE

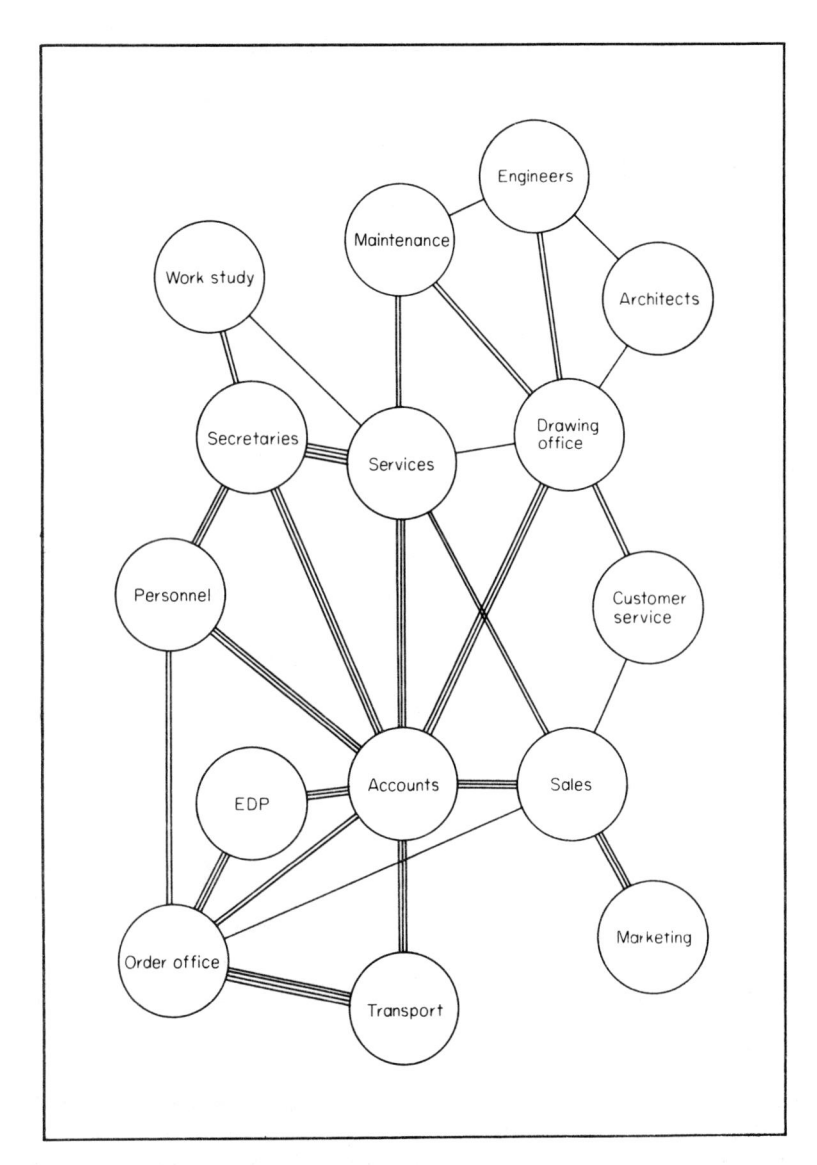

Figure 17.2 Relationship diagram

department. Figure 17.4 shows a typical open-space office. A high degree of flexibility is achievable and the reorganization of departments can be accomplished by moving a few pieces of furniture. Shoulder-high freestanding screens and boxes of indoor plants are used to provide privacy and freedom from undue distraction. Communications are good as there are few barriers to inhibit conversation or discourage meetings.

	OPEN SPACE	OPEN PLAN	CELLULAR INDIVIDUAL	CELLULAR SHARED	HALF-HEIGHT PARTITION	CARREL
Privacy	**		***	*	*	**
Freedom from distraction	**		***		*	**
Communication	***	***		*	**	*
Flexibility	***	**			*	**
Supervision	**	***		*	*	
Work flow	**	***		*	*	
Space utilization	**	***		*	*	**

Figure 17.3 Characteristics of office layout

SETTING UP A NEW OFFICE

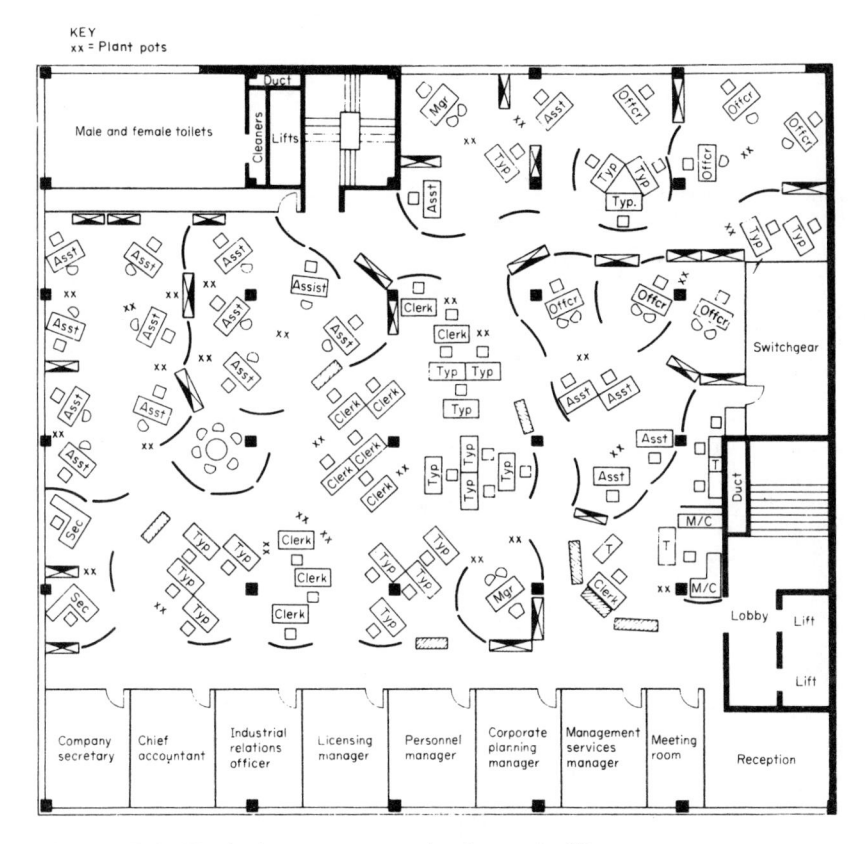

Figure 17.4 Typical open-space or landscaped office

Acoustics play an important part in the success of this type of layout. Noise levels must be such as to provide adequate masking without creating too much distraction. This will be promoted by using a large room which is as deep as possible and can accommodate at least fifty people. Nevertheless, several successful open-space offices have been created for as few as twenty people. The minimum number of people which is acceptable will be influenced by the number and intensity of noise sources and the individual need for freedom from distraction.

Figure 17.5 illustrates an open-plan office, which is particularly appropriate for many routine paper-handling departments or drawing offices. No fixed partitions are used and there is little if any screening. Space utilization can be very high and the flow of paper is good; however, it is difficult to achieve any degree of privacy. It is usual with this layout to accommodate managers in separate offices so that they will not have undue distraction. In drawing offices, the bulky furniture that is used tends to

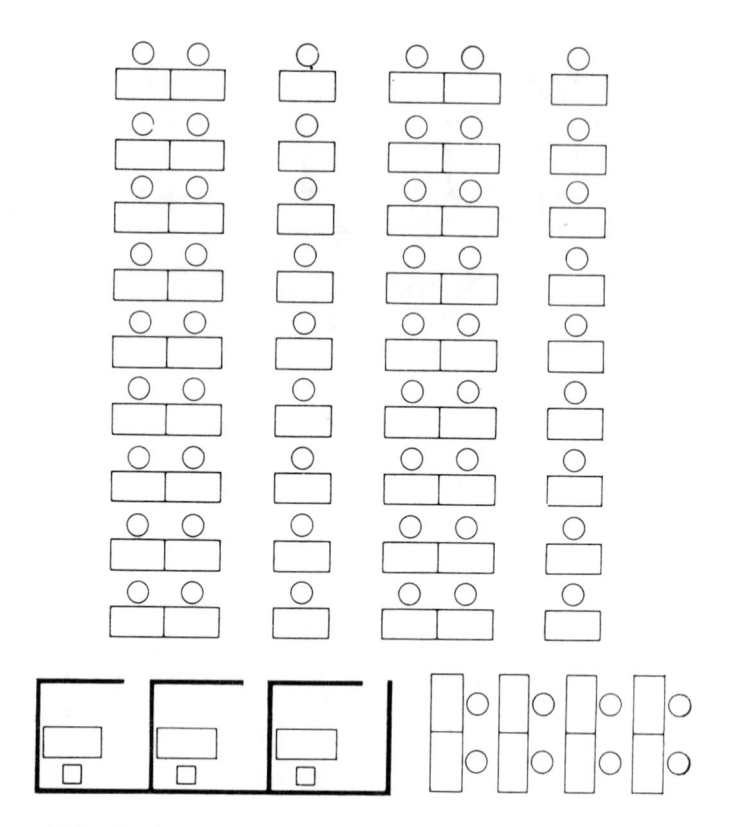

Figure 17.5 Typical open-plan office layout

break up the pattern of sound and the drawing boards provide some degree of screening.

Cellular offices when used by individuals achieve a high degree of privacy and freedom from distraction. However communications are not good and relationships tend to become more formalized. Flexibility of use is low, and any change of office staff may require a large number of partition moves. Space utilization is usually poor when the building module dictates large offices. Spare space is often wasted when it becomes available in the wrong part of the building.

A cellular office which is shared by several people has the worst of all worlds. It has the disadvantages of inflexibility, poor space utilization and bad communications. At the same time, because of its small size, it gives the highest levels of distraction and lack of privacy. However, the design of the building or special company requirements may dictate its use.

The half-height partition layout is a compromise between the cellular and open-plan office. Fixed partitions from four to six feet high are installed and

SETTING UP A NEW OFFICE

staff work in the boxes which are created. This layout tends to give a false feeling of privacy.

A new type of layout, which is being promoted by many furniture suppliers, is the carrel. This consists of a number of individual or paired work stations. The furniture is designed to provide an integrated system of work top, storage and screening, which forms two or three sides of a square. Some systems are designed as a complete square or rectangle with a small entrance way. This provides more flexibility than a cellular layout, and more privacy than an open plan. Considerable storage is close at hand, but communications are not good, which indicates that this is more appropriate for research or similar activities.

Service requirements

The provision of services is often one of the last items to be considered when companies move to new offices. Consequently telephone and power outlets are often in the wrong place or unavailable, causing undue expense and inconvenience. The planning of the telephone system should be started early in the project as delivery of equipment can be very long. During the initial investigation into individual requirements, it is important to determine the detailed telecommunication needs of each department and function. The British Telecom and other equipment suppliers undertake surveys of telephone traffic to form a basis for the future planning. There are now so many systems and new developments in this field that some time spent in discussion with suppliers or other experts will be well repaid.

Cabling. The proliferation of computer terminals, word processors, personal computers, local printers etc. has created additional problems for office designers. The amount of cable running round an office these days can pose considerable restrictions on layout if not properly managed. In addition to power and telephone cables, device networking cable will often need to be accommodated, e.g. for local area networks. Power cable must be kept separate from communication cables so that signal interference is avoided and fire hazard is minimized.

Flexibility of layout, ease of change, and basic safety are all further reasons why cable must be considered carefully and channelled effectively. Integral channels with removable covers should be used in preference to conduit which is difficult to access. There are several methods available to the designer, such as:

1. Channelling through the acoustic screens which form the basis of some workstation systems
2. Passing cable through the false ceiling, and down pillars to the workstations (but be sure there are enough points at which to drop cable

— it is dangerous and unsightly to drop cable without anything to which it can be attached on the way down)
3   Channelling through specially-designed floor and carpet tiles

It is interesting to note that cable management has assumed such importance of late, that the British Standards Institute has issued a code of practice on the subject (BS6396).

Working environment

The introduction of the Offices, Shops and Railway Premises Act in 1963 and the Health and Safety at Work Act in 1974 made management much more conscious of the influence of environmental conditions on staff efficiency and welfare. However, the standards that are set out in the Acts have been overtaken by current good practice. When determining environmental requirements for new offices, it is sensible to set two standards. A target standard should be established which would create good working conditions for the staff. In addition, a threshold level should be set, below which there is a significant drop in office efficiency or staff acceptance. If a proposed office does not meet the minimum standard then it should be rejected. On this basis a target figure can be used when looking for new accommodation, and the threshold level is known so that unsuitable offices can be identified at an early stage.

Figure 17.6 lists in a simplified form many of the standards that are commonly used. This list is only a general guide, as it may be possible or even desirable to depart from these figures under some circumstances. An example of this variation is shown in the tables. Noise levels need to be adjusted in line with the type of activity that is being performed. For instance, a typing pool can usually tolerate a noise level of 55dBA, whereas a private office will probably have a noise level of about 35dBA. Professional advice should be used for setting these standards and for ensuring that they are met, but the following notes on lighting, noise, heating and ventilation may provide food for thought when assessing real requirements.
Lighting. An important factor in the comfort of office workers is the way in which their work place is lit, and how well the balance between natural and artificial light sources is maintained.

Effective illumination is less concerned with the power of light sources, but more with the resultant illumination on the work surface and equipment. Combined with this is the need to ensure that light is not directed towards the eyes, causing glare; conversely, the avoidance of shadows over the work area must be an objective. The following guidelines may help:

1   Artificial light sources should always be diffused
2   Contrast between light source and background should be minimized

SETTING UP A NEW OFFICE

	CELLULAR OFFICE		OPEN-SPACE OFFICE	
	Threshold	*Target*	*Threshold*	*Target*
Temperature (°F)	68–80	68–75	68–80	68–75
Ventilation (cubic feet of fresh air/hour/person)	750	1200	750	1200
Humidity (per cent)	35–60	40–55	35–60	40–55
Lighting (Lux)	400	450	600	600–800
Acoustics (average noise level in dBA)	35–60	30–50	55	45

Figure 17.6 Environmental standards

3   Shiny work surfaces should be avoided
4   VDU screens should not face, nor back on to a window
5   VDU screens should be positioned so that ceiling lights are not reflected on them. If this proves to be a problem, due to the nature of the office, anti-glare filters are available for most sizes of screen

A problem brought about by VDU screens being used for *part* of a person's job, is the need to provide different degrees of illumination for different aspects of work. VDUs can be difficult to read if the office is as light as necessary for most other jobs. This problem can be converted to a money saver by using a two-tier lighting system. The overall lighting can be reduced significantly if a second light source can be controlled at, and applied to, the workstation. This can be achieved by table lamps, so long as they are flexible enough to direct the light to the area of the work surface where it is required. Alternatively uplighters fixed to acoustic screens serve the purpose well.

Noise. A moderate and steady level of background noise is not really disturbing (*cf* the habit of many people to have the radio on whilst reading or writing), and even noises made by office machines can be accepted, after a while, as background noise. Sometimes background noise can have a positive effect; surveys have indicated that complete silence causes its own type of discomfort. However, excessive noise (particularly if intermittent) is most undesirable.

Noise should be dealt with in three stages: you should first try to control it, failing which you should try to absorb it. If all else fails you must isolate it.

An example of noise *control* in one company, was the removal of the public address system used for calling errant staff to the phone. The trouble with such systems is that they cause unnecessary 'noise' to all but the subject of the search. In effect a new switchboard, with an automatic transfer of calls facility, meant that fewer calls failed to reach the person concerned anyway. A simple paging system (with individuals carrying their own receiver) supplemented the switchboard facility, thus totally eliminating the need for loudspeakers.

Absorption of noise was traditionally achieved by carpeting the floors, putting pads under typewriters and using sound-absorbing materials in screening and even wall panels and ceiling tiles.

All these methods are still available of course, but some of the noises are now louder and demand more drastic attention. The appearance of matrix and daisy-wheel printers throughout an office does tend to be noticed, but for all the wrong reasons! Fortunately acoustic hoods are available for most printers, and should certainly be used. A more expensive (at the moment) alternative reverts back to eliminating the noises by using non-impact printers (ink-jet propulsion or laser, for example). However, it would probably be difficult to justify the use of such high-volume/high speed printers for general office applications — they are useful for producing mailshots and sales promotion material, but these functions would normally be the responsibility of a print department.

This last point brings us to the third aspect of 'noise management', that of *isolation*. Most unavoidable noise will probably be already isolated, simply by virtue of its function: printing machines (of the offset litho variety) in the print department; high-speed line printers in the computer room: noisy mailing equipment in the postroom. If a source of noise is not isolated in such a way, there may well be a good reason, so great care must be exercised before proposing expensive isolation measures.

Heating and ventilation. Good heating distributes the heat uniformly throughout the office, without blowing hot air into somebody's face — which should be avoided even if they like it! An often forgotten fact is that local computing power can disrupt a balanced heating system, in that the machines themselves can give off a fair amount of heat. This should be considered when determining the layout, but it may be relevant to bear it in mind at this stage.

Effective ventilation is essential, not only for physical well-being, in that

SETTING UP A NEW OFFICE

it minimizes the dangers of infection. It also provides fresh air and clears smells (such as smoke) without causing a draught.

Timing

The preparation of a specification of requirements is often undertaken in two phases. In the first, sufficient information must be assembled for a search to be made for new accommodation and to assess its suitability. This is usually a matter of some urgency. During the search period, there is then time to assess the company needs in full, so that detailed planning can start as soon as a building is found.

Information required for the building search can be summarized as:

1. Net usable space requirement
2. Types of layout
3. Departmental relationship patterns
4. Main service requirements
5. Outline environmental requirements
6. Location requirements
7. Special facilities such as computer room, catering area or banking hall

This information is used as a basis for the selection of a shortlist of buildings. These would be separately assessed and a final selection made.

BUILDING ASSESSMENT

The selection of a new office building commits the company to it for a number of years. It is imperative, therefore, that the company's short and long-term requirements are used as the basis for comparison between alternatives. This requires an analysis of the building design and facilities to ensure the most cost-effective result.

The assessment may be best illustrated by the example summarized in Figure 17.7. Company requirements have been established in outline showing that during the next five years a total of 250 staff will have to be accommodated. In order to provide adequate working areas, together with space for other office functions and circulation, 37 500 square feet of net usable space is required. This has been calculated on the basis of 70 per cent of the area being used for open offices and 30 per cent for cellular offices. A number of service requirements and environmental standards have been fixed at both the target and threshold levels.

During the five-year period of occupation, it is anticipated that 10 per cent of the staff will move each year because of internal reorganization. It is also considered desirable to have additional space available for a 20 per cent

	COMPANY REQUIREMENTS	BUILDING 1	BUILDING 2	BUILDING 3	BUILDING 4
Staff	250				
Net usable area (square feet)	37 500	41 000	37 000	39 000	47 000
Net lettable area (square feet)		45 000	39 000	42 000	54 000
Layout	70 per cent open	*	–	–	*
	30 per cent cellular	*	*	*	*
Services	Telephone grid	–	–	–	–
	Power grid	*	–	–	*
Environment:	THRESHOLD / TARGET				
Temperature (°C)	68–80 / 68–75	Threshold +	Target	Threshold +	Target
Ventilation (cubic feet/hour/person)	750 / 1200	Threshold +	Threshold +	Threshold +	Threshold +
Humidity (per cent)	35–60 / 40–55	Threshold +	Target	Threshold +	Target
Lighting (lux)	600 / 750	Target	Target	Target	Target
Acoustics (dBA)	55 / 45	Threshold +	Threshold +	Threshold +	Target
Flexibility	10% Annual change	*	*	*	*
	20% Expansion after 5 years	–	*	*	*
Initial costs					
Conversion		£360 000	£312 000	£420 000	£810 000
Fitting out		£315 000	£273 000	£294 000	£378 000
Annual costs		£675 000	£585 000	£714 000	£1 188 000
Interest on capital at 14%		£ 94 500	£ 81 900	£ 99 960	£166 320
Rent and rates		708 750	819 000	504 000	405 000
Running costs		45 000	42 000	38 000	51 000
Maintenance costs		12 000	10 500	13 500	17 500
Staff cost differential		25 000	37 500	37 500	12 500
Total annual cost		£885 250	£990 900	£692 960	£652 320

Figure 17.7 Building assessment

SETTING UP A NEW OFFICE

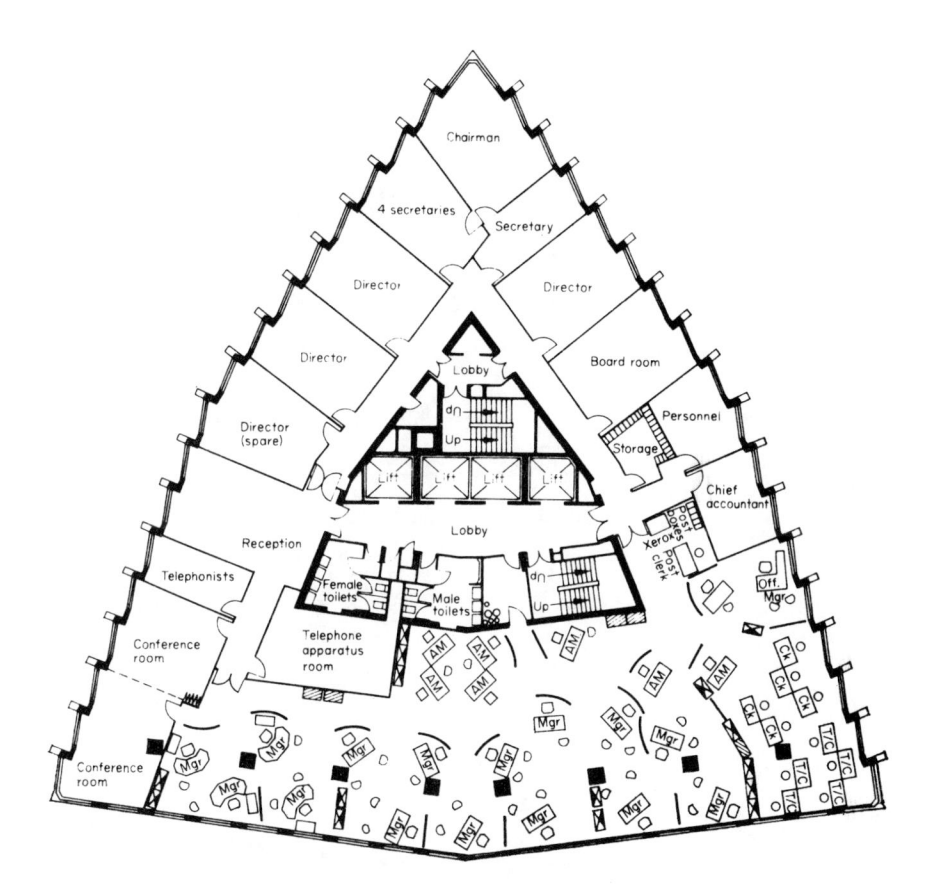

Figure 17.8 Office floor for a company headquarters

expansion after the five-year period. This additional space may be in the form of floors that have been sublet on a short-term lease or areas which have not yet been converted for use.

Four buildings are considered in this example. Buildings 1 and 2 are conventional postwar offices which have been built by a developer. Building 3 is a prewar office which was designed for another occupant. Building 4 is a warehouse which can be converted to office use.

The net usable area is calculated on the basis of company requirements and individual space standards, as described earlier.

The net lettable area within a building is the total area inside the walls excluding the service areas and vertical circulation, and is the figure usually used for lease documents.

These two figures are not directly comparable, and a utilization factor must be used to convert 'lettable' to 'usable'. This factor is normally between

Figure 17.9 Open-space layout

80 and 95 per cent, but it is not uncommon for it to be as low as 70 per cent. The size of this factor is controlled by the internal shape and layout of the building, the partition modules and inactive space. This is illustrated in Figures 17.8 to 17.10.

Figure 17.8 relates to layouts used on a floor of an office building in Wembley. The requirements for the chairman and directors of this company are for offices of 200 square feet each, plus 35 square feet for corridor space, making a total of 235 square feet. In practice, because of the internal dimensions of the building and the necessity for a one-sided corridor, the directors have offices of 320 square feet with corridor space of 80 square feet making a total of 400 square feet. Thus there is a loss of 165 square feet for each director which is reflected in the availability of space. Figure 17.9 shows an open-space layout on a lower floor of the same building. In the latter case 79 people have been accommodated at an average of about 105

SETTING UP A NEW OFFICE 351

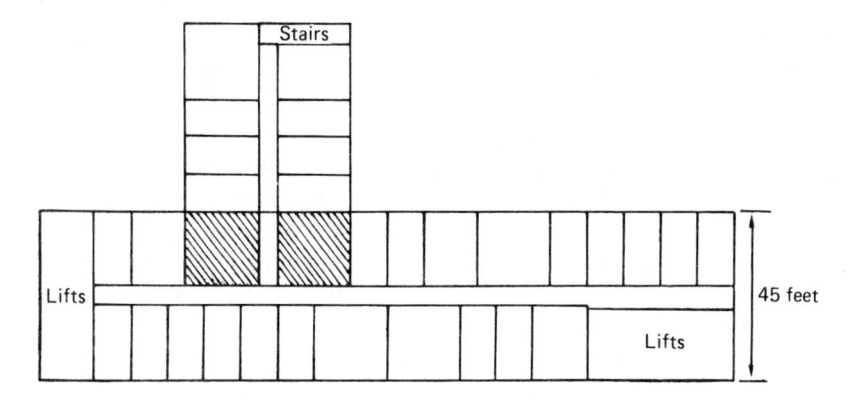

Figure 17.10 Cellular office layout

square feet per head, whilst on the upper floor there was room for only 56.

The building illustrated in Figure 17.10 has a more conventional shape and size than the previous example. The internal building depth is 45 feet and the window and partition module is 5 feet. On this basis, offices can be constructed with widths which are multiples of 5 feet. Because of the internal depth of the building, the individual offices will be 20 feet deep. Therefore the smallest usable office is 200 square feet. Increments can be made in steps of 100 square feet only. These figures are most unlikely to coincide with the company space standards which would have been previously established. An additional loss of space can be created in the shaded area of the plan, which can be used only for meetings or storage. However, it is likely that the requirement for these facilities would be spread in an uneven fashion throughout the building with a consequent waste of space.

These two examples illustrate the necessity to calculate a utilization factor when assessing the suitability of a building. If this is not done then it will probably be found that the new building does not provide enough space for all the activities which are to be accommodated. The process of establishing the utilization factor can be complex and should be undertaken with care.

In the comparison illustrated in Figure 17.7, each building area has been reduced by this factor to establish the net usable area.

The estimated capital cost for preparing each building for occupation has been calculated in this example on the basis of £8 per square foot for buildings 1 and 2, £10 per square foot for building 3 and £15 per square foot for building 4. This would provide lighting, power, telephones, other services, partitions and so on. The fitting-out cost for internal fittings, furniture and equipment has been estimated at £7 per square foot for each building.

Annual costs are based on interest and amortization charges, rent, power, heating, cleaning, maintenance and other running costs. In order to compare the buildings on a common basis, a staff cost differential should also be calculated. This is a reflection of the greater efficiency that can be expected from the provision of good working conditions for staff. If it is assumed that a new building has been designed to optimize working conditions and provide the most appropriate layout and staff space standards, then existing buildings will incur additional cost as a result of any variation. Information in this field is not yet conclusive, however there is evidence to suggest that this differential can be as high as 5 per cent of staff costs. For the purpose of this example, differences 1, 2 and 3 per cent have been used.

The totals for the annual costs give a cost comparison for the four buildings. This, together with the comparison of facilities, services and other factors, forms the basis for choosing the most appropriate course of action. In practice it is likely that these cost calculations would be based on discounted cash flow or other sophisticated accounting techniques.

FURNITURE

At an early stage in any project, the vexed question of whether to buy new furniture or retain the old is raised. In many cases, this question answers itself when the furniture is old and in a bad state of repair. In others, arguments are heard about the need for a uniform appearance or a good design image. Valid as these arguments may be, in most companies it all comes back to economics — is there an economic case for investing a significant sum of money in new office furniture and equipment? In this light, a decision can be reached based on facts and estimates instead of opinions and hunches.

During the early part of the project, considerable information will have been gathered about the methods of operation within departments and sections, and individual requirements. When selecting furniture a number of factors have to be considered.

Working surface

The size and shape of this is determined by the needs for reading, writing and meetings. The large majority of functions require space for reading and writing, no more than 36 inches by 24 inches. When additional reference material is used, this can rise to 60 inches by 30 inches. These sizes assume that suitable storage is available to each person which removes the need to use the work surface for storing papers, files, books or equipment.

If there is a need for meetings to be held at the work place, this should be reflected in the design of the work top. The conventional rectangular design is most appropriate for formal discussions between a small number of

SETTING UP A NEW OFFICE

people. It is possible to encourage a more informal and relaxed atmosphere by the use of a table which is circular or hexagonal. The more a person is surrounded or protected by his furniture, the more this creates a barrier between him and his visitor.

Storage

The first requirement of any system is that all items can be easily retrieved. This means not only that retrieval must be physically simple but also that the items should be readily identifiable. An efficient system ensures that items are stored in batches and that marker tags are visible so that the information can be identified quickly.

The amount of space available for storage is critical. Too little space results in overcrowding and the use of the work top for storage purposes. This leads to inefficiency and delay for other activities. Too much space encourages bad storage discipline. Many items are kept which should be destroyed or placed elsewhere, and important items are lost in the crowd.

The speed with which each category of information is needed and the use of storage by other people must be established. These factors can be used as the basis for deciding which items should be stored at the work place and which stored elsewhere.

Communication

This factor is often overlooked when choosing furniture, although it can have a significant effect on design. For instance, the carrel type of furniture layout mentioned earlier, which consists of a small screened area with the work top and storage hung on the screen, is an efficient means of providing storage. However it discourages person-to-person contact on an informal basis. Therefore the needs for working space and storage must be balanced against the individual requirement for communication.

The second point associated with communication is our old friend cabling again. Once the cable has arrived at the workstation, the second half of the problem arises. Means have to be found to feed the cable into the workstation, and cope with any excess cable. Hollow slabs as end panels on the workstation can solve both problems, but sometimes excess cable is accommodated by neatly securing it to the modesty panel (but only in the top half where it cannot be kicked free). Work surfaces should have holes through which cable can be fed.

General

Consideration should be given to the ergonomic and anthropometric suitability of each design. In other words, it must function efficiently and easily, and it should fit the range of anatomical measurements for office staff. Both the British Standards Institution and the Furniture Industry Research Association have published data on this subject.

An analysis, as set out above, makes it possible to compare the overall advantages of different designs of furniture, and to compare them in turn with the existing furniture already in the office. It should be remembered that it requires a very small increase in staff efficiency to repay the cost of furniture. For instance, a 1 per cent increase in efficiency would save £40 to £50 per year for each junior member of the staff, and this can be more than doubled for middle and senior staff.

IMPLEMENTATION

Layout planning

Once the furniture has been chosen, a building leased and all detailed requirements established, it is possible to carry out the detailed layout planning. This also serves as the basis for the allocation of services, the erection of partitions, and the design of all the interior.

The first step in the detailed planning process is to create a block diagram for the building. This allocates all the available space to individual departments, functions and reserve areas.

This is followed by the development of a detailed layout, which is a very critical phase. It is at this point that the immediate working environment for each individual in the organization is decided, and the result will have a significant influence on his ability and inclination to be efficient. For instance, if distraction is too high he will certainly work more slowly or make more mistakes. In a shared office, the layout for each person has an influence on all those others adjoining him, and therefore each individual's need for privacy or freedom from distraction must be considered.

When preparing the layout, it is most important to visualize it in all three dimensions. The height of screens and storage units can be forgotten when viewed on a normal two-dimensional plan. It is quite common to provide totally inadequate privacy for this reason. Another point to remember is that no one within the office will ever see the layout from the same bird's eye view as is shown on the plan. Therefore the temptation to create pretty patterns or strict regularity should be resisted. Groups must be identified clearly so that each person feels part of the team, but at the same time a feeling of individual treatment must be retained.

Some general guidelines concerning layout may be useful at this point. Where possible desks — or whatever form the workstation takes — should be positioned with the following in mind:

1   Natural light should come from the left for right-handed people and from the right for left-handers
2   The team, or people whose jobs most interact, should be located together. This not only applies to teams or sections within one department, but to whole departments too. It is important that the formal and informal communications structure is reflected in the office layout
3   Each individual should have his own defined work area so that he cannot allow the contents of his desk to wander on to anyone else's (and vice versa of course)
4   Overcrowding is counter-productive. It is impossible to generalize about an individual's space requirements these days, simply because the amount of equipment used is so variable. At one time it was advantageous to minimize the distance between people in a 'flow' line, but with less physical carrying (of card trays etc.), distance is now less important. In fact loss of privacy and increased distractions are two of the main disadvantages which manifested themselves when 'open plan' became established. These days, the availability of better information tends to present an argument for more space, in that more 'ad hoc' meetings occur to discuss the information and make decisions at the work place, rather than in long formal meetings at a central location

The layout will be affected by the availability of services such as telephone and power, as well as the interior dimensions of the building. Thus a number of priorities — some of which may be in conflict — must be balanced, as the result has a major influence on staff efficiency.

Control

In order to prepare the offices for occupation, the layouts and other planning decisions must be defined carefully in the form of a specification, so that contracts can be negotiated. If the work is likely to cost more than £15 000 it is advisable to use the services of a professional office planner or interior designer. He should check the feasibility of the company's decisions, carry out the detailed planning and design work, negotiate contracts with suppliers and other contractors, and supervise the completion of the work on time and within the cost estimates. However, before employing a professional adviser, it is important to establish clearly with him that the cost of his services will be more than recovered by the development of more cost-effective design solutions, the negotiation of larger discounts or an increase in staff efficiency.

A number of contractors and suppliers provide a design and planning service which can be used by client companies. These services are often supplied free of charge, and their cost recovered through the sale of goods.

Therefore it is most important when considering the use of such advisers that the total cost of the contract including services is established at an early date.

Co-ordination and planning

The importance of starting a detailed plan for occupation, at as early a stage as possible, cannot be overstated. Ideally a network analysis should be drawn up and the critical path calculated. This will force the planner to find out equipment delivery lead times and costs, estimated times for each site preparation job, and which jobs depend on others being completed before they can start. It should also determine which contractors have to be mutually exclusive (carpet fitters and false ceiling installers are the obvious examples) and what work is not dependent on knowledge of the detailed desk layouts (fire and burglar alarms, external work etc.).

The services of a property manager who can judge quality of work and reasonable timescales for the many different jobs may well be worth considering. His/her supervisory influence may make the difference between hitting and missing deadlines. Remember that the number of contractors on site at any one time may include decorators, electricians, carpenters, telephone engineers, partition builders and many more.

These days the planning involved in setting up a new computer room and installing the computer can and should be a project in its own right. Special fire precautions have to be taken, not to mention the air conditioning, security locking on the doors, and the cabling needed to install the machine itself. Preparations must be made to cater for the time the computer is non-operational, particularly if it usually runs for twenty-four hours a day. Close liaison with the computer operations manager and the manufacturer(s) is vital for a successful move.

Finally it is useful to involve certain official bodies at the planning stage so that their requirements are known and taken into account. The local fire officer, environmental health officer and your insurance company surveyor all fall into this category. Sometimes the crime prevention officer will also be a useful contact. Certainly the more advice is taken at the planning stage the lesser will be the problems of official acceptance at the end.

The move

The week of the move can be a traumatic experience with lost files, damaged equipment and disgruntled staff. However, this need not be if proper planning has been done. In the first place the layout and location of departments must be settled well in advance, and all staff notified. Visits to the new building by members of the staff can go a long way to winning their cooperation during the very sensitive period prior to the move.

At an early stage in the project when filing and storage requirements are first being determined, the entire company should be directed to examine all their filing to see what items can be disposed of or put into an archive store. This will usually reduce the total requirement by at least 25 per cent. This initial operation is likely to have taken place six to twelve months before the move date. If in the week immediately before the move the exercise is repeated, it is probable that an additional 10 per cent can be saved. However, it should be emphasized that in determining space requirements allowance must be made for growth, even though the base figure may have been successfully reduced.

Selection of the removal company is another important decision. As with all best laid plans the unexpected will certainly happen and the ability of people on the spot to respond positively is essential. An experienced removal firm will make all the difference in this respect, and they should want to be involved in planning the move as well as actually carrying it out.

The layout plans for the new offices should be clearly marked with room numbers and floor codes. If large open offices are used, a coded grid should be devised so that each desk or other piece of furniture can be located by a map reference code. Each member of the staff should then be notified of the code for his new location in the building and all items of furniture, equipment and paperwork should be clearly marked with this code. This will enable the removal team to assemble items together and ensure that they are taken to their right location. It is almost inevitable that some items will go astray during the move and this coding system will enable them to be rerouted.

Throughout this period, it is most important that a senior member of the staff has overall control of all operations and is present throughout the move.

CONTINUING ADMINISTRATION

The planning and other work that has been carried out should have resulted in the efficient occupation of the building. However, it must be remembered that this is right only for this company and at this point in time. Every company is constantly changing in size, organization and techniques. Therefore within a relatively short period of time, a number of changes will be necessary in order to ensure continuing efficiency. These changes must be closely controlled or the result can quickly deteriorate into a form of accommodation anarchy. It is of the utmost importance that a senior man, probably the office manager, has direct responsibility for all alterations to furniture, layout and services. He should have been closely involved during the planning of the new offices, so that he is fully aware of the planning philosophy and operational requirements for each department. If individual departmental managers are allowed to make major changes to their own accommodation this can affect the accommodation of other departments and is almost certain to result in a reduced space utilization.

The office manager has a major effect on company overhead costs. An office is a very expensive and highly complex management tool which must be used with intelligence and foresight. It is important that every member of the staff knows how to use the furniture and equipment they are given. It is rare to see desk drawers being used effectively, or chairs being adjusted to the right height. The office manager's role should be much closer in attitude to the production manager's role than is normally the case. He must be aware of the cost effectiveness of the decisions which he takes and he should not necessarily go for the cheapest solution. For instance, the cheapest item may also be the one which will wear out or break down first, or the cheapest service facility may have an adverse effect on staff efficiency. All these considerations must be taken into account if the new offices are to continue to meet the long-term requirements established at the beginning of the project.

FURTHER READING

The BWC Partnership, *Business Property Handbook*, Gower, Aldershot, 1982.

P. Manning (ed), *Office Design* (A study of environment), Pilkington Research.

M. Mogulescu, *Profit through Design*, American Management Association, New York, 1970.

Office Building (*Architects' Journal* handbook), series published 1973−5.

Planned Open Offices (Cost Benefit Analysis), Department of the Environment, Whitehall Development Group, London.

B. Robichaud, *Selecting, Planning and Managing Office Space*, McGraw-Hill, New York, 1958.

18

The Role of O & M

J M Alastair Gibson

Effective organization of a company is as essential to its success as the technical, professional or other expertise on which the company is based. Similarly, a company requires effective systems and procedures for handling the control information used in its operations and decision making. Administration depends on two factors: organization — by which work is divided among individuals or groups and the working relationship between them is defined — and the office function — which in its widest sense covers the means of handling the information of a company and which provides the system of communications by which it is controlled. A company has to adapt its organization to its changing needs and circumstances and will correspondingly find it necessary to adapt its office systems and methods. Failure to do so may limit its success or its growth.

WHEN IS AN O & M DEPARTMENT NECESSARY?

In a very small company, problems of organization and methods, while not unimportant, are relatively minor. The lines of communication are short, most communication is direct and relationships are face to face and unformalized. Paperwork tends to be at a minimum and the boss and his few staff may run the company with only the most elementary of systems and little in the way of formal procedure. As a company grows in size its operations usually become more complex. The organization necessarily becomes more defined and formalized even though it may be structured in such a way as to retain as far as possible the advantages of flexibility of the smaller concern. The office functions which prove necessary to this increasing size are accompanied by defined systems and procedures and more sophisticated methods of processing information whether in handling orders, keeping the accounts or planning production.

Before the Industrial Revolution business consisted for the most part of a few employees and a single owner/manager. Of course even today this is not an uncommon arrangement, particularly in agricultural, professional and small business organizations. In this type of environment, the few people involved are usually, but not always, intimately aware of the reactions of other members within the organization. The need for an orderly process for making decisions is important but the need for detailed written procedures may not be critical. While a systematic approach is required in almost any organization the need for formal systems does not necessarily become necessary until the organization becomes relatively complex. As business units grow larger, and personnel turnover becomes significantly higher, the need for the development of detailed procedures to handle routine activity becomes more important. The organization is likely to be using costly office machinery and employing specialists to analyse and design its systems, and anything approaching a reasonably detailed knowledge of the whole organization and its systems may well be beyond the capacity of any one individual.

WHY SHOULD O & M BE NECESSARY?

In the main, O & M is necessary in any organization because of its very nature. Line management, whilst realizing that all may not be right, do not have the time to devote to a detailed study to discover the reason for this. Therefore a specialized service has the following advantages:

1 Time
2 Independence
3 Ability to take objective views
4 Wider experience and training

There are several reasons why a business should take stock of its administration (organization and systems) and why it should consider the use of a specialist or specialist section to do so:

1 The growth of the business
2 The phenomenon of clerical work which covers:
 (*a*) the ease of starting new paperwork
 (*b*) the deterioration endemic to clerical work

(c) fluctuating load
(d) exceptional cases
(e) interdependability of clerical work
(f) problems of determining standards of efficiency in an office
3   Growth in size of the clerical force
4   Administrative savings as a direct contribution to profits

Whatever its size or stage of development, to be efficient a company needs to keep its organization and methods under regular review. It should, in addition, make a complete reappraisal every few years. The means by which this is done are likely to depend on the size of the company concerned. In the smaller company it may be a responsibility of the secretary, accountant or office manager. Larger companies will probably employ a full-time specialist in organization and methods whose job is to advise the management of the company in this field. In the largest companies and groups there is likely to be a management services department acting as an internal consultancy service and including on its staff specialists in general organization and methods, operational research, computers and data processing, and management accounting and control.

There is a considerable difference in practice between the continuing review and improvement and the periodic major review and reorganization. The former tends to deal with only a section or department at a time or with partial aspects of an overall system. The latter, however, to be effective, must be concerned with the business as a whole and it follows that the scope and level of the work involved may be substantially different. Both kinds of review, but especially the latter, should be carried out by someone who has the necessary general knowledge and experience of business and the specialist knowledge of organization and methods, office machinery and equipment and work measurement.

A company of sufficient size will employ its own O & M department or management services department which will deal with the process of continuous review and improvement and, provided it is of the right calibre and is properly placed, will also undertake major reviews. Smaller and medium-sized companies which are members of a larger group may have access to a central O & M or management services department. In those which have to rely on their own resources it is advisable that a person in a position of senior administration, for example the company secretary or chief accountant, should be charged with the responsibility to keep abreast of developments in the field of O & M and maintain a continuous review of the company's organization and office methods, not only to ensure that improvements are made but to recognize when there are problems or opportunities which require either the time or specialist knowledge which cannot be made available from within. In these circumstances such assistance and advice can be sought from external consultants.

O & M and management services departments can, as a rule, be supported only by the larger companies. It is nevertheless a fact that the larger companies commission most of the work done by external consultants. In spite of the impression of the predominance of large businesses in Britain, the majority of companies in the country are small to medium-sized and employ a large proportion of the working population. For this reason, the rest of this chapter deals with the needs of small and medium-sized companies. It is intended to convey an appreciation of the subject to enable them to judge whether and when to set up an O & M department and how to organize it, and to know how to go about using consultants.

ORGANIZING AN O & M DEPARTMENT

The way in which an O & M department comes into being will vary from one company to another. In some it will grow out of a department having some special concern with office systems and methods such as internal audit. In others it will be set up from scratch as a result of a recognition by the board of the need to improve administrative efficiency and not infrequently following a recommendation by consultants.

Preliminary considerations

The way in which O & M is first set up is likely to influence considerably the scope of its work, the level at which it subsequently operates and, at least initially, the acceptance of its role in the company. It is essential, as with any other function, that it should not be set up in accordance with preconceived ideas or in imitation of another company. It should meet the particular needs of the particular company and although different companies will frequently have similar needs, they will seldom be identical. It follows that before setting up O & M the board should thoroughly understand what O & M is and should have a clear idea of the kind of work and scope of operation for O & M in their particular company. In particular they should decide whether their need is to improve the management structure and overall administration of the business, to redesign major company systems, to improve the methods and organization of work in individual departments or sections, to improve the productivity of clerical employees, or to do all of these.

It is difficult to generalize about when a company can or should set up an O & M department and the number of staff that will be required. Some quite large companies have simple organization structures and employ relatively few office staff. In contrast the organization of some small companies is very complex and their office employees may outnumber the manual and technical employees. In practice it is unlikely that a company having say twenty office employees could use a full-time O & M officer; a company with

THE ROLE OF O & M

eighty office employees might well justify one and it would be exceptional if 200 office employees could not profit from the services of a full-time practitioner.

Definition

The generally accepted definition of O & M is usually:

> To review and improve the efficiency of organization and methods of clerical work and to achieve economies by studying the work to be done, giving advice on the way improvements might be made and helping in the planning and design of new work

Placing the department

The placing of O & M in an organization plays a large part in enabling it to operate effectively. The best reporting structure will differ from one company to another. It is important that O & M should report to a sufficiently senior person so as to enable it to operate through all departments; it is unwise therefore to attach it to any particular department where it might be used only as a tool for that department and where its impartiality might be questioned. O & M needs to be sponsored preferably by a board member who understands the role and scope of the function and who can ensure that it is given the chance to operate at the required level. The board member should keep a watch on general progress and ensure that the climate and working relationships are right. In practice the sponsor may be the managing director or some other senior official having an interest in overall administration.

The main value of O & M, as with all advisory work, is the ability to take a fresh and independent view of a problem and to take the time to study it properly. O & M must therefore be advisory in character but should wherever possible be involved in implementing proposals that have been agreed.

Relationships with other management services

The O & M practitioner is in the field of improving office and administrative efficiency. This may mean working alone in a company or being one of a team comprising a management services department which may include work study, operational research, data processing or other specialists.

There is a developing need for a much closer link between O & M as it has operated in the past in many companies and 'Systems' as such a function now operates in many companies. *Problem recognition, identification* and *definition* is now more than ever vital before a decision is made to use a computer at all. It is probable that this is best done by a team who are in sympathy with, but not of, the computer. The most important task, these days, is the recognition, identification and definition of the user requirement before work is considered as a computer application. This requires the study to be carried out in a logical sequence, using an engineering or scientific approach. Each job must be assessed critically in terms of pay-off before any consideration to put the task on the computer.

Selecting staff for O & M

When setting up O & M for the first time, the choice of the person to start and establish the function is more critical than the subsequent selection of staff. Where a department is being established as a result of recommendations by consultants, it is likely that they will advise on the selection and will assist in establishing the department in its early operations. Where O & M is being set up in response to some particular major problem or development, such as the installation of data processing equipment, the need for specialist knowledge or experience will influence the choice. In all cases a sound general practitioner experience coupled with breadth of outlook will prove most valuable in the long run. Subsequent staffing may be both from outside and from the company's existing personnel.

It is seldom wise to employ a person in O & M until he has had several years of practical business experience; not for the particular experience, but in order that he shall have gained a reasonable background of how business is organized, a knowledge of commercial procedures and an understanding of and maturity in dealing with people at work. People in O & M coming from different backgrounds in terms of education, training and experience can, given the opportunity to acquire the particular knowledge and expertise, do equally well. What characterizes the successful O & M practitioner is more the personal qualities than the specialized expertise. Personal qualities to be sought are common sense, a real interest in solving problems and improving the way things are done, good power of observation with the requisite analytical ability and the feel for a constructive and workable solution, tenacity, the tact to deal with people at all levels and, finally, clarity of thought and expression and the ability to sell his ideas but to negotiate to a realistic compromise when necessary.

For many people nowadays, a few years spent in O & M or some other branch of management services is looked on as a useful means of enlarging their experience and giving them a wider view of a company. Others may wish to make their careers in management services and after a few years in a company may wish to move on to greater responsibilities in a larger concern or join a firm of consultants. Whenever practicable it is of advantage to employ both kinds and to anticipate and provide for movement into and out of the department.

Training staff

O & M is an intensely practical job and formal training is no substitute for sound and varied experience in the field. Such experience is normally best obtained by working on assignments with a senior practitioner or as a member of a small project team. This kind of training may be difficult to arrange in a small company but may be compensated to an extent by the range of problems likely to be encountered in a shorter time. Further training in general O & M and in specific techniques can be obtained through courses run by technical colleges, professional institutes and consultants. Such training should be supplemented by attending exhibitions of machines and equipment and the meetings of professional societies and institutes. Visits to other companies and exchange of experience with other practitioners are of great value.

USING CONSULTANTS

The use of management consultants by all kinds of business, commerce and public service, has been increasing year by year. The reasons for seeking their services are as diverse as the assignments they undertake and their contribution to the continuous improvement in the standards of business management and to increasing productivity has been considerable.

Firms of consultants range in size from the one-man concern or small partnership to the handful of very large firms which employ several hundred consultants. Some are general management consultants covering the whole field and of these some are particularly strong in certain fields or techniques. Some are primarily specialists, but may offer supporting services in related areas. Several of the well-known firms of accountants have established management consulting branches. In addition there are also consultants who specialize in dealing with the smaller company.

Apart from dealing with technical, manufacturing or marketing activities, consultants are frequently employed to advise on organization, administration and office methods, computers and the use of techniques such as clerical work measurement. The circumstances in which consultants may be called in might include:

1. To deal with a specific problem area such as the installation of better production control or management accounting methods and systems
2. To improve staff productivity by improving methods and using clerical work measurement
3. To undertake an overall review of offices and administration when a company has outgrown its present systems and these require major change including, possibly, installation of data processing machinery

4   To carry out a general audit of the administration of the company on the basis of a periodic check-up, possibly as part of an overall review of the company
5   To carry out a specific project when the company has no staff of its own with either the time or the expertise

Consultants' fees amount to a significant expenditure by the company that decides to employ them. It is therefore important to choose carefully, to know what can be expected of them and, no less important, to know what the client should do in order to make best use of them.

The decision to seek the help of a consultant should have been preceded by thorough and careful consideration of the problem to be dealt with and should be agreed by the whole board. The reason for seeking their advice should be set out clearly to provide a firm basis on which preliminary discussions can be carried out.

Unless there is prior knowledge of the particular consultants best suited to the job, it is wise to get in touch with two or three firms. The problem should be clearly stated, followed by a discussion of what their appoach to it would be. This discussion should also elicit some indication of their previous work. Consultants do not advertise. The Management Consultants Association, of which not all are members, gives general advice on the basis for selecting a consultant and a list of member firms. The BIM and CBI maintain a register of consultants but neither of these bodies will recommend a particular firm. It is, however, usually possible to find companies which have used particular consultants and get an appreciation of what kind of work was done and how well it was carried out.

The consultants initially approached should be given the opportunity to make a preliminary survey, which may take from a few days to a few weeks, and should be asked to submit outline proposals of how they would handle the assignment, how long it would take and their estimate of the costs, savings and benefits. They should also say what staff they would assign to the project. The proposal should set out their terms which are usually based on a time rate either hourly, weekly or monthly and normally includes the cost of supervision. It should also set out the arrangements for cancelling the assignment at short notice.

To get the maximum benefit from consultants, it is essential to appreciate that their role is primarily advisory and that their main value to the client is in taking the time to study a problem fully, in giving an independent view and in having appropriate specialist knowledge and supporting resources. The client should therefore, following necessary preliminary survey and discussion, set down the agreed terms of reference clearly and ensure that these are thoroughly understood by both parties. Before the consultant *or* the internal O & M practitioner starts it is vitally important that the staff and any unions involved should be well briefed about the nature, scope and purpose of the assignment and it is usually advisable to appoint a senior staff member to look after liaison and generally assist the consultant in making the internal arrangements necessary to smooth working. There should be regular discussion on progress and regular progress reports and meetings.

Best results come from a partnership between client and consultant and where the recommendations emerge and are agreed during the study, rather than coming entirely in the final report. It is advantageous to both client and consultant that the consultant should himself assist in implementing whatever proposals are agreed and that the criteria by which the success of the project are to be judged should be clear. Where practicable the consultant should be given the opportunity of maintaining contact after completion to assess the success of the project.

FURTHER READING

Mills and Standingford, *Office Administration*, Pitman, 1977.
Harold T. Smith, *The Office Revolution*, Administrative Management Society Foundation, Willow Grove, Pennsylvania, 1983.
Willoughby and Senn, *Business Systems*, Association for Systems Management, Cleveland, Ohio, 1975.
And as background: John Naisbitt, *Megatrends*, Warner Books, 1982.

19

The Design and Control of Forms

Rod Revell

One may be forgiven for querying the relevance of such a chapter as this when all around seem to be talking about the paperless office. However, it is difficult as yet to imagine the paperless society.

People would still rather pick up a newspaper than read the news from a TV screen; they would still prefer to handle a £5 note than a piece of plastic; and they still prefer to fill in a form to order goods, apply for insurance, or deal with officialdom in its many guises. Forms can be a nuisance to the public but on the whole they beat learning how to use a keyboard and VDU, and trusting to luck that the computer on the other end will understand the information it is given!

Until significant numbers of the population change these views paper will continue to flourish as a primary means of communication. So let us consider just what is the purpose of a form?

Its main objective is to convey information from one person to another. It is a means of recording, moving and storing information in a standard format. Consequently there are four key factors in the effective use of forms:

1   Their creation, design and use must be tightly controlled
2   They should be easy to understand and simple to fill in
3   The completed version should be easily understood by the recipient
4   They should be easy to handle whichever way they are processed

The design and control of forms has always been a more important function than many have recognized, but in this age of high technology it is even more

THE DESIGN AND CONTROL OF FORMS

crucial than before. Speed of input to computer systems is often critical and the accuracy of databases created from that input is the cornerstone of an organization's administrative effectiveness and efficiency.

This chapter examines the factors to be considered when designing and controlling documentation.

FORMS CONTROL

The control of business forms, like their design, has been neglected in many organizations, due in part to ignorance of the benefits. What are these benefits and, by implication, the objectives of setting up a forms control function?

First it should be recognized that forms are the physical expression of a company's business system, computerized or otherwise. Inefficient and often ineffective systems are the product of poor documentation; conversely inadequate systems can be highlighted by frequent changes and/or additions to the range of documentation. In this respect it is logical and good sense to employ the O & M department to control and design forms, as they can take advantage of both aspects of the situation.

Second, lack of control results in the same function being performed differently and inconsistently in various parts of the organization. For example, a large building society with a nationwide branch network discovered it used over 3000 forms, the majority of which were found to be local variations of about 100 basic designs.

Third, as a consequence of the above stockholding costs and print operation costs would be considerably higher than necessary. A large part of the cost of producing a form is in the preparation of artwork and in making plates from that artwork. When the time spent designing the form is costed and added to those figures, the size of the problem begins to make itself clear.

Finally, and to put the above point into perspective, surveys indicate that for every £1 spent on creating and producing a business form, £40 is spent on using it in the company.

Clearly there is a case for controlling the proliferation of paper, but how should you go about it?

Forms register

First, ensure the involvement of O & M in the design and production of *all* new forms. This can be achieved by making the print department turn away any changes or new forms for which the order form does not contain an O & M approval stamp/signature. Then set up a forms register containing the following for each form the company uses:

1. *Sample* form, including copies (if any)
2. *Department* of origin, and other interested parties
3. *Unique reference* number for the form, incorporating month and year of origin, or last revision or review date
4. *Title* of the form
5. *Brief description* of the function(s) of the form, and reference number(s) of any form(s) with which it is associated
6. *Brief outline of each procedure* in which the form is used, *or* reference(s) to procedure manuals showing where the procedure(s) can be looked up
7. *Physical attributes* (if not obvious from the sample), e.g. 'pads of 50 sets', official colours of ink and paper, weight and type of paper used (for each part, if a set), size etc.
8. *Stocking* instructions — economic ordering volume, usage volume, minimum stock level in print department (if you have your own print department), minimum stock level in the user department. Note that in calculating the stocking levels, lead time for printing *and distribution* must be taken into consideration
9. *Name of printing company* (if not produced in-house)
10. *Comments* and instructions for *next* time the form needs reprinting, and who has requested the changes
11. *Number sequences* if serially numbered

A useful exercise in forms design would be to design the above register!

The register should be maintained in reference number order, but cross references by *function* and by *department* should be kept on index cards. Alternatively forms control provides an ideal application for a microcomputer.

All requests for new forms should be accompanied by a questionnaire based on the register information. The opportunity is then provided for O & M to question why the form is necessary, whether it replaces one or more other form(s), and to test whether the proposed procedure in which it is to work really is made more effective by it. The initial project to set up the register must ask all these questions and thereby eliminate straight away a considerable amount of waste.

All requests for *changes* to an established form can be investigated in a similar manner.

Standards should then be created for achieving specific functions, e.g. bankers order form, claim form etc., regardless of area of business. New forms can then be designed with some consistency and a company style will begin to emerge.

The initial task of setting up these controls will be an important exercise. However the opportunity must be taken to use the exercise to establish responsibility for future control. The O & M department, or whoever has been elected, should become the recognized experts on documentation so

THE DESIGN AND CONTROL OF FORMS

that people will contact them for advice in the future. This is far better than relying solely on imposed instructions.

Computer output control

The advantages of a coordinated and professional approach to the control and design of business documentation cannot be overstated. The forms register and cross-referencing indexes provide the basis of such control. But why stop there? Surely it is a logical argument to apply similar controls to *computer output*? After all, each report, even if it is only printed on plain listing paper, is a form, and so has its place in the forms register. The argument for strict control of such reports gains considerable momentum when you examine the subject in more detail. For instance, consider the following:

1. Once a computer has been programmed to produce a particular report, it needs a specific action to suppress printing in future months
2. People often ask for particular information, but they rarely say they *don't* need something they are receiving
3. At speeds of 1100 lines per minute, the computer can produce considerable volumes of printed reports quite quickly. However, after keyed input, printing is still the slowest activity carried out, and expensive computer time is tied up while it is happening
4. It is often inconvenient to carry out stationery changes between different jobs on the computer, especially if it only involves changing from one-part to four-part paper. The temptation is for the operator either to leave four-part stationery running for *all* jobs (creating and distributing four copies which somebody will undoubtedly file!), or to use one-part and print as many times as are necessary
5. Filing of computer printout is very expensive, both in terms of equipment and space. In spite of this, most of the 'just in case' filing is computer printout. There appears to be something sacred about the stuff, as though it can't possibly be thrown away because the computer produced it — at great cost!
6. Retrieval from computer printout is painfully slow, and the more there is the worse it becomes

The above list is not exhaustive, but it serves to remind us that forms control must include computer output. In one organization it was proved that several regular and lengthy reports were unnecessary simply by suppressing the printing of the reports. After three months no complaints were forthcoming. Several other reports were not recognized when presented to the user. Of the reports which were found to be useful all but two were acceptable on microfiche, and the two remaining ones were destroyed after a short but useful life. The resultant savings were considerable, but not unusual for a survey of its type.

FORMS DESIGN

The design of good business forms should be a bi-product of effective forms control. The control provides the opportunity to specify accurately:

(a) what forms are needed and for what purpose
(b) what standards are required in terms of content and presentation
(c) who will use each form, who will receive it, and where it will be used

This information serves as the base on which the design work is built — design for ease of completion, design for ease of use and design for ease of handling.

Production cycle

A brief guide to the cycle of events involved in the design and control of forms is listed below:

1 Request received from user department
2 Analysis of requirement, including procedure
3 Design of form/set
4 Initial entry in forms register
5 Draft produced — as accurate as possible using fine tipped pens, e.g. Rotring, and/or élite typewriter
6 Discuss with printer, or directly with the artwork company, who will advise on typefaces, thickness of lines etc. Try to avoid using more than two different typefaces on the same form
7 Artwork produced
8 Artwork proofread by designer *and* user department and corrected if necessary
9 Printing master plates produced
10 Forms printed
11 Complete the entry already started in the forms register

Paper sizes

Metrication in the paper trade is virtually complete in writing and typing papers, but imperial sizes are dying hard in forms. It is amazing to look at a file of incoming invoices to see how many are non A4 or A5. Some are the old imperial quarto or foolscap, some were designed to fit computer systems (how to make metric sense from a sheet of 15⅜ inches wide by 11 inches deep is an interesting problem, but it seems that IBM, when they held 80 per cent of the world's computer business, standardized on that size, so the difficulties and expense of changing the fanfolded paper throughout the world to metric become apparent).

THE DESIGN AND CONTROL OF FORMS

Wherever possible standardize non-computer forms on A4 or A5.

$$A4 = 210mm \times 297mm \ (8\tfrac{1}{4}'' \times 11\tfrac{3}{4}'')$$
$$A5 = 148mm \times 210mm \ (5\tfrac{7}{8}'' \times 8\tfrac{1}{4}'')$$

Paper types

There are generally three main paper types: plain, sensitized or coated and translucent, and there are certain advantages and disadvantages to every type and reproduction method. Take plain paper first.

Airmail paper (under 45 gsm) is suitable for export invoices and similar documents, but unless of best quality (and that means generally more expensive paper) it tends to curl and makes machine feeding more difficult.

Bank or typing copy paper of 45 gsm to 61 gsm is generally used for padded sets, interleaved with carbon paper. It is also used for continuous forms produced by typewriter, accounting machines or computers. Once again, cheap paper can give problems with the ancillary machines and equipment used for decollating the carbon paper, or bursting to separate the individual webs of continous sets into single forms, even though the weight of paper may be correct.

So use the best quality that the form will justify. Although machine handling demands good quality it may be assumed that hand completion does not, but allow for handling, perforating, posting, filing etc.

Forms that need to present a good top copy to the customer should use 80 gsm but this cuts down the number of copies which can be produced at one typing.

Sensitized or coated paper such as NCR, Corafax, Duscript, Action Paper etc. are generally treated with a pressure-sensitive coating on one or both sides so that one writing or typing produces 3 to 8 copies. One hazard is that it stays sensitive so that any further writing, even inadvertently under other papers, will show through. Also some coatings can be removed by water, heat or strong sunlight.

Translucent paper is used as a diazo or photocopy master. It can be printed with a form outline from which masters can be made by filling in the variable data, and then produced on diazo paper (which can be coated for semi-dry, heat or ammonia development) or to photocopy or xerox on coated or plain copy paper.

Completely transparent film can be used in the same manner, with one or more sheets being used as overlays one on top of the other to add or delete details on a form outline for various copies.

Make-up

If you are unfamiliar with the make-up of forms sets, approach a specialist.

There are a number of forms printers who will advise you and, in some cases, carry out an investigation into your form design requirements. Of course, you only get what you pay for, but 'doing-it-yourself' can be a costly way of finding out the problems involved.

However, it is useful to know the various kinds of forms sets which can be obtained. These range from simple, two or three copy forms, interleaved with carbon before completion to six-part sets. The carbon paper can be varied according to whether hand writing, typing, machine or computer completion is required.

Generally machine or computer sets have 'one-time' carbon (this is carbon paper used only once and thrown away afterwards) already interleaved, and requiring removal or decollation afterwards. Sometimes carbons can be cut to shape so as to delete information in certain areas of the form in some copies.

Alternatively sets can be made up with 'spot carbon'. In this case certain areas have carbon grafted during the production process to the reverse of the form, again only on certain copies to permit copying only in that area.

Pads and sets of forms. Should forms be made up into pads or sets as part of the printing process? Without doubt these methods are valid at times but the increases should be justified, particularly that of padding. Forms made into sets are frequently useful and of value when the forms are printed on sensitized paper. For example, if an invoice is in a five-part set it is much easier for the user to pick a set out of a box than to collate separate sheets.

Regarding sensitized paper, ensure that the paper is suitable for the job by testing it. Note particularly the following points:

> Will a copying machine copy it?
> Does the paper soil the fingers? (Important if the form has to be handled frequently)
> Are copies readable?
> Is it possible to write notes on the paper?
> Do filed copies curl?
> Will exposure to light affect copies?
> Can copied information be erased? (Answer should be No)
> Remember that qualities will vary from one supplier to another

Preprinted forms

You should also take into account the fact that your proposed form may require a specific layout to conform to government and/or international regulations.

To overcome this, there are often preprinted forms available, perhaps from the department concerned or from specialized stationers. One of the

THE DESIGN AND CONTROL OF FORMS 375

best examples of this is the shipping master documents available from SITPRO (the Simplification of Trade Procedures Organization), 12 Waterloo Place, London SW1.

EASE OF COMPLETION

The objective must be to design a form which people will *want* to fill in. It must be inviting, pleasing to the eye, unambiguous — in fact a pleasure to complete. There are certain principles to observe in this respect.

Provide adequate *space* for the required information to be entered. Take care not to provide too much space, but at the same time bear in mind that too little will cause 'crushing' and consequent illegibility (a good guide is four lines to the inch, and four characters to the inch for handwritten forms).

If the form is to be completed on a typewriter, allows six lines to the inch and either ten or twelve characters per inch. The spacing must be consistent all the way down the form so that if entries are made at the top and bottom, no resetting of the line spacing on the typewriter is necessary. Similar considerations must be borne in mind when the form is to be completed by a computer printer. The avoidance of boxes is advised here so that registration problems are minimized. A useful idea when designing forms for printers to fill in, is to obtain a piece of paper on which the machine has printed an 'x' in each print position and which shows line and column numbers (see Figure 19.1). The grid will guide the design of the form, and enable you to advise computer programmers as to which print positions to use for the entries.

```
Line      Col.       Col.  Col.
          10         20    25

01xx5xxxx1xxxx5xxxx2xxxx5xxx ......
02xx5xxxx1xxxx5xxxx2xxxx5x ..
03xx5xxxx1 .............
04xx5xx .............
05xx5x ..........
```

Figure 19.1 Spacing for computer printers

Always aim for maximum *clarity* as to the information which is required. Use precise but unambiguous captions, left justified, and avoiding questions. Use a clear typeface, and possibly in a colour different from the entry; avoid unnecessary ruled lines.

Instructions to internal staff should *not* be shown on the form. A procedure manual should cater for that problem, but it is sometimes useful to show brief instructions on the cover of padded forms.

Ensure a *logical sequence* of entries is used, particularly if the form is being completed in stages (perhaps even by different groups of people) and/or information is being entered from a separate reference point, e.g. model number and price.

If a series of similar forms is produced such as quotation forms for various types of insurance, requesting common items of information, then the sequence and position should be the same on each form. This will prevent confusion and possible errors due to incompatability and should speed up the completion of all the forms, as people will not have to concentrate on *which* one (and order) they are completing.

Wherever possible use *tick boxes* rather than asking the 'form filler' to write out the information. For example:

    Preferred colour   Blue ☐
                                  Red   ☐
                                  Green ☐
    rather than
    'Which colour would you prefer?'........................

The first method also has the advantage of defining the limits of the answer. There is no point in allowing them to enter 'purple' if 'purple' widgets are not available!

If the selection of a particular form by the user also means certain items of information are automatically determined, then preprint those items on the form. A common example of this is a computer system 'transaction code' or 'type of business code', e.g. selection of a proposal form for house contents insurance may mean that the 'type of business' must be 'HC' (house contents). This also has the added advantage of ensuring legibility of at least some of the information.

If a form could be filled in simultaneously with another, then clearly it would be the quickest and easiest method of completion. Clever use of hatching and carbon patches in multipart sets can allow this, so long as there is sufficient common information on the forms concerned.

An example is the payslip which is printed *within* its envelope, by a computer. The envelope displays basic identification details which are repeated on the payslip, but it is hatched to hide the payments and deductions which are also printed. This enables both to be printed at the same time, and keeps the sensitive information concealed throughout.

Perhaps a more traditional application is in multipart shipping documentation. Suppliers, agents, carriers, customs officials and recipients all require various details of a consignment of goods. Multi-entry sets of forms eliminate transcription error and drastically reduce completion time, not to

THE DESIGN AND CONTROL OF FORMS

mention the contribution they make to security, in that alterations to copies can and should be noticeable.

A condition of multi-entry methods is that the forms concerned must have been aligned, i.e. the entry spaces must be so arranged as to correspond. Thus, when the top one is completed, the different form underneath is completed, or part-completed automatically.

A second means of completing two forms for the price of one does not involve carbon, nor alignment of the forms. A line printer takes the same time to print a full line as it does a part of a line, so if the loaded stationery incorporates two forms side by side, and the same print line(s) is/are used, both can be printed at the same time. An example of this is a cheque and payment advice.

A method that deserves to be better known is the 'alternative sheet method'. It has considerable possibilities for such forms as cumulative daily returns. Assume, for example, a branch return of a common form, listing sales by department as in Figure 19.2.

Department	To yesterday	Today	To date
A B C etc.			

Figure 19.2 'Sales by department' forms

To yesterday	Today	To date

and

To date	Today	To yesterday

Figure 19.3 'Sales by department': alternative sheet method

It is possible to print alternative sheets (of possibly different colours, or printed in different coloured ink) where these columns are headed as in Figure 19.3.

Before totalling 'to yesterday + today = to date' a carbon is inserted and the closing figure 'to date' is thus copied automatically on the next day's sheet to produce the opening figure.

If a form looks good, it encourages completion. For instance, the paper and ink used present a wide range of colour combinations, some more attractive than others.

The aesthetics of a form are particularly important if it is to be used by people outside the organization. Application forms, proposal forms, mail order stationery, are all examples of forms filled in by customers, or prospective customers. In these cases it is important to consult the marketing department when designing any forms. Company image may also have to be portrayed.

As a general principle it is wise to avoid ruled lines on a form, but if they are necessary then use faint lines, perhaps dotted rather than solid. Boxes invite completion, as opposed to open spaces leaving the 'form filler' to guess where to start writing (but make sure the boxes are big enough). Varying thicknesses of column separators help to indicate the relative importance of the columns, and can be used to indicate 'total' columns. Different thicknesses of line also give the illusion of different colours of ink (e.g. pink through to dark red) which can be useful, and keep the cost down by avoiding two or more colour runs when printing.

EASE OF USE

Let us now consider the viewpoint of the form's recipient. If we are to design forms with ease of mind, it is worth considering the main roles which forms can fulfil. They may be a simple record or they may be used by keyboard operators to key information into a computer. Alternatively they may spark off a series of processes each contributing to the overall activity of, for example, credit vetting, or underwriting a life policy. They may be used to invite a reply, the reply being part of the form, such as a renewal notice for insurance.

Each of these uses stimulates comment about design and as many forms combine two or more of the uses it is worth listing the principles to be observed when designing for easy use.

If the form is to be used as a record, either immediately or after some processing, the reference number to be used in retrieval must be prominently displayed. Also the quality of the paper may be determined by the frequency of retrieval (and thus handling) and the length of the retention period.

If it is to be used as an input document, even if only in part, the input must be highlighted on the form and grouped together in the right sequence. Input should be boxed, to improve legibility, using half dividers for each character, and full ones at the end of each field, as in Figure 19.4.

It is easier to key from vertically arranged data rather than long lines of horizontal data (see Figure 19.5).

Highlighting of input data (as opposed to other information on the same

THE DESIGN AND CONTROL OF FORMS

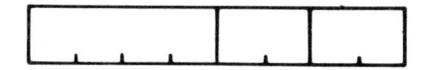

Figure 19.4 **Example of boxed input**

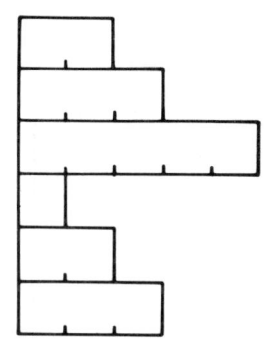

Figure 19.5 **Vertical boxed input**

form) is useful, particularly if it is not practical to group it all together. Highlighting can be achieved by having a coloured background with white boxes for the data.

If the form is to generate a sequence of operations, ensure that the sequence of the entries matches the 'flow' of work. In following the sequence of operations it often becomes necessary to allow for information to be added to the form *en route*. This has to be merged with information which is already there, preferably without affecting the sequence. A way round this problem is to divide the form into two parts (see Figure 19.6). The 'office' part is completed using the information supplied by the customer, but punching could be from either area.

Thus the form serves to prompt action, to generate further information, and as an input form. Undoubtedly it would be filed as a legal document as well in this case, being a proposal form for life assurance.

There are other ways of easing use with multi-purpose forms. Instead of *adding to* originator's information (as above) copies can be ingeniously combined as seemingly different forms (providing they have a certain amount of common information). The classic example is the invoice set which incorporates packing note and advice note — the warehouse can work from a form it knows will virtually guarantee an accurate and speedy invoice being sent out.

The preparation of this type of multi-purpose form is aided by the following devices designed to provide selective reproduction of detail on the different copies:

M O H LIFE ASSURANCE COMPANY

PROPOSAL FORM

OFFICE USE ONLY

Details of the Life Assured

Name
Address

Current No. (if any)

Post code

Date of Birth — DAY MONTH YEAR

Occupation

Occupation Code

Health   Weight   st   lb
          Height   ft   in

Cigarettes per day

Serious Illnesses — please tick as appropriate if you have suffered any of the below:

Heart Disease ☐   Nervous Disorder(s) ☐

Health Rating

Liver Disease ☐   Bronchitis ☐

Details of Cover Required — please tick as appropriate

Endowment ☐
Term   ☐   yrs
Whole Life ☐

Contract Type

Sum Assured   £

Figure 19.6   Example of two-part form

(a) different sizes of forms
(b) different sizes of carbon paper
(c) selective carbon coating
(d) blocking out, not recommended for forms that go to outside users, but which is effective in applications such as payslips produced in their envelopes (which have hatching to disguise pay figures) and which use the name, employee number etc. from the payslip

THE DESIGN AND CONTROL OF FORMS

Yet another type of multi-purpose form is typified by a 'tear off and return' slip. This is used for mailshots, renewal invitations for insurance, and bankers order forms, to name but a few applications. The important points to remember here are:

1. Ensure clear instruction is given to return the tear-off slip
2. Ensure that information shown on the slip is sufficient to process the document on its return without further work (if possible)
3. If the slip is to indicate choice of some kind, ensure that choices are clear and unambiguous, where possible by using the ballot box method

Great advantages are currently to be gained by using an OCR (optical character recognition) machine to read such reply slips, but this can only be achieved if the font used to print the slips is one recognized by the machine.

Having discussed multi-purpose forms, it should be emphasized that you should have as many forms as are really necessary — no more, no less. Too many forms confuse and slow down preparation, but it is equally wrong to attempt to do too much with one form.

For example, a motor parts company supplies spares to

(*a*) users — usually one or two items
(*b*) agents — on average 10–20 items per invoice

Any attempt to deal with these two types of customer on one form must result either in sending users large invoices with vast blank spaces, wasting paper with unnecessary folding etc., or in sending agents annoying multi-page invoices, involving excessive typing or printing, upsetting preprinted numbers etc. This problem may be solved, according to circumstances, by having *two* invoice forms, or an additional form on which agents' deliveries are listed. In this case the invoice would state 'spares as per list attached' and show the total value.

In deciding the number of copies a form should have, remember that if one copy can serve more than one user, and if the delay this causes to subsequent users is of little importance, then avoid extra copies. If time matters, use separate copies, but endeavour to cut down filing time and space by filing only one of any identical copies. Other departments can cross off on a number list and destroy. Always avoid 'defence records', i.e. those kept only to lay the blame at someone else's door!

One or two general considerations should be borne in mind when looking at ease of use.

It is easier to add figures if they are in a vertical column. This may sound unnecessary, but there are a surprising number of forms which still use horizontal calculations.

Similar looking forms (proposals for instance) should be distinguishable, perhaps by using different coloured ink, or a colour flash in one corner. Quick routeing of documents is critical in high volume situations, and colour can be an easy way round the problem. Use sensible colours in a shade which will be easily available in future.

EASE OF HANDLING

In addition to making forms easy to fill in, and easy to use, it is increasingly important to make them easy to handle. The computer age has brought high-speed printing to the desk top and forms which used to be typed or hand-written now have to be fed through a wide range of sophisticated printers.

Early attempts at local printing (by word processors, for example) merely introduced the evils of continuous stationery to everyday letter writing and form filling. Quality of print improved, but the stationery, with its perforation marks and cumbersome loading, did not really do it justice. Fortunately there are several alternatives nowadays, but each has its own advantages and disadvantages.

Continuous stationery has one big advantage — it is cheap. Designed for high-speed, high-volume line printers, it is the only stationery capable of the necessary speed of throughput. However, removal of sprocket holes, bursting and decollating multipart stationery needs expensive machinery. Unless this can be justified, use of continuous stationery on local terminals means that those auxiliary procedures have to be done manually. The alternatives are listed below.

1   *Peel-off sprocket holes.* By heavy scoring instead of perforating, the process of sprocket hole removal can be made much easier, and a clean edge is left, thus improving the presentation of the form. (The scoring is applied to the horizontal join between the forms as well.) The disadvantage is cost and that it is more difficult to apply to two or more part stationery
2   *Carrier-fed stationery.* The principle here is that cheap continuous paper is used as a carrier for better quality stationery sets. The good set is attached (by a narrow strip of gum for easy removal) to the carrier and fed through the printer. Again the main disadvantage is cost, but other points to look out for are registration, and movement of the quality set as it travels through the printer. Much depends on the individual printer and stationery used.
3   *No-carbon-required (NCR) stationery.* This eliminates removal of carbon paper of course, but again is expensive, particularly if produced with peel-off sprocket holes

A common disadvantage of continuous stationery of any kind is the time and effort involved in changing the stationary. This may be acceptable if

THE DESIGN AND CONTROL OF FORMS

most printing is to be done on a common form, or if high volumes can be run at each session. However, if frequent changes to stationery type are needed (such as from letterhead to quotation form and back again) further options should be considered.

4   *Single sheet feed.* A printer with such an attachment permits ordinary multi-part set to be used. Each set is individually fed so as many types as are necessary can be used. The disadvantage is of course the comparatively slow process. It is important to note here that all forms designed for such a process must have the same 'print area', i.e. line 1 column 1 must be in the same place exactly. If it is not so, the printer will need to be reset for every form

5   *Hoppers.* Many word-processing printers use a hopper to feed individual forms. This overcomes the problems of decollating, bursting and sprocket-hole removal, but still creates the possibility of frequent stationery changes. Also it is important to check the hopper's ability to pick up multi-part set if necessary — some are more able than others. Hoppers which can select from a number of different forms are being developed, but how selection will be made (extra print instructions to be keyed in?) and at what cost, are factors for further investigation

Several general points should be made concerning forms and printers:

Alignment. Stationery changes can be made easier by designing forms so that they line up against a constant left-hand margin. Each form should also have a 'top of form' marker to match the printer's line 1 setting.

Supplier. It is advisable to use a printing supplier with proven computer stationery experience. Most problems you encounter will have already arisen elsewhere, and an experienced supplier will be able to help solve them.

Sequence of printing. The ability to 'fill in' large numbers of forms very quickly on a printer often overshadows what has to be done with them *after* printing. If the forms concerned are just to be signed and posted, there may not be a problem, but what if there are enclosures to be sent with 6 letters out of 100? Finding those 6 could prove a difficult and lengthy exercise; printing them separately at the beginning or end of the run would solve the problem. As a general rule, printing should be in the order in which it will be used.

Finally, when designing any form, remember the following simple practicalities of handling:

1   Forms should be neither too big nor too small, and where possible standard 'A' sizes should be adhered to

2   Handling guides should be printed, such as fold marks, and guide marks for addresses to fit window envelopes
3   Forms usually need filing at some point in their life, either temporarily during a process or permanently at the end of the process — sometimes both. Consider how and where the form will be filed and provide for it in the design, e.g. punch holes, or leave a filing margin
4   NCR sets save the mess of carbon paper, but unless you supply some kind of hard backing plate, sets will be spoilt
5   It is easier to tear a form off a gummed pad than off a bound stub with perforations

CONCLUSION

It has been shown that a company can and perhaps should be judged on the effectiveness of its documentation. As a primary vehicle for the communication of information throughout the organization it ought to receive far more attention than it usually does. Only by adopting tight controls, and by giving due consideration to those who will complete, utilize and handle documentation, will it serve its purpose well.

FURTHER READING

P. Baily, *Purchasing Systems and Records*, 2nd edition, Gower, Aldershot, 1983.
The Design of Forms in Government Departments, HMSO. Although first published in 1945, and now in its 4th reprint, much of the information is still valid for manually produced forms.
G. Mills and O. Standingford, *Office Administration*, Pitman.
O. Standingford, *Simplifying Office Work*, Pitman.

20

Data Processing

Philip Goacher

Over the last decade the rapid development of computing facilities has provided many powerful tools for business management.

Today, management in most companies regard the digital computer as a valuable aid to business control and increasingly are becoming directly involved in the installation and development of computing facilities. Good computer systems do not happen by accident, but are the result of careful planning, to ensure that the machine's capabilities meet the needs of the user.

The computer itself (the 'hardware') is only part of any system. The most important part is the 'software' — programs that instruct the computer to carry out the required operations to process data for a particular task.

Traditionally, data processing has been thought of in terms of major computer operations under the control of computer departments in large companies. Recent developments have put sufficient power into desk-top computers that it is now becoming popular for users to control their own computing rather than to rely on a central company service.

THE HARDWARE

The computer industry has grown up with its own mystifying jargon. Today's equipment or 'hardware' can vary greatly in power and price — becoming increasingly cost effective. A machine which required a medium-sized room to house and cost £1000 per month to rent in 1970 can now be matched in performance by a desk-top computer which can be purchased for little more than £1000 — a direct result of miniaturized semiconductor technology.

Although machines can vary dramatically in size, they all work in a similar way. At the heart of any machine is the central processor, which contains the arithmetic unit. This unit carries out pre-programmed instructions accurately and rapidly; indeed, the computing power of large machines is often measured in millions of instructions per second (mips).

In conjunction with the central processor there is a main memory where instructions and data may be stored during processing. Typically a computer memory can store from several thousand to several million items of data, depending on the size of the machine. For more permanent data storage a backing store is used, usually a magnetic disk or tape. Again disks and tapes can vary greatly in storage capacity.

Up to this point the hardware described is capable of miniaturization, with small floppy disks and mini-tapes, to provide small yet powerful desk-top machines. However, the user needs to get data into the computer for processing and retrieve results in a readable form and for this there are a variety of peripheral devices. The size of these devices is usually the limiting factor in reducing the overall size of a microcomputer installation.

Large amounts of data are usually keyed into a data preparation system which writes a magnetic tape or disk that can be read quickly by the computer. This has largely superseded the relatively slow punched card and card reader method of data entry. For small amounts of data, particularly on desk-top machines, the user will often key data directly into the machine through a keyboard with a TV-like visual display unit (VDU).

Data may be outputted to a variety of peripherals. The most common is the lineprinter used on larger machines to print lines of data at a time. Using more recently developed laser technology, printers can be run at very high speeds creating even large output documents very quickly. The more modest computer systems and desk-top machines tend to use printers based on modern typewriter technology. Other output peripherals include VDUs and plotters for drawings, typesetting devices for high quality printing, synthesizers for music and so on.

In recent years communications and local area networks have become popular. With appropriate communications facilities data may be extracted from or sent to remote peripheral equipment. Local area networks (LANs) allow one computer to handle many peripherals located throughout a building. For example, a word-processing computer system might have many screen/keyboard/printer workstations located in individual offices sharing a single central processor and data storage unit.

USING A COMPUTER

How might a company benefit from using a computer? Given an efficient installation of hardware and suitable software for specific applications, the company might expect:

1 More timely and accurate management information
2 Information not previously obtainable
3 Greater accuracy in record keeping, and
4 Reduced costs of processing company data

The data processed by most companies falls into three classes:

1 Historical records
2 Current business operations
3 Predicting future trends

Much of the historical record keeping is for statutory reasons — past accounts, payroll, contracts etc. Although these are important, keeping such records will not generally help to make the company perform any better.

The current business of the company will probably require several application packages (suites of programs related to a specific business area such as order processing, stock control, accounting, production scheduling etc.). Such packages can provide assistance in managing the day-to-day business of the company more effectively.

Using all available data for projecting future business has become one of the growth areas in business computing. Here a range of useful applications such as financial modelling, statistical analysis and company modelling can be used to plan short-term strategies and to try 'what if' analyses on longer-term plans, perhaps to determine the effects of growth by acquisition or diversification of product.

A computer can obviously benefit a large company, and smaller companies can also benefit if only to keep their accounting accurate and up to date.

Suitable applications

It is important for the potential user to determine what applications are suitable for computer processing.

For a company new to computing it might be sensible to start with a smaller application — a simple operation which would provide experience in using new methods and give confidence to those who would then become involved in the more complex applications.

Where a company already has some experience or is confident in its ability to cope with the introduction of a new computer, it is probably best to install the application which gives the maximum pay-off for the business.

Selecting a computer

When considering the acquisition of a new computer, consider the following questions:

1. Is a computer the best way to tackle the requirement?
2. What software will do the job best?
3. What computer can run the software?

The more complex or repetitious the job, the more likely it is that a computer can prove to be cost effective. There are likely to be a number of useful applications that must be considered and for each one suitable software will need to be identified.

When a large computer is to be installed a short-list of leading manufacturers is a good starting point. Each will almost certainly have a range of software that can fulfil the user requirements to some extent and will be able to offer a configuration of hardware to give an acceptable performance.

If a desk-top microcomputer solution is envisaged, perhaps for a limited range of applications, it is best to identify the software packages first and then find a suitable computer on which to run them.

Small computers are now comparatively inexpensive, so there is a limited financial risk in making a mistake in the selection process. A large computer is a different proposition however. It has to last a reasonable length of time in order to repay the investment. The software must be sufficiently flexible to run for some time as it can be quite disruptive to change from one application package to another.

Before committing the company to getting its own machine it might be sensible to evaluate the alternative services offered by the computer bureaux (see below).

Evaluating software and hardware

To get the best advice on which software to use and on the most suitable hardware configuration, it is best to use not only the expertise existing within the company but also to employ a suitably qualified and unbiased consultant to assess the options.

Before approaching any manufacturer it is advisable to carry out a feasibility study to determine your objectives. The volumes of data to be processed, the frequency of particular operations and the relationship between operations need to be identified so that the company can properly define its requirements and invite tenders.

The requirements should be clearly stated in a tender document with a list of all the relevant facts that are needed for the company to make a decision. Demonstrations should be requested and any manufacturer should be able to offer visits to reference sites to show similar applications in operation.

Software should be selected that is flexible enough to withstand most planned (and unplanned) changes in operating procedures, so maximizing its useful life.

The hardware performance must be sufficient for immediate use and a planned growth over a period of time. Most manufacturers can now offer incremental power and capacity upgrades to meet increased workloads. The exact parameters relating to workload can only be determined from a careful analysis of the business requirements and a knowledge of the equipment being considered, and it is in this area particularly that the use of a suitable qualified consultant is recommended.

A consultant is especially useful where the company has no experience of buying from a major manufacturer as the response to tender is usually a voluminous proposal which often seems to be written in order to conceal the most relevant facts. It is the job of any consultant to involve the company management so that they understand the issues and make the relevant decisions. The more closely involved the management is, the more successful the installation is likely to be.

PAYING FOR A COMPUTER

This is a simple matter for small machines where outright purchase is usual. With more expensive computers, rental, leasing or hire purchase is normal, with most sites opting for rental. The decision is one for the finance director or company accountants based on the company's normal practice and the finance rates being offered. It is important to consider the likely requirement for upgrading the machine configuration sooner than anticipated due to unexpectedly rapid growth in its use.

Careful budgeting is necessary for the installation of a large computer. The machine itself is only part of the overall cost of the exercise. A computer room with controlled environmental conditions may be required. There is the cost of the initial evaluation, acceptance trials and parallel running (with current manual or mechanized system) following the installation of the equipment. Operations staff and users must be trained and the ongoing costs of the computer department and computer supplies must be reckoned.

Where the computer is replacing an existing machine, or is a significant upgrade, some of these costs will be incremental, but are usually considerable.

Acquiring a new computer is a complex project and it should be given sufficient priority within the company. Overall objectives must be decided at the outset with target budgets and timescales and the company management must control the project, keeping it on schedule and monitoring the cost implications throughout.

DEVELOPING APPLICATIONS

Sometimes no manufacturer has just the right software suitable for a particular business application, or the package being used is no longer flexible enough for an expanding business. In these circumstances the only course is to develop specific application software. This can be done in-house provided the company has the relevant staff or the job can be given to a 'software house' which specializes in bespoke software systems.

Firstly an overall definition of requirements is needed. From this a detailed specification can be developed by a systems analyst which will be expressed in terms that a team of computer programmers can understand and turn into computer programs comprising the applications 'package'.

Most companies find that they can use a number of proprietary packages for standard applications such as database management, payroll, stock control, accounting and so on, but they develop their own software in-house for the operational side of the business. This implies that a team of analysts and programmers needs to be established to develop and maintain in-house software.

COMPUTING STAFF

A computer department manager (often called the data processing manager or DPM) is responsible for the computer installation, its maintenance and continued enhancement in line with company requirements and manufacturer's developments. He is also responsible for running a wide variety of applications for users in the company. His staff are therefore usually split between computer operations and application or user support. In addition he is likely to have a software development team.

Operations

An operations team carries out both the daily and longer-term planning for the operation of the computer. Certain applications will be run on a regular basis, daily, weekly, or perhaps monthly. These applications are usually run in 'batch' mode, which means that the data to be processed are batched up into one or more streams of jobs.

It is necessary to schedule this work together with the ad hoc use of the computer system by users with their own workstations. In practice the batch

DATA PROCESSING

jobs will be allocated part of the computer resources and be run in the 'background' whilst current users share the remaining available resources in the 'foreground'. To a workstation user this is perfectly satisfactory provided that there are sufficient computing resources available. If not, the machine becomes overloaded and the response time to even trivial requests from the user becomes frustratingly long. When this happens regularly it may be possible to re-tune the balance of resources to overcome the problem, failing which an upgrade to a more powerful system may be necessary.

The operations manager has to balance the resources required for batch and online work and take the growth in machine load into account when planning future upgrades to the computer and ultimately its replacement.

At the other end of the scale, junior to senior operators are required to keep up to date a library of tapes and disks with stored data and to load these on to the system as required to maintain the flow of jobs through the machine. There is also a considerable amount of 'housekeeping' work associated with running a computer system.

System support

Every computer department needs at least one or two staff to support the 'system software' that runs the computer and supports other applications. All manufacturers regularly update their system software to improve it and to overcome outstanding problems. System support staff are usually programmers skilled in the low-level languages in which system software is written and their job is to maintain a working computer system for close to 100 per cent of its operational life.

Applications support

Staff are usually required to support the manufacturer's packages, giving user training and assisting users who have difficulties. Many large companies have set up their computer operations as information centres, with both proprietary and in-house software packages to support management information, planning and control systems. An essential part of such a centre is the availability of a user support service.

Applications development

Where a company needs to generate its own software a development team is established comprising systems analysts and programmers. It is the job of the systems analyst to understand the business application for which a new program is required and to design the software system. He expresses the design in such a way that the programmers can write the code to instruct the computer. This code is traditionally written in a 'high level' language such as

COBOL, PL/1 or APL for business systems and FORTRAN or BASIC for engineering and other technical systems.

Choosing staff

There is an obvious temptation to buy ready-trained staff from the outside market with skills in the right computer languages, familiarity with the same machine and a knowledge of the company's type of business. Such a person can bring valuable outside experience. However, often the most rewarding option is to promote existing computer staff and to retrain others from outside the computer department who already know the procedures used and can identify with the company. Such a use of in-house resources usually improves company morale, particularly in the computer department itself.

Salary levels vary markedly depending upon specific skills, experience and location. A guide to current levels may be readily obtained by inspecting the advertisements in the national and specialist computer press.

It has been suggested that using a consultant might be helpful at various stages of selecting and installing a new computer system. Suitably qualified people are probably best obtained through recommendation or by approaching a reputable consultancy. A consultant is likely to be a member of a professional body such as the British Computer Society or the Institution of Electrical Engineers and will therefore subscribe to a code of practice aimed at protecting his clients.

COMPUTER SERVICE BUREAUX

Where the initial use of a computer would be limited, or a company cannot immediately afford to install their own machine, a computer bureau may provide the answer.

A computer bureau is the equivalent of a computer department, operating a large computer and having many useful applications in various business areas.

It is usual to have one or more data input/output workstations linked by telephone lines to the bureau for batch or online use. Work is organized by the user as if using an in-house computer, but the machine itself is remote and user support is generally given by telephone. In the case of bureaux located overseas, local dialling access is usually provided and in most countries a local office would provide support.

The benefit of using a bureau is a much reduced cost associated with gaining experience in using computers, having less hardware to install and fewer specialist staff. Against this the lack of flexibility in both software and hardware compared to an in-house installation must be taken into account.

It is essential, however, that at least one person is responsible for maintaining a link with the bureau staff to avoid misunderstandings and costly re-runs and to keep control of work done by the bureau for the company.

As the volume of work at the bureau grows, it soon becomes more cost effective to install an in-house machine dedicated to the company's own work. However, certain specialist applications may continue to be run at the bureau if they are more cost effective.

SMALL OR LARGE COMPUTERS?

Until recently it was necessary to operate a large computer for most business applications. With the advent of small, powerful machines it is now possible to run many office applications on inexpensive computers, perhaps dedicated to a single task, e.g. word processing or accounts.

Where a company can split its applications between small machines and a central computer, it is possible that the entry level for the large machine will be at a much lower cost.

An advantage of smaller machines, dedicated to particular applications, is that they are often much simpler for the user to learn to operate, and all the more effective for that. Also they are generally more tolerant of the environment in which they are used.

Smaller computers can also be replaced outright at less than the cost of developing even a small application on a large machine. A microcomputer can often repay the investment in months.

FUTURE DEVELOPMENTS

The problem in predicting the future in computing is that by the time you have written your prediction it has happened.

Clearly the microcomputer, so popular today, is becoming more and more powerful. It will only be limited as a 'personal' computer by the sophistication required of its peripheral devices — better and faster printers, graphical output etc.

The next revolution is likely to be in the development of software. At the present rate of growth in computing worldwide there will clearly be a chronic shortage of programmers if we pursue conventional methods of producing software. As computers become more powerful yet less expensive, the necessity for programming efficiency becomes less important and software tools will be further developed to aid programmer productivity to the required extent.

Business applications for such uses as payroll, accounting and stock control are well understood and are the basis of most computer operations.

Perhaps more important, however, is the growing amount of sophisticated software being developed for business management in planning and control using operational and statistical techniques.

Artificial intelligence (AI) is a subject in which much research is being done. A practical development from AI is seen in the rapid growth of expert systems which operate with databases encapsulating knowledge of a process and rules which govern it. Successful expert systems operate in such diverse fields as medicine and engineering. Perhaps the business expert system will be the next management tool to exploit the power of the company computer.

FURTHER READING

David Harvey, *The Electronic Office in the Smaller Business*, Gower, Aldershot, 1986.

Dennis Jarrett, *The Electronic Office*, Gower, 2nd edition, Aldershot, 1984.

R.S. Welsby, *How to Buy a Business Microcomputer*, Gower, Aldershot, 1985.

Part Five
The Company and its Employees

21

Employment Law

F W Rose

SOURCES OF LAW ON EMPLOYMENT AND ITS ENFORCEMENT

The law governing employment is to be found in the general principles of law relating to contract, tort and crime, as it has emerged over the years from a number of decided cases. Increasingly Parliament has intervened to pass many statutes in this area, many of which will be mentioned in this chapter in the abbreviated form set out below. These statutes are:

    Trade Union and Labour Relations Act 1974 (TULRA)
    Employment Protection Act 1975 (EPA)
    Employment Protection (Consolidation) Act 1978 (EPCA)
    The Equal Pay Act 1970 (E Pay A)
    Sex Discrimination Act 1975 (SDA)
    Race Relations Act 1976 (RRA)
    Employment Act 1980 (EA 80)
    Employment Act 1982 (EA 82)
    Trade Union Act 1984 (TUA)

Legal problems connected with employment are considered by the ordinary courts of law, but some are referred to specially constituted tribunals for a decision. Each tribunal has a legally qualified chairman appointed by the Lord Chancellor and two lay members, one with knowledge and experience in business and another with knowledge and experience of trade union interests. Appeal lies to the Employment Appeals Tribunal comprised of

High Court, Court of Session and Court of Appeal judges and other members with special knowledge or experience of industrial relations. A further appeal will lie from the decisions of the Employment Appeals Tribunal to the Court of Appeal, and thence to the House of Lords. Any issue involving infringement of an individual statutory right may be passed on to a conciliation officer if both parties to the complaint agree, or if the conciliation officer considers that he has a reasonable prospect of successfully intervening. Additionally, either party to the issue may refer it direct to the conciliation officer without first referring it to a tribunal.

CONTRACTS OF EMPLOYMENT

A contract of employment is subject to the general principles of the law of contract; thus the essential elements of a contract must be satisfied, namely agreement (offer and acceptance), intention to create legal relations, consideration, capacity, legality and compliance with formal requirements.

If a contract of employment is illegal neither party thereto can enforce it by legal action, for this would be contrary to public policy. In Napier v National Business Agency Ltd (1951), Napier was employed by the National Business Agency at a salary of £13 weekly from which tax was deducted, plus £6 weekly for expenses from which tax was not deducted. Both parties knew that expenses rarely exceeded £1 a week. This agreement to avoid payment of income tax was contrary to public policy and illegal, consequently Napier's action for wages of £13 in lieu of notice failed.

A contract of employment is not a contract *uberrimae fidei* (of utmost good faith), consequently there is no obligation on the employee to inform his prospective employer of factors that might result in the employer declining to make an offer of employment. It is the duty of the employer to discover the facts for himself by question and inquiries. In Hands v Simpson Fawcett & Co. Ltd (1928) an employee engaged as a travelling salesman did not inform the employer at the time of contracting that he had been imprisoned for drunken driving. On discovering this fact the employee was instantly dismissed. It was held that the dismissal was wrongful at common law and the employee could claim damages for wages lost by failure to give the requisite period of notice terminating employment or wages in lieu of notice.

To avoid this type of situation, the employer should ask all questions relevant to the kind of job vacancy being filled, then secure the applicant's signature to a copy of his answers. Untruthful answers will permit the employer to rescind any contract made on the basis of those answers and, if relevant, also claim damages for deceit in respect of any loss suffered.

Terms of the contract

The employer and employee are free to negotiate whatever terms are regarded as appropriate in the circumstances, but in fact many important terms may have been settled already by a collective agreement to which the employer and a trade union, representing a section of the workforce, are both a party. Here the union has negotiating rights with the employer to fix such important issues as rates of pay, hours of work, holiday entitlement and settlement of grievances connected with employment. Although the employee is not a party to the collective agreement and therefore cannot seek implementation of its terms against his employer, nonetheless these terms may be legally binding and enforceable on and by the employee in the following situations:

1. Where the contract of employment expressly states the terms of employment shall be those agreed upon with the union in the currently operative collective agreement
2. Where the employer has in the past always conceded the new, improved terms of the collective agreement to his employees once he has negotiated with the union. The danger here is that the collectively agreed terms may only be regarded as a preliminary stage in determining future contractual provisions for the employee, rather than a final and binding agreement. To avoid these doubts it is better to have an express statement in the contract of employment where it is intended to concede collectively agreed terms

Obligations incorporated into a contract of employment

Often a contract of employment fails to cover an important matter affecting the relationship between the employer and employee. In order to fill that gap the court may be able to introduce a term into the contract based upon a well understood custom in that particular trade, by ascertaining the presumed intention of the parties, or by incorporation of a statutory provision on such issues as race relations, sex discrimination or health and safety at work.

The more important implied contractual obligations imposed upon an employee are set out below. Failure to observe them may permit the employer to dismiss the employee instantly, without notice, where a serious breach of duty occurs:

1. To carry out the contractual duties competently and not commit negligent acts causing loss to the employer
2. To obey lawful instructions
3. To behave in a manner consistent with the type of conduct expected in the employment undertaken

4   To carry out contractual duties imposed with good faith and not act dishonestly

There are also implied duties imposed on the employer:

1   To set up as safe a system of work as possible in relation to the type of work being done
2   To pay the agreed remuneration at the time agreed
3   To provide work for the employee to do
4   To indemnify the employee for losses suffered in the course of discharging the contractual duties

Indemnification

There is an implied term that the employer will indemnify his employee in respect of all liabilities arising while the employee is acting in the course of his employment, provided that the liability was not caused by the employee's own wrongful conduct. In Re v Famatina Development Corporation Ltd (1914), a consultant engineer was ordered to prepare a report on company affairs for submission to the board of directors. The report included defamatory comments about the managing director who unsuccessfully sued the engineer for libel. Costs awarded to the engineer were irrecoverable since the managing director was now insolvent. It was held that the employee's losses were recoverable from the company. Having been engaged to make a full report on the company's activities, the defamatory remarks were clearly made within the scope of his employment.

Provision of work

The general principle used to be that an employer did not commit any breach of the contract of employment if he refused to supply his employee with any work, provided the salary agreed upon was paid over. If the employee was dissatisfied with the situation he could terminate the contract by giving notice. There were always exceptions to this general rule. Thus, the need of entertainers to receive publicity by a public appearance, the need of skilled workers to practise their skills, preservation of contacts and reputation in a trade or profession, the need of apprentices to work, have all given rise to a duty to supply work. It now seems to be the rule that there is a duty to provide work in all types of employment if there is work to be done (Langston v AUEW (1974)). It is necessary for the court or tribunal involved to examine all the circumstances and decide whether, owing to the nature of the employment, a term should be implied to the effect that an obligation exists to provide work suitable for the employee in relation to his status (Breach v Epsylan Industries Ltd (1976)).

Restraint clauses

The contract of employment may include an express term whereby the employee promises (or covenants) not to work for a rival employer or set up a rival business on termination of the employment. In the absence of an express term there are implied restraints protecting the employer.

To be legally enforceable an express restraint must be reasonable, that is, no wider in scope than is necessary to protect the proper interests of the employer, and also, reasonable as far as the general public are concerned since it is advisable for everyone to use their abilities for the common good.

An employee may, subject to this reasonableness test, expressly protect his proprietary interests by restraining the former employee from:

1 Utilizing his knowledge relating to a trade secret, a secret manufacturing process, a secret design or a special method of construction belonging to the employer. After termination of employment, however, some information in the employee's knowledge ceases to be regarded as confidential, e.g. knowledge of the names of suppliers of raw materials
2 Soliciting former clients to transfer custom to his new employer's or his own business, in relation to work where the employee's close and regular contact may cause those clients to place confidence in his skill and judgement. In this context the restraint covers a limited geographical area for a defined period of time. The court balances these two restraints against each other to ensure that in total they are reasonable and not too wide
3 Preparing a list of the names and addresses of clients to use for the purpose of soliciting custom. In the absence of an express restraint the employer may rely on an implied duty of good faith to restrain from such activities. This implied duty is limited in scope and will not prevent the employee from circularizing his former employer's clients whose names he can remember without compiling a list, though he must not deliberately memorize such a list. Further, the employee can provide an efficient service with the ultimate aim of attracting those clients to transfer orders after termination of the current employment

When drafting restraint clauses it is vital to subdivide the clause so that only one restraint is covered in each subclause. The court may be prepared to sever a subclause that is not reasonable but leave reasonable subclauses standing and therefore enforceable.

FORM OF THE CONCLUDED CONTRACT

A legally enforceable contract of employment exists before, or at the time when, employment commences, in verbal or written form, or sometimes a combination of both. Although an oral contract can be legally binding, it is advisable nonetheless to use the written form with the employee's signature attached. In practice it is also advisable to explain the effect of the written terms to the employee in simple, clear language before he signs, to prevent any later assertions that he was misled as to his contractual duties. In this written contract the employer can embody all the written particulars that must be supplied within the first thirteen weeks of employment required under the EPCA *ss*1-7. The employer should appreciate that once the contract is concluded then, subject to exceptions noted later, he cannot alter its terms, unless the employee agrees and permission may not be given if the employee's rights are affected detrimentally. The employer should therefore take all the powers he needs at the outset in written form, e.g. restraint clauses, which reasonably limit the employee's competitive activities when the employment has terminated. It may be wise expressly to reserve, in writing, a right to permit the employer to vary unilaterally, without the employee's consent, some of the terms of the employment thereby avoiding the problem of seeking consent. The employer may wish to reserve unilateral power to change location, hours, type and method of work and perhaps the manner of ascertaining wages for work done. An employee refusing to accept proposed changes on these issues cannot claim that, as a result, there is no further work for him to do, thus entitling him to redundancy compensation. For example, there may be no further work for him at the usual location of his job, but work may be available on another work site some seven miles further away where the employer is directing him to work in future.

Even in the absence of contractual clauses expressly permitting variation at the employer's request, the courts seem prepared to accept that variations that are neither unusual nor onerous will be permitted where the employer is seeking to reorganize his business affairs to secure greater efficiency.

Statutory written particulars of employment

Under the EPCA, every employer, within thirteen weeks from the beginning of the employee's period of employment, must give the employee written particulars of his work, unless contained in a written contract of which the employee has a copy, or in some document which he has a reasonable opportunity to read in the course of employment. These particulars must state:

1   The name of the employer
2   The name of the employee
3   The date upon which employment commenced
4   The rate of remuneration, or the method used to determine entitlement to wages

5. The intervals at which wages are payable for example, weekly, monthly or quarterly
6. Hours of work, with reference to meal breaks and requirement of overtime (if any)
7. Entitlement to holidays, holiday pay and holiday pay accrued in respect of holidays not yet taken when the employment terminates
8. Terms and conditions relating to incapacity for work because of sickness and provisions for sick pay (if any)
9. The right to a pension (if any) and details of the pension scheme, except where pension rights are governed by statutory provisions requiring new employees to be informed of their rights
10. The length of notice required by each party to terminate the employment. Where the contract is for a fixed term, for example, five years, this fact should be stated and the date of expiry of employment given
11. The title of the job which the employee is employed to do
12. Details of any disciplinary rules applicable to the employee or reference to a document, which is reasonably accessible to the employee, specifying those rules
13. Reference to the person to whom the employee can apply if dissatisfied with any disciplinary decision relating to him and also the person to consult when seeking redress of any grievance relating to his employment and the manner in which such applications should be made. Details must be given of further steps to follow if such an application is made or reference to a reasonably accessible document to explain them

Changes to the employment particulars

Any changes in the terms upon which the employee is engaged must be communicated to him in writing within one month of that change becoming effective. Alternatively he may be given a reasonable opportunity of reading about the changes during the course of his employment, for example, from a notice prominently displayed on a noticeboard.

Legal effect of employment particulars

The statutory written particulars given to the employee do not constitute a contract of employment, nor are they conclusive evidence of the terms thereof. If the terms of any written contract drawn up differ from the particulars in the written statement, then the former probably prevails.

An employee may report his employer's failure to supply written particulars to a tribunal to determine what particulars ought to be given and any contract of employment may be legally unenforceable by an employer not observing the statutory requirements.

Importance of continuous employment

It must also be stated in the statutory written particulars whether any period of employment with a previous employer, such as the previous owner of a business now being acquired, counts as part of the employee's period of continuous employment with the present employer, that is the party taking over the business. The longer the period of continuous employment, the greater the sum payable to an unfairly dismissed or redundant employee by the employer. A year of continuous employment is made up of fifty-two normal working weeks in which the employee works for sixteen hours or more in normal circumstances. If, for a five-year period, an employee works less than sixteen hours a week but over eight hours a week, employment beyond that five-year period is treated as if it were sixteen hours a week or more, so that it is regarded as a normal working week for the purpose of computing a period of continuous employment. A number of factors may prevent a person actually working during a given week, but nonetheless the continuity of employment is not interrupted and the weeks not worked may be counted as if they were normal working weeks. Such factors are:

1 Absence through illness of not more than twenty-six weeks, since any longer absence does break continuity plus any contractual sick leave entitlement
2 Paid holiday, or unpaid holiday with the employer's consent
3 Absence by leave, or custom, or without leave where this is not regarded by the employer as a termination of employment
4 Absence caused by pregnancy or confinement in accordance with the EPCA
5 Absence caused by temporary lack of work
6 Working less than sixteen hours a week but still over eight hours a week, provided it does not extend beyond a twenty-six week period
7 Cessation of work caused by a strike or lock out, but the weeks out of work are not counted in the computation in this case
8 Unfair dismissal followed by reinstatement or re-engagement as ordered by a tribunal

A change in the ownership of a whole business, or a distinct and separate part of it, does not break continuity of employment of employees who work for the new employer. Any compensation for unfair dismissal or redundancy payable by the new owner is based upon the period of employment with the previous and present owner.

RACE RELATIONS ACT 1976

The Commission on Racial Equality has a duty to eliminate racial discrimination and promote equality of opportunity between different racial groups. An employer infringes the statute if a wrongful act is committed by his employee, for example, discrimination in recruiting new workers, unless it can be shown that the employer neither knew nor approved of what was being done and had taken reasonably practicable steps to prevent the wrongful act.

Meaning of racial discrimination

It is unlawful to discriminate against individuals or racial groups on the basis of colour, race, nationality, ethnic or national origins by:

1   Treating them less favourably than others

In Re v Commission for Racial Equality ex parte Westminster County Council (1984), an employee's job as refuse collector was terminated because of racial prejudice among fellow workers and trade union branch representatives' objections to the appointment. The Commission investigated the issue and the court held that the Commission had properly issued a non-discrimination notice. The dismissed employee had been treated less favourably by reason of his race or colour, although the employer had been motivated by a desire to preserve relations with the trade union and with their agreement help to eradicate racial prejudice.

2   Requiring a member of a racial group to meet a requirement as a prerequisite to employment or promotion etc., less easily satisfied by those members than other persons who are not members of the group. In effect there must not be any material difference in the relevant circumstances between persons within and outside the racial group. The requirement imposed must be unjustified irrespective of the racial origins of the person concerned. It must be to the person's detriment that he cannot comply with the requirement

In Hussein v Saints Complete House Furnishers (1979), the employer ran a furniture store in the centre of Liverpool. It was company policy not to employ youths living in the city centre, since they attracted their unemployed friends who congregated at the store entrance, thereby deterring customers from entering the shop. Hussein was not interviewed for a job because he lived in the city centre. It was held that Hussein had been unjustifiably discriminated against contrary to the RRA. In the city centre 50 per cent of the population were black or coloured, whereas in the outer areas it was only 2 per cent. The employer's selection policy excluded a larger proportion of black and coloured persons than white persons. The tribunal made a recommendation under s56 that the employers alter existing recruitment practices and take practical steps to alleviate the adverse effects of their pre-selection methods.

In Singh v British Rail Engineering (1985), it was held that a Sikh had not been unlawfully discriminated against when he was obliged to take less well paid work following refusal to wear a safety helmet. The job could not be discharged safely without wearing protective clothing, but this necessitated removal of his turban which he was required to wear for religious reasons.

A person who has given evidence or information concerning a discriminatory act is protected against less favourable treatment, that is victimization, by the employer accused, unless the allegations were made falsely or in bad faith.

Discrimination on employment matters

It is unlawful to:

1 Publish a job advert indicating an intention to select on a discriminatory basis
2 Have practices not discriminatory as such, but effectively causing discrimination, as by discouraging applications from immigrants where it is well known that they will not be selected by a particular employer. Here the immigrant does not apply and is not directly discriminated against as such
3 Instruct an employee, such as a personnel manager, not to select immigrants thereby committing a discriminatory act
4 Induce or attempt to induce anyone to act in a discriminatory way, such as calling a strike over the appointment of an immigrant as a foreman

Only the Commission can bring an action in respect of these wrongs.

It is also unlawful to discriminate against a person in the manner prohibited by the Act:

1 In arrangements made for ascertaining the person to be offered a job
2 In the terms governing any employment offered which operate once employment begins
3 By refusing or deliberately omitting to offer a job
4 In giving opportunities for promotion, transfer or training
5 By dismissal

Permissible discrimination

Membership of a racial group may constitute a genuine occupational qualification for a job, thus the employer may choose an applicant accordingly in the following situations:

1   To give authenticity to dramatic or entertainment performances, for example, insisting that a black actor plays Othello
2   Work as an artist's or photographic model for reason of authenticity, for example, posing for a Caribbean holiday poster may require West Indian models only
3   Work in a bar, cafe or restaurant where the setting requires an employee from a particular racial group for authenticity, thus only Chinese waiters may be eligible for work in a Chinese restaurant
4   Where personal services for a certain racial group can most effectively be provided by other members of that group, for example using an Indian social worker to work amongst other Indians

Enforcing race relations law

The 1976 Act has considerably strengthened the power of individuals and the Commission to secure effective observance and enforcement of the new legislation.

The person who believes that he has been discriminated against may question the employer on his actions and the answers given may be used in evidence when a claim is presented to a tribunal within three months of the wrongful act. A discriminatory act may be inferred if no reply is made, or the reply is evasive or equivocal. In complex cases the Commission may attempt to settle the matter, or advise, or provide legal representation to a claimant. A conciliation officer will attempt to reach a settlement if both parties wish it, if either party so asks, or on his own initiative, thereby removing the need to take further action where the intervention is successful.

Where a complaint is just and equitable the tribunal may make an order declaring the parties' rights; or award compensation up to £8000; or recommend remedial action such as promotion improperly withheld plus an award, or compensation, or increased compensation, for unreasonable failure to comply with directions given.

Allegedly unlawful acts may be formally investigated by the Commission in an attempt to promote racial equality. The employer to be investigated may make written or oral representations with the help of a legal adviser to show that such investigations are unnecessary. If the investigation proceeds the employer must supply, as specified, written and oral information and produce documents in his possession. A court order will compel compliance in cases of refusal to cooperate. To promote equal opportunity, the employer may be directed to change his policies or procedures as a result of the Commission's report on its investigation.

A non-discrimination notice may be served on an employer committing unlawful discriminatory acts requiring their discontinuance and specifying any changes in practice required. The employer must be given at least twenty-eight days' notice of the commission's intention so that he may make oral or written representations in an attempt to prevent its issue. Within six weeks after issue of the notice an appeal lies to a tribunal which may quash any requirement placed on the employer which is unreasonable or incorrect on a finding of fact. The public may inspect the register of final, non-discrimination notices.

At the instance of the Commission an injunction may be granted by the county court to restrain likely persistent discrimination occurring within five years of the issue of a non-discrimination notice, or some act declared to be unlawful by a tribunal.

SEX DISCRIMINATION ACT 1975

The Equal Opportunities Commission has a duty to eliminate discrimination in employment based on considerations of sex. An employer infringes the statute if a wrongful act is committed by his employees, for example, where a personnel manager commits an act of discrimination in recruiting new workers, unless the employer neither knew nor approved of what was being done and had taken reasonably practicable steps to prevent the wrongful act.

Meaning of sex discrimination

Direct sex discrimination arises where the employer treats a woman on grounds of her sex less favourably than he treats a man, after comparing her treatment with that of a man with comparable experience and qualifications. In Morris v Scott & Knowles (1976), the employer was forced to increase the wages of female employees in pursuance of the E Pay A. Women employees had a note inserted in their pay packets which stated that 'owing to the great increase in wages ... we will be forced to put all full-time women on a 30-hour week and make them part-time casuals'. It was held that Morris and other female employees had been directly discriminated against unlawfully on grounds of sex. The tribunal recommended restoration of their right to work the same number of hours as before receipt of the notice cutting their working hours, plus compensation for wages lost while working the reduced number of hours.

Indirect sex discrimination arises where the employer applies certain qualifying conditions to both men and women applicants, but the number of women able to comply is considerably less than the number of men able to do so, thus a female applicant is treated detrimentally. In Price v Civil Service Commission (1978), Mrs Price, a thirty-five-year old married woman, successfully complained of discrimination in a Civil Service Rule requiring candidates for the post of executive officer to be between the ages of 17½ and 28 years, on the ground that, due to family commitments, the proportion of women able to comply with the age requirement was considerably smaller than the proportion of men. In Kidd v DRG (UK) (1985) in a redundancy situation, the employer selected part-time workers first, who were mostly married women, in preference to full-time workers, who were mostly single women. It was held that such selection was not indirect sex discrimination. It was unsafe to assume that a greater proportion of women than men and married women than single women were precluded from full-time work by the child-caring role.

These rules are also available for the protection of a man, less favourably treated than his female counterpart, and also when a married person, male or female, is discriminated against in comparison with a single person and vice versa. In North East Midlands Co-operative Society v Allen (1977), the employer pursued a policy of dismissing all female employees when they married. It was held that Allen had been unlawfully discriminated against on grounds of sex and marital status.

Discrimination on employment matters

An advertisement for a job vacancy with a description carrying a sexual connotation, such as 'sales girl', is evidence of an intention to commit an unlawful discriminatory act, unless the advertisement states that the job is open to both men and women.

It is also unlawful to discriminate in relation to the terms and conditions of work offered, or by refusing, or deliberately omitting to afford access to, opportunities for promotion, transfer, training or other benefits. However, where work for an employer is done exclusively or mainly by one sex, it is lawful to provide facilities for training in that work to members of the other sex and encourage them to take advantage of the opportunities so offered.

Victimization is a separate, unlawful act, arising where the employer treats another person, male or female, less favourably because the person victimized has brought proceedings or given evidence against the discriminator, or anyone else, under the SDA or E Pay A. Less favourable treatment of a person who made a false allegation in bad faith is not victimization.

Lawful discrimination

An employer may concede special treatment to women in connection with pregnancy, childbirth, death or retirement and payment of pensions.

Sometimes a person's sex is a genuine occupational qualification for a particular job, then men only, or women only, need be engaged, for example:

1 Where the essential nature of the job requires either a man only or a woman only for physiological reasons, other than physical strength or stamina, for example, modelling clothes or performances in the entertainment media

2   Where there are considerations of decency or privacy because the job involves contact with persons of one sex only in a state of undress or using sanitary facilities
3   Where welfare, educational or similar personal services can be most effectively provided by a man only or a woman only
4   Where legal restrictions prohibit employment of women, for example, only men may be engaged on late-night shifts at factories
5   Where the employee must live on premises provided by the employer, as on a trawler, and the only sleeping and sanitary facilities available are for one sex only, unless the employer can be reasonably expected to provide separate facilities
6   Where the employee would have to work in foreign countries where women lack status in matters of employment and responsibility, for example, the Gulf States

Enforcing sex discrimination law

A successful complainant to an industrial tribunal may be awarded:

1   Compensation reflecting expenses incurred and other losses, up to a maximum of £8000
2   An order declaring the rights of the parties
3   A recommendation that the employer takes a particular course of action, for example, stating that a woman should be promoted to a higher grade. Compensation may be awarded for failure to follow the recommendation or compensation already awarded may be increased. The limit is £8000

An industrial tribunal may declare a practice discriminatory, but it has no power to order its discontinuance.

The Equal Opportunities Commission may issue a non-discrimination notice while investigating a breach of the SDA or the E Pay A, but the employer may make oral or written representations to prevent the issue. He may appeal to a tribunal against any requirement embodied in a notice that has actually been issued in an attempt to get it quashed for unreasonableness. The Commission may apply to the county court for an injunction to restrain any further discriminatory act which it believes may be committed within five years of the notice becoming final.

MATERNITY RIGHTS

An employee is entitled to time off work with pay for ante-natal care where she is pregnant and has an appointment for care made on the advice of a

EMPLOYMENT LAW

registered doctor, midwife or health visitor. The employer may ask for a certificate from the person giving the advice and the appointment card, but this condition does not apply where it is the employee's first appointment during pregnancy for which she seeks permission to take time off.

If time off, or payment for time taken, is not forthcoming, a complaint may be made to a tribunal within three months after the time off should have been granted. The tribunal may make a declaration stating the employee's rights and also make an order for a sum that would have been received as wages if time off had been given as appropriate, or payment of a sum that should have been paid where time off was granted.

Unfair dismissal when pregnant

Certain types of heavy work may be dangerous or unsuitable to an employee when she becomes pregnant. Dismissal for this reason is unfair under *s*60 of the EPCA and compensation may be claimed if the employer fails to transfer that employee to other suitable work in respect of which there is a vacancy. It is a prerequisite to an unfair dismissal claim here that the employee has been continuously employed for at least fifty-two weeks provided that she works 16 hours or more per week. If such alternative work is not available the dismissed employee is still entitled to maternity pay and reinstatement in her old job after giving birth, provided the conditions as set out below in *ss*33 and 34 of the EPCA are satisfied. In Martin *v* BSC (Footwear Supplies) (1978), a female warehouse 'puller and checker' became pregnant. In her condition the 'pulling' work was too heavy, but it was not feasible to put her onto full-time checking. Her subsequent dismissal with six weeks' notice was held to be unfair. She should have been offered a temporary vacancy in display packaging until the usual employee engaged on that work returned, or until she went on maternity leave, whichever event happened sooner.

An employee engaged temporarily to discharge the work of the permanent employee on maternity leave cannot claim for unfair dismissal when the temporary job terminates, provided a written warning of this contingency was given at the time of being engaged as a temporary.

Maternity pay

An employee absent from work because of pregnancy or confinement is entitled to statutory maternity pay for an 18-week period provided that:

1 She is still pregnant, or has been confined, at the 11th week before the expected week of confinement
2 Her average weekly earnings are not less than the lower earnings limit for payment of National Insurance contributions
3 She has been continuously employed for at least 26 weeks continuing into the 15th week before her baby is due

4 She has stopped working

An employee must also give her employer at least 21 days' notice of her absence from work.

There are two different rates of statutory maternity pay. The higher rate is 90 per cent of average weekly earnings and is paid for the first six weeks; after this, SMP is paid at the lower rate, which is set each year. Details of qualifications for the higher rate are given on pp.526-7.

Return to work

Not earlier than forty-nine days after the beginning of the expected week of confinement, an employer may ask in writing for the employee's written confirmation that she intends to return to work. The employee has no right to return to work unless she gives this confirmation within fourteen days of receiving it, or as soon as it is reasonably practicable thereafter. The employee may return to work up until the end of a twenty-nine-week period beginning with the date of confinement, under her original contract of employment, on terms as favourable as those that would have prevailed if she had not been absent. If this is not practicable she is entitled to re-engagement by her employer, or associated employer, in another occupation on suitable terms and conditions appropriate for her in the circumstances. The new contractual provisions as to her capacity and place of employment must not be substantially less favourable to her than if she had returned to work under her original contract of employment. In McFadden v Greater Glasgow PTE (1977), a grade CG3 clerk took maternity leave, but on her return was transferred to another depot as a supernumerary CG3 clerk since a permanent replacement had taken over her previous job. It was held to be a case of unfair dismissal since her new status and terms of work were less favourable than those applicable before she took maternity leave. She did not have her own desk, there was no assurance of a day's work being provided and in a redundancy situation her new job was at risk.

At least twenty-one days' written notice must be given to the employer, or associated employer, of the proposed date of a return to work. The employer may postpone the proposed return by up to four weeks, provided the employee is so notified. The employee may postpone her return for a similar four-week period by producing a medical certificate supporting her incapacity to return.

Where an employee has exercised her right to return to work, but has not been permitted to do so, she may claim compensation for unfair dismissal and also a redundancy payment, as if continuously employed up until the date notified by her for a return to work.

An employee is not entitled to return to her original job after confinement, nor claim unfair dismissal, if it is not reasonable to reinstate and she accepts, or unreasonably refuses, suitable alternative employment. The provisions of this alternative contract as to status, location of work, and terms of employment must be substantially as favourable to her as under her former job.

EQUAL PAY ACT 1970

If a woman's contract of employment does not include an equality clause in it, whether directly or by reference to a collective agreement or otherwise, then the contract is deemed to embody such a clause. Under the equality clause women are entitled to equal treatment with male employees, when engaged on the same or broadly similar work as men (s1 E Pay A). The Crown is bound in the same way as the private employer, except in relation to the armed forces.

Women are also entitled to equal treatment with men if their job, though different in nature to the man's work, is rated as equivalent following job evaluation.

In effect, the E Pay A did not provide any grounds for a claim where typically male and typically female jobs were covered by different job evaluation schemes, or alternatively, where the claimant's job and the job it was being compared with had not been subject to any evaluation at all. The Equal Pay (Amendment) Regulations 1983 provide that, as from 1 January 1984, women are to be paid the same wages for work of equal value, though the employer has not undertaken a job evaluation scheme to establish such equality. Industrial tribunals can appoint independent experts to help in deciding whether a woman's job is of equal value to that of the man with whom she seeks to compare herself. The expert's task will not necessarily be a formal job evaluation, but will require comparison of a man's with a woman's work in relation to such issues as effort, skill and decision making. Where an 'equal value' claim is upheld, the claimant will be entitled to equal benefits, terms and conditions as well as equal pay.

Equal treatment is unnecessary where the terms of a woman's employment are restricted in order to protect her, as by prohibiting employment in an active mine, or where women are more favourably treated than men in connection with giving birth (maternity leave and benefits), marriage, death or retirement (which is usually five years earlier than for men).

An employer or employee may refer to a tribunal a claim either for up to two years' pay arrears on failure to implement entitlement to equal pay, or for damages on failure to comply with an equal pay clause. Such claims may be brought during the continuance of the employment to which it relates, or within six months after its termination. The Secretary of State for Employment may refer an equal pay issue to a tribunal if the employees concerned are not protected by union representation or a potential claimant is apprehensive about reprisals by the employer.

The Central Arbitration Committee of ACAS will remove discriminatory pay clauses in collective agreements or wages orders if the issue is referred to them.

The equal pay directive of the EEC, article 119, grants women an enforceable legal right to equal pay with men for equal work, maintainable by a High Court action. Article 119 does not grant any other protection against sex discrimination. Where an inconsistency exists between United Kingdom law and Community law, the latter prevails.

VICARIOUS LIABILITY

This section deals with torts committed by an employee for which his employer may be responsible. A *tort* is a civil wrong committed by one person that causes harm to another person, giving rise to an action in damages as compensation for the loss suffered, for example, a negligent act causing personal injury. The person causing the loss is the *tortfeasor* and the wrongful act is referred to as a *tortious* act.

Liability of employer and employee

If an employee causes injury to a third party by his tortious act, then an action lies at the instance of the third party against both:

1 The employee responsible, as the actual tortfeasor
2 The employer, if in the circumstances he is deemed to be vicariously liable for his employee's act

The injured party may prefer to sue the employer, since he is more likely to be able to satisfy any award of damages made.

The employer's responsibility for a wrong that he did not commit personally is justifiable on the following grounds:

1 He is in a position to control the actions of his employee
2 He derives the profit from his employee's work, thus he should also bear the losses consequent upon the employee's tortious acts
3 He should choose only those persons as employees who will discharge their duty with care. If they are not careful this is the fault of the employer, who must then pay damages to the party injured

To protect himself against the consequences of vicarious liability, it is usual for an employer to take out appropriate insurance.

Exclusion of liability

An employer may effectively negative his liability to the public for the tortious wrongs of his employees either:

1 By displaying a notice at some appropriate place warning the public that liability is excluded, as by displaying a notice in a car park used by the employer's customers indicating that responsibility is not accepted for loss or damage to the car or its contents, caused by employees or other persons, provided it is reasonable to do so in the circumstances of the individual case
2 By incorporating, in a written contract between employer and customer, an express term which limits or totally excludes the employer's liability for any wrongful actions of employees. Under the Unfair Contract Terms Act 1977, an employer cannot exempt himself from liability arising in the course of his business, or from the occupation of premises used for business purposes, if death or personal injury results to someone, other than the employee, usually a customer as a consequence of the employer's negligence. Under the Law Reform (Personal Injuries) Act 1948 the employer is prevented from excluding his liability for injuries sustained by an employee in the course of his employment caused by a fellow worker's negligence

Establishing vicarious liability

To establish vicarious liability it must be proved:

1 That the relationship of employer and employee existed under a contract of service, as opposed to a contract for the services of an independent contractor
2 That the employee committed the wrongful act in the course of his employment

If the employer expressly authorized the employee's wrongful act then he is liable for issuing wrongful instructions. It is not a case of vicarious liability.

Express prohibition by the employer of the wrongful act

If the employee is carrying out those tasks that he is employed to do, even though he is doing them in a wrongful manner, it is no defence for the employer to show that he had expressly forbidden the act in question. For example, where contrary to his employer's instruction, a bus driver injured a third party by racing with buses run by rival companies in an attempt to be first at the bus stop to pick up passengers waiting there (Limpus v London General Omnibus Co. (1862)).

If this defence were possible, an employer could frequently evade liability in tort by giving restrictive instructions to his employees.

Employee's acts outside the scope of his employment

Where the employee has expressly ordered his employee not to act in a stated manner, the employee's failure to observe this direction may mean that he acts outside the scope of his employment. The employer is not liable to a third party for injury suffered as a result of the employee's wrongdoing if his acts are independent of and distinct from his employment, as when he either:

1 Does something alien to the job he is employed to do, for example, where a bus conductor drives the bus and causes injury to a pedestrian (Beard v London General Omnibus Co. (1900)), or
2 Stops working to indulge in an act for his own personal convenience, e.g. where a driver parks his employer's vehicle and causes an accident while crossing the road to take refreshment at a roadside cafe (Crook v Derbyshire Stone Ltd (1956))

An employee's improper performance of his duties

The employer is liable for the employee's tort, if it is within the scope of his employment, even though it is a negligent and improper way of performing the duties he is employed to perform. For example, when a driver delivering petrol lit a cigarette and caused an explosion that wrecked a garage. Lighting a cigarette is a personal act for the employee's own convenience, but the employer is responsible for the harm caused where the act is committed by the employee simultaneously with the execution of his duties, rather than separately and distinctly after employment for the day is over or during a meal or rest break (Century Insurance Co v Northern Ireland Road Transport Board (1942)).

Employer's duty to insure against vicarious liability

An employer is under a legal duty to insure vehicles used in the course of his business in respect of death or bodily injury to passengers and third parties, caused by an accident in which the vehicle is involved (Road Traffic Act 1972, ss143 and 148(3)). Any agreement between the passenger and its owner is ineffective if it attempts to negative or restrict liability for injury or death to the passenger in the event of an accident. It is a criminal offence not to take out compulsory insurance, the penalty being a fine and/or imprisonment. The owner and driver of the vehicle, if they are different persons, are both liable to prosecution. An employee driving a vehicle in the course of his employment is not liable if he neither knew nor suspected that the vehicle was

EMPLOYMENT LAW

not insured against the risks in question. If an employee is sued by a third party or passenger for injuries caused while driving his employer's uninsured vehicle, then he may claim an indemnity from the employer for any compensation payable.

Where compulsory insurance is required by law, the third party or passenger injured in an accident involving a vehicle driven by an employee in the course of his duties may require the insurer to meet any loss suffered where the employer has been sued and been judged vicariously liable for the injury caused. The employer's liability to pay must be for a compulsory risk covered by the policy. The insurer is not liable to pay the third party or passenger if, when the accident occurred, the vehicle was being used by the employee for a private purpose, but insured only for business purposes. In such cases the employee is personally liable to the injured person, but not the employer, since the employee was acting outside the scope of his employment at the relevant time.

The employer may be vicariously liable to a third party for damages to his property caused by a vehicle driven by an employee acting in the course of his employment, unless he has taken out a comprehensive insurance policy to cover the risk. There is no legal requirement to insure against this type of risk. The employee alone is liable if the damage was inflicted while he was driving his employer's vehicle, but acting outside the scope of his employment at the relevant time. The employee may take a journey in the course of his employment, but then deviate from the direct route most appropriate. It is then a question of degree as to how far the deviation could be considered to be a separate, unauthorized journey, such that the employer is not vicariously liable for damage to the property of a third party during that deviation. If the employee's journey while using his employer's vehicle is private and unauthorized, its character is not changed if during that journey he performs some act benefiting the employer, as by collecting goods on his employer's behalf.

An employer is still liable for an employee's torts committed in the course of employment when the employee uses his own vehicle in execution of his duties, even though he was ordered to use the employer's vehicle. If the employee's vehicle is uninsured, the employer is liable for any loss suffered by a third party.

If an employee is driving his own vehicle to or from his place of work along a public road and carrying a fellow employee as a passenger, any injury to that passenger, driver or a member of the public caused by negligent driving will be the employer's responsibility only if it can be proved that the employees were acting within the scope of their employment at the relevant time.

Assaulting a third party

Any assault on a person by the employee while carrying out his employer's business will render the employer liable in damages for the injury suffered by the person harmed in circumstances where:

1. The employee is overzealously executing his duties, for example, where a railway porter instructed to ensure that passengers travel on the correct trains forcibly removed a passenger from a train in the mistaken belief that he was on the wrong train. The porter had been given a discretion as to how he should perform his duties and the employer could not escape liability when he exercised that discretion improperly, provided that his acts were not so excessive that he stepped outside the scope of his employment (Bayley v Manchester, Sheffield and Lincolnshire Railway Co. (1873)). The employer is not liable however, if the employee steps outside the course of his employment when committing the assault. In Warren v Henley's Ltd (1948), a pump attendant thought that Warren, a customer, was about to drive away without paying for petrol supplied to him. After an argument Warren threatened to report the attendant to his employers, whereupon the attendant assaulted Warren. It was held that the defendants were not vicariously liable, since the assault was an act of personal vengeance not committed by the attendant in the course of his employment or within the class of acts he was employed to do
2. The employee is protecting the employer's property from damage or theft, even though the precautionary measures are excessive in relation to the danger and outside the scope of the employee's normal duties (Poland v John Parr & Sons (1927))

Criminal and fraudulent acts

An employer is liable at civil law for injury suffered by a third person because of his employee's fraudulent conduct in the course of employment though the wrong is committed solely for an employee's personal and proprietary benefit, where, for example, goods are stolen by an employee entrusted with them in the course of his employment. In Lloyd v Grace, Smith and Company (1912, House of Lords), at the instance of Sandles, a managing clerk employed by a firm of solicitors, Lloyd, an elderly lady, signed papers believing that this would enable her property to be sold. In fact the documents were conveyances to Sandles, who then sold the property and absconded with the proceeds. The firm was held liable in damages in respect of Sandle's fraud since, by advising Lloyd, Sandles was fulfilling the job he was employed to carry out.

Joint liability (Civil Liability (Contribution) Act 1978)

The injured party may sue either the employer only or the employee only, but he can if he wishes bring an action against both of them jointly. If, in a joint action judgment is given in favour of the injured part, then:

EMPLOYMENT LAW

1 The full amount of the damages awarded may be entered against both employer and employee, and
2 Execution for the whole amount (or any part thereof) may be levied against either employer or employee, provided not more than the total amount awarded is recovered

Separate actions. If the injured party successfully sues one joint tortfeasor only (the employee), this does not bar a later action against the other joint tortfeasor (the employer). A second action is useful if the first judgment cannot be satisfied because of lack of funds.

Contributions between joint tortfeasors

If the injured party recovers the full amount awarded by way of judgment from the employer, then a contribution may be claimed from the employee by way of a separate action, so that the employer wholly or partially recoups himself for the loss suffered. The employer could, when sued by the injured party, join the employee as a co-defendant to avoid the necessity of a separate action later.

The contribution of each tortfeasor is a matter of discretion for the court. It is a just and equitable sum having regard to the extent of the responsibility for the damage caused.

INDEPENDENT CONTRACTORS

An employer may have to engage an independent contractor under what is called a contract *for* services, when his own employees working for him under a contract *of* services are unable to cope with the task to be completed, perhaps due to pressure of work or lack of the necessary specialist knowledge. The mutual rights and liabilities of the employer and any person working for him will depend upon the status of the worker involved, and for this reason it is vital to draw a distinction between employee and independent contractor. For example:

1 Redundancy compensation payable under the EPCA is payable to employees, but not to independent contractors
2 The statutory duty to give particulars of a contract of employment is inapplicable to an independent contractor, though a written contract usually exists setting out such details
3 The precise sum payable as a contribution under social security legislation depends upon whether the insured party is an employee or an independent contractor
4 An employee can claim statutory sick pay and disablement benefit from the State in relation to any injury he suffers at work, provided he falls within the scope of the detailed regulations governing the payment of

such benefit. A claim cannot be substantiated by an independent contractor injured during the course of his work on the premises of the person engaging his services

5   Unfair dismissal protections do not cover independent contractors

In many cases it may be obvious whether a person is working as an employee or as an independent contractor, but sometimes it is difficult to reach a clearcut decision either way. The simplest solution is for the parties themselves to label their agreement as one 'of service' or 'for services' in accordance with their wishes, but it is still open to the court to draw their own conclusions on the matter after examining the substance of the agreement reached.

When is a worker an independent contractor?

1   A person is deemed to be an employee if he is controlled by his employer as to the time, manner and type of work he carries out. Although the 'control' test can be effectively applied to unskilled work, many employers, like hospital boards, lack the specialized knowledge necessary to instruct staff in the exercise of their professional skills

2   In the last twenty-five years, other tests have been applied though the element of control retains special significance. Under the 'multiple' test, reference may be made to four criteria, namely, who exercises the power of appointment and dismissal, who pays wages earned and who controls the work carried out

3   Under the 'organization' test, persons who are integrated into an undertaking are considered to be employees, but not those performing related work. In Whittaker *v* Ministry of Pensions and National Insurance (1966), a trapeze artiste, injured during her performance, was held entitled to industrial injuries benefit as an 'employed' person, on the ground that she was contractually bound to act, *inter alia*, as an usherette as well. She could not act independently, but was an integral part of the circus company since she also helped to move it from site to site. By way of contrast, a builder employed to erect new factory premises will be an independent contractor

4   A person will usually be an employee if the number of hours he works, the period during which he works, his entitlement to holiday, and the period during which it may be taken, are fixed by the person engaging him. An independent contractor will probably be able to make his own arrangements on these matters

5   A person who always works on the premises of the party engaging him is often an employee, for example, a factory hand working one specific machine. In contrast, the independent contractor may be able to work partly or wholly on his own premises, e.g. an engineer constructing machinery to meet the employer's own specifications, prior to its installation

EMPLOYMENT LAW

6   Where one party provides large-scale plant, machinery and equipment for another party to use this is indicative of employment under a contract of service. On the other hand a person is probably an independent contractor if he supplies his own equipment when executing those tasks he has been engaged to carry out, especially if his remuneration depends on his own efficiency, and the risks of a business failure rest on him

Employer's liability for an independent contractor's torts

When an employer has engaged an independent contractor to complete an agreed project, it may be necessary to determine who is responsible for any damage caused by the negligent acts of persons employed by the independent contractor to execute the task in hand. As a general rule an employer engaging an independent contractor is not liable for collateral or casual acts of negligence committed by employees working for that contractor in the course of the work they are employed to do, subject to the exceptions discussed below:

1   Where the tort is authorized or later ratified by the employer
2   Where an incompetent contractor is chosen
3   Where full information necessary to complete the task properly has not been given to an otherwise competent contractor
4   Where the employer has failed to take adequate safety precautions and work delegated to an independent contractor is of a dangerous nature
5   Where the employer personally interferes with the completion of the work
6   Where an independent contractor's negligent acts in leaving the employer's premises in a dangerous condition after carrying out repair or cleaning work there, causes injury to a lawful visitor to those premises, as where slippery patches are left on floors after polishing or scrubbing. A notice on the premises purporting to exclude the employer's liability for personal injury or death in these circumstances is ineffective if the employer himself is negligent in not rectifying any dangerous situation created by the independent contractor (Unfair Contract Terms Act 1977). Where the employer engages an independent contractor reasonably believed to be competent, there is no liability for injury to lawful visitors where the employer is unable personally to check and rectify the contractor's mistakes, as where a lift is serviced by an outside agency and left in a dangerous state thereby injuring its users. However, if the injured party is the employer's own worker he is liable even in this case, since a higher duty of care is owed to workers than other lawful visitors using the premises. Liability arises in respect of any defect in the equipment installed by an independent contractor whether manufactured by the contractor or another party (Employer's Liability

(Defective Equipment) Act 1969), or faulty installation by an independent contractor of equipment that has been safely manufactured

At the time of engaging an independent contractor it may be expressly agreed with the employer that any civil or criminal liability incurred during execution of the work delegated to the contractor will be his sole responsibility. If the employer is sued by, and pays damage to, third parties for the independent contractor's wrongful acts, then the employer may claim reimbursement under the indemnity clause. Even in the absence of such an express agreement, the employer may claim full or partial reimbursement of any damages he is liable to pay for the contractor's wrongdoing if an accident is attributable to the contractor rather than the employer (Civil Liability (Contribution) Act 1978).

Employer's liability for an independent contractor's safety

The general rule is that an employer is not liable for injury to an independent contractor or his workers, suffered while executing a task on the employer's premises. It is assumed that a contractor discharging specialist skills appreciates and guards against any safety risks that are inherent in the job being undertaken. There are important exceptions to this principle, however:

1. An employer may be criminally liable for a breach of duty owed under the Health and Safety at Work Act 1974 which requires him to provide a safe system of work. The same situation may also give rise to a civil action for damages. For example, where there are several contractors working simultaneously on one site, the employer must effectively co-ordinate their various functions to prevent one contractor creating a danger on the premises which causes injury to another contractor
2. An employer may be civilly liable in damages for injury to a contractor following a breach of duty owed to that contractor as a lawful visitor to make the premises safe to use under the Occupier's Liability Act 1957, s2. The injured party's knowledge of a danger does not automatically absolve the employer from his responsibility. Where work is being carried out by the contractor however, in many cases there will be a risk of injury because of the very nature of the work involved and the contractor may lose some or all of the damages awarded to him if his injuries are the result of his own contributory negligence or consent to running the risk of injury (*volenti, non fit injuria*)

TERMINATION OF CONTRACT

If an employer improperly terminates the employment contract, an employee may choose to sue for damages for breach of contract in the

EMPLOYMENT LAW

ordinary courts and/or claim unfair dismissal under statute in a tribunal. If both claims are brought, then one claim may be set off against another, but more usually the employee chooses the remedy most advantageous to him in the particular circumstances that have arisen.

INDEFINITE CONTRACTS

Many contracts of employment do not specify the period for which the contract is to last, since the parties contemplate a continuing relationship until some event occurs which brings the agreement to an end, such as dismissal, giving notice, or death of the employee.

The period of notice to be given by employer to employee to lawfully terminate the contract at common law is determined by reference to the following rules. The employee may rely on whichever of these provisions is most favourable to him in requiring the employer to give the longest period of notice:

1 The minimum periods specified by the EPCA, that is, one week to an employee with continuous employment of less than two years, and one week's notice for each year of continuous employment between two and twelve years
2 The period, if any, expressly stated in the contract of employment
3 Whatever period is 'reasonable' in the circumstances, which is determined by examining such factors as the employee's status, intervals between wage payments and whether he was engaged on a permanent or temporary basis
4 The period that is required by custom in the type of employment under consideration

Even if the employee is given the period of notice which is appropriate in the prevailing situation so that there is no remedy at common law, his dismissal may still be regarded as unfair under statutory rules in the EPCA giving rise to a right to reinstatement, re-engagement or compensation.

The employer is entitled to receive notice from his employee ascertained by reference to the following rules:

1 The statutory period of one week where the employee has been continuously employed for over four weeks, or
2 The period stipulated expressly in the contract of employment, if this is longer

DISCIPLINARY PROCEDURE

The employee must follow any agreed procedures if they are a part of his contract of employment, even though he lacks confidence in them. The procedure should clearly state who is entitled to give an informal warning.

The employee should be told when formal procedures are under way. As a sanction for established misconduct he may be given an oral warning first, with a written warning signed by the person authorized in cases of serious misconduct. After a second offence there might be a final written warning specifying what will happen if further breaches occur, for example, suspension or dismissal. In all cases, except that of an oral warning, the employee should be given, and also informed of, his right of appeal against any proposed action.

Written details of the charges should be handed to the employee to permit him to prepare his reply. He must be given an opportunity to state his case at a hearing before an independent body of persons previously unconnected with the issue. Representation by a union official or other employee should be allowed. The employee should be allowed to appeal to a member of higher management, or to an independent arbitrator. A decision to dismiss or take other disciplinary action should be recorded in writing and a copy handed to the employee and/or his representative. There should not be a dismissal for a first offence, unless it is a case of serious misconduct.

Disciplinary action

An employer will wish to avoid a successful action by his former employee, thus he should set up fair, internal, investigatory procedures within his own establishment to examine breaches of discipline and proposed dismissals to ensure that any action taken is proper and justifiable in the cicumstances. This procedure may avoid a hasty dismissal which a tribunal or court may subsequently hold to be improper. Often disciplinary action is a prelude to, and later justification for, a dismissal following further misconduct. The employer should follow the Code of Practice on disciplinary procedures. Though not legally binding, and observance will not automatically ensure that a dismissal will be fair, nonetheless failure to follow the guidelines will reflect adversely on the employer in any subsequent tribunal proceedings.

An employer must supply the employee with details of any disciplinary rules applicable to the employee, or reference to a document which is reasonably accessible to the employee specifying those rules. It is advisable to hand over a rule book, with the employee signing a receipt and acknowledging that he understands the contents therein and their applicability. The employer may wish to consult and seek the approval of any trade union involved.

Disciplinary rules state the type of conduct which will give rise to some form of sanction; such as theft, malicious damage and misconduct. The scope of the term 'gross misconduct' should not be delimited, so that it will cover every conceivable type of wrongful action that may possibly be carried out. An individual employer may have to impose rules and sanctions to prevent a specific form of wrongdoing which cannot be tolerated in that particular job, such as a 'no smoking' rule where there is a high risk of fire or penalties for fighting at work where this may become a frequent occurrence.

Suspension

The contract of employment should include an express power to suspend without wages for established misconduct, followed by resumption of the employer-employee relationship at the end of the suspension period. If an express power to suspend has not been included in the contract of employment, the employer may be able to fall back on an implied power.

If suspension is not legally justified, the employee may recover wages not paid during suspension and sue for wrongful or unfair dismissal, since the suspension constitutes a constructive dismissal.

Suspension may also be a precautionary measure while alleged misconduct is investigated. It may not be prudent to continue the contract of employment during an inquiry, if the employee can inflict harm on the employer during this period through further wrongdoing. The Code of Practice states that suspension here should be on full pay, a sound suggestion if an internal inquiry can settle the issue with some speed. Where the inquiry is through some outside body, it could be a lengthy period of time before the issue is resolved. If there is suspension without pay and the employee is cleared of misconduct and reinstated, pay for the period of suspension can be paid over. Where grounds for dismissal are revealed by the inquiry this may be effected and lost pay will have been justifiably withheld. If the inquiry's finding does not justify dismissal, forfeiture of pay during suspension may be confirmed as a lesser penalty.

REASONS FOR DISMISSAL

Where an employee is dismissed he may ask his employer for a written statement specifying the reasons for dismissal, within fourteen days of the request, if on the date of dismissal he had already been continuously employed for twenty-six weeks. The employee is now aware of the alleged case against him and may challenge the dismissal as being unfair or contrary to common-law principles.

Fixed-term contracts

A contract of employment may last for a stated period of time at the end of which it automatically terminates, without the necessity of either side giving notice. Neither employer nor employee can give notice to the other to terminate the contract before the agreed time, unless one party acts in breach of the terms set out and liability to pay damages may arise for losses incurred. Thus, if the employee fails to carry out his duties as set out by the express contractual terms, then after two years a fixed-term contract for five years may be repudiated by the employer and the employee is liable for any losses caused to the employer by reason of his failure to fulfil that agreement. An improper and premature repudiation of the contract by one party also entitles the other party to claim damages. So, if the employee has not behaved improperly, but is dismissed after a two-year period, he may claim damages from the employer equivalent to the salary he would have earned during the next three years, if the contract had operated normally and not been terminated by the employer's wrongful repudiation. The employee has a duty to seek suitable, alternative work, and if he fails to take up another similar job open to him during the three years he should have been working for his previous employer, then a sum is deducted from the damages he receives equivalent to what he could have earned in that other work. The amount recoverable as lost wages for premature termination of a contract with several years to run will often exceed the maximum claimable under statute for unfair dismissal.

Sometimes a fixed-term contract may include a 'break clause'. This means that the anticipated duration of the contract, say five years, can be terminated at any time during that agreed period if either side gives the agreed length of notice, say six months. This contingency permits either side to be relieved of their obligations where they have been unexpectedly onerous or unpalatable. On termination without the proper notice eiher side can be compensated for breach of contract only by reference to damages relating to this shorter notice period.

Dismissal without notice

An employee may be dismised instantly without notice, or payment of wages in lieu of notice if by his conduct he commits a serious breach of the contractual arrangements with the employer which undermines the essential purpose of the contract. If the employer establishes that he correctly interpreted the seriousness of the employee's wrongdoing, then liability for damages for wrongful, instant dismissal or a remedy for unfair dismissal cannot be sustained by the employee.

The employer should inform the employee of the reason for the summary dismissal at the time it occurs or shortly afterwards. The right to dismiss is waived by continuing the employment of an employee guilty of alleged misconduct. When sued for wrongful dismissal at common law reliance may be placed on the employee's misconduct as justification for that dismissal, even though the employer was unaware of the wrongdoing when he effected that dismissal (Devis & Sons v Atkins (1977)).

Incompetence

By accepting a job the employee asserts that he has the required skills and knowledge to complete work assigned to him. If the employee proves to be incompetent, then the employer is justified in dismissing him without notice or wages in lieu of notice, since effectively this constitutes a breach of contract. In practice an employer may prefer to give notice and permit the employee to seek more suitable work elsewhere, where continuance of the contract during notice is not inconvenient to the employer.

Negligence

Occasional negligence by an otherwise competent and skilled employee does not justify instant dismissal, unless it is sufficiently serious to strike at the root of the whole contract, as where an experienced printing press manager fails to adjust the machine before use, thereby causing extensive damage (Baster v London & County Printing Works (1899)). Conversely, a series of individual, less serious negligent acts may justify dismissal if they occur frequently.

Disobedience

A lawful order must be obeyed by the employee, otherwise he may be dismissed without notice or payment of wages in lieu of notice. If he is required to act beyond the scope of employment the order becomes unlawful, as where the employee is exposed to the risk of physical injury or serious infection by obeying an order. An isolated act of disobedience may justify dismissal, if it is serious, as where an insurance risk is underwritten in defiance of a definite order not to do so. A single act does not always suffice. In Laws v London Chronicle (1959), Laws disobeyed an order from the chairman of the company not to follow her boss after the latter had left the room in a fit of temper. Her subsequent dismissal, without proper notice, was held to be unlawful.

Misconduct

This depends upon the nature of the employment and the duties of the employee, a higher standard being expected where there is close personal contact with the employer. In general it means behaving in a way that is inconsistent with the standard of conduct expected. Behaviour outside working hours is considered as well, if this affects the confidence placed in an employee during working hours. Dishonesty usually justifies instant dismissal, as where a betting shop manager takes money from the till, intending to replace it, and in fact replacing it, but knowing that the employer disapproves of such conduct since replacement may not be possible if money borrowed is used for a bet that results in loss of the stake money (Sinclair v Neighbour (1967)).

Illness and injury

An employee's illness may make him permanently incapable of discharging his contractual duties. The commercial purpose of the contract of employment is frustrated and the employee may be dismissed without notice or wages in lieu of notice. On the other hand the employer cannot claim damages from the disabled employee for breach of contract, though the monetary loss incurred may be considerable where a highly paid employee has special skills.

If the illness or incapacity is of temporary duration, the contract of employment is discharged only if the incapacity makes a fundamental difference to the employer, by going to the root of the contract, making performance, when resumed, fundamentally different from that originally contemplated. The express terms of a contract of employment may provide for its termination if absence through illness extends beyond a stipulated period of time.

In Harman v Flexible Lamps Ltd (1980), it was stated as a general principle that in the employment field the concept of discharge of a contract of employment as a result of frustration is normally only relevant in long-term service agreements which cannot be terminated by notice. Where a contract is terminable by notice, if it is necessary to replace a sick employee the appropriate period of notice should be given.

CONSTRUCTIVE DISMISSAL

An employee may leave his employment without giving notice and regard the contract as breached in the following situations:

1 Employer's wilful neglect to carry out the contract properly, as by failing to pay wages due, or failing to provide satisfactory working conditions
2 Where the employee's life and health are at risk in circumstances not envisaged when the contract was made, for example, risk of infection, or risk of injury where civil war or acts of terrorism break out
3 Where the employer himself, or the employee's own superior officer, is guilty of assault on the employee

In these situations the employer's actions repudiate the contract and the employee may accept that repudiation by refusing to work in a situation alien to the basic concepts of the agreed terms. A claim may be brought for unjustifiable dismissal at common law and/or a statutory remedy for unfair dismissal.

When an employee goes on strike he may give appropriate notice to terminate the contract of employment, then he ceases to be an employee when the notice expires, but the employer cannot claim a remedy for breach of that contract. Often the employee withdraws his labour without giving proper notice. This constitutes a breach which in theory, though not often in practice, permits an action for damages by the employer to recover losses incurred as a result. The employer, in both of these situations, is not liable to any claim for wrongful common-law dismissal, statutory unfair dismissal or redundancy.

REMEDIES FOR BREACH OF CONTRACT

Damages

For breach of contract, whether by the employer or the employee, the usual remedy is damages for loss suffered, if it was contemplated in the circumstances. An employee wrongfully dismissed may recover damages for the wages he would have earned during the period of notice that he was entitled to, but he must seek alternative employment and try to mitigate his loss. If the employee leaves his employment without giving notice, the employer must try to fill the vacancy. The cost of finding a replacement and loss of production is the reasonably foreseeable loss suffered that may be recovered by way of damages. Substantial damages may be claimed where a responsible post is vacated in this way.

A breach of contract may be anticipatory, occurring before the date agreed upon for performance of the contract, and then the party detrimentally affected can sue for damages immediately. It is unnecessary to wait for the due date of performance.

Injunction and specific performance

A contract of employment is not directly enforceable at the employer's request. The court will not order an employee specifically to perform those tasks that he has contractually bound himself to undertake. It would be impossible for the court to supervise effectively the actions of the employee to ensure that he observed a decree of specific performance. Further, it is undesirable to keep persons tied together in a business relationship when the tie has become odious, thus turning a contract of service into a contract of servitude. The employer is limited to a remedy in damages.

Contracts of employment for a fixed period of time often embody positive promises, such as a promise to carry out various duties stipulated. There may also be negative promises, such as a promise not to work for competitors for the duration of the contract. If the employee refuses to carry out his positive promise, a decree of specific performance will not be granted to make him carry out his work. On the other hand an injunction may be granted to prevent him working for his employer's competitors until the period of the contract expires.

Injunctions are usually issued only against an employee with specialized skills earning a high salary, such as a director, engineer or designer. For example, a company may employ a highly qualified and well-established engineer for a fixed period of time, say five years, to assist in a proposed scheme of expansion. He may be contractually bound to give the whole of his time to the company's business and not to work for any other person as an engineer while the contract of employment is in existence. This contract will not be specifically enforced. Further, any injunction granted to restrain his breach of contract by preventing him from working for the employer's competitors, during the period of the contract of employment, must be limited in its effect to the type of work specified in that contract, namely engineering.

The engineer is free to engage in other remunerative activities, though presumably less highly paid, during the period of restraint. There is reluctance to grant an injunction the effect of which is to compel the employee to perform his contract or starve. Since the employee will usually wish to work only on his own specialized field, he will be induced to fulfil the original contract of employment.

If an employee agrees to give the whole of his time to his employer during the term of his employment, a clause that is not unusual in many contracts of employment, this is a purely affirmative contract for personal services. A negative promise will not be implied to prevent the employee from serving another employer in his spare time, provided such work does not compete with that of his employer.

UNFAIR DISMISSAL

As a general rule, an employee who has worked for two years or more may claim reinstatement, or re-engagement, or compensation if he can prove unfair dismissal. An employee will be regarded as having been dismissed if:

1. His contract of employment is terminated, with or without notice
2. A fixed-term contract for two years or more expires without renewal, excluding cases where the employee has voluntarily agreed in writing to forgo his statutory protection on expiry of the fixed term
3. He terminates his employment, with or without notice, for some justifiable reason, for example, constructive dismissal

Statutory definition of fair dismissal

Dismissal is fair in the following situations:

1 Where the employee lacks the capability or qualifications for carrying out the job
2 Where the employee has misconducted himself by being dishonest, incompetent or disobedient etc., thus permitting a dismissal to be fair under statute if it is justifiable at common law. An employer cannot rely on misconduct of which he was unaware at the time of dismissal as a justification for that dismissal. Nonetheless the issue can be taken into account when assessing a basic and a compensatory award for that dismissal
3 If caused by redundancy
4 For refusal to join a trade union in a closed shop situation. A recognized trade union, enjoying support from a substantial number of the employees in a particular workforce, may approach the employer with a view to the imposition of a closed shop. This means that if an employer and an independent trade union so agree, it may require all the employees working for that employer as part of a particular section of workers, e.g. those engaged on assembly line work, to join the specified trade union. An employee may be fairly dismissed for refusing to become, or remain a member, or refusing to comply with a requirement that on failing to become or remain a union member he would make a payment in lieu (i.e. to charity). The closed shop agreement must have been 'approved' by a ballot among employees affected, held within five years preceding dismissal. That ballot must be secret and, as a general rule, either 80 per cent of those entitled to vote, or not less than 85 per cent of those who did in fact vote, had voted in favour. When imposing a new closed shop it must be approved by 80 per cent of those entitled to vote, though in subsequent ballots to confirm approval the general rule applies
5 If continued employment in the present job held by the employee would be a violation of the employer's statutory duties, for example, dismissal of a foreign worker who no longer holds the necessary permit to work here
6 Some other substantial reason. This widely drafted phrase enables the tribunals to look at various, diverse types of conduct to ascertain whether in the individual circumstances of the case there was a justifiable cause for a dismissal

If the employer proves that he has a 'fair' reason for dismissal, the tribunal will ascertain whether or not it was 'reasonable' to regard that reason as constituting a sufficient reason for dismissal, taking into account the equity and substantial merits of the case and the size and administrative resources of the employer's undertaking. For example, in a redundancy situation it may be 'reasonable' for a small firm whose profitability has decreased sharply to make an employee redundant with immediate effect, whereas a larger company may be expected to wait and see if trade improves before dismissing since the cost involved is more easily absorbed.

Statutory definition of unfair dismissal

A number of situations are specified in which dismissal will be regarded as unfair:

1 Where the worker was, or proposed to become, a member of an independent trade union, or to take part at the appropriate time in its activities, or refused to become or remain a member of a trade union which was not independent. It is unnecessary for the worker to show any continuous employment before claiming protection. Taking part in trade union activities does not cover indulging in various forms of industrial action contrary to the contract of employment
2 On grounds of redundancy, where other workers employed by the same employer have not been dismissed, and the real reason for dismissal is related to union matters discussed above. Alternatively, where agreed redundancy procedures have been contravened without justification, as where a shop steward is allegedly made redundant, but the employer's true motive is to dismiss him for his union activities
3 If the reason, or principal reason, was the employee's participation in a strike or other industrial action, where other 'relevant' employees of the same employer were not dismissed, or, if dismissed, were offered re-engagement before expiry of three months from the dismissal date. A 'relevant' employee is one directly interested in the trade dispute in contemplation or furtherance of which the strike occurred. For example, thirty workers go on strike. If all are immediately dismissed and not reinstated, then an unfair dismissal claim is not possible. If three are reinstated within three months of the date of the dismissal then the other twenty-seven may claim unfair dismissal. It is necessary to wait for three months after the date of dismissal to see whether any reinstatements take place. If there is a reinstatement shortly before the end of this three-month period, then there is a further three-month period in which to institute an unfair dismissal claim. If after the elapse of three months after dismissal of all thirty strikers, three of them are reinstated, then the other twenty-seven cannot claim unfair dismissal
4 If a female employee is dismissed because of pregnancy (see 'Maternity Rights')
5 For refusal to join a union in the closed shop situation in the following

circumstances, even though it has been approved by employees affected:
- (*a*) where the employee has a genuine objection on grounds of conscience and other deeply held personal convictions, such as religious beliefs, to being a member of either any trade union, or a particular trade union. He may disapprove of policies pursued by a particular union which has militant attitudes
- (*b*) where he was already working for the employer when first required to join a union under a closed shop agreement, provided he has not been a member of the relevant trade union in the past under that closed shop agreement
- (*c*) where the closed shop was set up after 14 August 1980, after approval by a ballot of affected employees, with the employee being entitled to vote in the first or only ballot, provided that employee has not been a union member under the closed shop agreement since the ballot
- (*d*) if the employee had a complaint before a tribunal alleging unreasonable exclusion from a trade union, or if the tribunal has already declared his right to be a member, unless the employee has failed to become a union member by reason of his own default in not applying for, reapplying for, or accepting membership
- (*e*) where the employee holds qualifications relevant to that employment, is subject to a written regulatory code and has refused to join, or remain a member of, or been expelled from, the union for refusing to strike, or take other industrial action contrary to that code. This claim may only be used in the absence of available relief on grounds of conscience or other deeply held personal convictions, or unreasonable exclusion or expulsion from the union

Pressures exercised by a trade union

An employer may be forced to dismiss and compensate an employee who is a satisfactory worker because of union pressure, as where the employee refuses to join the union in circumstances where he is not required to do so since a closed shop agreement does not exist, or, if it does exist, the employee can lawfully refuse to join the appropriate union. In ascertaining whether the dismissal was fair, no account must be taken of those pressures in the form of calling, organizing, procuring or financing a strike or other industrial action or threatening to do so. However, that union may now be financially liable, thus apportioning blame and resultant liability between union and employer in proportion to their respective degrees of fault. In extreme cases the tribunal may order the union to indemnify completely the employer.

DISCRIMINATORY ACTION SHORT OF DISMISSAL

An employer must not suspend, or stop wages, or refuse to promote an employee in order to:

1. Prevent or deter him from being a member of an independent trade union, or from taking part in its activities at any appropriate time outside working hours, or within working hours where permitted by the employer, or penalize him for so doing
2. Compel him to be or become a member of any trade union in accordance with a closed shop agreement, if he has the statutory right to refuse
3. Enforce a requirement, however imposed, that he must make a payment (i.e. to a charity) on failing to become, or ceasing to be a trade union member. In this instance a deduction from wages to meet the payment is regarded as discriminatory action

If any complaint of such conduct is well founded, the employee may be awarded compensation. The employer or complainant may join another party to such proceedings, usually a trade union. The tribunal may order that third party to make a contribution towards compensation awarded, as the tribunal thinks fit, if that third party pressurized the employer into taking the action complained of, by way of calling, organizing, procuring or financing a strike or other industrial action or threatening to do so.

DETERMINATION OF DISPUTES

Unfair dismissal claims must be referred to an industrial tribunal. A claim must be presented:

1. Within three months of termination of the employment, or
2. Such further period as the tribunal considers reasonable where it was not reasonably practicable to present the complaint within three months

Many claims are settled by intervention of the conciliation officer.

A dismissed employee may be reinstated in his old job or re-engaged in comparable or suitable alternative employment. When making either of these orders the tribunal must consider the complainant's wishes, the practicability for the employer who may have appointed a permanent replacement if a reasonable period elapsed after dismissal before a claim for reinstatement or re-engagement was made, and whether it is just to do so if the complainant caused or contributed to his dismissal. The tribunal may award:

1   Arrears of pay for the period between termination of employment, and reinstatement or re-engagement, less wages paid in lieu of notice, *ex gratia* payments from the employer or remuneration from other employment
2   Restoration of employment rights, including seniority and pension rights
3   Improved terms and conditions of employment granted during the period of unfair dismissal to other employees in the same grade

Compensation, which is increased annually, may be claimed where reinstatement or re-engagement is not ordered by the tribunal, or where the employer completely or partially refuses to implement such an order. A basic award is calculated as follows:

1   For each year of continuous employment (maximum 20 years) between the ages of 41-64 (59 women) (inclusive) 1½ times a week's pay (maximum £155 a week)
2   For every year of continuous employment (maximum 20 years) between the ages of 22-40 (inclusive) 1 times a week's pay (maximum £155 a week)
3   For every year of continuous employment (maximum 20 years) between the ages of 16-21 (inclusive) ½ times a week's pay (maximum £155 a week)

The sum awarded is reduced to reflect the employee's blameworthy conduct, compensation already awarded for sex or racial discrimination, unreasonable refusal of reinstatement or re-engagement, any redundancy payments received, and misconduct before dismissal not discovered until after making a decision to dismiss which could not be used to justify the dismissal as being fair (Devis & Sons Ltd *v* Atkins (1977)).

A compensatory award is a just and equitable amount reflecting the dismissed employee's losses, such as expenses reasonably incurred in finding a new job. Also included is compensation for any loss which would have resulted from a benefit reasonably anticipated by the employee had he not been dismissed, such as a pay increase due after the time of the dismissal, together with immediate loss of wages, loss in relation to the manner of dismissal making the employee less acceptable to a potential employer, future loss of wages, loss of the benefit of continuous employment giving protection against unfair dismissal and loss of pension rights. The following deductions may be made from any award, which must not exceed £8000, a sum reflecting the employee's failure to mitigate his losses by seeking alternative, suitable work elsewhere, earnings in new employment since dismissal, the amount by which a redundancy payment made, if any, exceeds the amount of a basic award for unfair dismissal, any excess payment or ex gratia payment by the employer, unemployment benefit received, liability for income tax, and a sum reflecting the employee's own wrongful conduct, if any, which may have contributed to the dismissal.

If a tribunal orders reinstatement or re-engagement and the employer refuses to comply, though it is practicable to do so, then an additional award of between 13-26 weeks' pay (maximum £155 a week) is also payable. This is increased to between 26-52 weeks' pay (maximum £155 a week) where the reason for dismissal is an unlawful act of racial or sex discrimination.

Instead of an additional award, a special award will be made when an unfair dismissal is related to independent trade union membership or activities, or non-membership of any trade union, or for one of these reasons but disguised as redundancy. The complainant must have requested reinstatement or re-engagement, but the tribunal decided not to make such an order, as where it was not practicable for the employer to comply. The special award is one week's pay × 104, or £11 000 whichever sum is greater, up to £22 000 (maximum). Where the complainant is not reinstated or re-engaged in circumstances where it is practicable for the employer to comply with the direction of the tribunal, then the special award is increased to one week's pay × 156, or £16 500, whichever sum is greater, thus there is no maximum sum under this head – it all depends on the weekly salary. Engagement of a permanent replacement for a dismissed employee is only regarded as making reinstatement or re-engagement impracticable where it was the only course open to the employer. The increased special award may be reduced:

(a) by a just and equitable amount to take account of the complainant's misconduct
(b) if the applicant is over the age of 64 (59 for women), by one-twelfth in respect of each month over that age, until the special award is eliminated altogether at the age of 65 (60 for women), being the age of retirement

Interim relief

An employee alleging unfair dismissal for being a member of an independent trade union or taking part in its activities at any appropriate time may claim interim relief until the tribunal decides his unfair dismissal claim. If the employee's allegations are substantiated after a preliminary consideration, the employer may be requested to reinstate or re-engage pending a full investigation. If the employer fails to attend the hearing, refuses to reinstate or re-engage, or if the employee reasonably refuses re-engagement in a different job, then continuation of the original contract of employment will be ordered, failure to comply leading to a compensatory award.

TESTIMONIALS

An employer is not under any duty to provide an employee with a reference or testimonial, unless there is a term in the contract to that effect. If a reference is given, however, the employer must not defame the employee. A statement is defamatory if it tends to lower the plaintiff in the estimation of right-thinking members of society. The person making the defamatory statement may be liable for damages in tort, for either slander, in respect of spoken words, or libel, if the defamation is in some permanent form, like writing.

To succeed in any action, the employee has the burden of proving that the statement was defamatory and that it referred to him. There must also be publication, that is communication to a party other than the person defamed. No action lies for defamation in an open reference handed to the employee personally, for any subsequent publication must be by the employee himself. In cases of slander there is the additional burden of showing either an imputation of incapacity in relation to the employee's trade, profession or occupation, or special loss, such as loss of a position that might otherwise have been secured.

Defences to an action for defamation

The employer may have one of the following two defences to any action, and if the defence is successful it will negative liability: first, that the statements made about the employee were substantially true, for no one is entitled to a reputation that is unwarranted. This is a defence of justification. Secondly, there is the more usual and useful defence of qualified privilege, where, for example, an employer provides a reference for the guidance of a potential employer who might offer the employee a situation. Here the statement is made to someone having a justifiable interest in receiving it. An employer will not be in breach of duty to his employee, if the reference is not entirely true, provided it was not made maliciously. The defence of qualified privilege is lost, however, if the employee establishes malice, as by proving one of the following factors: that the employer did not himself believe the statement to be true, or that he made a false statement with spite, or that it was published to someone with no justifiable interest in receiving it.

If an employer gives a good reference, but later rescinds it, the second communication is also privileged. Where the employer supplies a reference unrequested he will have to bring in stronger evidence to show good faith than in cases where a reference is requested.

Liability for a false reference

An action in deceit will lie if an employer recommends an employee by making untrue statements fraudulently, that is knowing of their untruth, or without belief in their truth, or recklessly not caring whether they were true or false. The misconduct of the employee recommended renders the employer at fault liable, though the employer acted without malice or hope of gain. Further, following the House of Lords decision in Hedley Byrne and Company Limited v Heller and Partners Limited (1963), liability is established where a reference is merely misleading, if for example it contains careless mis-statements, causing monetary loss to the person relying on the reference.

FURTHER READING

John Bowers, *Employment Law*, 1st edition, Financial Training.
Hepple and O'Higgins, *Encyclopedia of Labour Relations Law*, Sweet & Maxwell, updated six times a year.
N. Selwyn, *Law of Employment*, 5th edition, Butterworths, London, 1985.
Fraser Younson, *Employment Law Handbook*, Gower, Aldershot, 1987.

22

Working Conditions

Patricia George

Good working conditions not only minimize, if not prevent, accidents at work, they make a significant contribution to the health and wellbeing of the staff, thus enabling better standards of work to be attained.

Recent research in France suggests that pregnant women who work in stressful jobs (long hours, monotonous and noisy environments) are more at risk of premature births. Research in Denmark has linked infertility and menstrual disruption with noisy work.

More organizations are now developing workplace health promotion programmes, which can include measures ranging from staff counselling to more healthy food on the menu of the staff restaurant.

Stress at work can be costly for the employer. Symptoms of stress are many and include headaches, higher absentee levels and deteriorating relationships at work.

Stress can be caused in many ways:

1. Poor workplace layout resulting in staff not being able to find the tools they need, or knocking into equipment
2. Poor lighting for close work, such as VDUs or draughtsmanship
3. Poor job design – routine office and factory tasks are not interspersed with interesting ones, nor shared out
4. Shift systems
5. Insufficient rest pauses, for example when sitting at a typewriter or VDU
6. Temperature
7. Inadequate briefing of the tasks to be undertaken

In recent years the moral responsibility of management to provide reasonable working conditions for their employees has, more and more, been taken over by legislation. No one would deny that the objectives of such legislation are well founded, but so much has been produced (with so many changes) that a concise summary will help to ensure that readers obey the letter, as well as the intent, of the law.

HEALTH AND SAFETY AT WORK ACT 1974

One of the main purposes of this Act is to provide a comprehensive and integrated system of law to deal with the health, safety and welfare of people at work. Based on the concept of a general duty of care, the Act has been drawn up in such a way that it can be changed, expanded and adapted to cope with risks and problems in industry for many years ahead. It has been described as the most significant statutory advance in this field since Shaftesbury's Factory Act of 1833. The Act applies to all people working in any capacity: employers, employees (except domestic servants in private employment), manufacturers, contractors, self-employed and to certain members of the public.

The basic obligations of all employers and all employees, which the Act deliberately couches in very general terms, are given below.

Basic obligations of employers

The employer must ensure, so far as is reasonably practicable, the health, safety and welfare at work of all his employees. To assess what is reasonably practicable, the employer must balance the risk against the cost of measures to prevent or minimize the risk. If the risk is clearly established as dangerous it is likely that even the most expensive measures would be deemed to be reasonable. The employer's duty includes the provision of (and maintenance of, as appropriate):

1　A safe, healthy working environment with adequate facilities and arrangements for welfare at work
2　A safe, healthy place of work with safe means of access and egress
3　Safe, healthy plant and systems of work
4　Means, etc., to use, handle, store or transport articles and substances without risk to health or safety
5　Information, instruction, training and supervision necessary to ensure the health and safety of the employees
6　Written statement of the employer's current general policy for the health and safety of the employees, and the organization and arrangements for carrying out that policy

Employers must, in specified circumstances, allow their employees to appoint their own safety representatives, consult with them and, if so requested, set up safety committees.

Directors will be required to give information in their annual reports to shareholders on what their companies are doing in this field. The Companies Act 1967 was amended accordingly by $s79$ of the Health and Safety at Work Act on 1 April 1975.

Additionally employers have a duty to ensure the safety of persons other than employees who enter their premises and to ensure that their activities do not endanger anybody outside their employment.

Basic obligations of employees

Every employee has a duty to take reasonable care for the health and safety of himself and of others who may be affected. He must co-operate with his employer to enable the duties and requirements of the Act to be carried out.

Many processes or activities are now, or will be, governed by regulations or approved codes of practice. In general contravention of the appropriate regulation will be an offence. A person will not however be open to criminal proceedings for failing to observe a particular code of practice but in the event of criminal proceedings any relevant code of practice is admissible in evidence.

HEALTH AND SAFETY ADMINISTRATION AND ENFORCEMENT

The Health and Safety Commission, Executive and Inspectorate

In general, the Commission is responsible to the Secretary of State for Employment for making whatever arrangements are appropriate for the general purposes of the new legislation. It has an information, education and advisory role and the power to carry out investigations and inquiries within the health and safety field.

The Health and Safety Executive, responsible to the Commission, is its operational arm and has been set up to carry out the Commission's functions under the Commission's direction. In its turn, the Executive is empowered to appoint inspectors to carry out its enforcement and advisory functions. Inspectors of factories, mines and quarries, nuclear installations, alkali and clean air and explosives have been transferred to the Executive for this purpose.

Inspectors can enter an employer's premises at any reasonable time (at any time in a situation which in their opinion is, or may be, dangerous) to carry out their functions.

Improvement and prohibition notices. An inspector will be able to issue improvement and prohibition notices. An improvement notice requires the employer to remedy a contravention of Act or a regulation under it within a specified period. A prohibition notice requires the employer to stop (immediately if necessary) any activity which carries risk of serious personal injury.

There is a right of appeal to an industrial tribunal against these notices. Improvement notices will be held in abeyance pending the appeal, but prohibition notices will remain in force unless the employer satisfies the tribunal to the contrary, by application prior to the hearing.

Employment medical advisory service

In addition to having an advisory role, the Act:

1   Authorizes a medical adviser to carry out a medical examination of employees whose health is believed to be in danger because of their work, provided the employees themselves consent
2   Requires an employer to inform the local careers office when recruiting a person aged less than eighteen to work in a factory, specifying the nature of the work the employee will be doing

Disclosure of information

The Commission can serve a notice on any person to reveal information affecting health and safety.

An inspector can in appropriate circumstances inform the employees at a workplace of matters affecting their safety, health and welfare.

The Safety Representatives and Safety Committees Regulations 1977 require employers to make certain information available to safety representatives.

Enforcement of the Act

The Executive is required to make adequate arrangements for enforcement except where regulations made by the Secretary of State place the duty on local authorities or other bodies.

Responsibility for fire prevention and fire precautions. Section 78 amends the Fire Precautions Act 1971 so that the fire authorities and the Home Office can deal with general fire precautions (means of escape in case of fire, fire-alarm systems, fire-fighting equipment and so on) under the Act. The Commission and Executive remain responsible for control over risks of fire associated with particular processes or the use of particular substances, and for all fire precautions in certain scheduled premises (which will include major hazard factories).

Offences. Section 33 lists the offences and the type of penalty which may be imposed for each: fines and/or imprisonment.

Action by management. Management should:

1. Prepare and issue a written safety policy statement
2. Set up an accident prevention programme
3. Provide training in safety policy and practice
4. Designate line and functional responsibilities for health, welfare and safety

The main provisions of the Act came into force on 1 April 1975 and largely replace most of the existing law on safety and health in industry. Among the Acts which will eventually be replaced or mainly replaced are the Factories Act 1961 and the Offices, Shops and Railway Premises Act 1963. For the time being many of their provisions remain in force.

THE FACTORIES ACT 1961

Many of the provisions of the Factories Act 1961 and the regulations made under it still remain in force. The Act applies to all factories as defined in $s175$, as well as to certain other premises, such as building sites, which are not factories in the normal sense of the word. For the purpose of the Act, a factory is defined as a place to which the employer has right of access or of conrol and where two or more persons are employed in manual labour, by way of trade or for the purpose of gain in any of the following operations:

1. Making any article or part of an article
2. Altering, repairing, ornamenting, finishing, cleaning, washing, breaking up or demolishing any article
3. Adapting an article for sale
4. The slaughtering of cattle, sheep, swine, goats, horses, asses or mules
5. The confinement of such animals while awaiting slaughter at other premises provided those premises are not maintained primarily for agricultural purposes and do not form part of the premises used for the holding of a market in respect of such animals

Furthermore, whether or not they fall within this general definition, $s175(2)$ specifically applies the Act to the following groups of premises, provided that persons are employed manually in:

1. Packing articles, washing or filling bottles or containers incidental to the purposes of the factory

2 Sorting articles prior to work in a factory
3 Printing or bookbinding carried out as a trade or incidental to a business
4 Making up or packing of yarn or cloth
5 Laundering carried on as an ancillary to a business or public institution (ordinary commercial laundries are factories within the general definition quoted above)
6 Constructing, reconstructing or repairing vehicles, locomotives, or other plant used for transport purposes, when ancillary to a transport, industrial or commercial undertaking (other than running repairs to locomotives)
7 Production of films (it would be wise to assume that the production of recordings on videotape might be treated as coming within this definition, though the point could lead to much legal argument)
8 Making or preparing articles for the building, fishing and engineering industries, the theatre and for films
9 Premises in which mechanical power is used to make or repair metal or wood incidental to business for trading etc.
10 Dry docks in which ships are constructed, repaired or broken up
11 Gas holders of over 140 cubic metres

Certain sections of the Act also apply to electrical stations and substations, warehouses, docks, wharfs, ships and sites where building and civil engineering are carried on.

Premises that come under the definition of a factory but are used by public authorities or charitable institutions may still be subject to the Act even though they are not actually operated 'by way of trade or for the purpose of gain'. The same applies to factory premises occupied by the Crown or a local council.

A place sited within the factory precincts is not a part of that factory if it is used solely for a purpose different from the processes carried on in the factory, for example the office buildings in the factory may not be part of the factory.

The principal matters legislated for under the Factories Act are: drainage, cleanliness, overcrowding, temperature, ventilation, lighting, sanitary conveniences, washing facilities, drinking water, seating and accommodation for clothing.

Drainage

All floors liable to become wet must be drained.

Cleanliness

Dirt and refuse must be removed daily from floors and benches in workrooms and from staircases and passages. Workroom floors must be washed

WORKING CONDITIONS

or otherwise cleaned at least once per week. All inside walls, partitions and ceilings must be periodically washed, painted, whitewashed or otherwise treated as prescribed by the Factories (Cleanliness of Walls and Ceilings) Regulations 1960, amended by SI 1974 No. 427. Factories must be kept free of effluvia from drains, sanitary conveniences etc.

Overcrowding

Workrooms must not be so overcrowded as to be dangerous to health. The employer must allow at least 11 cubic metres of space for every person employed excluding any air space more than 4.2 metres from the floor.

Temperature

The temperature must be reasonable. If a substantial proportion of the work in a particular room is done sitting and does not involve serious physical effort, the temperature must be at least 16°C after the first hour and at least one thermometer must be provided in every such workroom. However, SI 1980 No. 1013 restricts heating to a maximum temperature of 19°C, unless certain industrial processes require more heat.

Ventilation

Fresh air must be circulated to provide adequate ventilation, and measures taken to protect employees from inhalation of dust, fumes or impurities which may be injurious or offensive.

Lighting

Lighting, artificial or natural, must be sufficient and suitable.

Sanitary conveniences

The Statutory Rules and Orders 1938 No.611, as amended by SI 1974 No. 426, setting out the minimum requirements for factories can be obtained from the Stationery Office. The conveniences must be maintained, kept clean and effectively lit. The general scale is one convenience for every twenty-five men or twenty-five women, but when employing more than 100 this scale may be varied by the substitution of urinals for water or chemical closets.

Washing facilities

Must include a supply of clean, running hot and cold or warm water, soap and clean towels or other suitable means of cleaning or drying and be suitable and adequate for the number employed.

Drinking water

The employer must provide an adequate supply of drinking water, with an upward jet convenient for drinking or with suitable drinking vessels and facilities for rinsing them.

Seating

The employer must provide suitable seating where an employee (male or female) has reasonable opportunities for sitting without detriment to his/her work.

Accommodation for clothing

Adequate and suitable accommodation must be made for clothing not worn during working hours, with arrangements where practicable for drying such clothing. The risk of theft is an element which must be taken into account in deciding whether accommodation is suitable.

Safety

The Factories Act also provides for safe conditions of workplaces, including floors, stairs, passages and gangways, and the means of access to places where people have to work. The requirements for handrails and fencing are stipulated for means of access, for workplaces, and for openings in floors.

Precautions must be taken against dangerous fumes, dust and other health and safety hazards, protection of eyes and restrictions on lifting heavy weights.

There is a requirement for fencing on dangerous machinery and parts of machinery which are in motion or use, restriction on cleaning machinery by persons under eighteen and women, training and supervision of young persons required to operate certain machines.

Safe construction and operation of cranes, hoists and other plant with special hazards is also a stipulation.

The Act imposes restrictions on the employment of women and young persons, including limitations on normal hours, overtime and holiday work.

Statutory registers are required to be kept and statutory reports made, regarding (for example) accidents and industrial diseases, inspection of factories, lists of homeworkers in certain trades and other administrative matters.

In addition to the requirements of the Factories Act itself, many specific processes are subject to special regulations made by statutory instruments under the Act. These include detailed requirements for certain types of machinery, for example woodworking, and for certain types of industrial employment, for example building operations and works of engineering construction.

OFFICES, SHOPS AND RAILWAYS PREMISES ACT 1963

Many of the provisions of the Offices, Shops and Railways Premises Act 1963 remain in force for the time being. The Act extended to such premises some of the requirements formerly applied only to factories. Section 1 details what premises are covered but these can be briefly summarized as follows:

1   Office premises: a building which is used solely or principally for office purposes from filing or telephone operating to the preparation of material for publication. Premises used in connection with office premises, such as storerooms or canteens, are also subject to the Act even if they are not physically part of the office premises
2   Shop premises: in addition to a shop of the ordinary kind, the term is defined to include any building or part of a building
    (a) of which the sole purpose or principal use is the carrying out of retail trade, for example the sale to the public of food or drink for immediate consumption, retail sales by auction and the lending of books or periodicals for the purpose of gain
    (b) occupied by a wholesale dealer or merchant who keeps goods there for sale
    (c) which members of the public visit to deliver goods for repair etc. or to carry out repairs etc. for themselves
    (d) used to sell solid fuel

The Act does not apply to:

1   Offices in which the total number of man hours worked does not exceed twenty-one a week
2   Moveable office structures in which people work for less than six months
3   Permanent buildings in which persons work for less than six weeks
4   Premises where only the husband, wife and/or immediate family work

The Offices, Shops and Railway Premises Act is mainly concerned with the following:

1   Physical working conditions:
    cleanliness, ventilation, lighting, drinking water, seating, accommodation for clothing;

overcrowding: the employer must allow at least 40 square feet of floor space for each person normally employed in a room, or where the ceiling is lower than 10 feet, 400 cubic feet per person. Furniture, fittings, machinery and other items should be ignored when measuring the size of the room;

temperature: unless the room is used by the public and it is impracticable to do so, a reasonable temperature must be maintained. Where a substantial proportion of the work does not involve severe physical effort the temperature must not be less than 16°C (60.8°F) after the first hour but not more than 19°C (66.2°F). The employer must provide a thermometer on each floor in a conspicuous place for the use of the employees;

sanitary conveniences and washing facilities: the Sanitary Conveniences Regulations 1964, SI 1964 No.966, and the Washing Facilities Regulations 1964, SI 1964 No.965 lay down the minimum requirements

2   Constructing, maintaining and keeping reasonably free from obstruction floors, stairs, passages and gangways
3   Restrictions on lifting heavy loads
4   Fencing dangerous machinery, restricting the cleaning of certain machines by persons under eighteen and training and supervising persons using certain prescribed machines which are registered as particularly dangerous
5   Registration of offices and shops with the local council, obtaining a fire certificate from the fire authority, and other administrative matters
6   Eating facilities for those working in shops
7   Safe construction and safe operation of hoists and lifts

THE SHOPS ACTS

The Shops Acts are designed to ensure that shop assistants do not have to work excessive hours and that they are allowed adequate periods of rest and leisure.

REGULATIONS

As noted earlier, many regulations have been made for special processes and industries. They are too numerous to quote here, and most apply only to a few specialized processes, but mention should be made of the regulations for safety representatives and safety committees, building operations and canteens.

Health and Safety (First Aid) Regulations 1981

These regulations require an employer to make adequate first-aid provisions for staff and to inform them of these arrangements. Help and guidance concerning arrangements including first-aid boxes, kits and other equipment, first aiders and appointed persons are provided in the Approved Code of Practice and Guidance Notes prepared by the Health and Safety Executive.

The Safety Representatives and Safety Committees Regulations 1977

These regulations provide for the appointment of safety representatives, describe their functions and give them the right to certain time off to carry out their tasks and for training. The representatives are also empowered to carry out inspections and have access to certain documents and information. The setting-up of safety committees is also prescribed if at least two safety representatives make such a request in writing.

Safety Signs Regulations 1980 (SI 1980 No.1471)

All safety signs must comply with these regulations.

The Reporting of Injuries, Diseases and Dangerous Occurrences Regulations 1985 (SI 1985 No.2023)

Employers must, under these regulations, report major injuries, accidents/conditions, diseases and dangerous occurrences to the relevant enforcing authority and keep various records for at least three years.

Noise

It is likely that regulations will be published in the near future on exposure to noise.

Building operations

Regulations apply not only to the erection of new buildings but to the repair and maintenance of existing buildings, including redecorating, repointing and external cleaning of buildings. They thus affect firms who, without being engaged in the construction industry, employ their own teams of maintenance workers. The main requirements for such operations are contained in four sets of regulations:

> The Construction (Working Places) Regulations 1966
> The Construction (Lifting Operations) Regulations 1961
> The Construction (General Provisions) Regulations 1961
> The Construction (Health and Welfare) Regulations 1966
> and Amendment 1974

Building regulations

Part III of the Act, which will be the responsibility of the Secretaries of State for the Environment and for Scotland, extends the power to make building regulations governing the structure of buildings.

Canteens

Staff and works canteens are included under Food Hygiene (General) Regulations 1970, made under the Food Act 1984. These regulations include provisions for cleanliness (and personal cleanliness) and other precautions against the contamination of food. A canteen within the curtilage of a factory and used by employees working on the manufacturing process is also subject to the Factories Act. A staff canteen used by office workers, whether part of the office premises or not, is subject to the Offices, Shops and Railway Premises Act.

A guide to these regulations can be obtained free of charge from your local Health Education Unit or Environmental Health Officer.

CODES OF PRACTICE

Regulations will, where appropriate, be supplemented by Codes of Practice. These will not be statutory requirements but nevertheless may be used in criminal proceedings as evidence that statutory requirements have been contravened.

Codes of practice have been issued on the appointment and time off for training of safety representatives, on the establishment of safety committees and first aid.

EMPLOYERS' LIABILITY (COMPULSORY INSURANCE)

The Employers' Liability (Compulsory Insurance) Act 1969 prescribes that all employers must insure against liability for personal injury and disease sustained by their employees and arising out of, or in the course of, their employment. The Social Security Act 1975 does not exempt the employer from taking out this insurance.

FIRE PRECAUTIONS ACT 1971

There must be means of escape in case of fire, adequate in regard to the circumstances and number of people employed, and suitable fire-fighting

WORKING CONDITIONS

equipment and systems must be available. Inspectors from fire authorities have the power to enter and inspect premises. Application must be made to the local authority for a certificate that these requirements have been met.

NOTICES TO BE DISPLAYED

In the following list of statutory notices which have to be displayed, where relevant, the numerical references are to the sections of the Factories Act (FA) and the Offices, Shops and Railway Premises Act (OSRPA) in which the requirement appears. An asterisk against an item indicates that the notice displayed has to be in a prescribed form, copies of which can be obtained from the Stationery Office.

1. Statement showing the health and safety policy and the organization and arrangements that are in force for carrying out that policy must be brought to the attention of all employees
2. *Prescribed abstract of the Factories Act (FA 138). The employer is required to show on this the addresses of the employment medical adviser and the district inspector
3. *Prescribed abstract (or a copy) of any statutory regulations made under the Factories Act and applicable to the premises (FA 139)
4. *Prescribed abstract of the Offices, Shops and Railway Premises Act, unless every employee affected has been given a copy of the prescribed booklet containing the same information (OSRPA 50)
5. *Notice in each factory workroom showing the maximum numbers of persons permitted to work in that room unless the factory inspector exercises his power to exempt a factory from this requirement (FA 2)
6. Notice giving the locations of first-aid equipment and facilities and the name(s) and location(s) of the staff involved
7. *Notice of any exemption for or granted under the Offices, Shops and Railway Premises Act (OSRPA 46)
8. Notice showing the hours of work, times of meal breaks etc. for women and persons under eighteen (FA 88, 90, 94 and 115)
9. *Cautionary placards required to be displayed under regulations for certain special processes, for example, chromium-plating and power-press regulations
10. Placards showing the recommended treatment for electric shock, if electricity is used at voltages above 125v ac or 250v dc
11. Notice in sanitary conveniences used by persons handling food, requesting them to wash their hands (this is a requirement of the Food Hygiene Regulations 1960)
12. Notice showing the piecework rates payable for certain prescribed

operations (FA 135 and orders made under the Act) unless every employee is given a written note of these rates
13 Fire regulations and drill may be required to meet the terms of the fire certificate
14 Certificate of insurance against liability to employees for injury or disease incurred whilst at work
15 One thermometer in every workroom in a factory in which a substantial proportion of the time is spent sitting and the work does not involve serious physical effort, and on every floor in an office

It is an offence for any person to deface or pull down a notice displayed under the Acts.

NOTICES TO BE SENT TO FACTORY INSPECTOR OR OTHER AUTHORITY

The following notices must be sent to the district inspector of factories, unless otherwise stated. The numerical references are to the relevant sections of the Factories Act (FA) and the Offices, Shops and Railway Premises Act (OSRPA). An asterisk against an item shows that the notice must be sent on a prescribed form obtainable from the Stationery Office.

1 *Notice that premises are to be used as a factory (FA 137)
2 *Notice to local council that premises are to be used as offices or shops (if the offices are to be on factory premises, the notice must be sent to the factory inspector instead; if at a mine or quarry it must be sent to the inspector of mines and quarries) (OSRPA 49)
3 *Application to the fire authority for a fire certificate for a factory, office or shop. Small factories, offices and shops are exempt
4 Notice to fire authority when material structural alterations are made to premises, or number of employees materially increased, after fire certificate has been granted (FA 41 and OSRPA 30)
5 Notice to the local careers officer of the Youth Employment Service when recruiting a person under eighteen (a requirement under the Health and Safety Act, Part II) to work in a factory
6 Notice of any fatal accident or major accident, injury/condition to any person, whether or not an employee, and of dangerous occurrences, accidents causing more than three days' incapacity for work, certain work-related diseases, and certain gas incidents should be notified to the relevant enforcing authority as set out in the Reporting of Injuries etc. Regulations. Reporting accidents and dangerous occurrences should be notified to the Health and Safety Executive or other authority of it by the quickest possible means (usually by telephone) and confirmed by a written report within seven days

Free leaflets on when and how to make these reports are available from the Health and Safety Executive area offices
7 *Notice to factory inspector and also to employment medical adviser of any cases of industrial disease. These diseases are prescribed in s82 of the Factories Act and in various orders made under it
8 *Notice of intention to employ women or young persons on overtime (FA 90)
9 *Notice of intention to employ women or young persons at different times from those stated on routine notice posted in factory (FA 88)
10 *Notice of intention to take advantage of permitted exemptions to the legal hours for women and young persons allowed in certain industries (FA 99 to 112)
11 *Notice of intention to employ persons in an underground room, i.e. one with at least half of its height below ground level (FA 69)
12 *Biannual return to local council (in February and August) of any outworkers working on certain processes (FA 133 to 134)
13 *Intention to begin building operations or works of engineering construction expected to last for six weeks or more (FA 127)

The special regulations for certain processes also contain the requirement that the use of such processes shall be notified to the factory inspector.

REGISTERS TO BE KEPT

Most of the following records and registers must be kept on the prescribed forms, published by the Stationery Office:

1 General factory register. This provides a record of young persons employed, periodical painting or limewashing of the factory, accidents and dangerous occurrences, cases of industrial disease, persons trained in first aid, testing of fire-warning systems, and any exemption granted by the factory inspector concerning the hours worked by women and young persons (FA 140)
2 Certificates etc. attached to general registers. Reports and certificates of various examinations and test of plant required by the Factories Act and regulations made under it are, in most cases, required to be entered in or attached to the general register. The fire certificate issued by the fire authority must also be attached to the general register
3 Records must be kept of accidents, dangerous occurrences, reportable diseases and gas incidents
4 Health registers. The regulations for certain special factory processes require the medical examination of workers engaged in them; the results of these examinations must be recorded in the prescribed health register for the process

5   Register of overtime. This must be used to record overtime worked by women and by persons under eighteen (FA 90)
6   Record of hours worked by van boys etc. This must be used to record the hours worked by young persons employed outside the factory on business connected with the factory, for example as van boys or messengers (FA 116)
7   Register of homeworkers in certain trades

ADVICE AND FURTHER INFORMATION

There is a public enquiry point between 10 a.m. and 3 p.m. at the following offices of the Health and Safety Executive:

Baynards House, 1 Chepstow Place, London W2 4TC. Telephone 01-229 3456
Magdalen House, Trinity Road, Stanley Precinct, Bootle, Liverpool L20 3QZ. Telephone 051-951 4000
Broad Lane, Sheffield S3 7HQ. Telephone 0742 752539

Advice on health and safety can also be obtained from local offices of the Health and Safety Executive, which are represented by HM Inspectorate. A list of their addresses is given below.

Health and Safety Inspectorate addresses

Area	Address	Local authorities within each area
1 South West	Inter City House, Mitchell Lane, Bristol BS1 6AN Tel. 0272 290681	Avon, Cornwall, Devon, Gloucestershire, Somerset, Isles of Scilly
2 South	Priestly House, Priestly Road, Basingstoke RG24 9NW Tel. 0256 473181	Berkshire, Dorset, Hampshire, Isle of Wight, Wiltshire
3 South East	3 East Grinstead House, London Road, East Grinstead, West Sussex RH19 1RR Tel. 0342 26922	Kent, Surrey, East Sussex, West Sussex
4 London NW	Chancel House, Neasden Lane, London NW10 2UD Tel. 01-459 8844	Barnet, Brent, Camden, City of London, Enfield, Hammersmith, Harrow, Hillingdon, Hounslow, Kensington & Chelsea, City of Westminster
5 London NE	Maritime House, 1 Linton Road, Barking, Essex IG11 8HF Tel. 01-594 5522	Barking, Hackney, Haringey, Havering, Islington, Newham, Redbridge, Tower Hamlets, Waltham Forest

WORKING CONDITIONS

6 London S	1 Long Lane, London SE1 4PG Tel. 01-407 8911	Bexley, Bromley, Croydon, Greenwich, Kingston-upon-Thames, Lambeth, Lewisham, Merton, Richmond-upon-Thames, Southwark, Sutton, Wandsworth
7 East Anglia	39/43 Baddow Road, Chelmsford, Essex CM2 0HL Tel. 0245 84661	Essex except the London Boroughs in Essex covered by Area 5; Norfolk, Suffolk
8 Northern Home Counties	14 Cardiff Road, Luton LU1 1PP Tel. 0582 34121	Bedfordshire, Buckinghamshire, Cambridgeshire, Hertfordshire
9 East Midlands	Fifth floor, Belgrave House, 1 Greyfriars, Northampton NN1 2LQ Tel. 0604 21233	Leicestershire, Northamptonshire, Oxfordshire, Warwickshire
10 West Midlands	McLaren Building, 2 Masshouse Circus, Queensway, Birmingham B4 7NP Tel. 021 236 5080	West Midlands
11 Wales	Fourteenth floor, Brunel House, 2 Fitzalan Road, Cardiff CF2 1SH Tel. 0222 497777	Clywd, Dyfed, Gwent, Gwynedd, Mid Glamorgan, Powys, South Glamorgan, West Glamorgan
12 Marches	The Marches House, The Midway, Newcastle-under-Lyme, Staffs ST5 1DT Tel. 0782 610181	Hereford and Worcester, Salop, Staffordshire
13 North Midlands	Burkbeck House, Trinity Square, Nottingham NG1 4AU Tel. 0602 470712	Derbyshire, Lincolnshire, Nottinghamshire
14 South Yorkshire	Sovereign House, 40 Silver Street, Sheffield S1 2ES Tel. 0742 739081	Humberside, South Yorkshire
15 West & North Yorkshire	8 St Pauls Street, Leeds LS1 2LE Tel. 0532 446191	North Yorkshire, West Yorkshire
16 Greater Manchester	Quay House, Quay Street, Manchester M3 3JB Tel. 061-831 7111	Greater Manchester
17 Merseyside	The Triad, Stanley Road, Bootle L20 3PG Tel. 051-922 7211	Cheshire, Merseyside
18 North West	Victoria House, Ormskirk Road, Preston PR1 1HH Tel. 0772 59321	Cumbria, Lancashire
19 North East	Arden House, Regent Centre, Regent Farm Road, Gosforth, Newcastle-upon-Tyne NE3 3JN Tel. 091 2848448	Cleveland, Durham, Northumberland, Tyne & Wear

20 Scotland East	Belford House, 59 Belford Road, Edinburgh EH4 3UE Tel. 031-225 1313	Borders, Central, Fife, Grampian, Highland, Lothian, Tayside and the island areas of Orkney & Shetland
21 Scotland West	314 Vincent Street, Glasgow G3 8XG Tel. 041-204 2646	Dumfries and Galloway, Strathclyde, and the Western Isles

Many employers' organisations, trade associations and trade unions can also provide guidance, as do the British Safety Council and the Royal Society for the Prevention of Accidents. Detailed information about the responsibilities of employers in regard to working conditions and liability to employees will be found in the following standard works.

FURTHER READING

R. Birnbaum, *Health Hazards of Visual Display Units with Particular Reference to Office Environments,* TUC Centenary Institute of Occupational Health, London.

P.A. Chandler, *Croner's Health and Safety at Work*, Croner Publications, New Malden, looseleaf, updated guide to the law.

European Foundation for the improvement of living and working conditions, '*Physical and Psychological Stress at Work: Summary Report*', Shankill, Co. Dublin, 1984 (seminar held in Dublin, 3-4 September, 1981).

I. Fife and E.A. Machin, *Health and Safety at Work Excluding Factories and Mines*, Butterworth, London, 1980.

I. Fife and E.A. Machin, *Redgrave's Health and Safety in Factories*, Butterworth, London 1976 and Supplements 1979 and 1981.

M.J. Goodman (ed.), *Encyclopaedia of Health and Safety at Work*, Sweet and Maxwell, London, looseleaf, updated.

E. Grandjean, *Fitting the Task to the Man: An Ergonomic Approach*, Taylor and Francis, London, 1980.

A. Melhuish, *Work and Health*, Penguin, Harmondsworth, 1982.

V. Orlans and P. Shipley, '*A Survey of Stress Management and Prevention Facilities in a Sample of UK Organisation*', Birkbeck College Stress Research and Control Centre, London, 1983.

HM Stationery Office publishes the texts of all Acts and regulations, the prescribed forms, codes of practice, guidance notes and various advisory booklets. Details are given in the publications catalogue available from the Health and Safety Executive. Many employers' organizations, trade associations and trade unions also publish booklets and guidance notes.

23

Salary and Wage Management

Keith G Cameron

Managing the reward of employees can be complex and difficult. Putting to one side the statutory requirements for tax and social security deductions, the discretionary elements require judicious control.

The simplest and most comprehensive approach is to view the subject as reward – a combination of wages, salaries and benefits. However, the topic of benefits is so wide ranging (from company cars to private medical health provision) and variable that it should be left outside the scope of this chapter.

The distinction between salaries and wages is being eroded. The Wages Act 1986 removed some of the obstacles to paying manual workers via the bank transfer system, a restriction previously embodied in the Truck Acts. In terms of pay management the executive and the company need to manage carefully the relationship between the wage and the salary systems, as the factors which kept them separate disappear.

The astute manager should have a pay policy which incorporates the policies applicable to salaries and wages and the relationship between them.

Having made the point, it is still appropriate to approach the subject of pay management from the two subheadings of salaries and wages as the overwhelming practice is to operate two different systems.

I SALARY MANAGEMENT

NEED FOR A SALARY POLICY

Companies which employ up to fifty staff normally have an informal salary policy — and rightly so. However, when total staff exceed this number, anomalies begin to appear in the system and some form of framework is necessary. This is particularly so when rapid expansion is taking place.

Although there must be an overall coordinator, the responsibility for salary management is that of line management. What is needed therefore is a salary policy laying down administrative parameters within which discretion may be exercised and providing salary ranges based on simple job evaluation.

Involvement of line managers at this point is essential in order that they recognize the need for regularizing salary management and make a positive contribution towards drawing up a salary policy.

Example of a salary policy statement

Introduction. The aim of this document is to set down the company's policy with regard to salary. It is the responsibility of all who apply it to explain it fully to their subordinates.

Aims. The aims of the company's policy are:

1 To recognize the value of all jobs relative to each other within the company and in comparison with similar jobs outside
2 To recognize the value of the individual to the company and to relate this to the salary range applicable to his or her job

The foregoing is subject to government legislation, as appropriate.

Salary structure. The salary structure will be based on job evaluation. Each job will have a declared minimum and maximum salary range and it is the company's policy to pay at least the minimum for each job.

Job evaluation. It is the policy of the company to ensure that staff are fully involved in job evaluation, including representation on the job evaluation committee.

Job evaluation is a continuing process and once salary grades have been established, the committee will meet regularly to deal with re-evaluating existing jobs as well as evaluating new jobs.

Initial salary. In determining an individual's salary on appointment, no differentiation is made on the grounds of sex. In addition, the following features are taken into account:

1 The value to the company of the relevant experience he or she brings
2 The individual's value in the outside market

3   The individual's value in comparison to existing staff who hold similar jobs

Performance appraisal. An integral part of salary management is the regular appraisal of staff. This is the basis on which management counsels individuals in order that everyone has maximum opportunity to develop his or her own potential. In order that individuals utilize their abilities to the full, short and longer term objectives will be mutually agreed with management.

Salary reviews. It is the policy of the company to review quarterly the salaries of all staff under the age of eighteen years. At age eighteen years and over, all staff salaries will be reviewed annually. Performance increases, if any, will be effective from 1 April.

Promotion. When an individual is promoted to higher-grade work, his or her salary will be increased by 10 per cent or he or she will be paid the minimum for the new grade, whichever is the greater. If the individual fails to measure up to the needs of the new job, he or she will be made aware of his or her shortcomings and given an opportunity to improve and, failing this, to move to a more suitable job. If this results in moving to work of a lower grade there will be no salary decrease. Instead there will be a salary standstill until the rate for the new position equals that of the old.

Progression within salary range. Everyone will know the salary range for his or her job. Those who do their job particularly well will reach the maximum for their salary range within four years.

Long-serving staff who are already on their salary ceiling will be subject to a salary review every third year to a maximum of six years.

Grievance procedure. Anyone who feels that his or her salary indicates that an injustice has been done has the right to appeal first to his or her manager and then to the managing director whose decision will be final. The individual has a right to bring along a colleague to help support his or her appeal.

Communication

As important as the preparation of a salary policy is the need to communicate it to everyone concerned: indeed there is no reason why every staff member should not have a copy of the actual policy statement.

By far the best way of passing on information is for each departmental manager to call a briefing meeting with all his or her staff to explain what the policy covers and, more important, how it will affect each individual. Care should be taken that each employee's questions are answered sympathetically and honestly. Employees should also be fully aware of the company's intentions regarding possible salary anomalies.

JOB DESCRIPTIONS

In every company there are formal and informal arrangements about who reports to whom and how work is done. It is important, therefore, to establish and seek agreement on an organization or accountability chart. Job titles can be very misleading and some renaming may be necessary. This in turn involves the writing of *job descriptions*.

A job description is a basic statement covering such features as:

Job title
Department
To whom responsible
Date
Tasks/areas of responsibility
Job titles of subordinates
Training and/or experience required for job

The completed description must be agreed by both the job holder and his supervisor. (Where disagreements arise, the grievance procedure should be operated.)

A specimen job description follows.

Specimen job description

Position: Secretary to chief mechanical engineer
Department: Project engineering

Date:

Overall aim: To provide a complete secretarial service to chief mechanical engineer by organizing the routine aspects of his work

Daily tasks:

1 On receipt of mail, sort into order of priority, attach previous correspondence, if any, and type routine letters for signature
2 Take dictation from chief mechanical engineer and deal also with urgent correspondence dictated by senior mechanical engineers
3 Against a tight timetable, type complicated statistical tables connected with department's project work

4   Deal with department's travel arrangements and prepare travel itineraries
5   Maintain simple time records concerning progress of experimental projects. Ensure that progress charts are kept up to date
6   Act as an assistant to chief mechanical engineer by dealing with the more routine aspects of his work
7   Act as a 'shield' by dealing with callers personally and on the telephone

Weekly tasks:
1   Prepare for accountant short summary of personal expenses incurred by department during previous week, and allocate to individual projects

Monthly tasks:
1   Collect brief reports prepared by senior engineers on their respective projects and type draft of progress report for the project engineering director

Six-monthly tasks:
1   Transfer old files to basement and make out new files for next six months

Annual tasks:
1   Type statement of account showing income over expenditure on previous year's projects

Minimum age:	Twenty-one years
Educational qualifications:	Five 'O' levels (including English language) and secretarial college training
Experience:	Three years' practical office experience including one year in a similar firm
Induction:	Three months
Other information:	The chief mechanical engineer is frequently off site and the job holder is expected to deal with all routine problems arising during such absences

JOB EVALUATION

Many companies avoid installing job evaluation because they feel it is either too costly or too sophisticated. This need not be the case. Two methods should be considered as practicable:

1   Ranking
2   Job classification

Ranking involves the study of each job description and placing it in order of importance. Note that it is the *job* which is being graded and *not* the person doing it. Here is a likely plan of attack.

1   Constitute a committee of, say, three people who have a good knowledge of all the jobs being covered
2   Select about 15-20 jobs as being a good representative sample of all the jobs being covered. These are the benchmark or key jobs and form the basis of job evaluation
3   Write job descriptions of the benchmarks
4   Separately rank those jobs in order of importance and seek agreement with other committee members
5   Design a job questionnaire (see Figure 23.1)
6   Brief all employees on how they should complete the questionnaires (see 'Specimen briefing notes' below)
7   Ensure that all questionnaires are agreed by the respective supervisors
8   The committee finally slot in jobs according to benchmarks to reach an overall rank order

Specimen briefing notes

Introduction. Job evaluation is a method of looking objectively at jobs and ranking them in order of importance. By comparing them one with another, each job will be placed in a salary grade relative to its worth. However, it must be stressed that it is the *job* which is being considered and *not* the individual.

A job evaluation committee has been formed under the chairmanship of Andrew Brown, the company secretary. The other members of the committee are Alan Garnett and Jill Pepperell.

The scheme. After a great deal of investigation, the committee has decided to use a classification or grading scheme, a copy of which is described later in this chapter.

Completing the questionnaire

1   *Overall objective.* One sentence will normally suffice here. It should be concise and give the reason for the job's existence in order that the committee has 'something to hang its cap on' before looking at the job in depth. For example:

> Process all orders ensuring that departmental computer data codes are included and that the VAT figure is correct

SALARY AND WAGE MANAGEMENT

Job title	————————————
Department	————————————
Responsible to	————————————
Agreed by ———————————— Date ————	

1 What is the overall objective of the job?

2 Draw up a family tree showing the job in perspective

3 Give a concise description of the main areas of responsibility in the job. Take it area by area and stress the important features
   Daily tasks

   Weekly tasks

   Monthly tasks

   Quarterly tasks

Figure 23.1 Job Questionnaire

Half-yearly tasks
Annual tasks
4 Give the titles of the jobs which you *directly* supervise
5 Contacts — With what levels of people in other departments and/or outside the company do you have contact in order to carry out the job effectively? Is contact by telephone or in person? Comment on the reason for contact *Internal*
External
6 Comment on the qualifications and/or previous experience necessary to do the job effectively
7 Other information

Figure 23.1 (*concluded*)

SALARY AND WAGE MANAGEMENT

2 *Family tree.* A clearer picture of your job is given if you draw up a family tree of your department showing your job in relation to all other jobs.

3 *Job description.* It is always difficult to write one's own job description: consider therefore that you are transferring to another department in the company and that you must prepare a note for your successor covering the main elements of the job. Describe the job as it is now and not how it should be. Do not be afraid to go into detail.

Write down the area headings first, such as correspondence, planning, queries, staff; and describe the responsibility involved under each heading. For example:

> Correspondence — on receipt of mail, decide what can be delegated to subordinates and retain non-routine letters. Where necessary give instructions regarding the handling of particular letters.

4 *Supervisory responsibility.* Supervisory responsibility can only be assessed fairly by examining carefully the job descriptions of those jobs under his or her jurisdiction. By looking at the situation as a whole, the supervisory aspect should be accorded its proper degree of responsibility.

5 *Contacts.* The strength of the company lies in the service given to customers. This does not diminish the value of internal contacts. What is important is the level at which contact is normally made and the reason for contact in the first place.

6 *Qualifications and/or experience.* Comment should be made here regarding the minimum qualifications and/or experience which must be brought to the job *before* it can be done effectively. It may be possible to state an actual qualification or the job may simply call for 'an aptitude for figures'. Experience required must be quite specific. For example: six months' practical experience in credit control.

7 *Other information.* No questionnaire can possibly cover all aspects of a job and since it is important that every member of staff has the opportunity to comment on all areas of the job which are important, space is provided for this. For example:

> Large proportion of work is concerned with meeting tight time schedules

These comments should cover features which are an integral part of the job and not temporary difficulties.

Completion date for questionnaires. All questionnaires must be completed and returned to Jill Pepperell by Monday 29 January.

Completion date for job evaluation exercise. With the cooperation of everyone, the committee hopes to complete the evaluation exercise by 15 March.

Right of appeal. Any member of staff who feels his or her job has not been fairly evaluated has the right to appeal to the committee through his or her head of department. The individual can then expect to be invited, along with his or her head of department to discuss the job in detail with the members of the committee.

Paired comparisons

An extension of ranking — *paired or forced comparisons* — should be considered. Each job is compared with every other job and a decision is made about which job is the more important. An example of a paired comparison is given in Figure 23.2.

	Accounts clerk	Invoice typist	Receptionist/ telephonist	Wages clerk	Messenger	Costing clerk	Director's secretary	Shorthand typist	Stock clerk	Sales clerk
Accounts clerk	X	1	0	0	2	0	0	0	1	0
Invoice typist	1	X	0	0	2	0	0	0	1	0
Receptionist/ telephonist	2	2	X	1	2	1	0	1	2	1
Wages clerk	2	2	1	X	2	1	0	1	2	1
Messenger	0	0	0	0	X	0	0	0	0	0
Costing clerk	2	2	1	1	2	X	0	1	2	1
Director's secretary	2	2	2	2	2	2	X	2	2	2
Shorthand typist	2	2	1	1	2	1	0	X	2	1
Stock clerk	1	1	0	0	2	0	0	0	X	0
Sales clerk	2	2	1	1	2	1	0	1	1	X

Figure 23.2 Ranking chart

SALARY AND WAGE MANAGEMENT

Director's secretary	2	2	2	2	2	2	2	2	2
Receptionist/telephonist		2	2	2	2	1	1	1	1
Wages clerk		2	2	2	2	1	1	1	1
Costing clerk		2	2	2	2	1	1	1	1
Shorthand typist		2	2	2	2	1	1	1	1
Sales clerk		2	2	2	2	1	1	1	1
Invoice typist							2	1	1
Stock clerk							2	1	1
Accounts clerk							2	1	1
Messenger									0

Figure 23.3 Job evaluation matrix

A word of warning. Fifty discretely different jobs is the maximum number which can be ranked manually.

Once this is done, a matrix is drawn up showing the jobs in rank order (see Figure 23.3).

Grading/classification

Grading/classification is a means whereby jobs are separated into natural/homogeneous groups on a whole-job basis. This is achieved by:

1 Writing 15-20 benchmark job descriptions
2 Ranking them
3 Marking natural 'break points' between those groups of jobs which have the same relative work
4 Defining in short paragraph form the common features of those jobs in each group
5 Writing job descriptions for the remaining jobs and matching them against the appropriate grade/classification definition

Example of a grading or classification scheme

Grade 1. Tasks are simple and conform to clearly laid down procedures. No training or experience required. Continually supervised. All written work and calculations are checked. Up to a few weeks' training required.

Grade 2. Tasks are subject to laid-down procedures but can involve a limited measure of initiative. Work subject to spot checks. Up to six months' training or experience required.

Grade 3. Tasks are carried out and decisions made in accordance with standard procedures, subject to infrequent supervision. Routine contact, externally and internally, up to own level to obtain and provide information. Probably minimum of two years' experience.

Grade 4. After specific direction, plans and arranges work within main work programme with little or no supervision. Only non-routine problems referred to superior. May have supervisory responsibility. Can have contact at higher level than own, externally and internally, to obtain and give information which may be of a confidential nature. Specialized knowledge may be required. Probably four to five years' experience.

Grade 5. After general direction, plans and arranges work with little or no supervision. Tasks can involve work of a non-routine nature requiring an original approach as to planning and method. Would normally have contact at a higher level than own, externally and internally, to obtain and give information which may be of a confidential nature. Can be required to make decisions as to daily action and direct work of subordinates. More than five years' experience required.

Analytical job evaluation

The methods of job evaluation described so far are relatively simple and are known as non-analytical schemes because they look at jobs as whole entities and compare them without analysis and comparison of the elements within jobs. For example, in the approaches previously described, information about a job will be garnered under a selection of headings (contacts, experience needed etc.) but comparison of jobs by comparative analysis of the individual components is not a feature.

If job evaluation is being used to provide not only order and control for management but a perception of fairness for the employees, the non-analytical systems of ranking and grading/classification may be thought to be too arbitrary. In this case, a simple form of analytical job evaluation, culminating in a points score for each job can be designed and introduced in the following way.

Example of analytical job evaluation scheme

1   Constitute a committee with good knowledge of the jobs to be evaluated

SALARY AND WAGE MANAGEMENT

and representative of the various functions/areas of the organization

2 Select a set of factors to be measured for each job which cover the important elements in the set of positions to be evaluated. Although these will vary from company to company, a typical list of factors can normally be selected from the following:

training, knowledge, skill, experience, contacts, accountability, complexity, working conditions

3 Using the same principle described under the paired comparisons scheme, prepare a questionnaire for each committee member to complete which compares each selected factor with the others chosen for the scheme (see Figure 23.4)

Knowledge	v	skill	K
Accountability	v	contacts	A
Experience	v	knowledge	E
Knowledge	v	accountability	A
Contacts	v	skill	S
Experience	v	accountability	A
Knowledge	v	contacts	K
Accountability	v	skill	S
Skill	v	experience	S
Experience	v	contacts	C

Figure 23.4   Example of comparative questionnaire

4 Define the importance of the factors by each committee member deciding which factor is more important when forced into comparison with the other factors, counting the frequency with which the factors appear as choices and allocating a range of points per factor in line with the factor's number of 'wins' in relation to the total number of choices. In Figure 23.4, accountability 'wins' three times out of ten. If this was replicated by the other four committee members, then accountability would score 15 out of a maximum of 50

5 Derive the points range per factor. Continuing with the same example, a multiplication factor of 20 could be used for convenience. This would make the theoretical maximum score for a job 1000 points (50 × 20) and produce a maximum score of 300 for accountability, 100 for contacts (1 win × 5 committee members × multiplication factor 20)

6 Evaluate each job in committee, each member awarding points per

factor on the derived points scales, then averaging, or preferably, arriving at a consensus score per element. The total of the agreed points per factor is the score for the job and the total points bands can be defined to produce grades, or the points can stand in their own right and be used to determine pay

This analytical job evaluation method can be used for manual jobs as well as managerial, professional and administrative. The facility to choose and weight factors according to the circumstances of the organization provides the maximum scope and flexibility.

SALARY BANDS/GRADES

Five grades ought to suffice up to and including supervisory level. To have more will mean that differentials between grades will be reduced and staff will see little financial advantage in taking on more responsibility. Alternatively, the salaries coordinator will be faced with an excessive number of appeals for upgrading each time there is a slight increase in responsibility.

In general, jobs will tend to fall into broad groups but there are bound to be some jobs which will cause much soul-searching. The establishing of grades completed, the jobs on either side of the break point must be scrutinized carefully to ensure they are in the right group. In the event of appeals being raised, it is likely that they will spring from this grey area.

Salary ranges

Now comes the problem of allocating actual cash to each band or grade. A number of structures is possible, but a structure like that in Figure 23.5 is recommended for its flexibility.

Grade	
1	5 000—6 600
2	5 800—7 800
3	6 800—9 100
4	8 000—11 000
5	10 000—15 000

Figure 23.5 Salary structure

As will be seen, the salary ceiling is roughly a 30/50 per cent addition on the base figure and the base for the next grade starts at approximately the midpoint of the previous grade. This means that on promotion an employee may move easily from one grade to another. It also recognizes that an employee on his or her ceiling on a grade 3 job is worth more than one about to start on grade 4 work with less experience of the company's business.

SALARY SURVEYS

Although salary comparison is a continuing exercise, a particular effort must be made to obtain factual information when designing a new salary structure. This can be done in four ways:

1. By consulting national or local salary surveys
2. By telephoning your opposite number in other companies in the area and exchanging information
3. By sending to selected companies a job description from each grade and asking for a comparison.
   (It is wise to telephone personally to inquire if the company is willing to take part.) This must be followed up by sending to the participants details of the survey but excluding actual company names
4. By inviting four or five opposite numbers in your area to form a Salary Comparison Club with the first meeting on your premises. An agreed agenda should be drawn up stating the jobs to be discussed in order that salary information is forthcoming

Even at this point, the salary ranges cannot be thought conclusive until a thorough internal costing is completed.

USE OF GRAPHS

The use of graphs is invaluable when creating a new salary structure. Only when the situation is presented visually do anomalies stand out. Using a bar graph to study the number of people in each grade for instance a crude distribution curve will be obtained, i.e. the bulk of the jobs will likely be in the middle grades.

As an *aid* to determining what jobs should finally be in which grade it is helpful to do a scattergram (see Figure 23.6). Here is how it is done:
1. On a graph plot each job holder by basic salary and grade. This will give you the scatter on your current salary structure
2. Draw a (curved) line through the centre of the scatter so that there are roughly the same number of points above as below the line. This will give you the mid-point of each new salary range. (The technical description for the line is 'line of best fit')
3. The pure approach is to fix 15-25 per cent above and below the line the minimum and maximum salary figure for each new salary range
4. The jobs falling above and below the minimum and maximum are, of course, anomalous in the new structure

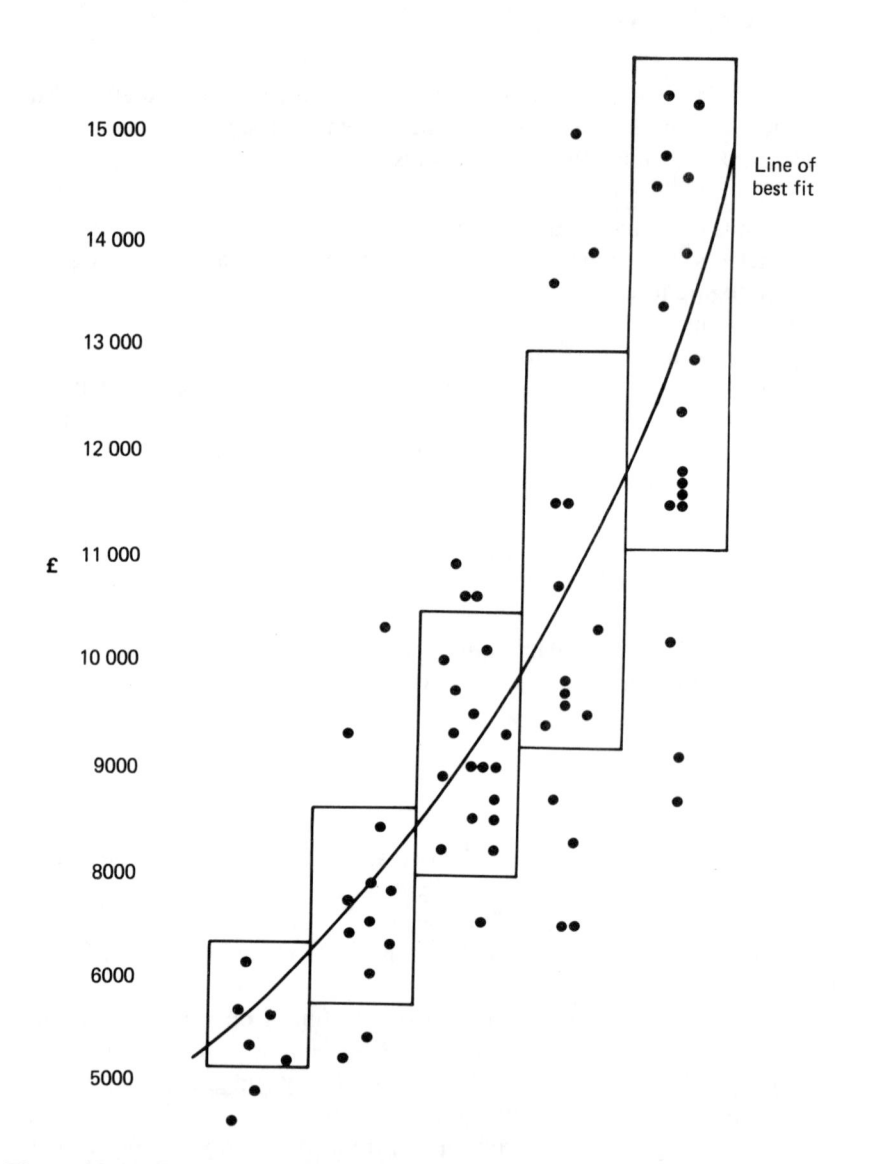

Figure 23.6 Comparison of old and new salary structures

DECIDING HOW MUCH TO PAY

You now have (*a*) an external salary survey; and (*b*) a formal salary structure which reflects accurately the *current* company position. It is likely these two aspects require reconciliation.

SALARY AND WAGE MANAGEMENT

Three terms are used to describe your own position in the marketplace — lower quartile, median and upper quartile. In simple terms, let us say that you have surveyed eight different companies' rates for, say, a wages clerk. These rates are then placed in rank order. Starting from the bottom rate, rate two is the lower quartile, rate four is the median and rate six is the upper quartile. In a bigger sample, the median figure approximates to the average rate as well.

As a *general* rule, the company which chooses to be in the lower quartile tends to have a poorer calibre of staff and consequently more of them to cope with normal business pressures. The reverse is the case with the higher quartile company. Labour turnover is a costly factor not to be viewed lightly.

RATE FOR AGE

Few companies find it useful to retain a rate-for-age scale. It is the experience of a large number of organizations that the inflexibility of such a system, even with merit rating on top, can result in a rapid turnover among staff of high potential.

If however a rate-for-age scale is maintained, care must be exercised to ensure that, on the eighteenth birthday, recognition is made of both the increase in social security contributions and rail travel (if applicable). Otherwise young adults should be paid at least the minimum of the grade applicable to their job.

SALARY ANOMALIES

Once salary grades have been established, it will be found that the majority of staff will be on a salary within the new grade boundaries. However, there will probably be a number of staff who are either over or underpaid. Those underpaid should be brought up to at least the minimum for the grade. Apart from explaining the situation to those staff who are over the maximum for their job grade, the following should be considered:

1 Promotion to higher-grade work
2 Rearrangement of job content in order that some higher-grade work is included
3 Salary standstill until the new rate catches up with the old

EMPLOYEE BENEFITS

The subject of employee benefits is covered in Chapter 24, but it is worth mentioning that when designing a new salary structure, consideration must at the same time be given to the adequacy and cash value of existing employee benefits. When conducting a salary survey, therefore, employee benefits must also be taken into account.

Staff accept fringe benefits as a fact of life but different social groups within the company and indeed within the area will view different benefits with varying degrees of interest. Young people are more attracted to a company by the promise of a realistic salary than by the offer of a generous sick pay or pension scheme. Assisted house purchase, membership of a hospital scheme and profit sharing is likely to appeal to management.

In designing the salary structure, therefore, it is important to consider how much influence employee benefits need have on the salary ranges.

DEPARTMENTAL BUDGETS

Every department should have a budget and within this there should be an agreed figure for salaries. This should be decided one year in advance and should take into consideration staff retirements (with recruitment on a lower salary level), promotions and increases in staff complement. It should also take into account a figure to be set aside for salary increases. This can either be an arbitrarily agreed lump sum or, more usually, something like 3-4 per cent, excluding cost-of-living increases.

SALARY REVIEWS

Most organizations conduct reviews of salaries in a systematic and regular manner, but there are many differences in the way they go about the process.

Frequency and scope

The most common practice is an annual review of salaries. The anniversary date of the review will vary from company to company and may be related to the end of the organization's financial year or a convention (or formal agreement) within the particular industry. Two-year pay programmes are, however, growing in popularity for salaried staff as well as manual workers. The two-year programme enables the employer to plan and control costs better and is more acceptable during times of low inflation. Six-monthly salary reviews for organizations do exist although their incidence is greater during times of high inflationary pressure.

The 'rolling review' system is also used by organizations and entails individuals having their salaries reviewed on the anniversary of their starting date with the organization or appointment to the present job. Although this method gears increases to a full year's review and thus is very specific, the administration and budgeting is intricate where more than a handful of people are involved.

The salary review may not apply to two groups of people: those who are on a different programme, for example young staff who may be given rises every six months, and those who do not justify a pay increase. Some systems, however, do not recognize the latter category.

Salary review methods

Putting to one side the 'fixed increment' system, for example the Civil Service, and formally negotiated salary reviews, the conventional methods are the general increase, general increase plus merit increase, and merit increase only. The general increase is a fixed amount or percentage for the group or for each category within the group. The other two approaches require a method for varying the amount to be paid to different people and this entails assessment of individual performance.

Performance appraisal

Performance appraisal is a valuable technique in its own right. A formal method of relating performance to expected standards and goals enables managers to examine rationally and agree upon corrective action in those areas where training may be required and where there is scope for development and promotion. Additionally, the majority of companies wish to reward individual performance and so link the results of appraisal to salary increases. The 'general plus merit' approach entails payment of an increase to all those eligible based on a generally applicable indicator like cost-of-living movement or, more frequently now, changes in the pay market which will have been quantified by the salary survey methods described earlier.

Some companies gear salary increases entirely to individual performance and this can be achieved by adjusting fixed percentage increases to the particular appraisal or merit ratings. For example, the performance appraisal system may have five categories, with A defined as 'Fails to meet the requirements of the job', B being 'Fails to meet some requirements of the job' through to E which states 'Achieves considerably more than is required by the job'. Against such an A to E scale the company could award the following increases to the base pay of individuals: A-0 per cent, B-2 per cent, C-5 per cent, D-8 per cent, E-11 per cent. Control of the amount available for the salary review is vested in the regulation of the numbers in each performance category. Using the example above, the cost of the review should be 6-7 per cent as the bulk of employees would be in C with a significant minority in D. There should be relatively few individuals in A or B as most cases of poor performance should have been dealt with by management action during the year. Similarly, *E* should house relatively few people if the targeting standards for individuals are properly set. The suggestion that there could be significant numbers in *D* is based on the assumption that the company is meeting its fiscal targets and this constitutes an improvement on the previous year. Although such an approach relates reward specifically to performance, it can have an adverse compounding effect if the base salary to which the percentage increase is applied is low. In these circumstances an increase of 8 per cent to a £8000 salary for good performance yields £640 while 5 per cent for standard performance on £12 000 means £600. Both individuals could be in the same grade with a midpoint of range of £10 000. A matrix can be developed to account for the individual's position in the salary range as well as the merit rating but, without being so elaborate, companies can take account of this factor by being flexible with the standard percentage for each rating and shading this up or down slightly.

For the administration of a merit-based salary review a form similar to Figure 23.7 should be used.

Name	Job title	Date appointed to job	Date of last increase	Amount	Present salary	Grade	Salary range	Performance rating	Increase proposed	New salary

Figure 23.7   Merit-based salary form

II WAGE MANAGEMENT

DESIGNING A COMPANY WAGE POLICY

The wage structure must be linked to what the company is trying to achieve. It is not unusual to find a company with a wage structure in direct conflict with the company's overall objectives. For example, a company may plan to produce a high-quality product while at the same time it may have a direct incentive geared to quantity. These questions must be asked:

Apart from profit, what are we in business for?
Where are we going during the next two to three years; in the next five to ten years?
How do we plan to get there?
What influence will these plans have on our wage structure?
How can the wage structure aid the company in meeting its objectives?

From this a business plan is built up, in simple terms, expressing the company's short and long-term objectives and how these will affect specific areas. It may be, for example, that in two years' time a massive capital investment is planned. In terms of human resources this will probably affect the way work is organized, manning arrangements and job demands. Care must be taken, therefore, to ensure that the new wage structure will form a satisfactory springboard to cater for future developments. Consideration must also be given to the spin-off which will affect the whole company.

Management style

It is necessary to identify the company's management style. Is it predominantly autocratic, paternalistic, participative or *laissez-faire*? Incompatibilities arise if a wage structure is implemented in isolation of this important consideration. An autocratic management style for instance is in conflict with a Scanlon/Rucker plan. Since the pay structure expresses to employees how the company values them, a real attempt must be made to draw up a declared wage policy. A framework for a policy statement is given on p.494.

CHANGING A WAGE STRUCTURE

The desire to change a wage structure usually springs from an existing structure which management no longer controls. Common features are that the present structure suffers from wage drift, that it has numerous rates which are inequitable in terms of individual contribution and there has been a gradual build-up of 'special' allowances.

Most companies, when faced with the need to change their wage structure, begin by looking for alternative incentives. In reality this is prejudging the issue. The first step should be an initial investigation to ascertain the pressure points which exist in the present structure. Only by discovering the 'lumps and bumps' in the present system will the way ahead seem clear. A discussion with the senior wages clerk will be an enlightening experience since that individual, more than anyone else, is fully aware of the inadequacies and inequities of the existing system.

Wage analysis

This should be based on a thorough examination of the gross pay earned department by department, for, say, a 'typical' week at two points in the year. All special allowances should be examined and the totals expressed as a percentage of labour cost. Consideration should be given to the effectiveness of the incentive element.

Overtime

The number of hours overtime should be broken down and scrutinized to see what indicators exist. Excessive overtime working usually means an unrealistic basic hourly rate. What, for example, would be the result if overtime working were curbed? If overtime earnings were consolidated in the basic rate on the understanding that productivity was maintained, would the need for overtime working cease? And would this be socially acceptable in your locality?

Work study

One of the main reasons why a company decides to change its wage structure is because work study values have worked loose and wage drift has become a dominant feature. For example, is the pace of working closely related to that shown on the time sheets? Too often top management assumes that because performances are high on paper, all is well. If the company's present work study team cannot cope with the situation, the use of consultants should be considered. An alternative is to employ experienced work study personnel on a short-term contract.

Labour turnover

Annual figures should be produced and broken down by department. These figures are normally associated with the social aspects of employment but it is not by any means unknown for a definite correlation to be established between them and the method of payment. For example, it is possible that a very low labour turnover linked to a very high rate of absenteeism indicates that earnings may be unusually high for the area but working conditions are intolerable, leading to low morale: the employees cannot afford to leave. In other words, it is just as problematic to grossly overpay people as to underpay.

Age and sex

On a departmental basis, figures should be produced for both men and women grouping them by age, for example 16-18, 19-25, 26-40, 41-50, 51-60,

61-65, 65+. Men and women in particular age groups have different attitudes to work and how their pay packet should be made up. Additionally, they will have fairly specific ideas about what they are prepared to do to earn £x per week. It is doubtful, for example, whether a middle-aged male workforce would be enthusiastic about the introduction for the first time of direct incentives.

Attitude survey

Ideally an attitude survey should be made to ascertain what needs have to be satisfied through a wage structure. What are the employees' attitudes towards the current pay structure and what are their deeper expectations? The pay structure to a large extent determines and reinforces attitudes. Two of the areas a survey ought to highlight are the reasons why employees work for a particular company and what motivates them. Every company has a reputation as an employer and if it has achieved, for example, a 'quick buck' image, it will attract a particular type of employee. Thought must therefore be given to the kind of image the company wants to have and how it plans to achieve it.

What motivates people in your geographical area? What kind of incentives are socially acceptable, for instance? The whole of the Midlands is almost incurably on direct incentives and a firm that works otherwise is viewed with suspicion. In a free bargaining situation, a company introduced a new incentive scheme which theoretically should have increased take-home pay — and the impact was nil! An investigation highlighted the fact that the social custom was for young people to lay their unopened pay packet on the kitchen table each pay day and to receive in return a fixed amount of pocket money. A little unusual in the 1980s, perhaps, but knowledge of this factor would have saved the company much time and trouble.

The survey should be done by an outside specialist in order to gain the confidence of the workforce.

Influence of production method

Insufficient consideration is normally given to the link between the technological aspects of production and how people are paid. It is obvious that this is important and yet many operatives in a machine-controlled situation are on direct incentives intended to make them work faster! Similarly, it is not unusual for a company specializing in one-offs to have a direct incentive scheme which entails on-the-spot bargaining between, say, a rate fixer and a shop steward for every unit produced: the result is a hardening industrial relations climate.

These questions should be asked:

1 Are runs short, long, one-offs?
2 How important is quality, quantity, accuracy, consistency?
3 Is the operation operator- or machine-controlled? And what happens in *practice*?
4 What are the capital investment plans for the next 3-5 years? Will these developments influence pay structure?
5 What are the market pressures? Are there seasonal fluctuations?
6 Can buffer stocks be kept or is the product perishable?
7 How must is lost through scrap? (If the material is reconstituted, cost this.)

JOB EVALUATION

Job evaluation is an essential exercise if a company is to be truly in control of its wage structure. Certainly it is the only answer to leapfrogging pay claims and escalating special allowances.

Job evaluation can be as difficult or as expensive as a company likes to make it. Ranking is quite satisfactory: the basis of job evaluation is ranking anyway and all other methods are, in simple terms, administrative systems which are an aid to maintaining the original rank order of the benchmarks. Points rating is the most commonly used system, however.

Nowadays it is normal for a joint management/union committee to introduce job evaluation though this depends to a large extent on the industrial relations climate. It is important, however, for the committee to be trained before embarking on an exercise.

At the other end of the industrial relations scale, however, is the multi-union situation, or long-established union militancy, or a combination of both. In such a situation, the unions should be consulted regarding their role but they will probably prefer to let management make all the decisions while they reserve the right to object on behalf of their respective members. In any case, such unions are probably accustomed to an autocratic management style and a large dose of participation is just as difficult for the unions to countenance as for line management. Obviously, union participation simplifies the situation but involvement does not guarantee instant success: there will still be appeals. What is important is that job evaluation is regarded as a quite separate situation from negotiating actual rates.

The Industrial Society's book entitled *Job Evaluation* is useful.

COSTING

The basis of a carefully considered wage structure is sound costing. The company accountant, therefore, has an important role to play. Here are the major areas to be scrutinized for key indicators:

SALARY AND WAGE MANAGEMENT

1. Budgeted labour cost for the coming year
2. Trend of total labour cost over the last five years
3. General breakdown of cost of the various wage components which contribute to the labour cost for, say, the last two years
4. Earnings distribution for each department for two typical weeks
5. The unit cost of producing each selling line and the proportion of labour cost attributed
6. Cost of employee benefits. Frequently overlooked, these benefits are nonetheless part of the total labour cost
7. Cost of labour turnover. As a rule of thumb, a routine factory worker who leaves after, say, three months, has probably cost the company approximately £750. This figure includes recruitment costs, interviewing time (allowance must be made for the average number of interviews to fill each job), initial training and a scale linked to the likely contribution an individual will make as his skill and know-how increases. A new employee does not begin to function as a member of a team until one or two weeks have elapsed
8. Cost of absenteeism. (Absenteeism is being used in a wider context than simply illness.) It is a useful pulse to take: if, say, absenteeism is running at a steady 20 per cent, possible causes are overmanning, overpaying or simply low morale. The cost of morale is not a balance sheet item but it is nonetheless an important hidden cost which must not be ignored

FINANCING THE WAGE STRUCTURE

It is inflationary to set out to design and implement a new wage structure without first agreeing with the unions concerned that the increase in the wage bill must be found from within the company's resources. The actual cost of changing a wage structure is about 5 per cent of the wage bill, excluding cost-of-living for example. At first glance this figure will appear to be high: in effect a redistribution of cash and control is taking place with a short-term gain for the operatives involved and a medium-term gain for management. In a stable economy, no matter how sophisticated a company's techniques and know-how, it is possible to find savings to cover this cost. Of prime importance at the beginning of the exercise is agreement by management and unions on how the savings are to be achieved and shared.

Running concurrently with the initial investigation should be the operation of productivity groups or quality circles bent on finding savings. These groups under the leadership of their supervisor should comprise *operatives* meeting on a sectional or departmental basis during working hours or at the end of a shift (on overtime). Their remit should be a broad one where they may discuss every aspect of the organization and planning of the work in their immediate working area.

While the structure of the groups will depend on the size of the section or department, the numbers meeting at any one time should not exceed eight to ten. A simple record of decisions made should be kept by each group for the sake of continuity and an effort made to communicate this within the group. Training will be necessary to help the groups to assess each problem, devise probable solutions and make recommendations. Many companies underestimate the wealth of untapped potential which exists at shopfloor level. However, companies who have attempted a similar exercise have discovered that operatives are quite capable of using simple problem-solving and costing techniques, for example. Provided the groups understand in essence the services provided by, say, the company's work study or production engineering specialists, the groups will ask for expert advice if the need arises.

DESIGNING THE WAGE STRUCTURE

Having established the realities of the existing structure, the next step is to design one which will meet the company's needs. The trend is for a company to have a two-tier wage structure: a basic hourly/job rate tier accounting for 80-85 per cent of the wage bill and an incentive tier (if any) accounting for 15-20 per cent.

Number of grades

The trend is to have four to six grades covering all factory personnel. The more straightforward the production process, the less reason for numerous grades. Without prejudicing the situation in the early stages of the investigation, there should be at least £7.50 per week differential between each grade. To have less will act as a disincentive to internal promotion. In effect this means reducing the number of grades to a point where the differential is a significant demonstration that work in a higher grade really is more important to the company. If the pay steps are too small, management will be faced with numerous requests for regrading jobs every time a fraction of responsibility or a grain of dirt is added to the job.

The decision regarding the break point for each grade is largely arbitrary. It will probably be a negotiating point. On the whole, jobs tend to fall into homogeneous groups but no matter where the break points are made, 'grey area' jobs on either side of the line will give rise to much tooth-sucking. It is from this area that job evaluation appeals usually spring.

As an aid to deciding where the break points might be, it is useful to produce some scattergrams showing how, for example, the results of job evaluation compare in relation to job holders' basic rates as well as gross pay (see Figure 23.8). The next step is to determine the 'line of best fit': in simple terms a line is drawn through the centre of the points already plotted. It is

SALARY AND WAGE MANAGEMENT 483

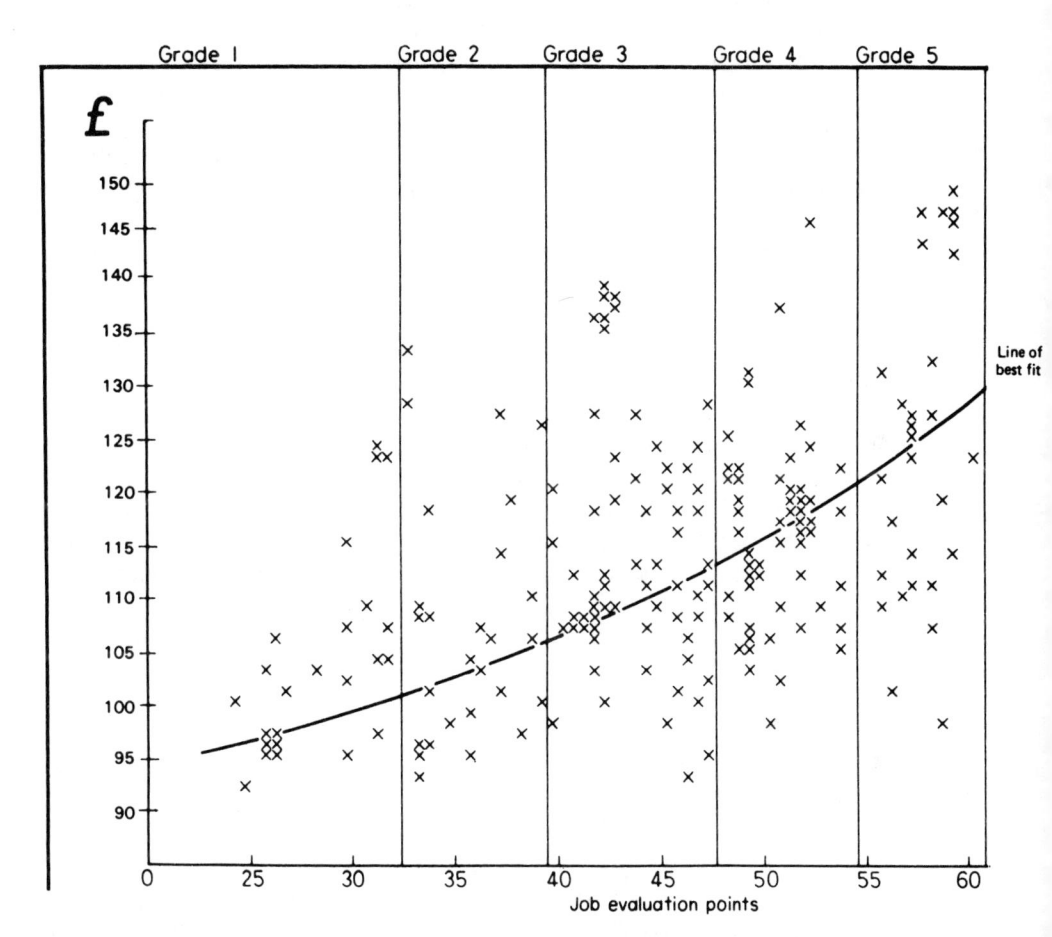

Figure 23.8 Scattergram of total earnings (excluding overtime) related to job evaluation points

then possible to determine roughly what the pay steps might be. In practical terms this is a quite considerable exercise and it may be that a 30 per cent sample, say, of all jobs might suffice.

Yet another statistical aid is the use of bar graphs. In most companies the bulk of the jobs will be in the middle two grades with roughly the same number in the bottom and top grades.

Deciding the basic rate

Traditionally, manual workers have been in a position where the ratio of basic rate to incentive was 2:1. However, this ratio now tends to be nearer 4:1

largely because companies moving towards single (staff) status are rightly challenging the concept that a manual worker's earnings should fluctuate with the company's production throughput.

The case for greater security of earnings should therefore be considered as a matter of course. If nothing else, a proportion of 2:1 is a prime cause of wage drift. Theoretically, a wage survey should be conducted with other firms but since the make-up of gross pay is so variable from company to company, it is difficult to establish any meaningful form of parity. A company must examine its own costing system in terms of budgeted labour cost and the relationship this bears to unit cost. In other words, management must decide how much of the budgeted labour cost should be attributed to basic rate and how much to incentive, if any. Since this is negotiable, management should also know in advance the influence on unit costs of different break points or alternative basic rates.

One company employing about 1000 people avoided this problem by taking the budgeted labour cost for the coming year and giving to the unions concerned three different 'mixes' of total wage cost. This was broken down into 3, 5 and 7 grades complete with incentive calculated at 80, 90 and 100 BSI. (80 BSI is a good average rate of working.) The unions were told that they could produce another option still coming to the same total if they so desired. The company in question, while unused to this level of participation, had a history of good industrial relations. Obviously some unions will question the budgeted labour cost but this does not detract from the principle proposed.

Dealing with anomalies

Once the job evaluation exercise is completed and new basic rates determined, a scattergram will pinpoint those jobs which are likely to be over or underpaid in relation to the new rates. Provided the old structure was not completely out of control, the bulk of the jobs will be just about right with roughly the same number over as underpaid. The options open to management are:

For overpaid employees

1   Retrain the individuals concerned in order that they can take on work of a more responsible or skilful nature and therefore justify the new level of payment
2   Make the difference between the old rate and the new a personal allowance which would be eroded each time a new basic rate was agreed. In time the new rate would catch up with the old
3   As for 2, but the old rate — sometimes called a Red Circle Rate — is retained for ever and ever. This is not advised. In time this becomes a thorn in the side of other employees

4 Buy out anomalies by paying a lump sum comprising the difference multiplied by a negotiated figure. This is a strong negotiating area. What must be considered is the percentage of employees involved and whether or not the majority of differences will be swallowed up within twelve to eighteen months anyway

For underpaid employees. There are no options here: the individual's pay must be brought into line.

INCENTIVE ELEMENT

The word 'incentive' is synonymous with the word 'effort' in the minds of many. But this is not so. An incentive is some form of financial encouragement recognizing a particular contribution made by the workforce. It is, in effect, a sum of money additional to the basic rate which a company pays to ensure that its most important production aspects are being optimized. For example, a capital-intensive company might have an incentive linked to machine utilization; a company making diamond-tipped tools might put particular emphasis on a low scrap value while still maintaining quality. Nonetheless many companies insist that effort is the only factor to recognize despite the fact that automation is very much with us.

Thought must be given to the *cost* of maintaining any one incentive: how many work study personnel, bonus clerks, tally clerks and inspectors are required to maintain standards? Can it be done in a more simple, effective way? Need there be an incentive? Will people only work on a carrot and stick basis? Will you, the reader, only work on this basis or are you different? What contribution does first-line supervision make to motivating people? Will the system encourage or stifle the growth of tomorrow's supervisors?

The basic decisions to be made about the incentive element are whether or not it is going to be individual, group, department or company based or a combination of these. The other important feature is whether the incentive is to be based on a straight-line formula (the more units produced the more earned *ad infinitum*) or on a curve where rather less is earned proportionately the more units produced, sometimes with a cut-off point to limit production and thereby restrict bonus. Yet another approach is to have a cut-off point beyond which any bonus earned is placed in a common pool. This in turn is used to help finance basic rates when these are renegotiated.

Direct incentives

Definition. A method of payment whereby a bonus is paid in direct relation to effort.

Advantages

1. Appropriate where a high level of physical effort is necessary and it is difficult to supervise workers effectively
2. Can generate substantial motivation as payment occurs shortly after achievement
3. Flexibility in allocating added reward for added effort
4. Introduction can mean a reduction in labour
5. Can be useful in the short term to increase the pace of working as an interim step to moving on to a more sophisticated system

Disadvantages

1. Management is not in control of production
2. Tendency to ignore avoidance of waste
3. Supervisors in time may earn less than their subordinates, skilled less than semi-skilled
4. People learn how to achieve earnings without undue effort, for example by qualifying for special allowances, avoiding promotion to non-lucrative jobs, embarking on slow-downs during 'testing' of new rates
5. Can ruin industrial relations
6. Mobility of labour becomes virtually impossible
7. Supervisors become good progress chasers but rarely good managers

Measured daywork

Definition. Measured daywork is a stabilized direct incentive system where the incentive element is consolidated in the basic rate, thereby achieving a high, non-fluctuating weekly wage or salary.

It is based on sound training, sophisticated work measurement techniques and sound management. It is still payment by results except that the underlying philosophy is one of trust — that an individual will work at an agreed pace provided work is available for him or her. The most common types are:

High day rate, which is suitable in an assembly-line situation. Each new employee is fully trained before starting work on the factory floor. He or she will be expected to produce work of a specified standard and to maintain a fixed working pace of, say, 90 BSI. The aim is to achieve a controlled work flow: those individuals who have a naturally high pace of working would normally be transferred to indirect work. Those who have a naturally slow pace are subject to warnings and then either transferred to indirect work or dismissed, following reasonable warning.

Advantages

1   Simplified pay structure usually based on job evaluation
2   Considerable operating flexibility
3   Trust and responsibility given proper emphasis
4   Management is in control of production and uses work study standards as a condition of employment as well as for management information

Disadvantages

1   Not always possible to elicit acceptable levels of performance without the 'pull' of a direct incentive
2   Sophisticated control techniques, such as daily computer data, are necessary
3   High calibre of supervision is essential
4   Disputes can be tougher than in direct incentive plants as employees can slow down without impairing earnings

Philips premium pay plan is suitable where individuals can control the pace of work. The same principles as those for high day rate apply except, perhaps, the problem of disputes since PPP is based on individual effort.

The pay structure is a simple one, usually based on job evaluation, but unlike high day rate, it is graded in steps according to the pace of working (see Figure 23.9). Each individual contracts through his supervisor to work for a period of three months at a particular pace. If this pace is not maintained and the fault is not that of management, a warning is given. If the pace of working does not meet the agreed standard during the following three months, he or she is either retrained or moved back to a lower pay band. If he or she is unable to maintain an acceptable pace, he or she is liable to dismissal.

	SALARY AND WAGE ADMINISTRATION		
GRADE	80 BSI	90 BSI	100 BSI
	£	£	£
I	113.00	122.00	131.00
II	104.00	112.00	120.00
III	95.50	102.50	109.50
IV	87.50	93.50	99.50
V	80.00	85.00	90.00

Figure 23.9   Example of a wage structure of the Philips premium pay plan type

Group/departmental incentives

Definition. A method of payment whereby a bonus is paid either equally or proportionately to individuals within a group/department as a result of, say, *output achieved* over an agreed standard.

Advantages

1   It encourages team spirit
2   It breaks down demarcation lines
3   The group disciplines its 'slackers'
4   Job satisfaction is achieved through seeing the complete operation within the group area

Disadvantages

1   Management is not in control of production
2   The bonus ceases in time to be an incentive and management might as well consolidate the rate
3   Individual effort is not rewarded

Plantwide incentives

There are three main types:

Factory throughput. Linked to, say, tonnes leaving the factory, the bonus is distributed either equally or proportionately according to skill. Basic concept is that workers become more closely associated with the company's aims.

Advantages

1   Improved atmosphere
2   Demarcation less pronounced
3   Employees are aware of the production targets the company plans to achieve

Disadvantages

1   Individual effort is not recognized
2   Employees find it difficult to associate themselves directly with the bonus
3   To safeguard against bad weeks/months, companies sometimes maintain a bank, so that the bonus becomes an employee benefit

SALARY AND WAGE MANAGEMENT

4   If a bad week/month is experienced it's always the fault of 'other' departments

Scanlon plan. An alternative name is share of production plan. The nub of the system is the formation of a joint management-union productivity committee which has *executive authority*. The bonus is based on productivity improvements and is usually calculated monthly.

Rucker plan. An alternative name is cost reduction plan. The basic theory is that there is a constant relationship between wages and production or added value. A joint management-union productivity committee is formed but it has *advisory authority* only. Savings made by reducing costs are shared either equally or proportionately and are usually distributed on a monthly basis.

In a nutshell, Scanlon is strong on industrial relations and weak on mathematics and Rucker vice versa. In practice, the best of both methods is adopted. The share-out is usually about one-third of total savings. The basic concept for both is that manual workers have very much more to offer to a company than simply effort.

Advantages of Scanlon/Rucker plans

1   Can encourage better use of resources and raw materials and thereby produce substantial savings
2   Focuses attention on cooperation and teamwork to reduce costs
3   Trust and responsibility given proper emphasis
4   People accept change more readily
5   Normally covers direct and indirect workers and can include staff directly linked with production
6   Work group has a stake in how well management performs — and has freedom to criticize poor decisions: it therefore keeps management on its toes

Disadvantages of Scanlon/Rucker plans

1   Cannot in themselves create a willingness to cooperate or a management capable of exploiting cost reduction
2   Some groups have more control over results than others and some contribute more than they receive
3   Parochialism can result: good communication is essential
4   Success largely hinges on sophisticated cost control techniques over a long period — and deciding on the 'right' calculation for distribution of savings

Profit-sharing

Definition. On the basis of company profits, employees either receive an annual cash bonus or actual company shares. Basic concept is participation.

Advantages

1. Thrives in non-union firms
2. From management's point of view, extra rewards are allocated only when they can be afforded
3. Improved teamwork and cooperation. However, to optimize this, management must communicate the economic facts of life
4. The system is self-adjusting although the method by which profits are calculated or the form in which the money is distributed may come under attack

Disadvantages

1. Workers have little control over final profit achieved
2. An industrious worker does not necessarily achieve extra payment
3. Tendency to withhold part of the profit to be shared against less fortunate times, thus making it a handout or employee benefit
4. Many schemes do not pay sufficient money to make an impact on motivation

Merit-rating

Definition. A method of payment based on management decisions about an individual's personal *qualities and aptitudes*. Basic concept is that management reserves the sole right to pay people individually.

Advantages

1. Supervisors regularly consider each subordinate's contribution
2. Method of payment is flexible
3. Employees feel they are being treated as individuals

Disadvantages

1. Because it is usually a subjective assessment, it is difficult to discuss problem areas without an element of emotionalism — always supposing they are discussed at all
2. Economic pressures often result in the system being bent with everyone ending up at the top end

3 Supervisors find it easier to pay everyone the same so that it effectively becomes an employee benefit

ADDED VALUE

It is a well-established fact that in a *stable economy* there is an almost constant relationship between labour costs and added value. It follows, therefore, that this provides a useful formula on which to calculate savings: these in turn can be used to fund annual wage increases on a plantwide basis.

For example, assume that unions and management agree (as a result of information provided by the company's auditors) that over the last five years labour cost has been 34 per cent of added value.

	£
Sales	100 000
Less raw materials, utilities and depreciation	55 000
Added value	45 000
Labour cost	15 300
Labour cost: Added value	34%

It is agreed that any savings made in labour cost beyond this reference point of 34 per cent will be shared equally between management and unions.

Assume that sales increase 20 per cent and that with no additional increases in basic cost the cost of providing raw materials is a further £11 000, and that labour costs increase by 10 per cent. The situation would appear thus:

	£
Sales	120 000
Less raw materials, utilities and depreciation	66 000
Added value	54 000
Labour cost	16 830
34% × £54 000	18 360
Saving in labour cost	1 530
Proportion contributed to plantwide increases	765
A total of 4.5 per cent on the total wage bill	

It will be obvious that companies will be required to open their books if the operation of the added-value concept is to maintain credibility. Set against this is the fact that the more information which can be produced prior to negotiation, the less conflict there will be between management and unions. Approximately half of all disputes leading to stoppages are caused by friction over wage rates. A removal in part, even of some of the reasons behind these stoppages would give both management and unions more time to contribute to other important areas.

PRODUCTIVITY AGREEMENTS

A productivity agreement is a statement jointly agreed by management and unions on how work and people may be more effectively organized to mutual benefit. Two types of agreement are:

1 An agreement using the 'buying out' principle on the basis of quid pro quo. In effect, this type of agreement covers immediate wage increases in exchange for relaxation of rigid demarcation lines; elimination of tea breaks; forfeiture of mates; reduction in manning levels
2 An agreement which lays down a framework for allowing savings to be accumulated over six to twelve months. These savings are normally shared equally between management and shopfloor employees

In a nutshell, the difference between the two is 'jam today or jam tomorrow'. In selecting the right approach, a company must consider what will best match its industrial relations climate *and* its overall company objectives. It may be that its lack of operating flexibility demands a 'buying out' agreement in the short term but its longer-term objectives require phased steps towards a position where greater participation will fund wage increases as well as strengthen the company's future. But it must be *planned*.

In times of high unemployment, productivity agreements of the buying-out type are not popular with unions. In any case, it is narrow to assume that increased productivity can *only* be achieved through a reduced labour force: there are numerous options which are equally valid. For example, what would be the effect of better machine utilization, improved work flow, reduction in scrap value, introduction of shift work? It is rather a question of selecting the right tools in order to make the best use of human resources.

Whatever form the agreement takes, it is, in effect, a *statement of intent* signed by both parties: what must not be overlooked is that it is not a once-and-for-all effort but a document calling for positive action throughout its term with regular progress reviews properly communicated. All too often companies negotiate excellent productivity agreements but fail to follow them through.

SINGLE STATUS

Employee or fringe benefits provide an element of security, a security which up until the last few years was the preserve of staff and management only. With the trend towards removing the differences in conditions between blue- and white-collar workers, unions are becoming increasingly aware of the value to their members of negotiating, for example, increased pensions. If the incentive element influences employee attitudes, how much more that of employee benefits? Sometimes overlooked, the Equal Pay Act requires equality in particular employee benefits as well as pay. If single status is the ultimate aim, a phasing operation must be planned in order that costs may be absorbed. The point being made is that employee benefits are part of the total labour cost and must be taken into account when looking at overall pay and conditions.

COMMUNICATION

An important area not stressed sufficiently is the need to communicate effectively. *The need to know* what is happening must be satisfied. Managers are often as starved of information as operatives! Will your present system cope? It is not the shop stewards' job to communicate management's intentions. Can your supervisors brief their subordinates face to face? What can you do to help them? Above all, every individual affected by the new pay structure must *understand* how it works. Could a simple booklet be produced? These are the main points concerning communication but since it is vital to the success of the whole project, readers are strongly advised to read the Industrial Society's booklet on 'Communication' in the *Notes for Managers* series.

SUPERVISORY STRUCTURE

Because many companies are attempting to move away from direct incentives, it is wise to comment on the need to investigate the existing supervisory structure and to consider the calibre, in effect, of first-line managers. Whatever management decides in terms of a new structure, first-line supervisors will be required to manage more effectively. Apart from training needs, the span of control must be examined. If a supervisor is to manage effectively, the most he can control and motivate is fifteen to twenty operatives. The successful implementation of a new wage structure hinges on how carefully this aspect is handled.

EXAMPLE OF A WAGE POLICY STATEMENT

It is the intention of management that this document is issued to every employee whom it concerns. It is the responsibility of first-line management to explain it fully to their subordinates. Should anyone feel that any aspect of this policy is not operating in practice, he should as a first step discuss this with his supervisor.

Aims. The aims of the policy are:

1   To recognize the value of all jobs in relation to each other within the company
2   To take account of wage rates paid by companies of similar size, product and philosophy
3   To ensure stable earnings
4   To enable individuals to reach their full earning potential as far as is reasonably practicable
5   To ensure employees share in the company's prosperity as a result of increasing efficiency

Job evaluation

The basis of a sound wage structure is job evaluation. It is in the interest of both unions and management that this is carried out on a joint basis.

Job evaluation is a continuing process and therefore must be maintained if it is to retain its usefulness. To ensure that the scheme is still relevant, it will be reviewed jointly by unions and management at the end of its third operating year.

Wage structure

In designing the wage structure, the company aims to make the best use of its employees in order to achieve the company's short and longer-term business objectives. By achieving these objectives the company hopes to remain a leader in its field, thereby ensuring greater job security for all concerned.

Rate for the job

No one will be paid less than the recognized rate for the job. Equal pay is in force on the basis of 'equal pay for work of equal value'. While the company recognizes the right of the unions' joint negotiating panel to negotiate on behalf of its members, management believes that first and foremost rates should be linked to the company's prosperity.

The company does not aim to pay the top rates in the area but rather to place the emphasis on good working conditions, security of employment and an atmosphere in which individuals may reach their full potential. Nonetheless the company aims to be in the top 15 per cent as far as total earnings are concerned. (Total earnings includes employee benefits.)

Number of grades

The number of grades will be as few as possible in order that differentials are of a sufficiently high level for real differences in responsibility and/or skill to be recognized.

Incentives

The company does not accept that its employees will work only on a carrot and stick basis: neither does it believe that its employees will give of their best if earnings fluctuate from week to week. This policy is reflected in the company's wage structure which is based on measured daywork.

Every employee should, wherever reasonably practicable, have the opportunity to reach maximum earnings for his grade. Provided work is available, employees are expected to work at a mutually agreed pace. Where work is not immediately available, employees will not lose financially but will be expected to move to alternative work in order to maintain production.

Where individual targets are not maintained, and management is not responsible, an employee must expect to be counselled, disciplined if necessary and, as a last resort, dismissed.

Work measurement

The basis of the wage structure is work measurement. The company aims to use the most advanced methods available. However, it does not intend to wrap these methods in a jargon not easily understood. All production managers (including first-line supervisors) and shop stewards will attend jointly sponsored appreciation courses in order that any disagreement over standards is discussed in full knowledge of how the system works.

Indirect workers

Indirect workers such as maintenance, cleaning and catering employees play an important support role in the overall production process. It is not possible to apply work measurement techniques to indirect jobs at an economic cost. An enhanced day rate will therefore be payable to employees in this category.

Minimum earnings

No employee will receive less than £80 for a 40-hour week. This ensures that lower-paid employees are paid a 'living wage', but employees in other grades must not expect that established differentials will necessarily be maintained.

Overtime

The wage structure is designed to ensure that excessive overtime is both unnecessary and unattractive. Overtime is a requirement which will only arise in very exceptional circumstances. Since it is management's responsibility to plan work effectively and determine manning requirements, 72 hours' notice will be given of the need for overtime working, except in very exceptional circumstances.

Promotion

The company operates a policy of internal promotion, wherever possible. When a promotion takes place, the individual will immediately take the 'rate for the job'. However, if the individual is on maximum earnings for his old grade, he will retain the old rate for three months until he has established himself in the new grade.

In exceptional cases where the individual fails to maintain a satisfactory level of performance, he will be transferred to lower-grade work. He will, however, retain the higher rate until the annual negotiation of wage rates when his personal rate will be eroded.

A similar policy operates for staff promotions.

Single status

It is company policy to remove progressively all differences in employee benefits for blue- and white-collar employees. To this end, the cost of such benefits will be included in overall labour costs. The ultimate aim is to move towards a 'package' concept negotiated annually.

Share of prosperity

The company believes that employees have a right to share in the company's prosperity. It also believes that increases in its labour bill should not be passed automatically to its customers. A special formula has therefore been agreed between management and unions whereby all savings made as a result of shopfloor participation will be divided on a 50/50 basis and used to finance increased wage costs.

SALARY AND WAGE MANAGEMENT

Negotiating information

The company believes that only by providing its recognized unions with sound, factual information can a positive industrial relations climate be fostered. Agreed information will be issued quarterly to the joint negotiating panel.

CHECKLIST: CHANGING A WAGE STRUCTURE

The following checklist is intended to provide a starting point for discussion before installing a new wage structure. The list is by no means exhaustive but answering such questions should enable managers to decide the direction in which they plan to go in the short and longer term.

Company objectives

1   Apart from profit, what are you in business for?
2   Where are you going during the next two to three years; in the next five to ten years?
3   How do you plan to get there?
4   What influence will these plans have on your wage structure?
5   How can the wage structure aid the company in meeting its objectives?

Product

1   Are runs short, long, one-offs?
2   How important is quality, quantity, accuracy, consistency?
3   Is the process operator- or machine-controlled?
4   What are the capital investment plans for the next three to five years? Will these developments influence the pay policy?
5   What are the market pressures? Are there seasonal fluctuations?
6   Can buffer stocks be kept or is the product perishable?
7   How much is lost through scrap? (If the material is reconstituted, cost this.)

Work measurement

1   Are measurements loose, tight, or a mixture of both?
2   Is pay related to effort? Is this what you want anyway?
3   To what extent are you subject to wage drift, that is, increasing labour costs with little or no increase in productivity?
4   Do your supervisors and shop stewards understand the principles of work measurement?

5   Have you enough industrial engineers to ensure that three separate studies are made before each standard is decided?
6   Are your existing studies sufficiently accurate to allow you to consider the introduction of synthetic ratings?
7   How about method study?
8   Will it be necessary to employ contract work-study personnel? Or experienced industrial engineers on a short-term contract?

Wage analysis

1   How many wage rates exist?
2   Where do national agreements fit in?
3   Is there a 20 per cent differential between supervisors' pay and the average gross pay (less overtime) of those they supervise?
4   What is the budgeted labour cost for the coming year? Does it include the cost of employee benefits?
5   What is the trend of *total* labour cost for the last five years?
6   How many elements make up gross pay? How many of these do you wish to consolidate? Or bring out?
7   What is the earnings distribution for each department for two, separate, typical weeks?
8   What trends are indicated from a breakdown of overtime worked?
9   What is the cost of producing each selling line and the proportion of labour cost attributed?
10 What is the cost of labour turnover?
11 What is cost of absenteeism?

Job evaluation

1   What is the simplest possible method you could use which would satisfy the company's and the job holders' needs?
2   Should there be a joint job evaluation committee?
3   Should it be a full or part-time exercise?
4   To what extent can you involve the job holders?
5   Who should write the job description? The job holder, a job analyst or a member of the job evaluation committee?
6   How much information are you prepared to give to job holders about the scheme? Do you mean, for example, to tell each job holder the number of points allocated to his job? Could you give everyone concerned a copy of the scheme?
7   Will your existing appeals procedure match the needs of a job evaluation exercise?
8   Could you time and cost in advance the implementation of job evaluation?

SALARY AND WAGE MANAGEMENT

Financing the wage structure

1. Can you finance from within the increased cost of the new wage structure?
2. Could you negotiate initially the share-out between company and employees of any savings made?
3. How can you communicate effectively the aims of the exercise?
4. What training will you have to be undertaken?
5. How can you involve your supervisors in order that they make a major contribution to the exercise?

Social aspects

1. What is the age and sex distribution by job and department?
2. What motivates your employees? What are their aspirations? Would an attitude survey be useful?
3. What kind of image does your company have? Is it what you want?
4. What kind of incentives are people used to in your geographical locality? Would your proposals cut across the expectations of your employees? What can you do to engineer the change?
5. How do you rate your industrial relations? How can this exercise improve them?
6. What is the company's predominant management style? Will the new wage structure alter this in any way? How can you involve middle and senior management in order that they are party to the proposals?
7. What plans have you regarding such things as security of employment and earnings; single status?
8. How important is a stable work force to the company? Is it company policy to promote from the shop floor? Will the new pay structure influence or detract from this?

Designing the wage structure

1. From scattergrams of the existing situation, what anomalies exist? How many of these can you hope to get rid of first time around?
2. Using the scattergrams, how many grades ought you to have in the short term? What are you aiming for in the long term?
3. How can you involve your company accountant in order that the exercise is properly costed?
4. Is an alternative incentive planned? Do you need incentives anyway? If you do, will they be individual, group or company based? Or a combination of these?
5. What effect will the incentive element have on your products, the way you plan work, the way you manage people, employee attitudes?
6. Could you work out three possibilities for, say, a 3, 5 or 7 grade structure

complete with differentials and incentive element, if any, each coming to the total budgeted labour cost?
7   How competitive would these rates be locally?
8   What is your policy on equal pay?
9   What will your unions be expecting at the negotiating table?
10 What kind of productivity agreement do you need? To what extent can you make it a charter for the future?
11 How far can you go in giving information to your unions in order that negotiation may be constructive?
12 How will you handle pay anomalies?

Implementing a wage structure

1   How can you improve your methods of communication in order that everyone *understands* what is happening?
2   Do senior managers understand how the new pay structure might affect them? Marketing and sales, for example?
3   What training can you give to your supervisors in order that their status and respect is strengthened and not weakened by the demands of the new pay structure?
4   Is your supervisory structure adequate in relation to the needs of the new pay structure? Can you give your supervisors more scope for decision making without reference to the next level? Is their span of control about right in view of the demands which will be put on them?
5   What training should you give to shop stewards in order that they are aware of the implications of the new structure?

AUDITING THE PAY SYSTEM

Although the mechanisms already outlined provide rules and, in many cases, checks to ensure that the wage and salary systems operate correctly, there is a need for an auditing method.

The purpose of the audit should be not only to validate the accuracy of the pay process but also to provide information about the appropriateness of the systems in use. So although the salary review process incorporates a check on the pay levels in the marketplace by salary surveys and other comparisons, a sensible auditing system will complement this activity. For example, a check on the occupancy levels of various grades compared to the distribution of jobs within grades from the previous year may indicate 'grade drift' if there has been an upward migration without a change in the company structure to justify such a position.

SALARY AND WAGE MANAGEMENT

Establishing the audit process

There may be considerably more detail available and required than described in the outline below and, if this is the case, the requirements for data should increase. The critical elements of any audit are the power of the process — senior management endorsement — and the positive recommendations for change and improvement which stem from the data.

The steps in the process are as follows:

1. Appoint a senior manager to be in control of the audit process. The manager should be conversant with the process of pay and have sufficient authority to secure all the necessary information. The manager should not, however, have daily responsibility for pay otherwise the critical and distanced stance is unlikely to be achieved
2. Inform all the individuals and groups who may be involved in the process, including union or staff representatives as well as all administrators
3. Define and agree the rules. In addition to the 'accounting' rules there needs to be agreement on the approach. What is going to be audited on a given date and what is going to be reviewed over the last twelve months?
4. Locate the information required. In addition to the obvious places, information should be gathered from other sources such as management control reports
5. Collect and plot data on rates and earnings levels
6. Collect and plot information on pay-related matters, for example labour turnover, exit interview results
7. Monitor structural aspects of reward, for example membership of grades
8. Pay special attention to bonus schemes and other methods of variable reward with a particular view to changing aspects of scheme design
9. Identify interfaces with other systems and monitor the effectiveness of the system and methods in use
10. Summarize the findings in a formal report and ensure that the findings are presented and there is endorsement or rejection of the findings

The audit should be a powerful tool in keeping the salary and wage system dynamic, which is an essential element in its successful operation. The process of salary and wage management is not completed with the introduction of various systems and techniques. Monitoring and adjustment to reflect changes in the company is an integral part of the process.

FURTHER READING

A.M. Bowey (ed.), *Handbook of Salary and Wage Systems*, 2nd edition, Gower, Aldershot, 1982.

T. Lupton and A.M. Bowey, *Wages and Salaries*, 2nd edition, Gower, Aldershot, 1982.

24

Employee Benefits

Peter Mumford

It is not too long ago that an individual was paid a straight fixed amount of money for coming to work or for producing a given amount of work.

Through a variety of causes, ranging from welfare, the need to attract scarce staff, and pay policies which prevented most forms of motivational rewards an enormous range of rewards, bribes and perquisites have been developed to provide a total benefits package approach.

Whilst various governments have sought as part of their social engineering policies to create conditions of equity or to relate reward to effort, they have invariably, by taxation policies, created the circumstances where fringe benefits and perks become of increasing importance. Indeed, reading some job advertisements, one might be forgiven for thinking that the type of car provided is of greater importance than the salary.

So far as the organization is concerned, the purpose of a benefit scheme is firstly to attract the required calibre of people and secondly, to keep and motivate them to a desired level of performance at the lowest cost.

ATTRACTING STAFF

This objective appears not to be too much affected by comparatively plentiful supplies of applicants for particular jobs. Once the benefits have been established, it is extremely difficult to get rid of them unless taxation rules are so drastically changed that it becomes worth the organization's while to buy out with a particular factor, perhaps a straight salary increase.

There have been many recent instances where a company has bought out benefits which are either proving ruinously expensive to maintain or are shown to be no longer as attractive to new recruits.

However, high unemployment has meant that, except in certain specialist categories where demand still exceeds supply, there has been little need to create new forms of benefit to attract staff away from their existing jobs.

KEEPING AND MOTIVATING

Whilst Herzberg correctly postulated that salary is not a true motivator and may be a cause of dissatisfaction and demotivation, he also recognized that the reward system must be seen to be adequate before good management can get on with the job of motivating people.

Arising largely from the time when government pay policies restricted wage and salary increases, a number of elements were added to the reward package to retain and reward staff to get round the restrictions.

In addition to these, periods of high inflation eroded the value of wages and salaries to such an extent that other benefits were frequently used as a direct incentive to attract staff or assist with the rising costs of direct expenses associated with working. These included assistance with travel, higher subsidies on meals and refreshments, and clothing allowances.

To these so-called fringe benefits must be added higher levels of state provision resulting from an increased social awareness and care for individuals. Many of these, paradoxically, are not available until an individual stops working either temporarily – unemployment and sick pay, or permanently – disability or retirement pensions.

However, they do have to be paid for by both the employer and the employee and so, on the one hand, they form part of the cost of an employee and part of the cost of working to the individual. On the other hand, since the average employee is only concerned with his take-home pay, these deductions serve to increase the expectation of the size of the total reward.

Inflation has further increased the cost of providing what are now regarded as adequate pension rights and safeguarding their value in the future.

To the employer, the net result is usually an employee cost running at least 30 per cent above the nominal salary level, rising to very much higher levels for senior managers and directors.

The elements of the benefit or, as it is sometimes called, compensation package, arise from a variety of causes. Much as the work of dispensing these would be simplified if wages or salary were the only element, this is hardly likely to be attained. It is worth, therefore, examining the major factors in these packages to try and establish some comparison between their actual and assumed benefits.

BASIC SALARY

This is the main factor in any package and, in most cases, the key to all the others; for example, the type of car is frequently related to the salary band.

According to the type of job and the possibilities of enhancing performance through additional variable rewards, the basic wage or salary may represent the main element in the benefits packages or, as in the case of some sales and production workers, only a small element in it. The key issues in this balance have usually been the assumed effect that individual effort can have on performance and the ease with which that effect can be measured.

This creates many anomalies. For example, a foreman, whose performance in arranging work, repairs and maintaining good relationships can have a material effect on the output of many workers, may be paid a fixed salary whilst they can earn bonus. The foreman has to go sick to obtain tangible benefit from the fixed salary.

BENEFITS AND SALARY

Good benefits can sometimes make up for a poorly planned salary structure, but unless they are used flexibly enough to suit a variety of needs, they may exacerbate problems even more.

The offer of further benefits in attempts to overcome these feelings or to placate groups will only result in added costs. It is much sounder policy to get the basic salary anomalies ironed out and then build a series of benefit packages which meet the real needs of the employees and the organization and give a positive return on top of this. The basis for developing an effective salary policy is given in Chapter 23.

Many unions have recently recognized that so-called fringe benefits can be just as attractive to their members as straight wage increases, especially when these would create the risk of advancing into a higher tax bracket. Recent examples which have caused consternation amongst some other unions have included private health scheme membership and share schemes.

The boundaries between blue- and white-collar workers are becoming even more blurred under pressures of social change, the desire for increased status and the well publicized approaches of Japanese companies setting up local manufacturing plants. They bring with them their own concepts of equality in dress, canteens etc.

All these pressures make it even more imperative that the basic salary and wage structure are soundly based, felt to be fair and administered openly. Openness is a fairly new concept to many organizations, but where the benefits of more open styles of management are being sought, it is anomalous to preserve secrecy over the rewards for greater involvement and commitment. Resentment and jealousy are far more a product of assumption made about another person's earnings for a perceived level of work than awareness of what different scales and pay brackets mean.

It is worth noting that in local government, where salary scales are well publicized, there is little cause for comparing one individual's earnings with another. There might, of course, be discussion about how an employee was promoted to a particular salary bracket, but this is on a far smaller scale than might be the case in private industry, where frequently such matters are surrounded in secrecy and hence prime grounds for speculation.

COMPANY CAR

Chief of the benefits currently being offered is the company car. Starting from the basis of an essential tool for representatives and others who genuinely have to travel to do their jobs, the company car has developed into an essential perk for all jobs above quite a modest level and an important status symbol for middle- and senior-level managers. As such, it can become a major time waster and cause of friction among those employees who seek to get into a better car bracket, or who have more extras than the next person, or merely spend hours of work time discussing the merits of one type or another. In addition, if a car is provided it must be seen to be essential, so it has to be used with the result that many executives spend much time as drivers when they could be more productive.

Taking into account the capital, running and repair costs, as well as the savings on travel to work, a company car is probably worth an average of £5,000 pa to the recipient, a significant factor in any benefits package.

As well as the financial benefit, there is the status effect of the company car, and the subsequent two-car family which it makes possible. Since some 50 per cent of cars on the road are company owned, it is very unlikely that this item could be replaced by other forms of benefit. Certainly the level of salary increase required to provide the equivalent value would be very high and, because of this, it would undoubtedly set off a chain reaction of pay claims to restore previous differentials.

PENSIONS

Pensions represent another area where the distinction between blue- and white-collar workers is being eroded and most organizations now offer them right across the whole spectrum of employees.

Pension schemes usually impose restrictions on age and service to avoid the starting up of a multitude of small agreements with little hope of survival. This is particularly important in the light of current regulations for portability which could present major administrative problems where there is high labour turnover.

At present there are some nine million employed people who are not covered by company pension schemes. The intention is that everyone in full-time employment shall be entitled to a personal pension to which they and their employers may contribute and which may be taken with them, without loss of benefit, each time they change job.

From 2000 onwards the value of these will, to some extent, be offset against reductions in the present supplementary earnings-related pension (SERP) scheme which, because of the ageing of the population, will become an increasing burden on those who are working.

The basis of most company pension schemes is a contribution of 5-6 per cent of salary by the employee, backed by contributions of around 6-8 per cent by the employer. The pension due at retirement age is calculated at 1/60 of the final or average of three final years' salary for every year of service, with a maximum of 60 per cent. Schemes vary enormously from those to which the employee does not contribute, to 'Top-Hat' policies for senior executives and directors, giving particularly generous terms.

In education and other parts of the public service, 1/80 of final salary is more common, but the apparent meanness is offset by better index-linking arrangements. In time of high inflation these are most valuable.

The cost of pension provision is bound to increase as living standards improve, expectations are higher, retirement age falls and life expectancy increases.

LOANS AND MORTGAGES

Access to loans and mortgages at cheap or nil interest rates are a special incentive to younger staff who may be setting up home or buying the first car, and hence have good attraction power. They are more generally the province of organizations in the finance business, banks, building societies, finance houses etc., but in times of high inflation they are often used by other companies to attract staff. Local authorities will often offer these facilities also. They can, of course, have a prison effect whereby employees will be reluctant to leave because of the high cost of obtaining a new loan.

DISCOUNTS ON GOODS AND SERVICES

Discounts can be particularly valuable and attractive where the services or goods are desirable consumer products. Of particular interest are low-cost travel for airline, rail and shipping staff, and semi-luxury goods. Control must be exercised on these to prevent abuse by friends and relations of employees.

In times of full employment it was not unknown for staff to plan a progression of jobs through various organizations in order to set themselves up with possessions at substantial savings.

MEALS AND ENTERTAINMENT

It is doubtful if anyone has ever worked harder because of a good canteen or the provision of subsidized meals. However, these facilities – often provided at great cost in terms of staff and space as well as running expenses – are undoubtedly a great incentive to people to join the organization, especially where outside catering facilities may be remote or expensive.

It is at least arguable that where signs of malnutrition are reappearing in the population, because of over indulgence in junk foods, absentee and sickness costs could be reduced by the provision of attractive real food at unrefusable prices. Communal dining facilities also provide opportunities for discussion of work problems, often between staff who would not normally meet. In the case of senior managers, substantial saving of time can be achieved by use of dining rooms where visitors can be entertained rather than by taking them to expensive restaurants outside.

However, staff and works canteens, like railway sandwiches, have a reputation for poor quality which is frequently undeserved and is often caused by the behaviour of the staff rather than the quality of meals. A Tom's café arrangement in a works, serving little more imaginative than egg and chips, can enjoy a very high rating because of Tom and his staff.

It is possible for a canteen to become a negative benefit, the subject of endless niggles and involvement by personnel who would be more profitably employed on other activities. To overcome this problem one organization successfully reduced overheads by turning over the management of the canteen to the staff association. The subsidy was maintained at the prevailing level, but in all other respects the staff had total control. The benefit rapidly became tangible and, as a side issue, the staff association became more willing to appreciate the management's point of view on other issues. One leading retail organization is so convinced of the value of adequate canteen and refreshment facilities as an aid to productivity and quality that it advises and assists its suppliers to improve theirs.

The alternative, where in-house facilities cannot be provided or the attractions outside are too great, is to provide luncheon vouchers. Whilst the amount is limited by tax rules, they do provide a small incentive when recruiting and help to encourage staff to eat at lunch time, with consequent health benefits.

Entertainment as a specific benefit is usually confined to executives, but attractions such as subsidized social clubs could also be considered under this heading. With increased varieties of entertainment available elsewhere, however, the attractions of sports and social clubs have diminished. It is likely that a comparatively small number of staff will use the facilities, and therefore the cost will be high in terms of the returns.

As a by-product of publicity and advertising activities, many executives and even in some cases the whole of the staff, are able to benefit from sponsorship of sporting or cultural activities. The provision of hospitality at major sporting and social events, membership fees for golf and other clubs, are all seen as legitimate business activities and an attraction and incentive to the users.

GIFTS AND SPECIAL BONUSES

These often represent a carry-over from the days of paternalism, but many organizations still use gifts or bonuses in cash or kind, as a means of maintaining good relations, rewarding special efforts or expressing general goodwill, for example the case of wine at Christmas. In sales and marketing departments it is quite common to find events such as 'salesman of the year' which are rewarded by gifts, a special bonus or holidays. An underlying, but frequently very powerful motivator, is the fact that by involving wives and families in the largesse and rewards, they will exert pressure for, or accept the penalties of additional efforts.

Cash bonuses, paid at regular intervals, should ideally relate to the profitability of an organization, otherwise they are taken for granted and may cause illwill if for any reason they have to be omitted or reduced on occasion.

HEALTH INSURANCE

The NHS is fine for emergencies, but in many areas non-acute treatment can be protracted, involving long waits to see specialists or for admission. Private medical care, therefore, has become an increasing attraction both to the recipient who can obtain speedy treatment by the desired specialist and also to the organization in terms of recruitment and perhaps, more important, earlier return to fitness by key staff.

If the organization does not want, or is unable, to carry the cost itself, the formation of a group scheme provides substantial savings to staff who participate. The negotiation of this benefit for all their members by a trade union was at once a measure of the progress of equality and a source of annoyance to other unions.

In terms of the growth of a more prosperous, less socially divisive workforce, it is undoubtedly a move to be encouraged by managements.

SABBATICALS

Although the concept of sabbaticals has been part of the academic scene for a very long time, they are an innovation for industry and commerce and may take many forms. The traditional one is a period of leave in which to study something related to the individual's job or development and/or the needs of the organization.

It may also be used as a reward or period of recovery from an exceptionally demanding or valuable piece of work, or even as a privilege to recognize rank. In some cases the sabbatical has already progressed through these stages to become an extra period of leave after a given length of service which can be aggregated over several years and used for almost any purpose, such as an extended trip abroad.

One leading organization has used the concept, if not the title, to combine a number of benefits to extend the interests of an individual, perhaps in preparation for retirement, to meet the organization's social or community objectives and to reduce an excess of staff at particular levels, caused by changes in the structure.

Whilst retaining full salary, the individual works for the charity, community project or other activity seen to be socially desirable by them and their organization.

A few companies are recognizing the benefits of staff exchanges with, for instance, the services, police, education or government departments. An extension of this idea which could be particularly valuable would be an exchange between supplier and retailer or customer.

TRAINING AND DEVELOPMENT

Although this subject will be developed more widely in Chapter 29, the benefits to be gained by both trainees and the organization from a properly designed training and development programme are difficult to overestimate.

Whilst there is always the risk that a person who has received expensive training may seek the opportunity to exploit these abilities elsewhere, there is a great benefit to the organization not only to have the skills available, but no less important, to ensure that it makes effective use of the staff it has trained and so retain their services.

Some companies have set up open learning centres where staff may study, especially through CAL programs, courses which are nothing to do with, and far exceed, the companies' expected needs. They believe this provision acts as a powerful motivator, a generator of goodwill and togetherness in the organization.

SHARE OWNERSHIP

This has been hailed by many as the cream of benefits, giving all employees a stake in their organization and its success. It is assumed that commitment and dedication will increase as a result. Government backing has been given to these schemes through tax relief and there are now some 2500 in British industry, with a further 1000 odd profit-sharing or savings-related share schemes.

They will be given a great boost when further proposals to allow a proportion of earnings related to company profitability to be tax free are accepted. The ultimate in owner schemes is represented by British Freight and the Baxendale Company where employees are owners of the whole company, either as a result of a buyout or by gift. In both cases results justify all the claims made for the system.

But what will happen when profit share forms a major component of earnings and the organization has a bad year? This may well be in spite of the best efforts of the staff and could result in frustration and large pay claims to restore the level of earnings at a time when the organization is least able to support increased costs.

The following conditions must prevail in order for these schemes to be successful:

1 The organization must be well managed and forward thinking
2 There must be good relationships
3 Staff must be able to have a material influence on results
4 Results should not fluctuate too widely from year to year
5 Staff should be trained to interpret results
6 Staff should be committed and informed

As a subdivision of employee shareholding schemes there are executive share options. This is perhaps the fastest growing area and is now seen as an essential element in attracting high calibre senior executives.

Against the enthusiasm for share participation it must also be admitted that a recent survey by the wider Share Ownership Council is at least open to the interpretation of a less than fully enthusiastic response to the value of such schemes.

KEEPING UP TO DATE

As needs and fashions change, it is essential to review the benefits package so that its cost brings the best return in terms of increased peformance, attraction of staff, length of service, commitment to organizational aims, reduction in disputes or whatever the objectives of the policy are.

When reviewing its benefits policy, an organization should take the preferences of staff into account through individual consultation, through negotiation with employee representatives or by opinion surveys. Whilst there is no point in increasing costs unnecessarily, a company which is aware of the needs and aspirations of its employees will be able to be proactive and gain much goodwill, rather than have to react under pressure and be perceived as old-fashioned or mean – a reputation which can be gained at very great expense.

Some preferences expressed by groups of employees might appear to be predictable – young employees would be less concerned with pension benefits than older ones who are nearer to retirement age. A recent survey in a large retail organization showed very definite preferences by staff for various types of benefits. The overall order of preferences was:

1 Pension scheme
2 Profit share scheme + Christmas bonus
4 Staff discount
5 Private health scheme
6 Commission
7 Staff canteen
8 Extra holiday entitlement
9 Clothing allowance
10 Mortgage assistance
11 Free hairdressing
12 Interest free credit + Free uniform
14 Luncheon vouchers
15 Long service award
16 Extra sickness leave
17 Company car
18 Time off for study
19 Businesswear discount scheme
20 Personal loans
21 Holiday discount scheme
22 Relocation assistance
23 Subsidized chiropody service
24 Sports facilities
25 Social club
26 Season ticket loan

It is interesting that in the case of the first choice, the percentage of staff opting for this varied according to age. Also worthy of note is the high preference expressed for commission as opposed to higher salaries:

Age group	Percentage
16-30	67
30-45	100
45-55	100
55+	71

This survey was carried out in a store where most of the staff lived within reasonable travelling distance. It is likely that for a London-based organization, the twenty-sixth choice, season ticket loan, would have been much higher up the scale.

These factors confirm the need to investigate which items are going to be voted most valuable by recipients, and hence more likely to represent value for money for the organization.

In structuring the benefits package it is also important to ensure that there is no discrimination on account of race, sex etc. Following a recent European Court ruling, differences in retirement ages and pension benefits between men and women will probably be eroded, allowing either sex greater freedom of choice in the matter.

Statistics indicate greater longevity for women than men and a strong correlation between longevity and the age of retirement. It would seem logical, therefore, to reduce the minimum retirement age for men rather than increasing the age for women. A number of organizations have already lowered the normal retirement age to sixty-three. Such moves will have important implications for the cost of funding pensions which will be likely to start earlier and go on longer.

The subject of benefits has become such a complicated and important area of personnel management that many companies have set up separate employee compensation or benefits package departments. This brief insight should indicate that opportunities exist for both the organization and its employees to gain significant benefit from the costs which can be involved. Conversely, unless those benefits are applied with discretion and are well thought out and planned, they can become just a drain on profits for very small return.

FURTHER READING

A. Bowey (ed.), *Handbook of Salary and Wage Systems*, 2nd edition, Gower, Aldershot, 1982.

G. Copeman, *Planning Employee Share Schemes*, Report of a conference on choosing right incentives, Gower, Aldershot, 1981.

G. Copeman, P. Moore and A. Arrowsmith, *Shared Ownership*, Gower, Aldershot, 1984.

F. Green, *Unequal Fringes: Fringe Benefits in UK*, Bedford Square Press, 1984.

D. Lock and N. Farrow (eds.) *The Gower Handbook of Management*, 2nd edition, Gower, Aldershot, 1988.

T. Lupton and A. Bowey, *Pay and Benefits*, CCH editions, 1985.

I. Smith, *The Management of Remuneration: Paying for Effectiveness*, IPM/Gower, Aldershot, 1983.

25

National Insurance

Information Division,
Department of Health and Social Security

Britain's social services grew up piecemeal and it was not until the 1940s that the various schemes were reviewed by a committee under the chairmanship of the late Lord (then Sir William) Beveridge and remodelled on the recommendations contained in his report. The present social security schemes have, therefore, existed only since the end of the Second World War. The present unified system began in 1948 — the National Insurance Act 1946 unified all state insurance and improved the benefits; the National Insurance (Industrial Injuries) Act 1946 replaced the old system of workmen's compensation; the National Health Service Act 1946 created a medical service for all which was reorganized into its present form in 1974.

Since 1948 the schemes have undergone considerable modification and extension in the light of experience. In 1961 a graduated addition to flat-rate retirement pension was introduced and in October 1966 a system of earnings-related supplements to employment and sickness benefit and widow's allowance began.

In September 1971, more favourable rates of payment for the chronic sick were introduced. An attendance allowance for severely disabled people was introduced in December 1971.

The Social Security Act 1975 introduced, from 6 April 1975, a new system of national insurance contributions to replace the previous system of flat-rate and graduated contributions. From 6 April 1975, Class 1 contributions are related to the employee's earnings and are collected with PAYE income tax, instead of by affixing stamps to a card. Class 2 and Class 3 contributions remain flat-rate, but, in addition to Class 2 contributions, those who are self-employed may be liable to pay Class 4 contributions on profits or gains between certain figures, which are assessable for income tax under Schedule D. Class 3 contributions are voluntary and may be paid only to secure entitlement to certain benefits.

Under the Social Security Pensions Act 1975, rights to additional (earnings-related) retirement, widows' and invalidity pensions began to build up from 6 April 1978. Employees who are members of an occupational pension scheme which meets the necessary requirements can be contracted-out of the additional pension for retirement and part of the additional pension for widowhood. Where this happens they and their employer pay a lower rate of contributions to the state scheme.

In August 1966 a new Ministry of Social Security was set up to administer the existing schemes of national insurance, industrial injuries, family allowances and war pensions. The Ministry also became responsible for a new scheme of supplementary benefits and the National Assistance Board was abolished. On 1 November 1968 the former Ministries of Social Security and Health were merged to form the Department of Health and Social Security.

Cost of the health and personal social services. The total cost of health and personal social services in Great Britain in 1986-7 will amount to over £22 694m, most of which is met from general taxation. The separate national health service contribution is estimated to produce about £2190m in 1986-87 (in Great Britain). Other sources of income are local rates for personal social services and health service charges for such things as prescriptions, spectacles, dentures and dental treatment.

Administration. To provide people with ready access, the nation's social security benefits are at present administered by 491 local offices of the Department of Health and Social Security grouped for control under six regional offices in England and Wales with a central office for Scotland, with a controller in charge of each. The local offices deal with claims for benefit and give advice on social security problems.

Unemployment benefit offices are run by the Department of Employment which acts as agent of the Department for the payment of unemployment benefit.

A central office at Newcastle houses the central records of British social insurance. Within the central office a records branch contains social security details of every contributor. Before 6 April 1975, cards bearing stamps or other details of the flat-rate contributions were sent in annually for clerical recording on record sheets. Graduated contributions were collected with PAYE income tax on the deduction card and recorded in a computer system. From 6 April 1975 earnings-related Class 1 contributions are similarly collected with PAYE income tax, on deduction cards, which are forwarded

NATIONAL INSURANCE

at the end of each income-tax year by the employer. These contributions are recorded by a highly mechanized system using magnetic tape and microfilm and are stored in a computer — Class 2 and Class 3 contributions are still collected by means of stamped cards or by direct debit of a bank or National Giro account, but the contributions are recorded in the computer.

WHO IS COVERED BY THE SCHEMES?

National insurance extends to practically the whole population aged 16 or over and under pension age. Arrangements are made for children reaching school-leaving age to be allocated a national insurance number. Persons over school-leaving age are liable for contributions where they are employed and their earnings reach the lower earnings limit of £39.00 (1987/88) or are self-employed. If they are non-employed they can pay contributions voluntarily, to establish entitlement to certain benefits. An employer also pays contributions once an employee's earnings reach the lower earnings limit of £39.00 (87/88). The State supplements the contributions paid by employees and employers, from general taxation. Contributions and supplement together with interest on investments form the income of the National Insurance Fund from which benefits are paid. There are four classes of contributions:

Class 1. (Payable by employed earners and their employers.) Employed earners are:

1   Persons gainfully employed in Great Britain under a contract of service or in an office (including elective office) with emoluments chargeable to income tax under Schedule E
2   Certain persons who are treated as employed earners by the regulations; this includes anyone who is employed:
    (*a*) As an office cleaner or in any similar capacity
    (*b*) Through an agency where the agency has a continuing financial interest in the employment and the person supplied to do the work renders or is under obligation to render personal service and is subject to supervision, direction or control or to the right of supervision, direction or control in the manner of the rendering of the service
    (*c*) For the purpose of trade or business by his or her spouse
    (*d*) Lecturers. teachers and instructors
    (*e*) Certain ministers of religion

A company director, being an office holder, is included in the category of 'employed earners' where his emoluments are chargeable to tax under Schedule E.

Class 2. (Payable by self-employed earners.) A self-employed earner is one gainfully employed otherwise than as an employed earner whether or not he is also an employed earner in relation to some other employment.

Class 3. Payable voluntarily by non-employed persons and others for the purpose of providing entitlement to certain benefits.

Class 4. Payable by the self-employed in respect of a limited range of profits or gains taxable under Case I or II of Schedule D.

NATIONAL INSURANCE CONTRIBUTIONS FOR EMPLOYEES

National insurance contributions for employees are related to their earnings and are collected under the income-tax PAYE procedure. They are payable, whether or not the employee actually works during a week, if earnings are paid, e.g. during sickness.

Employee's contributions are at one of three rates:

1 Standard rate payable by most employees
2 Reduced rate payable by certain married women and most widows entitled to national insurance widow's benefit
3 Nil rate where the employee is over pension age (65 for a man and 60 for a woman). In such cases, only the employer's contribution at the non-contracted-out rate is payable

From 6 October 1985 changes were made to the assessment of national insurance contributions. The main changes were the abolition of the upper earnings limit for employers' contributions and the introduction of several lower percentage rates of contributions for low-paid earners and their employers. The percentage rate payable depends on the 'earnings bracket' in which the total earnings fall. Figure 25.1 shows the rates and earnings brackets for the 87/88 tax year.

Earnings limits 1987/88

Weekly lower limit	£38.00
Weekly upper limit	£285.00
Monthly lower limit	£164.62
Monthly upper limit	£1235.00
Annual lower limit	£1976.04
Annual upper limit	£14820.00

Table C of the Contracted-out Tables (CF392) is for use only in cases where the employer holds form RD950 in respect of *contracted-out* employment.

NATIONAL INSURANCE

Not contracted-out employment

Total earnings	Employee		Employer
	Standard	Reduced	
£ 39.00 to £ 64.99 weekly or £ 169.00 to £ 281.99 monthly or £2028.00 to £ 3379.99 yearly	5%	3.85%	5%
£ 65.00 to £ 99.99 weekly or £ 282.00 to £ 433.99 monthly or £3380.00 to £ 5199.99 yearly	7%	3.85%	7%
£ 100.00 to £ 149.99 weekly or £ 434.00 to £ 649.99 monthly or £5200.00 to £ 7799.99 yearly	9%	3.85%	9%
£ 150.00 to £ 295.00 weekly or £ 650.00 to £ 1279.00 monthly or £7800.00 to £15340.00 yearly	9%	3.85%	10.45%
over £ 295.00 weekly* or over £ 1279.00 monthly or over £15340.99 yearly	9% of £295.00 or equivalent	3.85% of £295.00 or equivalent	10.45%

Contracted-out employment

Total earnings	Employee				Employer	
	On first £39.00 or equivalent		On earnings over £39.00 or equivalent		On first £39.00 or equivalent	On earnings over £39.00 or equivalent
	Standard	Reduced	Standard	Reduced		
£ 39.00 to £ 64.99 weekly or £ 169.00 to £ 281.99 monthly or £2028.00 to £ 3379.99 yearly	5%	3.85%	2.85%	3.85%	5%	0.9%
£ 65.00 to £ 99.99 weekly or £ 282.00 to £ 433.99 monthly or £3380.00 to £ 5199.99 yearly	7%	3.85%	4.85%	3.85%	7%	2.9%
£ 100.00 to £ 149.99 weekly or £ 434.00 to £ 649.99 monthly or £5200.00 to £ 7799.99 yearly	9%	3.85%	6.85%	3.85%	9%	4.9%
£ 150.00 to £ 295.00 weekly or £ 650.00 to £ 1279.00 monthly or £7800.00 to £15340.00 yearly	9%	3.85%	6.85%	3.85%	10.45%	6.35%
over £ 295.00 weekly* or over £ 1279.00 monthly or over £15340.99 yearly	9%	3.85%	6.85% up to £295.00 or equivalent	3.85% up to £295.00 or equivalent	10.45%	6.35% up to £295.00 or equivalent and 10.45% thereafter

*Employees do not pay contributions on any earnings over £295.00 a week or the monthly or yearly equivalent

Figure 25.1 Rates and earnings brackets for 1987/88

*Table C of the not contracted out tables (CF391) should be used (*a*) for *all* employees who have reached age 65 (60) and (*b*) where the employer holds form RD950 in respect of a *non-contracted-out* employment.

(Where the employee is age 65 (60) and not contracted-out Table C must be used.)

Surcharge exempt rates were abolished on 1 October 1984.

Special groups

Married women and widows. The Social Security Pensions Act 1975 abolished the right of married women and certain widows to make a fresh choice of reduced contribution liability although in general a woman may continue to have reduced liability if on 11 May 1977 she already had such liability. Reduced liability will automatically come to an end, however, if throughout two consecutive tax years after 5 April 1978 the woman is neither liable to pay Class 1 contributions nor self-employed.

Persons over pension age. Persons over pension age (65 for a man and 60 for a woman) are not liable for contributions. An employee who is over pension age should obtain a certificate of age exemption to give to his employer.

Calculation of Class 1 contributions

Class 1 contributions are always calculated on gross pay. Normally this will be the same as the amount of pay entered on the deductions working sheet for income-tax purposes. But where a net pay scheme is operated for tax purposes, national insurance contributions should still be calculated on the gross pay. Details of what should and should not be included in gross pay figures are given in the *Employer's Guide to Pay As You Earn* (P7) and in the *Employer's Guide to National Insurance Contributions* (Leaflet NP15).

The contribution payable depends on the date the payment of earnings is made (not the period over which it was earned) and the length of the shortest regular earnings period. If the employee is regularly paid weekly, the earnings period is a week; or if monthly, a month. If an employee works for more than one employer then contributions are payable in each employment, but there are provisions which enable the employee to obtain a refund of contributions paid in excess of a prescribed annual maximum. The employer's contributions, however, are not refundable.

The employer is responsible in the first instance for meeting the whole cost of the contribution payable by himself and the employee. The employer may recover the employee's contributions provided he deducts it from wages or salary at the time the wages are paid. Where, however, an under-deduction is made he may recover such underpayments during the current tax year so long as the total deduction is not more than twice that which would normally be made from that payment of wages.

An employer may calculate contributions either (*a*) exactly by applying the

NATIONAL INSURANCE

prescribed percentages (see Figure 25.1), or (*b*) by reference to contribution tables supplied by the Department of Health and Social Security. He may use only one method for any employee during a tax year, unless otherwise authorized.

Contracting-out. Employees who are members of occupational pension schemes which meet specific requirements can be contracted-out by their employers of the additional part of the retirement pension and the additional part of widow's pension. Once earnings reach or exceed the lower earnings limit, employees and their employers are liable for contributions at the appropriate standard rate on earnings up to and including the lower earnings limit, plus a lower rate of contributions on earnings between the lower and upper earnings limits. The employer is also liable for contributions on all of the earnings above the employee's upper earnings limit because the upper earnings limit for *employers* was abolished on 1 October 1985.

Exact calculation. An employer who uses this method must calculate the employee's contributions separately from his own, and round each calculation to the nearest penny (£0.01), ½p being rounded down.

Contribution tables. Tables are provided covering earning periods of one week and one month. There are five main tables, each bearing its own distinct category letter.

Not-contracted-out
    Table A is for use where the employee is liable for standard-rate contributions
    Table B is for use where the employee is liable for reduced-rate contributions
    Table C is for use where the employee is not liable and only the employer's contributions are payable

Contracted-out
    Table D is for use where the employee is liable for standard-rate contributions
    Table E is for use where the employee is liable for reduced-rate contributions
    Table C is for use where the employee is not liable and only the employer's contributions are payable

Instructions on the calculation of national insurance contributions and use of the tables are given in leaflet NP15 and on form P8 (Blue Card).

Recording national insurance contributions (NIC)

A record must be kept of NIC and statutory sick pay (SSP) and Statutory maternity pay (SMP) each time an employee is paid. If you use the official Deductions Working Sheet P11 (87) a separate sheet should be used for each employee and the items you need to record in respect of NIC are:

> The contribution table letter in use and any subsequent change of table letter
> The earnings on which employees contributions are payable
> The total of employee's and employer's NIC
> The total of employee's NIC
> The earnings on which employees contributions at the contracted out rate are payable (only when you use table letter D)
> The part of the employee's NIC paid at the contracted-out rate (only when you are using table letter *D*)
> Statutory sick pay
> Statutory Maternity Pay

If you use a computer to record NIC an end-of-year return must be submitted on magnetic tape for each employee. A more detailed instruction on the ways of recording NIC is given in leaflet NP15 issued in April 1987.

Monthly payment to Inland Revenue Accounts Office

Within fourteen days of the end of each tax month, the employer must pay to the Inland Revenue the total of the employer's and employee's NIC deducted during that month. The employer can deduct from the NIC any statutory sick pay and/or any statutory maternity pay paid to the employees during that month (or earlier months if not yet recovered) plus an amount to compensate for the NIC he has paid on the SSP and/or SMP. The Collector of Taxes (Accounts Office) will send the employer a payslip booklet P30CB(Z) to enable him to make monthly payments. Tax and NIC can be paid on one payslip provided they are recorded separately. A more detailed explanation of recovering SSP and NIC compensation can be found in leaflet NI227 Statutory Sick Pay issued in October 1985.

At the end of the tax year

At the end of the tax year the employer should ensure that every P14 (end-of-year return) shows, where possible, the employee's NI number, surname and first two forenames, sex, date of birth and address. The totals from columns 1*a*, 1*b*, 1*c* 1*d*, and 1*e* of the P11 (87) should be transferred to a P14 and a separate total should be shown in respect of each contribution table letter if there has been a change in the year. If no contributions have been paid throughout the tax year use letter 'X' to denote this. Send parts 1 and 11 of

NATIONAL INSURANCE

the P14 (bundled separately) to the Inspector of Taxes together with the completed form P35 (employer's annual statement). The balance of any tax and NIC due should be sent with a payslip to the Collector of Taxes (Accounts Office). Leaflets NP15 April 1987 give full details of the end-of-year procedure.

Form P60. The employer is required to give every employee for whom he holds a deductions working sheet, a certificate of pay and tax deduction (form P60 or P60 substitute) after the end of the income-tax year. Any statutory sick pay and/or statutory maternity pay paid to the employee can also be recorded on the P60.

National insurance numbers

The Department of Health and Social Security allocates national insurance numbers to all contributors. Generally, young people will have a national insurance number allocated to them on reaching school-leaving age and will be given a national insurance number card. Anyone who has not been given a number must, when he comes liable for contributions or wishes to pay Class 3 voluntarily, apply to the local social security office.

Employers should ask any new employee for his national insurance number. If he does not know it, he should be told to apply to his local social security office. New employees changing jobs will normally produce a form P45 on which his national insurance number should have been entered by his previous employer.

If an employer is unable to obtain the national insurance number of a new employee, he should not delay sending form P46 to his Inspector of Taxes, who will endeavour to trace the number from his records or from Department of Health and Social Security records. *It is essential that the correct national insurance number is obtained and entered on all deduction cards for employees so that the contributions can be posted to the employees' accounts in the computer.*

Company directors

Prior to April 1975, generally only those company directors employed under a contract of service were in Class 1 employment. From April 1975, liability for Class 1 contributions extends to all company directors whose emoluments are chargeable to tax under Schedule E. All directors have an annual earnings period from 6 April 1983. Details of how to work out NIC for company directors are shown in leaflet NI35 obtainable from your local social security office.

National insurance contributions for self-employed persons

Class 2 contributions payable by self-employed earners are at a flat rate. The rate for 1987/88 is £3.85 and contributions may be paid either by means of a stamped card or by direct debit of a bank or National Giro account.

Those whose earnings from self-employment are expected to be less than £2125 a year (rate current during 1987/8) may apply for exemption from liability to pay Class 2 contributions. Married women and certain widows who are self-employed and currently have reduced contribution liability do not have to pay Class 2 contributions.

Class 4 contributions are payable (in addition to the flat-rate Class 2 contributions) by self-employed persons at the rate of 6.3 per cent of annual profits or gains between £45.95 and £15 340 (1987/88) which are assessable to tax under Case I or Case II of Schedule D. The contributions, which are generally collected along with Schedule D tax, do not attract benefit.

People who have two or more jobs at the same time

A person who derives his earnings partly from employment and partly from self-employment is liable for both Class 1 and Class 2 (and, where appropriate, Class 4) contributions. Similarly, where a person has more than one employer, Class 1 contributions are due in respect of each employment in which the lower earnings limit is reached in any given pay period. If he pays more than a specified amount during a tax year, the excess if over £19.50 (87/88) will be refunded automatically by the DHSS.* Where he has a Class 1 contribution liability, he may apply to have any Class 2 and Class 4 liability deferred until after the end of the tax year so as to avoid any unnecessary refund action.

Payment of Class 3 contributions

Married women and certain widows who have reduced rate contribution liability cannot pay Class 3 contributions.

Class 3 (voluntary) contributions are at the flat rate of £3.75 (1987/88) a week. They may be paid on a regular basis in a similar way to Class 2 contributions, by stamped card or direct debit. Or they may be paid by an employed person who wishes to make up his record for entitlement to certain benefits, in which case payment may be by remittance after the end of the year.

BENEFITS

	28 July 1986 to April 1987
Sickness benefit under pension age	£29.45 a week†
over pension age	£37.05 a week†

*Smaller refunds of £1.77 or more can be made if applied for.
†Increases of benefit are payable in addition for dependants

NATIONAL INSURANCE

28 July 1986 to April 1987

Invalidity benefit	
Basic invalidity pension	£38.70 a week*
Invalidity allowance:	
— higher rate	£8.15 a week
— middle rate	£5.20 a week
— lower rate	£2.60 a week
Unemployment benefit under	
pension age	£30.80 a week*
over pension age	£38.70 a week*
Maternity benefit	
Maternity grant	£25.00
Maternity allowance	£29.45 a week* (18 weeks)
Widow's benefit	
Widow's allowance	£54.20 a week*
Basic widowed mother's allowance	£38.70 a week*
Basic widow's pension	£38.70 a week*
Basic retirement pension on own	
insurance	£38.70 a week*
Retirement pension on husband's	
insurance	£23.25 a week
Non-contributory retirement pension	
for people over 80	
(i) Man, single woman, widow	£23.25 a week
(ii) Married woman	£13.90 a week
Child's special allowance	£8.05 a week for each child
Death grant	£30.00 (adult)
Guardian's allowance	£8.05 a week (plus child benefit)
Child benefit	£7.10 a week
Age addition payable with pension of	
those over 80	25p a week

Flat-rate sickness benefit

Flat-rate sickness benefit is payable for up to twenty-eight weeks to insured people who are incapable of work because of illness.

Men and women normally receive £29.45 (from 31 July 1986) a week standard benefit plus £18.20 for one adult dependant.

If the illness continues beyond twenty-eight weeks, sickness benefit is then replaced by invalidity benefit, which consists of an invalidity pension made up of a basic pension, an additional pension based on earnings from 6 April 1978, increases for dependants on a par with those for retirement pensioners,

*Increases of benefit are payable in addition for dependants

and an invalidity allowance payable at one of three rates depending on the person's age when his illness began. Invalidity allowance is not payable to men whose illness began at age 60 or over (55 in the case of women).

When and how to claim sickness or invalidity benefit depends on whether the claimant is working for an employer when he or she falls sick. If he or she works for an employer the employer will generally pay SSP fo periods of illness. Sickness or invalidity benefit cannot be paid for days for which there is entitlement to SSP. If the employer finds that no SSP is payable he will give the employee a form on which to claim sickness or invalidity benefit instead. Fill in the form at once and send it to the local social security office together with any doctor's statements (often referred to as sick notes). Claim quickly otherwise benefit may be lost.

If the claimant is self-employed, unemployed or non-employed claim on form SC1 which can be obtained from doctor's surgeries, a hospital or a local social security office. Doctors do not issue sick notes for the first week of illness so form SC1 is treated as evidence of incapacity for the first week. If illness continues after the first week the claimant should visit his or her doctor to obtain a sick note as evidence of continuing incapacity.

On receipt of the claim the local office have to obtain the claimant's contribution record, normally from the central records at Newcastle, to establish his entitlement to benefit. Benefit is usually paid weekly by Girocheque. The claimant should send in further doctor's statements as each one expires. There are time limits for claiming, and benefit may be lost if statements and claims are not sent in promptly. Benefit for dependants has to be claimed separately. Sickness benefit is not paid for the first three days in spells of sickness separated from each other, or from spells of unemployment, by more than eight weeks.

Maternity allowance

Statutory maternity pay (SMP) is available from employers for the first 18 weeks off work provided the woman has been employed by the same employer for at least 6 months ending in the 15th week before the expected week of confinement and her average weekly earnings in the 8 weeks leading up to that week were at or above the amount where she has to start paying National Insurance contributions. She can qualify even if she has paid the reduced rate of contribution. There are 2 rates of SMP. If she has been in the same employment for at least 2 years, or part-time for 5 years for at least 8 hours per week, she will get a higher rate of SMP which is 90% of her average earnings, for the first 6 weeks of SMP. After that, she will get the lower rate which is £32-85 for the remainder of her SMP period. If she has been in the same employment for between 6 months and 2 years, she will get the lower rate throughout the SMP period. She has to pay tax and National Insurance contributions on SMP.

NATIONAL INSURANCE

SMP can be paid for up to 18 weeks. Payment is made for a 'core period' of 13 weeks starting with the 6th week before the baby is due. She can usually choose when to take the other 5 weeks.

Women who are not entitled to SMP may qualify for maternity allowance if they have been employed or self-employed for at least 26 of the 52 weeks ending in the 15th week before the expected week of confinement. The weekly rate is £30.05 which is payable for up to 18 weeks. A woman who is still working up to the start of the 11th week before the baby is due will have the same choice of the payment period as for SMP. Maternity allowance is not taxable or subject to deductions for National Insurance.

A woman wishing to receive SMP or claim MA should obtain a maternity certificate (form Mat B1) from her doctor or midwife between the 14th and 11th weeks before the week in which her baby is expected, even if she intends to continue working for a time. If she does not have an employer, she should send the certificate to her local office of the Department of Health and Social Security with a claim form MA1. If she has an employer but is not entitled to SMP, she should also enclose form SMP1 from her employer.

Unemployment benefit

Unemployment benefit is payable to those who become unemployed through no fault of their own and are capable of and available for further employment. The contribution and other conditions are set out in Leaflet NI12 on Unemployment Benefit which is available from unemployment benefit offices. Only Class 1 contributions count for unemployment benefit which is payable for a maximum of 312 days (a year, excluding Sundays) in a period of interruption of employment. Claims for benefit should be made on the first day of unemployment at the nearest unemployment benefit office.

For unemployment benefit (see under sickness benefit) Class 1 contributions must have been paid or credited (for weeks of sickness or unemployment) on earnings of at least 50 times the lower earnings limit for contributions in the relevant tax year — that is, the last complete tax year ending before the benefit year (starting on the first Sunday in January each year) in which the period of interruption of employment starts.

There are special conditions for certain categories of people: seasonal workers, share fishermen, students, and occupational pensioners over age 60. Relevant leaflets are available at unemployment benefit offices.

Retirement pension

If the contribution conditions are fully satisfied, a basic pension of £39.50 a week (as from 6 April 1987) is payable from age 65 on retirement, or at age 70, whichever is the earlier (at age 60 or 65 for a woman). For a married couple, where the wife has not herself been paying standard-rate contributions, the pension is £63.25 (as from 6 April 1987). The pension is subject to an earnings rule during the first five years following minimum pension age. For pensioners reaching pension age on or after 6 April 1979, there may also be an additional (earnings-related) pension based on their earnings as employees from April 1978. This part of the pension is not affected by earnings after retirement.

Extra pension. By deferring retirement after age 65 (60 for a woman) extra pension may be earned. This is an increase of 1/7th per cent of the pension rate (ie the rate excluding increases for dependants) for every six days (excluding Sundays) for which a person has not drawn his pension or another benefit, between the ages of 65 and 70 (60 and 65 for a woman).

Graduated pension. Every £7.50 (£9 for a woman) that a man paid in graduated contributions up to 5 April 1975, when these contributions ceased, gives rise to one unit of graduated pension. Any odd half unit or more in the final total counts as a whole unit.

Up to 5 April 1987 each unit was worth 5.06p; from 6 April 1987 it rose to 5.17p. The value of the units will be increased at the time of future general benefit upratings.

Industrial injuries

After 30 July 1986

Disablement benefit (payable at the end of the injury benefit period and depending on the degree of the disablement)	
Ranging from 100 per cent to 20 per cent after a period of 15 weeks (90 days) has elapsed since the date of the accident or 90 days from the first day you were disabled by the disease and	£63.20 a week (£38.70 aged under 18 with no entitlement to dependency benefit) £12.64 a week (£7.74 under 18 with no entitlement to dependency benefit)
Gratuities of up to £4200 for 19 per cent are payable for assessments below 20 per cent	

Additional allowances are payable with disablement benefit where because of the accident or the prescribed disease the person is unable to follow his regular occupation, requires constant attendance, is exceptionally severely disabled, is unemployable or requires hospital treatment. Additions are payable for dependants with unemployability supplement.

Industrial death benefit

Death benefit (payable for dependants of the deceased where death results from an industrial accident or a prescribed disease).

Widows:

	From 6 April 1987
First 26 weeks of widowhood	£55.35 a week
Thereafter, higher permanent rate	£40.05 a week
lower permanent rate	£11.85 a week

Allowances are payable for children of the deceased. For other adult dependants the benefit is a pension, allowance or gratuity according to their relationship to, and the extent to which they were maintained by, the deceased at the time of death.

Widow's benefit (if contribution conditions are satisfied)

Widowed mother's allowance — widow with qualifying children: Basic of £39.50 (as from 6 April 1987) with additional pension based on late husband's earnings from 6 April 1978

Widow's pension — widow of age 50 at date of husband's death or over age 50 when widowed mother's allowance ceases: Basic pension of £39.50 (as from 6 April 1987) with additional pension based on late husband's earnings from 6 April 1978. Widows aged 40-50 at that time are entitled to a pension with both the basic and additional pensions scaled down according to their age

Increases of widow's allowance and widowed mother's allowance are payable for dependent children.

SPECIAL DUTIES OF EMPLOYERS UNDER THE INDUSTRIAL INJURIES SCHEME

An employer is required to take reasonable steps to investigate any accident notified by or on behalf of an employee to him or his servant or agent as having arisen during the employment. If the employer is unable to reconcile the circumstances notified with those found by him, he should record the facts as found. The purpose of the requirement to investigate an accident is to ensure that the facts are confirmed by a responsible person while they are still fresh in the minds of any witnesses, so that, if a claim for benefit is made, the inquiry from the local social security office can be answered readily.

Accident book

Every owner or occupier (being an employer) of any mine or quarry or of any premises to which any of the provisions of the Factories Act 1961 applies and every employer by whom ten or more persons are normally employed at the same time on or about the same premises in connection with the employer's trade or business, is required to keep readily accessible an accident book in a form approved by the Secretary of State. Supplies of a suitable book (form B1510) can be obtained from the Stationery Office or through any bookseller.

All accident books must be preserved for three years from the date of the last entry.

The purpose of this arrangement is to facilitate the giving of notice of accidents by injured persons, and any entry in the book by an injured employee or by someone acting on his behalf is to be regarded as sufficient notice to the employer, of the accident, for the purposes of the Social Security (Claims and Payments) Regulations 1979.

POWERS OF INSPECTORS

An inspector appointed by the Secretary of State under the Acts has power to enter at all reasonable times any premises (except a private dwelling house not used for trade or business) where he has grounds for supposing that anyone is employed; and to make such examination and inquiry as may be necessary:

1 To ascertain whether the provisions of the Acts are being complied with
2 To investigate the circumstances of any industrial injury or disease giving rise to a claim for benefit

He may examine anyone found in the premises and call for the production of all documents required, to ascertain whether contributions are payable or have been payable or paid by or for any person, or whether benefit is or was payable to or for any person. He may also exercise such other powers as may be necessary for carrying the Acts into effect.

An inspector has a certificate of appointment which he must produce, if required to do so, on applying for admission to any premises. It is an offence under the Acts wilfully to delay or obstruct an inspector in the exercise of any of his powers or to refuse or neglect to answer any question, furnish any information or produce any document when required to do so.

The powers of inspectors, as broadly defined above, are retained by the Social Security Act 1975 which came into effect on 6 April 1975.

SOURCES OF INFORMATION

The administrative headquarters of the Department in London consist of a number of separate divisions each responsible for a particular section of the social security schemes and arrangements. On the social security side, the day-to-day administration of social security benefits is exercised through a network of about 500 local offices under the control of ten regional offices with central offices for Scotland and Wales.

Any employer who is in doubt about the social security provisions should consult the local social security office for advice. The address of the local office is obtainable from any post office or telephone directory.

The Department publishes a range of over 100 detailed leaflets and there are a number of posters designed for display on employers' notice boards.

Calculating earnings-related contributions

The employee's and the employer's contribution is read off from the appropriate contribution table: Category A, standard-rate basic contribution; Category B, reduced rate basic contributions; or Category C, employer's contributions only. Contributions are payable on all earnings, provided at least £38.00 a week is earned, up to £285. For other earnings periods multiply the weekly or monthly lower and upper earnings limits and earnings brackets by the number of weeks/months in the earnings period. If the exact gross pay figure is not shown on the tables, the next smaller figure should be used. (For information on earnings periods, etc., see leaflet NP15.)

It is the employer's responsibility to pay both his and the employee's contributions but he may deduct the employee's contributions from his pay.

Precise calculations

Employers may calculate earnings-related contributions on the basis of exact percentages instead of using the tables. See 'Payment of earnings-related contributions', above.

Entry of the PAYE deduction card. The final contribution must be rounded to the nearest penny (£0.01), except where the employer, as he is entitled to do, has already rounded the separate elements before addition. If either method of rounding produces a figure greater than is specified in the appropriate contribution table, the figure shown in the table is the one payable.

How to use the tables

Find in the first column of the table, the gross pay figure for the income-tax week or month (as entered on the PAYE deductions working sheet P11 (87)), or, if the exact gross pay figure is not shown in the table, the next smaller figure shown. Then read off from the table the corresponding contribution figures. The amount of the employee's contribution is to be entered in column 1(b) of the P11 (87). The total of the employer's and the employee's contribution is also entered on the P11 (87) at column 1(a).

The amount of the employee's contribution paid at the contracted-out rate on earnings lying between the lower and upper earnings limits should be entered in column 1(c) (an entry in this column is required only in Table D cases). This information is required so that the employee's benefit can be calculated where the contribution is paid at a mixed rate; and for calculation of the guaranteed minimum pension and any contributor's equivalent premium that may become payable.

26

Administering Redundancy

Peter Mumford

The Redundancy Payments Act, which set out to assist employees who were dismissed because of redundancy, came into force in 1965. Since then, many hundreds of thousands of people have been affected by redundancy situations.

No reliable or comprehensive figures for the numbers involved seem to be available. The Department of Employment, which is the responsible ministry having incorporated the 1965 Act into the Protection of Employment (Consolidation) Act 1978, maintains several sets of figures:

1. Records of notifications of impending redundancies — these do not include cases where less than ten workers are to be dismissed. Nor will all the anticipated redundancies actually take place
2. Records maintained by local employment offices following up statutory notifications with the employers concerned. They are more reliable than the original notifications, but still do not include cases where less than ten are dismissed at one time
3. Finally, the department maintains records of the number of claims for payment. There is a very marked difference, however, between these figures and the others because people under twenty, or with less than two years' service, do not qualify

This situation is often compounded by 'last in, first out' policies which ensure that those with less than two years' service are first to go again. There are, therefore, in the total figures many who have suffered multiple redundancies.

January 1981	Statutory notifications 120 349	Confirmed redundancies Employment office figures 41 300	Redundancy payments 52 348

	Confirmed redundancies all industries	
1984	237 343	
1985	227 328	
January 1986	14 282	(provisional)
February 1986	11 770	(provisional)

Figure 26.1 Redundancy statistics

Some statistics

Officially or unofficially recorded according to the Act, first time or 'Oh God, not again', the total presents a massive pattern of industrial change and disturbance. Even more it represents enforced change on the lives of the people directly affected and also their families and associates.

Redundancy, however recorded, is a major factor in current society and for those in industries which are subject to constant change, it is seen as an ever present threat. However, it need not always be so. For many individuals, as well as organizations, it can be an opportunity; an opportunity to get out of a situation or a straight jacket which is no longer appropriate to changed circumstances and which releases potential for new activities and achievement of new objectives.

The degree to which this more satisfactory situation can be achieved will undoubtedly depend to a very great extent on external economic, environmental or political circumstances, for example, changes in oil prices, government policies on nationalization etc. But these effects can be anticipated or, at worst, reacted to swiftly and with maximum consideration for those likely to be affected by the organization with an effective policy for dealing with redundancy. The requirements of the Redundancy Payments Scheme will ensure a high degree of fairness and make financial and other provision for those affected, but it cannot anticipate or plan in advance to take positive advantage of a developing situation. To do this, the organization needs its own strategic planning and forecasting system with built-in manpower planning and including a comprehensive redundancy policy.

The policy will have two broad objectives: the continued health and success of the organization, and the safeguarding of the interests of individuals affected by any possible redundancy situation.

It is necessary, therefore, to examine two aspects of the redundancy situation: the statutory requirements and benefits of the Employment Protection Act and the organization's own plans for forecasting and controlling its manpower requirements.

EMPLOYMENT PROTECTION ACT 1978

The Redundancy Payments Act 1965 was later embodied in the Employment Protection Act 1978. It covers nearly all classes of employees between the ages of eighteen and sixty for a woman or sixty-five for a man who have been continuously employed by the same employer for a minimum of two years (full-time employees). For people working between eight and sixteen hours per week, the qualifying period is five years. A few categories of employed people cannot claim redundancy payments: these include civil servants, registered dock workers, merchant seamen, share fishermen and the self-employed.

Note. To be entitled to payment, an employee must be formally dismissed because of redundancy. Entitlement will be lost if an employee leaves voluntarily because of anticipated or threatened redundancy.

WHAT IS REDUNDANCY?

The Act defines redundancy as dismissal due solely or mainly to:

(*a*) the fact that his employer has ceased, or intends to cease, to carry on the business for the purposes of which the employee was employed by him, or has ceased, or intends to cease, to carry on that business in the place where the employee was so employed, or
(*b*) the fact that the requirements of that business for employees to carry out work of a particular kind, or for employees to carry out work of a particular kind in the place they were so employed, have ceased or diminished, or are expected to cease or diminish

It should be noted that whilst it is the employee who is dismissed, it is the lack or change of work which is the criterion. Employees cannot be made redundant for reasons of poor work, discipline or ill health.

If there is a reduction in overtime working or rearrangement of working hours and workers are dismissed for refusing to accept the new arrangements, they are not considered redundant so long as the same number of that grade of worker is employed.

LAY-OFFS AND SHORT-TIME WORKING

Employees may claim redundancy, however, where

(*a*) they have been kept on short-time working or laid off (less than half a week's pay per week for four or more consecutive weeks)

(b) they have been kept on short-time working or laid off for six weeks or more in a period of thirteen weeks of which not more than three were consecutive

The employee must give written notice of an intention to claim within four weeks of the last day of the lay-off or short-time working.

The employer may make a counter claim in writing within seven days that there is a reasonable expectation of full-time working resuming within four weeks and continuing within thirteen weeks. Lay-off or short-time working caused by a strike or lockout does not count for this purpose.

PROOF OF REDUNDANCY

Employers have to prove that dismissal is not due to redundancy if an employee makes a claim.

SELECTION

Where a choice has to be made from a number of employees, this must be based on custom and practice in the organization or the industry, an agreed procedure or, last-in first-out, where this is customary.

NOTICE OF REDUNDANCY

Each employee to be dismissed is entitled to notice on the following scale according to length of service:

Continuous service	*Notice*
4 weeks	1 week
2 years	2 weeks
3 years	3 weeks
at the rate of 1 week per year up to a maximum	
12 years or over	12 weeks
or pay in lieu	

Employees may leave during this period without forfeiting payment or compensation, providing they obtain their employer's consent.

CONSULTATION

To give adequate time for consultation, the employer must give the following warning of impending redundancy to the Secretary of State for Employment on form HR1 and also to the recognized trade unions according to the following scale:

If 100 or more are to be dismissed within a period of 90 days or less	90 days of the first dismissal
Between 10 and 99 employees within a period of 30 days	30 days
For 10 or fewer employees	Consultation must begin as soon as possible

The following information must be given to trade unions involved, whether or not the employees actually belong to the union:

1 The reasons why the employees have become redundant
2 The numbers and descriptions of employees whom it is proposed to dismiss as redundant
3 The total number of employees of any such description employed by the employer at the establishment in question
4 The proposed method of selecting the employees who may be dismissed
5 The proposed method of carrying out the dismissals, including the period over which the dismissals are to take effect

In the course of consultation the employer shall consider any representations made by the trade union representatives and reply to them and state the reason, if any of their representations are rejected.

COMPENSATION

Compensation is payable at the following rates to those dismissed:

Age of employee	Scale for each complete year of employment
18–21	½ week
22–40	1 week
41–59/64	1½ weeks

For the purpose of this calculation, only full years of employment count.

Working back from the date of dismissal, any part of a year's employment which falls into a high wage scale is calculated at the lower rate.

Earnings above £155 per week do not count for compensation. Compensation under the Redundancy Payments scheme is free of tax up to the maximum of £4650. Occupational pension payments made at the time of, or shortly after, redundancy may be offset against redundancy payments.

REBATES TO EMPLOYERS

The enormous drains on the redundancy fund have meant that from 1 October 1986 only employers with less than ten employees may claim rebates from the redundancy fund. Thirty-five per cent of the payments made may be claimed. Claims must be made within six months of the payment, and the following information is required as well as a receipt for payment from the employee:

1   The employee's name and sex
2   The employee's national insurance number
3   The employee's income tax reference number
4   The employee's date of birth
5   The date on which the employee commenced his period of continuous employment
6   The date on which notice was given to the employee
7   The date on which the employment was terminated
8   The reason for the termination of employment
9   The amount of a week's pay calculated in accordance with form RPL 2 (Rev)
10 An indication of how the payment has been calculated

INSOLVENCY

Claims for redundancy payment against employers who are insolvent should be made by the employee to the employer's representative, who may apply to the redundancy fund for payment. Payments should include other outstanding items of pay, such as maternity and medical suspension pay covered under the Bankruptcy Act of 1914, as well as the following:

1   Arrears of pay up to a rate of £155 a week for a period not exceeding eight weeks. Pay includes salaries, wages, statutory sick pay, commissions, guarantee payments, medical suspension payments, payment for time off to look for new work or to make training arrangements and remuneration under a protective award

2   Holiday pay up to a rate of £155 a week up to a limit of six weeks according to entitlement in the last year
3   Any payment outstanding in respect of a basic award, by an industrial tribunal, of compensation for unfair dismissal
4   Pay in lieu of notice up to the statutory minimum entitlement under the Employment Protection (Consolidation) Act 1978
5   Reimbursement of apprentice's or articled clerk's fees

APPEALS

Employees who feel they have been unfairly treated by selection for redundancy, or for entitlement to compensation, may claim to an Employment Appeals Tribunal in the normal way. Claims may also be made for insufficient notice and failure to consult.

An employee may make claims for payment for redundancy and compensation for unfair dismissal at the same time.

Procedures for making claims are set out in the following leaflets:

Form IT1	for employees seeking decisions on their entitlement to compensation and the amount due
Form IT17	for employers seeking a decision on their entitlement to rebate against redundancy payments
Form IT18	in all other cases

ALTERNATIVE EMPLOYMENT

Employees may be offered alternative employment to avoid redundancy. The alternative offered must be reasonable, i.e. the work itself; pay and conditions should not be substantially different from the original work, nor should travel or access be significantly more difficult.

An employee is entitled to a trial period of four weeks, plus an agreed training period if this is relevant. During the trial period, either the employer or employee may give notice to terminate the new contract, and the employee will then be considered as having been made redundant under the original terms. The employer is entitled to claim that the refusal was unreasonable.

TRIBUNAL AWARDS

A tribunal may make:

1   An order for reinstatement in the original job

2   A protective award covering an individual or a group of employees who shall be paid for a period up to ninety days if 100 or more employees are affected, thirty days if ten or more employees are affected, or twenty eight days' pay in any other case
3   Compensation under the redundancy payments scheme.

Claims must be made by individuals or trade unions on their behalf on form HR1.

COMPANY POLICY

Most organizations will consider these statutory requirements as a minimum and will have a far more comprehensive approach to redundancy as a part of their overall manpower policy and planning. To some extent a redundancy situation may be seen as a failure of manpower planning.

In practice, however, changes may arise over which organizations have no possible control and inadequate warning may occur, which makes redundancy essential for the survival of the organization. In these cases, protection of the organization becomes of prime importance and redundancy policies must have adequate arrangements for reducing numbers and/or costs rapidly in those categories and activities affected.

In other circumstances, the organization may stand to benefit from changing the structure of its workforce, for example by adoption of new technology. Under these conditions it is reasonable that those adversely affected should be treated more generously.

CORPORATE PLANNING

Organizations which have adequate corporate planning will be geared towards future development, taking advantage of new situations and circumstances. They will protect their investment in the future — whether it be in equipment, in premises or, most important, in people — by effective monitoring of the success of their plans, by changes in the total environment in which they operate and by interpretation of the impact of these changes.

An effective company redundancy policy should include the following:

1   Objectives
2   Social and corporate considerations
3   Methods of avoiding or reducing the impact of redundancy
4   Selection methods
5   Consultation
6   Compensation

7 Re-engagement
8 Assistance to those dismissed

Both the legal requirements of the Employment Protection Act and the human aspect must be taken into account when drawing up the policy.

Objectives

It is essential to clarify company objectives in order to guide the decisions to be made when framing the policy and, even more important, implementing it if a redundancy situation should occur.

Objectives should be formulated, therefore, in the following areas:

> Protecting the economy and development of the organization
> Safeguarding the interests of the employees
> Avoiding adverse effects on the local community

The priority given to these objectives may vary according to whether the redundancy is forced on the organization because of outside circumstances, or whether it plans it to achieve greater profitability, new products or business.

Social and corporate consideration

If the efficiency of the labour force were the only consideration, it would probably be desirable to use redundancy as an opportunity of getting rid of the unwanted, the trouble makers, the least able, the least adaptable and the least hard working. It is arguable that if management had allowed any significant number of these categories to continue in employment until the need for redundancy occurred, the task of recovery would be particularly difficult for them. At the same time, using redundancy as an excuse in these cases is neither legal nor desirable.

Management must also consider the social implications of their actions, both upon individuals and the community in general.

So far as individuals are concerned, the chief considerations must be the comparative degree of hardship they will suffer, which will be affected immediately by their commitments and family responsibilities and, in the longer term, their age, fitness and the employment situation locally which will affect their ability to find alternative employment.

In a community where there is a shortage of various categories of labour, the release of suitable staff by one organization would obviously be welcomed. But where there is already unemployment and redundancy, as in so many communities, where one organization is a major or sole employee, those redundancies will have far-reaching consequences on the community.

Where the redundancy is foreseeable, as part of changes which will benefit the organization, consideration should be given to the possibility of timing, either by speeding up or delaying the dismissals to suit the circumstances in the community.

The prospect of substantial redundancies should be notified to the chairman of the regional economic council, any government department having special responsibilities for the industry, and local authorities. Particularly in development areas, the Department of Trade and Industry should be advised also, in addition to the statutory notification to the Department of Employment. These notifications should take place as early as possible, so that the authorities concerned have the maximum time in which to assist in finding suitable alternative employment.

The enormous efforts made by organizations such as British Steel and British Coal, who have had to handle massive redundancies over long periods, are classic examples of attempts to meet community interests.

Avoiding or reducing the impact of redundancy

In a period of economic recession for the organization, it is still possible to avoid or reduce the impact of redundancy if sufficient advance warning is available.

Methods which can be used include:

1. Identifying and attempting to sell surplus capacity even at marginal cost in order to retain skilled staff
2. Bringing subcontracted work into the organization's own workshops
3. Stopping overtime so as to share out the work available
4. Restricting recruitment and filling vacancies by internal transfer and retraining wherever possible
5. Dismissing employees who have been allowed to work on past normal retirement age
6. Dismissing part-time workers, assuming there are full-time employees available with the required skills
7. Short-time working for a limited period
8. Stocking up if the down turn is likely to be short lived. In a period of rising costs, holding stock may be cheaper than paying compensation to long service staff
9. Transfers. The numbers to be dismissed can often be reduced, or a valuable person retained in the organization, by transferring staff from one department to another or even to another company in a group
10. Voluntary retirement is a useful method of reducing the impact of redundancy which has the added attraction of relieving the employer of the need to make the choice between individuals. It has been used extensively by large organizations to reduce a surplus of senior staff who

would otherwise clog the avenues of promotion for younger people who must be developed for the future.

By making a direct financial appeal to the individual, it has been possible to break through the total resistance to any job losses which some trade unions have tried to enforce. This depends for its success on generous cash payments and subsidy of pension funds to ensure that the income available will be adequate.

There is no reason why the voluntary principle cannot be extended to earlier age groups. Many staff will welcome the lump sum and the opportunity of an early start in looking for other work.

Selection methods

The most controversial aspect of any redundancy is the method for selecting those who are to be dismissed. The simple solution is last-in first-out (LIFO), based purely on length of service. This is favoured by many unions, is easy to operate, understandable and allows people to know fairly accurately where they stand. The redundancy payments scheme itself favours this method by making it more expensive to dismiss long-service employees.

If all employees were of equal worth and if all sections of the organization were equally affected, then this policy could satisfy most needs. In most redundancies, and particularly in those caused by technological or product changes, it is unlikely that all departments or all grades of staff will need to be reduced by the same amount, and even in those departments whose overall numbers have to be reduced, there will be certain key jobs for which skilled workers are in short supply and whom it would be quite wrong to dismiss.

There will also be problems created by hardship cases, the registered disabled, those under training for skills required in the future and, perhaps most important of all, the future age structure of the company.

The effect of a number of even small-scale redundancies can be to bias significantly the age structure upwards, which may in turn create difficulties, in, say, five years' time.

From the broader social point of view, there is also a danger of creating a category of workers who will always be first out and who, through no fault of their own, will never be able to build up any service to qualify them for redundancy payments.

Where LIFO is used, it is essential that jobs are categorized within departments so that selection can be made within a group of skills, rather than across the whole department which may include skills which are still required. Arrangements must also be made to ensure that key personnel, whose absence could affect the output of other sections, are not dismissed purely because of seniority.

An ideal selection method would strike the balance between the requirements of the organization and the social needs of individuals. Factors to be taken into account would be:

Organization needs. Types and variety of staff and skills, as shown by the corporate and manpower plans; the worth of each individual in terms of their potential contribution to those plans; the cost of their replacement, and development.

Individual needs. Commitments and needs; age; service; likely difficulty in obtaining new work or retraining.

Such an approach would firstly enable each individual to know where they stood and, more important, enable them to improve their relative security rating by greater effectiveness and higher skill. For the organization, it would enable it to recognize people more easily as the valuable asset which they are and treat them accordingly. Whatever selection methods are used, it is essential that they are known and agreed beforehand with the representatives of the people likely to be affected.

Consultation

Although management must make the decision about the need for redundancy and the scale of it, the more employees are consulted about the way in which they are to be treated, the better.

Employees need to be advised about current and future business prospects and changes likely to affect them. This information can, of course, be interpreted in a number of ways and, indeed, exploited. It is therefore essential that the information is carefully presented and that staff are able to interpret it in a positive way. This, in turn, will depend on a build-up of trust and confidence between senior management and staff.

Once the decision has been taken on the need to reduce staff, full consultation on timing, methods, selection and so on, must take place. The existence of a detailed and agreed procedure will greatly reduce the need for ad hoc negotiation and bargaining.

In federated firms, the vehicle for consultation will be the convenor, shop stewards' committee, or their equivalents, as appropriate.

For the large numbers of firms with no union representation, staff committees or meetings of representatives from appropriately sized departments or sections should be instituted. Such representations will have far wider uses than consultation on redundancy, and they should be set up so that they are recognized and working well in normal, as well as emergency, circumstances.

Consultation involves notification that redundancy is likely. The Act requires that minimum periods of notice be given, so that the consultation process may begin. In cases where the changes can be foreseen in advance, it would seem reasonable to give longer notice of intention than is legally required. Should, however, such announcements precipitate a rush of key workers to secure first place in the queue for scarce jobs in other organizations, so putting the continuance of the existing methods in jeopardy, then little will have been accomplished.

Staff can, of course, be encouraged to work out their notice by a system of premium payments, and may lose their entitlement to redundancy payments under the Act if they do not obtain their employer's permission to leave before the expiry of their notice. Even so, a severe unemployment situation locally can make it more attractive for individuals to secure the long-term advantage of another job than a once-only cash payment.

The best policy is to restrict formal notice to the requirements of the Act, but to give notice of intention as part of the consultation procedures as early as possible. This will maintain good faith with employees and prevent the spread of rumour and loss of confidence.

Compensation

Many employers consider that the statutory level of payments represent a minimum and supplement them by scales of their own, usually related to length of service. A simple way of doing this is to add a fixed percentage to the statutory payment.

It is much easier to justify more generous treatment where the redundancy is due to circumstances from which the company will benefit and there is, therefore, merit in making additional payments in these circumstances only. Certainly in the extremes of redundancy where the organization is insolvent, only the redundancy scheme scale can be applicable.

An alternative method of supplementing payments is to make weekly and monthly payments, again on a scale according to service, until the employee has either used his entitlement or obtains alternative employment. To avoid reducing entitlement to unemployment benefit, these payments must be limited to one-third of normal earnings. Occupational pension payments which commence within a short time of redundancy can normally be offset against these payments.

The transferability of pension rights already earned, but not yet due for payment, must be protected in the normal way.

Re-engagement

Should circumstances change more rapidly than anticipated, it may be possible to re-engage those dismissed; the fairest way being to re-engage in reverse order to dismissal.

Before re-engagement takes place, the question of service must be clarified. If payments under the redundancy payments scheme have been made, then clearly service under the re-engagement can count only from this date and similarly, if payments against pension rights have been made, then pensionable service must restart from the date of re-engagement.

Providing no payments have been made, it is usual to count service for pension purposes as continuous if the period between dismissal and re-engagement does not exceed one year. Thereafter, it is preferable to regard any re-engagement as a completely new period of service for all purposes.

Assistance to those dismissed

The increasing recognition of social, as well as commercial, objectives by organizations of all types has encouraged greater attention to assisting employees who have been made redundant.

Assistance includes:

1   More generous compensation
2   Counselling
3   Assistance with job hunting
4   Assistance with setting up in business
5   Retraining

Severance packages greatly exceeding the statutory requirements are now common and may include enhancement of pensions, as well as ensuring the legal portability of pension rights already earned.

Although the incidence of redundancy has been so high in recent years, it is still a traumatic experience for most people, especially those in mid career or too young even for early retirement. Skilful counselling to determine needs and aspirations can be of immense benefit in opening up the range of options available in many cases, creating the opportunity for entirely new careers or occupations. In addition, counselling will help to rebuild the essential confidence and morale. Many specialist organizations now exist to carry out counselling and job search programmes on an individual or organizational basis.

With high levels of unemployment in many areas, job hunting is a skilled and demanding activity. In addition to requirements for time to seek new employment, assistance through contacts, use of services, identification of skills, guidance in writing CVs, interviewing skills and use of typing services, are all of extreme value. A number of self-help groups have been set up with a high degree of success.

For many, compensation or the availability of marketable skills, point to self-employment. In some cases where the organization still requires part of the service, a part-time consultancy agreement, leaving the individual free to build up business elsewhere, works well. Grants are available under the enterprise scheme of the Manpower Services Commission.

To enable individuals to acquire skills more in demand, or update existing ones, training schemes are run in some cases by the organization, by colleges or specialist agencies and are invaluable. For skills in high demand, grants may be available from the Manpower Services Commission.

Many of these activities are costly and time consuming for the organization, but their value in rebuilding morale and faith in the organization by remaining staff and the community in general, will usually more than justify this.

EMPLOYMENT SERVICES AND AGENCIES

The Manpower Services Commission is responsible for providing a wide range of services to industry and individuals including:

- Advice on manpower planning and forecasting methods
- Assistance and advice in documentation for redundancy
- Guidance on alternative employment available for dismissed employees
- Temporary employment subsidies
- Guidance on assistance and service available to help those dismissed
- Advice on retraining facilities
- Advice on appeals and industrial tribunals

Where large numbers of staff are to be dismissed, an employment office can be set up within the organization's premises.

Initial contact with the services should be made to the local department of employment office. The larger offices have specialist departments for dealing with all aspects of redundancy.

The following leaflets are available:

- RPL1   Offsetting pensions against redundancy payments
- RPL2   Ready reckoner for payments
- RPL4   Service calendar
- RPL5   Calculation of a week's pay for employees on shift and rota work
- RPL6   Summary of information for employees

FURTHER READING

T. Carew, *Get Up and Go Job Search*, Percy Coutts & Co.
Croners Reference Book for Employers, pp. 146 i−y, pp. 131−132.
Employment Protection (Consolidation) Act 1978, chapter 44, HMSO, 1979.
S. Golzen and P. Plumbley, *Changing Your Job*, Kogan Page, 1981.
S. Golzen, *Working for Yourself*, Kogan Page, 1981.
Guidelines for the Redundant Manager, 2nd edition, British Institute of Management, 1981.
F. Kemp et al, *Focus on Redundancy*, Kogan Page, 1980.
P.A. Mumford, *Redundancy and Security of Employment*, Gower, Aldershot, 1975.
Walsh and Blackburn, Edward Arnold, 1984 (for use by employees).
C. Waud, *Redundancy and Unfair Dismissal*, Penguin, Harmondsworth, 1982.

27

Employee Relations

J L Cookson

This chapter deals with regulating the working relationship between the employer and the employees collectively. It is an unrealistic and oversimplified view of management that sees managers making decisions and issuing instructions for others to obey. The conception, shaping and implementation of executive action in organizations is a complex process that depends heavily on employee consent. This consent is ceded to managers by employees individually, as they decide to accept rather than decline an offer of employment, as they work with enthusiasm rather than apathy and direct their activities towards the objectives of organizational success that managers determine.

Consent is also, however, ceded to managers by the employees collectively who give, implicitly or explicitly, a mandate to managers to make decisions and issue orders. There are many ways in which managerial action can be frustrated by collective employee resistance which would be beyond the scope of employees individually. There are not only the extremes of industrial action but cooperative or uncooperative working within the guidelines of union agreements, the degree of enthusiasm with which changes are accepted and implemented, the care with which safety routines are followed, flexibility on manning arrangements, and many more.

Whatever the level of national unemployment and economic gloom, and no matter how rightly collective agreements are worded, managers depend on the collective consent of employees to *allow* and *support* them in their duties. That consent can perhaps be required or even forced in some situations for a short time, but sustained and productive consent has to be won: it is won by managers who earn it through paying close attention to the working relationship.

The most recent empirically-based research findings (published in 1985 and 1986) attest to the continuing importance of employee relations. Despite recession and technological change, workplace trade union organization has proved durable and workplace employee relations stable. There is no evidence of decline in the importance which senior management attaches to employee relations and, to personnel practitioners, it remains pre-eminent — the activity upon which they spend most time and to which they assign most importance.

TRADE UNION RECOGNITION

When a trade union has recruited a number of members in an organization it will seek recognition from the employer in order to represent those members. What is recognition? It involves first of all that the employer singles out that trade union from others, so that the step of recognizing by an employer means that, while he will have to take seriously the representations of one union, he will not usually have to deal with others as well for the same group of employees. There are exceptions to this, especially when the number of union members is low, but it is a normal component of recognition. The second aspect is that the employer has to allow the recognition to affect his behaviour by taking seriously what the union representatives say to him. This does not necessarily mean agreeing to their claims, but it does mean taking time to talk with them to seek accommodations. It is an important, irrevocable step away from all decisions lying unilaterally with management. There are three points to consider about recognition:

1   The timing of recognition — when to recognize
2   Identifying the people, or groups of people whom the union should represent
3   Deciding which topics should fall within the scope of recognition — what to recognize

Reasons for recognition

Why should an employer recognize a union at all? Is there any advantage or is it simply an unfortunate yielding to pressure? The answer to that question lies in the wishes of the employees. If they collectively want trade union representation it is unlikely that they will cooperate with the employer who refuses it. They will want recognition partly because of their general experience and beliefs about working life and partly because of their particular experience with the individual employer where a recognition claim is brought. Manual employees tend to regard trade union representation as normal and necessary, managerial employees tend to regard it as abnormal and unnecessary, and administrative and clerical employees lie between these two extremes.

A more positive reason for recognition is the benefits which can flow to the employer from having representatives with whom to discuss plans and problems. It offers at least a useful method of communication and can be a way of contriving improved working relationships, hastening necessary change and developing trust in the motives and competence of the management.

When to recognize a union

The time at which to recognize a union is a fine judgement for managers to make. If it is too soon there will not be enough support among employees, who may feel that what should be their decision is being made for them. A union with only 5 per cent of the employees in membership has a small and potentially clique-like constituency, recognition of which might antagonize the majority. At the other extreme, the refusal to recognize a union which has 95 per cent of the employees in membership would be antagonizing the majority of the labour force in a different way, possibly with more serious results.

In the days when unions could seek recognition by legal means if an employer refused, the Advisory Conciliation and Arbitration Service (ACAS) often recommended recognition when the proportion of union members was below 40 per cent. The factors influencing the decision of when to recognize are the degree and efficiency of union organization, the number of representatives, the size of constituency and the degree of opposition. Nonetheless the key indicator is obviously the number of union members. It may be useful to ballot the employees to determine their wishes, although the greatest stimulus for a management to recognize union A is often the fear that union B may start recruiting members. Only recognition by management can check that move towards multi-unionism.

Identifying the groups of people to be represented by a recognized union

Another judgement to be made is to define the group of employees to be represented by the union. If the group is too large its members do not have enough interests in common for representation to be feasible. If it is too small there may be other employees, outside the group, who claim the same treatment as the union members because the terms and conditions of employment are similar. The employer either concedes the same benefits and antagonizes the union members who regard the others as 'riding on their backs' or the employer refuses and antagonizes the non-union members. The normal test is to consider what different groups of employees have in common.

Some of the more common boundaries are between manual and white-collar workers, where members of the two groups are seldom represented by the same union or involved in the same procedures and agreements. Another boundary is manual skill, where union membership or *grade* of membership is often jealously guarded on behalf of those who have completed a craft apprenticeship or other preparation that is acknowledged to justify special representation. In some situations the Amalgamated Union of Engineering Workers may represent employees who are skilled as well as those who are semi-skilled and unskilled, but the grade of membership would be different and arrangements with the employer would recognize that difference. The same union, through its Technical and Supervisory Section, may well represent white-collar employees in the same company, but that would be through a different section of the union, with different officials and different agreements.

More difficult boundaries are those connected with status in the organizational hierarchy. Should the supervisor and those he supervises be represented by the same body? In manufacturing industry it seems that he will usually be represented separately, to cope with the problem of the union member seeking representation against the management action of his supervisor, who is a member of the same union and entitled to the assistance of the same union official. In local government it is quite common for the chief officer in an authority and the most humble clerical personnel all to be members of the National and Local Government Officers Association.

What to recognize

A union can seek recognition on anything that might be covered in a contract of employment, but the employer may agree to recognition for only a limited range of topics. The basis is to recognize a union to represent the grievances of members. That excludes any consultation on payment, terms and conditions, working practices and the other potential ingredients of a recognition agreement. It may be that an employer will proceed progressively with recognition, so that the range of topics grows with familiarity in the negotiating relationship. It should be noted that the potential benefits for management from a recognition arrangement come only when recognition is on a wide basis. Also, if the employees are up in arms on an issue, it may be pedantic to refuse discussion because it is not covered by the recognition agreement.

The legal position on recognition

The fragmented structure of collective bargaining in the UK is partly attributed to the traditional abstentionist policy of the state, departed from only in the statutes prescribing the structures of nationalized corporations. During the 1970s, however, both major political parties were agreed upon the necessity for statutory machinery to resolve recognition disputes. The purposes embodied in the recognition provisions for the Industrial Relations Act 1971 were largely frustrated by the policy of non-cooperation on the part of the labour movement.

The Employment Protection Act 1975, *ss*11-16, represented an attempt by the state to steer a course between legalism and voluntarism in this area. These sections permitted a recognition issue to be referred by an independent union to ACAS for examination, inquiry and report. In the event of an employer failing to comply with a recommendation by ACAS for recognition and of conciliation failing to resolve the dispute, the union could present a claim for specified terms and conditions to the Central Arbitration Committee (CAC) for unilateral arbitration. Any terms and conditions awarded by the CAC would thereafter take effect as part of the contracts of the employees.

During their currency, these provisions were subjected to several criticisms:

1 The statutory processes culminating in unilateral arbitration could only be invoked by the union side
2 Inquiry procedures were protracted
3 ACAS's functions were capable of being seriously impaired by the absence of any requirement that employers should cooperate in inquiries, and by judicial review of ACAS's exercise of its powers
4 The ultimate sanction fell short of requiring an employer to recognize a union

The response of the Conservative government elected in 1979 to these criticisms (in the Employment Act 1980) was to repeal *ss*11-16, which thus represented a return to voluntarism in union recognition.

Despite the dismantling of the statutory recognition machinery, recognition disputes continue to be referred to ACAS and to represent a significant element (approx 14 per cent) of the service's collective conciliation activity.

The closed shop

In some ways, the logical development of union recognition is the 'closed shop' which is an agreement whereby all employees in a particular category should be members of the recognized union, as a condition of employment.

Perhaps nowhere is 'the dilemma between the function of the law to protect the individual and its function to help adjust power relations in society' (Kahn-Freund) more clearly demonstrated than in the debates which have raged since 1970 over the issue of the closed shop in British industrial relations and the extent to which the state should extend or restrict its operation. At the level of public policy, the issue is whether, given the ostensible commitment of the political parties to the system of collective bargaining, it is appropriate to provide individuals with a statutory right of disassociation and, if so, in what circumstances.

The provisions of the Industrial Relations Act 1971, heavily influenced by doctrines of individual rights which paid little heed to the realities of collective labour relations, aimed to outlaw the closed shop notwithstanding a pledge of support for the principle of collective bargaining. In the event, research has shown that established closed shop arrangements remained largely unaffected by the 1971 statutory measures, and it came as no surprise that the incoming labour government of 1974 should remove the right of disassociation from the statute book, thereby relegalizing the closed shop though providing limited statutory protection for religious objectors. Undoubtedly, statutory support for union membership agreements during the period 1974-1980 reinforced the willingness of employers (based upon administrative convenience) to conclude such agreements to the extent that, currently, approximately one-fifth of British employees and two-fifths of trade union members are covered by some form of closed shop arrangements.

The Employment Act 1980 is calculated, if not to render closed shops unlawful, at least to limit their operation and restrict their future development. The 1980 Act significantly narrows the circumstances in which employees may be dismissed fairly for not being a union member. It is now unfair to dismiss an employee:

1 Where the employee genuinely objects on grounds of conscience or other deeply-held personal conviction to being a member of any trade union whatsoever or of a particular union. Interestingly, the courts have held that a deeply-held personal conviction does not require that the objection be based on conscience, but may cover dissatisfaction with the performance or conduct of the union (see Home Delivery Services Ltd *v* Shackcloth, AT, 1984; Thorpe *v* General Motors Corporation, Bedford tribunal, 1984)
2 Where the employee was a member of the class of employees covered by the closed shop agreement before it took effect and has not subsequently been a member of a union which is party to such agreement
3 Where the closed shop was introduced on or after 15 August 1980 and has not been approved by a secret ballot of affected employees showing that at least 80 per cent of those entitled to vote supported the agreement

Employers may also require a union or other person to be joined as a party in unfair dismissal proceedings where the employer claims that the dismissal was the result of pressure exerted by such union or person calling or threatening industrial action because of the complainant's non-membership of the union. The 'joined' party may be ordered to contribute towards the compensation awarded if the complaint of unfair dismissal is upheld.

A further significant feature of the Employment Act 1980 is the restoration of statutory recourse to law for individuals who, in relation to employment subject to a union membership agreement, are unreasonably excluded or expelled from membership of a specified union.

Further statutory reform of the closed shop laws is embodied in the Employment Act 1982. Given the practical importance of the closed shop in British industrial relations and the doubts, based upon the experience of 1971-74, concerning the extent to which longstanding practices can be eradicated by law, the Conservative government's intention has been not to outlaw closed shops altogether but to impose further restrictions upon their operation. The Act provides:

1. Increased compensation for unfair dismissal for refusal to join a union. The 1982 Act introduced, for unfair closed shop dismissals, a minimum basic award of £2000. The dismissed employee will also be entitled to receive the conventional compensatory award. Most significantly, an employer, who dismisses an employee unfairly in a closed shop situation and who refuses to implement a tribunal reinstatement order, is liable to pay to the employee a further special award of three years' pay or £15 000, whichever is the greater.

   The government's expressed rationale for these increased levels of compensation is that they provide more adequate compensation for an individual who loses his livelihood unfairly. They appear also calculated to cause employers to think more carefully and to exercise greater reserve both before entering into new closed-shop arrangements and before dismissing objectors.

2. A dismissed employee may 'join', as a party to tribunal proceedings, the union that has contributed to the dismissal by exerting pressure on the employer. An award may be made against, and be recoverable directly from that union

3. Periodic ballots at five-yearly intervals to ascertain current support for continuance of existing closed shops. It will be unfair to dismiss an employee refusing to join a union not receiving the support of 80 per cent of those covered or 85 per cent of those voting

4. Compensation may be payable by the Secretary of State to victims of closed shop agreements who were dismissed under legislation passed by the last Labour government and who would have been protected as existing non-union members or conscientious objectors if the EA 1980

closed-shop provisions had been in force
5   It is unfair to dismiss an employee for not being a union member in a closed shop which took effect before 15 August 1980, unless in the five years preceding dismissal it had been supported in a ballot by 80 per cent of the employees covered or 85 per cent of those voting
6   Control of the exertion of pressure on a contractor, by the person engaging his services, to employ only union labour, since this requirement can involve conscription into unions of disinterested employees. Thus

   (*a*)   any clause in a contract is void if it requires the employment only of persons who are members of a union, or persons who are not members
   (*b*)   it is unlawful to discriminate, in inviting tenders, or making contracts, to require that those employed to perform that contract should be trade union members, or alternatively should not be members
   (*c*)   immunity is removed for industrial action which interferes with performance of a contract primarily on the grounds that those employed to do so are, or are not, union members

The impact, to date, of the new closed shop laws has been mixed. In the private sector, existing union membership agreements have rarely been subject to balloting and remain largely unimpaired. In the public sector also there has been little balloting activity, but three major employers (British Rail, British Gas and The Post Office) have announced their abandonment of long-standing union membership agreements.

ARRANGEMENTS WITH TRADE UNIONS

Within the framework of a recognition agreement, which may or may not have closed shop features, there are a number of arrangements to put management/union relationships on a satisfactory footing.

Collective procedures

Procedures provide a structure within which the parties can engage each other in discussion, problem solving and negotiation at the same time as exercising some degree of control over each other. Some actions are laid down to be followed and others to be avoided, so that it is commonplace for a procedure to state that an employee with a grievance about his employment will seek redress first from his immediate superior. It is also typical for a procedure to state that industrial action will only happen when procedural steps are exhausted and that changes in payment or other major terms and conditions of employment will not be made without prior consultation.

The essence of a procedure is to predetermine how matters shall be handled, so that all know what the next step is if they cannot solve a problem or reach agreement. There is a similarity to legal procedure, with its clear path from court to higher court, but it is an area of industrial relations activity that remains free from law. It is quite possible for employer and union to make legally-binding agreements, but most unusual.

The most common procedures are for discipline and grievance. The law relating to the contract of employment assumes that there will be a grievance procedure and the law on unfair dismissal assumes that there will be a procedure for discipline, so these are becoming almost universal, although the degree of sophistication is seldom great. The next most common are procedures for negotiation and consultation, which only exist when employer and union have reached the stage of recognition that embraces more terms and conditions of employment. There is also a frequent link with a procedure operated by an employers' association on a regional or national basis. Procedures are likely to bring clarity, fairness and consistency to employee relations, but they have limited effectiveness in altering the custom and practice of the workplace and they can make change difficult.

Rights of employee representatives

An inevitable consequence of recognizing trade unions is the need for union representatives to have some facilities.

Conventional industrial relations wisdom holds that the conduct of collective labour relations is improved by ensuring that employee representatives are informed and enjoy those facilities which they require to perform their functions. Thus it has been an aim of public policy in recent years to strengthen the quality of workplace representation primarily as a means of contributing to the creation of more orderly employee relations.

Under $s27$ of the Employment Protection Consolidation Act 1978, officials (including shop stewards) of independent, recognized unions have a right to take time off from work with pay to a reasonable extent and subject to reasonable conditions, in order to carry out their duties concerned with industrial relations between the employer (or associated employer) and the employees, or for the purpose of undergoing training relevant to those duties. Such training must be approved either by the TUC or the official's own union. For safety representatives, an analogous right is provided by the Safety Representatives and Safety Committee's Regulations. Under the stimulus of the statutory provisions, basic courses for workplace representatives have doubled in number. Further/advanced courses have trebled and health and safety courses have increased by four times.

Disputes concerning whether these rights have been denied are ultimately determined by industrial tribunals, which may seek guidance from the recommendations of the ACAS Code of Practice 3, *Time Off for Trade Union Duties and Activities* (1978). This jurisdiction has forced tribunals to the heart of workplace industrial relations in so far as disputes concerning time off require close consideration of both the structures of collective bargaining and of the functions which it is appropriate for shop stewards to perform.

The code of practice (para. 13) gives examples of union officials' duties, though the list is not intended to be exhaustive:

1. Collective bargaining with the appropriate level of management
2. Informing constituents about negotiations or consultations with management
3. Meetings with other key officials or with full-time union officers on matters which are concerned with industrial relations
4. Inteviews with and on behalf of constituents on grievance and discipline matters
5. Appearing on behalf of constituents before an outside official body such as an industrial tribunal
6. Explanations to new employees, whom he or she will represent, of the role of the union in the workplace industrial relations structure

The code offers no guidance however upon whether, in the case of multi-site organizations, time off with pay should be afforded to allow stewards from one site to consult with those from another. This has been the central issue in much of the case law to date. Tribunals have usually applied a restrictive interpretation of the statutory provisions, though more recently the Employment Appeals Tribunal (Good *v* GEC Elliott Process Automation Ltd) rejected the contention that an official's duties can only be those which fall within the area of recognition. And in Beal *v* Beecham Group Ltd (1982), the Court of Appeal held that attendance at a union-representatives-only meeting, called to discuss matters of an industrial relations nature *and* to plan a co-ordinated union strategy, constituted a duty concerned with industrial relations.

The courts have also demonstrated a willingness to place a liberal construction of 'relevant' training for workplace representatives. In Young *v* Carr Fasteners Ltd (EAT 1979) it was held that training may be 'relevant' under the statutory provisions if it relates to a subject which may, in the future, form part of the representative's duties.

Perhaps the most important recommendation in the code of practice (para.10) is that employers and trade unions should reach agreement on arrangements for handling the time-off facility in ways most appropriate to their particular situations.

Disclosure of information

During the 1970s, public policy supported the view that disclosure of information by employers to employees and their representatives is conducive to sound industrial relations and improves the processes of bargaining. Subsequent experience, however, reveals a marked lack of consensus from both British employees and trade unions concerning what information should be disclosed, how information might be used if it is disclosed and why/how its disclosure would assist bargaining and influence its outcome.

The Employment Protection Act 1975 substantially re-enacts the disclosure provisions of the Industrial Relations Act (never activated) by imposing a duty upon an employer to disclose (on request) to representatives of an independent, recognized union information relating to his undertaking or that of an associated employer without which the representatives would be materially impeded in their conduct of bargaining and which it would be good practice to disclose.

ACAS was required to produce a code of practice for the guidance of the parties. The code on disclosure, published in 1977, represents a disappointing gloss on the statutory provisions. Noting that the relevance of information is determined by the particular structure within which collective bargaining takes place, ACAS rejects the possibility of formulating a list of items which is universally relevant and disclosable. Instead, it provides examples of items of information which could be relevant in particular situations. These cover pay and benefits; conditions of service; manpower; performance; and finance. The central recommendation of the code is that the parties should reach voluntary agreements on what information is to be disclosed, when and in what form.

The scope of the statutory duty to disclose is restricted by the provision of certain safeguards for the employer, who is not required to disclose information communicated in confidence or which relates to an individual unless consent is given and, most importantly, which would cause substantial injury to the employer's undertaking.

Upon complaints of failure to disclose, the Central Arbitration Committee is empowered to declare what information an employer should disclose and by what date. As formerly with recognition claims, the ultimate sanction for failure to comply with such declaration is for terms and conditions to be determined by unilateral arbitration.

The Employment Protection Act provisions on disclosure are less stringent than the obligation of US employers to bargain in good faith under which certain information is presumptively relevant and disclosable. Nor do they make provisions for disclosure to individual employees.

Perhaps the most striking feature of the statutory disclosure machinery, since its establishment, has been its low utilization by trade unions, which suggests either that they feel no need to invoke the machinery to obtain the information they wish to have (because they can get it in various other ways) or that they continue to be suspicious of company-provided information, especially that disclosed to support an 'ability-to-pay' bargaining position. Thus, the impact of the disclosure measures appears to have been minimal though the existence of the statutory measures and the recommendations in the code of practice *may* have had a beneficial influence upon the attitudes of more reticent employers.

FURTHER READING

Kevin Hawkins, *A Handbook of Industrial Relations Practice*, Kogan Page, 1979.

28

Industrial Relations Law

F W Rose

Current statute law on industrial relations is embodied in the following:

1. Trade Union and Labour Relations Act 1976 (TULRA)
2. Employment Protection Act 1975 (EPA)
3. Employment Protection (Consolidation) Act 1978 (EPCA)
4. Employment Act 1980 (EA80)
5. Employment Act 1982 (EA82)
6. Trade Union Act 1984 (TUA84)

TRADE UNION MEMBERSHIP

Some employers in conjunction with a particular trade union operate a closed shop, ie on joining the workforce the new employee's membership of that union is a condition of continued employment. Refusal to allow an individual to join a particular union, or expulsion of an existing member, may affect that person's ability to earn a livelihood, thus fair and proper rules should exist governing the right to join, take part in the affairs of, and remain a member of a union.

The rules of a trade union must be strictly observed since they are a contract between that union and its members. The rules may state the description of workers who are entitled to join and also persons who are ineligible for membership. Clearly a union formed to protect the interests of mineworkers will wish to restrict membership to workers of that particular type.

The TUC has set up a non-statutory Independent Review Committee of a legally qualified chairman and two trade unionists to determine an employee's appeal against refusal to admit, or expulsion from, a particular union where membership is a condition of employment. The committee is empowered to recommend admission or readmission and the union is expected to accept and act upon any decision so made. Unions should settle these matters themselves as far as possible by setting up investigatory internal procedures. An appeal to the committee will only occur in cases of continued difficulty and disagreement.

The Employment Act 1980, *ss*4-5, has introduced new procedures to reinforce, but not to replace, the voluntary review procedure set up by the TUC. In a closed shop situation an employee must not be refused union membership on unreasonable grounds, and if already a union member he must not be expelled unreasonably. On refusal to admit, or subsequent expulsion, the employee may complain to a tribunal within a period of six months, even if use of the voluntary procedures has not been exhausted. The complainant must prove 'unreasonableness' of the union's actions, as by establishing that the decision was reached contrary to the union's own established procedures or in defiance of the rules of natural justice.

Where the union is deemed to have acted improperly, the tribunal will make a declaration as to the complainant's rights, subject to appeal on law or fact to the Employment Appeals Tribunal. If the complainant is admitted or readmitted to union membership in accordance with the tribunal's declaration, a further claim, if relevant, may be made for monetary losses suffered, when four weeks have elapsed since the declaration, up until six months after the date of the declaration. Compensation will be awarded at the tribunal's discretion for wages lost through inability to work, where union membership is a condition precedent to gaining employment. There is an appeal on a question of law relating to compensation to the Employment Appeals Tribunal.

If, within four weeks of the declaration, the union refuses to admit or readmit to membership as ordered, then within six months compensation may be claimed at the discretion of the EAT.

The union cannot exclude the application of these statutory provisions by any agreement with its members or applicants for membership, but a binding settlement of any dispute by a conciliation officer precludes tribunal proceedings. Compensation awarded may be reduced to reflect the complainant's own contributory behaviour to refusal to admit or expulsion.

Exercise of disciplinary powers

Union rules governing internal discipline and exercise of the power to fine or suspend a member must be followed to the letter, otherwise the decision may be challenged however slight the irregularity. The union's decision cannot be made final and binding. The aggrieved member may test an alleged irregularity in the procedure by appeal to the ordinary courts, even though union rules purport to exclude such an appeal. Further, a union cannot take any form of disciplinary action unless the necessary power has been expressly granted by union rules.

There are no statutory rules requiring trade unions to observe the principles of natural justice when disciplining members, nonetheless it is arguable that the common law rules are still applicable. This means that the member concerned must be notified of the charges against him, given an opportunity to prepare a reply and be allowed to attend a hearing to state his case before persons hitherto unconnected with the dispute.

Termination of membership

There is an implied term in every contract of membership of a trade union permitting a member to terminate membership on giving reasonable notice and complying with any reasonable conditions, such as paying arrears of subscriptions. A person may wish to resign from a union if he disagrees with its policies or does not wish to obey directions to go on strike ($s7$, TULRA).

Political funds

If a trade union spends its funds on political objects it must ballot members every ten years for permission to continue to do so. Thus a union which has not held a ballot in the nine years before 31st March 1985 will need to do so before 31st March 1986 ($s12(2)$, TUA).

Secret ballot for union elections

Under the Trade Union Act 1984, every voting member on a union's national executive committee must be elected by a secret ballot among all union members held within the last five years ($s1$). This does not include a purely federal or representative body. Every person entitled to vote should receive a voting paper through the post and be given an opportunity to return it by post without incurring any direct cost. Votes cast must be fairly and accurately counted. A member must not be unreasonably prevented from standing for election, nor required to belong to a particular political party ($s2$). As an alternative, a workplace or semi-postal ballot may be held where the union is satisfied that this equally enables members to exercise their entitlement to vote. Every person entitled to vote must be supplied with a ballot paper, or one must be made available during working hours, and be given a convenient opportunity to vote by post or at his workplace during working hours or at a more convenient place ($s3$).

An executive committee which has not been duly elected still has full capacity to conduct union business. However, a union member can apply to the certification officer and/or the High Court for a declaration that the union has failed to observe the above obligations imposed. The High Court may issue an enforcement order and failure to comply with that order renders the union liable for contempt proceedings by a member.

ADVISORY, CONCILIATION AND ARBITRATION SERVICE (ACAS)

ACAS is a body independent of the government with the general duty of improving industrial relations and encouraging the extension and reform of collective bargaining between employers and trade unions. When so requested, or on its own initiative, ACAS may give advice on the following matters:

1   The organization of workers or employers for collective bargaining purposes
2   The recognition of trade unions by an employer
3   Negotiating machinery and joint consultation
4   Disputes and grievance machinery
5   Questions relating to communications between employers and workers
6   Facilities for officials of trade unions
7   Procedures for termination of employment
8   Disciplinary matters
9   Manpower planning, labour turnover and absenteeism
10 Recruitment, retention, promotion and vocational training of workers
11 Payment systems, including job evaluation and equal pay

ACAS itself, or one or more of the parties to a trade dispute, may seek help from a conciliation officer or other person provided by the service so that a settlement may be achieved, where procedures agreed between the parties to settle disputes have failed. Arbitration may be used if conciliation fails, or, where there is an important issue requiring a direct reference to arbitration without intermediate conciliation, for example, where it is essential to attempt to settle a potentially damaging strike affecting the country as a whole.

Codes of practice have been issued giving practical guidance on the way in which to implement legal provisions, dealing with disciplinary procedures, disclosure of information to trade unions for collective bargaining purposes, time off for trade union duties and activities, closed shop agreements and picketing.

LEGAL STATUS OF AN EMPLOYERS' ASSOCIATION

A number of employers all engaged in the same or related areas of work may form an association to protect their mutual interests. In effect, they are an employers' trade union and consequently have the same position in law as unions acting for employees. An employers' association is a permanent or temporary organization of employers, or a number of affiliated organizations, with the principal purpose of regulating their relations with workers or trade unions (s28(2), TULRA). Unlike trade unions, such employers' associations may be incorporated or remain unincorporated.

LEGAL STATUS OF A TRADE UNION

A trade union is a permanent or temporary organization of workers formed with the main objective of regulating their relations with their employer. Since a temporary organization falls within the scope of this definition, it covers bodies such as committees of shop stewards setting themselves up as separate entities on becoming disenchanted with the policies of their own union.

All bodies traditionally regarded as trade unions will be allowed to register as such with the certification officer. A registered trade union may claim important tax concessions in respect of its provident benefit income. The certification officer has power to certify that a trade union is 'independent' and issue a certificate to that effect, subject to later withdrawal if the union ceases to be independent. The trade union concerned may appeal to the Employment Appeals Tribunal against refusal to issue or withdrawal of a certificate. An independent trade union is a body not dominated or controlled by an employer or subject to his interference through the provision of financial or other material support for that union which, if withdrawn, will affect its continued, effective functioning. Thus, staff associations which provide for the welfare of employees and are wholly or partly financed by the employer will not qualify as being independent. The advantages of being independent may be summarized as follows:

1 It is unfair to dismiss an employee for wishing to join such a body or for taking part in its activities, or for refusing to join a non-independent trade union (EPCA)
2 Disclosure by the employer of information concerning his business on such matters as profits and losses, orders for goods and planned expansion or reduction of the workforce. This enables unions to negotiate pay structures that are realistic and reasonable in the light of the employer's financial position. If there is a refusal to disclose, the Central Arbitration Committee may make an award granting improved terms of employment which will become an implied term of the individual worker's contract of employment (EPA)
3 An employer must not take action against his employee such as

suspension or stoppage of wages, or refusing to promote, in order to prevent or deter him from being a member of an independent trade union, or from taking part in its activities at any appropriate time outside working hours, or within working hours where permitted by the employer (EPCA)
4 Members may claim time off work for union activities, though not necessarily with pay, and they may seek interim relief if allegedly dismissed for their union activities (EPCA)
5 Officials are entitled to time off work with pay to discharge their union duties or to be trained on industrial relations matters (EPCA)
6 Representatives must be consulted on future redundancies (EPA)
7 Ability to make a closed-shop agreement with an employer requiring all employees of a specified description, for example, drivers of vehicles, to join the independent trade union negotiating the agreement (EPCA)
8 Securing public funds, when made available, to hold secret ballots on a number of issues affecting union matters, such as whether to go on strike and requiring the employer to make his premises available for this purpose (EA)
9 Power to conclude a collective agreement with the employer embodying a promise not to strike for a stated time period (TULRA)

Union recognition and the closed shop

Where some members of a workforce belong to the same trade union, that union may approach the employee and ask him to concede negotiating rights to the union. This means that the terms and conditions of work of members of that workforce, whether or not they are union members, will be fixed by discussions between the employer and the union so 'recognized' through the medium of a collective agreement.

A recognized trade union, enjoying support from a substantial number of the employees in a particular workforce, may approach the employer with a view to the imposition of a closed shop. This means that if the employer and independent trade union so agree, all employees working for that employer as part of a particular section of workers, for example, those engaged on assembly line work, must join the specified trade union. The code of practice on closed shop agreements does not impose any legally binding obligation, but its observance will be considered in legal proceedings and will support a party's claim to have acted properly and fairly. Failure to observe the code may be indicative of wrongful conduct. The more significant provisions are listed below:

1 Closed shop agreements, like collective agreements, require the participation of both parties. Employers are under no obligation to agree to a closed shop and should expect a very high level of union membership before considering its introduction

2 The employer should consider the interests of staff who, as members of professional associations, are subject to their own code of ethics or conduct, where the obligations imposed by that ethical code may be in--compatible with the full range of union activities, such as participation in industrial action endangering health or safety
3 Before seeking a closed shop, a union should be 'recognized' and should already have recruited voluntarily a very high proportion of the employees concerned, which may be in excess of 80 per cent
4 The parties should agree that an alternative to union membership would be the payment to a charity by individual non-unionists of a sum equivalent to the union membership subscription
5 Closed shop agreements requiring union membership before seeking employment (the pre-entry closed shop) may infringe the freedom to work. No new agreements of this type should be contemplated and where they currently exist the need for their continuation should be carefully reviewed

COLLECTIVE AGREEMENTS

Wages and working conditions may be settled by negotiations between an employer, or group of employers, and one or more trade unions representing the workers involved, recognized by employers and workers as having the right to negotiate collectively in this manner. Collective agreements are conclusively presumed not to be legally enforceable, but binding in honour only. This means that the agreed terms may be violated without any legal redress. An express statement in a collective agreement may make it wholly or partially enforceable in law to the extent so indicated. Trade unions are against legal enforceability especially if it inhibits strike action.

Some terms in a collective agreement, usually on matters such as wage rates and hours of work, may become part of the individual worker's contract of employment by virtue of a clause in that contract providing that certain terms governing working conditions will change automatically as each new collective agreement is negotiated. It is provided however that any term in a collective agreement, irrespective of when it was made, prohibiting or restricting a worker's right to strike or take other industrial action, such as a procedure for discussion and possible settlement of the dispute, to precede industrial action, does not form part of any worker's individual contract of employment and bind him in law, unless that collective agreement:

1 Is in writing
2 Embodies a clause expressly stating that the term in question may be incorporated into a worker's individual contract of employment as part of it

3   Is readily accessible at the place of work, for the worker to read and discuss
4   Is an agreement where each trade union which is a party thereto has the status of independent trade union

As an additional requirement the worker's individual contract of employment must expressly or impliedly permit incorporation into it of terms from the collective agreement.

SIGNIFICANCE OF LABOUR RELATIONS LAW

The aims and aspirations of trade unions, its officers, representatives, members and workers not belonging to a union, are often achieved by recourse to various forms of industrial action such as a strike, go slow or overtime ban. Such actions frequently involve commission of legal wrongs for which the employer and other parties affected may seek redress by bringing an action for infringement of laws governing contract, tort and crime. To prevent industrial action being thwarted by legal action in the courts, statute confers exemption from preceedings in certain, well-defined situations upon the trade union itself, its trustees, officers, members and persons coming within the statutory definition of the term 'worker'. A worker is a person who works or seeks work under:

1   A contract of employment or apprenticeship, or
2   A contract for the services of an independent contractor, excluding professional services, for example an accountant
3   A contract to provide some of the professional services under the national health scheme
4   Employment with a government department, excluding the police and the armed forces

The concept of a worker embraces a person who 'seeks work', for example unemployed persons organized into a group in order to secure work, or redundant workers taking industrial action after breaking away from their own union following what they consider to be an unsatisfactory handling of a redundancy situation with their former employer.

Trade disputes

Acts otherwise legally wrongful, such as inducing a breach of contract, picketing, and conspiracy, may not give rise to legal action if committed in contemplation or furtherance of a trade dispute, as where one worker induces another to go on strike and violate the express terms of his contract of employment. A trade dispute is a dispute between either employers and workers, or workers and workers, connected with matters affecting working conditions such as pay, hours of work, redundancy, demarcation disputes, disciplinary matters, facilities for trade union officials, recognition of a trade union and negotiating procedures.

TRADE UNIONS AND INDUSTRIAL ACTION

Under s15, EA82 a trade union may be sued in its own name for damages, or an injunction, in respect of the unlawful acts specified below, if authorized or endorsed by:

1   Its principal executive committee
2   Its general secretary or president, or
3   Any official authorized under the union rules to call industrial action
4   Its employed officials, or any committee to which they report, unless union rules impose a prohibition on so acting, or repudiated in writing by the executive committee, president or general secretary, as quickly as is practicable with the repudiators, not acting inconsistently with that repudiation. In Express & Star v NGA (1985) the general secretary of the NGA, in order to comply with an injunction granted to the proprietors of the Express & Star newspaper, sent out a circular instructing members not to breach their contracts of employment by refusing to implement introduction of new technology. It was held that the NGA were vicariously liable for continued disruption instigated by union officials, since the acts in question had been authorized by the union. The union was fined £7500 for each of the two wrongful acts. A repudiation of the official's acts required open disavowal to be communicated to the employer suffering the effects of disruption.

The unlawful acts are:

1   Any form of industrial action which results in commission of a tortious wrong by the union, unless acting in contemplation or furtherance of a trade dispute
2   Calling industrial action if there is no dispute between an employer and his own employees, or if the dispute is not wholly or mainly about pay or conditions of work, or does not involve any employer or if the dispute relates to matters occurring overseas. A remedy may be sought by the employer who is detrimentally affected by this secondary action
3   Unlawful secondary action
4   Secondary picketing
5   Defamation, trespass, negligence, or nuisance, whether or not

committed in contemplation or furtherance of a trade dispute, as where a trade union makes a defamatory statement about the employer's activities while he is currently in dispute with his employees

When damages are awarded against a trade union, $s16$ states the upper monetary limits: £10 000 if the union has less than 5000 members, or £50 000 if the union membership is between 5000-25 000, or £125 000 if the union membership is 25 000-100 000 and £250 000 if the union membership is 100 000 or more.

A trade union may be liable in damages without limit in the following cases:

1 An action for breach of contract, as where a member of a trade union claims damages from a union alleging wrongful expulsion in contravention of the union rules
2 Wrongful expenditure of union funds on an unlawful purpose
3 Misapplication of union funds by trustees who must restore money misappropriated
4 Any tortious act of negligence, nuisance, breach of common law or statutory duty resulting in personal injury to any person, or
5 Breach of duty connected with ownership, occupation, possession, contract or use of property

This means that injury to a person employed by a trade union during the course of his employment will still give rise to a tortious liability if it is the result of a failure to provide a safe system of work at common law or, where appropriate, under the Factories Act 1961, Offices, Shops and Railway Premises Act 1963 and the Health and Safety at Work Act 1974.

Some trade union property is protected under $s17$ from being used to satisfy an award of damages, costs of expenses, namely, personal property in its political fund or provident benefit funds.

Secret ballot on strike action

Immunity from legal action is removed where a union fails to hold a secret ballot before authorizing or endorsing a call for a strike, or other form of industrial action, which either breaks or interferes with the contract of employment on those taking part. A majority must vote in favour of the proposed action and the ballot must be held no longer than four weeks before it begins ($s10$ TUA). Entitlement to vote must be given only to those members that the union reasonably believes will be called on to take part, otherwise the result of the ballot is nullified. Immunity will also be lost if any member is called on to strike after being denied entitlement to vote. The question on the ballot paper must require a 'Yes' or 'No' answer, and state whether the voter will be involved in a breach of his contract of employment. The detailed result of the ballot must be made known to those entitled to vote. Every person entitled to vote must be supplied with a ballot paper, or one made available during working hours and be given a convenient opportunity to vote by post or at his workplace during working hours or at a more convenient place (s11 TUA).

A trade union is not liable for purely unofficial industrial action, unsupported either morally or materially by that union.

CONDUCT PROTECTED AGAINST LEGAL ACTION

Set out below are details of conduct that normally gives rise to some form of sanction if committed by an ordinary individual, but which will be immune if committed in contemplation or furtherance of a trade dispute.

Inducement to break a contractual promise

An employee may, in concert with others, go on strike, after lawfully terminating his employment by giving the proper period of notice or by acting unlawfully, for example withdrawing his labour without proper notice. In the latter case the employee may be sued for damages to make good the employer's losses suffered by the breach of contract. TULRA s13(1) does not remove this liability.

If an employee is persuaded to break his contract of employment by a fellow worker, trade union, or a union official, then the employer so harmed may sue the person responsible for the successful inducement for damages in tort to recover losses suffered. An action in contract is not available, since there is no contractual relationship between wrongdoer and employer. However, such a claim would prevent the effectiveness of industrial action. Thus, under TULRA s13(1), certain acts committed by a trade union, its officials, employees, or even someone not directly connected with the dispute are protected against a tortious action if committed in contemplation or furtherance of a trade dispute. The protected acts are:

1 Inducing an employee to breach his contract of employment, as where a union official calls for strike action
2 Inducing breach of a commercial contract, as where a union official induces suppliers of goods to an employer to withhold deliveries
3 Interference with proper performance of a contract of employment, as where a union official induces a supplier to withhold credit facilities to the employer in dispute
4 Inducing another person to interfere with the proper performance of a contract of employment or commercial contract, as where a union

official induces the driver working for a supplier not to deliver goods to the employer by crossing picket lines
5 Threatening that a contract will be breached, whether a contract of employment or a commercial contract, as where a union official merely threatens, but does not yet intend to execute that threat, to call a strike
6 Threatening to induce a beach of a contract of employment or a commercial contract, as where the union official merely threatens to try to effect a strike
7 Threatening to interfere with performance of a contract of employment or commercial contract, or threatening to induce interference with that performance. Here there is a mere threat of interference with the contract rather than a direct breach involved

In Hadmor Productions Ltd and Others v Hamilton and Others (1982) Hadmor made television films for sale to television stations for transmission using freelance technicians who were members of ACTT (Association of Cinematograph, Television and Allied Technicians). The union's national organizer assured Hadmor that the union would not prevent the programmes being televised, but a local branch resolved otherwise. There was a threat of redundancy if ready-made programmes were bought from facility companies, instead of using programmes made by the TV station itself employing ACTT members. Hadmor unsuccessfully sought an injunction against three union officials to restrain them from preventing transmission. It was held that the union officials were acting in contemplation or furtherance of a 'trade dispute' for the purposes of $s13(1)$, TULRA ie the fear of redundancy. Under $s13(1)$ there was immunity for the union officials from legal action for threatening to induce employees to break their contracts of employment by not transmitting programmes, an act in contemplation or furtherance of a trade dispute, thereby harming Hadmor.

In all the situations discussed above, there is no immunity from tortious action if unlawful means, such as threats of violence, are used to induce the contracting parties to act in breach of an existing contract.

A strike called for political reasons is not a trade dispute. In BBC v Hearn (1977) the Association of Broadcasting Staff, a trade union, threatened to ask technicians to prevent overseas transmission of the FA Cup Final, unless the BBC agreed not to relay the programme to South Africa. Technicians acting in this manner would be liable to an action for a breach of their individual contracts of employment with the BBC. The court held that, since there had not been any attempt by the trade union to renegotiate the terms and conditions of employment of its members with the BBC, there was no trade dispute between the employer and union. The blacking of the relay to South Africa could not be an act in contemplation or furtherance of a trade dispute, with the result that it was not protected under TULRA and could give rise to a legal action for damages. An injunction was granted to restrain the union from directing its members to breach their contracts of employment and from inducing the BBC to breach its contracts with other countries to relay the match.

Picketing

TULRA $s15(1)$ states that it is lawful to picket in contemplation or furtherance of a trade dispute for the purpose of peacefully obtaining information, communicating information, or persuading a person to work, or persuading a person not to work, by attending:

(a) at or near one's own place of work, or
(b) in the case of a trade union official, usually a full-time official, at or near the place of work of a member of that union whom he represents and is accompanying. An official representing only a specific group of employees, such as a shop steward, usually a part-time official, can picket only alongside the limited number of employees on whose behalf he acts. The object of these provisions is to permit officials to exercise some form of control to ensure orderly picketing

An unemployed person may lawfully picket his former workplace in furtherance of a trade dispute connected with his dismissal, but ceases to have this right on securing other work.

There is no protection for criminal or civil wrongs committed in the course of picketing, such as assault, battery, breach of the peace, obstruction of the highway, carrying offensive weapons, nuisance or threatening behaviour. The police frequently bring actions for such conduct committed during the course of picketing that falls outside the scope of $s15(1)$. In Moss v McLachlan (1985) striking miners, travelling in a convoy of vehicles, were stopped by police within four miles of Nottinghamshire collieries and informed that to continue their journey would obstruct the police in the execution of their duties. An inspector told the miners that he believed that they intended to demonstrate at the pit head and would cause a breach of the peace. Some miners then blocked the road with their vehicles. It was held that the orders given by the police were lawful.

'Secondary picketing' is illegal. The mass picket involves persons acting as pickets who are not employed by, and thus not striking against, the employer concerned. It may also involve employees of the employer in a trade dispute picketing premises belonging to his supplier or customer to pressurize their employees to join the strike, or persuade the supplier or customer to suspend commercial dealings with the employer. If an employer suffers as the result of secondary picketing, he may seek a remedy in tort by way of an injunction to restrain those activities, or claim damages for the loss that he has suffered as a result against the person responsible for organizing the picketing ($s15(2)$

TULRA). The trade union involved can also be proceeded against by virtue of $s15$ EA82.

Code of practice on picketing

The code's provisions are not legally binding, but their observance will be considered in legal proceedings and will support a party's claim to have acted properly and fairly. Failure to observe the code may be indicative of wrongful conduct. The more significant provisions are listed below:

1. The police may do whatever is reasonably necessary to ensure peaceful and orderly picketing, which includes enforcing the criminal law by limiting the number of pickets where otherwise there is reasonable cause to fear disorder or breach of the peace. Enforcement of the civil law, such as restraining picketing in pursuance of an injunction issued by a court, is not the function of the police, except by assisting officers of the court where there may be a breach of the peace
2. A mass picket is unlawful since the object is obstruction and intimidation, not peaceful persuasion. Pickets and their organizers should ensure that, in general, the number of pickets does not exceed six at any entrance to a workplace and frequently a smaller number will be appropriate
3. An experienced person, preferably a trade union official who represents those picketing, should always be in charge of the picket line
4. Disciplinary action should not be taken by a union against a member because he has crossed a picket line which the union had not authorized, or a picket line somewhere other than the member's place of work. Expulsion from a union in a closed shop on such grounds may be held to be unreasonable
5. Pickets should ensure that their activities do not cause distress, hardship or inconvenience to the public, and that the movement of essential goods and supplies, essential maintenance of plant and equipment, and the provision of essential services are not impeded, still less prevented

Sit-in on work premises

Employees may 'sit in' at work premises, often where the employer intends to introduce wide-scale redundancies. This is a trespass against the occupier usually the employer, giving rise to an action in damages. However, the employer may be more interested in regaining possession under Rules of the Supreme Court Order 113, which permits summary proceedings though the identity of the employee is unknown.

It is a criminal offence to resist or obstruct a court officer enforcing an order for possession, or to use or threaten violence to persons or property to gain entry to premises knowing that a person inside is resisting entry. Having entered premises as a trespasser, it is a crime to be there with a weapon of offence.

Secondary action

Action may be taken against innocent employers who are not involved in an existing trade dispute, to increase the pressure by widening the effects of a strike, so that the employer directly involved will meet the demands being made on him. Legal liabilities imposed by $s17$, EA80 to curb secondary action, expose trade unions, union officials and other persons involved to an action in tort at common law, for interference in some way with performance of a commercial contract outside the limits of permissible secondary action. Such persons lose the protections conferred on them by $s13$, TULRA against legal liability while acting in contemplation or furtherance of a trade dispute. Anyone detrimentally affected by illegal secondary action may rely on the appropriate common-law action to give relief.

However, immunities against legal liability provided by $s13$, TULRA will protect secondary action with the principal purpose of directly preventing, or disrupting, the supply of goods and services during the dispute, under a contract existing at the time when the secondary action is taken, between the employer in dispute and his first supplier of goods, or his customer who buys his goods, provided the secondary action is likely to achieve that purpose. In Dimbleby & Sons Ltd v National Union of Journalists (1984), a trade dispute existed between T Ltd and the NUJ. D Ltd had a printing contract with P Ltd, a subsidiary of T Ltd. The NUJ successfully instructed its members working for D Ltd not to complete material which was to be printed by P Ltd, consequently D Ltd sought to restrain the NUJ's actions. It was held that the NUJ had committed the tortious common-law wrong of inducing D Ltd's employees to break their contracts of employment. The NUJ had also threatened to interfere unlawfully with the contract between D Ltd and their printers, P Ltd. TULRA $s13$ could protect otherwise unlawful acts committed by the NUJ if directed against T Ltd, and also protect secondary action against its first customers and suppliers since there was a trade dispute between the NUJ and T Ltd. However, D Ltd was not a first customer of T Ltd, having a contract only with, and thus being a customer of, P Ltd, a separate company and distinct legal entity from T Ltd. The NUJ's action directed against D Ltd and P Ltd was unlawful secondary action, there being no dispute between the NUJ and these two companies.

Injunction

An employee may seek the court's help in restraining threatened action by a trade union by issuing an injunction. Such an injunction must not be granted against a trade union or its officials, apparently acting in contemplation or furtherance of a trade dispute, unless the court is satisfied that reasonable steps have been taken to ensure that the union or official has been given notice of the application, as by serving a written notice together with a copy of the application, and an opportunity to be heard in court proceedings.

Where an application is made by an employer for an interlocutory injunction, the court, in deciding whether to accede, shall have regard to the likelihood of the union establishing a defence at trial of the action based upon ss13 and 15, TULRA by proving that it was 'acting in contemplation or furtherance of a trade dispute'. The court should consider whether on a 'balance of convenience' granting an injunction to the employer would cause more loss to the union than the employer would be able to pay, or, conversely, whether refusing an injunction would cause greater loss to the employer than the union restrained would be able to pay.

In Mercury Communications v Stanley (1983) British Telecom and its employees were in dispute about government privatization plans, in the course of which the union 'blacked' work for Mercury Communications. An interlocutory injunction was granted restraining the blacking. Job security for British Telecom workers was not an issue, since there was an agreement covering this problem. It was not, in law, a 'trade dispute', but was motivated by extraneous matters involving government privatization policies. It was unlikely that the union would make out a case to show the blacking was lawful and, further, it could not adequately compensate Mercury Communications by payment of damages for loss suffered by disruption of work.

FURTHER READING

I. T. Smith and J. C. Wood, *Industrial Law*, Butterworths, 3rd edition, 1986.
Bryn Perrins, *Trade Union Law*, Butterworths, 1985.
Davies and Freedland, *Labour Law*, Weidenfeld & Nicholson, 2nd edition, 1984.

29

Industrial Training

Derek Torrington

A report published in 1985 by the Manpower Services Commission included the following two statements:

> Britain's future international competitiveness and economic performance will be significantly influenced by the speed with which substantial improvements can be made in the scale and effectiveness of training by British companies.

and

> Few employers think training sufficiently central to their business for it to be a main component of their corporate strategy; the great majority did not see it as an issue of major importance — a few openly stated as much.

Those responsible for training in companies often regard their work as vulnerable. If times are hard, training programmes are among the first to suffer cutback. It was partly to change this situation that the Industrial Training Act 1964 was introduced to boost the provision of training in companies. That intervention was only temporarily successful and the more rigorous circumstances of recent years have shifted government priorities in the UK towards provision for the unemployed, and companies are less constrained by the requirements of industrial training boards.

Company training budgets remain vulnerable because training is often regarded as an optional extra: 'without proper training we may not be here in five years, but without more productivity and cash in the bank we won't be here next week'. Sadly some training programmes are indeed expendable because they are not geared to real organizational needs and are of dubious effectiveness. The purpose of this chapter is to make a case for training and then to review some methods of putting it into practice.

THE NEED FOR TRAINING IN COMPANIES

The advantages of training range from more effective use of resources to considerations of the overall purpose of the enterprise.

Resources

The people in an organization are its main resource. If they are not appropriately trained for the work they have to perform they will not do it as efficiently as they could and operations will not be as profitable as they might be. Some degree of investment in training can make the human resources at the disposal of the management more productive and more profitable.

Fragmentation of work

Specialization is growing so that the work to be done within the undertaking is constantly being broken up into smaller parcels. New departments are set up to specialize in a particular aspect of the company's affairs, and each employs people to work in a specialized rather than in a general field. In the management ranks this produces the functional specialist who can do one or two things well, replacing the gifted amateur who could do many things with reasonable competence. This means that each employee needs training to undertake his duties, and this need is likely to become greater.

New skills and knowledge

One consequence of specialization is obsolescence in skills and knowledge. Many people in the financial and administrative field, for example, have forced themselves through the traumatic experience of accepting electronic data processing in the last decade. This acceptance has made it necessary for them to take some training so that they understand the monsters that are spewing forth information at such an alarming rate. The arrival of the computer has rendered obsolete some of the established administrative skills. This effect of technological development is apparent in every part of commercial and industrial activity. Few if any people will still be practising at forty the skills they learned at twenty. The new skills have to be taught.

It is short-sighted, expensive and impractical merely to hire new people who happen to have picked up the new skills elsewhere. The challenge of retraining the adult has to be faced, both by the employer and by the individual concerned. With managerial staff especially, there is the even more demanding need constantly to develop new understanding of the environment in which the organization is functioning. Changes in law, economic circumstances and in the community outside the organization have great influence on affairs within the organization, and knowledge of the environment is essential to managers.

On-the-job training

Some people counter this sort of argument by saying that training should take place outside the field of employment, and that the substantial proportion of the gross national product channelled into further education should take care of industrial training needs by training people in colleges and government training centres in the whole span of skills and areas of knowledge that are developing. Those who make this point would usually be surprised by the extent of what is done in this way, but still the training that is done off the job cannot be completed off the job. Just as a person learning to drive has to sit in the driving seat and drive along the street during his training, so the apprentice engineer, the trainee typist, laboratory technician, supervisor, personnel officer, sales manager and other industrial trainees all have to get their academic training in practical perspective, which is best done in the working situation. Also much necessary training is in routines which are peculiar to one company, so that although a supervisor may learn much of great value on a supervisor's course at the local college it will be equally important for him to learn his own company's disciplinary procedures, and obviously this can come only from an agent of the employer.

Employee expectation

There is a standard of expectation which prospective employees have about what the company provides for its recruits. They will expect canteen facilities and locker rooms. Many will expect pension provision and sick pay. If these basic expectations are not met, they will not come and work for the company unless they have no choice, or unless they are likely to earn much more money than they would elsewhere.

Employees who have no choice of employer may not be influenced by the training that is provided, or not provided, but those who can afford to be selective are much influenced by the training opportunities that a particular opening offers. Here is a comment from a twenty-five year old expert in information technology:

> When I came out of university all the employers were trying to outbid each other on the money and the perks, but that's not what you want. The non-contributory pension scheme means nothing to you until you're on your way out and who needs free medical insurance? I went for a job that was worth doing and where there was proper training so that I could do it well. Some of my friends who were attracted by the money are in their third and fourth jobs now, but getting nowhere: they're just ripping off one company after another without making any sort of future for themselves.

A well-run training scheme will be an aid to recruitment. Complete lack of training will be a disincentive to prospective recruits.

Social purpose

All administrators and managers have a view of the purpose of their enterprise that goes beyond mere survival and profitability. One of management's many objectives is that the company should be a place worth working in, and that the people working there can to some extent achieve personal fulfilment. Assuming that a company has a personnel policy which recognizes its employees as people rather than simply resources, then the requirements for industrial training are the requirements of the people employed as well as the requirements of the employer.

ADMINISTERING THE TRAINING FUNCTION

The passing of the Industrial Training Act led to many companies taking the concept of specialization too far, and training departments were set up where the managers reported directly to the managing director or to the general manager quite independently of the personnel department. The reason for this was usually the calibre of the incumbent personnel manager, or the alarm of the managing director at the prospect of being 'fined' by his industrial training board for not meeting their requirements. In the mid-1960s many personnel managers were limited in their thinking to aspects of employee welfare such as canteen, lavatories and record-keeping rather than taking the broader view of personnel which is common today. As a result this type of personnel manager was not considered the appropriate person to be responsible for training with its new levy sanction, and most of the bright, keen training officers who started emerging were not prepared to report to that type of company executive.

This produced a split in the personnel function. Fortunately this practice is now less common except in the largest organizations with substantial training requirements, but it is important to appreciate that personnel work is an amalgam of many activities including training, employment, payment, trade union recognition, discipline, grievances, the design of jobs and consultative arrangements. Each of these interlocks with the others and they have to be co-ordinated and administered under an overall personnel policy. One cannot be isolated from the rest without risks. Effective training depends on effective selection, improved industrial relations often require new training programmes and training innovations frequently influence the industrial relations environment. In considering how the training function is administered, it is therefore of primary importance to see it as part of personnel work.

The personnel function should not usually report to a line manager. If the responsibility for any aspects of personnel comes under, say, the production manager, then managers in marketing, R & D and other areas will regard it as a specifically production function — as may the production manager. It must be seen to be available to, and necessary for, all company functions. Furthermore the responsibility of the training specialist does not interfere with the line authority of the manager. The training officer provides a specialist service to all line managers in the organization. His particular usefulness lies in his understanding of the requirement of the training board for the relevant industry, his expertise in the skills and the knowledge needed to administer a training programme, his awareness of how people learn, his knowledge of courses and potential visiting lectures. He has a general responsibility for the quality of training provided in the organization, but the individual line manager remains responsible for the performance and competence of his own staff. The line manager needs to appreciate what the training function can do for him in developing that competence: he cannot wash his hands of the responsibility and 'leave it to personnel'. They can only provide him with some services that he has to understand and use.

Integration with other functions

Responsibility for specialist training services needs to be integrated with the whole of the personnel function, which must in turn be integrated with the management of the enterprise. Personnel and training are actively concerned with ensuring that the organization meets its business objectives, not some parasitical unnecessary growth imposed by an outside agency.

Objectives

Corporate objectives need to be reappraised to consider the place of training within the total personnel activity. What are its objectives? How do these fit in with the existing business objectives? What targets have to be achieved? This procedure sounds obvious, but it is perhaps the aspect of training which is most often ignored, with the consequent vulnerability of the training arrangements.

Identification of training needs

The person responsible for training has first to establish the training needs of the organization. He will consider two aspects of this. First he will investigate the operational efficiency of the organization. Later he will look at the training needs of individual people, and the need of the organization for people to be trained. In considering operational efficiency, he will seek to identify those jobs within the organization that appear to be holding back the achievement of proper levels of performance and where training may help to lift this level to one that is acceptable. He will take note of the various indicators which personnel people use to 'take the temperature' of working groups.

Absenteeism, labour turnover, punctuality, sickness, changes in output level, complaints and labour troubles can all be indicators of the state of morale in a department, and low morale may be caused by inadequate training. There may be data available from work study officers who feel that the work standards in a particular department are not satisfactory. Conversations with managers and supervisors will suggest other areas requiring attention. The training officer's own experience and training will suggest others, as will the officers of the industrial training boards.

The training officer will therefore collect a mass of information about the training needs that exist within the company, and can then begin to draw up proposals about what training should be done and in what order, the priority usually being determined by the likely pay-off. He may suggest, for example, that the training of typists could be altered to enable newly recruited school-leavers to reach an acceptable level of proficiency in half the time now considered as necessary, at a saving of £x a year, followed by specially designed programmes of operator training in selected departments to reduce the level of labour turnover and to boost output. He might suggest middle managers attending courses at a business school, or supervisors having a series of discussions on the implications of recent legislation. Whatever the particular proposals, he will draw these up and require them to be endorsed by his management colleagues or superiors, so that he has a mandate to start work.

Implementation of the training programme

When the training officer has received his mandate he will also be empowered to spend some money to implement his programme. This will be based on his prediction of how much he can produce in the way of operating economies. The expenditure will come broadly under two headings. First

INDUSTRIAL TRAINING

there will be expenditure on hardware and fees, which are outgoings that would not be incurred if the training were not done. Hardware can range from boxes of chalk to overhead projectors, teaching machines and fully equipped, soundproof lecture theatres. Fees will be either the fees payable for employees to attend courses, or payable to outside experts to come and take part in internal courses. The training officer, like any other executive submitting a budget for approval, is likely to ask for more than he needs under this heading, as he expects those who have to sanction his budget to cut it. It may be sensible for a newly established training function to start off with a minimum of equipment and to invest more heavily when experience has been gained. The reason for this is that most training programmes change fundamentally after a spell of running in and the benefits of experience. Heavy initial investment can result in an accumulation of expensive equipment that is unused, and a dearth of equipment that is needed but not available because the budget has been overspent.

The second category of expenditure is salaries and wages of trainees, where the administrator perhaps needs to scrutinize proposals closely. Employees away from work on training courses are still being paid. In the case of most managers and supervisors this adds nothing to the cost of their duties being carried out. Someone else will deputize for them in their absence, they will catch up with their work when they return, and that is that. In some other cases, however, there may be expenditure of either increasing the establishment for a department so that people absent for training can be covered, or arrangements for colleagues to work expensive overtime to make up the shortfall. The training is necessary, but this type of consideration needs to be thought of before the training begins so that the cost implications are fully appreciated.

As well as hardware, the training officer will need some space to run his schemes in. Some training will be done on the job or in a training section of the normal job environment, such as the apprentice bench in an engineering shop. Some training will be carried out away from the premises altogether, as when a young manager goes to the nearby polytechnic to take a management course. But there will also be a need for some of the training programme to take place away from the job but on company premises. Typists are often trained in a small school within the company, and a number of short courses may be run to give managers or others an appreciation of a subject or to give training in certain skills that are needed.

Evaluation of training effectiveness

Finally in setting up a training function, there is a need for some means of evaluating the training, and this is one of the most nebulous and unsatisfactory aspects of the training job. The starting point is to compare the results achieved with the original objectives and, where possible, to measure the degree of improvement. This can be done in such areas as labour and material utilization, or the reduction in the number of despatch errors being made in a warehouse. It can only be guessed in the more difficult areas such as the quality of supervision by a foreman before and after a training course. This often depends on a subjective assessment that may be influenced by the reactions of the trainee.

Another possible means of evaluation is to measure the benefits that are set as objectives at the beginning of the programme. It might be a drop in labour turnover and other measures of improved efficiency and employee morale. There may be fewer accidents or reduced levels of overtime. It is also important to attempt some evaluation of the intangibles, such as atmosphere in industrial relations, customer satisfaction, self-confidence among managers and so on. To some extent this can be done by the use of an outside adviser who can come along for a day to examine the situation relating to training within the organization and then report upon it, rather like an auditor.

It is useful from a training point of view to carry out some form of regular performance appraisal among employees. If this is done systematically over several years, the validity of training arrangements will be confirmed — or otherwise.

TRAINING FOR DIFFERENT CATEGORIES OF EMPLOYEE

Operators

The largest single grouping in the employed population is the operator on the shop floor who has no craft skills — the general worker. His job may require such a small amount of skill and knowledge that he needs no training other than a short period of 'being shown how' by his supervisor. There are, however, very few jobs which genuinely fall into this category. Most would be done better by more satisfied employees if they were preceded by a period of training, which covered induction to the organization and the place of the job in the manufacturing process, as well as the mechanics of how it should be done.

As operator jobs in manufacturing are usually specific to each employer, the training needs to be set up and run within the company. There is no outside body either with the understanding of the job or any alternative source of supply of trainees. The training officer will need to study the operations and to use a process of skills analysis to devise a programme of training to be carried out by an instructor instructing trainees. Seldom is the training load large enough to justify a full-time instructor and it is usual for an experienced operator in each department to be trained in instruction so that he does all the instruction needed by new recruits. Another method is for the foreman to be trained so that he inducts and trains all those in his department. This may be the best method as long as the training job is not going to take up too much of his time.

Clerical

Most organizations provide very little training in clerical duties although the practice is spreading and companies are finding that it pays big dividends in cost savings and employee satisfaction. The practice of clerical training is similar to that for operator training, although there are certain more general occupational skills involved, so that the further education system is more helpful. Widely available is a course in office skills which is taken by young people on leaving school. They attend technical college for one day a week and learn simple office skills and routines to fit in with the working experience they are beginning to acquire. There are also many courses in shorthand and typing, although the demand for shorthand is declining and the word processor is rapidly replacing the typewriter as a professional tool. Technical colleges still have some difficulty in equipping their classes with word-processing facilities for student practice, but equipment suppliers provide on-the-job training when they put in a new installation. Many secretaries are still left to struggle with the manual when a new piece of office machinery is delivered, and manuals often seem designed to confuse more than instruct.

The important development marked by the word processor is that this is a way in to computing skills. Many ex-secretaries are now manipulating numbers and elaborate programs with the same facility that they initially acquired by mastering the discipline of the word-processing package.

Craft

One of the first areas to repay attention is the training of craft apprentices, as this is a long and expensive business. Some training boards gave the largest amount of their attention to this area in the first few years of their operation.

Apprentices are recruited at the age of sixteen on leaving school and serve an apprenticeship of several years before being accepted as craftsmen at the end of their training, usually at the age of twenty-one or twenty-two. Most apprentices are young men, although some young women follow apprenticeships, but these are heavily concentrated in hairdressing. Many companies follow the customary practice of binding apprentices by indentures, under which the apprentice is obliged to stay with the employer until finishing his 'time' and the employer agrees to provide his training.

A greater part of the apprentice's time is spent in further education at a local college, learning the theoretical background of his craft and some manual skills. While with the employer, he needs to practise the skills he is learning and to develop them by applying his knowledge and ability to a growing range of work. Traditionally this has been done by watching, helping and copying a craftsman at work. Gradually this method is being replaced by systematic and full-time training under an instructor in charge of a group of apprentices.

If an organization is not big enough to warrant the services of a full-time instructor, it is often possible to join a group training scheme, in which a number of small and medium-sized companies pool resources to employ a training officer who organizes the training of the apprentices in all those companies. In return, the individual company pays a relatively modest fee to the group scheme. Also, the individual apprentice has a better training as he probably moves from one firm to another in the group.

There are usually national agreements between employers and trade unions regarding the employment and training of apprentices.

Technician

A category in which the number of employees is growing is that of technician, who is one step up from a craftsman and is likely to be concerned more with design than with manufacture. In the field of engineering, the fitter is the craftsman and the draftsman is the technician, although there are many others classified as craftsmen and technicians respectively in that industry. To some extent the training needs are common, as the basic technology is the same, but the technician's training needs go further. He is likely to have better educational qualifications at the outset and his further education will go to a higher theoretical level. His practical training will tend to lie in conventional white-collar rather than manual operations. It is usually carried out in close conjunction with a qualified man.

Technologist

It is difficult to distinguish between technicians and technologists and in many industries such a distinction cannot be drawn at all. A rough and ready identification would be by the word 'professional'. In engineering, for example, the technologist is the professional engineer who has achieved membership of one of the constituent bodies of the Council of Engineering Institutions. This requires a high level of academic qualification together with the appropriate working experience.

In this category will be the ex-technician who has taken the HNC/HND route through day release or evening courses, as well as the technical graduate who starts his working life in his early twenties. These are the people on whom the technical competence and progress of the organization will depend. The HNC/D method of qualification has been replaced by the scheme of the Technical Education Council (TEC). Courses for technical graduates now have the interesting development of a small number of courses in selected universities that combine engineering and management studies, usually over four years.

The man who comes up through the ranks will need facilities to pursue his academic studies, either by day release or by sandwich course. His practical expertise will be acquired almost incidentally as long as he has reasonable opportunities for varied working experience, rather than being classified as a trainee who cannot be given a proper job because he has not finished his education.

The technical graduate who joins industry in his early twenties with academic qualifications of a high order but no practical experience usually needs some form of graduate apprenticeship while he spends a number of months acquiring the practical experience that is needed to go with his theoretical grounding.

Management

Training managers is a very different matter from training other categories of workers in industry. This is largely because a smaller proportion of the manager's job content can be isolated and taught. To be effective a manager needs to learn management techniques, such as various methods for the quantification of data so that decisions may be soundly based. He also needs knowledge in such areas as the behavioural sciences so that he can understand how employees may react in certain situations, and so that he may plan sensibly for the future. Beyond this, however, there is still a large area of training or development needed for the individual management trainee, so that he acquires the stature and confidence needed for the job of leadership, gains judgement and determination and develops good timing and a sensitive awareness in handling people.

Largely because of the difficulty and lack of definition in the task of management training, most large organizations separate this particular aspect of training and give the responsibility to management development officers within the training function. The body of knowledge and some of the skills can come from the educational system. In addition to the business schools, which cater for a small fraction of the total amount of management training, there are a number of polytechnics and universities with management departments running courses with recognition from some professional body. The most widely recognized management qualification available in the field of further education is the Diploma in Management Studies, run under the auspices of the Department of Education and Science. It is operated at a limited number of centres and provides a broadly based management education for the well-qualified entrant with limited practical experience. There are also courses run under the aegis of, for instance, the Institute of Personnel Management and the Institution of Industrial Managers which provide a broad management education with particular emphasis on the specialism that the professional body represents.

In conjunction with further education, the trainee manager will need controlled working experience and career development so that he can apply his developing skills and knowledge. He may also need careful coaching to help him develop qualities such as judgement and timing. All managers need constantly to bring themselves up to date with new techniques or with new knowledge. Thus, professional bodies like the British Institute of Management and many firms of professional consultants conduct admirable short courses, running for a few days or a few weeks, to update the experienced manager. Typical of these have been the endless variety of courses and conferences to brief managers on unfair dismissal legislation, safety and health, or negotiating skills. The next chapter deals with management development in more detail.

Supervisory

Training of first-line supervisors is generally unsatisfactory in the United Kingdom, and the foreman has more than once been referred to as the forgotten man of British industry. Much of the problem lies in the uncertainty about the nature of the job. In the early years of this century the foreman was a man of considerable power and authority in a factory, with extensive discretion in decision making, and was often a general manager in all but name. Since then we have seen the professionalization of management and the development of shop steward authority. The professionalization of management has spawned countless middle managers who have taken bits of the foreman's job away from him, like the production engineer and the training officer. The development of shop steward authority has largely done away with the foreman's role as representative of shopfloor feeling, and he is constantly bypassed as shop stewards negotiate with middle and senior managers at meetings he is not invited to attend.

As the position of first-line supervisor is so difficult to define, training for it presents obvious problems. The most useful approach is probably the in-company course which aims to inform foremen of the changes taking place around them and give them an understanding of company procedures together with an introduction to such vague but necessary subjects as leadership and human relations. An attempt to establish a course for foremen within the further education system has not received widespread support.

Administrative

The term 'administrative' covers an amorphous group of people who are lumped together because their work is neither clerical nor managerial. They are such people as cost accounts, computer programmers and systems analysts, salesmen and O & M staff.

INDUSTRIAL TRAINING

For the cost accountant, training will usually be on the job as a cost clerk while he makes his way through the further education courses for cost and management accountants, perhaps after starting with an Ordinary National Diploma in Business Studies while he is making up his mind about the area in which he wishes to specialize.

The training of computer personnel operates at various levels. Most courses in management include some elements of computing, even if only at the appreciation level, and there are a number of degree courses in computation. Computer operators and data input personnel are still mainly trained by computer manufacturers or specialized private agencies.

Shop stewards

The final category is shop steward. It is the joint responsibility of management and trade unions to train shop stewards. The best courses for stewards are provided by the trade unions, and an introductory course for newly elected shop stewards is run at many educational centres under the auspices of the TUC. It is difficult for many employers to provide satisfactory courses of their own, as stewards are likely to be suspicious of them, but this field of training will no doubt develop.

TRAINING METHODS

Teaching someone to *do* something requires a different approach from teaching someone to *understand* something. This broad distinction between training in skill and training in knowledge has been refined by research in the training field to produce a division of all types of learning into five basic types.

Some learning involves theoretical subject matter: knowing how, why and when certain things happen. This is *comprehension*. Examples are the laws of thermodynamics, the currency structure of the EEC, or the arguments justifying the recognition of trade unions. *Reflex* learning is involved when skilled movements or perceptual capacities have to be acquired, involving practice as well as knowing what to do. Speed is usually important and the trainee needs constant repetition to develop the appropriate synchronization and co-ordination. Typing is one of the many jobs that requires reflex learning. *Attitude* development is concerned with enabling people to alter their attitudes and social skills. *Memory* training is concerned with learning how to cope with varied situations and *procedural* learning is very similar except that the drill to be followed does not have to be memorized but located and understood. This categorization produces the mnemonic CRAMP.

Learning for comprehension requires the whole subject to be treated as an entity and the lecture or training manual are appropriate methods. Attitude change is typically handled by group discussion, but reflex learning is best handled by part methods, which break the task down into sections, each of which can be studied and practised separately before putting together a complete performance. Memory and procedural learning may take place either by whole or part methods, although memorization is usually done by parts.

FURTHER READING

B. M. Bass and J. A. Vaughan, *Training in Industry*, Tavistock, London, 1968.

Industrial Training Research Unit, *Choose an Effective Style: A Self-instructional Approach to the Teaching of Skills*, ITRU Publications, Cambridge, 1976.

J. P. J. Kenney and M. Reid, *Training Interventions*, Institute of Personnel Management, London, 1986.

MSC/NEDO, *A Challenge to Complacency: Changing Attitudes to Training*, Manpower Services Commission, Sheffield, 1985.

R. B. Stammers and J. Patrick, *The Psychology of Training*, Methuen, London, 1975.

I. Winfield, *Learning to Teach Practical Skills*, Kogan Page, London, 1979.

Part Six
The Management of Physical Assets

30

The Administration of Commercial Property

Philip Westwood

The company secretary or office manager may be required, as part of his duties, to administer the property within which the company carries out its business, or to advise the directors in matters related to the company's buildings or land.

In normal circumstances, a company secretary will take over the company property from his predecessor, and many of the decisions discussed in this chapter will have been made for him. But like all other aspects of the company's activities, the continuing suitability of its premises should be reviewed regularly. This chapter is intended to aid that process and assist in the correct decisions being taken as the company expands or contracts to meet changing circumstances.

All proprietary interests in land are at law 'real' property, as distinct from other property including chattels, animals, stocks and shares etc., which are 'personal' property. Thus 'real estate' includes freeholds and easements, which are rights by virtue of land ownership over the land of others, e.g. a right of way.

The nature of a company's real estate will depend on its activities. It may consist of retail outlets, administrative offices, warehouses, garages for the repair and maintenance of the company's transport, factories, research and development facilities, leisure and training facilities, and company houses for the accommodation of its staff. If a great deal of property is involved, then the company would be best advised to employ its own staff with professional expertise in the selection and maintenance of its buildings. A small company may feel unable to afford such help, and will look to the office manager or company secretary to fulfil these duties, whilst taking professional advice when the need arises.

FACTORS AFFECTING THE SELECTION OF A BUILDING

Selecting a building to suit the needs of a company will involve the review of a number of factors, including the location of the building, choice of site, type of building proposed, and the extent of refurbishment, repair, or new building work needed to meet the company's requirements. The choice of freehold or leasehold purchase is dictated by the availability of suitable buildings and will generally have little affect on the decisions taken.

Location

A modern business should be sited where it can achieve the most efficient use of its resources. Traditionally, businesses are located near their markets, their raw material, or the labour and power necessary for the conversion of that material into goods for sale. In the nineteenth century, the development of the railways allowed the increased separation of these elements and introduced the additional need for proximity to railway depots and marshalling yards. Many heavy industries had their own railway sidings. The decline of the railways coupled with improvements in the road network and suitable vehicles has resulted in the transfer of a greater part of raw materials and goods distribution to the roads. Docks and airports are vital for businesses entering the export market. As trade becomes more international, the availability of alternative means of fast distribution remains an important consideration in the location of a company's premises.

The location of industry and commerce is therefore dependent upon easy access to raw materials, easy delivery of products to markets, docks or airports, and the availability of a suitable labour force.

Commercial undertakings generally begin in locations which favour the small scale of the enterprise. As the company grows the commercial environment may alter to such an extent that the factors which worked in its favour in its early development are either neutralized or begin to work against its interests. It should be borne in mind that relocation could be a solution to the problems of inefficiency resulting from labour problems, unavailability of space for expansion, or the need for reorganization of production lines without interruption of output.

Selecting a site

A company wishing to establish itself on a new site, either by conversion of an existing building or by building afresh, will find its choice limited by planning legislation, which controls the location of commercial and industrial development. This control, as well as preventing certain types of development in particular areas, also encourages the establishment of special commercial and industrial zones or estates. Sites within such zones are available for light industrial use, allowing the letting of existing purpose-made factory or office units, or the erection of buildings to the company's own design. The government, in partnership with local authorities, also attempts to direct the location of new business to areas of high unemployment. Tax and rate allowances are available in favour of some regions, particularly the North-east and South Wales and in areas such as London's 'Docklands' where 'enterprise zones' have been established and special provisions apply. For example, rate 'holidays' for the first year of trading in the area. If the business is large or politically important enough, local authorities will generally be prepared to consider proposals for new development and negotiate special terms, e.g. low interest loans, rate reductions etc., in order to attract the business to its area. Similar opportunities apply abroad, particularly within the EEC. A company considering relocation would be well advised to explore all these options before settling on a suitable site.

New towns have been established over the past fifty years or so, to take the overspill population from the larger cities. They were designed as self-contained economic units, with their own industrial and commercial centres. The sites for these new towns were generally chosen to take advantage of good communications and other facilities, and offer many amenities to attract business and labour.

The long-term benefits to companies of relocation include continuing rate and insurance bills lower than in city centres, and a more contented workforce, not hidebound by traditional working practices.

Here is a checklist of factors to be considered when choosing a building location:

1   Communications
    (a) standard of trunk roads
    (b) proximity of railhead
    (c) access to international airport
    (d) access to seaport
    (e) average distance from suppliers and consumers (as small as possible)
2   Services
    (a) electric power available without restriction
    (b) Mains gas supplies
    (c) Adequate water supplies
3   Climate and topography
    (a) temperate climate throughout the year
    (b) area/site well drained and free from flood danger

    (c) site sheltered from high winds and extreme weather
    (d) surrounding area pleasant; good outlook from site
4 Government and local authority
    (a) area scheduled as development area (or enterprise zone) and eligible for investment grants
    (b) planning restrictions in the area minimal
    (c) friendly and cooperative local authority
5 Labour and labour relations
    (a) local branches of trade unions moderate and cooperative
    (b) key staff willing to move into area
    (c) good supply of skilled or suitable work people already living in the area
6 Amenities
    (a) housing prices low, good supply of houses of all types (private and local authority)
    (b) good schools, with possibilities in the area for higher education
    (c) good local transport facilities for commuters
    (d) good local health services and hospitals
    (e) adequate recreational facilities in the area
    (f) theatres, cinemas and other entertainments
    (g) police and fire services efficient
    (h) churches of all denominations accessible
7 Specific site factors
    (a) means for disposal of waste/effluent
    (b) access on good local roads
    (c) as required by the particular industry

Choosing a building

The choice of building will depend on a number of factors which must be considered carefully together.

The activities and processes which are to be undertaken within the building should be analysed so that their requirements can be satisfied in its design. A report of the requirements of manufacturing processes, the storage of raw materials and finished products and the methods of packing and distribution should be requested from the managers responsible. The difficulties encountered in setting up a new office are dealt with in Chapter 17. All must be considered and a brief prepared to enable the appropriate building to be sought.

Unless the requirements of the firm are extremely specialized, it is likely a choice will be made from among a number of buildings with varying degrees of suitability. The first consideration is whether the firm wishes to rent or purchase the property and, if the latter, whether an existing building is being sought or specially built premises are required. The time factor is very important — a new building may take one or two years to complete, depending on its complexity, after all necessary consents are to hand. The design stage may add a further six to twelve months to the process. If the company can afford to purchase the freehold the building will represent a valuable asset and surety against the rent reviews inevitable in leases.

Any building which is taken over either by lease or purchase will probably require considerable capital expenditure in adapting it to the needs of the company. These may range from a complete refurbishment − installation of air conditioning, improved insulation and modern welfare facilities − to minor redecoration work and carpeting. If the use of the building is to be changed, work may be needed to meet the requirements of special legislation or a licensing authority, and planning permission obtained.

PROFESSIONAL ADVICE

At this stage it is wise to consider appointing a professional who will be able to advise on the selection, conversion or construction of suitable premises. This appointment should be made at an early stage in order to avoid problems which may arise from the purchase of a building which is ill fitted to the company's requirements for technical reasons. There are many considerations which require professional expertise in their assessment, e.g. the suitability of the structure to carry the loads required, the capacity of the drains to cope with the increased use envisaged and the requirements of the fire authorities.

The range of suitable qualified professional help has never been wider. In the past the architect has dominated this area, and may well be the only professional who springs to mind when considering building work. Of recent years the emergence of the surveyor, particularly of the building surveyor, as an expert in conversion and refurbishment work, has allowed the client greater choice and a range of skills which go beyond that offered by the architect.

Building surveyors and quantity surveyors are able to offer a full range of services which include structural surveys, cost feasibility studies, advice on the appointment of contractors and the design and supervision of the conversion work. Building surveyors are usually graduates who qualify under the examinations of The Royal Institution of Chartered Surveyors. They use the title Fellow (FRICS) or Associate (ARICS). Architects must be registered with the Architect's Registration Council of the United Kingdom (ARCUK) and are usually Fellows (FRIBA) or Associates (ARIBA) of the Royal Institute of British Architects. Both the RICS and the RIBA publish registers (available in most public libraries) of practitioners.

The correct choice of someone who is going to be closely linked with major expenditure on a company's behalf is of vital importance. It would be prudent to interview prospective candidates. References from recent clients should be sought, and work in progress or recently completed should be inspected.

The architect/surveyor may be appointed to carry out the complete task, from advising at the inception of the scheme to the final handover of the completed work, or appointed to deal with specific stages of the work, perhaps for the feasibility study only, or up to the selection of the contractor to carry out the work. The scale of fees would be varied accordingly.

He, or she, will require a brief of the company's requirements, with particular emphasis on any special areas of concern. For example, special provision will have to be made for areas of high fire risk, loads such as safes or heavy equipment, and ventilation and air conditioning. Account must be taken of any constraints upon the layout of offices and workshops arising from working practices, manufacturing production lines, open-plan or individual offices etc., vehicular access and parking for staff and deliveries, catering facilities and special service needs requiring high voltage electrical substations or generators (for computers or large machinery).

Selecting a contractor

One of the architect/surveyor's duties will be to advise on the selection of a contractor to carry out the building work. Since it is particularly difficult to control building costs associated with conversion work, that selection process must produce a contractor and price for the works which can be relied upon. The traditional method of choosing a contractor is by a process of competitive tendering, whereby a number of contractors are selected to bid for the work. The contractor offering the cheapest price is generally awarded the contract. The architect/surveyor will normally invite contractors capable of undertaking work of the type and value required, selected prior to the tender itself. A list of suitable contractors circumvents any difficulties which may arise if an unknown contractor submits the lowest price in an open tender. The additional confidence in a contractor chosen by this selective tender process, and the time saved in the selection may well be worth the possibility of a higher contract price.

Other systems of selection and contracting are available which may be used where suitable. These will now be discussed briefly in turn.

Management fee contracts, whereby the contractor undertakes to manage the contract for a fee established in advance. This allows the appointment to be made at an early stage in the design process and the introduction of an important new member to the professional team. The intention is that the contractor cannot be said to gain from increases in the value of the work, a useful factor if major refurbishment is contemplated.

Package deal and turnkey systems are those where the whole of the design and construction work is undertaken for a total cost, the client being handed the key to the building on completion ('turnkey'). Contracts of this type are offered by companies with an interest in providing a standardized form of construction and are often used for standard factory or warehouse units on industrial estates. They are therefore more suitable for new building work rather than for refurbishment, but they may be used for extensions to existing buildings, or for new work within an existing site.

Design and build contracts are similar to package deal contracts, but with a greater emphasis on the client's special design requirements.

Separate contracts or the Alternative Methods of Management system (AMM) involve the use of the architect/surveyor as usual, but the various aspects of the work are let to individual contractors, as appropriate, thus avoiding the appointment of a single main contractor. The architect/surveyor manages the contract. The client selects a number of contractors who each carry out their own part of the work. Refurbishment work could be carried out using this sytem.

Project management contracts place the responsibility for all the various aspects of the work, design, supervision and performance, on one organization. No single profession has emerged as the legitimate leader in this type of contract. Architects, surveyors and main contractors are all conducting contracts of this type at present. Essentially the functions of each are being carried out by a team consisting of architects, surveyors and contracting staff, but all under the one contract. It generally depends on the professional background of the team leader as to which profession claims to be the project manager. Advantages of the system include the removal of the litigious barriers between the members of the team, who can all be seen to be working together for the good of the project.

The British Property Federation System is a client-based alternative system. It is biased towards the interest of the client, which may mean that better contractors will avoid it. The system contains many previously untried processes, and may not prove as advantageous to the client as it at first appears.

Remember that the cheapest initial price may not prove to be the cheapest final contract figure. Costs arising from delays, claims, or the bankruptcy of contractors caused by the enforcement of onerous contract conditions may not be assessable or recoverable. It is worth spending some little time ensuring that the right designer, supervisor and contractor are chosen and that the building requirements are fully worked out and understood before work is started on site.

BUILDING LEGISLATION

There are approximately 200 Acts of Parliament and nearly 300 regulations affecting building operations.

Of course, not all the legislation applies to any particular building. Many types of building or uses to which a building may be put have their own specific regulations, but some of the general legislation, such as the building regulations, applies in most cases, and should always be considered.

Many of the regulations apply only to particular classes of building, or to buildings used for special purposes. For example, the Asbestos Regulations apply only to premises where asbestos processes are carried out.

There are twenty-six Acts and regulations for buildings in general and if the building is of some architectural or historical significance, a further eight apply. The number of items applicable to commercial buildings depends on the proposed use of the building. Offices and shops for general purposes have eighteen Acts and regulations, in addition to the twenty-six mentioned above. If it is a food shop or market, a further eight must be added, and if it sells medicines, another nine. Industrial buildings have twelve general Acts or regulations, a further twenty-two if it is a general factory, nine more for the manufacture of medicines.

Residential buildings are also covered by Acts and regulations depending on use. Private domestic housing does not have many, but there are twenty-eight Acts or regulations to do with housing improvement grants and home insulation grants, some of which are applicable to private as well as public housing.

In addition there is legislation on fire precaution, town and country planning and health and safety.

Legislation affecting particular commercial and industrial applications would normally be well known to a company working in that field. It is therefore proposed to discuss only the more important items of legislation of general concern to building owners.

Planning control

The use to which a building may be put is controlled by planning legislation exercised by the local authority under the Town and Country Planning Act 1971. The Use Classes Order 1972 categorizes a number of uses for land. Although land, and the buildings on the land, may continue to be used for purposes within the same use class, any change in use class constitutes development and requires planning permission. For example, a greengrocers may become a newsagents, but not a fast food restaurant; a factory producing clothing may switch to the assembly of electronic components or other light industrial use, provided no noxious emissions result from the process.

Planning permission can be sought in two stages. Initial application can be made for outline planning approval. A prospective user can explore the likelihood of permission to use land for his purpose without the need to fully develop the scheme, even before he has obtained any legal interest in the site. Care needs to be taken here, since the value of the land may increase considerably if planning consent is given. For this reason, consent is generally given to a particular individual or company and may lapse if that company sells its interest to another party. Before development can take place, detailed proposals must be put forward and full planning consent obtained.

As well as the nature of the use of the development, the local authority will be concerned with the appearance and height of the building, means of access, car parking provision and, increasingly, the employment opportunities offered by the development.

If it is felt that planning approval may be required, the advice of the planning authority should be sought. Planning permission cannot be awarded retrospectively. The local authority is required to order the removal of any building for which planning permission is not obtained and the restoration of the land to its former use.

Building control

Any development which involves the construction of new work or alterations or extensions to existing buildings may have to satisfy the requirements of the building regulations. Building control is also exercised by the local authority and it is common practice to submit plans for building regulation approval at the same time as an application is made for planning approval. The practice of submitting plans for scrutiny and approval prior to the commencement of building work has been criticized in the past as causing unnecessary delay, particularly in circumstances where the work required is straightforward and simple, e.g. the installation of a washbasin or the erection of a small shed. Since November 1985 alternative procedures have been available whereby the local authority is notified that the work will be carried out and inspection takes place on site, without the prior approval of plans. The building owner loses certain protection afforded under the older system, but gains time in circumstances where the risk of failure to comply with the regulations is less likely. A third method, using inspectors approved under the Approved Inspectors Regulations instead of the local authority inspectors, has also been introduced, but at present the only approved inspectors are the National House Builders Registration Council, who deal with private housing developments.

The Building Regulations lay down standards of design and construction mainly in the interests of public health and safety, and to conserve power and water supply. Sections of the regulations deal with structural strength, means of escape in case of fire, drainage and sanitation, ventilation, thermal insulation and water supply.

In all the alternative inspection systems now available, the building owner is held responsible for compliance with the building regulations. Failure to do so can lead to a fine, and an order to put right or remove offending work.

Fire precautions

Fire precautions are an important part of the safety of premises and are dealt with in two ways. New building work is dealt with primarily under the building regulations, but existing buildings are dealt with under the Fire Precautions Act 1971 and related legislation.

The Act deals with the adequate provision of means of escape in case of fire. It includes the provision of fire-fighting equipment, alarm systems etc. It is primarily concerned with the protection of life, but the measures necessary to meet the requirements will provide some protection to property in the event of fire. There is also a requirement to instruct staff on necessary action in case of fire, and records must be kept of fire drills, alarm tests, maintenance checks and incidents involving fire. Registers are provided for the purpose. The provision of special equipment, sprinkler systems and the like, may be used in order to prolong the time available for escape and to protect property where there is special risk. Sprinklers and smoke-detection devices may be required in special circumstances, e.g. basements and storage areas for inflammable materials.

In order to invoke its powers, the minister must place before Parliament a designating order, which brings the types of buildings specified by the order under the Act. The Act was intended eventually to cover all buildings which fall into one of the following categories of use:

1 Recreation, entertainment or instruction or for any club, society or association
2 Teaching, training or research
3 Institutions providing treatment or care
4 Any purpose involving the provision of sleeping accommodation
5 Any use involving access to the building by members of the public, whether on payment or otherwise
6 Since the enactment of the Health and Safety at Work etc. Act 1974, the use of the premises as a place of work

At present there have been only two such designating orders. The first dealt with hotels and boarding houses, the second with premises previously covered by the Factories Acts and the Offices, Shops and Railway Premises Act. In both cases there is a minimum size related to the number of people on the premises below which certification is not required.

Other categories of building are presently covered by further regulations with respect to fire control. For example, nursing homes and residential care homes may come under the Act with the introduction of a future designation order. At present the fire officer's requirements in this area are covered by the Residential Homes Act 1984 and the Residential Care Homes Regulations 1984. In this case the registration by the area health authority under the Act includes the requirement to satisfy the fire officer in the same areas of concern covered by the Fire Precautions Act.

Under the Fire Precautions Act the owner of premises in a category designated by an order must make application to the fire authority for a fire certificate. The fire authority is required to inspect the premises and advise on necessary standards. If necessary, he may provide written notice of the steps required to achieve a certificate and stipulate a time to carry out the work. After the specified period of time, a final inspection takes place. If the work is carried out to the satisfaction of the fire officer, a fire certificate is issued. If not, the business must cease trading. If the owner feels that the schedule of requirements, or any decision of the fire officer, is unreasonable, an appeal must be made within twenty-one days.

The provision of fire protection systems may be prudent in situations not at present covered by the Fire Precautions Act. Suitable detection and control systems can prevent serious damage from fire by early detection and local control and may allow normal business to recommence more quickly after a fire. Constant vigilance and inspection is necessary to maintain standards and ensure that the measures taken are not undermined by careless action. Recently a fire which broke out in a basement storeroom of a leading oil company's head office in London, caused £100 000 damage despite almost instant detection and the attendance of the fire service after less than two minutes. The subsequent disruption caused by repair work added a further £200 000 to the bill. Fire doors had been wedged open and communication ducting and air conditioning conducted the smoke as far as the tenth floor.

Insurance companies will look favourably on an organization with a sound fire prevention policy. Whilst it is unlikely that there will be a reduction in premiums, the additional premiums required to cover high risk areas or materials may be avoided.

FUTURE ALTERATIONS AND EXTENSIONS

When reviewing the suitability of a company's property due allowance for future expansion should be made. If considering the purchase of existing property the possibility of taking over adjacent property in the future, or of buying a building with a greater floor area than present requirements demand, should be explored. The extra space may be let on a short lease until required. If a new building is contemplated the architect or surveyor responsible for the design should be informed of future plans so that he may make allowance within his design. The additional cost of building stronger foundations and structural members to take an extra storey in the future will be minimal compared to the cost involved later. The choice of location of the building may be influenced if site investigations show that the extra loads take the design beyond the bearing capacity of the ground, or likely planning restrictions inhibit the anticipated development. The incorporation of larger capacity service mains may also be considered.

A company is entitled to extend its property within normal planning constraints up to 10 per cent of the original development without further planning approval being required. If an extension of less than the full 10 per cent is made, further expansion up to the total of 10 per cent of the original development is possible. The stated limits relate to the building, not the occupier, and care should be taken to establish if the development allowance has been used up by earlier owners. Where expansion beyond the gross 10 per cent is contemplated, new planning approval must be sought.

For leasehold property the lessor's consent will be required and at this stage it should be considered whether notice should be served under the Landlord and Tenant Act 1927, to protect the tenant's position at the end of the lease.

DISPOSAL

In considering the initial design, alteration or extension of any building it is advisable to have in mind the possibility of eventual disposal. The more specialized a building in design the more difficult it is to sell, as it cannot easily be adapted for use other than that for which it was originally intended. An extreme example of this would be a steelworks; although such buildings as Thames-side warehouses have been converted into flats. In office buildings partitioning arrangements will almost certainly be unsuitable to a subsequent occupier and open office floors should be subdivided by partitions that are easily removed or adapted.

MAINTENANCE AND REPAIR

An important aspect of property management is maintenance and repair. Buildings consist of materials of varying durability, with 'lives' ranging from a few years to centuries. Some, such as timber joinery, can be protected by impregnation at the manufacturing stage or the application of surface treatments (paints, stains or varnishes) throughout their life. Others, such as heating appliances, wear out after a number of years' use, and need overhaul or replacement well before the rest of the building deteriorates.

Failure to carry out repair and maintenance at the appropriate time can lead to a considerably more expensive replacement later, or even danger to the building occupants — for example, if a faulty gas appliance continues to be used.

Whilst not all equipment and materials need to last the whole life of the building, those which are used in parts of the building which are difficult to reach without severe disruption should be designed to do so. However, the replacement of a boiler may provide an opportunity for a review of the heating and ventilating requirements of the property, resulting in the introduction of more efficient systems. Very few buildings over twenty-five years old still retain the same heating system, or even the same internal layout, as envisaged in their original design.

When evaluating the suitability of any building, ease of maintenance should be a prime consideration. There are a number of hidden costs associated with maintenance which may be overlooked when comparing alternative materials. In addition to the work itself, there is the cost of disruption to the normal routine whilst the work is carried out. The cost to the company of misplaced documents or files because they were moved to allow the painters in, or of a vehicle access blocked by scaffolding may be extremely high. Also, the additional security risk of unauthorized access via scaffolding cannot be overlooked. Some of these maintenance costs cannot be avoided entirely, but choices taken during the design or refurbishment of premises at the time of purchase can reduce their effect or frequency.

In some cases the initial cost of incorporating materials or design requiring low maintenance into a building will be greater than would otherwise be required. The loss of earnings or interest on the extra capital should be balanced against the expected savings in the future. Maintenance is an area which is particularly vulnerable to the company's financial circumstances. It is all too easy to delay maintenance to save costs. For this reason the temptation of agreeing to a cheap specification and relying on future maintenance being carried out on a regular basis should be avoided, but the idea of spending money today in anticipation of problems which may not arise for twenty or thirty years is a difficult one, particularly if a board of directors or shareholders has to be persuaded. It can be argued that companies are more concerned with current expenditure than future expense, but the value of designed maintenance is becoming better appreciated and may be reflected in the value of the property if it comes to the market before the maintenance is required. A compromise between designing a cheap specification with high maintenance costs or an expensive specification with little or no maintenance must be reached, and the architect or surveyor should be able to advise here. The terms 'costs in use' or 'life-cycle costing' may be used and they describe procedures where, on paper, future expenditure is discounted to present values for comparison purposes.

Maintenance programmes should be prepared by the prudent building owner. In order to identify the requirements of the building it is necessary to carry out a survey and programme of maintenance appropriate to the materials and design incorporated within its construction. This programme can form the basis of a maintenance budget which should be approved at the highest level, particularly in view of the vulnerability described above.

The varying needs for maintenance in different parts of the building must be established. Little used or carefully used rooms and corridors require less frequent redecoration with consequent savings in the maintenance budget. Reception areas and other prestigious parts of the building require redecoration more frequently than is strictly necessary for the protection of the fabric, in order to maintain or promote the corporate image of the company. Also, where the fabric of the building is exposed to corrosive processes or where hygiene requirements must be considered, for example in food preparation areas, more frequent redecoration will be required.

Provided the building is in a good standard of repair when purchased, expenditure on maintenance should not be great in the first few years of occupation. If low maintenance materials are incorporated, maintenance will be limited to the repainting of external painted surfaces every three to five years and redecoration internally as required. Longer term planning for the replacement of boilers or electrical rewiring can be included within an annual maintenance budget.

Labour for maintenance may be provided by a contractor whose selection was described earlier in this chapter. The contractor may carry out specific tasks in accordance with the previously agreed maintenance programme, or cope with emergencies. Minor repairs and the replacement of consumable equipment like fluorescent light tubes is usually carried out by staff directly employed by the company. In some areas of high office concentrations, it is now possible to obtain such services from specialist maintenance contractors who will undertake a twenty-four-hour comprehensive service.

LEASEHOLD PROPERTY

A high proportion of commercial property is leasehold, and most leases contain a clause which allows the rent to be reviewed at fixed intervals during its term. At each review date the current market rent is assessed and substituted for the rent previously payable. The dates or interval between reviews should be expressly stated in the lease, together with the procedure which must be followed. Recent court decisions have been concerned with the rights of the parties if the procedure is not followed, for example, where the landlord does not give notice of the review at the time stipulated or implied by the lease. The view is that the landlord will forfeit the right to a review until the next review date if time is of the essence of the agreement. Time will only be of the essence if it is expressly so provided in the terms of the lease, or if there is some indication in the lease or in the surrounding circumstances that time is to be of the essence. Generally, surveyors or valuers acting for each party meet and negotiate the new rent. Provision is usually made within the lease for the appointment of a third independent surveyor to settle the matter by arbitration if agreement is not reached.

Full repair covenants

Leases for commercial property may contain a full repair covenant, which requires a tenant to leave the property newly decorated and in a condition of good repair at the end of the tenancy. Even if in disrepair at the commencement of a lease having a full repairing covenant, a tenant must put the premises into good repair and so hand them back at the end of the term.

The law of dilapidations is complex and a subject for experts; but the principle should be borne in mind that the measure of dilapidations when they have to be valued is the amount of injury to the landlord's revisionary interest. If it is the landlord's intention to demolish the building for redevelopment, he will fail in a claim against the tenant if the building is in disrepair, as he has suffered no loss.

A tenant of business premises may be entitled to a new lease on the expiration of an existing lease should he desire to continue in occupation under the terms of the Landlord and Tenant Act 1954. The rent of the premises is subject to review under the new terms and the landlord can regain possession, thus avoiding granting of a new lease, if he proves intention to redevelop the premises or requirement for his own occupation. Provision is made in the Landlord and Tenant Act 1927 for compensation for tenants making improvements, or establishing goodwill in business premises at the end of the term of the lease. Alternatively a new lease may be granted.

VALUATION

The valuation of freehold or leasehold property should be carried out by an expert who is familiar with the value of similar properties in the same market. The value depends on the purpose of the valuation. Valuation for insurance purposes will be the full cost of rebuilding on the existing land and consequently should not include the value of the land. The cost of rebuilding should include the cost of site clearance, professional fees and legal expenses. Insurance should also be taken out to cover the cost of disruption to production or temporary accommodation required whilst the work is carried out. The value of a property for the purpose of sale or the setting of rents will depend on its location and the demand for property of that type and condition in the area. Perhaps surprisingly, it has no direct relationship to the cost of building, particularly where the advantages of the location may be overwhelming, and there is a scarcity of building land in the area. It is prudent to undertake a revaluation of a company's real estate at intervals, as it represents an asset which is often undervalued in the accounts with a consequential affect on the company's value in the market place.

RATING

The responsibility for valuing property for rating purposes rests with valuation officers of the Inland Revenue, who establish a gross value for the property or hereditament concerned. The rating authority levies a rate in the £ or 'rateable value' for each property, based on the valuation officer's assessment. Valuation lists for England and Wales contain all rateable hereditaments for each rating area together with their assessments.

Rates are levied on the occupier of a property, although the owner may be liable for rates on unoccupied premises.

The basis of the valuation is an estimate of the rent at which the particular property might be let according to the statutory definition defined within the General Rate Act 1967. The current valuation lists came into force on 1 April 1973, and any subsequent alterations to those assessments, or properties being assessed for the first time, should not exceed the value that would have been ascribed to the particular hereditament had it existed in the year prior to 1 April 1973. This is called the 'tone of the list' and it is important to ensure that should reassessment occur, for example as the result of building alterations, the addition in assessment is not excessive and the 'tone' has been properly applied.

Under the General Rate Act 1967 it was intended that a revaluation of the list would occur every five years. This provision was abolished by the Local Government, Planning and Land Act 1980. The further removed that 1 April 1973 becomes the more difficult it is to assess new buildings satisfactorily. Plans are in progress to revalue all commercial property with effect some time in 1990, the date still to be announced. A ratepayer has the right to seek a reduction in assessment at any time by making a proposal, although the operative date of any reduction in assessment can only be, at the earliest, from the beginning of the rate year in which the proposal was served, i.e. 1 April. The majority of appeals are determined by agreement negotiated between the ratepayer's professional advisers and the valuation officer. If agreement cannot be reached, the matter will be heard by a local valuation court. There is a right of appeal to the Lands Tribunal and on a point of law to the Court of Appeal and thence to the House of Lords.

Grounds frequently exist or arise where an appeal is justified, particularly if the valuation officer is not aware of special difficulties associated with the premises in question. For example the premises may be outmoded for their present use or irregular in shape. They may have difficult access, poor natural light, low headroom etc. The effect of building works either within the hereditament or adjacent to it can give rise to a temporary reduction in assessment. In view of the foregoing, and the high rate burden carried by the business community, it is sensible for a company to review its rating assessment at periodic intervals and appeal if grounds exist.

ADJOINING OWNERS

The owner and occupier of a property has a responsibility to his neighbours and the community at large in respect of his use of the site. Nuisance and negligence are legal torts which may arise between adjoining owners as the result of the use of property. Nuisance can arise in the generation of smoke, fumes, noise etc., by a neighbour causing grievance to a property owner. If a substance is dangerous, such as toxic chemicals, or is stored in a dangerous manner on a neighbour's land, for example a reservoir of water, he will be liable should it escape and cause damage. There is also a legal responsibility embodied in legislation such as the Health and Safety at Work Act 1974 and in certain planning legislation. Failure to comply can result in prosecution.

The boundary to a property is usually defined on the site by a boundary wall or fence. Disputes can often develop concerning boundaries, particularly about their ownership, maintenance and repair. The title to the property may define the ownership of the enclosure, but in the absence of such evidence, the convention is that the fence stands on the property of the owner, for example the posts are on the owner's side, and the face of the fence usually represents the boundary. Boundary walls may be built on the owner's land, or they may be party walls. Walls separating buildings are usually party walls, the law relating to which is well defined, requiring notice to be served by the party initiating works on the neighbours, and if the works are not agreed surveyors have to be appointed by both parties to negotiate agreement. A third surveyor may be required to arbitrate if agreement cannot be reached.

There may be rights of way across an owner's land in favour of an adjoining property. Such easements may be limited to a particular purpose or use and generally are limited to a predetermined path or route. It should be borne in mind that if an access is taken and used openly and as of right by a neighbour across an owner's land a prima facie right will be established in twenty years, which could become a burden and frustrate development. Rights of light can be acquired by the windows of a neighbour's building enjoying light and air across an owner's property for a period of twenty years. Such rights cannot be obstructed and may restrict an owner's future development of his property.

Disputes between owners of business premises are rare. When a neighbour is in residential occupation however, every consideration should be shown by the occupier of business premises as it will be seen that a business use could be very intrusive to the quiet enjoyment of residential property.

FURTHER READING

The BWC Partnership, *Business Property Handbook*, Gower, Aldershot, 1982.
Woodfall's Law of Landlord and Tenant, 28th edition, Sweet & Maxwell, 1978 with updating service.
C.A. Cross, *Principles of Local Government Law*, 6th edition, Sweet and Maxwell, 1981.
W.A. West, *The Law of Dilapidations*, 8th edition, Estates Gazette Limited, 1979.
Town and Country Planning (Use Classes) Order 1972, HMSO.
Fire Precautions Act 1972, HMSO.
Housing and Building Control Act 1984, HMSO.
The Building Act 1984, HMSO.
Guides to Fire Precautions Act 1971, HMSO.
The Fire Precautions Act in Practice, Architectural Press, 1977.
N. Taylor, *Property Managers' Guide to Fire Legislation in Commercial and Industrial Premises*, F.P.R. Distribution, 37 Dumbarton Road, Glasgow.
Fire Precautions Register, F.P.R. Distribution, 37 Dumbarton Road, Glasgow.
G. Underdown, *Practical Fire Precautions*, 2nd edition, Gower, Aldershot, 1979.
J. Franks, *Building Procurement Systems*, The Chartered Institute of Building, 1984.
Warning! Not using a Chartered Surveyor can put you at risk, Royal Institution of Chartered Surveyors, 1986.
J.M. Mole, *Landlord and Tenant*, 2nd edition, M & E Handbooks, 1984.

31

The Management and Maintenance of Buildings

John Cavilla

The management and maintenance of buildings can be defined as:

(*a*) maintaining the optimum working environment
(*b*) keeping the fabric and services in a condition matching or enhancing that in which they were originally handed over
(*c*) maintaining and improving safety and security, not only for the protection of the building and its contents but also the well-being of the occupants

Any strategy must be seen to operate at a reasonable cost and to achieve a good resale value at the end of the building's useful life.

Its importance within a company structure

Building management and maintenance are essential, regardless of the size of the company, the nature of its activities, or whether the estate is large or just a single property. What will vary is the extent to which set procedures described in this chapter may be required, and although some may not be appropriate to the smaller property owner the basic principles remain the same.

RESPONSIBILITY FOR BUILDING MANAGEMENT

The role of senior management

As a starting point there must be a definition of needs – and this is a task for top management – setting levels of environment, services and maintenance which they see as appropriate, in addition to those which are required by law. It is top management who control the resources and so it is right that they should make these important decisions. Their first hurdle is to appreciate that there are no obvious returns; these aspects of a company's operations are a charge against profits, so they must be as efficient and economical as possible to keep the cost to a minimum whilst maintaining the appropriate standards.

Whatever the size of the organization there is a need not only to take continual care of 'hygiene factors' so that its staff are able to work well, but also to forecast plans and operations so that these may develop with minimum restrictions being imposed by its buildings. Someone within the top team must therefore devote sufficient share of his time to ensure that building management policies are put into practice and monitored.

The building manager

The effective execution of policies requires foresight, planning and expertise, regardless of the company's size and must be managed, not just left to the caretaker! A building manager must therefore be appointed, responsible to the senior executive. This person has a key role in the organization and ideally should have qualities embracing technical skill, administrative ability, an awareness of how his actions may affect the company as a whole and the morale of its staff.

A POLICY PLAN

The initial task of the building manager is to assist top management to clarify their broad objectives, then set out to review the present state of things and draft a policy plan and budget which gives a balance between efficiency and cost. In practice, this balance will need adjusting as results emerge and so detailed records should be kept of targets, what is achieved and how much it costs.

Drafting the plan

When drafting the plan of action the requirements should be divided into convenient categories to give a framework for reference, for example:

Human requirements. Furniture, fittings, finishes, lighting, heating, cooling, ventilation, sanitation, degrees of privacy, resting facilities, safety, security.

THE MANAGEMENT AND MAINTENANCE OF BUILDINGS

Work requirements. Main services, drainage, lifts, conveyors, equipment (production lines, computers etc.)

Building requirements. Structural condition, condition of services, fittings, layout required, floor space, structural loadings, building and planning approvals, fire precautions, leasehold conditions.

Maintenance requirements. Company policy, standard to be achieved, statutory and legal requirements, labour.

Legislative requirements. Legislation covering working conditions, building works, safety of the occupants.

These categories may be further subdivided as the nature of the business demands. These demands may in turn suggest that expert advice is needed to assist with detailed studies in areas of importance; for example in the fields of ergonomics, plant maintenance, structural maintenance/alterations, fire precautions.

The analysis

Having established what is required it is necessary to review the building facilities which are actually available or obtainable and see how these compare with the ideal. The cost of achieving a match can then be assessed.

Estate records

To enable the building manager to carry out the analysis he must have to hand adequate estate records. These may include details such as capital value, size/area/layout, details of construction, services, master drawings, plant, fire precautions. These details may be consolidated in a form of 'owner's handbook' (see under 'Maintenance').

LEGISLATION

The building manager must be familiar with the considerable amount of legislation concerning working conditions and building works. He must also be aware of any local byelaws or regulations in force. Factory inspectorate, building control officers, fire prevention officers, local authority staff, for example, will advise on details and interpretations. The effects of the legislation can then be absorbed into the policy plan and subsequent analysis. The following legislation is relevant:

> The Building Regulations 1985
> Town and Country Planning Act 1971

Health and Safety at Work, etc., Act 1974
Offices, Shops and Railway Premises Act 1963
Public Health Acts 1936 and 1961
Fire Precautions Act 1971
Factories Act 1961
Occupiers Liability Act 1957
Defective Premises Act 1972

Records

Records of negotiations, agreements, certificates, consents, should be kept on file, together with copies of approved drawings. Remember that the approving bodies, for example local authority building control, will keep copies of all such documentation and will refer back to them when further work is proposed.

Minimum standards

The building manager should realize (and, indeed, encourage top management to realize) that legislation produces minimum standards; it is not designed necessarily to produce staff contentment or efficiency. Hence, policy decisions may have to be made. For example, does the company control heating to pre-set legal minimum temperatures, or should staff be given freedom to control their own temperature? The results could produce an interesting study in balancing costs of extra controls and potentially higher fuel bills against staff contentment and maybe better output.

BUDGETING

Classifying expenditure

For budgeting purposes it is useful to think in terms of 'fixed' and 'flexible' costs. Fixed costs are those over which management action has little effect; flexible costs are those which are variable and can, at least to some extent, be managed.

Fixed costs

Include items such as rent, rates, insurance and depreciation; other expenses such as the cost of meeting leasehold or statutory requirements may also be considered in this category.

Flexible costs

Depend on the scale of operations required to achieve the variable items

THE MANAGEMENT AND MAINTENANCE OF BUILDINGS

which have been identified in management's policy plan. They include maintenance expenditure and running costs of services, which are unavoidable but to some extent manageable from year to year, and may also include alterations/extensions, which are clearly optional but also in the long run unavoidable if the organization is to be free to progress and perform efficiently.

Long-term assessment of costs

So that top management can make reasoned budget decisions from year to year it must have clearly defined long-term objectives, with assessments of the costs of achieving them, together with estimates of the cost of maintaining the property to the standard set. The building manager should be able to plan work sufficiently far ahead to stabilize the workload of his own staff or of his contractors and thus obtain good and well-timed performance. So the management of 'flexible' costs should not become a convenience, otherwise they will be used as a tool for hiding inefficiency, waste will occur and faith in planning ahead will be lost.

Having assessed the 'fixed' costs and the desirable level of 'flexible' costs, management must then reconcile its objectives with its resources. By careful forward planning and estimating the building manager will be able to give a reasoned statement of the alternatives, and it is then up to top management to judge the priorities.

Budgetary control

The agreed budget should be seen as a provisional target which can be adjusted according to the organization's cash flow, progress within each element and the occurrence of unforeseen events or changes in circumstance. Regular monthly reporting and updating of forecasts (more frequently if a situation demands), will allow problems and deviations to be identified quickly and corrective action to be taken. The Building Maintenance Cost Information Service, 85–87 Clarence Street, Kingston, Surrey, has produced a convenient framework for recording and reporting purposes, and establishing good practice in budgeting and cost control. It gives examples of historical costs relating to case studies of various types of buildings.

THE BUILDING MANAGEMENT TEAM

To ensure that funds are used effectively requires a high degree of management skill and planning so that money is not wasted by panic judgements or failure to make provision for unforeseen circumstances.

The building manager should employ no more staff than is necessary for the normal level of activity in his department and should consider use of contract labour for jobs that 'peak' or are occasional or highly specialized. He should be allowed adequate numbers of properly qualified staff for all regular work, irrespective of whether it is being executed by direct or contract labour. Whatever form of labour is used it must be programmed adequately and supervised; staff must therefore embrace management and supervisory staff.

Directly employed labour or contract labour?

The question of employing direct or contract labour, or a combination of the two, is not one which can be pre-judged.

The structure of the team will depend on the size of the organization, anticipated workload, budget and the company's policy towards employing direct labour.

Even in the smallest firms there must be some direct employment of staff even if it is as part of, or in addition to, other tasks or duties. There must be someone on the premises who will replace a washer or a light bulb, and unblock a sink. In a large firm the department may have sufficient plant in its care to justify a full engineering team of fitters, electricians etc.

It may be economic to employ someone directly responsible for typical 'housekeeping' jobs; for example, periodic cleaning, putting up a shelf, touching-up paint, oiling door closers etc. However, much of this sort of work, and many other types of maintenance, needs to be carried out at weekends or outside normal hours. This can give rise to problems of supervision and recruitment of labour and it may therefore be preferable to have this work done by a competent contractor. For example this is particularly true with regard to buildings such as large schools where redecorations or work on toilets would be confined to vacation periods and hence put too heavy a workload onto the daily maintenance staff.

The advantages of directly employed labour are:

1. management has full control over movement and allocation of work; this will enable them to redirect labour to give quick response to emergencies
2. The labour force acquires an intimate knowledge of a building and its services, which helps speed up diagnosis and remedy
3. Management is able to allocate labour more effectively, taking advantage of individual abilities

The disadvantages of directly employed labour are:

1. There may be insufficient preventative maintenance to keep them busy

2   Low productivity; because of lack of incentives this can be as low as 65 per cent
3   Contract labour tends to be more efficient as they have targets set to meet; direct labour may be older age groups who have no desire for bonus work, *but* may be more reliable

The choice

The final decision regarding labour can only be made with a full assessment of the workload, together with feedback on productivity and costs from past projects. Also, remember that to the number employed as direct labour should be added supervisors in the form of chargehands and/or foremen, and the workforce should be balanced to give full employment to the supervisors.

SAFETY, FIRE PRECAUTIONS AND SECURITY

Safety

It is always good policy to observe the spirit of the regulations controlling the use of buildings as well as following them by the letter; a happier and more confident staff will be the result (see under 'Legislation')

There should be a periodic review of safety policy, maybe in the form of a safety committee, when the staff should be represented. Items for consideration might include:

(*a*) the building structure and services
(*b*) the safety of users and visitors to the property
(*c*) the safety of workers carrying out maintenance etc.

There will be regular inspections by officials of the fire brigade, the local authority surveyors and public health departments – these are occasions for obtaining advice.

The reporting of safety hazards (for example loose handrails to stairways) by all who use the building should be encouraged, and they should be informed that they have a statutory duty to do this.

Fire precautions

The local fire prevention officer will help to devise a thorough system of precautions. Fire stewards must be trained. It is no good hoping that all will be well, unless there has been forethought and practice. The whole staff must be informed and occasionally involved in training exercises. A post-mortem should be held after each exercise, so that slipshod methods do not become a habit.

The wedging open or obstructing of fire exits must not be allowed, attention of the staff being drawn to the location of such exits together with an explanation of how these are incorporated for their safety.

Fire extinguishers are often inadequately labelled. Adjacent to the appliance should be a simple reference to the *type* of fire that it will cope with, say 50 mm high lettering in a vivid colour (for example red); this is particularly important in a factory/warehouse complex.

Security

As technology advances the resulting products become smaller and more portable (for example calculators and microcomputers), hence security has taken on renewed importance. All doors, windows and personal storage should be lockable, with only selected personnel having master keys to general rooms of significance. In large offices it may be prudent to introduce a coded card system for staff/users, to allow entry to circulation areas after passing through reception. The card is inserted into a box which automatically opens entry doors when the card details have been verified.

MAINTENANCE

A policy for maintenance

For maintenance to be both effective and economic a policy must be agreed between the building manager and top management which should include:

1. The life-cycle requirements for the building fabric, divisions, fittings and services – these depend on the extent to which they satisfy performance requirements and future plans
2. The standard to which the building and its services should be maintained – the original standard may not be sufficient to meet changing needs
3. The reaction time considered necessary or desirable between a defect occurring and a repair being carried out. An early response to all service calls may be desirable, but it presupposes a reserve of labour and therefore the acceptance of extra costs. A system of agreed priorities and service intervals will help to avoid friction

Classifications of maintenance

Maintenance can be divided into several categories and from these an annual programme of work can be devised.

Recurring maintenance. Those items which recur at regular intervals, such as redecoration, cleaning finishes and fittings.

Non-recurring maintenance. Major repairs and replacements which are regular but infrequent, for example, structural maintenance, re-roofing, re-surfacing of car parks.

Preventive maintenance. This is carried out on a regular basis in order to prevent breakdowns. It is easy to overdo this and so the advice of suppliers or manufacturers should be sought as to frequency and extent of maintenance – shampooing a carpet itself creates wear, so does taking apart a machine.

Emergency maintenance. Maintenance left until there is a breakdown which is reported. Attempts to obviate *all* breakdowns by preventive maintenance can lead to uneconomic levels of servicing without success, so an economic balance must be found.

Minor works. Small alterations, upgradings and additions; for example, erecting a partition, erecting shelves, fixing pin-boards. These often form a large part of the work and a distraction from true maintenance, so each job must be justified, costed and given a slot in the programme of priorities.

The 'owner's handbook'

The building manager's task will be eased greatly by reference to an owner's handbook. This document should be compiled in such a way that it is easily understood by the layman – a set of the original construction drawings can be very difficult to read, even for the practised eye. With a new building the production of this handbook could be made a requirement of the designer's services.

A typical handbook should contain the following details:

1 The architect and other consultants (although approach may be best through the architect)
2 The main contractor
3 Construction details, with full set of drawings indicating structural importance, with explanatory notes
4 Identification/location of plant, with details of model, manufacturer's instruction manual, frequency of servicing required
5 Services layouts showing access points, valves etc. (all easily understood by the layman in an emergency)
6 Identification of finishes and manufacturer's cleaning recommendations

Item	Spr.	Sum.	Aut.	Win.	Spr.	Sum.	Aut.	Win.	Spr.	Sum.	Aut.	Win.	Spr.	Sum.	Aut.
Inspection (Int.)	●						●				●				●
Inspection (ext.)			●			●				●			●		
Int. painting				●								●			
Ext. painting		N/E				W				N/S					
Heating/A.C. plant		●				●				●				●	
Waste/Soil system			●				●				●				●
Gutters	●				●				●				●		
Brickwork										●					
Roof						●									
Car park														●	

Figure 31.1 Typical long-term maintenance programme

THE MANAGEMENT AND MAINTENANCE OF BUILDINGS

7   Suiting details of locks, sanitaryware etc.

An appendix may contain details of legal or tenancy agreements or any restrictions over the property such as easements or wayleaves.

Programming maintenance

For maintenance to run smoothly, economically and as unobtrusively as possible it must be properly programmed. A programme showing maintenance requirements and sequence over a period of, say, four or five years will enable management to plan the spread of manpower and to assess budget requirements (see Figure 31.1).

Within the long-term plan the annual programme of maintenance can be prepared as each year draws to a close. This will consist of:

(a) recurring and non-recurring maintenance shown in the long-term plan
(b) items prompted by inspections
(c) preventive and emergency maintenance

Of course the long-term targets will be reassessed at each annual review to ensure that the time is right for inclusion. It may be desirable to give certain elements priority, for example if the principal elevation is severely exposed it may be reasonable to repaint this every two years whilst expecting the others to last for three or four years.

Periodic inspections

The building management staff should be on the lookout for faults, signs of wear, signs of dampness, and encouraged to report them immediately. But this is equally applicable to *all* staff. It is too easy to look upon building defects and the work rate of maintenance staff as items of amusement — an alternative to the taking of positive action.

In addition, periodic inspection is necessary for building fabric, plant, fittings and contents. Some inspections, for example on lifts and boilers, will be as a condition of insurance and are legal requirements. Others will be made by the local authority. It will be prudent for technical inspections to be supplemented by professional inspections for structural and policy purposes to ensure that effective management and standards are being maintained. The building manager should be present, or well-represented, on such occasions.

The inspections should be incorporated in the programme so that the work arising can be planned and budgeted if major repairs are involved. Electrical inspections, including testing of circuits and earth continuity, are of particular importance since so many accidents and fires are caused by neglect of aged wiring and switchgear. The use of correct pattern and rating of fuses must also be periodically checked; hasty or 'do-it-yourself' repairs may well have resulted in make-shift solutions.

Cleaning

Cleaning should be an integral part of maintenance and controlled by the same management.

The rate at which surfaces or items become dirty or damaged should not be ignored at the design stage or when formulating building management policy, as they may affect the choice of finish. A decision will be needed on whether to have a durable surface which is cleaned regularly, with infrequent replacement; or whether to have a short-term finish which is replaced rather than cleaned or repaired.

Light fittings and glazing need regular cleaning to maintain good lighting levels. Sanitary fittings must be kept stain-free and in good working order whilst the associated wastes and drains should be regularly inspected and cleaned to prevent blockages.

It is worth considering how labour-saving features might be incorporated, for example keeping dirt out by efficient dust control at entrances, reducing the number of dust traps, shields to keep dirt out of machinery and moving parts.

Whether executed by direct or contract labour there must be a detailed specification of daily and periodic cleaning operations, and skilled supervision. Getting the right quality of work is difficult, as most labour is part-time and low paid. A good contractor will ensure that supervision is adequate but the building management team should check this regularly. Too often the contractor submits his monthly invoice whether or not he has been able to provide full staff and complete the work efficiently. Where sensible, the number of staff should be agreed with the contractor and they should be booked in and out.

Redecoration

A regular cycle of redecoration is required internally and externally. Advice can be obtained from reputable paint manufacturers regarding the right materials and their application. Modern paint finishes can stand up to severe conditions for several years, provided that cleaning is done carefully and with a good quality detergent. The standard of appearance agreed will determine the intervals at which redecoration will take place (see 'Programming maintenance'). But it should always be remembered that painting at longer intervals involves more preparation and extra coats of paint. The costs of a 'long cycle' policy should therefore be balanced carefully against those of a 'short cycle'. Within the analysis should be considerations for access and safety, such as scaffolds and hoists.

THE MANAGEMENT AND MAINTENANCE OF BUILDINGS

Again, forethought will help to avoid premature redecoration, for example buffers on trolleys, door stops to prevent handles hitting wall surfaces, horizontal rails fixed to walls to prevent chair-backs scarring wall finishes.

Unplanned maintenance and breakdowns

The need to attend to faults and emergencies should be covered by maintenance planning. To allow for them staff should not be overloaded with routine or programmed work. On the other hand, a close watch should be kept on the amount of unplanned work. To ensure a good balance, adjustment of maintenance periods or the interception of over fussy service requests may be required. Where action is needed, it should be timely and positive; prompt attention breeds confidence, neglect breeds complaints, reminders and unreasonable demands which clog the system and waste management time.

Cost control

The building manager must be able to keep costs under review and within budget and the accounting system should enable him to do so. He should be able to divide his cost control system into two forms, to allow control of the total budget for the financial year and to control the allocation of funds to individual jobs within the whole. The use of the two forms will also enable him to balance out any overspendings on some jobs against savings on others.

The costing of individual job sheets may not be practical or economic but some analysis of labour utilization should be considered. Obviously, the major budget items may offer the best source of savings.

Building management budgets, however, tend to be predominantly made up of a small number of 'fixed' costs and a large number of 'flexible' costs which cover a multitude of small jobs.

The building manager should therefore encourage his staff to look for ways of reducing costs. His task is to take a long-term view, not only of current and projected workload but also ways of obviating or simplifying maintenance, and projecting what improvements or alterations should be budgeted for.

Maintenance records and feed-back

It is important to establish a log so that a history can be built up of each maintenance item. To accompany this, a reminder system may be useful, prompting programmed work, noting unplanned work, and, if each item is crossed out on completion, providing a record of when the work was done;

memory can be very misleading and impressions different from facts. A job-sheet system which enables the manager to review what has been done and identify where his resources are being applied is likely to pay off. If a central materials store is established, stock cards, with details of reordering, should be kept to control waste and obtain a smooth flow of stores.

In addition, a 'feed-back' system would be of great help to the building manager. It would enable him to consider how to avoid repetition of defects, to incorporate improvements in future projects, and of course to provide information to assist maintenance staff. A typical system might also be used to assess in advance the probable replacement times for inclusion in forward programming.

ALTERATIONS AND EXTENSIONS

As an enterprise develops, the need for alterations or extensions to its buildings increases. These may be simply adjustments to layout and services or could be major adaptions/extensions requiring structural change.

Accordingly the approach may vary; adjustments to layout could be tackled by direct labour whilst structural or recurring alterations might be put out to tender. When deciding upon the most suitable approach it is important to ensure that such works are not allowed to interfere with the execution of priority maintenance work; they must be considered outside the maintenance programme and catered for separately.

In-house planning

With a large estate which brings a regular flow of work it may be worth setting up a central planning section, responsible to the building manager, within the building management structure.

This section would be responsible for assessing and updating estate records, carrying out feasibility studies (comprising survey/design/costs/permissions needed) of management proposals, preparing detailed plans/specifications, supervising. If the full range of expertise is not available within the organization, independent professional advice should be considered. However, it is not possible to lay down firm rules and the advice of a contractor who values your custom may be no less worthwhile than that of a consultant.

Programming

Great care must be taken with adaption work since it will be carried out within the confines of an existing building; therefore the designer, builder and building manager must be aware of the timing and sequence of the work

THE MANAGEMENT AND MAINTENANCE OF BUILDINGS

so that disruption to normal company operations can be kept to a minimum. An example might be alterations to bank premises, to include new screens and counters. This will require detailed programming and consultation to ensure that materials are delivered on time and the work is able to proceed out of opening hours with no loss of security.

Structure

Whenever structural alterations or extensions are proposed a fully detailed structural survey should be carried out, reinforced with information from the estate records. This will not only establish the means by which loads are to be supported and transferred to the foundations but also identify defects which require attention. The cost of putting the structure into good order must be taken into account when evaluating the viability of a scheme.

Services

The availability of services is important and obviously a new accommodation layout scheme should be detailed with these in mind so that, say, drainage connections are kept simple and major works to existing drains are avoided. Today we too often see an efficient air-conditioning system, or lighting system, in an 'open-plan' environment which is destroyed by new full-height partitions, erected in an attempt to create a 'cell' structure reflecting hierarchy.

Estimates

An estimate of the likely costs and time should be evaluated to give management a clear picture of how the proposals fit in with their priorities and budget; also to enable them to judge tenders. The estimate may be detailed or approximate, depending on the purpose for which it is required.

Approximate estimates are a quick and simple method of assessing costs based on past records plus inflation trends. Examples of this would be 'cost per floor area' (area in square metres of net floor space) and 'cost per element' (for example windows, doors, ceilings, related to the total floor area).

Again, depending on the level of expertise within the team, the advice of a consultant (a Quantity Surveyor) may be needed for the purpose of the estimating procedure.

FURTHER READING

The Chartered Institute of Building, *Managing Building Maintenance*, 1984. Property Services Agency, *The Estimating Handbook for Building Maintenance*, HMSO, London.

32

The Insurance of Company Operations

Commercial Union Assurance

The modern business has many opportunities to succeed. However, more than ever before it is essential for the businessman to protect his company. Competition, health and safety legislation, the complexity of products, environmental considerations and a whole host of natural disasters from fire to flood, and man-made catastrophes from burglary to fraud can spell disaster for any size of company.

Insurance is one form of protection against many of the accidental or natural disasters. For over 300 years there have been 'risk takers' who, for a fee called a premium, are willing to assume financial responsibility for losses incurred following a variety of events. The premiums of the 'many' pay for the claims of the 'unfortunate few'.

Not all business risks are insurable; some are pure business risks which involve the successful businessman in making good business decisions. 'Risk management' involves the appraisal of the risk which might affect the performance of the company. Once the risks have been established a business plan is designed to cope with them.

A number of risks are unavoidable and have to be catered for in business plans – obsolescence or overestimation of the market, for example – their remedy lies in research, development and marketing. Other corporate problems can be answered by advice from accountants, bankers and solicitors.

What about the unpredictable? This is where the insurance company or broker play their part in your company's prosperity. The purpose of insurance is to provide a financial indemnity against loss from accidental

THE INSURANCE OF COMPANY OPERATIONS

and unpredictable risks. Its aim is to put your company in the same position as it was before the advent of the fire, storm damage, burglary or other disaster.

What follows explores some of the factors involved in business insurances. It cannot do more than skim the surface of what has developed into a complex series of risks involved in business processes.

There are over 300 insurance companies and Lloyds who make up the UK insurance market today. Some of those companies handle only life or pensions business; those who handle both are known as composite insurers. They are predominantly the large companies, the nationally known names. All non-life and composite companies are limited liability companies. Lloyds, however, are different. Insurance is placed only by Lloyds insurance brokers with syndicates of individual underwriters who act for the syndicate members. The members have to satisfy Lloyds of their financial standing and integrity and are liable without limit to the full extent of their individual wealth. Most Lloyds syndicates specialize in specific classes of risk, for example marine, aviation, motor, or property etc.

INSURANCE LANGUAGE

Before looking at the insurance cover itself, it might be useful to look at some common expressions used in the insurance industry. While many present-day insurers attempt to produce contracts in a 'plain English' format, there are still some fundamental principles on which most insurance contracts are based. In addition, some words have developed a common usage within the insurance industry. The following glossary is an attempt to provide a basic understanding of some of those principles and terms:

Adjuster A specialist appointed by the insurer to investigate the circumstances and negotiate settlement of a loss. Usually an independent specialist whose fee is paid for by the insurer.

Assessor A person who acts on behalf of the insured at the insured's expense to negotiate claims with the insurer and, where necessary, the insurer's adjuster. An assessor can also negotiate on behalf of third-party claimants.

Average (non-marine) A principle of insurance (mainly insurance of property) where the insurer will only pay for the same proportion of a loss as the sum insured bears to the actual value of the property at the time of the loss. For example, if an item covered by the policy is 'subject to average' but is only insured for half its value at the time it is damaged, the insurer will only pay half of any claim for repair.

Betterment See *Indemnity*.

Broker, Insurance A professional insurance adviser who, following discussions of the cover required with his client, will negotiate and place the business with insurers. The broker must meet the standards required by the Insurance Brokers (Registration) Act 1977, which includes a statutory code of conduct, and they may be a member of BIBA (British Insurance Brokers Association).

NB: The description 'insurance broker' may only be used by individuals who have registered (if a company, enrolled) under the Act. Sometimes the term 'broker' is used colloquially. When the new financial services legislation comes into force it is likely that some brokers who specialize in life business only will 'deregister' and only be under the control of the regulatory organization set up under that legislation.

Code of conduct/codes of practice Brokers are required to follow a statutory code of conduct under the Insurance Brokers (Registration) Act. Other insurance intermediaries are required to follow a code of practice agreed between insurers and the Department of Trade and Industry. There are two codes – one for general (non-life) business and one for life business. Each code is in two parts which distinguish between those who sell and those who merely introduce ('introducers').

Days of grace When a non-life policy falls due for renewal, the insurer concerned is usually willing to hold cover under the terms for renewal, pending payment of the premium, providing the policyholder intends to renew.

Under motor policies, there are no days of grace. However, as it is necessary for a certificate of motor insurance to be delivered to a policyholder for it to be effective, insurers usually provide fifteen days' temporary cover beyond the renewal date to enable the insurer to date the new certificate from renewal date and deliver it within the period of temporary cover.

Should a life assured die in the days of grace specified under a life policy before the renewal premium is paid, the position must be ascertained from the policy or the insurer.

Debris removal	Under a policy covering buildings and/or machinery against damage, the cost of removing debris can be included providing the costs have been allowed for when deciding on the sums to be insured. If the costs are insured as a separate item under a policy covering commercial property, they are not subject to average. Similarly, debris removal of stock can also be insured as a separate item under a policy covering commercial property.
Disclosure	The rule of law whereby a prospective policyholder must tell ('disclose') the insurer any facts known to the prospective policyholder which are likely to affect acceptance by the underwriter or his assessment of the risks proposed. If the prospective policyholder fails to do this, the policy may not provide the cover required, or the policy may be invalidated altogether.
Excess	If expressed in money terms (which is usual), it is the uninsured amount for which the insured is responsible in the event of a claim. See also *Franchise*.
Ex gratia	Voluntary payment made by an insurer, without admission of liability under the policy, as a gesture of goodwill.
Fees, Professional (architects etc.)	Under a policy covering buildings, and/or machinery against damage, it is possible to insure fees incurred in the rebuilding/repairing of damage in a variety of ways. These are normally calculated as a percentage of the value of buildings or machinery, and are limited to the scales of professional bodies. If insured separately under a policy covering commercial property, such fees are not subject to 'average'.
Fidelity guarantee	This insurance protects employers against 'direct pecuniary loss' which they suffer by all acts of fraud or dishonesty committed by any of their employees. The term 'direct pecuniary loss' refers to the loss of monies, stock and other items of value belonging to the employer, which can be proved and the employee(s) responsible identified, though insurers do not insist on prosecution. Unaccountable deficiencies or losses are not covered.
Franchise	If expressed in money terms, there is no payment by the insurer if the total claim is below that figure; above that amount, the agreed claim is payable in full. Some policies, for example certain personal accident or

engineering contracts, may have time franchises. These operate similarly; thus, only if the time franchise is exceeded is the claim payable and the agreed amount will then be paid in full.

Indemnity Principle of common law by which the policyholder after a loss shall be put in the same financial position as he was immediately before the happening of the event insured against. In practice this often means that, in the event of a claim, payment is based first on what it would cost to replace new a lost or damaged item, but then an amount is deducted to take account of fair wear and tear. Such a deduction is sometimes called 'betterment'.

NB: This principle naturally does not apply to life assurance, permanent health or pensions contracts. Nor does it apply to personal accident and sickness cover, although medical expenses insurance does provide indemnity for costs incurred.

Insurable interest A policyholder has an insurable interest if the insured event would involve him in financial loss or diminution of any right recognized by law or any legal liability, or for the consequences of his own bodily injury or illness.

As regards life and personal accident policies, a person is deemed to have an unlimited insurable interest in his or her own life, or in the life of his or her spouse. Insurable interest may also exist between employer and employee, debtor and creditor and other cases.

Insurance agent An insurance agent is primarily the agent of the policyholder, not least when passing information to the insurer with a view to obtaining insurance cover. He can also be the agent of the insurer, in particular when collecting premiums due to the insurer.

An insurance agent can be in business either full time – such as an 'insurance broker' or an 'insurance consultant', probably acting for a number of insurers – or he may act for only one insurer, such as a company that specializes in the sale of industrial life business (where premiums are collected weekly/monthly from the policyholders' premises).

Insurance consultant A professional insurance adviser whose business is similar to that of an insurance broker (q.v.), but who has not registered/enrolled under the Insurance Brokers (Registration) Act. While unlikely therefore to meet the standards required under the Act, they are required to follow a code of practice agreed between insurers and the Department of Trade and Industry.

Introducer An insurance intermediary who merely introduces a prospective policyholder to an insurer, but who takes no part in the subsequent selling process.

Local authorities clause In the event of damage, current building regulations may well be applied to the structure, thereby involving additional expense when it is rebuilt. If the insurance is on a reinstatement basis, this clause can be added extending the policy to meet the additional expenses on rebuilding for the damaged portion, though the sum insured must have been increased to allow for such expenses.

Proposal form The form completed by a proposer. A completed life proposal forms the basis of the contract between the guarantor and the insurer.

Reinstatement
(a) Where property is destroyed, it means the rebuilding of the property if a building, or, in the case of other property, its replacement by similar property, in either case in a condition equal to (but no better or more extensive than) its condition when new.
(b) Where property is damaged, it means repair of the property to a condition substantially the same as (but not better or more extensive than) its condition when new.

The sum insured needs to represent what it would cost fully to rebuild/replace, at the time the property is actually rebuilt/replaced, and any under-insurance will result in a proportionate reduction of the amount paid in accordance with the average principle (see *Average (non-marine)*).

Renewal notice Form sent to insured advising the approaching renewal date and inviting renewal on payment of a stated premium.

The insurer is not bound to issue a notice, but it is the normal practice.

The renewal invitation is provided on the basis of information already given to the insurer. Other than for individual life, pension or permanent health insurance, if that information is affected by any change of circumstances or additional fact known to the policyholder, the

	insurer (or his authorized agent) should be told. It could be that, as a result of the additional information, the insurer will wish to revise the terms on which renewal is being invited.
Subrogation	The substitution of one person or thing for another so that the same rights and remedies which attached to the original person/thing attach to the substituted one.
Surveyor	Person who inspects property to advise the underwriter about the risk. He may also require or recommend improvements to the risk to lessen the likelihood of fire, burglary, or other incidents occurring, or to minimize the effects of them.
Time-on-risk charge	Premium charged for a period (often limited to a number of days) during which an insurer is holding a risk covered, for example, by means of a cover note.
Underwriting	The process whereby a risk is assessed for insurance purposes, on the basis of information supplied to the underwriter often by means of a proposal form. The underwriter will decide whether the risk is acceptable to the insurer, the terms on which it may be acceptable, and the premium to be charged, before issue of the policy.
Utmost good faith	Legal duty imposed on both parties to an insurance contract to disclose all facts material to the contract (see also *Disclosure*).
Warranty	A policy condition or requirement which, if not complied with, may have the effect of invalidating the policy. It may relate to woodworking in a motor garage or to the absence of certain property (for example no oil stored in the hardware shop or only certain types of oil kept).

Insurance cover

Let us now see what is involved in arranging insurance for your company. There are four basic categories:

1 Property protection
2 Loss of income
3 Legal liabilities
4 Personnel

PROPERTY PROTECTION

The insurance arrangement is essentially a complete form of protection where, if a loss occurs, within certain criteria, the insurer will resolve the problem by way of financial compensation. Such an insurance will include wide cover for your stock, machinery, fixtures and fittings and furniture, employees' belongings, and other items for which you may be responsible. The structure, if you own it, would come within this category, or, if you are a tenant, you can arrange for the insurance to cover that portion of the structure and interior decorations for which you are responsible. Specific requirements within a lease would obviously have to be complied with.

Fire insurance

There was a tendency in the past for companies to be selective in terms of which contingencies to insure against. It has now become almost standard practice for insurers to offer a package which includes the basic traditional calamities such as fire, lightning, explosion and so on. There are many special features and extensions on the market which are worthy of consideration.

Many insurers now refer to 'all risks' cover which could be more accurately described as accidental damage cover. 'New for old' cover is also offered which requires you to arrange your sums insured on a full reinstatement value.

Additional standard extensions include property which has been temporarily removed, architects', surveyors' and other specialist fees, removal of debris costs, special provision for local authority legislation, and even damage to the underground service pipes and cables on which your business might rely.

Theft

Theft and loss of money are now two of the prime security considerations in many businesses and cover will almost inevitably carry a proviso from the insurer that a certain degree of minimum security is observed. Certain manufactured goods, and even raw materials, have become prime targets to the criminal world and insurers require their policyholders to improve the safes, locks and alarm protections at their premises rather than rely solely on charging a higher premium for a risk as it stands.

Cash

Money cover carries a variety of limitations and requirements and particular attention should be paid to the observance of such conditions in the day-today business of the company. For example, certain safes will have insurance limits as to the amount of cash which can be kept in them overnight and there may be conditions relating to the sum which can be taken in transit on any one trip. Where large-volume cash transits are involved the use of security companies has become more prevalent. On a lower degree the insurer may require more than one of your employees to be present during a delivery of cash either to the bank or to a point of wages payment.

Loss of money as a result of theft should not be confused with fidelity guarantee insurance, which would be dealt with separately.

Glass insurance

Apart from the traditional concept of insuring against breakage of glass in doors, windows etc., extensions apply which include breakage of sanitary ware, damage to neon signs and burglar alarms, foil lettering, painting etc.

Again insurers expect policyholders to take positive steps to reduce risk in certain areas, for example by the use of grills or roller shutters. Large excesses could apply in areas where the insurers' experience has been particularly poor.

LOSS OF INCOME

This feature of the insurance portfolio protects the business when it is interrupted as a result of loss or damage under the above sections.

It covers loss of gross profit due to a reduction in your business income. It also covers increased costs of working incurred to reduce the loss of profit, so long as these do not exceed the loss of profit which would otherwise have been paid.

Once more, a variety of extensions are available to protect the business against financial loss and these include damage to property in the vicinity, causing denial of access to your own premises, or damage at the premises of any supplier. This extension would normally carry a limit in respect of any one supplier.

This particular style of insurance has its own special definitions, the principal one being 'indemnity period', which relates to the maximum period of time during which the business might suffer loss as a result of the interruption. Traditionally, the indemnity period has run for a period of twelve months following the incident, although longer periods are now commonplace.

Such insurance normally requires the service of a professional accountant should a claim arise and the insurer will usually include the professional accountant's charges as part of the sum paid.

Careful consideration should be given to the calculation of the sum insured in this context and future company projections should be taken into account. It is not appropriate to rely on your previous year's gross profit as a basis for fixing sums insured.

For example, if a two-year indemnity period were to be selected and the loss were to take place at the end of a particular insurance year, then at the expiry of the indemnity period it is possible that the original sum insured could be almost three years out of date.

To compensate for future projections the insurer will accept audited declarations in retrospect and adjust premiums to reflect the actual risk as compared with the projected one, paying appropriate rebates to the policyholder.

Following the rise in inflation insurers have developed more sophisticated means by which to adjust this cover. Consultation with a professional intermediary or insurance advisor is highly recommended in this context.

LEGAL LIABILITIES

If any one thing could bankrupt a company at one stroke it would more than likely be a heavy court award. No matter how far a company may consider that it can set aside the need for insurance this particular form is imperative.

The cover relates to legal liabilities to pay compensation:

1 *To employees.* For bodily injury, illness or decease arising out of and in the course of their employment in the company for an unlimited amount. Any person working for the company for the purpose of gaining work experience is automatically included. This cover is a statutory requirement of the Employers' Liability (Compulsory Insurance) Act 1969

2 *To members of the public.* For bodily injury, illness or disease or loss of or damage to material property, which arises in connection with the business, including liability arising from the sale of goods, for an amount of, say, up to £500 000 for any one occurrence. Increases on cover are available on the payment of an additional premium.

   In addition, all litigation costs and expenses are paid when incurred with the insurers' agreement

Certain extensions and special features include:

3 *Defective premises.* Cover for liability incurred by the company under $s3$ of the Defective Premises Act 1972

4 *Damage to rented premises.* Cover for damage to premises rented or

hired by the company (other than if liability is assumed by the company under an agreement which would not have attached in the absence of such agreement). The insured may be asked to pay the first £100 or thereabouts of each loss unless the damage was caused by fire or explosion

5 *Health and Safety at Work Act.* Cover for legal costs arising out of any prosecution under Part 1 of the Health and Safety at Work Act 1974, but excluding any fines or penalties imposed and any costs incurred as a result of a deliberate act of omission

6 *Contingent liability.* Cover for liability incurred by the company as a result of the use by any employee of his own vehicle on the company's business

As a result of the tendency in the US towards very large court awards, the UK insurance market is now particularly sensitive to this area. Therefore if your company is involved in the supply of materials or products to that part of the world your insurer should be informed.

It is common for insurers to exclude public liability claims which arise from motor vehicles licensed for road use, professional negligence, or for property which is held in the company's custody or control. Special arrangements should be made to cover these areas.

PERSONNEL

Personal accident insurance

This is the least expensive of the covers and takes one of two forms:

Occupational accident cover. This applies to all accidents at work including those not directly the fault of the employer. It is one of the cheapest forms of protection and can be extended to include accidents on the way to and from work.

24-hour accident cover. This applies twenty-four hours a day, every day of the year at home and at leisure anywhere in the world. Clearly, as the cover is extended, the costs increase and vary depending upon the occupation of the staff involved. They can be arranged either for specific members of staff by name, groups of staff or for all employees.

Personal accident policies usually include capital sums and weekly benefits. They can be either a fixed benefit or a figure related to the employee's earnings.

Capital sums are paid following accidental death or serious injury and may be in the form of compensation to the injured employee or to the firm to offset the very high costs of replacing a key individual (see 'Key man' assurance).

Weekly sums, usually for short-term absence by reason of accidents, are normally payable for 104 weeks only.

Personal accident and sickness insurance

The personal accident only cover can be supplemented in respect of sickness. This extension of the policy would normally provide a weekly benefit in the event of illness on the same lines as for personal accident only. There is usually a two-year limit (104 weeks) on the benefit payable.

Rates of premium are often based on a percentage of the wage roll and the rates vary according to occupation. In general, the employer would collect premiums and pay them in bulk to the insurance company. From the insurance company's point of view the group schemes covering most or all employees would be at a cheaper rate as there is a wide spread of risk among administrative as well as manual staff.

Personal accident insurance, including or excluding sickness, is renewable every year. This means that if there is a run of bad accidents or illness, the insurer may wish to revise the terms of the cover. For key employees permanent health insurance may be the answer.

Permanent health insurance

This has two advantages over personal accident and sickness insurance. Firstly, it provides regular monthly income for as long as the employee is ill, without limitation. Payments can continue, if necessary, right up to retirement age. Because the possible amount payable by an insurer is far greater, premiums are higher. To keep premiums at a reasonable level, it is usual for the first thirteen or sixteen weeks of disability, known as the waiting period, to be excluded from the cover. An employer will often pay full salary for the first six months of illness and there would be a duplication of payment if this was included in the permanent health cover.

The second advantage is that, once effected, the insurer cannot subsequently withdraw cover or change the terms of that cover however disabled the member of staff becomes through recurrent health problems. Furthermore, if the employee becomes totally disabled and takes an early retirement pension through illness, or has to take some lower-paid professional occupation, a reduction benefit will still be paid under the permanent health policy.

'Key man' assurance

There are certain members of staff who are particularly valuable to the company and whose loss, either permanently or temporarily, can affect its financial stability. Statistically, it is more likely that a forty-five-year-old businessman will die before he is sixty-five than that his business premises will suffer a serious fire in the same period. But while the businessman would not dream of failing to insure premises and contents against fire, very few take steps to combat the equally serious loss following death or illness of one of their key people.

Key man assurance can be made-to-measure to cover exactly what is needed and nothing more. It is specific to the individual and refers to his or her contribution to the company. Also, because no employer knows precisely what the future holds, benefits can be changed to suit changing circumstances.

To protect your profits against a key person's death. The cheapest way to offset the effect on profits of a key person's death is by means of term assurance or convertible term assurance. In either case, the policy is arranged to pay a lump sum in equal instalments spread over, say, ten years to minimize corporation tax. The sum to be assured will depend on the value of the employee.

With term assurance cover ceases after a set number of years. With convertible term assurance there is the option of converting at any time into a permanent whole of life or endowment policy, or a further term or convertible term policy, without the employee having to undergo a further medical examination.

For a small additional premium, many assurers will include a guaranteed insurability option which allows the sum assured to be increased without further medical evidence at certain intervals and within certain limits.

The premiums for life assurance are remarkably small, £100 000 cover on a ten-year term assurance, assuming a non-smoker, would cost approximately £300 per annum from which corporation tax would often be deductible.

Key man permanent health insurance. The long absence of key people through illness or injury can be as disruptive as their deaths. A regular income for the company whilst the employee is unable to work is best provided by permanent health cover. Statistically, there is a one in six chance of a forty-five-year-old key employee suffering long-term disablement through illness or accident during the next twenty years.

The policy is usually for a period of ten years, but a slightly higher premium will secure an option to extend for a further ten years without further medical evidence. Monthly benefits are usually limited to two years including the 'waiting period' of thirteen or twenty-six weeks. The loss of a key person may not be a problem in the very short term and, similarly, the firm might reasonably be expected to replace or retain by the end of two years.

The key man permanent health policy is designed to tide the company over the short-term financial difficulties arising from serious incapacity. If the key person is incapacitated more than once, benefits start again on the same terms as on the first occasion provided a different illness or injury is responsible. If there are separate periods of incapacity due to the same illness or injury, these are aggregated and benefits are paid for only two years in total, less the original waiting period. The waiting period is not repeated for related illnesses.

If, while in receipt of payments under the policy, the employee takes early retirement and a pension, or takes up some lower-paid occupation, a reduced benefit is payable during the remainder of the period.

Again, premiums are relatively inexpensive. For example, an employer would pay an annual premium of approximately £88 to provide a benefit of £10 000 per annum payable for 104 weeks less a waiting period of twenty-six weeks, assuming the employee was in an administrative or clerical occupation.

Medical expenses

Substantial discounts are available for groups of employees from firms specializing in medical expenses insurance schemes, such as BUPA and Private Patients' Plan. A common practice is for the employer to arrange such schemes on behalf of their employees, as an employee benefit, with premiums paid by the employee by deduction from salary.

The advantage to employees is that they obtain the benefit of private medical insurance at comparatively low cost because of the group discounts, whilst the employer has the advantage of faster medical attention available to his employees who can then resume work much more quickly.

The employee has the choice as to which plan he wishes to opt for, but it is recommended that as hospital accommodation charges form a large part of the claim it is better to assume hospital treatment at London rates rather than take up cover on the basis of provincial hospital charges.

'Death in service' benefits

Benefits following death from any cause are usually part of a company pension scheme (see Chapter 24). Nonetheless, provided it is arranged by the employer, cover can be paid for by deduction from salary or subsidized by the employer. There are two basic forms of 'death in service' schemes.

Capital sums. In this type of arrangement, a lump sum is payable which is either a sum directly related to salary, for example once, twice, three times, or a maximum of four times the employee's salary at death, or a sum which bears no direct relationship to the salary.

Widow's 'death in service' benefits. This scheme can be in addition to the lump sum benefits and provides an income to the widow or dependants of the deceased employee from the date of death until he or she would have reached retirement age.

Under both these schemes there are certain limitations laid down by the Inland Revenue. In respect of lump sum benefits the maximum is usually four times current salary, and in respect of widow's death in service benefits the maximum is normally 44 per cent of current salary.

The previous sections have attempted to cover the fundamental principles of insurance in relation to business practice. There are, however, many specialist forms of insurance which are designed to cater for whole of life or to end the huge variety of specialist activities with which the UK business community is involved. These include the insurance of fraud or dishonesty of employees, breakdown of computers, explosion of central heating boilers, breakdown of refrigeration implant, death of livestock... in fact the considerations are almost endless.

Insurance is now a highly competitive market which is no longer inhibited by tariffs or market agreements. As a result the need for specialist advice is paramount, particularly if your business has any degree of specialism in itself. The events against which a company insures itself were traditionally described as perils. Perhaps the greatest peril of all would be to ignore the existence of insurance altogether.

FURTHER READING

Association of Insurance and Risk Managers in Industry and Commerce (AIRMIC) (eds), *Company Insurance Handbook*, 2nd edition, Gower, Aldershot, 1984.

33

Managing Transport Services

Frank H Woodward

There are two basic activities which are the responsibility of a transport services function:

1   Movement of goods and material necessary for the business
2   Movement of personnel

In both of these, the objective is to achieve a cost-effective operation in order to reduce the impact of the additional cost burden on product price.

The transport function is called upon to provide a service to every function within industry. It is hard to name a function which at some time will not require goods, services or personnel to be moved. Because of this broad responsibility to give a service, those engaged in managing transport come into direct contact with all other departments within a company and will incur costs on behalf of those departments. With this licence to accept costs comes the added responsibility of ensuring that value is received for costs incurred, and of checking constantly costs and performance of all activities within the function against alternative services available.

ORGANIZATION STRUCTURE

The person responsible at board level for the control of transport operations can vary from the sales director to the company secretary, from the production director to the chief executive. With increased activity in the distribution of goods, and escalation of costs in all areas of transport operations, arguments continue over the rightful place of the transport function in a company organization. Despite the strength of many proposals, it has become increasingly obvious that there is no answer which would be suitable or acceptable as a general rule for all types of industry.

A company whose activity is centred around the packaging, warehousing and distribution of goods to retail outlets would find that 'transport', a word used in the broadest sense, is responsible for anything up to 40 per cent of annual turnover and would justify direct representation on the board of directors to ensure that a full account of this expenditure is presented at the highest level in the organization. A company whose transport requirement is only a few cars would not need such total executive responsibility. Unless a company 'sells' transport as a means of adding directly to the profit of the company, in other words, it is engaged in road haulage, then transport is a service function in exactly the same way as the catering activity of a company. The value of this service to the profitability of the company will determine its correct place in the organization structure.

Line or staff. Line management is that which is responsible for achieving the main objectives of the business. Staff functions are those which assist line management to achieve those objectives. Transport is primarily a line function, especially when applied to the movement of a company product. To manufacture goods and to leave them at the end of the production line is not 'achieving the objectives of the business'. They must be placed before a customer, and this implies movement or transportation of the product.

The management organization of a road haulage operation would be a line responsibility, in that the main objective of the business is to achieve profit by selling transport services. In the manufacturing industry, it all depends on who gives the instructions about the movements. If the manufacturing or sales function states where, when and how the goods are to be moved, then the transport function has no line responsibility and merely provides the service requested. On the other hand, if the transport function takes over the final stage of customer satisfaction and is able to decide the method of movement having been given instructions on where and when, then it is in a position of line responsibility, accountable for its own decisions. Figure 33.1 shows the distinction between line and staff functions in an industrial transport services activity.

Developing the organization structure

Figures 33.2 to 33.4 show different types of organization structure suitable for the transport services function of a manufacturing company. The transport services requirement is of a general nature and is not confined to a major warehousing or retailing operation. It is intended that the types of

MANAGING TRANSPORT SERVICES

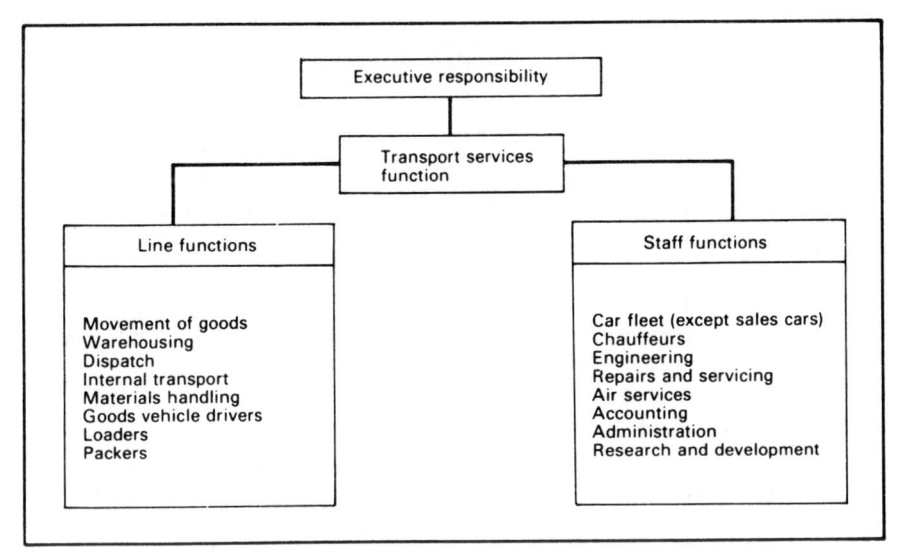

Figure 33.1 Line and staff functions within the transport services activity

Executive responsibility
Transport services function

Line functions:
- Movement of goods
- Warehousing
- Dispatch
- Internal transport
- Materials handling
- Goods vehicle drivers
- Loaders
- Packers

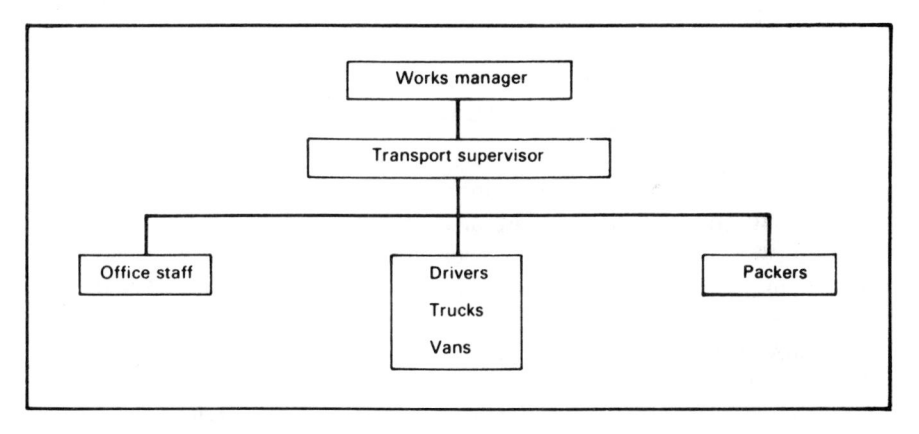

Staff functions:
- Car fleet (except sales cars)
- Chauffeurs
- Engineering
- Repairs and servicing
- Air services
- Accounting
- Administration
- Research and development

Figure 33.2 A simple organization for a small company

Works manager → Transport supervisor → Office staff | Drivers, Trucks, Vans | Packers

organization illustrated will assist readers to develop their own organization structure after taking into consideration their own special needs.

A typical organization for the transport services function of a single factory location of a small company with only a few cars and light vans and one heavy truck used on local deliveries is shown in Figure 33.2. Dispatches are by local carrier and rail. All vehicle maintenance is carried out at local garages. A dispatch section is established which is responsible for packaging and loading goods on to vehicles.

Organization for the transport services function of a medium-sized

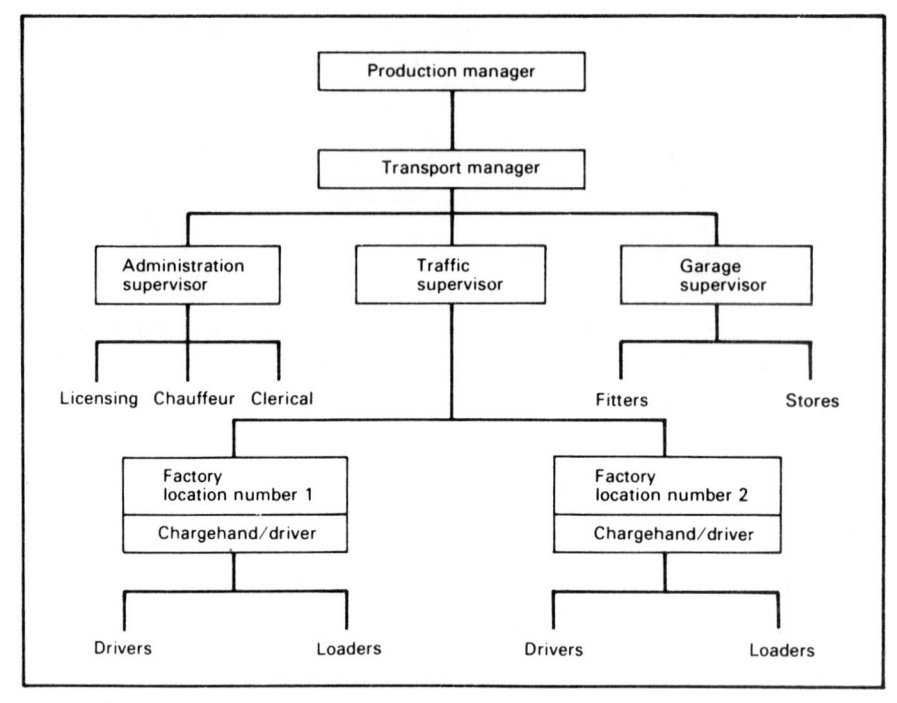

Figure 33.3 Transport services organization for a medium-sized company

company with two factory locations is shown in Figure 33.3. There are twenty cars for management and sales staff use, a number of light vans for customer after-sales service, four trucks for goods delivery to customers and a personnel carrier for personnel movement between factories. Distribution is by company transport and local carrier as well as by rail services. A company garage is available to service and repair the majority of company-owned vehicles.

Figure 33.4 shows the organization for the transport services function of a large group of companies with many factory locations spread across the UK. A mixed vehicle fleet of over 2000 has to be controlled and administered, consisting of executive and management cars, a large sales fleet of cars and light vans, and a truck fleet exceeding 200 vehicles. A full distribution service from all factory locations to customers is carried out using company vehicles. Local carriers are used to meet peak demands. Extensive use is made of rail facilities. Company garages are established in each transport location. The whole of the transport function is based on a regional organization with line responsibility for the movement of company products. A corporate air service is the responsibility of the transport services function.

MANAGING TRANSPORT SERVICES

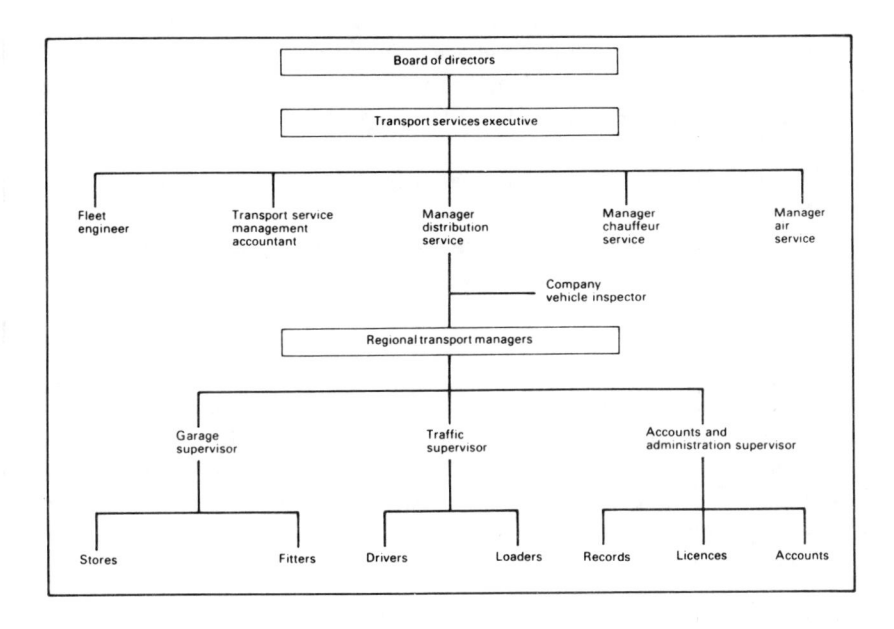

Figure 33.4 Transport services organization for a large group of companies

TRANSPORT MANAGEMENT

One of the conditions for the granting of an operators' licence is that the 'person' named in the application to manage that transport operation is 'professionally competent'. This means that managers in the road haulage industry have to pass an examination in order to obtain this standard, and a certificate will be issued stating that the person named therein is 'professionally competent'. Although this requirement for the granting of an operators' licence only applies to 'hire and reward' operations, the Certificate of Professional Competence is a qualification available to 'own account' transport management where the transport services are not offered for hire and reward. In recruiting or promoting managers to any transport operation, this 'certificate' should be the minimum standard qualification.

Before development of any vehicle plan, a number of questions need to be asked:

1 Does the distribution of the product, or movement of personnel need vehicles? Liquids and gases can be distributed by pipeline, personnel can communicate by telephone, closed circuit television, electronic mail etc.
2 If vehicles are needed, must they be road vehicles? Will railways, waterways or aircraft give a more efficient and economic service?
3 If road vehicles are needed, is the service of a haulier or contract distributor more efficient than the company operating its own vehicle fleet?
4 If road vehicles are to be operated by the company, should they be leased, on contract hire, or owned?
5 If it is finally decided to have company-owned vehicles, how should they be financed, how many are required, what types are needed, and where are they to be based?

These questions are vital. The answers will affect all future transport planning and must be based on sound commercial reasoning, taking into account not only basic costs, but also real costs, including service to the customer and the total value of the whole operation to the overall profitability of the company. The same questions can be used to test current transport policies and to change those policies should the 'answers' differ from the time those initial decisions were taken.

OPERATORS' LICENSING

The Goods Vehicles (Operators' Licences, Qualifications and Fees) Regulations 1984 (SI 1984 No. 176) is the statutory instrument for the control of goods vehicle operations by means of a licensing system known as operators' licensing.

Scope of regulations

Subject to certain exemptions operators' licensing applies to all goods vehicles and combinations used for the carriage of goods in connection with trade or business and which exceed 3.5 tonnes gross plated weight or, if unplated 1525 kg unladen weight. The weight of any trailer forming part of a vehicle combination which is not in excess of 1020 kg unladen weight is discounted in the calculation.

There are three types of operators' licence:

Restricted licence. Issued for 'own account' operators who carry only goods as part of their trade or business provided the business is not professional haulage. Goods must not be carried for hire and reward or in connection with any other business except that of a subsidiary or parent company. A

MANAGING TRANSPORT SERVICES

restricted 'O' licence permits operations both within the UK and abroad. The applicants for a restricted licence must satisfy the licensing authority that they are 'fit and proper persons' and 'have appropriate financial standing'. There is no requirement for the applicant to be, or to employ a person who is, 'professionally competent'. The holder of a restricted licence using a goods vehicle for hire and reward is liable on conviction to a fine of up to £500.

Standard national licence. Issued for professional haulage operators who carry goods for 'hire and reward' and to 'own account' operators who may from time to time carry goods for hire and reward. Hire and reward operators are limited to the UK but 'own account' operators issued with a standard licence may operate abroad subject to a restriction of carrying their own goods. Applicants for a standard national licence must satisfy the licensing authority that they are of good repute and have the appropriate financial standing *and* must be, or must employ someone who is 'professionally competent in national transport operations'.

Standard international licence. Issued to professional hauliers and to own account operators and permits the carriage of goods for hire and reward both within the UK and abroad. Applicants must be of good repute and have appropriate financial standard *and* must be, or must employ someone who is 'professionally competent in both national and international operations'.

Operating centres. An application for an 'O' licence has to be made to the traffic area in which the vehicle operating centre is located. An operating centre is defined as 'the place where the vehicle is normally kept'. This in effect is construed to mean where the vehicle is parked when not in use.

Applications for an 'O' licence. Applicants for an 'O' licence must advertise the intention to apply in a local newspaper in order that people living near to the operating centre can make representations against the granting of a licence. Full details of how to apply for a licence and the conditions to be met are contained in the Department of Transport publication, *A Guide to Goods Vehicle Operators' Licensing* (GV74).

The certificate of professional competence (CPC)

A person will be considered professionally competent if holding:

1. A certificate issued by the licensing authority prior to December 1979, conferring on the holder so called 'grandfather rights' after proving qualification by experience. This certificate will be accepted to support an application for both types of standard licence

2   Membership of one of the professional transport institutes confers the professional competence qualification according to grade of membership
   (a)   for national and international standard licences
      fellow or member of Chartered Institute of Transport
      member or associate member of the Institute of Transport Administration
      member or associate member of The Institute of Road Transport Engineers
      fellow or associate of the Institute of the Furniture Warehousing and Removing Industry
   (b)   for national operations only
      licentiate of Chartered Institute of Transport
      associate (by examination) of the Institute of Road Transport Engineers
      graduate or associate of the Institute of Transport Administration
      holder of the General Certificate in Removals Management issued by the Institute of Furniture Warehousing and Removing Industry
      Note   The above membership must be in the road haulage sectors
3   A certificate of competence issued by the Royal Society of Arts after taking the examination for proof of professional competence. Examination 'pass' certificates act as proof of qualification. The RSA examination is held at centres throughout the UK, usually four times each year. The examination is in two parts
   (a)   national transport operations
   (b)   international transport operations

VEHICLE MANAGEMENT AND VEHICLE STANDARDS

The object of setting vehicle operating standards is to obtain the most efficient utilization of a fleet of vehicles. This is the key to a minimum cost operation. Standing costs now account for more than half the total operating costs of a vehicle and it follows that the higher the utilization, the cheaper the cost per mile. Figure 33.5 shows the standing costs and running costs of various types of vehicle.

There are four main areas of vehicle operation where an attack on utilization can be made, and which can provide a basis for comparison of planned performance against actual performance.

	Rigid truck	Articulated trucks			Chauffeur car
	12.50 tonne GVW	24.19 tonne GCW	32.52 tonne GCW	38.00 tonne GCW	2.8cc (diesel)
Standing costs per year	£	£	£	£	£
Licences	430	1 200	2 500	3 150	100
Insurance	900	1 578	2 135	2 504	450
Depreciation	3 630	5 132	7 950	9 560	5 400
Driver costs (50 hrs)	6 447	7 544	8 025	8 426	9 200
Total	11 407	15 454	20 610	23 640	15 150
Running costs per year based on 36,000 miles					
Fuel	4 975	6 825	9 752	10 501	3 762
Lubricants	90	122	133	133	46
Tyres	1 210	1 850	2 401	3 744	240
Maintenance	5 443	6 034	7 168	7 704	670
Total	11 718	14 831	19 454	22 082	4 718

Figure 33.5 Standing costs and running costs of various types of vehicle

Vehicle preparation

This includes checking the vehicle before a day's work, driver administration and documentation. Work study techniques can be applied to this area of work, and standard times are easy to establish.

Vehicle loading and unloading

One way of achieving a higher productivity is to keep loading and unloading time to a minimum. The use of demountable 'swop bodies', containers and trailers are all ways of preloading vehicles while the motive unit is delivering another load. The size of pallet, side loading, double-deck loading, lower deck height, are all areas where a work study investigation may be applied with advantage. The use of vehicle-mounted handling aids such as tail lifts, cranes and special tracking, will speed up the unloading of a vehicle at customers' premises. Standard forms of label and consignment note, colour coding identification of depots, factories, warehouses or customer delivery areas will speed up the loading procedure and assist the driver to make an efficient delivery.

Vehicle running time

The running time of a vehicle between two points is governed by the speed

Type of road	Type of vehicle	Maximum legal speed	Acceptable average speed for route calculations
Restricted to 30 mph (built-up areas)	All	30 mph	22 mph
Dual carriageways (other than motorways or roads restricted to a lower limit)	Car-derived van or dual-purpose vehicle	70 mph	55 mph
	Rigid goods vehicle not in excess of 7.5 tonnes gvw	60 mph	45 mph
	Articulated vehicle or rigid goods vehicle in excess of 7.5 tonnes gvw	50 mph	38 mph
	Rigid vehicle and trailer in excess of 7.5 tonnes laden weight	50 mph	38 mph
Motorways	Rigid goods vehicle not exceeding 7.5 tonnes gvw and not drawing a trailer	70 mph	55 mph
	Rigid goods vehicle exceeding 7.5 tonnes, articulated vehicles and rigid goods vehicles drawing a trailer	60 mph	48 mph
Other roads (when derestricted)	Rigid goods vehicles, articulated vehicles not exceeding 7.5 tonnes gvw and rigid vehicles drawing a trailer where the aggregate maximum laden weight of the vehicle and trailer does not exceed 7.5 tonnes	50 mph	35 mph
	Goods vehicles including articulated vehicles in excess of 7.5 tonnes gvw and rigid vehicles drawing trailers with an aggregate laden weight in excess of 7.5 tonnes	40 mph	30 mph

Figure 33.6 UK speed limits for goods-registered vehicles

MANAGING TRANSPORT SERVICES

limit of the road over which that vehicle has to travel. Figure 33.6 shows the present speed limits in the UK and acceptable vehicle speeds used in transport operations as a basis for calculating time taken over road routes.

The working day of a delivery vehicle can be divided into three sections:

(a) proceeding to actual delivery area
(b) delivering the goods in the delivery area
(c) returning to base

The speed-limit factor will only affect the first and last sections. The main controlling factor in the delivery area is the number of delivery points and the number of units to be delivered at each point.

Delivering the goods

This is an area of uncertainty when trying to calculate standard times of performance and the approach to the problem will differ with each company and product. Calculations can be based on:

(a) the number of delivery drops
(b) a basic time allowance for each delivery point
(c) standard times for handling each parcel delivered
(d) an average speed for the vehicle when delivering in towns

The setting of vehicle and operating standards in a transport operation is called 'load assessment' and there are many ways of applying this technique. The object in every case is to establish a standard against which the driver's performance can be measured.

DRIVERS' HOURS AND RECORDS OF WORK

Drivers' hours

New regulations governing drivers' hours and rest periods came into force on 29 September 1986. EEC Directive 3820/85 sets out the drivers' hours rules for most goods vehicles with a gross plated weight in excess of 3.5 tonnes. The new rules are now the same for drivers engaged on national and international journeys and all the old duty restrictions contained in the Transport Act 1968 have been abolished for drivers of vehicles falling within scope of EEC Directive 3820/85.

From 29 September 1986 two sets of drivers' hours rules apply in the UK:

1. *National and international operations.* For national and international journeys applying to drivers of goods vehicles exceeding 3.5 tonnes gross

plated weight including the weight of any trailer drawn, not exempted under UK legislation and to passenger vehicles with a maximum of seventeen seats including the driver and operated wholly within the UK

2 *Domestic operations.* Apply to drivers of goods vehicles which are exempt from EEC rules including those vehicles below 3.5 tonnes gross vehicle weight

National and international operations. The following is a summary of drivers' hours rules for national and international journeys:
Daily driving. 9 hours maximum, extended to 10 hours maximum twice a week
Driving in any two consecutive weeks. 90 hours maximum
Consecutive days of driving. 6 days maximum
Definition of 'fixed week'. The period between 00.00 hours Monday and 24.00 hours Sunday
Continuous driving. Limited to 4.5 hours accumulated driving either in one block or a number of shorter periods of driving not separated by a legal break
Daily rest. 11 hours minimum, with a reduction to 9 hours on 3 days per week subject to an equivalent period of rest being taken as compensation before the end of the following week
Weekly rest. 45 hours minimum, with reductions to 36 hours at base or 24 hours away from base, subject to each reduction being compensated by an equivalent rest taken *en bloc* before the end of the *third week* following the week when the reduced rest was taken
Breaks from driving. 45 minutes minimum after an accumulated driving period of 4.5 hours or, three 15-minute breaks spaced out over and at the end of that period.

It is to be noted that under the new regulations there are no limitations on the duty hours which a driver can work.

Note EEC regulations allow member states to exempt certain other vehicles and operations at their discretion and to make special exemptions in particular cases, but generally the restrictions on maximum driving periods are applied without exception. Information on exemptions and variations are available from the Road Haulage Association or the Freight Transport Association.

Domestic operations
Daily driving.   10 hours maximum
Daily duty.   11 hours maximum

The above rules are the only limitations placed on the driving and working hours of drivers of goods vehicles exempt from the EEC rules. It is to be noted that there are no requirements to take a legal break during a driving or duty day, or daily/weekly rest minimum.

MANAGING TRANSPORT SERVICES

Drivers' records of work

The use of a tachograph to record the work and driving hours of goods vehicle drivers applies to all goods vehicles in excess of 3.5 tonnes plated gross weight which are not exempt from the EEC drivers' hours rules. Tachographs and compliance with EEC drivers' hours rules also apply to passenger vehicles constructed to carry more than seventeen persons including the driver. The relevant EEC Directive 3821/85 was brought into effect in the UK on 29 September 1986 and amended the previous rules which had been in operation since 1 January 1982. The revised rules do not apply to crew members other than the driver who is defined as 'any person who drives the vehicle even for a short period or is carried in the vehicle in order to be available for driving if necessary'.

Where a tachograph is fitted to a vehicle it must conform to the detailed specification as laid down in the EEC Directive. It must be able to record:
(*a*) distance travelled
(*b*) speed
(*c*) driving time
(*d*) other periods of work of the driver
(*e*) breaks from work and daily rest periods
(*f*) opening of the case containing the tachograph chart

The tachograph chart must also have a facility by which the driver(s) can continue recording driving and duty time in the event of the instrument becoming unserviceable during a journey. Once a vehicle has been fitted with a tachograph, the instrument must be calibrated and sealed at an approved centre.

The tachograph record. An employer must:

1   Issue each driver with sufficient charts for the journey
2   Organize each driver's work so that the relevant provisions of the regulations can be complied with
3   Take periodical checks to ensure that the provisions of drivers' hours and tachograph regulations have been complied with and, if infringements are found, take the appropriate steps to prevent repetition
4   Ensure that drivers return charts within twenty-one days of use
5   Retain tachograph charts for a minimum of one year after use and produce or hand over any charts on request by an authorized inspecting officer

The driver must:

1   Use a tachograph chart every day in which he is driving, starting from the moment he takes over the vehicle. The same chart should continue to be used until the end of that daily driving period

Key

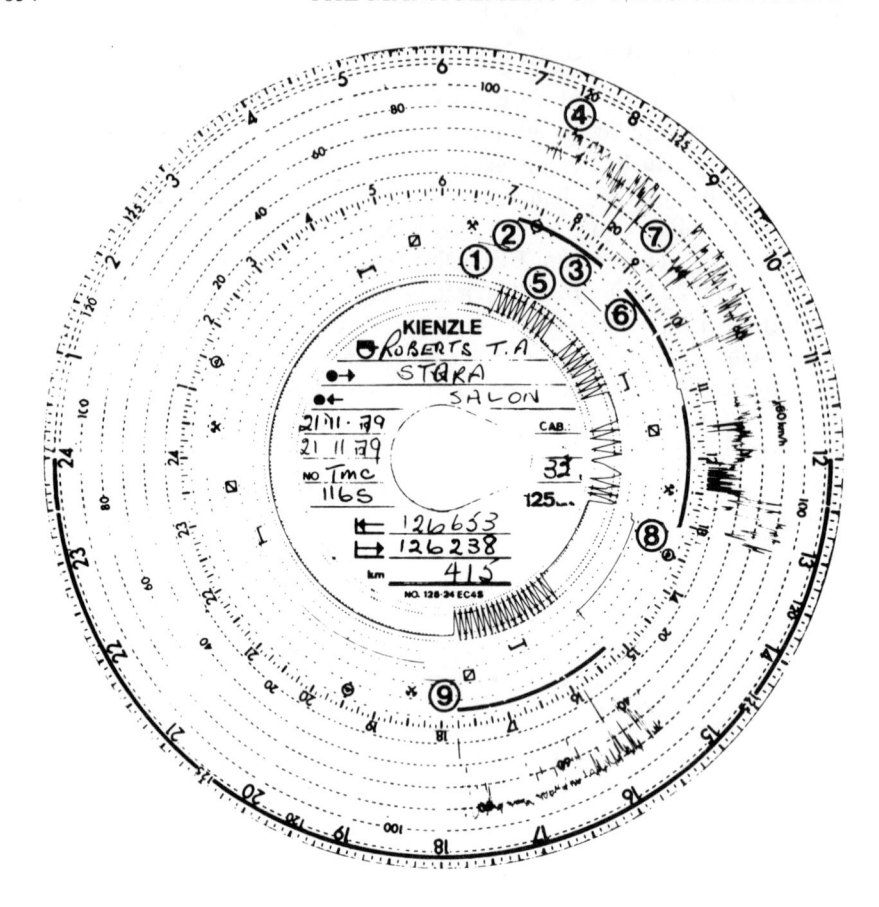

1 06.30 commence work
2 07.15 commence driving
3 First break from driving at 08.45
4 Maximum speed 82 kph
5 Distance covered between 07.15 and 08.45 — 90 km (each peak represents 10 km)
6 Recommence driving at 09.15
7 Length of break from driving 30 minutes
8 Long break from driving between 13.00 and 15.15
9 Driving and duty finished at 17.45

Analysis of driving

07.15 Start driving
08.45 Stop driving
09.15 Recommence driving
10.30 Stop driving, engaged on other duties
11.15 Recommence driving
13.00 Stop driving
15.15 Recommence driving
17.45 Stop driving
Total accumulated driving = 7 hours

Figure 33.7 Example of a tachograph chart

2   Enter on the chart
    (a) surname and first name
    (b) date and place where the record chart begins and ends
    (c) the registration number(s) of the vehicle(s) driven
    (d) the odometer readings: at the start of the first journey; at the end of the last journey; at each change of vehicle, plus the time at which a change of vehicle takes place
3   Produce charts for inspection if requested by enforcement officers of the Department of Transport
4   Retain charts for the current week *and* the chart for the last day on which he drove a vehicle in the previous week
5   Return the charts to his employer within twenty-one days of completion

A specimen tachograph chart is shown in Figure 33.7

Written records. Drivers of vehicles which are exempt from EEC drivers' hours regulations are required to maintain written records for vehicles over 3.5 tonnes gross plated vehicle weight, or if not plated, with an unladen weight in excess of 1525 kg. The record is required to be in a prescribed form and there is a duty on the employer to check and sign each record. There is no requirement to keep written records for those vehicles which do not exceed 3.5 tonnes gross plated weight or have an unladen weight not in excess of 1525 kg.

VEHICLE SELECTION AND DESIGN

The efficiency of any distribution operation depends upon the selection of the right truck for the job to be done. For the 'own account' user it is the essential element in achieving an effective customer delivery service, and for the haulier it provides the means to maximize profits. Selecting to meet a given set of criteria can only be achieved after full discussion with all functions within the total distribution chain – a full understanding of the size, weight and types of load to be carried is necessary as well as a knowledge of the routes over which the truck is to operate. As the product structure of a company changes, vehicles designed specifically to carry that product may become obsolete. Long-term planning is essential and a degree of flexibility needs to be built into the design features of any industrial fleet.

Setting the body specification

The body of a goods vehicle is that part on or in which the load is carried. This part of the specification must be set first, followed by a chassis specification to accommodate the body. The specification will cover:

1 Internal and external dimensions and floor height
2 Size, type and location of doors, shutters and tailboards
3 Materials to be used, including provision for insulation and temperature control equipment
4 Internal fittings and load security fitments
5 Load-handling equipment, vehicle mounted or carried
6 Requirements for carrying hazardous loads
7 Painting and company livery requirements

Truck design and legislation

The Motor Vehicles (Construction and Use) Regulations 1978, as amended, will determine the maximum dimensions and permitted gross weight of the chassis on which a truck body is to be mounted. A brief outline of the weights and dimension legislation is as follows:

1 Length:
   rigid vehicles – 11.0 metres
   articulated vehicles – 15.5 metres
   draw-bar combinations – 18.0 metres
   semi-trailers manufactured from 1 May 1983 – 12.2 metres*
   * This is the internal load space measurement, but the total length of the tractor and semi-trailer must not exceed 15.5 metres.)
2 Width:
   all vehicles – 2.5 metres
   (Under certain conditions a refrigerated vehicle is permitted to have a maximum width of 2.55 metres.)
3 Height:
   None specified except for articulated vehicles where the semi-trailer has a plated gross weight in excess of 26 000 kg and the total laden weight of the tractor and semi-trailer when driven on the road exceeds 32 520 kg. In such cases the vehicle is subject to a height limit of 4.2 metres
4 Maximum permitted gross weights:
   2-axle rigid vehicle – 16 260 kg
   3-axle rigid vehicle – 24 390 kg
   4-axle rigid vehicle – 30 490 kg
   Rigid vehicle and tow bar trailer (must be fitted with power assisted brakes) – 32 520 kg
   Articulated vehicles:
   tractor and semi-trailer with total of 3 axles – 24 390 kg
   tractor and semi-trailer with total of 4 axles – 32 520 kg
   tractor and semi-trailer with total of 5 or more axles – 38 000 kg

The above maximum weights depend upon meeting a number of conditions in respect of 'axle spread' and 'overall length', which should be checked carefully before setting a design specification for a truck.

Environmental legislation

With the increase in permitted vehicle operating weights up to 38 tonnes (38 000 kg), legislation has been introduced to meet higher safety and environmental standards. These include:

(*a*) sideguards
(*b*) antispray protection
(*c*) rear under-run protection
(*d*) noise levels
(*e*) minimum ground clearance

The choice of vehicles for the carriage of goods varies from a small van to a 38-tonne gross articulated vehicle. The design of vehicles within this range is just as varied. The use of unit load movements is an important element in achieving a high utilization of both vehicle and driver. Containers, demountable bodies, semi-trailers and draw-bar combinations are used in all types of distribution operations. The ultimate test of vehicle design is the efficiency of the vehicle to do the job it was intended for. In setting design specifications it is also necessary to ensure compliance with Health and Safety at Work Regulations.

ACQUIRING VEHICLES – THE FUNDING OPTIONS

The market place is full of package schemes to tempt industrial management to acquire assets, including vehicles, by different methods of funding. Many names are used to market these options, but within all the different methods there are only two ways by which to fund a vehicle: purchase or rental.

The Finance Acts give a clear definition of determining each basic option:

> If a company acquires plant etc. under a contract whereby that contract provides that it *may or will* eventually have title of such plant, then the equipment will be regarded as belonging to that company and will be a '*purchase*'.
> If the contract does not lead to or offer an 'option' to eventual title, then the contract will be '*rental*'.

Purchasing

The following options fall under the purchase heading:

1   Reduce current cash balances

2   Establish or increase a bank overdraft
3   Arrange a bank loan to be repaid over a predetermined period
4   Hire purchase, which is normally associated with a credit facility for a private purchaser. It has advantages for the smaller business and is usually referred to as a 'conditional sale agreement'
5   Lease with the 'option to purchase', which gives the lessee (the hirer) the option to purchase the vehicle at the end of the lease period and to acquire title by payment of a stated sum

Finance leases

A finance lease is a term generally used to mean the same as 'hire'. It excludes any option or agreement on the part of the lessee to acquire legal title. The repayment will be in the form of *equal rentals over a predetermined period*. The finance company will purchase the vehicle in its own title and the asset capitalized in the financial accounts. The lessee is responsible for all the costs of operating the vehicle, including road fund licence, insurance and maintenance. At the end of the lease period, the vehicle is sold and the lessee is usually credited with up to 95 per cent of the proceeds as a refund of rentals. In the case of trucks, a clause in the agreement may provide the lessee with the choice of continuing to lease for a secondary period at a nominal rental usually 0.5 per cent of the total rental payments per annum.

Contract hire

The growth in the use of the contract hire option by companies has continued to increase since 1980. It can best be described as 'paying a rental for the use of a vehicle over a stated period of time and/or miles'. A contract hire agreement will provide:

(a) supply of a vehicle ready for the road
(b) road fund licence during period of contract
(c) all repair and maintenance costs of the vehicle
(d) tyres/batteries/exhaust systems etc.
(e) replacement vehicle in the event of the contract vehicle being under repair
(f) roadside recovery and repair services

Many contract hire companies now offer insurance as part of the agreement. The objective is to provide the user of the vehicle with no liability for costs other than the monthly rental. Most contract hire agreements have a mileage limitation. If the mileage is exceeded, an extra cost is charged based upon a 'pence per mile' calculation. Contract hire agreements for trucks, especially for periods in excess of three years, usually have the maintenance element of the rental linked to an index or a clause providing for this to be reviewed each year.

Advantages of contract hire: fixed costs and cash flow over the period; simple and easy to forecast budgets; reduced administration; maximum availability of the vehicle; reduced downtime; no risks on residual value or maintenance costs.

Value added tax

Each funding option is affected in a different way as regards the treatment of VAT.

Purchase. Vehicles are subject to VAT based on the invoice price of the vehicle. This means that if higher discounts are obtained which reduce the invoice price, the VAT amount is less. VAT on goods vehicles is an input and recoverable through the VAT account on quarterly settlement dates set by HM Customs and Excise. VAT on cars, including dual purpose vehicles (estate cars) is not recoverable, so a reduction in the invoice price by negotiating discounts also reduces VAT and is a *real saving*.

Hire purchase. VAT is payable on the invoice price of the vehicle the same as if the vehicle had been purchased outright. No VAT is payable on the repayments of capital or on the interest element of the repayments.

Lease with option to purchase. No VAT is payable on the lease rentals when vehicles are acquired by any conditional sale agreement.

Finance lease. VAT is payable on all rentals and this requires additional funding. For those companies registered for VAT, the charge is recoverable as an input through the quarterly VAT account.

Contract hire. VAT is payable on all contract hire rentals.

VAT costs on finance lease and contract hire rentals is an additional cost to those organizations not registered for VAT, e.g. some local government departments, and when using these two funding options to acquire cars, VAT is being paid twice: on the invoice cost of the vehicle which is built into the rental, and then on the rentals paid.

Balance sheet disclosure

One advantage of selecting a lease option when funding assets was that the funding was 'off balance sheet', which improved the gearing ratios of a company. From 1987 SSAP21 (Statement of Standard Accounting Practices) requires certain leases to be shown within the balance sheet of a company. The test is *'whether the lease transfers substantially all the risks and rewards of an asset to the lessee'*. Vehicle finance leases fall within this definition and under SSAP21 are required to be recorded on the balance sheet as an asset. Where vehicles are acquired under a contract hire agreement, the lessor takes all the risks under the contract. Such leases are called *'operating leases'* and are not required to be treated as an asset in company balance sheets.

Effect on taxation on purchase, leasing and contract hire

An argument used in favour of leasing and contract hire is that the payments (rentals) are wholly allowable for tax purposes. This is true, but the fact is that tax is neutral. No matter by which method a vehicle is acquired, the payments, either revenue or capital, qualify for tax relief, the only difference is in the *pace* at which relief is given.

Capital allowances

Capital allowances are the means by which an asset acquired by purchase is depreciated by an annual writing-down allowance which is used to reduce the tax liability of a company. *Vehicles* come under the category of 'plant and machinery' and, from 1 April 1986, there is no difference in the way goods vehicles or cars are treated under the rules of capital allowances.

Annual writing-down allowance
1   Goods vehicles are eligible for an annual writing-down allowance of 25 per cent on a *reducing balance* from the date of acquisition. This is defined as the date the obligation to pay arises
2   Cars and dual purpose vehicles are eligible for an annual writing-down allowance of 25 per cent on a *reducing balance* from the date of acquisition, but restricted to a maximum of £2000 per annum. Example:

Invoice cost of car	£11 000	
Year 1 writing-down allowance	2 000	(restricted)
balance forward	9 000	
Year 2 writing-down allowance	2 000	(restricted)
balance forward	7 000	
Year 3 writing-down allowance	1 750	(25%)
balance forward	5 250	

MANAGING TRANSPORT SERVICES

The balance of capital expenditure carried forward after applying the first year annual writing-down allowance is transferred to a pool of qualifying expenditure for writing-down allowances.

De-pooling of short life assets. The Finance Act 1985 introduced a method of de-pooling for assets expected to be sold within five years of acquisition. The objective is to give companies the benefit of applying the total depreciation of the asset at the time it is sold. The rules of de-pooling are:

1. Applies only to assets previously eligible for 100 per cent first year allowances. This includes goods vehicles but excludes motor cars and dual purpose vehicles
2. Affects only assets acquired on or after 1 April 1986
3. Election to de-pool must be taken within a period of two years from the date of acquisition
4. If the asset is not sold within five years, any balance of capital is to be transferred to the asset pool of qualifying expenditure

Hire purchase. The Finance Acts provide that if a person incurs capital expenditure (including vehicles) under a contract whereby he becomes the owner, for example hire purchase or lease with option to purchase, then capital allowances may be taken on the total cost of the asset purchased at the date of entering into the contract.

Contract hire and leasing rentals. Because the ownership of the asset does not pass to the user under a contract hire or leasing agreement, no capital allowances are allowed to the user of the asset. The rentals under contract hire and leasing agreements are treated as revenue expenditure and the total rentals paid in any one financial year are allowed against taxable profits for that year. For cars costing more than £8000 retail, the tax relief on rentals is restricted using the following formula:

$$\frac{\text{retail price of car price} - (£8000)}{2 \times \text{retail price}} = \text{percentage rental disallowed}$$

Examples of the amount of tax relief lost on vehicles with a retail price in excess of £8000 are:

Retail price £	Percentage rentals disallowed
10 000	10.0
12 000	16.7
15 000	23.4
20 000	30.0
30 000	36.7
50 000	42.0

Timing of acquisition and taxation benefits. Tax benefits from allowances are usually received at the end of a company financial year following the year of entitlement.

Capital allowances claimed on assets purchased at any time during a tax year are allowable in full.

Recommendation. If the company has taxable profits acquire vehicles (purchase, hire purchase, or lease with the option to purchase) before the end of a financial year.

If no taxable profits are forecast, delay acquisition until the period immediately following the end of a financial year.

Revenue expenditure (lease rentals, contract hire rentals)

Only the amount of rentals paid are eligible for relief against taxable profits. The timing of the commencement of such agreements has little effect on the receipt of taxable benefits.

Capital budget planning. The timing of vehicle acquisitions and disposals is an area where real savings in total operating costs can be achieved. The disposal prices of vehicles are governed by the trade values in *Glass's Guide* and similar publications. Purchasing a vehicle in the last quarter of a calendar year is seriously reflected in the price obtained when the vehicle is sold. The guide uses the year as a bench mark for assessing the residual value and this value drops when the vehicle becomes a year older. Examples:

> *Vauxhall Cavalier 1600 GL (5 dr)*
>   registered December 1984
>   trade value May 1986 – £4325
>   registered January 1985
>   trade value May 1986 – £5000
>   difference of £675
> *Truck: Ford Cargo 0708*
>   registered December 1982
>   trade value May 1986 – £3250
>   registered January 1983
>   trade value May 1986 – £4200
>   difference of £950

Vehicle fleet management (VFM)

Fleet management is not an alternative funding option but simply the administration of the selected option by an outside agent for a fee. It is

MANAGING TRANSPORT SERVICES

usually associated with the company car fleet. The objective is to reduce costs and administration. A vehicle fleet management package will include:

1 Operational management of the vehicles:
    acquisition
    maintenance
    fuel credit cards
    licensing
    disposal
2 Financial analysis of costs:
    fuel
    maintenance
    depreciation
3 Advice and consultancy:
    vehicle make and models
    replacement policies
    funding options

What does VFM cost?
All purchases by the fleet management company on behalf of the user company are charged at cost, *plus* a set fee per vehicle per annum usually based on a percentage of the invoice cost of the vehicle.

MAINTENANCE POLICIES

Before an operator's licence can be issued an applicant must satisfy the licensing authority that vehicles will be kept fit and serviceable at all times when used on the public roads. The licensing authority may also request a copy of any maintenance contract or letter of agreement if the servicing and repair of vehicles is carried out elsewhere than in a company garage workshop, and in all cases may request examples of the forms used for vehicle safety inspections. It is also a requirement for the issue of an 'O' licence that proper arrangements are available for drivers to report safety faults in vehicles as soon as possible. The Department of Transport publication, *A Guide to Goods Vehicle Operators Licensing* (GV74 4/84), sets the following guidelines around which vehicle operators should formulate a vehicle maintenance policy:

1 Two separate vehicle checks and inspections should be carried out: daily running checks; vehicle safety inspections and routine maintenance at set intervals on items which affect vehicle safety, followed by repair of any faults
2 The daily check is normally carried out by the driver on basic items

including brakes, tyre pressures, lights, windscreen wipers and washers, and trailer couplings
3 Vehicle safety inspections and routine maintenance should be carried out at set intervals of time or mileage and should include wheels, tyres, brakes, steering, suspension, lighting and all safety components
4 Staff carrying out inspections must be able to recognize faults and be aware of the acceptable standard of performance and wear of parts
5 Records must be kept, for at least fifteen months, of all safety inspections to show the history of each vehicle. Where an outside garage carries out the safety inspections, maintenance records must still be kept
6 Adequate facilities must be available for carrying out the inspection, especially equipment for measuring braking efficiency and setting lights
7 Drivers must report vehicle faults to whoever is responsible for putting them right. The reports must be in writing
8 Users are responsible for the condition of hired vehicles and trailers. The user is defined as the employer of the driver
9 Where maintenance work is contracted out to a garage or other vehicle repairer, a written agreement must be entered into setting out the conditions and periods of safety inspections

Planned maintenance and inspection

A number of ready-made planned maintenance and inspection schemes are available to operators, all of which have been designed to ensure compliance with the legal requirements. Basically, each contains the following documents enabling a complete history of a vehicle's maintenance and inspection to be recorded and preserved:

(*a*) driver's defect report
(*b*) vehicle inspection check sheet
(*c*) servicing sheet for predetermined intervals of time or mileage
(*d*) stores requisition form
(*e*) work order sheet or job card
(*f*) servicing, planning and record chart
(*g*) vehicle history folder

No matter what method is adopted, in company premises by company employees, or by contracting out the entire task of maintenance, inspection and documentation, the onus of responsibility for the roadworthiness of the vehicle is always with the vehicle operator. He is still responsible in law even though an outside contractor providing the service and maintenance facilities has been neglectful.

The use of computers

There are many computer programmes designed to meet the requirements of all sizes of fleet. For under £3000 there are small 128K personal computers with printer and a fleet management programme which can handle all the records and maintenance control information for a fleet of up to 100 vehicles. It must be stressed that a computer does not replace the need for written records. The Department of Transport inspectors will require to see the original documents – invoices, service and repair sheets.

FINANCIAL CONTROL OF THE TRANSPORT FUNCTION

The only way to ensure a cost-effective operation is to establish a system of budgetary control and accounting responsibility which ensures that any overspending is immediately highlighted at the point where the cost was incurred. The best way to impose effective financial control on the transport services function is to make it an independent cost centre within the company.

The whole range of transport services is now on offer to companies who do not wish to invest in a fleet of vehicles. From the acquisition of company cars through to the distribution and storage of the company product range is available on contract terms. By setting up the transport services function as an independent cost centre, a correct evaluation of both cost and service can be carried out using 'in house' services or outside contractors.

A rate schedule for the carriage of goods within the company and to customers should be produced in the same way as one would expect to see from a haulier. Similar rate schedules can also be prepared for other services such as chauffeur-driven cars, allocated company cars, and even for the repair and maintenance of vehicles in company garages. These rate schedules should be fixed for the period of a company financial year and published to all departments to be used as a basis for determining the transport and distribution costs borne by the product. By adopting such a system, the transport function receives regular revenue for its services against which it incurs costs.

To be cost effective two requirements must be met: actual expenditure should be within the budgeted expenditure, and recoveries should equate to actual expenditure.

It is to be noted that recoveries should equate to expenditure – excess recoveries only add an unnecessary price burden on the product, and an under-recovery will indicate a loss due to an insufficient charge being made for the services provided.

To establish financial disciplines, it is necessary to keep adequate costing information for each vehicle and also to have a system of budgetary control in order that, over the whole of a financial period, regular checks can be

Vehicle costing record

Vehicle costing record		Speedometer reading	
Registration number C888 XYZ		Finish	29155
Make FORD CARGO 0813		Start	22108
Depot WATFORD		Miles	7047
Vehicle group 3/3/B			
Month MARCH 87			

Day	Fuel issues (Gallons) Bulk	Fuel issues (Gallons) Agency	Lubricant (pints)	Tyres £	Repairs and service (£) Workshop	Repairs and service (£) Agency	Miles
1	16						22121
2	32		4		39.60		22471
3		10					
4	14						23372
5	18					44.00	23768
6	26		2				24191
7							
8							24597
24							
25							
26	8				247.50	97.20	
27	24						26923
28		6	2				
29	22				8.40		28068
30	10		4				28508
31	16						28732
Total agency		28					
Total bulk	293						
Totals	321		16	247.50	145.20	44.00	

Figure 33.8 Layout of a simple monthly vehicle costing record

made on areas of excessive expenditure and corrective action taken by management if necessary.

COSTING THE OPERATION

There are two main components of vehicle costs:

1 Standing costs, which generally include:
    (a) depreciation cost of the vehicle, together with a charge equivalent to the interest which the capital invested in the vehicle can earn

MANAGING TRANSPORT SERVICES

  (b) licences, including road fund and operator's licences
  (c) insurance, for both vehicle and goods in transit
  (d) wages of the driver
2 Running costs, which are the result of operating the vehicle on the road and include:
  (a) fuel and oil
  (b) repair and maintenance
  (c) tyres
  (d) driver's expenses
  (e) driver's overtime

The most informative costs of own-account transport operation are the running costs of a vehicle.

Monthly cost record

The vehicle monthly costings record (see Figure 33.8) ignores all costs other than those directly associated with day-to-day operation.

Fuel. Issues from company bulk installations are shown separately from the fuel picked up from garages by means of agency cards or cash. This helps to control the amount of fuel picked up from outside sources and to maximize the higher discounts available by having bulk stocks.

Lubricants. Only issues during normal running are recorded. Oil changes will be recorded on maintenance job cards.

Tyres. Expenditure on new tyres is recorded from invoices received. Sale of old casings will be entered as credits.

Repairs. A distinction is made between repairs and maintenance carried out in company garages and repairs by outside agents.

Miles run. This is recorded from driver tachograph charts and gives a simple but clear picture of vehicle utilization.

This vehicle costing record also shows registration number or fleet number, make, vehicle group and operating base. Dividing a fleet into groups of similar vehicles, e.g. vehicles under 3.5 tonnes GVW, vehicles 3.5 to 7.5 tonnes GVW etc., also allows the costings to be arranged in groups and will highlight any variance within a group so that investigatory action can be taken.

VEHICLE DATA														
Reg. No.	C 888 X Y Z			Invoice cost (less tyres)	£18,473.									
Make	FORD CARGO 0813			Estimated life	300,000 ML.									
Cost group	3/3/B			Gross vehicle weight	7490 Kgs									
Date purchased	Oct. '85			Unladen weight	3979 Kgs									

STANDING COSTS	
Interest	£1,662.
Licences	£570
Insurances	£580
Total per annum	£2,812
per month	£234·33

TYRES	
Size	85 R 17·5
No. per set	6
Cost per set	£1,260.
Estimated life	40,000 MLS

ESTIMATED COST PER MILE	
Tyres	£ 0·0315
Depreciation	£ 0·0616
LAST DATE COSTS UPDATE	
January 1986	

Month	Mileage	Fuel Gallons	Fuel Cost (1)	m.p.g.	Oil Pints	Oil Cost (2)	Tyres Est. cost (3)	Tyres Actual	Servicing/repairs Work shop	Servicing/repairs Agents	Total (4)	Depreciation (5)	Total running costs (1–5)	Running costs per mile	Standing	Operational	Operational costs per mile
1985																	
Oct	4284	211	321	20·3	7	2·10	135	—	84·80	3·20	88·00	264	810·10	0·19	234·33	1044·33	0·24
Nov	4291	214	325	20·0	8	2·40	135	—	16·80	55·20	72·00	264	798·40	0·19	234·33	1032·73	0·24
Dec	4838	236	354	20·5	6	1·80	152	—	93·94	2·50	96·44	298	902·44	0·19	234·33	1136·77	0·23
1986																	
Jan	6083	297	445	20·5	14	4·10	192	—	182·60	4·20	186·80	375	1202·90	0·20	234·33	1437·23	0·24
Feb	2612	124	181	21·1	7	2·00	82	—	42·90	22·70	65·60	161	491·60	0·19	234·33	725·93	0·28
Mar	7047	321	469	22·0	16	4·75	222	247·5	145·20	44·00	185·20	434	1314·95	0·19	234·33	1549·28	0·22

Figure 33.9 Example of a vehicle operating cost record sheet

Vehicle operating cost sheet

A layout for a vehicle cost sheet is shown in Figure 33.9. All costs recorded refer to the direct operation of the vehicle. Overheads, rent, rates and wages are excluded as these would tend to reduce the value of the costings as a means of comparing the different types of vehicle. The following vehicle data is shown:

1. Registration or fleet number
2. Make, group, type, gross vehicle weight, unladen weight (3/3/B indicates the HGV driving licence class, the size of the vehicle in that class and 'B' denotes a box van)
3. The invoice cost of the vehicle, reduced by the value of a set of tyres and the expected life of the vehicle in miles
4. Details of tyre size and cost of complete set. The estimated tyre life is used as a basis for costing
5. Standing costs will include interest on capital invested, licences and insurance costs
6. Depreciation is calculated in terms of cost per mile, based on the actual cost and the estimated life of the vehicle in miles (18,473/300,000 = £0.0616)
7. Tyre costs per mile (1260/40,000 = £0.0315)

The details of running costs are taken from the monthly vehicle costing record and over the life of the vehicle a permanent record is built up. The following points are to be noted.

Fuel. Calculating mpg is suspect unless the tanks on the vehicle are full at the start and end of a monthly accounting period.

Oil. Calculating mpg or miles per pint serves no useful purpose. Excessive oil use can be seen quite easily from total usage each month.

Tyres. Calculations are based on the tyre wear. Actual purchases are shown and if the estimated mileages are correct, expenditure on tyres should balance the estimated costs over the agreed mileage.

Depreciation. Obtained by multiplying monthly mileage by estimated cost per mile.

Running costs. Total cost of fuel, oil, estimated tyre wear, repairs and depreciation, divided by miles run. This figure can be compared with the performance figures of other vehicles in the fleet within the same vehicle group, with its own performance figures over previous months and with cost tables published by the transport journals.

Standing costs. These are now added to the total running costs to give the total monthly operating costs. The total operating cost per mile is of little use as this depends entirely upon the mileage recorded for the period. It will be seen from the example that total operating cost per mile varied from 22p to over 28p, whereas the per mile figure of running costs was reasonably constant.

MOVEMENT OF PERSONNEL

The transport services function should be responsible for personnel movement in order to minimize the problems and increase the overall efficiency of the company by reducing the fatigue associated with people moving.

Sales and service function

The responsibility for the mobility of the sales force of a company comes within the function of transport services in that the provision of small vans, cars, and estate cars and the maintenance and servicing of such a fleet is the direct responsibility of the transport department of a company. The transport services function will need to advise on the choice of vehicle allocated to personnel of the sales and service force, and will need to know the difference of law and taxation in the use of this type of vehicle.

Law on small goods vehicles

A small goods vehicle is defined in $s60(4)$ of the Transport Act 1968 as:

> One which does not form part of a vehicle combination and has a gross plated weight not exceeding 3.5 tonnes including the weight of any trailer drawn or, if not having a plated weight, has an unladen weight not exceeding 1525 kg including the weight of any trailer drawn

The law for the small goods vehicle and its driver can be summarized as follows:

Operator's licences. Exempt.

Vehicle testing. An annual test for roadworthiness when three years old or more.

Speed limits

1   Dual carriageways other than motorways and not drawing a trailer − 60 mph

MANAGING TRANSPORT SERVICES

2   Dual carriageways other than motorways when drawing a trailer – 50 mph
3   Other roads – 50 mph
    (The above subject to the road not being restricted to a lower speed limit)
4   Motorways: not drawing a trailer – 70 mph; drawing a trailer – 50 mph

Trailers. Subject to the weight of the vehicle not being less than the weight of the trailer being towed, the speed limit on derestricted roads and motorways is 50 mph. A 50 mph disc must be displayed on the rear of the trailer, and the kerb weight of the vehicle and the maximum permitted unladen weight of the trailer must be shown on each.

Driving licences. Ordinary driving licences group 'A' or group 'B' if restricted to automatic transmission vehicles.

Drivers' hours. Goods vehicles with a gross plated weight not in excess of 3.5 tonnes including dual purpose vehicles (estate cars), are required to conform with the British Domestic Hours Rules which have been revised and simplified with effect from 29 September 1986. The rules are:

   Maximum daily driving – 10 hrs
   Maximum daily duty – 11 hrs

There are no regulations governing the hours of continuous driving, break periods, weekly duty or weekly rest periods.

Drivers' records. Completely exempt (written records and tachographs).

Servicing and maintenance of sales and service vehicles

Although this class of vehicle is exempt from the requirements of operator licensing, it is important to understand that any convictions against a company or a vehicle user for contravention of the Construction and Use Regulations 1978, or for instances of using, or causing to be used, vehicles which are found to be unroadworthy, may be taken into consideration when application is made for the renewal of, or the initial granting of an 'O' licence. A system of reporting defects by the driver of the vehicle is recommended and a suitable form is illustrated in Figure 33.10. Drivers should also be asked to send in weekly reports showing any work done on the vehicle by outside garages.

The company car

Mobility of personnel costs money. Just as the cost-effectiveness of a goods

```
                DRIVER'S REPORT OF VEHICLE DEFECTS

   Date _____

   This form to be used only to report defects and must be handed to the Transport Office
   IMMEDIATELY on your return. No verbal reports please

   Depot _____

   Registration number _____   Make _____

   NATURE OF DEFECT.  Faults must be reported at once, even if only of a minor nature



   Speedometer reading _____   If anything is wrong, don't be afraid to say so

   Driver's signature _____

   Date rectified _____   By _____
```

Figure 33.10 Form for reporting vehicle defects

distribution service is judged on its contribution to the total profitability of a company by giving an efficient customer service, the value of a fleet of company cars should also be assessed on its contribution to the efficient mobility of management and executives, as well as the part it plays in recruiting the right calibre of person to fulfil the needs of the company. There are many different approaches to determining a policy for the supply and allocation of cars to company employees. Each company will decide its own policy based on its own needs. For a medium-sized fleet, there are several ways of obtaining cars:

1   Outright purchase or hire purchase negotiating the best terms
2   Leasing, generally without maintenance but sometimes with the cost of the vehicle licence included
3   Contract hire, with maintenance cost, licences and a replacement vehicle included in the monthly rentals

Each of the above methods has advantages and disadvantages and, as stated in the section dealing with the purchase of trucks, it all depends on the financial position of a company, and how it views its cash flow. There is no doubt that, provided the cash-flow situation of a company will permit, outright purchase at the highest discount, followed by a direct disposal policy to trade outlets, is the most cost-effective way of obtaining cars.

A company car issued to an individual is considered as a benefit in kind and as such the user is liable to be taxed on the assessed benefit. The annual Finance Bill states the taxable benefit on types of car subdivided into groups either by engine capacity or retail cost. Fuel supplied to car users for private use is also liable to tax and full details are included in the Finance Act published after each year's budget.

Replacement policies

Any replacement policy will again depend upon the cash-flow situation of a company, and should take advantage of changes in secondhand market values, or impending price increases of new cars. It is possible to negotiate guaranteed buy-back prices for cars when they are purchased, but this type of arrangement tends to become less flexible and arguments will arise over delays and damage when vehicles are returned to the dealers. A well-tested policy with in-built flexibility is as follows:

1. Outright purchase of all cars after negotiating for highest fleet discounts
2. Replacement policy:
    (*a*) cars 1600cc and under, replace after two years
    (*b*) other cars, replace after 60 000 miles or three years whichever comes first
3. Disposal policy. Sell to the trade (not to the dealer who supplied the original vehicle) or through car auctions where special fleet terms are available

With the above policy, the transport services function will be carrying out a responsible task and obtaining every possible cost benefit for the company. It is flexible in that no firm contracts are entered into and the purchase and disposal dates can be delayed or brought forward for reasons of cash flow, to avoid heavy repair bills or to take advantage of minimizing the impact of taxation balancing charges which may become due at the end of a company financial year.

Chauffeur services

One of the neglected areas in a transport function is that of the provision of an efficient and well-managed chauffeur operation. Even the smallest company will have a driver, whose duties will include meeting visitors at airports and stations, and driving customers between company locations. Larger companies have chauffeurs allocated to directors and executives, whose duties may include tasks other than driving a company car. A chauffeur should be trained to keep himself and his car in immaculate condition, so as to portray an image of an efficient organization. Very often a chauffeur is the first contact a visitor will have with a company and the initial impression can be of vital importance.

Company air services

The company aircraft, owned and operated by a company for use by its personnel is now firmly established in the UK. Its justification on financial grounds is difficult to assess, but any cost exercise based solely on financial justification must fail. The task of the transport services function is to operate a service based on the highest standards of safety and also to minimize the additional costs which accompany the operating of a company aircraft. Safety, comfort, punctuality and reliability are the most important features. Safety means operating to a high standard and strict compliance with the current air navigation orders. Comfort of passengers should take into consideration cabin layout, quietness, facilities for reading and writing, temperature control, and above all, commonsense thinking of the crew to find a comfortable flying altitude for that particular journey. Punctuality and reliability are the two features which will test the efficiency of the service. Crews must ensure that the aircraft is always waiting for the passengers. Timings are important. Passengers should know the take-off and arrival times.

There are a number of ways to acquire the use of an aircraft:

Charter. Specialist companies will supply the aircraft and crew, and carry out all maintenance, route-planning and management.

Lease. An aircraft lease is available in two forms:

1. A finance lease for the aircraft only, including all the instrumentation required to meet the standards of the CAA. This will be written over a period of years at the end of which the aircraft can be made the subject of a secondary lease at a much lower rental
2. An operational lease which will provide an aircraft to the required level of specification, fully maintained to CAA standards and with the provision of the crew

The administration in both cases would be under the control of the company using the aircraft.

Purchase the aircraft and contract out all maintenance and management and also the provision of crews to an operating company.

Purchase the aircraft and employ your own crews as well as providing the necessary management and maintenance controls.

Operating the aircraft. Owning your aircraft does not give you the right to operate outside the public category, and if the crew is supplied by a charter company and not employed directly by your company, i.e. on the payroll, the operation will be subject to all the restrictions placed by the Department of Trade and Industry on a public-category operation. By employing your own crew to fly the aircraft, it is possible to operate in the private category using aircraft with an 'all up weight' not in excess of 1500 lb. All aircraft

MANAGING TRANSPORT SERVICES

above this weight are required to meet the full standards of operation as laid down for operating within the public category. It is always advisable to operate at the highest standards of safety irrespective of the type of aircraft used.

Selecting the aircraft and costing the operation. A wide variety of aircraft are available which are suitable for company operation, ranging from the single-engine helicopter which flies 'point to point' at speeds of up to 150 mph to the twin fan-jet aircraft capable of speeds approaching 600 mph. The approximate costs of operating helicopters and fixed-wing aircraft are as follows:

Helicopters: single-engine (turbine) – £325–400 per hour
twin-engine (turbine) – £700–850 per hour
Fixed-wing: twin engine (piston) – £175–200 per hour
twin engine (turbine) pressurized – £425–525 per hour
twin engine (jet) – £1000–1400 per hour

FURTHER READING

Commercial Vehicle Buyer's Guide, Kogan Page.
James Duckworth (ed.), *Kitchen's Road Transport Law*, 25th edition, Butterworths, 1985.
P.N.C. Cooke, *Financial Analysis of Motor Transport Operations*, Gower, Aldershot, 1974.
P.N.C. Cooke, *The Company Car*, Gower, Aldershot, 1980.
J. Gattorna (ed.), *Handbook of Physical Distribution Management*, 3rd edition, 1983.
D. Lowe, *Transport Managers' Handbook 1986*, Kogan Page, published annually.
D. Lowe, *A Study Manual of Professional Competence in Road Transport Management*, Kogan Page, 1978.
B.A. Thompson, *Croner's Road Transport Operation*, Croner Publications (by subscription, and kept up to date monthly).
B.A. Thompson, *Professional Driver's Guide*, Croner Publications 1985, revised every two years.
C.C. Toyne, *Motor Vehicle Technical Regulations*, 2nd edition, Liffon Engineering Services, London.
Tables of Operating Costs (annually), *Commercial Motor*, IPC Business Publications, London.
Frank H. Woodward, *Managing the Transport Services Function*, 2nd edition, Gower, Aldershot, 1977.
P.N.C. Cooke and Frank H. Woodward, *Controlling Company Car Costs*, Gower, Aldershot, 1985.
P.N.C. Cooke (ed.) *Car Fleet Administration and Finance 1985*, Professional Publishing Limited.

34

Security Policy and Administration

A J Slinn

The modern company, be it large or small, has to maintain a huge and ever increasing number of books, documents, records, and other sundry items, either because of statutory requirements, or in the interests of efficient administration. Some of these have to be retained permanently, for example minute books, registers of members, directors, certificates of incorporation and of business-name registrations, and the common seal; many will have to be kept for the full term of their viability — such as title deeds and leases, or for their term plus twelve years as in the case of correspondence and papers relating to property transactions, particular types of contract, and so on. In certain other matters, six years' cover has to be maintained, and into this category would fall sales and purchase ledgers with their associated records, wages and salaries registers etc.

Although the foregoing have little intrinsic value to make them attractive to a common thief, loss or damage could have serious consequences and absorb much time, money, and effort in their replacement — assuming replacement was actually possible.

Over and above the foregoing, items of actual cash value may be held at the company offices in the form of paintings, valuable silver for use on special occasions, trophies for sporting or musical competitions etc. The safeguarding of these may well fall within the company secretary's jurisdiction but it is almost certain that most of the documentary matter referred to would be his direct responsibility.

There is distinct virtue in having a periodic survey made or commissioned to ensure the right items are being retained for the right periods of time under the right conditions of security. Attitudes vary from having a total lack of security classification, to endorsing everything as 'secret', and of building up files of dust-covered documents which will never be consulted and never need to be. A survey list could readily be made summarizing, say:

1 The individual document, book or other item
2 Its proper retention period
3 Its security classification ('secret', 'confidential', 'unclassified' — or 'high', 'medium', or 'low') — this will largely determine the necessary degree of fire or other protection that should be given
4 Its custodian
5 Its present housing, for example safe (fireproof, fire-resistant, or thief-resistant), steel filing cabinet, steel or wooden cupboard, drawer, or open shelf etc.
6 Feasibility of reducing and storing on micro film or microfiche (this would be of use in evaluating space-saving or increased security proposals)

A list of this nature would enable any necessary or desirable changes in practice or housing to be highlighted and also pinpoint where a change of custodian should be implemented.

DOCUMENTARY LOSS

Fire is of course the greatest threat and the location and housing of irreplaceable and highly important documents should be considered with this in mind. Over and above the threat of damage from heat and flame, there is also that of water during the extinguishing of outbreaks.
   This may also apply in older premises with a risk of storm damage or other causes of flooding — frozen pipes in winter — so there could be merit in siting repositories in some cases above basement or groundfloor level.
   Specially constructed safes and fireproof cabinets are very expensive items and specialist advice should be taken when making purchases. The company's insurers will have such information readily to hand and should be consulted. In the areas of low fire risk, obsolete or obsolescent safes primarily designed to be burglar proof, may be suitable for the purpose since they carry ballast linings of a fire-resistant nature.
   Duplication is a reasonable precaution for essential matter so that the originals can be lodged elsewhere, perhaps in a safe deposit, and copies retained for daily use.
   Books, records and documents may be vandalized by thieves as a by-product of the efforts to steal, but they are rarely the targets of theft in themselves. The occasions when this is actually so are likely to be acrimonious industrial disputes, or when their contents are the targets of industrial

espionage. There is an unexpected source of risk associated with housing such papers inside small old safes, especially if these are sited on the ground floor. Many thieves prefer to take safes from premises prior to what might be a noisy operation in opening them and experience has shown that anything up to a tonne dead weight is liable to be removed. This can be circumvented by sinking rag bolts into a concrete base to match corresponding holes in the base of the safe which is then bolted down onto them. This is a subject where the advice of a police crime prevention officer, or an insurance assessor, would provide guidance.

Nevertheless, the most likely source of interference with the documents lies in the threat of theft of information from them.

THEFT OF INFORMATION

Provided a document is actually stolen, the law of theft can be applied; if, however, information is simply copied, photographed or memorized and used to the detriment of the owner, the law is vague in the extreme. Where an employee is obtaining the material for a competitor on repayment, it may be possible to prove corruption, which is criminally actionable, but the very few prosecutions under the Prevention of Corruption Act 1906 have been virtually restricted to public bodies and for purposes other than business espionage. Civil actions for redress are even less promising and more likely to benefit the lawyers involved than any other participants. It should be noted that cases have failed on grounds that a firm took no steps to ensure privacy of what it subsequently claimed to be important, nor did it emphasize to employees that the operations were regarded as being in any way secret.

Data Protection Act 1984

The Data Protection Act 1984, which was enacted in 1985, changed the situation, however, and brought the term 'reasonable security' into law. The Act provides for an independent registrar and there is roughly a three-year 'honeymoon' period during which various regulations come into force. The main provisions are as follows.

Data

1   Must be obtained 'fairly and lawfully'; must be held only for 'specified and lawful' reasons; must be 'adequate, relevant and not excessive' in relation to the specified purpose; must be accurate and kept up-to-date, and must not be retained for longer than is necessary for the specified purpose

2   Must be protected by 'appropriate' security measures to avoid unauthorized access, alteration, disclosure or destruction

Access. The data subject is entitled to access at 'reasonable intervals and without undue delay or expense', and he can, where appropriate, have the data corrected or erased.

Penalties

1   Refusal of registration where the registrar is satisfied 'that a breach of the data protection principles is likely'
2   Criminal prosecution (and probably very high fines) where there is failure to comply with any notice served by the registrar
3   Civil actions brought by wronged data subjects — the registrar's opinions will almost certainly be given a lot of weight by the courts in this event.

Exemptions

1   Most, but not all, police records
2   Specified data banks held by government departments
3   Data used for 'statistical or research purposes where there is a claim to legal professional privilege'
4   Data held for the assessment or collection of any tax or duty
5   Data held 'for the control of immigration'
6   Powers exist within the Act to provide exemptions in the case of health and social work data
7   Data held 'for the prevention or detection of crime'

The holding of personal data became a criminal offence in March 1986 (remember that under the Act a 'data subject' has been able to seek compensation through the courts for damage/distress in a limited sense since September 1985).

From March 1986. Registered data users became bound to operate within the terms of their registered entries, and liable to pay compensation in respect of damage or associated distress suffered as a result of any inaccuracy contained within the data.

From September 1987. The registrar's powers of supervision come fully into operation: any notices he has served before then, now take effect.

Take action now, if you have not already done so. Appoint a responsible member of staff as Data Protection Act CO. He or she should be within the security department or personnel department, should be computer literate and should be at a reasonably senior level. His first task should be to read the Act and the various critiques and information sheets which apply to it.

A methodical approach is essential and should cover the following:

1 Check all the personal data currently held. Why is it held? Where did it come from? Who is responsible for the collection/collation? How much requires a 'security' rating, or qualifies under the exemptions?
2 On the basis of the above, how does your company qualify under the Act, i.e. is your data secure, accurate, up-to-date, relevant etc? *Security* is important. Remember that data subjects will have the right to compensation if you lose, destroy, allow unauthorized access to, or unauthorized disclosure of the data. Ensure that your company's staff are aware both of the Act and its implications
3 Stay abreast of the subject. Keep a file of articles etc. relevant to the Act and make sure those of the staff who will have responsibilities covered by the Act are kept up-to-date too, which will almost certainly mean short courses or training. Be ready for the various sections of the Act as they come into force, for example when the first data subject under the meaning of the Act bangs on your door and demands to look at his file

Don't ignore the Act. While there are many exemptions, the Act still gives some basic rights to data subjects and there will surely be an assortment of test cases which will be based on the security of data bases and 'abuse' of personal information held. Apart from a copy of the Act, we suggest the following further reading:

The Data Protection Act 1984 — A Guide to the New Legislation, J.A.L. Sterling, CCH Editions Ltd, Bicester, £16.50

Out of the Inner Circle, Bill Landreth as told to Howard Rheingold, Penguin Books, London £8.95. This book is a real 'true confessions' style guide to how 'hackers' (people who break into firms' computer systems for the fun of it) work and it will — or should — stop you from making the most basic and idiotic security mistakes in setting up a computer system. Landreth reckons at least 80 per cent of the hackers' successes come from password abuse in the United States, and puts the figure at 95 per cent plus in the UK.

Finally, if the idea of computer security still seems akin to black magic, contact the National Computing Centre, Oxford Rd, Manchester M1 7ED. The NCC have set up a Security Circle to which more than 100 of the UK's biggest firms now subscribe. Valuable professional advice is available from a deep well of experience, and meetings are held on a strictly confidential basis.

Word processors

While on the subject of the Data Protection Act, remember that word processors — given the amount of information now stored, or capable of storage — may come within the meaning of the Act. Check the following points with regard to the security of your word processor:

1. How are the tapes and floppy disks stored? They should be in a secure safe or cabinet designed for the job, preferably a safe with a fire-resistance rating
2. How do you control access to the word processor in terms of both physical access and actual use of the machine? Too often they are in rarely locked (or even lockable) offices, and also too often they are available to anyone with the knowledge to use them
3. Does your processor have a lockable keyboard? Such systems are already on the market, one such in conjunction with an access control system manufacturer
4. Are you aware of exactly what is being stored and what type of information is being processed?

The word processor should be considered as a part of the established security chain, not a weak link within it. To establish the risk, begin with a typical survey, and ask:

1. What is the potential loss to the firm if, say, an unauthorized user with ill-intent, e.g. an industrial spy, gained access to the machine?
2. How much would it cost the firm if stored data were stolen or erased?
3. How often/easily could either of the above occur?

Basic security must therefore include control over who uses the machine, and when. It is vital to identify word processor users and to know what type of data they are handling.

A fire-resistant safe or cabinet would meet the 'reasonable security' requirement in order to protect tapes and floppy disks.

Physical protection of the machine can be achieved in a variety of ways, including anchoring it to a heavy desk. A lockable office, even a special room, may be considered, and after hours the machine should be covered by the building's intruder alarm system.

INDUSTRIAL ESPIONAGE

A company may not regard itself as a worthwhile target for any form of information theft and in many cases this may be almost true. Regrettably and increasingly the threat is becoming less fanciful. At least fifty companies manufacture electronic 'bugging' equipment and a similar number produce devices for detecting their use — including one leading UK manufacturer. In addition, 'Marketing Information Research' appears among the services offered by some organizations whose previous claimed capabilities have lain mainly in the private detective sphere. It is said that at least twenty such firms have been identified as having an active interest internationally in trade spying. A US survey showed that nearly 50 per cent of the private investigation agencies contacted admitted that they would do electronic eavesdropping themselves or would recommend others that did to clients. Finally, both the French government and the Institute of Directors in the UK have produced documents dealing with counter-espionage.

A simple test for any firm in doubt about its vulnerability is to ask itself two simple questions: (1) What, if anything, do we not want our competitors or other interested parties to know about our business? (2) What information would harm our industrial relations if it became generally known?

The initial answers might indicate that there is sufficient at risk to justify a board-level decision to undertake a more complete security survey which could pinpoint areas where precautions were necessary and establish the amount of effort and expense that is justified.

Potential target areas

These could include departments working on:

1   Plans for production and sale of new products
2   Plans for new advertising campaigns
3   Customer lists coupled with rebate and discount particulars
4   Marketing projections
5   Evaluations of possible acquisitions or mergers
6   Sources and costings of raw materials and components
7   Policy decisions on future activities, redeployments, closures etc.
8   Contractual or trading agreements, and customer contracts
9   Specifications and tenders
10 Research and development projects

Of less interest to competitors but more immediately embarrassing are those matters which can cause industrial unrest. Obtaining information about these may be more of a case of human curiosity than anything savouring of industrial espionage — but nevertheless can be crucially embarrassing if made general knowledge. They would include:

1   Rationalization and redundancy plans
2   Personal files and confidential reports
3   Wage-negotiation preparatory material

SECURITY POLICY AND ADMINISTRATION

4   Confidential instructions on industrial relations negotiations
5   Salary structures and job-weighting factors

Document classification

This is a basic requirement, and a simple system, used and understood by everyone, is required. If left to individuals, all sorts of terminology will be used, and the tendency will be to classify everything, no matter how innocuous. Fixing the degree of restriction is the responsibility of the originator, and the recipients should conform to his wishes, unless they have his permission to treat the material otherwise.

'Confidential' implies the sender's wish that the contents should not be general knowledge, but allows a discretion to divulge the information to those who need to act upon it or must know of it for their work. 'Secret' is much more emphatic and means not to be divulged (without the express permission of the sender) to anyone other than those upon the circulation list, which should be attached or marked upon the document.

Naturally an outer envelope which is marked 'secret' will attract attention and it is suggested that it should simply be marked 'personal' — which would convey nothing to a handler. Personal secretaries normally will open all mail, unless their supervisors decree otherwise, so that if an originator feels that the contents are such that they should be restricted purely to the named person, a second envelope may be put inside the external one and endorsed 'secret — to be opened only by. . . .'

For projects vital to the profitability of the firm, an authorized circulation list should be agreed, which can be expanded as the project develops. If necessary a code word can be given to a project and it should then always be referred to in this way, either in correspondence, or in telephone conversation. The specific number of document copies needed should be printed and marked sequentially with each person on the authorized circulation list allocated an identification number. Highest priority matter is best transmitted by hand and against signature by the recipient.

Production of documents and minutes

Highly sensitive papers should be typed only by trusted personnel who are informed of the importance of secrecy and, ideally, all copying should be done by the same people. This is not a job for temporary employees from an agency who conceivably might subsequently work for a competitor, or may realize the value of what is being handled and try to capitalize accordingly. A danger lies in recipients wanting further copies for their own use or for unauthorized dissemination to their subordinates or others; 'not to be copied', or some other endorsement should be overstamped on the originals and retribution follow any reproduction carried out without permission.

At present, many firms are working on paper which is impossible to photocopy. But only Rank Zerox have a *system*, using special paper and a security device fitted to the photocopier, which actually will prevent a photocopy from being made.

Plastic typewriter ribbons of 'once only' use should be burnt and spare copies, carbons, shorthand notes, or other sources of information should be put into a shredder. Fortunately, most firms only use longstanding and trusted employees for the sorting and movement of mail internally, but documents of prime importance should be passed to the office of the recipient so far as possible by hand. A risk that does arise lies in the fact that mail delivered to a department is likely to be dropped in an office tray at a designated reception point where a variety of people will have access to it; if they can recognize the importance of the particular envelope, it is then at their disposal.

Safekeeping of documents

All precautions can be invalidated by a careless executive who leaves his desk littered at night with confidential papers; or the secretary who is given them to file, then leaves them in an office tray until it is convenient to do so; or locks them away, then leaves the key to the cabinet in an unlocked drawer, the top of a typewriter, or the pull-out accessory tray in her desk.

Standard locks on the doors of offices likely to hold restricted information can be replaced by a master-keyed suite of locks of high security rating with restricted key-holding. Human nature being what it is, where such a system is instigated, inevitably it will be found the special lock becomes something of a status symbol which practically every manager or executive will find substantial reasons for having on the grounds of the importance of the material he handles.

Filing cabinets are rarely resistant to any forcible attack and have a major disadvantage in that the keys are usually fairly easily available for purchase from the number which is printed on the face of the lock. Despite the somewhat disfiguring effort, it is suggested these numbers be obliterated by drilling. Fire resistant cabinets are usually sufficiently substantial to offer some security protection, but they are expensive and the use of old safes may be found advisable.

Any discussions affecting documentary secrecy should include checks to ensure that important papers are not persistently left out on desks; a 'clean desk' end-of-work policy should be advocated, and practised, by all staff.

Destruction of papers

The importance of a document does not of necessity lapse when the project to which it refers is terminated. This is particularly true of industrial relations-linked matters. After being handled with every care and precaution during their lives they are then handed over for destruction to what may be the lowest paid and least skilled class of worker who is employed. It is asking too much to expect that such an individual will not be interested in any document which is stamped with 'secret', or some similar intriguing title. For immediate destruction small cheap shredders are available for departments or larger ones can be centrally sited; and in some industries the cost may be offset by the use of the shredded paper produced for packing purposes. The computer department is of special importance, although the print out material may be meaningless to most people; disintegrators are available to destroy printouts and tapes; these should be installed, either in the department, or in a suitable room closely adjacent.

Failing this, there are now specialist firms who will, for a fee, collect and destroy confidential material. Our advice on selection of such a firm is to choose that which allows you to observe its entire procedure, from collection through to destruction.

Potential forms of attack

Typical means of obtaining information unethically are:

1   Exploiting the carelessness, boastfulness, or negligence of employees
2   Corrupting employees, or forming an emotional attachment and inducing confidences
3   Inserting an agent into the workforce
4   Deliberately recruiting an employee from a position where he holds the requisite information
5   Holding a detailed interview of a knowledgeable employee for an advertised, attractive, financially wonderful, but non-existent job
6   Electronically 'bugging' telephones and offices, or using other specialized forms of surveillance
7   Entering premises to locate information either:
    (*a*)   as a visitor or
    (*b*)   as an intruder by force

Far and away the simplest method of operating is to walk in and see, if the target firm's procedures are so lax as to make this possible. A skilled observer, apart from possibly acquiring or having a sight of the paperwork, might recognize the processes and materials in use, the general level of activity, and innumerable other factors which will enable him to supply the information wanted.

If there are areas where there must be the strictest control on personnel entering, a constantly manned reception desk could be installed, or electronic control of access may be more economic. This could be a coded lock, magnetic card-operated lock, or combination of card and code, or even a card and code linked to a mini-computer which monitors and provides a permanent record of who goes where. A further variation has a pocket transmitter which causes an electronically controlled bolt to be automatically withdrawn when the carrier approaches. Photo-identity cards can be affixed to lapels for easy recognition, and colour variations in these can clearly indicate areas to which the wearer is entitled to have access. Control of entry to a computer room has a non-security merit — it prevents distraction and interference with the work of highly paid operators. But beware of systems which, even with busy, constantly used doors, require a card and/or code to open them. They *will* be abused — usually the door will be jammed open. 'A 'hands-free' for example radio activated, system is required. Access control, which uses signature verification, fingerprint, or even retinal scanning, is very much a specialist subject, especially given the power today inherent in centralized control systems. Access control systems can, for example:

1 Be linked with intruder alarm and/or closed-circuit TV (CCTV)
2 Control various environmental factors, e.g. lighting and heating
3 Provide a bewildering array of computerized options, from flexi-time working through to time zoning — cleaners allowed access only during specified hours, for example, from 6–8 pm.

Our advice is to seek specialist consultation.

Entry by subterfuge

This is one of the ploys of professional investigators engaged to obtain information. Latitude in asking questions and moving about premises is often given to persons claiming to be carrying out safety surveys or appreciation of equipment, or posing as prospective customers etc. Impersonation of telephone engineers, gas and electricity supply employees, laundrymen, window cleaners etc. have all been used. Preventive action is largely a matter of common sense and developing a suspicious mind. Most public utility employees will have identification cards to produce if challenged. A system of handling visitors efficiently should be devised and they should not be allowed to roam the premises unattended. Others worth bearing in mind are cleaners and temporary staff — the wastepaper basket remains one of the most prolific sources from which information can be gleaned. It may be possible to make special arrangements for the cleaning work in sensitive areas to be carried out when there is supervision on the premises. Every care should be taken to avoid the use of temporary staff on projects of importance; if this cannot be done reasonably, the supplying agency could be asked details of the person's service with them and the firms to which he/she has previously been allocated, so that there is at least an informed option to accept or refuse. If used, there is no objection to impressing on the incumbent the confidentiality of the position.

Electronic surveillance devices

The use of 'bugs' is not widespread in the UK; the extent to which they have been used is a matter for some speculation, but the publicity which has been given to them may lead to temptation to try them. They are easily concealed and can be fitted into table lighters, wall decorations, stuck under tables etc. A standard telephone bug is a transistorized oscillator which is powered by the telephone line current, using the line itself as an aerial. Variations can allow the microphone to be active even when the hand set is not in use. Offices can be checked visually, but this must be done thoroughly and patiently with a knowledge of what to look for, and where. Electronic detection equipment can be bought, but the best varieties are very expensive, and the limited number of the larger private detective agencies who provide a checking service also have charges which are very substantial.

Precautions checklist

1   Define key posts and areas, applying stringent selection and vetting to applicants for the former, and restricting entry to the latter
2   Establish classification, handling, copying and safe-keeping instruction procedures for documents etc.
3   Provide means of destroying the secret material and anything connected with its production, for example shredders
4   Restrict copying
5   Ensure wall charts, graphs, or other visual aids are not left where they can be freely seen
6   Instigate occasional out-of-hours checks upon offices for important papers carelessly left out
7   Indoctrinate staff
8   Instigate a policy for treatment of any person with access to secret information, who is to leave the company employment for any reason

Inadvertent disclosure

The unworldly scientist, who 'discloses all' in a learned paper for some technical journal or at some sophisticated symposium, is difficult to cater for; the best that can be hoped is that he will conform to the restrictions that may and should be contained in his contract of employment. However, ideas, inventions, and information in general may be released without thinking in the normal course of business.

As mentioned earlier in this book, it is possible to protect ideas and inventions by means of one or more patents, design registrations, registered trade marks and copyright, but it is also often the case that such protection is unobtainable or impracticable on the grounds of cost, or the idea lacking the right degree of novelty or inventiveness. At times it may be best to keep a good idea firmly under one's hat and in such instances the advice of a good patent agent is desirable and may prove invaluable.

Customers, students, prospective buyers and others may by tradition be shown around the factories and workshops with frank answers being given to their questions. Care must be taken, at the risk on occasions of causing genuine or simulated offence, to be judicious in what is shown and to decline to answer queries which would reveal too much of the firm's business. In one instance, a private detective posing as a potential (and bogus) customer's 'quality assurance expert' acquired secret process detail given in all good faith. The same care may be needed in dealing with market research questionnaires, intended student thesis projects and inquiries from the media. The basic question in such circumstances is 'Will my disclosure in any way be detrimental to my company?' Sadly, the answer today may well follow the pattern of the United States where leading firms, including many household names, famous for their tours of company plants, are now halting such tours and referring all inquiries for information to a press department briefed to protect vital secrets.

SECURITY POLICIES AND DISCIPLINE

A high proportion of disciplinary matters arise from incidents with security connotations and the process of enforcing security is as productive as any for industrial discord. It is therefore advisable to have clearly defined policies and procedures in those areas where ambiguity or opportunity could create controversy or a temptation to dishonesty. Such policies and procedures could include:

1. Action to be taken in respect of a criminal offence, where the firm is the complainant, committed:
   (a) by employees — suspension, dismissal, prosecution
   (b) by contractors — prosecution, expulsion from site, other alternatives etc.
   (c) by outsiders — prosecution, or other alternatives
2. The matters to be referred to the police and at whose discretion
3. Dealing with lost and found property
4. Working of notice by person who has been dismissed, or has resigned from a position of special risk
5. Permission of sales of products to employees and the procedures to be used

6   Work permitted for company staff utilizing company's labour on repayment
7   Use of firm's facilities for private purchase, ie discounts
8   Policies in respect of giving of references
9   Communication sources for media in the event of newsworthy items, ie accidents, industrial action and losses etc.
10 Policy towards losses by employees on premises — disclaimers, and permission for facilities for cash holding, ie collections in company safes
11 A policy to cope with drug abusers

Drug abuse

An effective company policy to deal with drug abuse is now vital in the UK as it is almost certain that medium-sized to large firms will harbour some drug abusers. In the USA, firms now routinely require job applicants to undergo urine/blood sampling for drug testing. Even the White House has a policy.

In the UK, the government 'crackdown' is summed up in legislation based on four key points:

1   Power for the courts to seize drug barons' assets
2   A reform of banking laws to allow closer examination of drug traffickers' financial records
3   A new offence, similar to that of handling stolen goods, or handling assets made from trading in hard drugs, and
4   A reversal of the burden of proof so that drug barons will lose homes, cash and luxury assets unless they can prove these were not purchased out of drug income. This is similar to the law now operating in the United States.

A policy on drugs, if not now essential, will almost certainly become so. Better, then, to use the current flurry of publicity to institute such a policy while it is on everybody's mind. A wise course, too, would be to involve the trade unions represented in your firm. Firstly, if you or your security staff want more information on the types of drug currently being abused, the effects of those drugs on users, the legal definitions and how to spot drug users, then see the January 1985 issue of *Security Times* magazine, the official journal of the International Professional Security Association, which had an excellent article on the subject by Benedict Weaver. Your local drugs squad should also be able to provide extensive information.

A written statement of the firm's policy on drugs (*all* drugs, including alcohol and drugs legally obtained) is the first step. The statement must set out graphically the firm's position on drugs, and the penalties awaiting staff found abusing them. It should also offer help to employees with problems, and contact with local social and advisory services should be established and maintained.

A typical statement should include the following:

1 Health considerations, pointing out not only the loss to the firm of staff taking days off 'sick,' but the disastrous consequences of drugs to the abuser
2 Safety considerations, particularly where machinery is being operated, where vehicles need to be driven or in any situation where one worker relies for his safety on the competence of another
3 Quality control, which affects not just the individual products being made by the firm, but eventually the jobs of all concerned
4 Security, not only in the short term, but also in the long term. The US has already seen horrific levels of so-called 'petty crime' by opportunists with a heavy drug habit to feed
5 Morale of the entire staff, which is not just a factor of drug abuse of course, but a general consideration on attitudes to slackness, lateness, dress etc.

What the firm expects of its staff, how they are expected to act while at work and what specific actions are intolerable should also be set out. Factors should include:

1 The firm's reputation, how it is seen by the public and how this in turn will affect what the firm expects of its employees. The higher profile in the marketplace, or the more trust placed by the public and/or customers in the firm, the higher the standards
2 The relationship between drug abuse and fitness for work; how the firm views acceptable/unacceptable standards
3 What help the firm is offering drug users. This may take the form of a confidential advisory service through a suggestion box-type method of getting employees to state their problem and then using, say, the company notice board to give replies/advice
4 Asking employees to help in the programme and to tell senior staff about abusers and particularly about pushers. Again, the suggestion box could work here, or a twenty-four-hour telephone answering machine such as the Metropolitan police have used with such success

A clear line must be taken as to 'legal' and 'illegal' drugs so that there is no confusion, no loophole in the firm's policy.

'Legal' drugs, such as alcohol or any which are prescribed by a doctor (and the latter can include heroin substitutes where the user is a registered addict), should be looked at in the light of whether or not they affect job performance. If they do, the easiest way is to treat abusers as being 'ill', which means sick leave. But this should only be temporary. Continued abuse of any 'legal' drug should subject the abuser to normal sanctions and penalties. Where alcohol is abused actually on the firm's premises, a very stern line needs to be taken.

'Illegal' drugs will include all those whose sale is restricted or prohibited or whose use or possession is restricted or prohibited. And the firm's policy should take the form of outright bans on the following:

1   Any employee arriving for work under the influence of any drug so that his work is adversely affected
2   Any employee found using the prohibited drugs while at work
3   Any employee found buying, transferring or possessing illegal drugs
4   Any employee found selling or offering to sell illegal drugs

In the latter case, and possibly others, the firm should reserve the right to bring in the police.

The most obvious penalty is immediate suspension pending an investigation. A team approach to the consideration of the individual problem is worth considering — security, personnel, safety, training and medical people should all be involved, as well as a representative(s) from the employee(s)'s trade union.

Enforcement of the penalties is absolutely essential. Once set in motion, an anti-drug policy has to be maintained, and all drug users should be treated equally. This means careful attention to such definitions as 'adverse job performance'. For instance, such a definition might include improper use of company equipment, incompetency, physical or mental incapacity, plain carelessness, negligence, lateness on the job, unauthorized absences from both the firm and the designated place of work, unwarranted abuse (verbal or physical) of other staff, especially senior staff, and so on.

Problems will include the possible abuse of cocaine by executives and especially by high-powered sales people, who feel that this drug can enhance their performance. The problem is particularly acute where such senior staff spend most of their time away from the office. The approach here probably comes best from an executive of the same, or higher, rank and it should be made clear to the abuser that the company policy applies to *all* employees.

Finally the questions of employees' rights and legal liability should be thoroughly researched by the company lawyer before the statement is formulated. Make sure, too, it reaches *all* employees, possibly through the company newsletter if you have one. Despite the government's proposed new laws, the profits from drug peddling remain so vast — and Britain remains such a soft target, along with most of Europe — that the plague will continue. Recommended reading is *Drug Abuse in the Workplace*, by Henry J. Balevic, Personnel Services Inc., 2303 W. Meadowview Rd., Greensboro,

NC-27407, USA, US$24.95, which gives an excellent outline of what currently faces American employers and how they are dealing with it

Theft by employees

It is most important to establish a firm line on how employee theft will be treated. Since this is likely to be associated with dismissal, no grounds should be allowed whereby an appeal can arise from a legal nicety. The types of serious misconduct meriting dismissal should of course be listed by a firm amongst its rules and that of theft is generally accepted by industrial tribunals as a perfectly valid reason (Trust House Forte *v* Murphy, 1977).

The following ruling is recommended in the light of changes in legislation and decided cases:

> If any act of theft, or attempted theft or other form of dishonesty, or criminal damage, is admitted, or on reasonable grounds found to have been committed by an employee in connection with company property, or the property of another employee, then the employee responsible will be dismissed and, where company property is involved, the company will exercise its discretion in whether the matter is to be reported to the police.

Discretion

A ruling of this nature does not cover all criminally actionable offences that may be committed, either on the firm's premises, or elsewhere and contrary to its interests. The inflicting of injuries, and sexual offences, for instance, are of rare occurrence, as are those involving customers, the consequences of which would be prejudicial to the company interests. Too wide definition would prove unwieldy and the nature of the other criminal actions which can be envisaged is sufficiently serious that dismissal for their commission would be an acceptable reason to a tribunal.

The definition as it stands leaves an ultimate discretion whether or not to prosecute and allows the taking into account of mitigating circumstances which could have bearing on the decision. The prime objective is to achieve consistency on the aspect of dismissal, rather than on that of prosecution.

Right of search

Even where a company includes a 'search clause' in its conditions of employment, there is no legal right of personal search without the consent of the individual being searched. Nevertheless, Employment Appeals Tribunal decisions have indicated that where such a condition is included, refusal can constitute reasonable grounds for dismissal; conversely, where it is not included, dismissal for refusal was found unfair, despite the fact that there were grounds for suspicion of theft. Whilst there are no publicized decisions to the effect, it would seem probable that any search productive of stolen property would be considered justified — dismissal of course being for the theft, not the refusal.

Dismissal without prosecution

This is an expedient to be applied with care in the current industrial climate. No avenue should be provided for a claim of unfair dismissal, but a successful prosecution is not a prerequisite for action by the employer. This has been made clear by several judgments, one of which — British Home Stores Limited v Burchell (20 July 1978), an Employment Appeals Tribunal decision on dismissal for suspected involvement of theft where there was no prosecution — is worth quoting in full.

> In a case where an employee is dismissed because the employer suspects or believes that he or she has committed an act of misconduct, in determining whether that dismissal is unfair an Industrial Tribunal has to decide whether the employer who discharged the employee on the ground of the misconduct in question entertained a reasonable suspicion amounting to a belief in the guilt of the employee of that misconduct at that time. This involves three elements. First, there must be established by the employer the fact of that belief; that the employer did believe it. Second, it must be shown that the employer had in his mind reasonable grounds upon which to sustain that belief. And, third, the employer at the stage at which he formed that belief on those grounds must have carried out as much investigation into the matter as was reasonable in all the circumstances of the case. An employer who discharges the onus of demonstrating these three matters must not be examined further. It is not necessary that the Industrial Tribunal itself would have shared the same view in those circumstances.

Burchell has become a definitive industrial appeal case in that W. Weddel Ltd v Tepper, Court of Appeal, 1980 declared its three-stage test should be used to determine whether an employee dismissed for *any* alleged misconduct had been fairly dismissed — not simply in cases of dishonesty.

Where there is an admission of theft, and the employer does not wish court proceedings, it is highly advisable that the admission is in a form that cannot be retracted for the purposes of an appeal against dismissal. It is suggested that a signed admission be obtained or one made under circumstances which would preclude any such retraction. This could be in the presence of witnesses or of the offender's own representative.

Dismissal in the face of a denial of guilt could lead to appeals causing cost and inconvenience beyond any normal police court proceedings and a tribunal is less restricted in the evidence that it will accept than criminal courts (Dockerty v Reddy — 28 September 1976); it is therefore recommended that instances where guilt is firmly denied should be referred to the police.

There are a number of points arising from other tribunal decisions which are worthy of note in this connection.

1. An opportunity must be given for an explanation of facts by the suspect before the dismissal decision is made
2. There is no necessity of a successful prosecution to justify dismissal
3. As shown above, it is adequate that those formulating the decision to dismiss have reasonable grounds for their belief in the facts before them when making their decision
4. The decision must be based on the facts that are known at the time of the decision, not those that may arise subsequently
5. There must be as much investigation as is reasonable before the dismissal is made

Suspension with or without pay

Suspension without pay, where such a power is not included in the contract of employment, is held to be tantamount to dismissal and therefore is subject to the normal appeal procedure.

Suspension with pay is reasonable in cases of strong suspicion pending the accumulation of all the available evidence bearing on a decision. However, if this suspension is extended to the termination of court proceedings it can be extremely expensive since the accused, by various ploys, can defer the hearing of his case interminably. In one instance five employees were suspended on average earnings for two years and six months. The evidence was such that they had to plead guilty, but the cost of their wages far exceeded the value of the theft.

No dismissal

There are cogent reasons why every instance of proven or admitted dishonesty by an employee against his firm should result in immediate dismissal. A company ruling of the type previously mentioned is invalidated if any exceptions at all to it are allowed — precedents are highly important to industrial courts and management could find great difficulty in explaining a variation in policy.

Other reasons of importance exist:

SECURITY POLICY AND ADMINISTRATION

1 Leniency could cause others to copy in the belief no retribution would follow
2 A repetition of the offence by the same person would invoke caustic comment from board level on the individual who has taken the lenient view (some would say the easy way out!)
3 Retention is unfair to the offender's colleagues and the atmosphere in a department would be impossible if a fellow worker's property had been involved
4 The offender will inevitably be the focus of attention should any further offences occur, even if he is not responsible, and his continued presence be an embarrassment not least to himself

POLICE NOTIFICATION

The reporting of a theft is not mandatory nor is the prosecution of an individual known to have stolen from a complainant, who is also legally allowed in making a decision to press charges or not, to take into account whether the loss or injury caused by the offence is to be made good or reasonable compensation paid — a matter which could of course be made quite clear to an offender. If the police are called in, they are unlikely to be familiar with procedures, persons, and places all of which might have to be explained. Their presence automatically attracts attention and workers may have to be taken from their jobs to be spoken to. The consequential loss may be out of all proportion to the effect of the offence which is being investigated. However, once they have been notified, it is highly advisable that the question of prosecuting should be left entirely in their hands — even if this causes embarrassment or inconvenience.

No prosecution

There are circumstances which can militate against a prosecution which at first sight might be justified by the nature of the offence. Amongst the considerations are:

1 Will the firm receive adverse publicity by:
   (a) a lax system putting temptation in the way of the employee?
   (b) having put a lowly paid man in a position where he is handling property of a value out of all proportion to his salary?
   (c) permitting the ventilation of a grievance in open court which would reflect adversely on the firm?
   (d) compulsorily disclosing matters in court which the firm would desire should not be known?
2 Will the prosecution spotlight a weakness in the security system which

could be exploited by others and which may be difficult or impractical to remove?
3 Is the end product of prosecution worth the effort and inconvenience; or considering the age, length of service, and good repute of an employee, would dismissal be a greater penalty than any the court might impose?

It must be remembered that malpractices, actual or alleged, by an employer have greater news value than routine theft by an employee.

PACEA

The Police and Criminal Evidence Act 1984 is now with us, and security people up and down the country have been thrown into confusion by it. Letters in magazines such as *Police Review, Security Times* and others have all asked to what extent this law will affect the position of security personnel and store detectives.

The main area of contention arises from $s66$ (codes of practice which replace the former Judges' Rules) and $s67$ (parts 9, 10 and 11). Section 67(9) of the Act states:

> Persons other than police officers who are charged with the duty of investigating offences or charging offenders shall in the discharge of that duty have regard to any relevant provision of such a code.

The code mentioned (in $s66$) covers stop and search, premises search, seizure of property, detention and treatment of persons and the identification of offenders.

The arguments revolve around whether a security officer can be said to be a person 'charged with the duty...' And if he is such a person, to what extent must he then abide by the codes of practice? For example, if a store detective detains a suspected thief, must he administer a caution? And how will that affect the suspect's right if and when the police are called in? What about statements and detention facilities?

The answer is, for once, fairly simple: *nowhere* in the Act is the security officer mentioned in any capacity. And the Act does not materially affect any security officer in as far as existing legislation is concerned; his/her powers remain the same. The Home Office, in a letter to the International Professional Security Association (IPSA) states:

> This Act does not alter in any way the position of security personnel and store detectives under law. They have no special power of arrest, search, entry or seizure. If they make an arrest it is a citizen's arrest which involves no power of detention for questioning and they must bring the person arrested before a Justice of the Peace or a police officer as soon

as reasonably possible. Security personnel and store detectives *are not charged with a duty of investigating offences within the meaning of section 67(9) of the Act* (my italics). However, the Codes of Practice represent good practice in the investigation of offences, and it is clearly desirable that people who may take it upon themselves, whether by virtue of a contract of employment or otherwise, to investigate a crime or a category of crime, should have regard to the standards set in the codes so far as in commonsense they are applicable to the work they do and the limited powers they have.

The Act does, however, give security personnel (and, of course, all of us as members of the general public) slightly wider powers. Section 24(4) and (5) outlines the circumstances where any person may effect a citizen's arrest, and subsections (1) to (3) define arrestable offences.

Give this basic advice to all security officers working in your firm. Use commonsense when interpreting the Act and its codes of practice. Involve police at a fairly early stage when such a course of action is necessary. Be fair-minded, and act fairly, and remember to keep your temper regardless of provocation. And make a note of everything said as soon as is possible.

Intruders

The considerations which apply to employees do not, however, apply to offences by non-employees. If these are involved in an offence of any consequence the police should be informed — particularly where identifiable property has been stolen and police assistance is the only means of recovery. Outsiders should be given no indication that they can steal from a firm with impunity; a consistent policy of prosecuting all should be followed as a deterrent to others.

Thefts from employees

Despite the fact that an offence may take place upon company premises the right to decide whether it should be referred to the police is vested in the loser and he is entitled to object if the company tries to interfere with this right. It follows that he also has the right to prosecute or not to prosecute should an offender be detected. However, this in no way affects the rule of dismissal for theft from company or employee. The employee himself may have pressure put upon him by friends of the offender not to presecute and he may so agree, but this does not invalidate the issue of dismissal.

Prosecution

The Law of England does not preclude any person or body from instituting or carrying out criminal proceedings in which the police will assist, but, unless there are very good reasons, there is little point in acting as a private prosecutor. Once notified, the police will ensure that all necessary statements are taken, the case is prepared and witnesses warned of the time, date, and place of hearing; the police solicitor will present the evidence and there can be no suggestion of bias in the conduct of the whole affair. In other words a minimum of inconvenience and cost is incurred by the firm.

Police procedure

A company secretary, with the legal overtones of his position, may find he automatically slips into the position of being a link-man with the police. It is as well therefore that he should have some idea of the action the police will wish to take should the company be the complainant in proceedings. This knowledge is particularly necessary where an offender has been detained by company employees.

The police officer attending will ask to be told, in the presence and hearing of the person detained, the evidence that that person has committed an offence. He will also want a positive identification by a competent witness of the property said to have been stolen, together with its value. Having received this information, the officer will then caution the suspect and ask him whether, having heard what has been said, he himself wishes to say anything. What he says, the officer will then record in writing. If then, in the officer's opinion, a *prima facie* case exists against the suspect, he will arrest and take him to a police station to be formally charged. Procedures differ in various parts of the country, but he may ask the witnesses to go with them.

At the police station, the evidence will be outlined to the officer in charge who will decide whether it is adequate and suitably credible for a formal charge to be laid against the accused. If so, he will make out a 'charge sheet' showing, amongst other detail, the offence in simple but precise language. Again, practice is not uniform, but the complainant may be asked to sign this sheet.

A written notice beginning with a caution and describing the offence is also prepared and given to the accused so that neither he, nor any legal representative he may instruct, will be in any doubt about the subject of the allegations.

High technology evidence

Before the end of the 1980s, police throughout the country will be using tape recorders during the interviews of all suspects, according to a report in the *Criminal Law Review*. At present there are six field trials underway, and police response has apparently been 'enthusiastic', in total contrast to the attitude of a few years back.

In the minefield of industrial relations, tape recording is an excellent idea. But in the past there have been problems of acceptability in the courts. The same has been true of video recordings. The advantages, however, are dramatic. If a tape recording is accepted as evidence, there is no way a smart lawyer can discredit it by clever cross-questioning.

The red tape which surrounds the handling of audio or video tape was looked at in depth by Kent Police some years ago when they pioneered the use of video (and established the first police television unit which made training films, taught senior officers how to handle themselves on television and much more). The following guidelines have been tested and accepted in courts throughout the country and are recommended:

Clean tape, i.e. has not been used before, should be used. However, erased tape is permissible as long as the person who erased the previous information has evidence to that effect.

The same person who draws the clean/erased tape from stock should place it in the recording machine and should remove it from the machine and there must be evidence to this effect.

The type and location of the recording machine must be noted. And once the recording has been made, it should be checked immediately to ensure that the interview is actually on the tape.

Lock it away and keep a record of this action. Any subsequent reviews of the tape should be kept to a minimum and carefully noted and copies should *not* be made unless absolutely essential. At this point it may be wise to hand over the tape to the police (if a criminal case is to be brought) or to your solicitor for safekeeping.

To summarize: the objective is to have a continuous flow of evidence from the moment the tape was placed on the machine to the moment it is presented in court. There must be absolutely no gaps in the flow, and it is thus better if one person is made completely responsible for the tape from start to finish.

Statements, attendance of witnesses, court proceedings

Statements. Most police officers, however, will take *written* statements from those competent to give evidence, which he will ask them to sign. They should check the accuracy of the contents before doing so — they have the onus of giving that evidence in court and it is essential the statement is what they can truthfully say — not what the officer thinks they can.

Court attendance by witnesses. Statements from witnesses in a prescribed form may now, with the agreement of the accused or his legal representative, be read in court without the personal attendance of the witness. However, apart from the accused, the court itself may require personal attendance to ask questions.

Bail. More frequently than not, a person who has been arrested by the police will be admitted to bail to appear before a court at some later date. If indeed he is kept in custody by the police, the court before which he subsequently appears for the first time may grant him bail. With the current pressures upon courts, there may be considerable delay before the offender appears even before an ordinary magistrates' court for trial. When he does so, he also has the right in theft charges to ask for trial before a jury at a crown court. The net result of this is that there may be a delay of months, in complicated fraud cases of over a year, before the offender appears for trial. This is a factor which a company must bear in mind when deciding on a policy for employees who are being prosecuted.

Retention and restitution of property recovered

Property recovered by the police in connection with a criminal offence may be retained by them until the final disposal of proceedings; then, if the accused has pleaded or has been found guilty, it will be returned to the loser. This is not, however, automatic. A convicting court *may* order it but is unlikely to do so if there is the slightest legal dispute over ownership — as could arise if the property has changed hands again after the theft. In straightforward circumstances the police will probably return it without seeking formal permission from the court. It is advisable if there is an indication of a counterclaim to obtain legal representation at an early stage.

Where an accused is found not guilty, he may be prepared to sign a disclaimer waiving his rights, if faced with the alternative of a legal action by the owner. The police or any claimant may apply to a court to make an order restoring the property to the person appearing to be the owner (Police Property) Act 1897). In the event of an appeal against conviction, the police will retain possession until it has been dealt with and will also do so during the period in which an appeal can be lodged.

Where stolen goods have been converted into other goods or cash, an order may be made that these other goods can be given to the loser on application and recompense can be awarded from any monies found in the thief's possession at the time of his arrest.

Compensation

Where loss has occurred from theft or damage, and a person is convicted of that offence, under the provisions of the Powers of Criminal Courts Act

1973, the convicting court *may* order compensation to be paid by him to the sufferer. The relevant section is self-explanatory and reads:

1 (1) Subject to the provisions of this part of the Act, a court by or before which a person is convicted of an offence, in addition to dealing with him in any other way, may, on application or otherwise, make an order (in this Act referred to as 'a compensation order') requiring him to pay compensation for any personal injury, loss or damage resulting from that offence or any other offence which is taken into consideration by the court in determining sentence.

'Offence' can be widely interpreted, the main exclusions are the ordinary road traffic offences and there is no power to award compensation to dependants of a dead person. The jurisdiction is extended to instances where stolen property has been recovered in a damaged condition — including motor vehicles. The amount which can be awarded in respect of an individual charge is limited to £1000, but there is no restriction, other than common sense, and the feelings of the court, on the number of charges which may be laid. To facilitate proceedings, it is conventional to allow offenders to have offences taken 'into account' without the preferring of charges and adducing of evidence; there is now power to make compensation awards in respect of these likewise, but the gross amount permitted is limited by the factor of £1000 and the number actually charged, ie five offences maximum compensation £5000 irrespective of the number 't.i.c.'. A substantial loser should definitely ask that his offence be the subject of a specific charge — if evidence to prove it is adequate.

An order *may* be made 'on application or otherwise', but there is no doubt that a court is much more likely to direct its attention to the issue of compensation if it has before it the loser's written notification of a desire for it which can most easily be done by incorporating the request in any written statement given to the police. This is an award made by a criminal court immediately after conviction, and in passing sentence; of course civil action can also be taken but any award then made would take into account that of the criminal court. An itemized account of the loss or damage sustained should be available including the cost of making good, not just cost of materials. Where large amounts are concerned, the court may desire that documents should be at hand to prove the claim.

In the past, companies have appeared to think it *infra dig*, too much trouble or pointless to pursue these claims, but there is a substantial deterrent effect upon prospective predators in doing so, especially those among their own employees. The operative word however remains 'may' — it can be expected that, if there is a contentious issue of any kind involved, the wrangling will be left to civil action, which, if undertaken, is often found infuriatingly tedious and frequently only of financial benefit to the legal fraternity involved.

COMPANY SECURITY STAFF

Where circumstances justify the employment of security officers it is essential that they should be good calibre, and properly trained and utilized. It is a total waste of money to follow the outdated practice of internal recruitment from redundant or ageing employees — worse, this gives an impression that security surveillance exists whereas the resultant inefficiency causes the reverse to be true.

Authority

Morale is increasingly important and an efficient security staff must be capable of earning the support and respect of the whole working community, while at the same time producing an image of authority which effectively deters dishonesty or non-cooperation on the part of the minority. This is a demanding role and one in which prevention is of greater importance than cure.

Duties

The duties required must be committed to writing in the form of 'standing orders', which in effect may be a much expanded and detailed version of their job description. The two combined, amongst other things, must specify what they are expected to do, their line of reporting and the degree of discretion allowed.

Fire-fighting and first aid are customary inclusions among responsibilities, but every firm will have others where continual presence of responsible men on premises can be utilized. The contribution that security staff can make in accident prevention is very relevant. It would be unrealistic to suggest that security staff should be given special training in this subject, except in very exceptional circumstances where recurrent risk may arise. Nevertheless, there are a number of things which may be temporarily overlooked by personnel intent on production where commonsense observation by a patrolling officer may be used to advantage.

Instructions should be given to deal with these matters tactfully to avoid apparent intrusion into the disciplinary authority of line management, bearing in mind also that a procedure that appears unsafe to the uninitiated may be one which has been considered and found acceptable.

If unsafe practices are seen, security staff should draw them to the notice of the supervisor and not approach the worker himself, unless the matter is one of immediate physical risk or serious contravention of works rules.

Responsibility for security

Every commercial and industrial concern should have a member of senior management who has designated responsibility for the security of its property and the safety of its employees and their belongings while they are engaged at work. The status of that person will depend on the size and importance of the concern and can range from a member of the board of directors downwards in the operating structure. For instance, at a factory engaged on government classified contracts it is likely a director will be responsible. In other circumstances, the senior man on the site, though he must have ultimate responsibility to board or shareholders, is likely to delegate routine supervision to a subordinate manager.

The amount of attention a person given the responsibility for security should devote to that job will depend on a number of factors which will also determine the degree of expertise in security practices and techniques which he should acquire. These factors will include, apart from the size of the organization, the known losses and unexplained deficiencies, the value of materials at risk, insurance requirements, the location and type of premises, and the calibre of employees. It could well be that security is included among other responsibilities. If so, and the incumbent has neither training nor aptitude for it, the attention he will give may be far less than he gives to his other duties. *Security is not the most popular job if incorrectly handled.* If the factors creating the need for a security function are cogent, the time has then arrived to consider the appointment of a qualified individual whose overriding responsibility will be that of security, bearing in mind there are other administrative spheres in which his presence can be utilized.

Such an individual can be titled security manager, security officer, or chief security officer if he is responsible for personnel engaged on security duties. The status to be given must reflect the importance the management attaches to his position, his responsibilities and the staff he controls. Normally he would be a member of the management structure which would assist him in dealing with all levels of employees. He would wear civilian clothes or protective clothing in the same manner as other managers.

Staff selection

For the actual operational implementation of day-to-day security, and advising or recommending where needed, an 'in-company' appointed security manager has advantages of familiarity with persons, places, products etc., but he has to be trained to a knowledge of essential law and security expertise. Perhaps most important, he has to think in terms of security priorities as having an importance he did not perhaps previously accord them, and develop a suspicious and enquiring mind that he did not previously need for his job. This type of appointment is best for a small firm with limited problems, or for a unit within a large organization with centralized security control and expertise which can be called upon for assistance and advice; training is however essential.

If the risk dictates that professional experience is called for, the main sources of supply are ex HM Forces SIB (Special Investigation Branches), ex police, existing senior security personnel in industry or the commercial security service supplying firms. Alternatively, an outside consultant can be retained for services as required — which is unlikely to be financially advantageous — and care has to be taken in checking ability and to carry out contractual obligations in the light of existing commitments.

Remember that security staff are *not* exempt from the Rehabilitation of Offenders Act, which means the potential security officer may have a criminal record which he does *not* (*by law*) have to disclose.

In the past many firms have appointed ex-senior police officers with the expectation they would, by virtue of the 'old boy network', have access to criminal records files. Now computerized, these files are closely maintained and serving officers who have complied with requests to 'check on so and so' have been suspended and dismissed as a result. Do not, therefore, rely on 'inside knowledge' of former police officers who may be on your security staff. Asking serving officers to risk their careers on an 'everyday' basis is not viable.

Selection from 'second career incumbents' can produce know-how but a judgement must be made as to whether the job is being taken with real interest or as a means of supplementing a pension with minimum personal effort and inconvenience.

It must be expected that someone being inducted from a disciplined service into commerce and industry will have problems of adjustment and it is advisable that colleagues, with whom the prospective incumbent will have closest contact, should have an opportunity to meet and assess short-listed candidates for compatibility before the appointment is made.

Training

Security heads are apt to be drawn from the older age bracket, especially when they are 'second career' selections. One possible danger is that they become agoraphobic in attitude with their interest limited to the physical perimeter of their responsibility. If this happens, their knowledge of law and practice becomes outdated, they do not learn from the misfortunes of others, and they miss the advantages of discussion with contemporaries. Arrangements should be made for at least 'brush-up' attendance at security courses and seminars, and they should be encouraged to develop liaisons within their own industry and locally for mutual advantage.

At security guard level, it is frequently forgotten that these employees need training as much as, if not more than, others — their potential to hurt the firm by unwise action through ignorance is greater than those of considerably higher status. Apart from instruction that is available on site, it is advisable that they should have basic instruction amongst others similarly employed, if a suitable course is available. Commercially organized one- or two-day seminars are occasionally held for senior security officers and management but few, if any, at the lower level. However, the International Professional Security Association, hold basic, intermediate and advanced courses throughout the country; these are essentially practical in nature, the lecturers are primarily drawn from members with specialized expertise who hold senior positions with industrial firms. Details of what is available at any given time can be obtained from the Secretary of the Association.

HIRING THE SERVICES OF A SECURITY COMPANY

Commercial firms provide a variety of services:

1. The transporting of cash to and from banks and if so required, at most branches, the making up and paying out of wage packets
2. Transporting computer tapes, data etc.
3. Security attention to premises, with or without guard dogs
   (a) continuously over twenty-four hours, seven days a week
   (b) for specified shorter periods
   (c) for visits at irregular intervals
4. To act as key holders of premises to reduce the inconvenience of having to attend them at all hours in consequence of some incident which requires attention
5. To protect especially valuable property on display at, for example, exhibitions and provide guards at sporting functions etc.
6. To survey premises and to recommend security measures
7. To provide a store detective service in retail premises and make check purchases
8. In some instances a facility to carry out internal investigations; in others to give a debt collection service

In addition to these, there are of course the alarm, lock, safe, television etc. specialist firms.

Transporting cash

When a contract is arranged for this service, it must specify the place at which the delivery is to be made. It is not sufficient to give just the address: the precise location of the transfer must be given, for example, the cashier's office on the second floor. Regrettably attacks during cash deliveries occur frequently, so the precise liability on the carriers at the time of the theft is important. The nationally known cash-in transit companies have adequate cover spread over several insurers, but positive written confirmation of that cover should be available and the wording of contracts carefully studied. Those with current national coverage are Securicor, Group 4 and Security Express, but other internationally known, and equally reputable ones, also operate in the larger cities.

A wage packeting service is available in many areas, for which the charges made vary little from one company to another. However, the level of these charges has risen to the point where internal make-up could be more cost effective.

Very firm arrangements must be made with the carriers, and with the bank authorities, to agree procedures for cheque submission, cash collection and delivery, with adequate means of identification of both signatures and persons, to preclude any possibility of fraudulent attack.

If an unknown person purporting to be from the security company attends premises to collect cash or anything valuable, his identity documents must be inspected and his employers telephoned to confirm his instructions — his documents might have been stolen or forged.

Cash-in-transit — own personnel

If it is intended that wages or, for that matter, any large sums of money, should be carried in circumstances where they are exposed to attack, the insurers *must* be consulted. They are not enthusiastic about sums in excess of £2000 being carried without extra precautions by way of guards and vehicles which probably will outcost the expense of a professional carrier. This of course is a reasonable ploy by the insurer since it transfers the period of greatest risk to someone else's insurance.

If, however, the amounts are relatively small, or a decision is taken to accept the risk, the advice of the police crime prevention department should be sought, and their recommendations strictly followed as to how the job should best be done. Special waistcoats, alarmed bags and others that deface the contents, or throw out clouds of smoke, are commercially available.

It is worthy of note that an employee carrying cash for his masters in an area where there was reasonable expectancy of attack, was successful in an action for negligence, in that no precautions had been taken or adequate instructions given to him, when he was so attacked and injured.

Cash-in-transit: security advice and checklist

This is too detailed to be dealt with here and reference should be made to *Practical Security in Commerce and Industry* (Wilson and Oliver, Gower, 4th edition, 1983).

SECURITY OF CASH IN OFFICES

Money in any form is just about the most attractive target for theft; it is normally non-identifiable, does not need the intervention of a receiver, and there is no delay in benefiting. Insurance against loss can be obtained either in transit or on premises; the cost is progressively rising, and premiums will be heavily loaded if claims are made — the first £100 or more will probably be excluded in any case.

The weight of claims has caused insurance companies to insist on rigorous security measures, including installation of burglar alarms, without compliance to which they will not offer cover. Even so, failure to observe elementary precautions may cause the refusal of a claim, such as has happened with an unguarded till in retail premises and failures to set alarms or to lock doors on delivery vehicles.

Cash on premises should be the minimum for needs; if it accrues to a greater than desirable amount, transfer arrangements to the bank should be made. Key holding for cash boxes and safes must be kept to an absolute minimum and locks must be changed immediately in the event of a key-loss. A spot check should be made on cashiers' petty cash holdings — often amounts in excess of insurance cover are kept for purely personal convenience.

Procedures are apt to become slack after spells without incidents; it is advisable therefore to review the situation periodically and repeat previous instructions if necessary.

Companies are apt to regard safes as continuing to fulfil their purpose long after they have become antiquated. It must be anticipated that if an insurance company insists on an examination prior to renewal of policies, many such safes will be condemned as unfit for the storage of cash, and insurance cover will not be extended to them. The surveyors have a classification which includes all types of safes in manufacture and equates them with the maximum amount of money the insurers are prepared to accept that they should hold. Before buying new safes, it is therefore essential to obtain confirmation that they will meet the insurers' requirements.

It does not follow that old safes should automatically be discarded. Most may still be serviceable for fire protection purposes, as mentioned earlier, and can be used to house confidential matter and documents of interest to prying eyes but not to thieves.

Petty cash and floats must not be left in locked drawers overnight but should be returned to safes and withdrawn again the following morning. Special care should be taken of cheque books, and the absolute minimum of presigned cheques be retained at any time. If possible, these should be restricted to the control of a single person. The value of pre-signed Giro cheques for payments to pensioners may be overlooked and a close check should be kept on these. All spoilt pre-signed cheques must be retained for audit purposes; the signature block and cheque machine should have separate holders and be kept under lock and key.

Cash in private possession

The company secretary will no doubt be involved in the drafting of policy instructions of various kinds, one of which may well relate to the keeping of money arising from football pools, clubs and collections of all kinds. It should be clearly spelt out to employees that the company will not accept responsibility for such monies kept on the premises, unless they are handed over to a responsible managerial person who is prepared to accept them and lodge them in suitable safe keeping. Any cases coming to notice where such monies are left in drawers should be the subject of verbal reprimand and, if a theft does occur, the opportunity should be taken to stress to everyone the importance of compliance.

Paying-out stations

Increasingly, attacks are being made on offices where money is in the process of being paid out. Shotguns and pickaxe handles are frequently used — and there should be no heroics in the face of a gun. It is strongly recommended that consideration is given to providing personal attack alarms (button or foot operated) in cashiers' offices and at pay points. Thieves are under strain and may be 'trigger-happy', so there should be no audible alarm at the scene but an indication at a safe point from which police assistance can be sought.

Where new positions are being constructed to act as pay points, thought must be given, and if necessary professional advice obtained, as to protection from violence, including the threat of firearms, for those paying out. The point must also be so devised as to prevent casual theft of wage packets through the pay-window. Complete armoured glass window and shelf units are available from specialist suppliers. It is also good practice to exhibit at each paying-out point a notice that clearly indicates that the recipient is responsible for his own wage packet after collection. Where control of the pay packets and pay points changes during a wage issue, proper checking and handing over should take place between the clerks concerned. The paying-out system itself should be such that the possibility of an employee being able to draw another's pay packet fraudulently is minimized. This can be done by issuing the payslips which authorize collection twenty-four hours before the pay-out. False allegations of an unauthorized packet collection are not infrequent where a firm has previously paid without query — all such claims should be thoroughly investigated before a repayment is authorized. Where packets of a type that allow checking of contents are used, no claims of shortage should be entertained if the packet has been opened.

Because of the 150-year-old Truck Acts, which allow employees to claim payment *in cash*, Britain leads the world in such payments. The government has announced an intention to repeal the Acts but as yet nothing has been done. Union compromises may well include installation of an automatic teller machine (ATM) or cash dispenser, run by the company and on company premises. There are specialist risks with regard to ATMs, especially fraud, and while already one firm is offering a private ATM 'package' operation, great care should be taken, and specialist advice sought.

BUILDINGS

A company secretary will inevitably be closely concerned with purchase of property and new buildings. He is therefore in a unique position to ensure that security considerations are borne in mind and the acceptability or otherwise of risks is given due emphasis.

Old property, though satisfactory in every respect of location, floor space and amenities, may be totally unsuitable for high-risk commodities. If this is suddenly realized after acquisition, considerable unbudgeted expenditure may be needed to rectify the condition and this will reflect on the foresight of those who conducted the negotiations.

New construction does not offer the same difficulties, provided that — from the draft-plan stage — civil engineers, architects, planners and builders have in mind what is at risk and the steps that can be taken to minimize it, without jeopardizing the essential functions of the building. If no company specialist is employed the police crime prevention officers will be delighted to give their views and advice — they regard this stage as the best time to utilize their services. Simple adjustments to plans can easily cut out avenues for walk-in theft, or such invitations to a thief as obscured windows or doors which may be forced at leisure. Indeed, some police forces are now appointing architectural liaison officers whose speciality is to advise on plans before building commences.

A few basic essentials: endeavour to keep all parking facilities outside the premises proper; provide maximum lighting on perimeters; restrict the number of entrances to a building or site to the absolute minimum (it is much harder to do so when employees have become accustomed to using them); ensure that persons using any entrance can be seen, either by a receptionist, or by occupants of adjoining offices; restrict keys to an absolute minimum and prohibit the making of duplicates. Do not overlook the possibilities of closed-circuit television which can survey several entrances from a central point and be coupled with remote control of locks by electronic means.

Alarm systems

The electronic alarm industry has grown to major proportions and several firms have nationwide coverage. Their equipment can be extremely sophisticated; its cost therefore should be in relation to the risk. Whole areas or selected danger points can be covered; warning can be by immediate bells, '999' connection to the police, or by direct line to the police (where this is still permitted) or to a central station operated by the alarm company. Delayed bells can be fitted so that the message can be transmitted to the police but loss restricted if for some reason their arrival is delayed. Reliance on bells alone is a dubious proposition — little attention is paid by the public. Facilities offered include ordinary door contacts, rays, pressure pads, tautened wiring, radar and sonic detectors; new conceptions are continually being developed. When costing such an installation, it is advisable to consult and seek estimates from at least three unconnected companies. Knowing that others are in competition, none will recommend an unnecessarily expensive system which might exclude their quotation. The police crime prevention officer may be willing to indicate those that have the local servicing facilities that are essential to eliminate waste of time. He cannot be expected to recommend any particular one.

A certain number of false alarms must be anticipated in the early teething stages of an installation but should clear within two or three weeks. The police will look with a jaundiced eye if false alarms continue thereafter since they implement a prearranged plan to cover the premises on each occasion as a priority to other duties; they also require key holders to be nominated who are conversant with the contents of the building, have means of transport, and preferably are available by telephone.

There are now three organizations whose aim is to safeguard customers and abide by BS4737, the British Standard on alarm installation:

1 *The National Supervisory Council for Intruder Alarms* (NSCIA) set up in 1972, the most powerful, and largest
2 *The British Association of Security Installers*, set up in 1985, based in south-east England (London and the Home Counties) and consisting of small firms, but with insurance company recognition
3 *The Inspectors Approved Alarm Installers*, based in the north of England, and with a grading system for small to large firms, again installing to BS4737

Of the three, it must be said that the NSCIA has the most 'clout' with insurers, but not necessarily the keenest-priced firms. Check with your insurers on *any* considered alarm installation firm.

Contracts should be carefully scrutinized before acceptance, liability restriction clauses and the precise supplier obligations under 'maintenance' merit special attention. An alarm log, showing dates and nature of work done on the system, and recording false calls with their causes should be kept.

Locks and keys

A lock is just as good as its price, and a key as good as the precautions taken to restrict the holders and the opportunity to copy it. For security purposes, a five-lever lock is the minimum insurance requirement and again the insurers' advice can be obtained in cases of doubt; for privacy the 'Yale-type' lock will suffice. The locking of internal doors can frequently result in excessive damage by intruders and it is a waste of time and money putting a first-class lock on a poor door. The same is applicable to padlocks — the best are close shackled and of hardened steel, and must be used with hasps of equal calibre. Both padlocks and ordinary door locks of all kinds can be 'master-suited', which implies that the keying is such that, for example: an executive will be able to open all doors within his jurisdiction with the one key he holds; his departmental managers will have access to the offices in their departments only; and individuals will be able to enter only their own offices. The same sort of arrangement can be implemented in research departments which contain areas of different security importance.

Duplicated locks on doors are not desirable, even with cheap locks, but the main danger is that of desk locks where it is not unusual to find a single key will open almost all drawers in an office. If the desk contains matters demanding privacy, the lock itself should be unique in its environment. To obtain a desk or filing cabinet which will resist forcing, even with limited violence, is wellnigh impossible — fire-resistant cabinets are the nearest available type and even the smaller substantial ones may reach £300 in price; old safes are preferable. Keys must always be kept in personal possession.

Use of dogs

Trained dogs can be a valuable aid for patrolling or guarding premises, particularly on dispersed sites. They afford protection and give confidence to those using them and their very presence is a formidable disincentive to potential intruders.

Liability for injury caused by them is governed by the Animals Act 1971, which lays down that a keeper is not liable for damage if *(a)* it is wholly due to the fault of the sufferer, *(b)* the sufferer has voluntarily accepted the risk (an employee is not regarded as a 'volunteer'), or *(c)* it is caused to a trespasser by an animal kept on premises and it is proved that either it was not kept there for protective purposes or if so used, it was not unreasonable to do so.

Section 1 of the Guard Dogs Act came into force on 1 February 1976. This lays down that a guard dog shall not be used on any premises unless:

1   There is a warning notice of its presence at each entrance
2   It is in the charge of a capable handler at all times, except 'while it is so secured so that it is not at liberty to go freely about the premises'

It seems unlikely that any other sections of the Act will now be brought into force and in any case they do not relate to the dog 'which is only used as a guard dog at premises belonging to its owner'. A divisional court case, Hobson v Gledhill (1977), did indicate that a handler was not always required when a dog was so tethered that a safe space was always available for the intruder to escape into, but also said that each case would be judged on its merits ... there have been very few prosecutions indeed.

Closed-circuit television

Closed-circuit TV is increasingly being found of value particularly in retail concerns for observation of purchasers and employees. It is possible to create permanent records for later scrutiny by means of video-tape recording (see 'High technology evidence'). The simple combination of fixed camera and monitor can be enhanced by special low light or infra-red lenses, pan and tilt facilities for the camera mount, all-weather protection, screen washing and wiping, heating units etc., all of which grossly increase the basic price, but make the installation much more multipurpose adaptable.

A further use, which could result in substantial manpower economies, is that of remote control of doors and gates by coupling TV observation with microphones for 'speak through' and electronic control of the entry lock thereby allowing an under-utilized receptionist to be more gainfully employed.

As yet, moving pictures cannot be sent via ordinary telephone wires. But a video picture can be built up, line-by-line. This technique, called 'Slow-Scan' TV, is especially valuable for monitoring remote sites at low cost. Pictures take from eight to sixty-four seconds to 'build', depending on what quality of reproduction the operator calls for, and remote telemetry, for example pan and tilt of cameras and even audio surveillance, is possible. The police used slow-scan (via the cellular radio telephone network) to track Margaret Thatcher and French Premier M. Mitterand in a vehicle convoy during the Channel Tunnel signing. There is no restriction on distance. For the price of a phone call, a security officer in the UK could monitor a remote site in Australia and, via the same phone, alert the Australian police.

It is advisable to point out reasons for installing a system to employees before doing so. To avoid employee opposition, it may be necessary to agree not to take any action if purely disciplinary matters are seen. Dummy cameras may be used apparently to extend a system and can be interchangeable with the genuine if necessary.

FIRE AND SAFETY

A company secretary may not have direct responsibility for the implementation of fire precautions and safety measures but he will, almost certainly, be the recipient of any summons issued against his firm for non-compliance with regulations. He will also be concerned with common-law claims in respect of injury and insurance after fire damage. It behoves him therefore to establish that there is a clear onus placed upon a specified person of managerial status to ensure that legal obligations are carried out, especially in connection with the health and safety at work legislation which is too detailed to discuss here, and too voluminous for most company secretaries' remit.

The creation of an immediate avenue of notification to the company secretary of happenings that might result in claims or proceedings is important. A fire assessor wants to know of damage as soon as possible after it has occurred so that he can survey it to ascertain extent and causation. Any delay in checking the details of an accident can result in essentials being missed and possible failure to inform the factory inspectorate of one of notifiable gravity. A standardized and comprehensive system of reporting should be instituted, especially in connection with accidents.

Fire prevention officers

Full use should be made of the services of the local fire prevention officer. Under the Fire Services Act 1947, the fire authority must maintain efficient arrangements for giving, on request, advice to firms in its area on fire prevention, means of escape, and the restriction of the spread of fires. Consultation with the fire prevention officer should always take place when building alterations or new buildings are contemplated, to avoid unnecessary work and later recriminations. Advice will also be given on the provision and siting of extinguishers and other means of putting out fires. Fire drills should be carried out at regular intervals — it is too late to do so after a tragedy. Very explicit instructions should be given so that all staff know exactly what to do in emergency, and appropriate notices should be displayed. The appointment of fire wardens to be given proper training to combat fire is well worth while, and again the fire prevention officer will be glad to cooperate.

Fire: security checklists

Detailed guidance is given in Eric Oliver and John Wilson's *Practical Security in Commerce and Industry* (Gower, 4th edition, 1983).

First aid

First aid requirements are also laid down in health and safety at work legislation; they refer to the equipment that should be provided and the trained first-aid staff that should be available on premises. This latter requirement should always be treated as one for security staff to cover where these are available, thus obviating difficulties during shift working of ensuring that first aiders are always present.

Delegation in all aspects of fire, safety, and first aid is advisable for the company secretary, in light of the extent of the legislation applicable.

PRECAUTIONS AGAINST TERRORIST ACTION

Regrettably, it has now become necessary for all firms to consider precautions against apparently indiscriminate and senseless acts of violence designed to achieve political ends. These are not entirely confined to the IRA or to the anti-Israeli organizations; others are being tempted to emulate, and terrorism — coupled perhaps with kidnapping — may increase before final containment. There is also ample evidence that criminal elements are involved in some aspects for financial gain.

Of the total of just over 3000 terrorist incidents in 1985, 986 were aimed at industry and commerce around the world, with 976 aimed at government, 946 at the police/military and 117 at political parties among the prominent targets.

Other than reasonable security for the firm, and stringent security for 'at risk' personnel, terrorism is a task for state and international agencies. On that front, at least, there is some movement and most encouragingly, under its American president John Simpson, and English secretary-general Raymond Kendall, the 138-nation-member Interpol (due to move from Paris to Lyons in 1988) is at last taking a much more active role following President Reagan's demands that Interpol should take on a more aggressive function.

Employee safety

The topic is board-level importance and the company secretary, at least in smaller companies, may be required to advise on policy, to draft instructions and perhaps initiate action. Not least, he should keep an eye on insurance implications, whether against terrorist or armed raiders' attacks.

'Reasonable security' is all that industrial tribunals will look for, following an appeal in 1986 to the Employment Appeals Tribunal, London, by Dutton & Clark of Raynes Park against an earlier decision by an industrial tribunal that a cashier, Mrs Karen Daly, who left her job following two armed robberies, was entitled to damages for constructive dismissal. Mrs Daly had asked her employers for a bullet-resistant screen, which would have cost £10 000 for an office making only £1 500 profit per year. The appeal was refused.

The ruling, by Sir Ralph Kilner-Brown, hinged on the notion that, like the bomber, the really determined armed robber or terrorist would always get through. An employer's duty to protect employees from armed robbery or other criminal activity was thus limited to taking 'reasonable steps'.

The problem now is who is to decide what is, and what is not, 'reasonable'? The only pertinent legislation is the Health and Safety At Work Acts, which provide little or no guidance. It is suggested that companies seek expert advice; be seen to have a scheme and to have followed it.

The threats and risks can take several forms, ranging from malicious telephone calls to explosive and incendiary devices, and letter bombs. The first steps that need to be taken are those of formulating and agreeing policies to deal with particular contingencies, giving due weight to the views of those who will be asked to carry out specific duties such as searching for suspect objects.

Bomb-threat calls

These may be by direct call, anonymous letter, or via a third party, i.e. the police or newspaper office; the IRA have used a code to the police to confirm the presence of a bomb but this is by no means an accurate yardstick of veracity. If sufficiently prevalent, and treated as needing automatic evacuation, these calls can disrupt a firm's activity almost as effectively as a device itself can. The decision is not easy and any individual, whatever his convictions about the validity of a message, will have at the back of his mind the consequences of ignoring a genuine call; this decision therefore must rest with the senior person available, who should be influenced by preconsidered guidelines (see Figure 34.1).

Bomb-threat policy

Fundamentally, there are three possible courses of action:

1 To evacuate and search before re-entry
2 To search without evacuation
3 To ignore the message

Amongst points to be considered are:

1 Nature of the call — apparent age of the caller, speech, attitude, general approach etc.
2 Recent history of such threats, genuine or otherwise, locally and nationally
3 Prevailing conditions of industrial tension, strikes and political unrest in the neighbourhood and at the recipient's premises particularly

Signal your supervisor and conform to prearranged drill for nuisance calls: tick through applicable word below, insert where necessary.

TIME.......................... DATE..........................

Origin	S.T.D.		Coin box		Internal
Caller	Male		Female	Adult	Juvenile

Voice	Speech	Language	Accent	Manner	Background
Loud	Fast	Obscene	Local	Calm	Noises
Soft	Slow	Coarse	Regional	Rational	Factory
Rough	Distinct	Normal	Foreign	Irrational	Road traffic
Educated	Blurred	Educated		Coherent	Music
High pitch	Stutter			Incoherent	Office
Deep				Deliberate	Party atmosphere
Disguised				Hysterical	Quiet
				Aggrieved	Voices
				Humorous	Other
				Drunken	

Text of conversation

Figure 34.1 Bomb-threat checklist

4   Any trading relationships between the company and countries whose opponents have used bombs
5   The implications and dangers of an evacuation

In all instances, police and fire authorities should be informed immediately, whether an evacuation is to be ordered or not. As a neighbourly gesture, adjoining firms should be told what is happening.

It must be anticipated that the police will be reluctant to take the initiative in advising on evacuation or otherwise — unless they have positive information.

Telephone operators

As first recipients of a message, it is important that operators have clear instructions on what to do so that there is a minimum of alarm and subsequent confusion about the content of the message. In addition to the instructions suggested below, a stereotyped form based on the checklist in Figure 34.1 could be provided to the operators, and its mere availability could relieve natural tension.

Guidelines to telephonists

1   Let the caller finish his message without interruption

2   Get the message exactly — bearing in mind the points shown
3   If it is possible to tie the supervisor or another operator into the conversation, do so
4   Ensure that senior management or a predesignated person are told exactly the contents of the call as soon as possible
5   If the caller is apparently prepared to carry on a conversation, encourage him to do so and try to get answers to the following:
    (a)   *Where* has the bomb been put?
    (b)   *What time* will it go off?
    (c)   *Why* has it been done?
    (d)   *When* and how was it done?

In general, if the caller is prepared to continue, try to get him to talk about possible grievances as they affect the firm, and anything which bears upon the truthfulness of the message and the identity of the caller.

It is essential that senior management should be told as soon as possible so that there is no delay in implementing policies and procedures.

Evacuation

Communications should be such that the general warning to evacuate is given simultaneously in all parts affected; otherwise there will be confusion, with people coming and going, difficulty in checking that everyone is out, and garbled messages being passed. If time permits the warning to be given verbally through a managerial chain, it should be on the lines 'At 2pm instruct your staff to begin evacuation; ensure that it is complete not later than 2 15pm'.

Based on experience in the USA, a clear radius of 100 yards should be allowed from the threatened area, 200 yards if a car bomb is suspected. Assembly points for evacuation will not of necessity coincide with those used for fire drills. Car parks are definitely not acceptable, for obvious reasons, and there are advantages in housing evacuated staff in substantial buildings if of suitable size and outside the prescribed distance. There must be facilities for checking employees to ensure complete evacuation, the passing of messages and for expediting the return to work. A handheld loud hailer will be found invaluable to those in charge.

In case of evacuation

1   Persons who are instructed to get out must, if time permits, collect and take their personal parcels, bags and other belongings to avoid complications during searching (particularly important in cloakroom areas and office blocks generally)
2   If the time-limit given by the warning permits, there should be a quick

search by supervisory staff and/or designated employees before the premises are vacated. A system should be devised to ensure that everyone is out. (Special provisions may be needed for disabled employees)
3   After the time-limit of the threat has elapsed, a reasonable margin should be allowed before a search by security/supervisory personnel, and employees are allowed to re-enter. (Searching of course is a voluntary matter but, in general, supervisors will cooperate)

No evacuation

A search should be made by security/supervisory personnel of likely 'planting' areas, i.e. entrances to buildings, cloakrooms and toilets, and the perimeter of buildings — with special attention to parked cars. Police and fire brigade should nevertheless be informed.

Search

1   Responsibility for search of premises lies with the occupiers. The police cannot be expected to accept this task by themselves, since they will be unfamiliar with buildings and likely contents, but they will almost certainly offer their assistance
2   Bearing in mind the multiplicity of forms that a bomb may take, it is the unusual object — not normal in the particular environment — which is suspect. Again the occupants are best qualified to identify
3   Any search made must be methodical with areas designated to individuals to ensure that the whole is covered, and with a co-ordinator to make certain that this is done
4   Unaccountable or suspect objects should not be interfered with. If such are found, the police should be advised and they will then instigate any necessary action

Recognition of explosive/incendiary devices

These can be encountered in almost any form. In retail premises, small incendiary packets put in pockets of clothing left in cloakrooms or among inflammable textiles may be one of the reasons why the arson rate has escalated over the past few years. From the terrorist point of view, they have the virtue of completely eliminating any sign of their existence.

Explosive types have been planted in parcels, suitcases, dustbins, post-boxes, biscuit tins, or where large bulk has been used, lodged in hijacked cars; on casual inspection, they may not be recognizable for what they are and it is not unusual for the obvious device to have been booby-trapped as a means of attacking anti-bomb personnel. A relatively new type is clearly identifiable and potentially very lethal to those nearby — a conventional

SECURITY POLICY AND ADMINISTRATION

bomb is placed with polystyrene padding between two cans of petrol and then lowered into premises where inflammable matter is contained, via a hole cut in the roof.

It follows that anything of a foreign nature — rough parcels, plastic shopping bags left in odd corners or near entrances, dustbins out of place etc. should be regarded as suspect. In effect, there is no easy way for a layman without special equipment to identify or otherwise a potential bomb, and at the risk of repetition, it is the unusual thing that just should not be where it is which should immediately arouse suspicion.

In the near vicinity of a suspect bomb, the military advise that personal or other types of radio intercommunication be switched off as a precaution against activating a sophisticated device.

General precautions

A general tightening of precautions in or around plant and offices can reduce the opportunity for incidents and at the same time have the added benefit of minimizing other sources of loss. For example:

1. If not already in existence, inaugurate a registration system for immediate identification of cars and motor cycles used by employees (helps quick location of owner when lights left on, tyres flat etc.)
2. Control entrance of visitors, suppliers and contractors to the site. Visitor and vehicular passes can be used to provide a record, and to check that the person or vehicle leaves (improves privacy of firm's operation)
3. Do not allow visitors to enter on any pretext without prior confirmation that they are expected/welcome (excludes unwanted, time-wasting callers and stops a common form of impersonation to get into premises to steal). Arrange collection from reception point in cases of doubt. Always check identity of purported public officials — gas, electricity repairmen etc. — who will be in possession of the necessary cards
4. Review physical protection of buildings, i.e. adequacy of fencing, external lighting, doors, groundfloor windows, fire escapes, alarms etc. (leads to strengthening of physical defences against intruders)
5. Ensure that the standard of housekeeping around buildings is such that unfamiliar objects will at once become noticeable
6. Restrict parking outside particularly important facilities such as computer installations, gas terminals and power substations
7. Establish a central control point which will not be evacuated unless there is a substantiated positive danger to it. This should have means of communication with outside authorities should the firm's switchboard be obliged to close down, and it should be easily accessible to incoming police and fire services
8. In the event of a bomb warning, small rough parcels and plastic-type

shopping bags left in odd corners or near entrances should be at once suspect, likewise unfamiliar cars parked haphazardly, especially those with Irish registration plates

Letter bombs

There is of course no warning given in respect of these; reasons can usually be thought of as to why a particular target has been selected but the senders are irrational, and immunity for lack of causation should not be assumed. It has been suggested in one instance of injury that the employers may be liable in that no guidance, appropriate to present circumstances, had been given to the person opening the mail.

Letters or parcel bombs mainly take the form of substantial envelopes not less than 3/16 inch thick or of parcels containing paperbacked books delivered through normal postal channels. The weight in letter form is unlikely to exceed 4oz.

General features

1   Letter bombs are made to withstand the handling that any normal letter or parcel would sustain during delivery; they are to all intents and purposes safe until steps are taken to open them, and can be handled normally until then
2   So far as is known, no letter/parcel bomb has been received which has borne a franking mark on the envelope or wrapping, but a franked stuck-on address label has been used on letter bombs originating on the Continent
3   Spraying with an aerosol of the Boots pain-killing type as used for sporting purposes or Holts 'Cold Start' (the first is the better) may make a manilla envelope or wrapping sufficiently transparent for contents to be identified enough to alleviate suspicion if not to establish dangerous nature
4   Conventional components include detonators, connecting wire and minute batteries; no device yet used has been known to have been activated when tested with a low-power metal detector or X-ray (a wide variety of hand-held metal detectors are commercially available). The military advise that if X-ray equipment is used, it should be operated by remote control
5   The police have already dealt with innumerable suspect but innocuous letters/parcels and may be able to give immediate clearance if provided with pertinent details, i.e. town of origin, size and shape, franking or other distinctive stamping.

SECURITY POLICY AND ADMINISTRATION

Points which may make unfamiliar material received suspect

1 The postmark, if foreign and unfamiliar
2 The writing, which may have an 'un-English' appearance, lack literacy, or be crudely printed
3 Name and address of sender (if shown), if address differs from area of postmark
4 'Personal'/'Only to be opened by' or 'Private' letters addressed to senior management under the job title, for example Managing Director
5 Weight, if excessive for size and apparent contents. Thickeness: 3/16 inch or more
6 Weight distribution, if uneven may indicate batteries inside
7 Grease marks showing on the exterior of the wrapping and emanating from inside may indicate 'sweating' explosive
8 Smell — some explosives smell of marzipan or almonds
9 Abnormal fastening — sealing excessive for the type of package. If such an outer contains a similar inner wrapping, this may be a form of booby trap
10 Damaged envelopes which give sight of wire, batteries or fluid-filled plastic sachets should be left strictly alone; those that rattle or feel springy should be treated with caution; and naturally, any ticking noise should be treated as a 'red' alert. Pinholes in the outer wrapping may indicate where devices for the safety of the bomb-maker have been removed. Where conventional paperback books have been used, the resultant parcel bomb may be discernibly softer in the centre than at the edges

If suspicions cannot be alleviated

1 Do not try to open the letter/parcel or tamper with it
2 Do not put it in water or put anything on top of it
3 Isolate it where it can do no harm with minimum handling, i.e. enclose it in a nest of sandbags but ensure that it is in a position for easy visual inspection
4 Open any windows and doors in the vicinity. Keep people away from it
5 Inform the police and seek their guidance: give them full details of the letter/parcel, its markings and peculiarities which have led to suspicion

KIDNAPPING

In Great Britain, this has not materialized other than in infrequent instances. In the Americas, it is sufficiently widespread for the term 'executive kidnapping' to be applied to a practice which is being used for both financial gain and political advantage. Some American security firms do tender advice on the precautions that should be taken, and insurance can be obtained against it from Lloyd's. If the company secretary is called upon to arrange an itinerary for a senior director in an area where instances have occurred, there is nothing to be lost by inquiring to the appropriate government department for guidelines to be followed. This advice is now available but the essential ingredients are — maintain low profile and minimum publicity, accept that there is a risk however unattractive a target you consider yourself, and use commonsense precautions in your behaviour and movements accordingly. The countries of current highest risk are the Argentine, Colombia and Italy, but publicity of success elsewhere could easily create new trouble points.

MISCELLANEOUS

The Rehabilitation of Offenders Act 1974 [mentioned earlier] is often misunderstood. Essentially, it is intended to prevent the stigma of criminal conviction attaching itself indefinitely to an individual. According to the severity of the sentence, after a specified period of time elapses from the date of conviction, he shall be treated for all purposes in law as a person of previous good character. For example, in applying for jobs he need not give true answers to questions indicating he has 'spent' or 'lapsed' convictions and cannot subsequently be dismissed for lying about them; it also penalizes unauthorized disclosure of such by any person. Briefly, sentences of over 30 months are excluded and never lapse; 6 — 30 months persist for 10 years; not exceeding 6 months — 7 years; borstal training likewise; fines — 5 years. Penalties on younger offenders have reduced periods. It should be noted that one of the objectives of the Act is 'to amend the law of defamation' and indiscreet wording of references should be guarded against.

An 'exceptions' order in 1975 listed jobs where a spent conviction remained adequate grounds for dismissing or refusing to employ, professions where it could be a bar to admission, and permits, licences etc. which could be denied. To date, the Act has had a trivial number of even mentions in courts and its importance is apt to be overstressed. But, remember, security staff are *not* exempt.

Picketing during strike action

Picketing in furtherance of an industrial dispute is lawful but certain acts if carried out during it are offences. There is no right to encroach on private land and police assistance can be called for the purpose of effecting removal; the police can order the limiting of numbers if they consider these are unreasonable and likely to cause a breach of the peace; violence to persons or property and the hiding of tools are offences, and the picketing of a place where a person lives is prohibited.

Relevant to you?

In a recent poll in the US conducted by *Venture Magazine* of New York, almost two in every three firms reported they had been hit by crime, and that their known losses were averaging US$114 000 annually. Those hardest hit were retailers (75 per cent reported losses) followed by manufacturers (70 per cent), wholesalers (69 per cent), service industries (60 per cent) and financial institutions (59 per cent). The most common problem was theft (cited by 40 per cent of all respondents), followed by embezzlement (16 per cent) and pilferage (14 per cent). Interestingly, only 3 per cent thought or knew they had been victims of industrial espionage.

On security measures only 40 per cent of the firms had taken some sort of measure to prevent the crime they had suffered from. The rest said they had applied security only after the fact. Steps taken included:

> more stringent accounting and auditing practices (43 per cent)
> better vetting of all prospective employees (25 per cent)
> various types of security equipment (19 per cent)
> security devices on computers (16 per cent)

Reflecting perhaps, on American trends in business, 10 per cent of those asked said they felt that certain illegal practices, including industrial espionage and the paying of bribes, were actually necessary to do business.

Advertising rewards for the return of stolen property

If such adverts are placed, they must not imply that no questions will be asked, or that no further inquiries or legal action will be taken, i.e. a promise of immunity to the person producing the stolen property. To do so is an offence punishable by a fine on both the printer and the inserter.

Trespass

With the exception of a limited number of offences created by the Criminal Law Act 1977 (mainly concerned with squatters) and those involving government lands or factories/stores containing explosives, trespass is primarily a civil wrong.

The casual trespasser can be invited to leave and almost always will do so; minimum force sufficient to effect removal can be used if repeated requests are ignored and the police can be called to assist if numbers of persons are concerned, or there is likelihood of a violent reaction. Deliberate and recurring trespass is best dealt with by seeking a court injunction to prohibit it.

Holiday checklist

Particularly applicable to Christmas:

1. The short days give villains longer 'working hours' of darkness
2. Both police and contracted-for security guards are at a premium because of the holiday
3. There are generally fewer people around, especially in industrial estates and parks, to deter intruders

The executive responsible for security should have made all necessary arrangements, especially if it is felt extra guards/patrols would be beneficial (check *now* as most contract companies will be under heavy pressure). But after the last office party, and as the site/building is closed down, we suggest you check the following, just in case:

The power. Make sure all unnecessary plugs are disconnected. Check that heating and lighting controls are set properly, particularly pilot lights/burners. Check/observe all frost and flood precautions.

Access control. Whatever system is used, be it standard locks with keys or the most sophisticated access control system, make sure that all cards/keys etc. are properly accounted for.

Company vehicles. If they are to be left on the site all vehicles should be immobilised, even if they are fitted with an alarm system. It should, too, be company policy to have lockable petrol caps to frustrate those whose idea of Christmas cheer is to pour sugar or water into fuel tanks.

Petty cash. And any other easily convertible/portable forms of ready money, e.g. postage stamps, should be securely locked away or banked. Make sure, too, that any pre-paid meters, for example staff telephones, are emptied before Christmas. And, where possible, leave safe doors open.

Storage tanks, particularly fuel of any kind (especially butane and other specialist gases) should be thoroughly secured. Fuel is expensive and a favourite target.

Small and valuable items such as computers, calculators and any other items easily 'fenced' should be locked away securely. Or, in some cases, ask staff to take them home.

Security lighting has always been an undervalued tool. For less than £20, an electronic randomly programmed time switch is available to deter thieves.

SECURITY POLICY AND ADMINISTRATION

Some form of 'surprise' lighting is also a good idea, and a useful aid to staff who have to turn up early while it's still dark. For about £50+ simple 40/60W light units activated by a built-in body-heat sensor are available for strategic entry/exit points (useful for external stores/sheds particularly). The better models of these will also drive up to 1000W of auxiliaries — flood/spot lights etc.

Windows and doors should be checked by the security staff of course, but it does no harm to have a last look yourself. If you have any worries (a lock which has been 'playing up', or a window with a broken or vulnerable catch, for example) sort them out now.

External stores must be properly secured, especially if they hold valuable tools, fuel containers or the like. Large stores, such as garages, can be further protected by parking a company vehicle across the door. The vehicle must, of course, be immobilised, and a visible form (such as the dreaded clamp used by London police and which is now commercially available) will signal the situation immediately to would-be intruders.

Climbing aids. The most obvious are ladders, which must be securely locked away out of sight. But such items as pallets and any other handy aid must not be overlooked.

Alarm system. Check that there are no problem areas where sensors continually false alarm (which is how the Buckingham Palace break-in happened) and which guards ignore. Make sure there are no by-passes on the system.

Finally be sure the police know how long your company will be shut down for; how they can get in touch with the keyholder(s) throughout that period, and anything else you can think of vital to your specific security, particularly if specified in your insurance agreement.

Cheque and credit card fraud

Estimated to cost £100m annually in the UK (neither banks nor firms will reveal exact figures), cheque and credit card fraud is on the increase.

The checklist which follows is by no means fully comprehensive; rather, it is designed to aid the setting up of a workable system which could save your firm thousands of pounds.

1 Do you have an internal reporting system for all fraud losses?
2 Is there a single executive responsible for fraud control?
3 Have you a training programme to teach staff what to look for with

regard to bad cheques, credit card fraud and telephone orders quoting a credit card number?
4 Do you get authorization on *all* credit card amounts, regardless of size?
5 Have you checked with the bank as to how much notice they will give on refuting claims and recharging on fraudulent credit card transactions?
6 What percentage of recharges are you able to reverse (it should be 90 per cent or more if you have a positive system)?
7 Have you direct links with those at the bank/credit card firms who are responsible for fraud control?
8 Are all employees who handle credit card and cheque transactions (*a*) thoroughly vetted; (*b*) bonded?
9 Do you check the signature on a credit card against that given on the charge slip on *all* transactions?
10 Do you ask for two forms of ID, for example driver's licence and one other, for credit card and cheque transactions?
11 Are employees instructed to rip up the carbons from credit card charge slips?
12 Do you get both home and business phone numbers on all mail-order and telephone sales, and then check those numbers on a routine basis?
13 Do you ask for the name of the issuing bank on all telephoned or mail credit card sales?
14 Do you then check with that bank that the customer's name and address are as given?
15 Where orders are not to the card holders or cheque issuer, but to a third party, do you ring the holders, just in case?
16 If you have any type of retail outlet, do you have a system to prevent the multi-imprinting, on blank charge slips, of credit cards by staff? And do you stamp the backs of cheques received not only with the bank guarantee card number but the customer's name and address?
17 Are employees who open envelopes containing cheques kept to a minimum?
18 Are envelopes containing cheques/cash opened and handled under a security procedure?
19 Do you have a special internal rubber stamp for cheques which are redeposited?
20 Do you maintain your own 'black file' of fraudulent names and addresses?
21 Are names from this 'black file' cross-checked, and removed from all mailing lists?
22 Is the same procedure adopted with names and addresses you may receive (*a*) from banks/credit card firms' security departments; and (*b*) bought-in mailing lists?
23 Do you use a 'letter of credit' instead of issuing a direct credit to customers due credit?

24 Do you have a system to avoid being debited twice for the same account?
25 Do you give every transaction an order number?
26 Do all your regular customers have their own 'customer reference number'?
27 Do you keep the documentation on every order, including any proofs of delivery, together and readily accessible?
28 Do you have a unified, integrated order-processing system, including a cross-index of credit card charge slips with sales accounts, which gives you control over orders from beginning to end?
29 Do you check that all returned goods and claims of non-delivery are reconciled with credits?
30 Do you issue and control credit card charge slips and their reference numbers under a security procedure?
31 Do you have a check procedure for all new, large, one-off or otherwise unusual transactions?
32 Have you read any books, or attended any seminars, on credit card and cheque fraud?
33 Have you contacted the police fraud squad and talked with them about current problems and trends?
34 Are you a member of any kind of crime prevention circle, or 'hot-line' system, with fellow traders in your field?

As said, the above is not a comprehensive 'system', but represents what you should be doing. Don't rely on credit card companies or even banks' own security checks. In 1986, in a case involving Nigerians and Kenyans staying in Britain, a swindle was described as 'laughably easy' by a QC in Inner London Crown Court. Finance companies had handed out dozens of credit cards to a fraudster without making even the slightest attempt to check back; even the bank account numbers put on application forms were fake, as were the names and addresses of the applicants.

Works closures

Regrettably, works closures have become commonplace during recent years. They bring with them security problems which are often unexpectedly serious. The risks start when the news of closure is announced, and can persist long after the intended closure date. By no means all work forces react badly, but there have been many incidents where ill will has led to theft, vandalism and fraud — to the extent that a group of senior security officers have produced guidelines for action during such periods to limit damage to disposable assets.

These guidelines, which are too detailed for inclusion here, are obtainable from The Secretary, International Professional Security Association, 292a Torquay Road, Paignton, Devon, TQ3 2ET.

FURTHER READING

Jack Bologna, *Corporate Fraud*, Butterworth, 1985.
Norman R. Bottom, Jr, and John Kostanoski, *Security and Loss Control*, Macmillan, 1983.
A. Evans and A. Korn in association with Percom Limited, *How to Comply with the Data Protection Act*, Gower, Aldershot, 1986.
Handbook of Security, Kluwer-Harrap Handbooks, London, 1974.
D. Hughes and P. Bowler, *The Security Survey,* Gower, Aldershot, 1982.
Oliver and Wilson, *Practical Security in Commerce and Industry,* 4th edition, Gower, Aldershot, 1983.
Oliver and Wilson, *Security Manual*, 3rd edition, Gower, Aldershot, 1979.
R. Post and A. Kingsbury, *Security Administration*, 2nd edition, Charles C. Thomas, Springfield, Ill., 1973.
Philip P. Purpura, *Security and Loss Prevention* Butterworth, 1984.
Michael Saunders, *Protecting Your Business Secrets*, Gower, Aldershot, 1985.
Walsh and Healey, *Protection of Assets Manual*, Merritt Co. (USA).
Walsh and Healey, *Industrial Security Management: A cost effective approach*, Merritt Co. (USA).
K.G. Wright, *Cost Effective Security*, McGraw-Hill, Maidenhead, 1973.

Index

accident book, 530
accounting:
  for inflation, 135
  for taxation, 161–2
accounts:
  annual, 121–36
  balance sheet, 124–7
  designation, 63
  disclosure, 127–8
  presentation, 122–8
  profit and loss, 122–4, 130–5
    presentation 122–4
    taxation, 124
acquisitions, *see* mergers and acquisitions
activity sampling, 323, 325
added value, 491–2
Administrator (ICSA journal), 12–13
Advance Corporation Tax, 157, 168–9
advertising code of practice, 304
Advertising Standards Authority, 304
Advisory Conciliation and Arbitration
  Service, 551
  advice, 564
air services, 673–5
alarm systems, 710–11
annual general meetings, 83–5
annual return, contents, 42–3
articles of association:
  adoption, 30–1
  alteration, 31
artificial intelligence, 394
assets:
  current, 125, 127
  fixed, 124–5
  replacement, 172–3
audit, and pay system, 500–1
auditors:
  duties, 40
  payment, 42
  qualifications, 41
  removal, 41–2
automation, offices, 331–2

balance sheet, contents, 124–7

bankruptcy, 259–61
Bargain Offers Order (1979), 304
Bell House Limited v *City Wall Properties Limited* (1966), 209
Bills of Exchange Act (1882), 206
bomb-threats, 715–22
bonds, foreign currency, 145
bonuses, 329
breach of contract, remedies, 429–30
building contracting, systems, 598–9
Building Regulations, 601–2
buildings:
  and adjacent properties, 609–10
  alterations, 624–5
  cleaning, 622
  costs, 330
  decoration, 622–3
  disposal, 604
  finance, 614–15, 623
  fire precautions, 617–18
  future requirements, 603–4
  inspections, 621–2
  legislation, 600–3, 613–15
  location, 594–6
  maintenance, 605–6, 618–24
  maintenance manual, 619, 621
  management, 611–12
  management team, 615–17
  policy, 612–13
  rates, 608–9
  records, 623–4
  safety, 617
  security, 618, 709–12
  selection, 594, 596–7
  surveyors, 597–8
  valuation, 607–8

campaigns, as incentives, 328
capital:
  need for, 137–8
  types, 138
  venture, 139
Capital Gains Tax, 170–3
cars, as fringe benefits, 506

INDEX

cash:
  security, 707–9
  transfer, 705–6
cash flow, and VAT, 186
Certificate of Professional Competence (CPC), 647–8
charges (on property), registration, 44–5
chauffeur services, 673
citizen's arrest, 696–7
City Code on Takeovers and Mergers, 195
City of London, 15
Clerical Standard Data (CSD), 323, 324
closed shop, trades union, 553–6, 566–7
closed-circuit television, 712
Commission on Racial Equality, 404–5
companies:
  annual return, 42–3
  articles of association, 30–1
  borrowing, 43–5
  capital, 28–9
  characteristics, 17
  close, 173–4
  and contracts, 208–14
  directors, 34–8
  and disclosure, 20–1
  documents, 25–6, 38
  formation, 18, 22–3, 21–3
  functions, 17
  gearing, 152
  goals, 14
  going public, 140–1
  guarantee, 46–7, 103–4
  liability, 28
  membership, 31–3
  names, 24–5
  nominal capital, 28–30
  and notification, 212–13
  objects, 26–8
  public and private, 21
  purchase, 22–3
  register of members, 32
  registered office, 25
  and two-tier boards, 14
  types, 18, 46–7
  unlimited, 46, 103
  unlisted, 138–9
Companies Act (1980), and company secretary, 5–6
Companies Act (1985), 18
Companies Registry, 20
company cars, 671–2
company secretary, 40–1
  and board meetings, 104–5
  and Companies Acts (1980), (1981), 5–6
  duties, 6–10, 40
  future, 14–16
  independence, 9–10
  legal status, 3–6

qualifications, 5, 11–13, 39–40
role, 3–4
compensation, and dismissal, 435–6
competition:
  attitudes to, 292
  and EEC law, 298
Competition Act (1980), 293–4, 296
competitions, 329
computers:
  applications, 390–2
  basics, 386
  benefits, 387
  bureaux, 392–3
  developments, 393–4
  forms, 382–4
  office management, 312–17
  operations, 390–1
  paper control, 371
  payment for, 389–90
  procurement, 388–90
  selection, 314–17, 388–9
  staff, 390–2
  use, 387–8
'concert party' (share dealings), 33
consultants, use of, 365–7
Consumer Credit Act (1974), 300–1
Consumer Protection Act (1987), 301, 304
Consumer Protection Advisory Committee, function, 300
consumers:
  and contracts, 222–3
  protection, 298–9
contractors:
  definition, 420–1
  employer's liability for, 421–2
  employment law, 419–22
contracts:
  and bankruptcy, 208
  breach of, 215–17
  capacity for, 207–14
  and companies, 208–14
  consideration, 206
  and consumers, 222–3
  and damages, 215–16
  and drunkenness, 208
  elements of, 203–6
  and European Communities Act (1972), 209–14
  illegal, 205–6
  indefinite, 423
  and injunctions, 217
  and mentally ill persons, 207–8
  and minors, 207
  and ownership of goods, 218–19
  restraint of trade, 220–1
  and specific performance, 216–17
  termination, 422–3
  see also employment contracts

INDEX

convertible loan stock, 79–80
copyright, 285–6, 285–8
  licensing, 287
Copyright Act (1956), 285
corporate planning, and redundancy, 540–7
corporate strategy, and training, 581–2
corporation tax:
  advance, 157, 168–70
  calculation, 156
  definitions, 175–6
cost reduction, space, 330–1
costs:
  offices, 318
  wage structure, 480–1
credit problems, 20
Currie v Misa (1875), 206

Daimler Company Limited v *Continental Tyre & Rubber Company (Great Britain) Limited* (1916), 3–4
data, types, 387
Data Protection Act (1984), 678–81
Davis Contractors v *Fareham Urban District Council* (1956), 205
death, industrial, 529
debentures, 143–4
  definition, 45
  holders, meetings, 104
debt collection:
  agencies, 251–2
  and court judgements, 256–8
  and court proceedings, 254–6
  decisions about, 252–4
  moratorium, 258–9
  solicitors, 252
designs, 285–8
  licensing, 287
Designs Act (1949), 285
Designs Register, The, 286
Director General of Fair Trading, 294
directors:
  appointment, 36
  companies, 34–8
  contracts, 38
  information about, 36
  interests, 37–8
  legal status, 35
  meetings, 99–103
  and national insurance, 523
  payments to, 122–4
  qualifications, 35–6
  register of, 37
  removal, 36
  report, contents, 128–30
  role, 35
  and *ultra vires* doctrine, 35
disciplinary procedures, 423–5
disclosure, annual accounts, 127–8

discrimination, against employees, 434
dismissal:
  and compensation, 435–6
  constructive, 428–9
  and discrimination, 434
  fair, 431–2
  and industrial tribunals, 434–6
  procedures, 424–9
  reasons for, 425–8
  and trades union, 433–4, 436
  unfair, 430, 432–3
  without prosecution, 693–4
divided mandates, 63
documents:
  classification, 683
  custody, 684
  destruction, 684–5
  loss, 677–8
  privacy markings, 683
  safety precautions, 684
  security policy for, 682–8
dogs, and security, 711–12
Doyle v *White City Stadium* (1935), 207
drivers' hours:
  legislation, 651–2
  records, 653, 655
drug abuse, 689–92
Dunlop Tyre Company Limited v *New Garage Limited* (1915), 216

EEC, competition law, 298
electronic offices, 309–10
electronic surveillance devices, 687
employees:
  benefits, 473–4
  liabilities, 414–19
  and patent rights, 269–70
  right of search, 692–3
  and safety at work, 441
  theft by, 692–3
employers:
  associations, legal status, 564–5
  duties to employees, 400
  liabilities, 414–19
  and references, 437–8
  and safety at work, 440–1
  and safety of contractors, 422
employment:
  continuity, 404
  contracts, 398–404
  statute law, 397–8
Employment Appeals Tribunal, 397–8, 562
employment contracts:
  form, 401–4
  obligations, 399–400
  restraints, 401
  terms, 399
  variations, 403

employment law, 397–410
  independent contractors, 419–22
Employment Protection Act (1978), 535
Equal Opportunities Commission, 408
Equal Pay Act (1970), 413–14
espionage, industrial, 681–8
European Communities Act (1972), 27
  and contract, 209–14
European Patent Convention (EPC), 263–4, 272, 275–7
expenses, taxation, 158–60
expert systems, 394
Export Credits Guarantee Department (ECGD), 149–50
exports finance, 149

Factories Act (1961), 443–7
fair trading:
  and civil law, 302–4
  codes of practice, 299–300, 304
  and criminal law, 301–2
  see also consumer protection and restrictive trade practices
Fair Trading Act (1973), 291, 293, 297
Fair Trading, Director General of, 293
Family Law Reform Act, (1969), 207
Felthouse v *Bindley* (1982), 204
finance:
  exports, 149
  long-term, 141–5, 148
  medium-term, 148–9
  short-term, 150–1
  sources, 137–53
Financial Services Act, (1986), 15
fire precautions, 602–3, 617–18, 713
Fire Precautions Act (1971), 450–1
fire prevention officers, 713
first aid, 713–14
flexible working hours, 333
forms:
  and computers, 382–4
  control, 369–71
  design, 372–5
  ease of completion, 375–8
  ease of handling, 382–4
  ease of use, 378–82
  layout, 378–80
  make-up, 373–4
  multipart, 376–7
  preprinted, 374–5
  production, 372
  purpose, 368–9
  register, 369–70
fraud:
  cheque, 725–7
  credit card, 725–7
fringe benefits:
  canteen facilities, 508

  costs, 327–8
  discounts, 507–8
  entertainment, 508–9
  health insurance, 509
  loans, 507
  mortgages, 507
  and recruitment, 503–4
  review, 511–13
  sabbatical leave, 510
  shares, 511
furniture costs, 330–1, 352–4

garnishee proceedings, 257
gearing, companies, 152
General Rate Act (1967), 608

Hadley v *Baxendale* (1854), 215
Hands v *Simpson Fawcett & Co. Ltd* (1928), 398
health and safety:
  advice, 454–6
  in offices, 344–7
Health and Safety at Work Act (1974), purpose, 440
Health and Safety Executive, 441–3
Health and Safety Inspectorate, addresses, 454–6
heating, offices, 346–7
holidays, security actions, 724–5
Hussein v *Saints Complete House Furnishers* (1979), 405–6

incentives, 327–9, 485–91
Industrial and Commercial Finance Corporation, 139
industrial tribunals, and dismissal, 434–6
inertia selling, 301–2
Infants Relief Act (1874), 207
inflation, 135
information:
  disclosure, 559–60
  obtaining by deception, 686–7
  theft, 678
information technology:
  convergence, 309
  office management, 310–17
injunctions, 429–30
  and contracts, 217
  trade disputes, 575–6
injuries, industrial, 528–30
insolvency, and redundancy, 538–9
inspectors, social security, 530
Institute of Chartered Secretaries and Administrators (ICSA), 5
  qualifications, 10–12
  strategic plan, 10, 16
Institute of Trade Mark Agents, 288–9
insurance:
  accidents, 636–7

cash loss, 633-4
cover, 632
definitions, 627-32
fire, 633
glass breakage, 634
health, 637
key personnel, 637-9
legal liabilities, 635-6
loss of income, 634-5
medical, 639
theft, 633
intellectual property:
 definition, 263
 marking of products, 287-8
 protection, 687-8
 rights, 263-90
International Convention for the Protection of Industrial Property, 277
International Convention, The (patents), 277-8
inventions, 264, 269-70

job descriptions, 460-1
job evaluation, 461-70, 480
 questionnaires, 462-6
job grading, 467-8
job ranking, 462, 467
Joint Stock Companies Act (1856), 17

Kelner v *Baxter* (1867), 211-12
keys (security), 711
Kidd *v* DRG (UK) (1985), 409
kidnapping, 721-2
know-how, 281-2

leasehold property, 606-7
LEO (Lyons Electronic Office), 310
licensing, 279-82
lighting, offices, 344-5
Limitation Act (1980), 217
limited liability, advantages, 18-19, 28
line managers, 493
liquidation, 261-2
locks (security), 711
losses, and taxation, 165-8

McFadden v *Greater Glasgow PTE* (1977), 411
maintenance, buildings, 618-24
management buy-outs, 139
Manpower Services Commission, 547
maternity allowance, 526-7
maternity leave, 412-13
maternity pay, 411-12
 statutory, 522, 523, 526-7
maternity rights, 410, 410-13
meetings:
 adjournment, 90, 98

agenda, 93, 100, 105-6
alternatives to, 332
annual general, 83-5
 organization, 109-113
chairman, 91-3, 101-2
class, 86
committees, 102-3
conduct, 82-116
debenture holders, 104
directors', 99-103
extraordinary general, 85-6
guarantee companies, 103-4
minutes, 97-8, 102
notice of, 88-91, 99-100
postponement, 98
preparation, 95-6
proxies, 96-7
quorum, 91, 101
resolutions, 87-8, 99, 102
 examples, 106-9
shareholders', 83-6, 113-15
unlimited companies, 103
voting, 93-7, 102
winding-up, 115-17
memorandum of association, contents, 23-4
Mental Health Act (1959), 208
mergers and acquisitions:
 checklist, 197-8
 definition, 190-2
 financing, 194-6
 human aspects, 196
 planning, 188-90
 procedures, 194
 reasons for, 192-3
 types, 190-2
merit-rating, 490-1
misconduct, and prosecution, 695-6
Misrepresentation Act (1967), 204, 303-4
monopolies:
 attitudes to, 291-2
 definition, 293-4
Monopolies Commission, 292
Monopolies and Mergers Act (1965), 292
Monopolies and Mergers Commission, references to, 294, 297
Monopolies and Restrictive Practices (Inquiry and Control) Act (1948), 292
Morris v *Scott & Knowles* (1976), 408

Napier v *National Business Agency Ltd* (1951), 398
National Freight Corporation, 139
national insurance:
 benefits, 524-6
 contracting out, 521
 contributions, 517-21, 531-2
 death benefit, 529

development, 515–16
and directors, 523
information about, 531–2
injury benefits, 528–30
numbers, 523
rates, 518–21
records, 522
and self-employed, 523–4
negotiation:
definition, 227
elements, 227, 230–2
examples, 248–50
leader, 240
objectives, 229–30
planning, 228–9
strategy and tactics, 232–9, 245–8
teams, 239–40
and time, 238–9
Newborne v *Sensolid (Great Britain) Limited* (1954), 211
Newlands v *National Employers' Accident Association Limited* (1885), 3
noise, in offices, 345–6
North East Midlands Co-operative Society v *Allen* (1977), 409
Northland Airliners v *Ferranti*, (1970), 203

O & M:
benefits, 360–2
consultants, 365–7
definition, 363
role in organization, 363–4
staff, 364
training for, 365
Office of Fair Trading (OFT), 298–300
offices:
automation, 331–2
cabling, 343–4
cellular, 351–2
computers, 312–17
cost reduction, 319–34
costs, 318
equipment, 307–8
health and safety, 344–7
heating, 346–7
information technology, 310–17
layout, 331, 354–5
layout patterns, 337–43
lighting, 344–5
minimum standards, 331
noise, 345–6
open-plan, 338–9, 341–3
planning, 356
removals, 356–7
setting up, 335–58
Shops and Railways Premises Act 1963, 447–8
space requirements, 336–7

specification, 355–6
work measurements, 321–7
organization and methods *see* O & M

Panorama Development (Guildford) Limited v *Fidelis Furnishing Fabrics Limited* (1971), 4–5, 210
paper:
control, 369, 371
sizes, 372–3
types, 373
Patent Cooperation Treaty, The, 277
patents:
agents, 288–9
costs, 289–90
definition, 265–6
disputes, 274–5
employees' rights, 269–70
infringement, 270–1
North America, 278–9
registration procedure, 272–6
specification, 264–5
types, 264
validity, 266–8
Patents Act (1977), 263
pay system, and audit, 500–1
pensions:
retirement, 527–8
schemes, 506–7
performance appraisal, 475–6
performance ratios, 132–3
Philips premium plan, 487
picketing, 573, 722
code of practice, 574
secondary, 573–4
planning legislation, 600–1
Police and Criminal Evidence Act (1984), 696–701
political funds, trades union, 563
powers of attorney, shareholders, 62–3
Powers of Attorney Act (1971), 62–3
Price v *Civil Service Commission* (1978), 408–9
productivity agreements, 492
profit and loss accounts:
contents, 122–4
example, 130–5
profit sharing, 329, 490
property management, 593–610
proxies meetings, 96–7

Race Relations Act (1976), 404–8
race relations, law enforcement, 407–8
racial discrimination:
definition, 405–6
examples, 406
meaning, 405–6
permitted, 407

INDEX

redundancy:
  appeals, 539
  claims, 538
  compensation, 537–8, 545
  consultation about, 537, 544–5
  and corporate planning, 540–7
  definition, 535–6
  fund, 538
  help to dismissed employees, 546–7
  impact, 542–3
  and insolvency, 538–9
  and Manpower Services Commission, 547
  notice of 536
  and re-engagement, 545–6
  selection, 543–4
  social implications, 541–2
  statistics, 534
  tribunals, 539–40
Redundancy Payments Act (1965), 533–4
references:
  employers, 437–8
  provision of, 437–8
Registrar of Companies, 18
Rehabilitation of Offenders Act (1974), 722
resale price maintenance, justification, 297–8
Resale Prices Act (1962), 292; (1964), 221, 292; (1976), 293, 297–8
resolutions examples, 106–9
restraint of trade, contracts, 220–1
Restrictive Practices Court members, 294
Restrictive Practices Court Act (1976), 293
restrictive trade practices:
  justification, 296
  scope, 295–6
  summary of legislation, 291–6
Restrictive Trade Practices Act (1956), 221, 292; (1968), 292–3; (1976), 293, 294–6
Rose v *Humbles*, (1970), 155
Royal British Bank v *Turquand* (1856), 210
Rucker plan, 489

safety:
  buildings, 617
  of contractors, 422
  enforcement, 441–3
  legislation, 448–51
  precautions, 713
  records, 453–4
  statutory notices, 451–3
salaries:
  anomalies, 473
  basis for, 505–6
  policy, 457–9
  reviews, 474–6
  scales, 470–1
  structure, 471–2
  surveys, 471

Sale of Goods Act (1979), 218–19, 302
Salomon v *Salomon Ltd* (1897), 20
Scammel v *Ouston* (1941), 203
Scanlon plan, 489
scrip issue, shares, 76–7
search, right of, 692–3
secondary actions, trade disputes, 575
secret ballots:
  strikes, 570–1
  trades union, 563–4
security:
  buildings, 618, 709–12
  companies, 705
  and discipline, 688–95
  precautions, 685–6
  staff, 702–5
    job descriptions, 702
    selection, 703–4
    training, 704–5
self-employed, and national insurance, 523–4
Sepon pool, 66, 71
sex discrimination:
  advertisements, 409
  meaning, 408–9
  permitted, 409–10
Sex Discrimination Act (1975), 408–10
shareholders:
  change of address, 55
  change of name, 56
  death, 56–62
  dividend mandates, 63
  powers of attorney, 62–3
  registration, 49–52
shares:
  capitalization issues, 76–8
  certificates, 52–4
  certification, 71, 76
  'concert party' dealings, 33
  conversion, 79–80
  disclosure of interest, 32–3
  documentation, 48–81
  equity, 34
  ordinary, 34, 143
  preference, 34, 48, 143
  register, 49–81
  rights issues, 79
  scrip issue, 76–7
  transfer, 29, 66–71, 80–1
  types, 33–4
Sidebottom v *Kershaw, Leese and Company Limited* (1920), 31
Singh v *British Rail Engineering* (1985), 406
sit-ins, 574–5
social security:
  administration, 516–17
  information, 531
  inspectors, 530

software packages, 390
space, and cost reduction, 330–1
specific performance (contracts), 429–30
Stacey and Company Limited v *Wallis* (1912), 25
standards, offices, 331
statutory maternity pay, 522, 523, 526–7
Steinberg v *Scala Limited* (1923), 207
Stock Exchange:
  issue, 145–7
  listing, 140
stocks:
  convertible, 144–5
  fixed interest, 144
  warrant, 144–5
stress, causes, 439–40
strikes, secret ballots, 570–1
Supply of Goods (Implied Terms) Act (1973), 221–3, 302
Supply of Goods and Services Act (1983), 225–6
surveyors, professional bodies, 597–8
suspension with(out) pay, 694

tachograph, 653–5
takeovers *see* mergers and acquisitions
Talisman system, 66, 71
taxation:
  accounting for, 161
  and annual accounts, 124
  assessment, 155
    appeals against, 155
  capital allowances, 161–5
  expenses, 158–60
  and groups of companies, 169–70
  rate, 158
  statutes, 154
telephones, efficiency, 333
terrorist actions, precautions against, 714
theft, by employees, 692–3
trade, restraint of, 220–1
trade associations, 299–300
Trade Descriptions Act (1968) and (1972), 301
trade disputes, 568–9
  injunctions, 575–6
  lawful acts, 571–3
  secondary actions, 575
  unlawful acts, 569–70
trade marks, 282–5
  agents, 288–9
  disputes, 283–4
Trade Marks, Register of, 283
trades union:
  closed shop, 553–6, 566–7
  collective agreements, 567–8
  collective procedures, 556–7
  discipline, 562–3

dismissals, 433–4, 436
  and industrial action, 569–71
  legal status, 565–7
  membership, 561–2
  political funds, 563
  recognition, 550–1, 552–3
  representation, 551–2
  representatives, 557–8
  secret ballots, 563–4
training:
  administration, 580–4
  for administrative staff, 588–9
  for clerical staff, 585
  and corporate strategy, 581–2
  for craft apprentices, 585–6
  identification, 582
  importance, 577–80
  for line managers, 588
  for management, 587–8
  methods, 589–90
  officers, 581–3
  for operatives, 584–5
  programme, 582–3
  for shop stewards, 589
  for technical staff, 586–7
transport services:
  financial management, 665–70
  licensing, 646–8
  organization structure, 642–5
  and personnel movement, 670–2
  planning, 645–6
  professional bodies, 648
  staff management, 642
trespass, 723
tribunals, redundancy, 539–40

ultra vires doctrine, 27, 209–11
  and directors, 35
unemployment benefit, 527
Unfair Contract Terms Act (1977), 224–5, 302–3
Unlisted Securities Market (USM), 140–1
Unsolicited Goods and Services Acts (1971) and (1975), 302

VAT:
  accounting, 183–4
  appeals, 186–7
  application, 178–9
  and bad debts, 182
  and cash flow, 186
  definition, 177
  and discounts, 181
  exemption, 182–3
  and groups of companies, 186
  invoices, 180
  legislation, 177–8
  penalties, 184–5

INDEX

    rates, 180–1
    records, 185
    and second-hand goods, 182
vehicles:
    design, 655–7
    environmental considerations, 657
    fleet management schemes, 662–3
    maintenance, 663–5
    purchasing schemes, 657–63
    running costs, 648–51
    speed limits, 650
venture capital, 139

wage structure:
    anomalies, 484
    design, 482–5
wages:
    cost, 481–2
    costing, 480–1
    policy, 476–7, 494–7
    structure, 477–80, 497–500
Wages Act (1986), 457
Wilson Committee (1977), 13
work measurement:
    offices, 321–7
    techniques, 322–5
works closures, security problems, 727

Young v *Carr Fasteners Ltd* (1979), 558